BRAHMS IN CONTEXT

Brahms in Context offers a fresh perspective on the much-admired nineteenth-century German composer. Including thirty-nine chapters on historical, social and cultural contexts, the book brings together internationally renowned experts in music, law, science, art history and other areas, including many figures whose work is appearing in English for the first time. The essays are accessibly written, with short reading lists aimed at music students and educators. The book opens with personal topics, including Brahms's Hamburg childhood, his move to Vienna and his rich social life. It considers professional matters from finance to publishing and copyright; the musicians who shaped and transmitted his works; and the larger musical styles which influenced him. Casting the net wider, other essays embrace politics, religion, literature, philosophy, art and science. The book closes with chapters on reception, including recordings, historical performance, his compositional legacy and a reflection on the power of composer myths.

NATASHA LOGES is Head of Postgraduate Programmes at the Royal College of Music, London. She has published articles on Brahms, concert history and art song in various volumes and journals including *19th-Century Music* and *Music & Letters*. She is the author of *Brahms and His Poets: A Handbook* (2017) and a co-editor of *Brahms in the Home and the Concert Hall* (Cambridge University Press, 2014).

KATY HAMILTON is a freelance researcher, writer and presenter. She has published on the history of the Edinburgh Festival, émigré musicians in Britain and variety shows at the Wigmore Hall. She is a co-editor of *Brahms in the Home and the Concert Hall* (Cambridge University Press, 2014) and has contributed to several other projects concerning nineteenth-century lieder.

BRAHMS IN CONTEXT

EDITED BY
NATASHA LOGES
KATY HAMILTON

CAMBRIDGE
UNIVERSITY PRESS

University Printing House, Cambridge CB2 8BS, United Kingdom

One Liberty Plaza, 20th Floor, New York, NY 10006, USA

477 Williamstown Road, Port Melbourne, VIC 3207, Australia

314-321, 3rd Floor, Plot 3, Splendor Forum, Jasola District Centre, New Delhi - 110025, India

79 Anson Road, #06-04/06, Singapore 079906

Cambridge University Press is part of the University of Cambridge.

It furthers the University's mission by disseminating knowledge in the pursuit of education, learning and research at the highest international levels of excellence.

www.cambridge.org
Information on this title: www.cambridge.org/9781107163416
DOI: 10.1017/9781316681374

© Cambridge University Press 2019

This publication is in copyright. Subject to statutory exception and to the provisions of relevant collective licensing agreements, no reproduction of any part may take place without the written permission of Cambridge University Press.

First published 2019

A catalogue record for this publication is available from the British Library

Library of Congress Cataloging in Publication data
NAMES: Loges, Natasha. | Hamilton, Katy, 1982–
TITLE: Brahms in context / edited by Natasha Loges, Katy Hamilton.
DESCRIPTION: Cambridge, United Kingdom; NewYork, NY : Cambridge University Press, 2019.
IDENTIFIERS: LCCN 2018048305 | ISBN 9781107163416
SUBJECTS: LCSH: Brahms, Johannes, 1833–1897. | Brahms, Johannes, 1833–1897 – Criticism and interpretation. | Music – 19th century – History and criticism.
CLASSIFICATION: LCC ML410.B8 B6837 2019 | DDC 780.92 [B]–dc23
LC record available at https://lccn.loc.gov/2018048305

ISBN 978-1-107-16341-6 Hardback
ISBN 978-1-316-61519-5 Paperback

Cambridge University Press has no responsibility for the persistence or accuracy of URLs for external or third-party internet websites referred to in this publication, and does not guarantee that any content on such websites is, or will remain, accurate or appropriate.

Dedicated to the memory of our dear friend Robert Pascall, whose brilliant scholarship and boundless generosity have been an inspiration to Brahmsians around the world.

Contents

List of Illustrations	*page* xi
List of Music Examples	xiii
Notes on Contributors	xiv
Preface	xxiii
List of Abbreviations	xxvi

PART I PERSONALITY, PEOPLE AND PLACES   I

1   Childhood in Hamburg   3
    Renate and Kurt Hofmann

2   The Schumanns   14
    Thomas Synofzik

3   Vienna   23
    Camille Crittenden

4   Leipzig and Berlin   33
    Karen Leistra-Jones

5   Personal Habits   44
    William Horne

6   Correspondence   52
    Wolfgang Sandberger

7   Holidays   60
    Inga Mai Groote

PART II IDENTITIES, ENVIRONMENTS AND INFLUENCES   69

8   Finances   71
    Jakob Hauschildt

viii *Contents*

9	As Pianist *Katrin Eich*	80
10	As Conductor *Walter Frisch*	88
11	As Arranger *Valerie Woodring Goertzen*	98
12	As Editor *Peter Schmitz*	114
13	As Teacher *Johannes Behr*	123
14	Private Music-Making *Katy Hamilton*	130
15	Concert Life *Laurenz Lütteken*	138
16	Genre *Matthew Gelbart*	149
17	Folk Music *George S. Bozarth*	164
18	Early Music *Virginia Hancock*	175

PART III PERFORMANCE AND PUBLISHING 185

19	Singers *Natasha Loges*	187
20	Conductors *Leon Botstein*	196
21	Pianists *Michael Musgrave*	206
22	Other Instrumentalists *Heather Platt*	215
23	Instruments *Anneke Scott*	227

Contents   ix

24 Publishers   236
    Peter Schmitz

25 Copyright   246
    Friedemann Kawohl

PART IV SOCIETY AND CULTURE   257

26 Politics and Religion   259
    David Brodbeck

27 Literature   269
    Natasha Loges

28 Philosophy   277
    Nicole Grimes

29 Visual Arts   286
    William Vaughan and Natasha Loges

30 Science and Technology   296
    Myles W. Jackson and Katy Hamilton

PART V RECEPTION AND LEGACY   305

31 Germany   307
    Johannes Behr

32 England   316
    Katy Hamilton

33 Analysis   324
    Heather Platt

34 The Era of National Socialism   336
    Ulrike Petersen

35 Editing Brahms   347
    Michael Struck

36 Recordings   357
    Ivan Hewett

37 Historical Performance   367
    Michael Musgrave

x Contents

38 Inspiration 376
Markus Böggemann

39 Mythmaking 384
Natasha Loges and Katy Hamilton

Further Reading 393
Index 395

Illustrations

1.1 City Map of Hamburg, 1846. Hamburg Edition vol. 3,   *page* 6
HHE 01019, Archiv-Verlag Hamburg.

1.2 City Map of Hamburg, 1882. Hamburg Edition vol. 1,   12
HHE 01014, Archiv-Verlag Hamburg.

3.1 Strauss II, *Seid umschlungen Millionen* Op. 443 (Berlin: 26
Simrock, 1892), frontispiece. Brahms-Institut, Lübeck.

3.2 Construction site of the new Court Opera on Vienna's   29
Ringstrasse with Heinrichshof building, c. 1863. Bildarchiv
Austria.

4.1 Elisabeth von Herzogenberg, photographed by Wilhelm   35
Robert Eich, Dresden, 1860s. Universitätsbibliothek der
Universität für Musik und darstellende Kunst Graz, kindly
supplied by Bernd Wiechert and Sven Nielsen.

4.2 Heinrich von Herzogenberg, photographed by Wilhelm   36
Robert Eich, Dresden, 1860s. Universitätsbibliothek der
Universität für Musik und darstellende Kunst Graz, kindly
supplied by Bernd Wiechert and Sven Nielsen.

10.1 Brahms conducting, drawn by Willy von Beckerath, 1895.   96
Alamy.

11.1 Autograph engraver's model of Brahms's arrangement of the   102
First Piano Concerto Op. 15 for piano duet, last page of first
movement, with revisions in ink in Brahms's hand.
The Library of Congress (Whittall Foundation),
Washington, DC.

11.2 Concert Programme, 29 November 1862, Saal der   109
Gesellschaft der Musikfreunde. Brahms-Institut
Lübeck.

11.3 Concert Programme, 14 March 1873, Grosser Saal des   111
Convent-Gartens Hamburg. Brahms-Institut
Lübeck.

List of Illustrations

12.1	Revision copy of Chopin's Barcarolle Op. 60 (prepared for the Chopin-Gesamtausgabe) with annotations by Johannes Brahms. Verlagsarchiv Breitkopf & Härtel Wiesbaden, Sig. N 35 <1>.	118
15.1	The 'Komponistenhimmel' in the Tonhalle, Zurich. Brahms-Institut, Lübeck.	140
17.1	Brahms, 'Ade mein Schatz, ich muß nun fort', German folk-song copied by Brahms into his handwritten collection of folk-songs from different countries, c. 1850 (Washington DC, Library of Congress. ML30.8b.B7 CASE).	168
22.1	Portrait of the Joachim Quartet. Beethoven Feier in Bonn, 11–15 May 1890. Royal Academy of Music, London.	220
22.2	Adolph Menzel's 1891 sketch of Mühlfeld as a Greek god. Alamy.	223
24.1	Assignation of Rights for Opp. 7–8. Handschriften- und Musikabteilung der Hessischen Universitäts- und Landesbibiliothek Darmstadt.	237
24.2	Breitkopf & Härtel Calculation List. Staatsarchiv Leipzig, Bestand Breitkopf & Härtel 21081. Sig. 6465, Bl. 110.	241
29.1	Adolph Menzel, *Joachim and Clara Schumann in Concert* (1854), pastel (now lost).	290
29.2	Anselm Feuerbach, *Iphigenia* (1862), oil on canvas. Held by Hessisches Landesmuseum Darmstadt.	291
29.3	Arnold Böcklin, *Isle of the Dead* (1880), oil on wood. Held by Kunstmuseum Basel.	293
34.1	Unattributed caricature of Brahms, c. 1938.	339
35.1	Part of an engraved metal plate for the old Urtext edition by G. Henle Verlag, Munich 1976 of J. Brahms, Intermezzo Op. 117 no. 1, middle section. Henle Verlag. Reproduction by kind permission of G. Henle Verlag Munich and the Brahms-Forschungszentrum Kiel.	352
39.1	Portrait of the youthful Johannes Brahms, a gift to Sir George Grove in the early 1890s. Royal College of Music/ ArenaPAL.	388
39.2	Portrait of the elderly Johannes Brahms. Royal College of Music/ArenaPAL.	389

Music Examples

11.1a   Brahms, Second String Quintet Op. 111, first movement, *page* 104
bars 57–69.

11.1b   Brahms, Second String Quintet Op. 111, arrangement for   105
piano, four hands, first movement, bars 57–69.

16.1   Brahms, Second String Quintet Op. 111, bars 1–19.   150

16.2   Mendelssohn, Octet Op. 20, bars 1–25.   152

16.3   Brahms, Motet Op. 74 no. 2, 'O Heiland, reiss die Himmel   155
auf', bars 18–36.

17.1   Transcription of melody handwritten by Brahms and   169
annotated by Reményi (Hamburg, Staats- und
Universitätsbibliothek Carl von Ossietzky,
Musiksammlung. BRA: Aa8).

17.2   Brahms, *Variations on a Hungarian Song* Op. 21 no. 2, bars 1–8.   170

22.1   Evolution of the solo violin line in the Violin Concerto Op.   217
77, first movement, bars 102–4, reproduced from B.
Schwarz, 'Joseph Joachim and the Genesis of Brahms's
Violin Concerto', *Musical Quarterly* 69/4 (Autumn
1983), 514.

22.2   Brahms, Clarinet Quintet Op. 115, second movement, bars   224
52–7.

33.1   Schubring's diagram of motivic relationships between the   326
movements of Brahms's Piano Sonata Op. 2.

33.2   Brahms, 'Immer leiser wird mein Schlummer' Op. 105   331
no. 2, bars 41–7.

33.3   Score reduction and Richard Cohn's analysis of Brahms,   332
Double Concerto Op. 102, first movement, bars 268–79,
reproduced from 'Maximally Smooth Cycles, Hexatonic
Systems, and the Analysis of Late-Romantic Triadic
Progressions', *Music Analysis* 15/1 (March 1996), 14–15.
Reproduced with permission of Wiley.

Notes on Contributors

JOHANNES BEHR, studied musicology and philosophy at the universities of Heidelberg, Vienna and Marburg. His Master's thesis (2000) examined the genesis of Brahms's piano exercises; his doctoral dissertation (published 2007) explored Brahms's different roles as an adviser, teacher and evaluator of younger composers. In 2006 he joined the team of the Johannes Brahms Complete Edition in Kiel. In addition to his editorial work, he has published several articles, mainly on aspects of Brahms philology.

MARKUS BÖGGEMANN is Professor of Music History at the University of Kassel. His main research interests focus on aspects of modernism in nineteenth- and twentieth-century music, compositional theory and practice, and contemporary music. He has written about Arnold Schoenberg and his school, *fin-de-siècle* Vienna and historicism. Recent research includes the early music of Anton Webern and the reception of Bach by contemporary composers.

LEON BOTSTEIN is President and Leon Levy Professor in the Arts and Humanities of Bard College. He is the music director and conductor of the American Symphony Orchestra and the Orchestra Now and co-artistic director of the Bard Music Festival. He was music director of the Jerusalem Symphony Orchestra (2003–10), where he serves as conductor laureate. He is artistic director of the Grafenegg Campus and Academy, has recorded extensively and edited *The Compleat Brahms* (1999).

GEORGE BOZARTH is Professor of Music History at the University of Washington. He specialises in nineteenth-century studies, particularly the music of Johannes Brahms and musical life in Boston. He is also interested in the early history of the piano. He was the founding Executive Director of the American Brahms Society, 1983–2014. He has published extensively on the music of Brahms, editing essay

Notes on Contributors xv

collections as well as correspondence and documents relating to Robert Keller and George Henschel. He has also edited the complete organ works of Brahms for the *Johannes Brahms Gesamtausgabe.*

DAVID BRODBECK is Professor of Music at the University of California, Irvine. Among his recent publications are '*Heimat* is Where the Heart Is; or, How Hungarian was Goldmark?' (*Austrian History Yearbook,* 2017), 'Music and the Marketplace: On the Backstory of Carlos Chávez's Violin Concerto' (*Carlos Chávez and His World,* 2015) and *Defining Deutschtum: Political Ideology, German Identity, and Music-Critical Discourse in Liberal Vienna* (2014).

CAMILLE CRITTENDEN completed a PhD in musicology at Duke University and is the author of *Johann Strauss and Vienna: Operetta and the Politics of Popular Culture* (Cambridge University Press, 2000). She currently serves as Deputy Director of the Center for Information Technology Research in the Interest of Society (CITRIS) at the University of California, where she writes on topics related to human rights, technology and new media, as well as applications and policy for civic engagement, government transparency and digital equity.

KATRIN EICH is member of the editorial board of the *Johannes Brahms Gesamtausgabe/New Complete Edition of the Works of Johannes Brahms* (Kiel University, Germany). She gained her doctoral degree with a dissertation about the chamber music of César Franck (2002). Her scholarly focus includes music from the nineteenth and early twentieth centuries, as well as editorial aspects. In 2010 she and her colleagues received the Brahms Award from the Brahms-Gesellschaft Schleswig-Holstein.

WALTER FRISCH is Professor of Music at Columbia University. His principal area of research has been Austro-German music of the nineteenth and twentieth centuries. His publications on Brahms include *Brahms and the Principle of Developing Variation* (1984), *Brahms and His World* (1990; rev. 2009, with Kevin Karnes) and *Brahms: The Four Symphonies* (1996/2003). He is also the author of *German Modernism: Music and the Arts* (2005) and *Music in the Nineteenth Century* (2012).

MATTHEW GELBART is Associate Professor of Music at Fordham University. He is interested in the ways that we classify sound to make meanings and identities from it. His first book, *The Invention of 'Folk Music' and 'Art Music'* (Cambridge University Press, 2007), explores the xvi *Notes on Contributors*

historical contingency of these large categories, and his forthcoming book on musical genre and romantic ideologies examines the tension between a drive toward originality and the need for familiarity and social belonging in music.

VALERIE WOODRING GOERTZEN is Associate Professor of Music History at Loyola University New Orleans. She has edited two volumes for the *Johannes Brahms Gesamtausgabe* containing Brahms's piano arrangements of works of other composers. Other recent publications include essays in *Brahms am Werk: Konzepte – Texte – Prozesse* (2016) and *Brahms in the Home and the Concert Hall* (Cambridge University Press, 2014). Goertzen is Vice-President of the American Brahms Society and co-edits the Society's Newsletter with William P. Horne.

NICOLE GRIMES is Assistant Professor of Music at the University of California, Irvine. She is the author of *Brahms's Elegies: The Poetics of Loss in Nineteenth-Century German Culture* (Cambridge University Press, 2019). Her co-edited volumes include *Rethinking Hanslick: Music, Formalism, and Expression* (University of Rochester Press, 2013) and *Mendelssohn Perspectives* (2012). Her research is focused at the intersection between music aesthetics and music analysis in repertoire from the late eighteenth century to the present.

INGA MAI GROOTE is Professor of Musicology at the University of Zurich. She studied musicology, history and Italian philology and has taught at the universities of Munich, Zurich, Fribourg/Uechtland and Heidelberg. She is the author of *Östliche Ouvertüren. Russische Musik in Paris, 1870–1913* (2014) and editor, with Iain Fenlon, of *Heinrich Glarean's Books* (Cambridge University Press, 2013). Her research focuses on the early-modern and nineteenth-century cultural history of music and the history of music theory.

KATY HAMILTON is a freelance researcher, writer and presenter. She has published on the history of the Edinburgh Festival, émigré musicians in Britain and variety shows at the Wigmore Hall. She is a co-editor of *Brahms in the Home and the Concert Hall* (Cambridge University Press, 2014) and has contributed to several other projects related to nineteenth-century German song. Katy has taught at the Royal College of Music, University of Nottingham and Middlesex University.

VIRGINIA HANCOCK, Professor of Music *emerita* at Reed College in Portland, Oregon, directed the Chorus and Collegium Musicum and

Notes on Contributors xvii

taught theory and history courses. She holds degrees in chemistry from Reed and Harvard and a doctorate in music history from the University of Oregon. She is the author of *Brahms's Choral Compositions and His Library of Early Music* (1983) and articles and book chapters on Brahms topics, particularly his choral music and songs.

JAKOB HAUSCHILDT is member of the editorial board of the *Johannes Brahms Gesamtausgabe/New Complete Edition of the Works of Johannes Brahms* (Kiel University, Germany). He gained his doctoral degree with a dissertation on the masses of Nicolas Gombert (2006). He is currently editing a volume of Choral Works and Vocal Quartets (*Chorwerke und Vokalquartette mit Klavier oder Orgel I*) for the *Johannes Brahms Gesamtausgabe*.

IVAN HEWETT has worked in music for over thirty years as composer, writer, promoter, journalist, lecturer and broadcaster. For nine years he presented BBC Radio 3's flagship magazine programme, *Music Matters*. He is Chief Music Critic for the *Daily Telegraph*, teaches at the Royal College of Music and is the author of *Music: Healing the Rift* (2004).

KURT HOFMANN, born in 1931 in Hamburg, has a background in political education work. Since the early 1950s, he has dedicated himself to the life and work of Johannes Brahms and over the years has amassed probably the largest private collection of Brahmsiana. This forms the basis of the Brahms-Institut founded in 1990 at the Musikhochschule Lübeck, which he led together with his wife, Renate, until 1999.

RENATE HOFMANN, born in 1941 in Wrocław, gained her Master's degree in musicology in Leipzig. She moved to Hamburg in 1981 as Lecturer at the music publisher Hans Sikorski. From 1990 to 1999 she led the Brahms-Institut together with her husband, Kurt, at the Musikhochschule Lübeck. The Hofmanns are authors of numerous publications on Johannes Brahms, Clara Schumann and their world.

WILLIAM HORNE is the Francisco M. Gonzalez M. D. Professor of Music at Loyola University New Orleans. His articles about Brahms and his music have appeared in *The Musical Quarterly*, *The Journal of Musicology*, *Journal of Musicological Research*, *NOTES: The Quarterly Journal of the Music Library Association* and various essay collections. He

xviii   *Notes on Contributors*

is a co-editor of the *American Brahms Society Newsletter* and a composer whose music may be heard on the Blue Griffin and Centaur labels.

MYLES W. JACKSON is Professor of the History of Science at the Institute for Advanced Study in Princeton. His works include *Spectrum of Belief: Joseph von Fraunhofer and the Craft of Precision Optics* (2000), *Harmonious Triads: Physicists, Musicians, and Instrument Makers in Nineteenth-Century Germany* (2006) and the *Genealogy of a Gene: Patents, HIV/AIDS, and Race* (2015).

FRIEDEMANN KAWOHL is a freelance musicologist based in Villingen-Schwennigen. He holds degrees in music theory (Hochschule der Künste Berlin) and musicology (Technische Universität Berlin) and his doctoral dissertation, *Urheberrecht der Musik in Preußen 1829–1840*, was published in 2003. From 2000 to 2003 he was a lecturer at the Centre for Intellectual Property Policy and Management at Bournemouth University. In the 1990s he was an orchestra manager and wrote for German-language national newspapers and public radio. He was an editor of the online Project Primary Sources on Copyright www.copyrighthistory.org/cam/index.php.

KAREN LEISTRA-JONES is Associate Professor of Music at Franklin & Marshall College. Her research interests include the history of musical performance, the Schumann-Brahms circle and musical representations of landscape, motion and travel. Recent publications have appeared in the *Journal of Musicology, Music & Letters, 19th-Century Music* and the *Journal of the American Musicological Society.* Her current project explores the rise of *Werktreue* performance as a cultural ideal in the nineteenth century.

NATASHA LOGES is Head of Postgraduate Programmes at the Royal College of Music London. She is the author of *Brahms and his Poets* (2017) and a co-editor of *Brahms in the Home and the Concert Hall* (Cambridge University Press, 2014). She has published chapters and articles in *Music and Literature in German Romanticism*, the *Cambridge History of Musical Performance, Music & Letters, Nineteenth-Century Music Review* and *19th-Century Music.* She is also a pianist, broadcaster, public speaker and critic.

LAURENZ LÜTTEKEN, born in 1964, studied at the Universities of Münster and Heidelberg. He completed his PhD on Dufay and

Notes on Contributors xix

his post-doctoral studies with a book on eighteenth-century music. In 1996 he was appointed Chair of the Department of Musicology at the University of Marburg. In 2001 he moved to the University of Zurich. His most recent work is *Mozart. Leben und Musik im Zeitalter der Aufklärung* (2017); an English translation of his book *Music of the Renaissance* (University of California Press) appeared in 2018; a translation of his book on Richard Strauss is forthcoming.

MICHAEL MUSGRAVE is author and editor of six books on Brahms, including, with Bernard D. Sherman, *Performing Brahms: Early Evidence of Performance Style* (Cambridge University Press, 2003). His editions for the *Johannes Brahms Gesamtausgabe* include the two orchestral Serenades Opp. 11 and 16, and he is currently editing *Ein deutsches Requiem* Op. 45 jointly with Michael Struck. Other editions include the *Liebeslieder* of Brahms in different versions for Carus Verlag and Edition Peters.

ULRIKE PETERSEN, originally from Hamburg, read Music and Musicology at Girton College, Cambridge, before pursuing doctoral studies in Music History at the University of California, Berkeley. Her doctoral dissertation, completed in 2013, examines the social, political and cultural impact of operetta in early twentieth-century Vienna. Her contribution to this volume is based on her Master's thesis.

HEATHER PLATT, Professor of Music History at Ball State University, is the author of *Johannes Brahms: A Research and Information Guide* (2011) and a co-editor, with Peter H. Smith, of *Expressive Intersections in Brahms* (2012). Platt's articles on the tonal structures, reception, and social context of Brahms's lieder have appeared in such publications as *Brahms in the Home and the Concert Hall* (Cambridge University Press, 2014), *The Cambridge Companion to the Lied* (Cambridge University Press, 2004), *Brahms Studies, The Journal of Musicology* and *Integral.*

WOLFGANG SANDBERGER is Professor of Musicology and Director of the Brahms-Institut at the Musikhochschule Lübeck. He studied as a cellist in Osnabrück/Hanover (1986) and gained a Master's in musicology, philosophy and history in Münster and Hamburg. His doctoral research was entitled *Das Bach-Bild Philipp Spittas* (which won the Hannelore Greve Prize of the Joachim Jungius-Gesellschaft der Wissenschaften). He has published widely on music history from the seventeenth to the twenty-first centuries. Areas of research, besides Brahms and his social

XX   *Notes on Contributors*

environment, are reception history and science-historical subjects. Sandberger also works as an author and host for various ARD broadcasting corporations.

PETER SCHMITZ, born 1979 in Leipzig, is manager of the Institute for Musicology at the University of Münster. Prior to this, he was employed at the Brahms-Institut at the Musikhochschule Lübeck from 2007 to 2008 (Deutsche Forschungsgemeinschaft project 'Brahms-Briefwechsel-Verzeichnis'). He researches and publishes on diverse topics from the late sixteenth to the early twentieth centuries, including music and death in the seventeenth century, the history of the music publishing industry and music in Rome.

ANNEKE SCOTT is a leading exponent of historical horns. In addition to a busy solo and chamber-music career she is principal horn of a number of specialist period instrument ensembles, including Sir John Eliot Gardiner's *Orchestre Révolutionnaire et Romantique*, with whom she has performed and recorded all of the large-scale orchestral and choral works of Brahms. Anneke teaches historical horns at the Royal Welsh College of Music and Drama and the University of Birmingham.

MICHAEL STRUCK, born in Hanover in 1952, is a music teacher, pianist, critic and musicologist. Following conservatoire studies, he gained his DPhil in musicology at the University of Hamburg with the dissertation *Die umstrittenen späten Instrumentalwerke Schumanns* in 1984. Since 1985, he has been a member of the editorial management of the new *Johannes Brahms Gesamtausgabe* (Kiel University). His publications span the music of the eighteenth to the twentieth centuries and include numerous editions. In 2009 he won the Schumann-Prize Zwickau (Germany) and, in 2010 (as member of the Brahms Edition team), the Brahms Award from the Brahms-Gesellschaft Schleswig-Holstein.

THOMAS SYNOFZIK studied musicology, German philology and philosophy, church music and historical keyboard instruments in Cologne, Dortmund and Brussels. From 1998 to 2005 he lectured at several different universities. He has published various books on Schumann and his circle, music of the early seventeenth century, and performance practice and interpretation. Since 2005 he has been the director of the Robert Schumann House in Zwickau. With Michael Heinemann, he is General Editor of the Schumann-Briefedition (which accounts for twenty-five volumes since 2008).

Notes on Contributors   xxi

WILLIAM VAUGHAN is Professor Emeritus in History of Art at Birkbeck College, University of London. He has published widely on romanticism and British and German nineteenth-century art. His monographs include *German Romanticism and English Art* (1978), *German Romantic Painting* (1980), *Samuel Palmer: Shadows on the Wall* (2015) and *Caspar David Friedrich* (2004).

Preface

Natasha Loges and Katy Hamilton

> Fiction, imaginative work that is, is not dropped like a pebble upon the ground . . . fiction is like a spider's web . . . attached to life at all four corners . . . when the web is pulled askew, hooked up at the edge, torn in the middle, one remembers that these webs are not spun in mid-air by incorporeal creatures, but are the work of suffering human beings, and are attached to grossly material things, like health and money and the houses we live in.
>
> Virginia Woolf, *A Room of One's Own*

It is unusual to write a book about a composer which does not focus on their works. However, putting those works to one side, as these essays mostly do, allows us to sense the web which attaches that composer to the world. If we have omitted repertoire, we have managed to include reading habits, religion and recipes. Our hope is to inspire new ways of understanding this endlessly fascinating figure. We have also sought to reflect the ways in which musical scholarship is changing and how the word 'context' is expanding ever outwards. To that end, we have drawn together scholars from different traditions, disciplines and countries, aiming for a balance between established and emerging figures, older and newer perspectives.

The chapters are organised in broad sections. We open with the people and places that were most important in Brahms's life, beginning with his family in Hamburg, taking in the pivotal meeting with the Schumanns and his settling in Vienna, and considering his extended circle of friends and colleagues in two other major cities. Next, we turn to more private matters: his habits, letter-writing, holidays and finances. The focus then shifts to his various interlocking professional musical roles aside from composition, the spaces for which he wrote music, the genres in which he wrote and the broad musical styles which shaped his work beyond his immediate contemporaries and predecessors. In order to convey the sense of interconnectedness which inspired the book, each essay includes copious cross-references to other essays in the volume and is also supplied with a short, xxiv

Preface

dedicated reading list of key texts (in both English and German) to encourage further exploration.

We have aimed to give a sense of the importance of Brahms's collaborators, the numerous fine musicians who brought his work to life across Europe and beyond. Those figures are one part of his public interface; others include the instruments of his day, his astute publishers and the state of copyright law during his lifetime, all of which shaped his life and music in subtle ways. The notion of context is then expanded still further outwards to confront, within this brief format, the vast topics of politics, religion, literature, philosophy, visual arts and science and technology – the grand sweeps of historical change which transformed the world in which he lived and worked.

The book closes with essays which consider Brahms's afterlife in different ways. Space only permits two explorations of reception history, but the idea of reception is stretched to include his contribution to the shape of musical analysis, the editing of his music today, the recent shifts in historical performance practice, the vast discography of his music, and the ways in which he has inspired more recent composers. The closing chapter aims to pull together on a small canvas various factual and less factual depictions of the man and his music.

Because the definition of context is limitless, a book of this sort can never be comprehensive. Apart from omissions we have not yet identified, we have had to exclude considerations of topics that other editors may regard as crucial: essays on Brahms's relationships with specific musicians such Clara Schumann, Franz Liszt, Richard Wagner, Anton Bruckner and others; the musical influences of such significant figures as Bach, Handel, Haydn, Beethoven and Schubert; issues of identity such as gender; the War of the Romantics; and we have not attempted to define what it meant to be a freelance musician in Brahms's lifetime. As the late nineteenth century recedes further from the present day, the notion of reception becomes infinitely more geographically and chronologically complex and diverse. Brahms societies exist in Japan, for example, but this volume only permitted considerations of Brahms's reception in Germany and England. In terms of later reception, we chose to focus on one pivotal historical moment – the period of National Socialism – but space limitations precluded detailed consideration of other major historical periods since Brahms's death. And, although this volume is in itself motivated by historiographical imperatives, we could only touch briefly on historiography itself. Nevertheless, we have covered what is hopefully a rewarding range of perspectives; for example, we have deliberately not reconciled the

Preface xxv

various translations of Schumann's seminal review article 'Neue Bahnen', but sought to retain each author's individual reading of this elusive text.

The following chapters were translated by Natasha Loges: 1. 'Childhood in Hamburg', 2. 'The Schumanns', 6. 'Correspondence', 7. 'Holidays', 8. 'Finances', 9. 'As Pianist', 12. 'As Editor', 13. 'As Teacher', 15. 'Concert Life', 24. 'Publishers', 25. 'Copyright', 31. 'Germany' and 35. 'Editing Brahms'. All work titles have been rendered in English except where the German titles are more familiar to an English readership in the original language, or where a translation results in loss of accuracy, e.g. the distinction between *Lieder* and *Gesänge*.

We wish to thank the following individuals and institutions for their generosity with assistance and permissions: the Brahms-Institut Lübeck, the Kiel Brahms-Forschungszentrum, the Universität für Musik und darstellende Kunst Graz, the Library of Congress, the Verlagsarchiv Breitkopf & Härtel Wiesbaden, the Royal Academy of Music in London, the Universitäts- und Landesbibiliothek Darmstadt, Staatsbibliothek Leipzig, the Hessisches Landesmuseum Darmstadt, the Kunstmuseum Basel, Wiley Publishers and the image libraries Bildarchiv Austria, Alamy Limited and ArenaPAL. Thanks are also due to James Gaddas-Brown, for setting the music examples; Wendy Baskett for preparing the index; Janos Darvas for providing a copy of his film documentary on Brahms, *Wären nicht die Frauen*; the Royal College of Music for invaluable financial support; and Victoria Cooper, Kate Brett and the excellent team at Cambridge University Press for their patience and encouragement.

Abbreviations

The following standard texts are presented with short titles throughout this book:

Avins	S. Avins (ed.), *Johannes Brahms: Life and Letters*, trans. S. Avins and J. Eisinger (Oxford: Oxford University Press, 1997)
Brahms Handbuch	W. Sandberger (ed.), *Brahms Handbuch* (Stuttgart: Metzler and Kassel: Bärenreiter, 2009)
Briefe	M. Kalbeck et al (eds.), *Johannes Brahms Briefwechsel*, 19 vols. (Berlin: Deutsche Brahms-Gesellschaft, reprinted and continued by Tutzing: Hans Schneider, 1974–95)
Heuberger	R. Heuberger, *Erinnerungen an Johannes Brahms*, ed. K. Hofmann, 2nd edn (Tutzing: Hans Schneider, 1976)
Kalbeck I–IV	M. Kalbeck, *Johannes Brahms*, 2nd edn, 4 vols. (Berlin: Deutsche Brahms-Gesellschaft, 1912–21, repr. Tutzing: Hans Schneider, 1976)
Litzmann I–III	B. Litzmann, *Clara Schumann, ein Künstlerleben nach Tagebüchern und Briefen*, 3 vols. (Leipzig: Breitkopf & Härtel, 1918–20)
May I–II	F. May, *The Life of Johannes Brahms*, 2 vols. (London: Edward Arnold, 1905)
SBB I and *II*	B. Litzmann (ed.), *Clara Schumann-Johannes Brahms. Briefe aus den Jahren 1853–1896*, 2 vols. (Leipzig: Breitkopf & Härtel, 1927)
Werkverzeichnis	M. McCorkle, *Johannes Brahms. Thematisch-Bibliographisches Werkverzeichnis* (Munich: G. Henle Verlag, 1984)

List of Abbreviations xxvii

Abbreviations for Scores from the *Johannes Brahms Gesamtausgabe*/New Complete Edition of the Works of Johannes Brahms

Johannes Brahms Gesamtausgabe (JBG): until 2011, ed. ***Johannes Brahms Gesamtausgabe*** e. V., Editionsleitung Kiel, in cooperation with Gesellschaft der Musikfreunde, Vienna; thereafter ed. the Musikwissenschaftliche Institut of the Christian-Albrechts-Universität, Kiel in cooperation with the ***Johannes Brahms Gesamtausgabe*** e. V. and the Gesellschaft der Musikfreunde, Vienna.

JBG, 1. Symphonie	*Symphonie Nr. 1 c-Moll op. 68* (Series I, vol. 1), ed. R. Pascall (Munich: G. Henle Verlag, 1996)
JBG, Violinkonzert	*Violinkonzert D-Dur op. 77* (Series I, vol. 9), ed. L. Correll Roesner and M. Struck (Munich: G. Henle Verlag, 2004)
JBG, Doppelkonzert	*Doppelkonzert a-Moll op. 102* (Series I, vol. 10), ed. M. Struck (Munich: G. Henle Verlag, 2000)
JBG, Arrangement 2. Klavierkonzert	*Klavierkonzert Nr. 2 B-Dur op. 83, Klavierauszug (Bearbeitung für zwei Klaviere)* (Series IA, vol. 6), ed. J. Behr (Munich: G. Henle Verlag, 2014)
JBG, Arrangements fremder Werke 1	*Johannes Brahms, Arrangements von Werken anderer Komponisten für ein Klavier oder zwei Klaviere zu vier Händen* (Series IX, vol. 1), ed. V. W. Goertzen (Munich: G. Henle Verlag, 2012)
JBG, Arrangements fremder Werke 2	*Johannes Brahms, Ein- und zweihändige Klavierbearbeitungen von Werken anderer Komponisten* (Series IX, vol. 2), ed. V. W. Goertzen (Munich: G. Henle Verlag, 2017)

PART I

Personality, People and Places

CHAPTER I

Childhood in Hamburg

Renate and Kurt Hofmann

'Today, my dear wife, née Nissen, successfully delivered a healthy boy. 7th May 1833. J. J. Brahms.' Thus, on 8 May 1833, Johann Jakob Brahms announced the birth of his first son Johannes in the local paper, the *Privileged Weekly General News of and for Hamburg (Privilegirte wöchentliche gemeinnützige Nachrichten von und für Hamburg)*. At a time when such announcements were the exception, this was a clear sign of pride.[1] Johann Jakob Brahms or Brahmst, as he also spelled it, was born on 1 June 1806 in Heide in Holstein, the second son of the innkeeper and trader Johann Brahms, who had moved to Heide from Brunsbüttel via Meldorf. His ancestors were from Lower Saxony. Johann Jakob completed a five-year apprenticeship as a city wait in Heide and Wesselburen, during which he learned the flugelhorn, flute, violin, viola and cello, then standard instruments. In early 1826, the young journeyman began his travels with his certificate of apprenticeship, received in December 1825. He arrived almost immediately in Hamburg where he hoped to earn his keep more easily than in the country.[2]

Initially it seems he played brass or strings in places of public entertainment in the Hamburg Berg, and also worked as a street musician in the city lanes and courtyards. However, he soon joined the Hamburg voluntary police (essentially a citizens' militia) as a horn player, a precondition of attaining the freedom of the city of Hamburg. The first high point of his career was in 1830, when he was made a citizen of Hamburg by taking the citizen's oath (written in Low German dialect) on 21 May; he could now settle within the city walls. Later, he played the flugelhorn until the dissolution of the militia in 1868.[3] His monthly wage in 1867 was 24

---

[1] O. Biba, R. and K. Hofmann, J. Neubacher, *'in meinen Tönen spreche ich ...' Für Johannes Brahms 1833–1897* (Heidelberg: Edition Braus, 1997), 74.

[2] S. Kross, *Johannes Brahms. Versuch einer kritischen Dokumentar-Biographie*, 2 vols. (Bonn: Bouvier, 1997), vol. 1, 11f.

[3] F. Ebrard, *Von Hamburger jungen Brahms. Sonderdruck aus der Schweizerischen Musikzeitung 75/11* (1 November 1946), 4.

3

Marks in Hamburg currency.[4] Upon his departure, he received the 'Silver Medal for faithful service' and a lifelong two-thirds pension as an 'Oberjäger'.[5]

On 31 May 1831, Johann Jakob was among the founders of the Hamburg Musikverein. By now, he was playing second violin in the sextet of the Alsterpavillon; he graduated to double bass in 1840, having mastered this instrument.[6] Henceforth, he worked primarily as a double bassist, between 1853 and 1861 in the State Theatre Orchestra, and between 1863 and 1870 as a regular member of the orchestra of the Philharmonic Concerts, for which he was also a valued flautist. He was a Freemason, and a Master in the St. Johannis Lodge 'Zum Pelikan', where he recorded his profession as 'music teacher' in 1868/9.[7] Enterprising, free-spirited, and with an earthy sense of humour, Johann Jakob aspired to nothing more than to provide for his own, while also fulfilling his own pleasures. He loved dancing throughout his life, and as an old man occasionally still played in the taverns of Hamburg's alleyway neighbourhood or 'Gängeviertel'.

After taking his citizen's oath, Johann Jakob was permitted to marry, so on 9 June 1830 he wedded Johanna Henrica Christiane Nissen. Seventeen years his senior, she lived with her sister and brother-in-law Christina Friderika and Diederich Philipp Detmering on Ulricusstrasse 37, in the Hamburg Neustadt 'Gängeviertel', and assisted in their haberdashery and laundry business. Johann Jakob was their lodger.[8] Christiane Nissen was born in Hamburg on 4 July 1789. Her ancestors were from Schleswig-Holstein. Among them were schoolmasters, pastors and aldermen, and some had been minor nobility in Schleswig-Holstein. Her father, Peter Radeloff Nissen, came from Tondern, her mother, Anna Margaretha von Bergen, from Itzehoe. When they moved to Hamburg, her father did an apprenticeship in tailoring.[9] Consequently, Christiane Nissen was a seamstress. Accounts of her suggest that she was hard-working, devout, interested in literature although not educated and, subsequently, sensitive to her son's burgeoning talent.

---

[4] K. Stephenson (ed.), *Johannes Brahms in seiner Familie. Der Briefwechsel* (Hamburg: Hauswedell, 1973), 17.

[5] *Ibid.*, 148. [6] Kross, *Johannes Brahms*, 15.

[7] *Verzeichniss der Beamten und Mitglieder der Provinzial-Loge von Niedersachsen zu Hamburg, so in der zu ihrem Sprengel gehörende St. Andreas- und St. Johannis-Logen, unter Constitution der höchstleuchtenden und hochwürdigsten Grossen Landes-Loge der Freimaurer von Deutschland zu Berlin. Für das Jahr 1868–1869*, 27.

[8] See the final letter of Brahms's mother in K. Hofmann, *'Sehnsucht habe ich immer nach Hamburg . . .' Johannes Brahms und seine Vaterstadt. Legende und Wirklichkeit* (Reinbek: Dialog-Verlag, 2003), 23f.

[9] Stephenson, *Der Briefwechsel*, 11.

Childhood in Hamburg

The newly-weds moved on St Martin's Day, 11 November 1830, to the Haus Cordeshof, Bäckerbreitergang, where Brahms's older sister, Wilhelmine Louise Elisabeth (called Elise) was born (rather soon after) on 11 February 1831. The same year, again on St Martin's Day, the family moved to an apartment in Specksgang 24 (after the road was widened, it was renumbered as No. 60). In a small room at this address, Johannes Brahms was born on Tuesday 7 May 1833. That autumn, the family returned to Ulricusstrasse, this time to a larger apartment in No. 15, where Brahms's younger brother Friedrich (called Fritz) was born. Following three further moves, the family finally settled at Dammtorwall 29 in autumn 1841 until spring 1850, making this address the true 'Brahmshaus'.[10] The young Brahms lived there from his eighth to his seventeenth year.

All these apartments were in the 'Gängeviertel', an area which stretched from the Michaelis-Kirche to the Alster. From the seventeenth century onwards, the gardens and courtyards behind the substantial half-timbered buildings were gradually built up. The buildings were connected by narrow, crooked alleys ('Gänge') which one accessed through the main house fronting the street. Thanks to an explosion in the city's population, even smaller buildings were raised by several storeys, so that little light penetrated into the alleyways. For the most part, these homes were occupied by middle-class, small tradespeople and respectable artisans. Nearby there were various drinking or dancing houses. The apartments surrounding the City Theatre on the Dammtorstrasse and the numerous other artistic and entertainment establishments were much sought after by musicians, singers, actors, theatre employees and so forth. After the great fire of May 1842, the need for accommodation in Hamburg was so pressing that even wealthy citizens, such as Brahms's teacher Eduard Marxsen (1806–87), rented an apartment in a *Gängeviertel*. The mixture of social classes would have been normal for the young Brahms. Contrary to the well-established myth, it is virtually impossible that he played the piano in taverns, since at his age he was not allowed to enter them, and his father's sense of class consciousness would never have permitted it.[11]

From spring 1850 to mid-1864, the family occupied three other apartments which document Brahms's father's social ascent through their location and rent. Around this time, Brahms's parents separated, the tensions

---

[10] Drawn from the record of residents maintained by the Hamburg militia. Staatsarchiv der Freien und Hansestadt Hamburg. See also Ebrard, *Von Hamburger jungen Brahms*, 2ff.
[11] Hofmann, *Sehnsucht*, 44ff.

Figure 1.1. City Map of Hamburg, 1846.

Childhood in Hamburg

arising from the age difference having become irreconcilable. The children suffered from this parental conflict, especially Johannes. This can be inferred from Christiane Brahms's final letter to him, which she wrote from 26 to 30 January 1865, shortly before her death on 2 February.[12] It is a devastating account of a demanding, patriarchal situation; she also revealed her suspicion that Brahms's father had long planned to leave the family and had siphoned off funds in order to do so. It also shows how little understanding Johann Jakob had of Johannes. For his father, Johannes's studies were too prolonged, and the seventeen-year-old should leave home: in his opinion, his son's musical training would not result in a sustainable career. When Johannes extended his stay with the Schumanns in Düsseldorf, his father declared: 'The boys [Johannes and Fritz] will come to nothing.'[13] These statements affected Johannes deeply, and it remained his secret goal to prove to his father that he could gain respect and status not only as a pianist but also as a composer.

The boy Johannes was a small, pale, dreamy youth, who liked playing with tin soldiers while listening to his father practise. He could easily and accurately repeat the melodies he heard. It was clear to Johann Jakob that the boy should follow in his father's footsteps, and he taught him his own instruments early on. But Johannes showed little inclination for the career his father intended for him, preferring the piano instead. His father finally capitulated and chose the best teacher that he could find in Hamburg, Otto Friedrich Willibald Cossel (1813–65). From 1839, Johannes went to elementary school, then four years later to the so-called 'Bürgerschule', where he stayed until 1848, and where he also had English and French lessons. School attendance was not compulsory then, and the Brahms family paid significant fees to educate their three children.

Brahms's lessons with Cossel began in 1840. Cossel himself had studied with Eduard Marxsen, who in turn had studied in Vienna with the renowned musicians Ignaz von Seyfried, Simon Sechter and Carl Maria von Bocklet. Cossel started with finger exercises and etudes but progressed to works by Carl Czerny, Muzio Clementi, Johann Baptist Cramer, Johann Nepomuk Hummel and Friedrich Kalkbrenner. He also acquainted Brahms with music by Schubert and J. S. Bach.

In 1843, a 'private subscription concert for the benefit of the further musical education of Johannes Brahms' was organised in the public assembly room 'Zum Alten Raben' near the Dammthor. Brahms played a virtuosic piece by Henri Herz as well as the piano part in Beethoven's

[12] *Ibid.*, 21ff.   [13] *Ibid.*, 27ff.

Quintet for Piano and Winds Op. 16, a piano quartet by Mozart and other solo pieces.[14] The concert was an artistic and financial success. One of its consequences was that an impresario suggested to Johann Jakob Brahms that the boy go on tour to the USA, where he would earn a fortune. This prospect tempted Brahms's father, but Cossel (whom both father and son greatly respected), protested vehemently and asked his former teacher Marxsen to take over the boy's lessons. Marxsen initially declined, but, when Cossel persisted, he agreed on condition that Cossel share the teaching. Soon afterwards, Marxsen took over Johannes's entire musical education for free.

Marxsen's lessons were aimed above all at a mastery of the Classical repertoire, and he also stressed the importance of transposition of substantial works at sight, a skill Brahms enjoyed exercising as a professional performer. The piano lessons with Marxsen lasted until 1847, the composition lessons with theory until 1848. Already in 1842, Cossel had complained that Brahms could be an excellent pianist if he would only leave aside his endless composing.[15] Brahms's childhood friend Louise Langhans-Japha also recalled that the twelve-year-old played her his own music, a piano sonata in G major.[16] But his teacher's goal was to make him a financially self-sufficient virtuoso pianist. On 20 November 1847, Brahms performed publicly for the first time as a pianist in another artist's concert, for which he was praised in the press; similar occasions followed. Alongside this he earned pocket money as a pianist in dance venues and pleasure gardens.

Brahms enjoyed his first countryside summer holiday in May 1847 in Winsen an der Luhe, on Lüneburg Heath between Hamburg and Lüneburg, and he returned there in 1848 and 1851. He stayed with an acquaintance of his father, the mill-owner Adolf Giesemann, and gave his daughter piano lessons. He also conducted a male-voice choir in the neighbouring village and composed several works for them – his first experience of working with an ensemble of this kind.

His formal schooling ended in 1848, and he was confirmed in the Michaelis-Kirche in Hamburg in the same year. On 21 September 1848, the fifteen-year-old gave his first concert alone, a programme dominated by virtuoso pieces but also including a Bach fugue. His second programme on 14 April included Beethoven's 'Waldstein' Sonata Op. 53 alongside some of his own works. From 1849, Brahms undertook work as an arranger for the

---

[14] *May I*, 59.
[15] J. Spengel, *Johannes Brahms. Charakterstudie* (Hamburg: Lütcke und Wulff, 1898), 11f.
[16] *Kalbeck I*, 35.

Childhood in Hamburg

Hamburg publisher August Cranz. The only piece which can be firmly identified as his is the arrangement *Souvenir de la Russie*, which Cranz published as Op. 151 under the collective pseudonym 'G. W. Marks'.[17] Other fantasies for piano on operatic themes by Meyerbeer, which appeared as G. W. Marks's Opp. 158 and 161, may also be Brahms's work, although such claims must be made cautiously. Brahms was playing Sigismund Thalberg's *Lucia di Lammermoor* Variations at exactly the time that G. W. Marks's Op. 160, a Fantasy on *Lucia*, appeared, suggesting – if it was by Brahms – that his performance inspired his own creative work. He was also working as a pianist and song accompanist at the Hamburg Thalia Theatre.

Around 1850, his main occupation was piano teaching, which gave him a regular income. [See Ch. 8 'Finances' and Ch. 13 'As Teacher'.] However, his chief interest was now composition. Around this time, he wrote the first works which would be published under his name and which he entered in his catalogue of compositions for 1851. These include the Scherzo Op. 4 and the song 'Heimkehr' Op. 7 no. 6.

Following the turmoil of revolutions across Europe in 1848/9, the Hungarian violinist Eduard Reményi (1828–98) had to flee his home and found himself in Hamburg in 1853. Waiting for passage to America, he hoped to fill the time with concerts and was seeking an accompanist for a small concert tour. He booked Brahms. They departed on 19 April 1853, going first to Reményi's acquaintance the violinist Joseph Joachim in Hanover in order to get letters of recommendation for the rest of the trip. They gave concerts in Celle, Lüneburg and Hildesheim and met Joachim again in Göttingen on 4 June. Upon his recommendation, they went to Weimar in mid-June to see Liszt, who received them warmly. They spent over a week in the company of Liszt and his pupils. Thereafter, Brahms and Reményi parted ways. The latter continued his tour, while Brahms returned to Joachim and spent the summer with him. In his view, he could only return to Hamburg when he had success to report – namely, a publisher for his compositions. To this end, Joachim urged him to visit Robert Schumann in Düsseldorf [see Ch. 2 'The Schumanns']. Initially, Brahms travelled to Mainz, and then on to Mehlem, where he visited the music-loving Deichmann family, and first studied Schumann's works. Deeply impressed, Brahms went to Düsseldorf and knocked on their

---

[17] *Souvenir de la Russie. Transcriptions en forme de Fantaisies sur des Airs russes et bohémiens composées pour le piano à quatre mains par G.W. Marks*. Op. 151. Hambourg chez A. Cranz. Reprint with preface by K. Hofmann (Hamburg: K. D. Wagner, 1971).

door on 30 September 1853 (fruitlessly, as they were not home). On 1 October he finally met them and played them some of his works. Schumann was completely enthralled by both the music and the personality of the young composer. In this spirit, he published his essay 'New Paths' in the *Neue Zeitschrift für Musik,* making Brahms's name famous at a single stroke but also inviting scepticism, since Brahms was unknown as both composer and pianist at this point [see Ch. 31 'Germany'].

Schumann also brokered the relationship between his young friend and the Leipzig music publishers Breitkopf & Härtel. Thus, Brahms's first works appeared as early as December 1853, and he could present them to his parents that Christmas. These early days were of life-changing significance. Schumann, as both the man and the musician, was henceforth infallible for him, possibly also because the older composer had an exemplary middle-class marriage and family which would have seemed impossible in Brahms's own home. Henceforth, Brahms belonged to Schumann's closest circle of friends.

In June 1859 Brahms began working with his so-called Hamburg Ladies' Choir, an association of young women from mutually friendly patrician families in Hamburg, for which Brahms composed and arranged sacred songs and folk-songs, performing them for their own pleasure and for invited guests. The small choir performed publicly only three times under Brahms's directorship, on which occasions his compositions were very positively received. And although Brahms did not settle in Hamburg, the musical and personal legacy of this informal group remained evident in his compositional work for the rest of his life.

In May 1861 Brahms stopped working with his Ladies' Choir and withdrew almost completely from Hamburg's concert life. He moved into an apartment outside the city limits, in Hamm, Schwarze Strasse 5 (now a suburb of the city). Here, he composed various early masterworks: both the First and Second Piano Quartets Opp. 25 and 26; the *Variations and Fugue on a Theme of Handel* Op. 24, the four-hand *Variations on a Theme of Schumann* Op. 23 and the first of the fifteen *Magelone Romances* Op. 33. He also began working on his Piano Quintet Op. 34, which was initially conceived as a string quintet. In early 1862 in Hamm, Brahms also worked on the opening movement of his First Symphony Op. 68, and he sketched his initial idea for the text of *A German Requiem* Op. 45.

In those years, the artistic and financial situation of Hamburg's Philharmonic Society was in decline. Friedrich Wilhelm Grund, co-founder and conductor of the institution, which had existed since 1828 and co-operated with the Hamburger Singakademie, was more than ready

Childhood in Hamburg

to lay aside his duties after thirty years. Thus, the committee of the Philharmonic Society, which relied on Grund's financial support to put on the six annual concerts, sought a strong successor. Brahms's friend and supporter Theodor Avé-Lallemant, a Society board member, planned to create an additional post of choirmaster of the Singakademie for Brahms and confided this to him. But he advised him, as Clara Schumann had,[18] to go abroad first and make his name.[19] Brahms thus went to Vienna on 8 September 1862 – but heard there, to his great disappointment, that the post of Director of the Philharmonic Society had been given on 26 November 1862 to Julius Stockhausen, a singer he regarded highly, and that he was no longer under consideration since the Singakademie would not, after all, have a choirmaster. He was deeply upset, even though he knew that he was not truly suitable for the post.

Brahms remained in Vienna for nearly eight months. He gave several successful concerts, grew close to several families and only returned to Hamburg on the eve of his thirtieth birthday. He spent the following period in a small house which still exists today, on the Elbe in Blankenese, today part of Hamburg. Here he composed his cantata *Rinaldo* Op. 50. And here he also received the news that he had been selected as choirmaster of the Vienna Singakademie for the 1863/4 season.

The secure middle-class existence for which he longed was now in reach. Yet, despite his success, he left the job after one season, since he was 'less occupied with musical matters than with other things . . . I have to concern myself too much with prima donnas, and a thousand other things which have nothing to do with me'.[20] With his first Vienna trip in September 1862, Brahms's Hamburg time ended; however, he remained closely connected to his home city.[21] He also left his library in Hamburg for an extended period; it was not until early 1883 that it was brought to Vienna.

Brahms's love for his native city remained evident throughout his life. His personality was truly North German: reserved, brusque and direct. Viennese manners were initially alien to him, although the open-minded Viennese charm soon won him over. Brahms's telegram of thanks for the conferral of freedom of the city of Hamburg on 23 May 1889 conveys better than any other document his closeness to Hamburg, as he expressed it to the Mayor, Dr Carl Petersen: 'I regard your message with gratitude as the

---

[18] Clara Schumann to Brahms, 29 August 1862, *SBB I*, 406. [19] *Kalbeck I*, 478f.
[20] Brahms to Adolf Schubring, 19 June 1864, *Briefe VIII*, 203.
[21] See also Brahms to Clara Schumann, 10 August 1855, *SBB I*, 120.

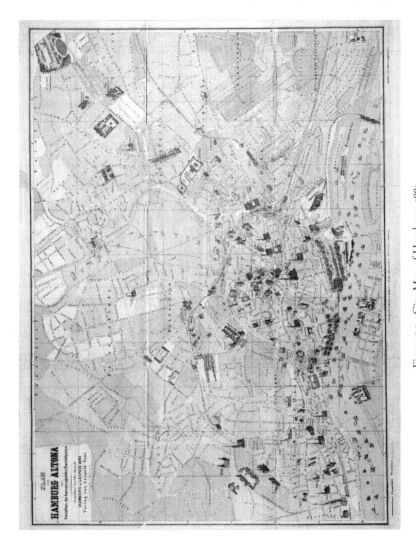

Figure 1.2. City Map of Hamburg, 1882.

Childhood in Hamburg

most wonderful honour and greatest joy which man can give me.'[22] In keeping with his personality, he moderated his emotional expression in his letter to Petersen. But in a letter to Richard Barth from Ischl on 6 July 1895, he wrote:

> I am truly an old-fashioned person, and I often long for home. But apart from the fact that I have practically no connections there, I also need all sorts of little household objects to combat this longing, like receiving the [Hamburger] *Fremdenblatt* every eight days! Also, I still have a truly impressive collection of Hamburgiana from old and recent times.[23]

Even in the last phase of his life, he liked showing his friends his 'Heimatschein', as he referred to his letter conferring the freedom of the city.

Further Reading

K. Hofmann, *'Sehnsucht habe ich immer nach Hamburg . . .' Johannes Brahms und seine Vaterstadt. Legende und Wirklichkeit* (Reinbek: Dialog-Verlag, 2003)
K. Hofmann, 'Brahms the Hamburg Musician 1833–1862', trans. M. Musgrave, in M. Musgrave (ed.), *The Cambridge Companion to Brahms* (Cambridge: Cambridge University Press, 1999), 3–30
W. Hübbe, *Brahms in Hamburg* (Hamburg: Lütcke & Wulff, 1902)
S. Kross, *Johannes Brahms. Versuch einer kritischen Dokumentar-Biographie*, 2 vols. (Bonn: Bouvier, 1997), vol. 1
K. Stephenson (ed.), *Johannes Brahms in seiner Familie. Der Briefwechsel* (Hamburg: Hauswedell, 1973)

---

[22] *Kalbeck IV*, 179.
[23] K. Hofmann (ed.), *Johannes Brahms in den Erinnerungen von Richard Barth* (Hamburg: Schuberth, 1979), 59.

CHAPTER 2

The Schumanns

Thomas Synofzik

Various books and films have been devoted to the friendship between Johannes Brahms and Clara Schumann, often overlooking the manifold connections Brahms also had with other members of the Schumann family. Listeners and performers have been intrigued by stories of love and romantically inspired works with secret encoded musical messages. Indeed, triangular artistic relationships like that of Robert and Clara Schumann and Brahms are fascinating for many reasons, rarely to do with music – but can Clara Schumann be compared to Alma Mahler-Werfel or Cosima Bülow-Wagner? In reviewing the relationship, with recourse to unpublished letters from Clara Schumann's correspondence with her family, the following focusses on the mutual artistic influences, dedications, Clara Schumann's performances and Brahms's editorial contributions to her complete edition of Robert Schumann's works.

Contrary to standard accounts, Brahms's first meeting with Robert and Clara Schumann most probably took place on 14 March 1850 in Hamburg, when Theodor Avé-Lallemant (1806–90), board member of the Hamburg Philharmonic Society, invited friends for a soirée. Among these were the Schumanns, who spent a fortnight in Hamburg for concerts, and Brahms. Apparently the sixteen-year-old Brahms showed some compositions to Schumann, but the older composer did not look through them.[1] Brahms did not dare to approach the Schumanns again until the summer of 1853, when he was travelling along the Rhine. He met various significant musical figures en route, including the violinist Wilhelm Joseph von Wasielewski in Bonn, and the composers Carl Reinecke and Ferdinand Hiller in Cologne. According to Robert Schumann's diary, Brahms arrived at their house in Düsseldorf on 30 September 1853. Schumann's daughter Marie remembered that on opening the door she found a young man 'handsome as a picture, with long blond hair'. As her parents had gone out, he had to return the

---

[1] W. J. Wasielewski, *Aus siebzig Jahren* (Stuttgart & Leipzig: Deutsche Verlags-Anstalt, 1897), 144.

The Schumanns

next day. Robert Schumann asked him to play some of his compositions – among which were the Piano Sonatas Opp. 1 and 2, the Scherzo Op. 4 and some lieder including 'Liebestreu' Op. 3 no. 1 (all of which would soon be published) – and after just a few bars, ran out, saying, 'Please wait a moment, I must call my wife.'[2] For the next month, Brahms stayed at the hotel *Römischer Kaiser* in Düsseldorf. He had the daily privilege of meeting Robert for a morning walk. Two kindred spirits had found each other – both deeply affected by Romantic writers like E. T. A. Hoffmann, and both sharing a profound interest for music of earlier times. On 28 October 1853, Robert praised Brahms in his article 'New Paths' in the *Neue Zeitschrift für Musik*, introducing him to the musical world at large – but the resultant expectations placed on the twenty-year-old composer were considerable [see Ch. 31 'Germany'].

After leaving Düsseldorf that November, Brahms went to another new friend, the violinist Joseph Joachim, in Hanover. Robert and Clara Schumann joined them there in January 1854, following a concert tour to the Netherlands. However, upon his return to Düsseldorf, Schumann had a nervous breakdown. On 27 February he tried to take his own life; a week later he voluntarily entered a private asylum in Endenich near Bonn. Brahms hastened to Düsseldorf and, from 3 March onwards, rented a room on Schadowplatz. During the following months he assisted Clara Schumann in every way, comforting her verbally and musically, helping with the seven Schumann children (including teaching them somersaults) and even taking over the regular entries in Robert's household diaries. Brahms and Joachim were the only two friends allowed to visit him regularly in Endenich.

There has been much speculation about the degree of intimacy which sprung up between Brahms and Clara around this time, for instance around the paternity of the Schumanns' youngest son, Felix. He was born in June 1854, when Robert was already in Endenich. In 1926, Alfred Schumann (pseudonym Titus Frazeni), a grandson of the Schumanns, published a pamphlet called *Johannes Brahms, the Father of Felix Schumann. A Very Serious Parody of the 'Recollections' of Eugenie Schumann*. (The Schumanns' youngest daughter Eugenie had published her recollections the previous year.) However, Schumann's diaries conclusively prove his fatherhood.[3] At Felix's baptism on 1 January 1855 Brahms stood godfather.

---

[2] E. Schumann, *Robert Schumann. Ein Lebensbild meines Vaters* (Leipzig: Koehler & Amelang, 1931), 357.
[3] T. Synofzik, 'Brahms und Schumann', in *Brahms Handbuch*, 71.

16   THOMAS SYNOFZIK

Already in October 1853 'Herr Brahms' had quickly become 'Johannes'
to both the Schumanns. On 10 October Clara wrote into her diary:
'I always call him Robert's Johannes.' From November 1854 onwards,
Clara addressed him in her letters at his request with the intimate pronoun
'Du', justifying this in her diary: 'I could not refuse, for indeed I love him
like a son.'[4] When Brahms called her 'dear Mrs Mama' or himself 'a well-
behaved child' in return, this seems to be intended as jokingly as his
allusions to a contract that he was to marry her daughter Eugenie.
In March 1855 he confessed, 'I love you more than I can express in
words.' Although his letters retained the formal address 'Sie'
until May 1856, by 25 June 1855 his closing sentences used the intimate
form, which probably reflects how they spoke to one another: 'Please go on
loving me as I shall go on loving you ('dich') always and for ever.'[5] Against
this, it must be remembered that Clara was not only fourteen years his
senior but also a renowned artist and the wife of a revered composer.
A letter to Joachim from 1854 illustrates Brahms's inner battles between
religious devotion, on one hand, and intimacy, on the other: 'I believe that
I do not have more concern and admiration for her than that I love her and
am under her spell. I often have to restrain myself forcibly from just quietly
putting my arms around her and even –.'[6] He did not dare to write the
word 'kiss', and it is open to question if they ever did kiss.

In October 1854, Clara resumed her concert activities. Brahms accompanied her as far as Hanover, then continued alone to Hamburg, where she
arrived on 7 November 1854 and met Brahms's parents during her stay. She
developed an especially close relationship to his mother, Christiane, who,
born in 1789, could have been her own mother.

After Robert's incarceration, the Schumann family was dispersed.
The older daughters, Marie and Elise, and the two older sons, Ludwig
and Ferdinand, were sent to boarding schools; Julie went to Clara's mother
Mariane Bargiel in Berlin. At Christmas 1854, Brahms moved into the
Schumann home at Bilkerstrasse, practising and composing in Robert's
room on the first floor. Browsing through Robert's library significantly
influenced the young composer. Six months later, Clara moved to
a cheaper apartment in the Poststrasse, and Brahms took a room on the
ground floor in the same building.[7] By now, Brahms had developed

---

[4] *Litzmann II*, 282 and III, 94.   [5] Brahms to Clara Schumann, 25 May 1855, *SBB I*, 116.
[6] A. Holde, 'Suppressed Passages in the Joachim-Brahms Correspondence Published for the First
Time', *The Musical Quarterly* 45/3 (July 1959), 314.
[7] E. Schumann et al., *Claras Kinder* (Cologne: Dittrich Verlag, 1995), 293. In this account by Marie
Schumann, she stresses that Brahms lived separately; however, a letter from 24 August 1855 to Clara

The Schumanns

a fatherly friendship with the children, composing and publishing a collection of folk-songs (*Volks-Kinderlieder* WoO 31), which he dedicated to them in 1858. He dedicated his Piano Sonata Op. 2 and *Variations on a Theme of Robert Schumann* Op. 9 to Clara. She had chosen the same theme for her own Variations Op. 20. While it was common practice to dedicate works to close friends or honoured colleagues, it is interesting to note how Brahms manages to include both the Schumanns, quoting not only from Robert's music, but also including a quotation from Clara Schumann in his tenth variation. Only one other friend, Joseph Joachim, received two printed dedications by Johannes Brahms but with an interval of more than twenty-five years, whereas the two works dedicated to Clara were both published in 1854.

On 29 July 1856 Robert died in Endenich. In subsequent letters to her family, Clara Schumann praised her friendship with Brahms, writing to her brother Alwin of her 'dear friend Brahms' living in her house, who was her 'faithful succour since Robert's illness', living only to 'cheer her up', and who was a 'wonderful genius'.[8] She and Brahms remained in Düsseldorf until September 1857, after which Brahms accepted a post at the court of Detmold, and Clara moved to Berlin.

They met frequently in Hamburg until Brahms went to Vienna in 1862. During her sojourns in 1860 and 1861, Clara sang in Brahms's Hamburg Ladies' Choir. In autumn 1861, she was accompanied by her fifteen-year-old daughter Julie. In this period, Brahms composed his *Variations on a Theme of Schumann* Op. 23 (based on the 'Ghost' theme), which he dedicated to Julie. Her coughing, which had already been a problem for two years, was worrying Brahms; eleven years later, she died of tuberculosis.

From 1855 onwards, Brahms and Clara often shared their summer holiday excursions. In the second half of July 1855, they went on a walking tour along the Rhine and the Main. In 1856, after Robert's death, Clara invited Brahms and his sister Elise for a journey to the Upper Rhine and Switzerland with the elder Schumann boys, Ludwig and Ferdinand. From 12 July to 5 September 1857, they stayed in Oberwesel and St Goarshausen, together with the younger children. In 1858, Clara Schumann invited him to join her, Marie, Elise, Julie, Eugenie and Felix in

---

Schumann indicates that on at least one occasion, he slept on the ground floor with the children. See *SBB I*, 134–5.

[8] E. Möller, *Briefwechsel Robert und Clara Schumanns mit der Familie Wieck* (*Schumann-Briefedition* I.2) (Cologne: Dohr, 2011), 350.

THOMAS SYNOFZIK

Göttingen. During this summer, Brahms fell in love with Agathe von Siebold.[9] On 14 September Clara Schumann left, probably not out of jealousy, but because Elisabeth Werner, the children's governess in Berlin, had returned from her holiday.[10] Brahms remained for another fortnight. Under pressure regarding his relationship with Agathe von Siebold in early 1859, he broke off their engagement. Clara disapproved of this course of events and also later tried in vain to suggest a suitable wife.[11] She appears to have had more motherly feelings for her close friend Johannes Brahms. But apparently, although a life with Clara was not feasible, Brahms was also unable to choose another woman in her place – his courting of one or other of the Schumann daughters may be seen as a sort of substitute love.

Probably deliberately, Brahms and Clara spent summer 1859 apart. In the summers of 1860 and 1862, Brahms visited Clara in Kreuznach, and in 1863 Brahms visited her for three days in Baden-Baden, where she had bought a house, for the first time. Clara was having a love affair with Theodor Kirchner at the time.[12] During the following three years, Brahms lodged in a nearby house for extended periods until October.

In 1866 their friendship suffered a crisis. Nearly two years later she wrote to him about this summer: 'You appeared to be so uncomfortable with us and were so disagreeable, not occasionally, which among friends would have been overlooked, but continuously and daily.' It seems that the main source of misunderstanding arose from Clara's family. Brahms did not get on with her mother, who was staying in Baden-Baden that summer, and he also exchanged unfriendly words with Clara's daughters when they tried to defend their mother against him.[13] Their friend, who earlier in 1866 had given a cookery book as a present to Marie (today in the Robert-Schumann-Haus Zwickau), had now become an unwelcome visitor.

It was not the first time that Brahms put on his notorious 'armour of irony and coldness'.[14] From October 1866 to April 1868, he and Clara did not see each other at all. Things worsened in early 1868 when Brahms tried to persuade her to abandon her concert career and settle in Vienna. She retorted that giving concerts was artistically fulfilling and not simply

---

[9] E. Michelmann, *Agathe von Siebold. Johannes Brahms' Jugendliebe*, 2nd edn (Stuttgart & Berlin: J.G. Cotta'sche Buchhandlung Nachfolger, 1930).

[10] E. Möller, *Briefwechsel Robert und Clara Schumanns mit der Familie Bargiel (Schumann-Briefedition I.3)* (Cologne: Dohr, 2011), 197.

[11] Clara Schumann to Brahms, 5 February 1860, *SBB I*, 297.

[12] See R. Hofmann, 'Johannes Brahms im Spiegel der Korrespondenz Clara Schumanns', in C. Floros et al. (eds.), *Brahms und seine Zeit. Symposion Hamburg 1983* (Laaber: Laaber Verlag, 1984), 53.

[13] See letters, 4 September 1868 and 15 October 1868, *SBB I*, 593 and 598.

[14] See Hofmann, 'Johannes Brahms im Spiegel', 52–3.

The Schumanns

financially necessary. Nevertheless, she travelled to Bremen for Good Friday 1868 to listen to the first performance of *A German Requiem* Op. 45. On 12 April 1868 she wrote to her daughter Marie:

> I could not stop thinking of your papa, who said (in his beautiful article on Johannes): 'once he waves his magic wand over choir and orchestra, then you will realise what he is.' It was an impressive vindication, when they all came and said: 'Schumann was right'. If only he could have heard it. Never in my life had I felt such a power over me in church.[15]

In November and December 1868, they met for concerts in Oldenburg, Bremen and Vienna. Clara already then knew of her daughter Julie's relationship with the Italian count Vittorio Radicati di Marmorito but told Brahms of this only after the official engagement in July 1869. She may have ignored Brahms's interest in Julie, which had probably arisen during the latter's stay in Hamburg in 1861. Clara noted in her diary:

> Johannes is quite altered, he seldom comes to the house and speaks only in monosyllables when he does come. And he treats even Julie in the same manner, though he always used to be so particularly nice to her. Did he really love her? But he has never thought of marrying, and Julie has never had any inclination towards him.[16]

Some days after the wedding, Brahms showed Clara his *Alto Rhapsody* Op. 53, calling it his 'bridal song', full of deepest sorrow in words and music, as Clara attested in her diary.

The tension seems to have eased when Brahms realised that he would not be accepted into the Schumann family as anything but a close friend. Clara saw Brahms regularly during her concert tours to Vienna in December 1869/January 1870 and November/December 1872. In 1871–3, Brahms returned for longer stays to Baden-Baden. In summer 1874 Clara Schumann and her daughters visited Brahms in Nidelbad am Zürichsee and, in summer 1875, in Ziegelhausen near Heidelberg.

In 1873–5, Clara Schumann had to interrupt her concert career for nearly eighteen months due to pains in her hand. It has been suggested that this arose from her playing of Brahms's First Piano Concerto Op. 15 in Leipzig in December 1873.[17] She only played this work twice; indeed, despite giving

---

[15] Robert-Schumann-Haus Zwickau 10468,37-A2. The quotation is from Schumann's 'Neue Bahnen', *Neue Zeitschrift für Musik* 39/18 (28 October 1853), 185–6.

[16] *Litzmann III*, 230 and 232.

[17] E. Altenmüller and R. Kopiez, 'Suffering for Her Art: The Chronic Pain Syndrome of Pianist Clara Wieck-Schumann', in J. Bogousslavsky, et al. (eds.), *Neurological Disorders in Famous Artists – Part 3* (Basel: Karger, 2010), 109.

the premiere of ten of his keyboard works, Brahms's works make up only 2 per cent of the her solo and chamber music repertoire.[18] This may be because she found it hard to cope with the specific technical demands of Brahms's piano writing. In Brahms's concert repertory, on the other hand, Robert Schumann's music featured most prominently apart from his own compositions; he also occasionally performed works by Clara. And Robert's works, in their poetical and contrapuntal density, also challenged Brahms. It seems hardly coincidental that just like Robert, he wrote four symphonies, three concertos for one solo instrument and orchestra and one for a group of instruments and orchestra, three piano sonatas, three violin sonatas, three piano trios and three string quartets.

Brahms typically sent his compositions to Clara before publication, often asking for her judgement. Probably the most critical reply she ever gave concerned his song collections Opp. 69–72, on 2 May 1877.[19] Brahms had requested unreserved criticism from her as well as from their mutual friend Elisabeth von Herzogenberg; they were unanimous in their praise and disdain of certain songs. Clara tried to persuade him to publish just two collections of significant songs, rather than three including some she felt to be unworthy of his name, but as usual, Brahms – after consulting friends – changed nothing. He also gave several of his autograph manuscripts as gifts to Clara.

In 1879, another intensely personal event drew them together. On 16 February, Brahms's godson Felix Schumann died of tuberculosis. In 1873, 1874 and 1878, Brahms had set three of Felix's poems to music (Op. 63 nos. 5 and 6, and Op. 86 no. 5). Four weeks after Felix's death, Brahms visited Clara in Frankfurt for the first time since she had moved there in 1878, staying for nearly four weeks – his longest visit for decades.

In the late 1870s, Clara began working on a complete edition of Robert's works with the publishers Breitkopf & Härtel [see Ch. 12 'As Editor']. Brahms acted as an adviser, mostly in editorial matters, but also in questions of fees and contracts. He was involved in the edition of most of the piano works, of the First and Third Symphonies, several chamber music duos and trios and the *Requiem für Mignon* Op. 98b. However, he disagreed with Clara over the question of which works

---

[18] R. Kopiez, A. C. Lehmann and J. Klassen, 'Clara Schumann's Collection of Playbills: A Historiometric Analysis of Life-Span Development, Mobility, and Repertoire Canonization', *Poetics* 37/1 (February 2009), 56.

[19] *SBB II*, 96–9.

The Schumanns

to include; the plan of a supplementary volume was shelved and resumed only in October 1892.[20]

Shortly before, there was another severe crisis in their relationship. A week-long stay in March 1891 turned into a nightmare for Clara after an altercation they had on the first day over her pupil Leonard Borwick.[21] Then, in October 1891, Clara was surprised by a notice in the music journal *Signale* that Breitkopf & Härtel was going to publish an edition of the first version of Robert Schumann's Fourth Symphony (originally his second) after the manuscript in Brahms's possession. She protested in a letter that she would never have consented to this; however, the publication proceeded and their relationship was again damaged. In earlier cases, she had conceded to Brahms's wishes, and later on she also let him publish the first version of Schumann's *Andante and Variations* Op. 46 and three early songs in the supplement volume to her complete edition of Robert's works. But Clara wanted to be the definitive custodian of her husband's music.

Accordingly, in 1892, Brahms did not visit Clara in Frankfurt, as he had done nearly every year since 1879 (the exceptions were 1884 and 1888). Most of his visits were connected with concerts he was giving, so Clara had complained already on 14 June 1883 to her daughter Elise: 'Yesterday, Brahms was also here – so there is not much to say, we are nothing but a dosshouse for him – if only it would not make me so deeply sad each time.'[22] They met for summer holidays, as in Ischl and Berchtesgaden in 1880, and in Baden-Baden in September 1883, 1887 and 1889. Their last meeting took place in Frankfurt on 3 October 1895.

When Brahms received the news of Clara Schumann's death on 20 May 1896, he took the wrong train, missing the memorial in Frankfurt and only arriving at the funeral in Bonn. Before going to bed that evening, he is recorded as saying: 'Today I have buried the only woman I really loved.'[23] In 1880 Robert Schumann's tomb, for which Brahms had chosen the stone in 1857, had been replaced by a monumental tomb, for the inauguration of which there were two concerts directed by Joachim and Brahms. Brahms's Violin Concerto Op. 77 was the only work not by Schumann to feature in this programme – a public sign that Robert's hope of finding a successor in the Hamburg composer had been realised. In July 1896, Brahms sent Marie and Eugenie Schumann his *Four Serious*

---

[20] M. Heinemann, *Briefwechsel Clara Schumann mit dem Verlag Breitkopf & Härtel* (*Schumann-Briefedition* III.9) (Cologne: Dohr, 2015), 640.
[21] *SBB II*, 447, n. 2. [22] Düsseldorf, Heinrich-Heine-Institut: 84.5069.2.1.92.
[23] G. Ophüls, *Erinnerungen an Johannes Brahms* (Berlin: Verlag der Deutschen Brahms-Gesellschaft, 1921), 20.

THOMAS SYNOFZIK

Songs Op. 121 as a 'death offering to the memory of your dear mother'.[24] While Brahms always enjoyed, loved and respected Robert's music, he hoped in vain to fill Robert's place in Clara's life after his death. The fact that his love was not returned inevitably led to misunderstandings, but the friendship nevertheless endured.

Further Reading

G. Nauhaus, 'Brahms und Clara Schumann. Aspekte einer Lebens- und Arbeitspartnerschaft', in I. Fuchs (ed.), *Internationaler Brahms-Kongress Gmunden 1997* (Tutzing: Hans Schneider, 2001), 377–91

L. Roesner, 'Brahms's Editions of Schumann', in G. Bozarth (ed.), *Brahms Studies: Analytical and Historical Perspectives* (Oxford: Clarendon Press, 1990), 252–60

N. Reich, *Clara Schumann. The Artist and the Woman*, 2nd edn (Ithaca: Cornell University Press, 2001)

A. Schubring, 'Schumanniana No. 11. Die Schumann'sche Schule. Schumann und Brahms', *Allgemeine Musikalische Zeitung* 3/6 (5 February 1868), 41–2.

R. Schumann, *Tagebücher*, ed. G. Eismann and G. Nauhaus (Frankfurt am Main and Basel: Stroemfeld/Roter Stern, 1971–87)

E. Schumann, *The Schumanns and Johannes Brahms. The Memoirs of Eugenie Schumann* (New York: Dial Press, 1927)

---

[24] *SBB II*, 300.

CHAPTER 3

Vienna

Camille Crittenden

Brahms arrived in Vienna as an ambitious young musician, settled there in his early thirties and remained for the rest of his life. His flourishing career mirrored the dramatic transformation of the Habsburg Empire and its vibrant capital city during this period. Recent studies about creativity illuminate the historical, geographic and demographic circumstances that converged in late nineteenth-century Vienna to forge its special character. This chapter will explore the city where Brahms spent his most productive and influential decades, highlighting the unique opportunities the city and its intellectual elite provided to stimulate his greatest creative accomplishments.

Long an important crossroads of Europe, Vienna in the last half of the nineteenth century evolved rapidly as an urban metropolis and musical capital. Its population swelled nearly fourfold between 1857 and 1900, largely due to in-migration from farther reaches of the Habsburg Empire.[1] Attracted by jobs in construction and industry, as well as in services to the growing class of industrialists, bankers, real estate magnates and others benefiting from the growing city, new residents were themselves consumers of culture and goods. The city and empire enjoyed relative political stability under Emperor Franz Joseph, who ruled from 1848 until his death in 1916. However, the city's physical countenance changed dramatically, with the razing of the city wall, and creation of the Ringstrasse with its architectural tributes to the growing liberal class. Between 1860 and 1890, major civic buildings arose on the site of former battlements: City Hall (completed in 1883), Parliament (1883), the University (1884), as well as cultural institutions like the Court Opera (1869), Musikverein (1870), Burgtheater (1888) and the Museums of Art History and Natural History (1891). These edifices of civil society and the

---

[1] www.populstat.info/Europe/austriat.htm.

24   CAMILLE CRITTENDEN

arts would rival the existing monuments to traditional Austrian power centres: the Imperial court and the Catholic church.

Vienna also boasted a burgeoning cultural life to match these architectural monuments. Artists, musicians and writers flowed into the city, along with the business leaders and real estate investors who supported their activities. Brahms arrived in Vienna in autumn 1862, still hopeful that success abroad would lead to a job offer in his home town but, after failing to secure the directorship of the Hamburg Philharmonic for the second time, decided to make his home in Vienna in 1869. He wrote with trepidation to his father, who reassured him, 'Vienna is too important to exchange with Hamburg, where everyone has his eye only on business; [in] Vienna, [you will] find understanding and recognition to allow you to work and create. It is completely understandable that you struggle with yourself whether to live with us [in Hamburg]; this is your hometown.'[2] His father's death in 1872 strengthened Brahms's decision to settle permanently in Vienna. He accepted a position as director of the concerts of the Gesellschaft der Musikfreunde (where he served until 1875), and moved into a modest apartment in Karlsgasse 4, near the Musikverein, where he remained for the rest of his life.

Brahms enjoyed a wide and intellectually diverse circle of friends and acquaintances in Vienna. Physician Theodor Billroth, music critic Eduard Hanslick, composer Johann Strauss II, composer and critic Richard Heuberger, writers Ludwig Speidel and Daniel Spitzer: these were his closest friends in Vienna, and he maintained active correspondence with colleagues including Joseph Joachim, Clara Schumann, Hans von Bülow, Fritz Simrock and others throughout Europe. As he became more firmly established in Vienna, his social circles widened to include a range of civil servants, industrialists, lawyers, academics, artists and writers. Billroth, Hanslick and Strauss II were among Brahms's closest friends during the last decades of his life. An influential physician, Theodor Billroth was also a highly trained amateur musician and a kindred spirit to Brahms as a German Protestant making his home in Vienna; the two enjoyed a thirty-year friendship, despite some fraying in their relationship before Billroth's death in 1894. They sat side-by-side at countless dress rehearsals and premieres; Brahms sought Billroth's opinion on his own new works and dedicated his two String Quartets Op. 51 to him.

---

[2] Jakob Brahms to Johannes Brahms, 4 May 1869, K. Stephenson (ed.), *Johannes Brahms in seiner Familie. Der Briefwechsel* (Hamburg: Hauswedell, 1973), 160.

Vienna 25

Brahms, Billroth and Hanslick frequently attended evening musical salons and public performances together. Music critic for the *Neue Freie Presse* for thirty years, Hanslick became acquainted with Brahms soon after he arrived in Vienna in 1862, and Brahms surprised him by dedicating his Waltzes Op. 39 for piano duet to him several years later.[3] Hanslick fondly recalled playing four-hand arrangements with Billroth of Brahms's works in manuscript fair copy or as soon as they were published. He was also thrilled to be offered to address them with the intimate 'Du': 'It pleased me more than two medals!'[4]

Brahms and Hanslick were both close friends with Johann Strauss II, who lived only a mile from Brahms in Vienna's fourth district. Brahms always sought to attend premieres of Strauss's operettas and socialised frequently with him and his family in Vienna as well as on holiday in Bad Ischl. He admired Strauss's orchestration and technique as a conductor and introduced Strauss to his trusted Berlin publisher, Fritz Simrock, a relationship that proved rewarding for both parties. Brahms and Strauss remained pillars of Viennese musical life throughout the 1890s. At a birthday celebration for Strauss in October 1893, Brahms signed Adèle Strauss's fan with the opening strain of the Blue Danube Waltz and the comment 'Sadly, not by Johannes Brahms.'[5] Strauss attended the rehearsals of Brahms's new Clarinet Sonatas Op. 120 in January 1895, and Adèle invited Brahms to serve as a member of her daughter's wedding party the following year.[6] One of Brahms's last outings was to attend the premiere of Strauss's *Die Göttin der Vernunft* Op. 471 at the Theater an der Wien in March 1897. He died just three weeks later. An article in the *Neue Freie Presse* days after his death noted that Brahms died without heirs and cited the Strauss family residence as Brahms's second home.[7] Two years later Strauss's funeral would follow the same path as Brahms's, to the Evangelical Church and Central Cemetery, where they are buried in adjacent graves. The frontispiece of Strauss's *Seid umschlungen Millionen* Op. 443 shows a dedication to Brahms (Figure 3.1).

Brahms's extensive social circle may have played a role in his creative successes. In a theory first articulated in the early 1970s and popularised

---

[3] E. Hanslick, *Aus meinem Leben*, 2 vols. (Berlin: Hermann Paetel Verlag, 1911), vol. 2, 16.

[4] *Ibid.*, 94.

[5] Recounted in a report in the *Neues Wiener Journal*, Nr. 3 (1893), reprinted in F. Mailer (ed.) *Johann Strauss: Leben und Werk in Briefen und Dokumenten*, 10 vols. (Tutzing: Hans Schneider, 1983–2007), vol. 6, 450.

[6] *Heuberger*, 76 and 95.   [7] 'Johannes Brahms', *Neue Freie Presse* 11718 (6 April 1897), 5.

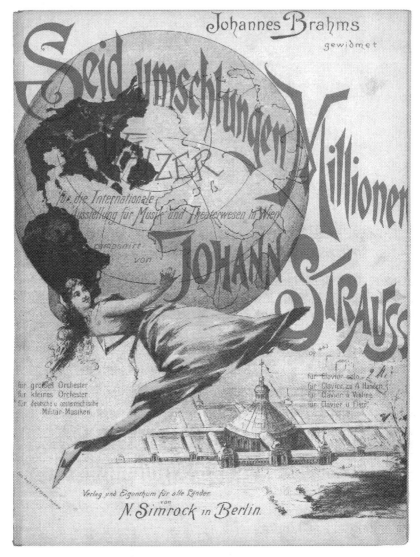

Figure 3.1. Strauss II, *Seid umschlungen Millionen* Op. 443 (Berlin: Simrock, 1892), frontispiece.

more recently by Malcolm Gladwell and others, creativity is enhanced by social networks that combine strong ties (close relationships with people seen frequently) and weak ties (a broader set of acquaintances from

Vienna 27

different social circles).[8] Studies devoted to the topic over the last forty years have added nuance, but the principle remains well regarded: 'The access to more non-redundant information and diverse social circles provided by weak ties should facilitate a variety of processes helpful for creativity.'[9] In Brahms's case, his intimate knowledge and love of Straussian waltzes or Hungarian and Czech folk music traditions surely encouraged him to incorporate these vernacular genres into his work. 'In addition, when an individual has connections with people who have different perceptions, expectations, or interests, he or she cannot easily, without reflection, make choices or come to decisions that are consistent with his or her contacts.'[10] Knowing that his works would receive a first hearing by friendly but knowledgeable critics such as Billroth, Hanslick and others would have encouraged Brahms to develop novel ideas. At the same time, strong ties like these provide trust to explore and develop new ideas with greater confidence.[11] Through his wide-ranging connections in Vienna, Brahms could scan the landscape for new ideas, test them with a range of potential audiences, and receive feedback from his inner circle.

Vienna also offered Brahms access to high-quality performances in a range of musical styles and genres: chamber music, opera, symphonic music, choral music, popular music, operetta and more. Brahms benefited directly and indirectly from artistic institutions like the Gesellschaft der Musikfreunde and Wiener Singakademie; they offered Brahms short-term appointments, performed his music and provided a lively cohort of fellow musicians. Many genres were accessible not only in public concerts but in the homes of friends and colleagues – reading through new string quartets, songs, piano reductions and other arrangements. Indeed, Brahms appreciated that music and culture were integral to city life in Vienna, a perception enhanced by his travels throughout German-speaking Europe. For example, he scorned the residents of Munich for caring only about beer and food and speculated that even artists born there lived as if in a foreign country. In 1885, he contrasted this attitude with that of the Viennese: 'I am interested in them and they are interested in me.'[12]

---

[8] M. S. Granovetter, 'The Strength of Weak Ties', *American Journal of Sociology* 78 (1973), 1360–80; M. Gladwell, 'Small Change: Why the Revolution Will Not Be Tweeted', *The New Yorker* (4 October 2010), 42–9.

[9] J. E. Perry-Smith and C. E. Shalley, 'The Social Side of Creativity: A Static and Dynamic Social Network Perspective', *The Academy of Management Review* 28/1 (January 2003), 94.

[10] *Ibid.*

[11] B. H. Kevyn Yong, 'Creativity and Social Networks: The Relational Advantage of Strong Ties', PhD thesis, Cornell University (2008), 7–8.

[12] *Heuberger*, 28.

Vienna supported a variety of venues for popular music: dance halls, suburban theatres, park bandstands and the like. In addition to the mainstream institutions of the Court Opera and Musikverein, theatres outside the Ringstrasse also had lively schedules. The Theater an der Wien, for example, featured operetta by local composers (Johann Strauss, Carl Millöcker, Franz von Suppé) and visitors (Jacques Offenbach), contemporary satirical theatre by Johann Nestroy, performances by visiting companies from France and Germany, and individual benefit concerts. Wagner gave afternoon concerts in December 1862 and January 1863, featuring pieces from operas that had not yet been produced in Vienna (*Die Meistersinger von Nürnberg, Das Rheingold, Die Walküre, Siegfried*). Brahms attended the Wagner concerts and expressed regard especially for *Die Meistersinger*.

No other city in Europe boasted such an abundance of musical professionals as in Vienna. Among European countries between 1650 and 1850, Austria was home to the most composers, both native and immigrant, proportional to its population.[13] This saturation also required an infrastructure of related artists, craftspeople and small businesses, such as teachers, instrument makers, publishers and sheet music vendors. Vienna was a centre of piano manufacturing: Graf, Stein and Streicher were based in the city, and Bösendorfer established headquarters there by mid-century . By 1800 some sixty piano makers had workshops in the city, providing instruments for homes and concert halls all over Europe. Makers of stringed and wind instruments were also prevalent in Vienna and other cities of the Austro-Hungarian Empire, evidenced, for example, by the list of exhibitors for the 1851 Great Exhibition in Britain.[14] Documentation of musical life was fuelled by a ravenous appetite for music criticism. Following the democratic uprisings of 1848, the number of newspapers and periodicals soared. As many as ninety daily newspapers were produced in Vienna during the latter half of the nineteenth century, many of which included arts criticism as a matter of course.

Keenly aware of musical heritage, Brahms was also attracted to Vienna for its historical resonances of Haydn, Beethoven and Schubert, whose manuscripts he avidly collected and edited for publication [see Ch. 12 'As Editor']. When he began lengthening his stays in Vienna in the early 1860s, he

---

[13] F. M. Scherer, *Quarter Notes and Bank Notes: The Economics of Music Composition in the Eighteenth and Nineteenth Centuries* (Princeton & Oxford: Princeton University Press, 2004), 122 and 133.

[14] R. Ellis et al. (eds.), *Great Exhibition of the Works of Industry of all Nations, 1851. Official Descriptive and Illustrated Catalogue*, 3 vols. (London: Spicer Brothers & W. Clowes and Sons, Printers, 1851), vol. 3, 1014–15.

Figure 3.2. Construction site of the new Court Opera on Vienna's Ringstrasse with Heinrichshof building, c. 1863.

remarked upon 'the sacred memory of the great musicians, whose life and work here one is reminded of every day. That's particularly true of Schubert, of whom one has the sensation that he is still alive! One keeps meeting new people who speak of him as a close acquaintance.'[15] Just months before he died, he recalled: 'It never occurred to me that these people had *written* all this down; when I came here and saw so many manuscripts by Schubert and Beethoven, it gave me a most uncanny feeling.'[16]

As exciting as it may have been to live in a city undergoing massive population growth and construction (see Figure 3.2), the stimulation was likely also stressful for Vienna's residents. The proximity of natural settings appealed to Brahms, who took long walks of up to eighteen kilometres at weekends in the wooded hills around Vienna (in Nussdorf and Rodaun). He enjoyed spending time in the nearby Prater park in evenings, strolling and listening to popular music by the Schrammel quartet and other local artists. The capacity to move easily between

---

[15] Brahms to Adolf Schubring, 26 March 1863, *Avins*, 276.   [16] *Heuberger*, 120.

urban and rural environments surely contributed to his creative and intellectual accomplishments.[17]

Still, despite Vienna's superficial conviviality, Brahms was also attuned to the sinister undercurrent of intolerance which threatened to overwhelm the cultural and artistic accomplishments of the city in the next century. He became increasingly disturbed by the emerging anti-Semitism and adherence to narrow Catholicism. As a Protestant [see Ch. 26 'Politics and Religion'], Brahms belonged to a smaller religious minority in Vienna than the Jews (roughly 10 per cent of Vienna's population in the late nineteenth century); he was also close friends with many prominent Jewish leaders and thinkers. In May 1895, he denounced the recent advances that Karl Lueger's Christian Social Party had made in the city government. At a dinner with Eusebius Mandyczewski, Victor von Müller zu Aichholz, Anton Door, Julius Epstein and Richard Heuberger, Brahms expressed outrage that Lueger had become vice-mayor and soon would become mayor. He said he had warned of this possibility in the past and his warnings were laughed off, but now the circumstance had come true: 'If there were an "anti-priest party" that would make sense, but "anti-Semitism" is nonsense!'[18] The leadership transition Brahms feared came to pass and Lueger became mayor of Vienna in 1897, shortly before Brahms's death.

Brahms took umbrage on behalf of his musical colleagues and friends who were slighted by the establishment on moral or religious grounds. Noting that neither a court or city official nor sitting or previous president of the Musikverein attended the fiftieth anniversary celebration of Johann Strauss II's career, he speculated that it was because Strauss had converted to Protestantism in order to divorce his second wife; therefore, some considered his marriage to his third wife Adèle illegal. Probably for this reason, too, Strauss received no medal from the city on the occasion.[19] Brahms also remarked with disdain on the Gesellschaft der Musikfreunde's decision to deny Gustav Mahler a director's post because he was Jewish.[20]

A combination of adherence to convention and civic pride compelled city and cultural leaders to overturn Brahms's instructions to be cremated and buried in Gotha, one of two cemeteries in Germany with a crematorium, and bury him instead in Vienna's Central Cemetery. The notice in the

---

[17] R. A. Atchley, D. L. Strayer and P. Atchley, 'Creativity in the Wild: Improving Creative Reasoning through Immersion in Natural Settings', *PLoS One*, published 12 December 2012, https://doi.org/10.1371/journal.pone.0051474.

[18] *Heuberger*, 82, note from 16 May 1895. Despite his protests, Brahms retained his German citizenship and would not have been eligible to vote in Viennese elections.

[19] *Ibid.*, 72.   [20] *Ibid.*, 83.

Wiener Zeitung on 4 April described his deathbed scene and announced that the funeral would take place two days later in the Evangelical Church. In the meantime, representatives of the Gesellschaft der Musikfreunde decided whether to follow Brahms's burial wishes.[21] According to an article in the *Neue Freie Presse* following the meeting, the men decided not to cremate the body: '[the notion of] *burning* [his corpse] was *abandoned*'.[22] Interestingly, discussion of cremation was already current in the 1870s, and Brahms and Billroth mocked the idea at the time,[23] yet Brahms requested precisely this in a letter to his publisher and executor Fritz Simrock, intending to amend his will seventeen years later. Although the letter's legality was contested and the settlement of Brahms's estate took many years, he insisted: 'Finally, as to myself, I wish that my body will be cremated. Arrange it so that the expenses, of course, will be taken from my wealth.'[24]

Recent theories regarding the relationship between cities and creativity have sought to identify common characteristics of the most vibrant urban environments: a combination of city hardware (urban infrastructure such as roads, sewers, buildings), software (human organisations and networks) and 'third spaces' (parks or cafés) that are neither home nor work.[25] These qualities aptly describe late nineteenth-century Vienna. The city was implementing new technology in civil engineering, design, electrification and communication; the relative political stability and centrality as capital of a vast polyglot empire attracted leaders to create and invest in new civic and cultural institutions; and, although the city would not be described as 'tolerant' for long, it managed to accommodate an enormous influx of people from the farthest reaches of the empire. Brahms and his circle benefited from these trends, and their legacy reflects the multiple linked contributions of the city's residents to its unique cultural history.

Further Reading

O. Biba, 'Brahms in Wien', in C. Floros, H. J. Marx and P. Petersen (eds.), *Brahms und seine Zeit: Symposium Hamburg 1983* (Laaber: Laaber Verlag, 1984), 259–71

[21] Anon, 'Kleine Chronik: Dr. Johannes Brahms †', *Wiener Zeitung*, 77 (4 April 1897), 3.
[22] 'Johannes Brahms', *Neue Freie Presse* 11717 (5 April 1897), 3. Emphasis in original. The passive voice of formal German syntax erases the agency of the men making a decision that contravened Brahms's expressed wishes.
[23] See correspondence of November 1874 in O. Gottlieb-Billroth (ed.), *Billroth und Brahms im Briefwechsel* (Berlin and Vienna: Urban & Schwarzenberg, 1935), 214–5.
[24] See *Kalbeck IV*, 228–30.
[25] C. Landry, *The Creative City: A Toolkit for Urban Innovators* (London: Earthscan, 2008), xxiii.

32   CAMILLE CRITTENDEN

L. Botstein, 'Time and Memory: Concert Life, Science, and Music in Brahms's Vienna', in W. Frisch and K. C. Karnes (eds.), *Brahms and His World*, 2nd edn (Princeton: Princeton University Press, 2009), 3–22

K. Karnes, *Music, Criticism, and the Challenge of History: Shaping Modern Musical Thought in Late Nineteenth-Century Vienna* (Oxford: Oxford University Press, 2008)

S. McColl, *Music Criticism in Vienna, 1896–1897* (Oxford: Clarendon Press, 1996)

M. Musgrave, 'Years of Transition: Brahms and Vienna 1862–1875', in M. Musgrave (ed.), *The Cambridge Companion to Brahms* (Cambridge: Cambridge University Press, 1999), 31–50

C. E. Schorske, *Fin-de-Siècle Vienna: Politics and Culture* (New York: Vintage Books, 1981)

CHAPTER 4

Leipzig and Berlin

Karen Leistra-Jones

Robert Schumann's 1853 essay 'New Paths' is famous for its prophetic introduction of the young Johannes Brahms to the wider German musical community. In this, his last piece of published criticism, Schumann presented Brahms, then a virtually unknown young composer, as a Messiah-like figure for a nascent musical era, one who would be called to 'give the highest expression to the times in an ideal manner'.[1] The final sentence of Schumann's essay has often been overlooked, but it is significant for the glimpse that it offers of the place that he envisioned for Brahms in the future: 'In every era there presides a secret league of kindred spirits. Draw the circle tighter, you who belong together, that the truth of art may shine ever more clearly, spreading joy and blessings everywhere!'[2] [see Ch. 31 'Germany'].

Schumann's article was prophetic, then, not only for the way it forecast Brahms's future centrality in German musical life but also for the way that it positioned him among what Schumann called his 'comrades', a league reminiscent of the older composer's earlier *Davidsbund* that was dedicated to advancing an ideal vision of art. Indeed, contrary to the common view of Brahms as a solitary Romantic figure, the composer throughout his life was embedded within various overlapping social circles that played a crucial role in his professional and creative life. Some of his most important and enduring friendships originated in the circle of musicians around the Schumanns in the 1850s, but over the years his network expanded across German-speaking Europe and came to include professional musicians as well as accomplished amateurs and members of other learned professions. Many of these friends were members of the educated elite of their respective cities, and, as Schumann had predicted, they felt a sense of kinship and mission through their idealistic view of music, in which Brahms occupied a key position.

[1] R. Schumann, 'Neue Bahnen', *Neue Zeitschrift für Musik* 39/18 (28 October 1853), 185.
[2] *Ibid.*, 186.

Particularly important in Brahmsian circles was the feeling of connection that the act of making music together afforded [see Ch. 14 'Private Music-Making']. Playing chamber music and reading through four-hand piano arrangements deepened the bonds of friendship, while enjoying Brahms's music in his absence engendered a sense of spiritual and emotional connection with him. In turn, such relationships provided the bachelor Brahms with personal and musical fellowship and with welcoming hosts and communities when he was on tour. Just as significant, however, was the work that these far-flung friends performed in advancing the cause of Brahms's music in cities where he may otherwise have been unknown or unwelcome. Such work included organisation and advocacy as well as musical performance, and it shows that the ideals of Schumann's imagined league were alive and well even decades after his death. This was particularly apparent in Leipzig and Berlin, two of the most influential German musical centres when Brahms was at the height of his career from the 1870s onward.

Notoriously, Leipzig had been the site of a major professional trauma in Brahms's early career. In 1859, he had appeared at the Gewandhaus as the soloist in his First Piano Concerto Op. 15, which had been received with outright hostility by the Leipzig public and critics. Hisses had greeted the young composer at the work's conclusion, and it was subsequently eviscerated in the Leipzig musical press. After one last unsuccessful appearance in that city with a performance of his Second Serenade Op. 16 in November 1860, Brahms completely withdrew from Leipzig; he would not appear there again until 1874. That year, however, marked a sea change in Brahms's relationship to the city. Following an unexpected invitation from the board of the Gewandhaus, he arrived in Leipzig to preside over a 'Brahms week' between 29 January and 5 February, at which several of his chamber, vocal and orchestral works were performed. By all accounts, the week was a critical and social success for Brahms and a crucial event that opened the door to his future presence in the city.[3]

But why the change in Brahms's status? Certainly, the widespread success of *A German Requiem* Op. 45 in 1868 had considerably improved his reputation in Germany. But as various biographical sources show, Brahms's new acceptance in Leipzig was not merely the result of the city's conservative musical establishment being converted through renewed

---

[3] *Kalbeck III*, 4–11.

Figure 4.1. Elisabeth von Herzogenberg, photographed by Wilhelm Robert Eich, Dresden, 1860s.

exposure to his music. Rather, the success of the Brahms week was the result of months of planning and promotion on the part of a select group of friends and supporters. Foremost among these were Elisabeth and Heinrich von Herzogenberg (see Figures 4.1 and 4.2). The couple had become acquainted with Brahms in Vienna in the 1860s and were both admirers of his music. In 1872 they had moved to Leipzig, where, as Max Kalbeck described it, Heinrich's thoughts quickly turned to 'paying public homage' to Brahms, the composer that 'he so enthusiastically revered, who so far had not yet been treated with honour in the concert rooms of "Little Paris"'.[4] One of the first steps in righting this injustice was his arrangement of a matinée in May of

---

[4] *Briefe I*, xviii.

Figure 4.2. Heinrich von Herzogenberg, photographed by Wilhelm Robert Eich, Dresden, 1860s.

1873 at which Brahms's Piano Quintet Op. 34 was performed, with Elisabeth, a musician of near-professional calibre, playing the piano part.

Significantly, though, the Herzogenbergs were not alone in their Brahms evangelism. Since their arrival in the city, they had cultivated social and professional connections among the city's musical elite, eventually assuming a central role. Indeed, in Kalbeck's telling, it was a 'small community of Brahms-worshippers' led by the Herzogenbergs that built on other developments in order to make the Brahms week happen.[5] This

---

[5] *Ibid.*, xix. Clara Schumann had played Brahms's First Piano Concerto Op. 15 at the Gewandhaus to a respectful audience in 1873; Karl Riedel had directed repeated performances of *A German Requiem* Op. 45 in 1873; and Hermann Kretzschmar wrote a series of appreciative articles on Brahms's music in the Leipzig *Musikalisches Wochenblatt* that appeared between January and March 1874 and discussed several of the works that were performed during the Brahms week.

Leipzig and Berlin

group, which Ethel Smyth, in her account of Leipzig's social life in the 1870s, called 'the Artists', was a rarefied set of connoisseurs within the larger circle of Gewandhaus subscription holders. It included the composer Franz von Holstein and his wife Hedwig, the orchestral director Alfred Volkland and the musicologist Philip Spitta, a friend and correspondent of Brahms. These men were professionally linked through their founding (with Heinrich von Herzogenberg) of the Leipzig Bach-Verein in 1875. The group also included the publisher Wilhelm Engelmann; Livia Frege, a friend of Clara Schumann's and a former professional singer who had married a wealthy banker; Lily Wach, Mendelssohn's youngest daughter; and her husband Adolf, a professor of law who was (in Ethel Smyth's words) 'notoriously musical'.

These people regularly gathered in each other's homes to make and discuss music, and the Holstein, Wach, Frege and Herzogenberg homes were particular centres of activity.[6] As Florence May implied in her biography of Brahms, advocacy in such elite homes was crucial to the acceptance of a composer in Leipzig; as she noted, Brahms's lack of a presence in the city during the 1860s can at least partly be attributed to the fact that during those years there was virtually 'no active "Brahms" propaganda in the houses of wealthy amateurs'.[7]

It is in this context that Elisabeth von Herzogenberg assumed an influential role. Kalbeck's account assigned her husband, Heinrich, central agency in converting Leipzig to Brahms, maintaining that Elisabeth's effect was limited by her primary status as a *Hausfrau*.[8] And yet it was precisely talents in the traditionally feminine realms of social diplomacy and private performance that were crucial to advocacy in these domestic circles. Elisabeth appeared often as a pianist in Leipzig's overlapping public and private musical spheres; her letters show that she was also an extraordinarily astute communicator *about* music; and accounts from her friends describe her as having a particularly endearing way of interacting with others, one that was often able to inspire devotion. She may not have (in Kalbeck's words) 'converted the unbelievers *en masse*' to Brahms, but in the exclusive world of Leipzig's *Bildungselite*, she undoubtedly had a profound effect in generating enthusiasm for his music.

These elites came together to celebrate Brahms's appearance in Leipzig; during the whole week, he was entertained and fêted in their houses.

---

[6] For a vivid description of this group's position in Leipzig social life at the time, see E. Smyth, *Impressions that Remained: Memoirs* (London: Longmans, Green, and Co., 1919), 184–200.
[7] *May II*, 134.   [8] *Kalbeck III*, 7.

Notably, though, his success among these circles did not translate immediately into widespread popular enthusiasm. Clara Schumann, who travelled from Berlin for the occasion, described the Gewandhaus audience as, 'like all our northern publics, dull, only in the songs and [Hungarian] dances did it become somewhat lively. Incidentally, one could say that Johannes's reception was good - the goodwill of musicians, and especially music-lovers - he was truly celebrated in private circles.'[9]

While the adulation in 1874 was limited to a small group, these circles clearly had a gradual broader effect on the acceptance of Brahms in Leipzig. The Gewandhaus concerts were a small world; tickets went almost exclusively to subscription holders, a group of about forty families linked to each other through marriage, business and social connections. Even in the open rehearsals, music was experienced in a relatively intimate setting: the hall's capacity in the 1870s was only around 500 seats. The reception of his First Symphony Op. 68 in Leipzig in 1877 shows how influential the enthusiasm of Leipzig's 'Brahms-worshippers' could be, especially when their ranks were augmented by other supporters. On this occasion, Clara Schumann, Amalie Joachim, Julius Stockhausen, Fritz Simrock and other Brahmsians descended on Leipzig. In the Leipzig *Signale für die musikalische Welt*, the critic Eduard Bernsdorf described how:

> an official Brahms-Party meeting was organised, in which the local supporters and devotees of the composer were joined by a fairly strong contingent from out of town. It is therefore a matter of course that the enthusiasm with which the work was received was enormous, and that the success of the symphony was one of only rarely occurring greatness in the annals of the Gewandhaus.[10]

To be sure, Brahms's success was far from universal: Bernsdorf's review of the symphony was cool, and even Florence May noted that the symphony's success was still 'not very warmly helped by the official patrons of the Gewandhaus'.[11] But nevertheless, the city had become a significant site in Brahms's career. Subsequently, the composer visited Leipzig every winter until 1882 and regularly thereafter, and chose the city for important early performances of many of his best-known works.

The 1870s also marked a turning point in Brahms's status in Berlin. While not outright hostile to Brahms, the city's musical establishment had been overwhelmingly oriented toward historical repertories, despite Hans

---

[9] Clara Schumann to Hermann Levi, 11 February 1874, *Litzmann III*, 310–11.
[10] E. Bernsdorf, 'Dur und Moll', *Signale für die Musikalische Welt* 35/7 (January 1877), 100.
[11] *May II*, 154.

Leipzig and Berlin

von Bülow's attempt in the 1860s to establish it as a centre for the New German School. Again, however, the enthusiasm and advocacy of Brahms's friends in Berlin proved crucial in securing his new prominence. During the 1870s several of Brahms's closest friends settled in the city, some of whom made Berlin their home for the decades to come. These included the singer Julius Stockhausen (1874–8), Clara Schumann (1873–8), Brahms's publisher Fritz Simrock (who moved his firm to Berlin in 1870), Philip Spitta (1875–94) and Joseph and Amalie Joachim, who moved to Berlin in 1868. In 1885 the Herzogenbergs also relocated to the city, and the 1880s saw the arrival of another powerful Brahms advocate in Hans von Bülow, who broadcast his new allegiance to Brahms through his piano recitals, his tours as director of the Meiningen Court Orchestra and later his programming as director of the Berlin Philharmonic. Promoting Brahms remained as much a concern in these Berlin circles as it did among the Leipzig Brahmsians, but their activities also reflected substantial differences in the cultural and demographic profiles of Leipzig and Berlin. At roughly eight times the size of Leipzig, Berlin at the time was well on its way to becoming a modern metropolis, and its establishment as the capital of the German Empire in 1871 also made it into an administrative and political hub. Thus, while Brahms advocacy in Berlin was pursued through many of the channels familiar from Leipzig, it also relied more heavily on public, institutionalised networks of power at a time when music was taking on a crucial role in defining the cultural identity of the young empire.

As in Leipzig, the members of the Berlin Brahms circle gathered frequently to socialise and make music in private and semi-private settings. Such settings could include intimate gatherings at each other's houses, but they also included larger occasions such as the renowned musical matinees held regularly at Simrock's house. At these events, a sizeable group of musicians and music-lovers would gather in the grand music room of Simrock's elegant residence in order to hear new music by composers associated with the firm – Brahms's music featured prominently – as well as other classic works.[12] These were serious, exclusive, yet convivial gatherings that had deep roots in Berlin's celebrated salon culture, and they reinforced the sense of group identity and shared values of those who participated. Central to this culture was the ideal of *Bildung*, an ongoing

---

[12] A detailed description of a matinee at Simrock's can be found in Robert Lienau's unpublished *Ich erzähle. Erinnerungen eines alten Musikverlegers* (1942), quoted in B. Borchard, *Stimme und Geige: Amalie und Joseph Joachim: Biographie und Interpretationsgeschichte* (Vienna: Böhlau, 2005), 289–90.

40 KAREN LEISTRA-JONES

and deliberate cultivation of an individual's intellectual, aesthetic and moral faculties through engagement with art and ideas. Bruno Walter, born in Berlin in 1876, described the importance of the *Bildungsideal* to Berlin's music-loving circles:

> Those were not yet the days of mechanical inventions, when the mere turning of a knob would provide a ready-made home delivery of Beethoven's Ninth Symphony ... Life's musical enrichment was a thing to be worked for. The raising of the cultural level through the ennobling influence of music was part of the educational program of almost every middle-class family. Musical appreciation was thus not only a general possession, but also a very personal and highly valued one because it had been gained by years of individual endeavour.[13]

Significantly, the middle-class *Bildungselite* that Walter describes often strongly identified with the aesthetic and expressive qualities of Brahms's music, music that needed to be studied and heard repeatedly in order to be understood, and whose contrapuntal and formal rigour seemed to affirm their values of reason and self-discipline. For this group, a love for Brahms was often cast in direct opposition to Wagner, who was thought to encourage a mode of listening based less on education and reason than on immediate emotional and sensual responses and thereby address a broader, populist audience distinct from the cultivated elites that Walter described. The existence of such circles proved a fertile ground for the introduction of Brahms's music by his friends; indeed, Walter described these same groups' 'quiet but determined repudiation' of Wagner which drew 'vital strength ... from a positive attitude toward Brahms, around whom they gathered and whom they had raised up as Wagner's counter-idol'.[14]

Joseph Joachim came to be a central figure in this world, and his activities show important connections between the Brahms-loving *Bildungselite* and the networks of political and economic power that formed in Berlin following the founding of the German Empire in 1871. In 1869, at the request of the Prussian Ministry of Education, he had founded and assumed the directorship of the Berlin Königliche Hochschule für Musik. The school was envisioned by Joachim and by the authorities who hired him not only as the training ground for musicians but as an institution that would raise the profile of musical life in Berlin, educating the people while carefully curating the tradition of

[13] B. Walter, *Theme and Variations: An Autobiography* (New York: Alfred A. Knopf, 1946), 25–6.
[14] *Ibid.*, 26.

Leipzig and Berlin   41

German music in the Prussian capital. The directorship of the Hochschule combined with Joachim's pre-existing fame evidently opened doors for him. Early on in his tenure, Joachim was invited to an intimate evening with prominent Berlin aristocrats and politicians, including Heinrich von Treitschke and members of the Bismarck family; in an account, he expressed surprise at how easily he was assimilated into this circle, and, indeed, throughout his career he demonstrated a notable ability to cultivate friends and patrons among those in powerful positions.[15] These private relationships helped to garner support for his work with the Hochschule, as can be seen from Joachim's account to his brother Heinrich of the first concert that he directed with the Hochschule Orchestra on 11 May 1871. He described the event as an enormous success among the 400 or so listeners who attended. Significantly, he noted that he himself had invited these listeners from a variety of spheres: military, academic, government, court, merchants and so forth. He mentioned this to his brother because, in his words, 'it is favourable for our endeavour that the highest circles are interested in it'.[16]

To Joachim, 'our endeavour' meant not only the success of the Hochschule, but the musical ideals that he wished to promote through it. With the support of these 'highest circles' in the new capital of the German Empire, Joachim was able to advocate effectively for his own vision of a German musical tradition, a vision that explicitly positioned Brahms as Beethoven's heir and successor and erected barriers against Wagnerism. He staffed the Hochschule with known Brahms supporters such as Spitta, Heinrich von Herzogenberg and the pianist Ernst Rudorff, and generally suppressed Wagner, Liszt and other 'progressives' in the institution's teaching and programming.

Furthermore, his celebrated 'Quartet Evenings' pointedly situated Brahms's chamber music within an emerging canon. From 1869 until his death in 1907, Joachim and his quartet appeared in an annual series of eight concerts at the Singakademie. These concerts were overtly 'classical' in their orientation, with repertory drawn overwhelmingly from Austro-German composers of the past. Beethoven was by far the most frequently performed composer, with 323 performances of his works, followed by Haydn (174), Mozart (108) and Schubert (63).[17] And, as Beatrix Borchard

---

[15] Joseph to Amalie Joachim, November 1871, J. Joachim and A. Moser (eds.) *Briefe von und an Joseph Joachim*, 3 vols. (Berlin: Julius Bard, 1913), vol. 3, 80–1.

[16] Joseph Joachim to Heinrich Joachim, [12 May 1872], quoted in Borchard, *Stimme und Geige*, 307.

[17] This data, along with the programmes that included Brahms's music, appears on the CD-ROM accompanying Borchard's *Stimme und Geige*.

has noted, works by contemporary composers were rarities, often consigned to 'novelty' evenings.[18] Brahms, however, was the crucial exception. His works were performed seventy-three times in the Quartet Evenings, and this included premieres of several of his chamber works. These works were not performed in 'novelty' evenings but rather were integrated into evenings devoted to canonic composers, often placed alongside Beethoven's music, and repeated over the years in order to give the audience ample opportunities to assimilate the works. Indeed, for Joachim, the 'mission' that his quartet fulfilled was clear: increasing understanding for Beethoven's late quartets and 'advocacy for Brahms'.[19] These, in the words of his biography that he co-wrote with Andreas Moser, were 'good services which Joachim rendered his "comrade-at-arms"'.[20]

Joachim's language is reminiscent of Schumann's league of kindred spirits in 'New Paths', and points to the larger cultural and political goals of these Brahms circles in Leipzig and Berlin. These groups were linked not just by an idea that Brahms's music needed to be given a hearing; they also shared the idea that the 'true art' his music represented needed to be fought for. Cities needed to be won over, and boundaries against lesser music needed to be maintained ('draw the circle tighter') in order for Brahms's music to prevail. Significantly, these groups coalesced when Brahms's position in an enduring pantheon of German composers was not yet assured, and their activities took place during decades in which Wagner, Liszt and the adherents of the New German School were articulating a compelling counter-vision for the future of German music and had their own geographic strongholds in locations such as Weimar, Munich and Bayreuth. This context sheds light on the rhetoric of struggle and border maintenance that we often find associated with these circles, from Elisabeth von Herzogenberg's discomfort at having Bruckner 'forced upon' Leipzig music-lovers like a 'compulsory vaccination' that needed to be resisted,[21] to Bruno Walter's impression, as a student in Berlin in the 1890s, that the Hochschule functioned as a 'fortress' of anti-Wagnerianism.[22] For these Brahmsians, advocacy for their master's music was nothing less than a battle for the souls of audiences and the right, in Schumann's words, to 'give the highest expression to the times'. They pursued their cause with passion, and that Brahms was ultimately able to fulfil

---

[18] *Ibid.*, 535.
[19] A. Moser, *Joseph Joachim, Ein Lebensbild*, 2 vols. (Berlin: B. Behr, 1898), vol. 2, 239.
[20] *Ibid.*, 240–1.   [21] Elisabeth von Herzogenberg to Brahms, 5 January 1885, *Briefe II*, 48.
[22] Walter, *Theme and Variations*, 25–6.

Leipzig and Berlin 43

Schumann's prophecies speaks as much to the zeal of these circles of friends as it does to the undeniable power of his music.

Further Reading

C. Applegate and P. Potter, 'Germans as the "People of Music": Genealogy of an Identity', in C. Applegate and P. Potter (eds.), *Music and German National Identity* (Chicago: University of Chicago Press, 2002), 1–35

P. Berry, *Brahms among Friends: Listening, Performance, and the Rhetoric of Allusion* (New York: Oxford University Press, 2014)

R. Eshbach, 'The Joachim Quartet Concerts at the Berlin Singakademie: Mendelssohnian Geselligkeit in Wilhelmine Germany', in K. Hamilton and N. Loges, *Brahms in the Home and the Concert Hall* (Cambridge: Cambridge University Press, 2014), 22–42

J. Forner, '*In Leipzig war's aber doch am schönsten': Johannes Brahms und seine Beziehung zu Leipzig* (Leipzig: Hofmeister, 2007)

M. Notley, *Lateness and Brahms: Music and Culture in the Twilight of Viennese Liberalism* (New York: Oxford University Press, 2006)

A. Ruhbaum, *Elisabeth von Herzogenberg: Salon – Mäzenatentum – Musikförderung* (Kenzingen: Centaurus Verlag, 2009)

M. Sumner Lott, *The Social Worlds of Nineteenth-Century Chamber Music: Composers, Consumers, Communities* (Chicago: University of Illinois Press, 2015)

CHAPTER 5

Personal Habits

William Horne

We know a great deal about Brahms's professional activities, thoughts about music and musicians, and general views on politics and culture, from his voluminous surviving correspondence. These letters and the reminiscences of his friends also trace his personal habits – what his daily routine was like, his enjoyment of food, drink, and tobacco, his delight in pranks and walking in the outdoors, his peculiar attire and occasional curmudgeonliness.

Generally speaking, Brahms was a man of simple and regular habits. The journalist Josef Viktor Widmann, a close friend in Brahms's middle and later years, provided a description of his typical summer routine in the Swiss Alpine town of Thun:

> Already up and about at the break of dawn, he brewed himself his first breakfast on his Viennese coffee machine ... The morning hours were dedicated to work, which turned out especially well in the Thun dwelling where a large porch and a suite of interconnected, spacious rooms permitted him to pace about thinking, undisturbed by anyone ... At midday Brahms took a meal, if the weather to some extent permitted it, in the garden of any old tavern; all his life he detested *table d'hôte* dining ...[1]

After lunch, Brahms would often go for a stroll, stop at a café to read the papers and dine in the evening with friends. His daily routine in winter was less regular owing to the demands of travel during the concert season, but when in Vienna he liked to eat with friends at simple places such as the restaurant *Roter Igel* and attend a play, a concert or an opera in the evening. He was a man of remarkable energy who often stayed out quite late. George Henschel recalled first meeting Brahms in May of 1874 at the Lower Rhine Music Festival in Cologne:

---

[1] J. V. Widmann, *Erinnerungen an Johannes Brahms* (Zurich: Rotapfel-Verlag, 1980), 55–6.

Personal Habits

> In the evening ... I found myself sitting with Brahms in a *Kneipe* [pub] – one of those cosy restaurants, redolent of the mixed perfumes of beer, wine, tobacco, coffee, and food ... Brahms was very fond of sitting with good friends over his beer or wine or his beloved *Kaffee* ... in the *Kneipe* till the small hours of the day.[2]

These are the habits of a man who enjoyed companionship. Sociable dining among friends was important to the lifelong bachelor, and even in his younger years he enjoyed being invited into the homes of sympathetic musicians, where he could discuss things that interested him more fruitfully than at his parents' board. Charlotte Avé-Lallemant, the oldest daughter of the influential Hamburg musician Theodor Avé-Lallemant, recalls that in the late 1850s and early 1860s, 'Often [Brahms] came to dinner in the summertime around four o'clock, then went strolling with Father and came back again to supper with Father. Sometimes they brought along knockwursts that Mother heated up for them; it was a favourite food of Brahms, and he looked forward to it like a child.'[3] Clara Brandt, daughter of the Hamburg merchant Carl August Brandt, whose wife Auguste served as chaperone for Brahms's Hamburg Ladies' Choir, recalled how he would come frequently to dine in their home: 'One time the meal brought forth *Kartoffelfrikadellen* with prunes, and this dish met with so much approval from Johannes that he later said several times on entering the house: "I smell it, I smell it, today there are *Kartoffelfrikadellen*," whereupon these were then immediately prepared for him.'[4] (Kartoffelfrikadellen are a versatile dish made from mashed potatoes, eggs and butter, spiced, if desired, with onions and garlic, combined with other ingredients such as salami, bacon or tomatoes, shaped into thick, biscuit-sized pancakes and baked or fried. Fortunately, Clara Brandt preserved the recipe that Brahms enjoyed.)

Brahms always delighted in such plain fare. Later in his career, the opulent homes of prominent aristocrats, princes of banking and industry and distinguished, upper-middle-class writers and intellectuals were open to him. Florentine ('Flore') Luithlen-Kalbeck, daughter of Brahms's friend and biographer Max Kalbeck, and later a concert singer who appeared in Vienna with such renowned conductors as Bruno Walter and Ferdinand Löwe, recalled such gatherings from her childhood:

---

[2] G. Bozarth, *Johannes Brahms & George Henschel: An Enduring Friendship* (Sterling Heights, Mich.: Harmonie Park Press, 2008), 13.

[3] Quoted in R. and K. Hofmann, *Johannes Brahms Privat: Tafelfreuden und Geselligkeit* (Heide: Boyens, 2002), 11.

[4] *Ibid.*, 11–13.

46 WILLIAM HORNE

> In my mind's eye I see a well-stocked table full of variegated glasses and
> bottles. Father walks about and keeps on filling the guests' glasses . . . There
> at the head of the table sits the uncle with the long, white-flowing beard.
> The laughter with which he signs receipts for jokes roars its way out to us.
> Yes, Uncle Brahms can drink and eat! Mother would have a big herring salad
> made for him and he would spoon the whole dish empty, because he loved it
> so.[5]

Florentine Kalbeck's childhood moniker for 'Uncle Brahms', doubtless instigated by her parents, the preparation of special dishes for him, seating him at the head of the table – all indicate the extent to which friends provided a sense of family for the childless and often lonely composer in his later years.

From the diary of Olga von Miller zu Aichholz, wife of the wealthy Viennese industrialist Viktor von Miller zu Aichholz, we glimpse a typical summer visit by Brahms to their villa in Gmunden, with its gathering of sophisticated friends around a generous table: '3 [August] Thursday. Beautiful weather. Around a half-hour before one, Brahms, the Kalbecks, Grün, and Privy Councillor Wendt, fetched from the train station by Viktor, [arrived] from Ischl. [Everyone was] very cheerful, [and] Brahms very well disposed. (Menu: French soup, trout, baked ham, mussels with crabs, venison, custard, etc.).'[6] Long before he became Brahms's biographer, Kalbeck was a prominent journalist, librettist, editor and poet; Jakob Moritz Grün was the concertmaster of the Imperial court orchestra in Vienna; Gustav Wendt authored several important translations of classical texts and was the director of the Grand Ducal Gymnasium at Karlsruhe. Notably absent from this party were any members of the nobility, despite the fact that nearby Ischl was the official summer residence of the Austrian Imperial Court. Brahms liked the company of people of accomplishment who could bring interesting things to a conversation and was generally either bored or vexed by aristocratic table companions. (The one significant exception was Brahms's warm friendship with Duke Georg II of Saxe-Meiningen and the Duke's wife, Helene Freifrau von Heldburg, whose company he valued for their personal warmth and refined artistic judgement. Helene von Heldburg, born Ellen Franz, was a pianist and actress.)[7]

---

[5] Quoted in R. H. Schauffler, *The Unknown Brahms* (New York: Dodd, Mead and Co., 1933), 87.

[6] I. Spitzbart, *Johannes Brahms und die Familie Miller-Aichholz in Gmunden und Wien* (Gmunden: Kammerhofmuseum der Stadt Gmunden, 1997), 36.

[7] See R. & K. Hofmann, *Johannes Brahms auf Schloß Altenstein* (Altenburg: Verlag Klaus-Jurgen Kamprad, 2003).

Personal Habits

As the lavish spread described by Frau Miller suggests, the main meal of the day was taken early in the afternoon. The evening meal was lighter. This *Abendessen* might consist of bread and soup, cold cuts or *Mehlspeise*, a category of baked goods, vast in variety, that basically consists of sweet dumplings or pastries filled with fruit. Brahms was very partial to *Mehlspeise*. When he ate supper alone at home, he reverted to simple, even frugal fare. The British art journalist Amelia Levetus reports that 'When [Brahms] was not invited out to supper he provided his own, of German sausage, sardines, or such like; his drink being half-a-litre of ordinary Italian table wine, cheap and weak.'[8]

Brahms delighted in pranks and jokes. Walter Hübbe recounts a party in Hamburg during which the young Brahms impersonated a piano-playing machine and the Hamburg composer Karl Grädener, its attendant.

> Carried into the room and set before the piano by Grädener, his inner workings were wound up and the playing began. But soon the machine all of a sudden, right in the midst of the piece, stood motionless. It would just have to be oiled. Immediately then it continued playing exactly in the same place until at last it fell down from the stool and, lying on the ground, comically continued to finger the air.[9]

Brahms's pranks often came with a cutting edge – in this case a malicious swipe at the empty virtuosity he despised. His practical jokes sometimes involved elaborate preparation. He once went to great lengths to try to fool Clara Schumann into believing that some of his recent piano compositions had really been written by her![10] Like many of his ruses, this one tested the discernment of the recipient, as did his elaborate plot to fool his friend, the Beethoven scholar Gustav Nottebohm, into thinking that a cheese he had bought from a Vienna street vendor was wrapped in a music manuscript by Beethoven.[11]

Brahms was also given to spur-of-the-moment wit, sometimes delivering deliciously ironic remarks with a perfectly innocent expression. On visiting the prolific, but not especially inspired composer Joseph Joachim Raff, Brahms was informed by Raff's wife that she had prevailed on her husband to take a daily stroll with their daughter and reduce his busy schedule of composing, whereupon Brahms replied, with a perfectly straight face, 'Ah,

---

[8] A. S. Levetus, *Imperial Vienna* (London: John Lane, 1905), 305.
[9] W. Hübbe, *Brahms in Hamburg* (Hamburg: Lütcke & Wulff, 1902), 34.
[10] E. Schumann, *The Schumanns and Johannes Brahms. The Memoirs of Eugenie Schumann* (New York: Dial Press, 1927), 158–63.
[11] *Kalbeck II*, 110.

that's good, that's very good!'[12] In the same vein, Brahms liked to quip that one should never be too critical of the works of aristocratic composers – since one never knew who might actually have written them.

As these anecdotes show, Brahms was often amazingly convivial, even playful, as though it pleased him to express himself without inhibitions – to be taken as he was. But when he was out of sorts, this meant that his hosts might be confronted with a moody, even rude guest. (Note the air of relief in Frau Miller's comment quoted above: 'Brahms [was] very well disposed.') Sometimes Brahms's temper was ignited by musical issues. In 1893 his friend, the composer Karl Goldmark, presented a new work, written to a text ostensibly by Martin Luther, at a concert of the Gesellschaft der Musikfreunde. Brahms believed (correctly) that the text was not by Luther, and he evidently could not let the matter pass. Several days later, at a dinner party in the home of the composer Ignaz Brüll, he announced loudly, in Goldmark's presence: 'Don't you think it strange that a Jew should set a text of Martin Luther to music?' Brahms probably intended this to be crudely funny, since it was common knowledge that Luther was virulently anti-Semitic. But he must have known that his remark would deeply offend Goldmark, who was sensitive about his Jewish heritage, and the incident so disturbed the other guests that it was reported by several of them, in slightly differing versions, in their reminiscences about Brahms.[13]

In this instance, Brahms's personal amusement came at the expense and discomfort of others, and such occurrences happened in private as well as in public. While visiting his friends, Heinrich and Elisabeth von Herzogenberg, he nicknamed the English composer Ethel Smyth, whom Elisabeth regarded as a daughter, 'the dung-fly', making a bad pun on the German pronunciation of her last name. Brahms heartily enjoyed the joke until the mortified Elisabeth demanded that he desist.[14] It goes without saying that Ethel Smyth, who had been brought up in a well-regulated English Victorian household, did not take kindly to Brahms's humour.

Brahms had a lifelong habit of vigorous walking out of doors. One of his letters to Bertha Porubsky (with whom he was then in love), suggests that this activity was not just recreational but was also important to him for thinking and composing:

[12] Bozarth, *An Enduring Friendship*, 29.
[13] See D. Brodbeck, *Defining Deutschtum. Political Ideology, German Identity, and Music-Critical Discourse in Liberal Vienna* (Oxford: Oxford University Press, 2014), 59–61.
[14] E. Smyth, *Impressions That Remained: Memoirs* (New York: Alfred A Knopf, 1946), 237.

Personal Habits 49

I want to chat a little with you, then it's off into the forest and not back before late in the evening ... It felt strange when I beheld the wooded heights once more and walked into the magnificent forest. I have not seen nature this beautiful for a year. Much has changed since then. Yet I am completely happy. I only thought music.[15]

Brahms enjoyed Alpine hiking in Switzerland and long strolls in his beloved Prater, Vienna's extensive city park, which Florence May described:

There is the Hauptallée, with its broad drive and shady walks, its open-air cafés and music of military bands ... There is the Würstelprater, the playground of children and other simple folk, where, in the fine weather season, a continual fair goes on with shows and games and entertainments of every kind ... There is the wild portion ... where the solitary walker may fancy himself in a forest far from human habitation.[16]

Amelia Levetus recalled:

It was the Wurstl Prater which Brahms preferred, and for the reason that he was very fond of children – that is, poor ones, for those of the rich did not interest him so much. In the Wurstl Prater he sought out the little ones he loved, paying for their seats at the marionette theatre, or for them to have rides on the 'merry-go-rounds.' He always had sweets in his pockets; they looked like stones, and when the children doubted, he only smiled and said, 'Try'.[17]

Brahms concealed the sweets in the pockets of his ill-fitting and worn-out coat. One of his distinguishing features was an indifference to niceties of dress. Eugenie Schumann recalled that 'The schoolgirl in me resented his neglect of appearances; his coloured shirts without collars, his little alpaca coats, and the trousers which were always too short, were a thorn in my flesh.'[18] In the 1930s Robert Haven Schauffler described some of Brahms's clothes in the Brahms Museum established by the Miller-Aichholz family in Gmunden: there were 'patches and mends on the right elbow of the alpaca coat ... Here and there it is faded from dark grey almost to light yellow ... The black trousers have an enormous brown patch on the seat and a black patch in front.'[19] Brahms did make concessions to convention; when he stayed at the Duke of Meiningen's opulent Altenstein castle, he regularly dressed for dinner. But he usually needed to

---

[15] 9 October 1859, *Avins*, 202.   [16] *May II*, 5–6.   [17] Levetus, *Imperial Vienna*, 305–6.
[18] Schumann, *Memoirs*, 116.
[19] Schauffler, *The Unknown Brahms*, 78. A great many photographs of Brahms in such garb appear in Spitzbart, *Brahms und die Familie Miller-Aichholz*.

50 WILLIAM HORNE

be in control in order to be comfortable, and his oddities of dress reflected his insistence on living life as much as possible on his own terms.

Brahms smoked avidly all his adult life. 'The enclosed Turkish tobacco', Joseph Joachim wrote to him in June of 1856, 'has led me astray into smoking; I roll cigarettes from it every day; it has an exquisite, agreeable aroma.'[20] Brahms's surprising reply was: 'Your Turkish tobacco is good. Frau Clara rolled cigarettes for me, since I can't do it.'[21] Joachim was up-to-date in his smoking preferences; Turkish tobacco came into vogue in Europe during the mid-1850s as British soldiers brought it home from the Crimean War. Widmann relates that in his later years Brahms preferred the dark, strong tobacco in French Caporal cigarettes. He also enjoyed cigars. According to Florence May, he abstained from them in the presence of ladies but was less ceremonious among close friends. Eugenie Schumann, a late riser, recalled that in her mother's Baden-Baden home:

> the nicest time of the day used to be breakfast-time. When I came down into the dining-room I saw nothing at first except thick clouds of tobacco smoke, pierced by Mamma's affectionate, good-morning glance. Brahms was more difficult to discover, and I read a slight disapproval of my late appearance in his look. He . . . often used to tell us in Baden, 'You don't know what you are missing when you are not in the woods by five o'clock.'[22]

Through the lens of our contemporary norms, some of Brahms's habits – rising early and exercising frequently – were healthy ones, while others, in particular his smoking habit, probably shortened his life. Today it would be unacceptable to disparage a Jewish person, and most people would contact authorities on observing an ill-dressed, bearded old man offering sweeties to other people's children in a park. But, aside from a few genuine idiosyncrasies, Brahms's personal habits were mostly ordinary in the context of his own place and time. He took his meals zestfully, enjoyed the Prater and followed an orderly schedule to facilitate his work, like many other urban professionals in Vienna.

Some of his habits flowed naturally from his character. He valued time with his friends – mostly men – who were as necessary to him as solitude. His simple attire, love for poor children and impatience with aristocracy denoted a fierce rejection of pretentiousness. His rudeness, difficult though it could be to bear, was rooted in relentless honesty. All this makes one recall the German proverbs he collected in the spring of 1855 in Düsseldorf. A few examples will suffice: 'Virtue is the highest nobility.' 'Enough is

---

[20] *Briefe I*, 153.   [21] *Ibid.*, 156.   [22] Schumann, *Memoirs*, 168–9.

Personal Habits 51

better than too much.' 'Morning is the golden time.' 'Old friends and old wine must be treasured.'[23]

Further Reading

G. Bozarth, *Johannes Brahms & George Henschel: An Enduring Friendship* (Sterling Heights, Mich.: Harmonie Park Press, 2008)

R. and K. Hofmann, *Johannes Brahms Privat: Tafelfreuden und Geselligkeit* (Heide: Boyens, 2002)

R. H. Schauffler, *The Unknown Brahms* (New York: Dodd, Mead & Co., 1933)

I. Spitzbart, *Johannes Brahms und die Familie Miller-Aichholz in Gmunden und Wien* (Gmunden: Kammerhofmuseum der Stadt Gmunden, 1997)

J. V. Widmann, *Erinnerungen an Johannes Brahms* (Zurich: Rotapfel-Verlag, 1980)

---

[23] See G. Bozarth, 'Johannes Brahms's Collection of *Deutsche Sprichworte* (German Proverbs)', in D. Brodbeck (ed.), *Brahms Studies* (Lincoln & London: University of Nebraska Press, 1994), vol. 1, 1–29, in Bozarth's translation.

CHAPTER 6

Correspondence

Wolfgang Sandberger

In the nineteenth century, letters functioned as bridges between people. Brahms as a correspondent was part of many interconnected social webs; thus, his letters offer a view into this world. The vicissitudes of lifelong friendships, such as that with Joseph Joachim, can be traced seismographically through his greetings: from the romantic, rapturous letters of the twenty-year-old ('Dear Friend of my heart!', 'Beloved Friend!') to the 'Dearest' he used until 1863, the reserved 'Dear Joachim' after the crisis in the Joachims' marriage (1883) or 'Most honoured one' (1886), until the restored intimacy of 'Dear Friend' (1894). Many of the composer's letters, beyond the lifelong, established correspondents like Joachim or Clara Schumann, also trace the Brahms network. They are interwoven into a synchronous toing and froing of letters, for example in the early correspondence between all the Schumann friends: Brahms, Joachim, Grimm, Dietrich and so forth, which can be read in parallel. That said, Brahms's correspondents are by no means homogenous, especially when considered over his lifetime, and so his correspondence can only be evaluated on a case-by-case basis.

As biographical testimony, Brahms's letters reflect – as with much everyday writing – aspects of personal opinion and aesthetic self-reflection. However, in comparison with other composers, such as Mendelssohn or Wagner, Brahms avoided expressing specific points of view in emphatic public or semi-public letters. Furthermore, the individual letters are more than just texts – they are physical objects encoding meaning. The epistolary message begins with the choice of paper, ranging from a brief word on a visiting card to extensive letters of dedication on manuscript paper with a decorative border. It continues with the choice of writing tool, the handwriting and spacing, and it ends when Brahms folds the paper, slips it into the envelope, addresses, franks and posts it. With this in mind, a complete digital edition presenting a facsimile alongside the edited letters would be of great value for research.

52

Correspondence

According to the Brahms-Briefverzeichnis (BBV), 6,897 of Brahms's letters have been preserved.[1] More will doubtless emerge from private collections and in auctions. The first surviving letter is from Brahms the nine-year-old piano pupil, a thank-you letter clearly guided by his parents, written on New Year's Day 1842 to his 'beloved teacher' Otto Cossel, in which Brahms apologises for his lack of diligence in practice.[2] The final dated document is a visiting card sent two days before Brahms's death to Albert Gutmann. In shaky writing, it states:

> Most honoured one. Could you not arrange, <u>also for my sake</u>, for Herr Nikisch to perform the Tchaikovsky symphony on the first evening, but on the second to begin with mine. And please apologise on my behalf – but because of great distress and exhaustion, I cannot write letters. Sincerely.[3]

Brahms's quota of letters was of average size. There are significantly fewer than 5,000 letters by Dvořák and Bruckner, roughly 5,000 by Schumann and Weber, 7,000 by Mendelssohn and over 10,000 by Wagner and Liszt. Even if these numbers reflect the duration of each life, Brahms was hardly the 'writing slacker' (*Schreibefaulpelz*) Schumann accused him of being.[4] The composer himself constantly joked about his aversion to letter writing – indeed, it is practically a leitmotif in his letters. Aged twenty-one, he wrote to Clara Schumann, 'Excuse my shameful handwriting, but I can hardly control my hand when forming the alphabets; I write notes better.'[5]

Brahms's letters are matched by over 4,000 surviving replies, although he probably received – and chose to destroy – many more. Within these 10, 921 items, Brahms's network is revealed: relationships to family, friends, colleagues, women and business correspondents. He had roughly a hundred correspondence partners; these included prominent musical personalities such as his early friends Clara and Robert Schumann, Joseph Joachim, Albert Dietrich and Julius Otto Grimm; conductors such as Hermann Levi, Otto Dessoff, Hans von Bülow and Hans Richter; and composers, choral directors, musicians and singers such as

---

[1] See W. Sandberger and C. Wiesenfeldt, *Brahms-Briefwechsel-Verzeichnis (BBV): chronologisch-systematisches Verzeichnis sämtlicher Briefe von und an Johannes Brahms, gefördert von der Deutschen Forschungsgemeinschaft unter Mitarbeit von Fabian Bergener, Peter Schmitz und Andreas Hund* (www.brahms-institut.de, 2010).
[2] Brahms to Otto Cossel, 1 January 1842, *Kalbeck I*, 24.
[3] Staatsbibliothek zu Berlin – Musikabteilung mit Mendelssohn-Archiv; Mus. ep. Johannes Brahms 233.
[4] F. G. Jansen (ed.), *Robert Schumann's Briefe. Neue Folge* (Leipzig: Breitkopf & Härtel, 1886), 331.
[5] Brahms to Clara Schumann, 21 August 1854, *SBB I*, 15.

Carl Georg Peter Grädener, Theodor Kirchner, Bernhard Scholz, Hermine Spies, Karl Reinthaler, Ernst Frank, Ignaz Brüll, Julius Spengel, Ernst Rudorff, Heinrich and Elisabeth von Herzogenberg and Julius Stockhausen. There were also doctors (Theodor Billroth and Theodor Engelmann), manufacturers (Arthur and Bertha Faber, Viktor von Miller zu Aichholz, Richard and Maria Fellinger), bankers (Rudolf von der Leyen), vineyard owners (Rudolf von Beckerath), publishers (Fritz Simrock, Jakob Melchior Rieter-Biedermann), painters (Anselm Feuerbach, Max Klinger), poets (Klaus Groth, Josef Viktor Widmann) and numerous scholars (Eduard Hanslick, Philipp Spitta, Carl Ferdinand Pohl, Gustav Nottebohm, Friedrich Chrysander, Gustav Wendt and Eusebius Mandyczewski). And even though Brahms's relationship to each person was unique, this wide correspondence reflects many more friendships than other composers.

Altogether, this suggests that the clichéd image of Brahms as an aloof, lonely bachelor must be at least partially revised. He was certainly egocentric and reserved, yet his unconventional personality was attractive. And there are also surprises; two letters from Wagner, for example, asking him for the return of the original manuscript of the reworked second scene of *Tannhäuser* which Brahms had received earlier from Cornelius (6 June 1875). Brahms responded, and on 26 June Wagner thanked Brahms for sending the manuscript.

Contrary to the stereotype of Brahms as a careless correspondent, he generally replied promptly. The extent to which he observed middle-class notions of good correspondence habits is revealed in his various complaints about other letter-writers. On one occasion, he warns that the singer Vogl, who was intended for a performance of *Rinaldo,* was 'apparently an unreliable, negligent letter-writer'.[6] Still, it was a sometimes struggle to keep up with his letters, and he did not always justify his haste and curtness as charmingly as he did to Elisabeth von Herzogenberg, in which the invoked intimacy of 'whispering' barely conceals the apology for his brevity:

> Dear, honoured friend! If I quickly whisper a few words in haste, believe me that from start to finish, it does not suffice for me. I wish I knew better how to thank you properly from the heart for your letters – partly excellent, but always so dear and friendly![7]

[6] Unpublished letter to Raphael Maszkowski, 28 April 1872, private collection.
[7] Brahms to Elisabeth von Herzogenberg, 3 February 1878, *Briefe I*, 49.

Correspondence

In summer 1877 Brahms acknowledged the consequences of late responses, as well as the issues raised by different types of correspondence, in the case of the publisher Breitkopf & Härtel. Regarding his 'agreement' to edit Mozart's *Requiem* K626, he admits that this had arisen through his laziness in responding: 'Härtel had to request my response via telegraph and so I couldn't explain that I didn't want to do it, and why.'[8]

In the second half of the century, the letter was supplemented by the correspondence card and the telegram. These new modes inevitably affected Brahms's writing style: address, grammatical terms, etc., are often lacking. Brahms himself humorously acknowledged the brevity of these formats when he described a particularly short response to his friend Hermann Levi as a 'telegram': 'Dear friend, this time I permit myself to respond with a telegram, although for so much kindness [on your side] I should have used a large sheet of paper.'[9]

Of the total, 27 per cent comprises correspondence with publishers, chief among which was his friend and publisher Fritz Simrock, to whom Brahms wrote 950 letters. Brahms could be stubbornly – and idiosyncratically – insistent, for example in a letter to Rieter-Biedermann regarding his demand for a fee of 100 Napoleons for *A German Requiem*:

> So that this can somehow be called a fee, I ask you to give me 10 Napoleons more as a small contribution to my costs . . . I won't count what I have worn through in terms of boots, walking through Winterthur and Baden to find the notorious organ pedal point [in the third movement].[10]

Within the private realm, the correspondence with Clara Schumann dominates at 12 per cent, despite much being destroyed. These letters also provided Clara Schumann with insights into her young friend's artistic biography. She confided to her diary on 16 October 1887:

> I wanted to extract from the letters everything relating to his life as an artist and a man for him, because they give a picture of his life and creations that no biographer could wish to be more complete. I wanted to put it all together, and only then give him the letters to destroy, but he didn't want this, and so I gave them to him today with wistful tears.[11]

---

[8] Brahms to Friedrich Chrysander, c. July 1877, in H. J. Marx, 'Johannes Brahms im Briefwechsel mit Friedrich Chrysander', in W. Sandberger and C. Wiesenfeldt (eds.), *Musik und Musikforschung. Johannes Brahms im Dialog mit der Geschichte* (Kassel: Bärenreiter, 2007), 242.

[9] Brahms to Hermann Levi, *Briefe VII*, 29.

[10] Brahms to Rieter-Biedermann, 24 May 1868, *Briefe XIV*, 153.

[11] 16 October 1887, *Litzmann III*, 497.

WOLFGANG SANDBERGER

This reveals that it was Brahms's idea to destroy their correspondence. According to Marie Schumann, Clara burnt her letters, and Brahms threw his into the Rhine. Of those remaining, Berthold Litzmann edited 760 letters in 1927 under Marie Schumann's supervision.

Bearing in mind Clara Schumann's idea of distilling a biography from the letters, Brahms's observations about the significance of letters are revealing. He himself distinguished between historically valuable letters and fleeting communications. He frequently spoke out against the

> bad habit of editing the letters of great men after their deaths. Earlier, when one still had the leisure to write real letters, their subsequent publication may perhaps have been justifiable, but then only if the letters had value for research and history. But today letters are mostly just the product of passing moments.[12]

Unlike Wagner, Brahms did not write with eventual publication in mind. Unlike Mendelssohn, for example, who wrote 'skilfully, indeed brilliantly',[13] his letters were not polished. Rather, they fluctuate between cosy chattiness and unsurpassable laconicism: 'Since I have so many letters to write, I send you a sample of my Scarlatti instead, which may interest you – and which completely delights me', he wrote in January 1885 to Elisabeth von Herzogenberg.[14] The superb grace, ease and brevity of the Scarlatti sonatas, of which Brahms owned a rare original edition, elegantly compensates for his short letter.

Despite his 'non-literary' approach to writing, anyone who has immersed themselves in Brahms's letters will agree with Ludwig Finscher's claim that Brahms was a 'great letter-writer in the nineteenth century of letters', indeed that he was 'perhaps the one who most virtuosically mastered irony, ambiguity, disguise and role-play'.[15] From the countless examples, one might select a letter to the publisher Rieter-Biedermann from January 1869, in which the composer responds to the publisher's request for a four-hand edition of his *Requiem*. He expresses himself ironically about the work, the tedious task of arranging and the publisher's request to create an easy

---

[12] V. Schnitzler, *Erinnerungen aus meinem Leben* (Köln: Tischer & Jagenberg, 1935), 53.

[13] W. Seidl, 'Die Briefe von Felix Mendelssohn Bartholdy. Einleitung in die Gesamtausgabe', in J. Appold and R. Back (eds.), *Felix Mendelssohn Bartholdy. Sämtliche Briefe*, 12 vols. (Kassel: Bärenreiter, 2008), vol. 1. *1816 bis Juni 1830*, 7.

[14] Brahms to Elisabeth von Herzogenberg, January 1885, *Briefe II*, 46.

[15] L. Finscher, 'Kunst und Leben. Bemerkungen zur Kunstanschauung von Johannes Brahms', in F. Krummacher, M. Struck et al (eds.), *Johannes Brahms. Quellen – Text – Rezeption – Interpretation* (Munich: Henle, 1999), 31.

Correspondence

arrangement, above all, not omitting allusions to the publisher's piano-playing daughter:

> I have devoted myself to the noble task of making my immortal work enjoyable for four-hand souls. Now it cannot perish. Incidentally it has come out excellently and furthermore very easy to play, really and truly, completely and thoroughly light and quick. Fräulein Ida will not only be able to conquer it more easily than the mountains with her papa, but her godlike, or rather 'götziger' teacher [punning on the name Herrmann Götz] will not even be able to keep her at an *andante* pace. Hell has been gone through [referring to the sixth movement, 'Hölle, wo ist dein Sieg?'], and I think I will send it to you soon.[16]

Brahms was also adept at historical phrases in letter writing, as shown by the tongue-in-cheek Baroque-style closing flourish to the following letter: 'With which I have the honour to be this and especially that, your most obedient servant to the honoured ladies, J. Brahms'.[17]

Although the correspondence reveals much about Brahms's works and their reception, it rarely offers glimpses into his working process. There are some exceptions: for example, the two letters between Brahms and the conductor Vincenz Lachner from summer 1879 concerning the details and significance of the Second Symphony Op. 73, in which Brahms described himself as a 'deeply melancholy person'.[18] More often, though, Brahms's statement to Clara Schumann in February 1858 holds: 'Never wonder, dear Clara, that I do not write about my works. I will not and cannot.'[19] Still, Brahms repeatedly sent new works around his social circle – to Clara Schumann, Joseph Joachim or Julius Otto Grimm, and later to Elisabeth von Herzogenberg. The ensuing dialogue, even if fragmentary, is revealing. Thus, for example, the mock-complacent response to Clara Schumann's criticism of his motet 'Es ist das Heil uns kommen her' Op. 29 no. 1 in which the fugal choral lines were the subject under discussion:

> Doubtless you've laughed a little at me on account of my suspensions in the choral motet? Your answer seems to me to be ironic – 'a little motive for a fugue', how ugly! A sweet little school mistress, at best, could have come up with that. You are a real scamp. First, one is expected to offer a full opinion, and then one gets one's nose boxed afterwards.[20]

---

[16] Brahms to Rieter-Biedermann, Vienna, 31 January 1869, in *Briefe XIV*, 172. [17] *Ibid.*, 173.

[18] Johannes Brahms to Vincenz Lachner, August 1879, in R. Brinkmann, *Johannes Brahms. Die zweite Symphonie* (München: Edition Text + Kritik, 1990), 75.

[19] Johannes Brahms to Clara Schumann, Hamburg, 24 February 1858, in *SBB I*, 217.

[20] Clara Schumann to Johannes Brahms, Godesberg, 5 October 1860, in *SBB I*, 330.

58 WOLFGANG SANDBERGER

Clara Schumann later envied Elisabeth von Herzogenberg née Stockhausen, who Brahms briefly taught before her marriage and to whom he preferentially sent his manuscripts for comment from 1877 onwards. In addition to her musicality, Brahms intermittently regarded her as a 'distant beloved', even if this friendship fluctuated greatly because of his complex relationship with her husband, Heinrich. An outstanding musician, she could respond to Brahms's music after a single hearing or play-through. Their exchange gives one of the deepest insights into his art.

Alongside biographical aspects, the philological significance of the correspondence can hardly be overstated. Apart from the communication with publishers and proofreaders, we often only learn details of the compositional process from the letters: for example, that the earliest roots of the 1864/5 Second String Sextet Op. 36 lie in 1855.[21] This is interesting from a biographical perspective, because many commentators have understood this work as a reaction to Brahms's love for Agathe von Siebold (in Göttingen in 1858), whose initials are coded into the main theme. The early sketch of the theme in a letter to Clara shows, however, that the roots of the Sextet pre-date that encounter. Letters also reveal vanished works, such as a Piano Trio movement in E♭ major, which was composed alongside the opening movement of the Second Piano Trio Op. 87 and which circulated among his friends; we know of its existence only through his correspondence with the surgeon Theodor Billroth as well as a remark in Clara Schumann's diary.

Brahms scholarship is hampered by the fact that the existing editions of the correspondence are both inaccurate and incomplete (around a third of the letters remain unpublished). For example, Kalbeck fed both irritation and speculation in his rendition of a letter from Brahms to Simrock, according to which the seven Fantasies Op. 116 originally consisted of 'three' and 'two' pieces.[22] In Litzmann's edition of the Clara Schumann–Brahms letters, another piece in C minor was also mentioned in the context of these Fantasies. Both these errors, along with inaccurate dating, led to much head-scratching about the original constitution of those piano pieces; the 'C minor piece', which does not correspond with any of the Fantasies, even received an entry in the *Werkverzeichnis* under lost works. However, Brahms had actually written 'three' and 'four' pieces, i.e. the number of pieces in Op. 116 was seven from the outset. The 'C

---

[21] Johannes Brahms to Clara Schumann, Düsseldorf, 7 February 1855, in *SBB I*, 75.
[22] Johannes Brahms to Fritz Simrock, Vienna, 20 October 1892, in *Briefe XII*, 79.

Correspondence
59

minor' was in fact 'E minor', and therefore clearly refers to the fifth Intermezzo in Op. 116. There are more examples of this kind. The first letter from Brahms to Rudolf von der Leyen in Krefeld, which recently resurfaced and which the addressee himself published in 1905, also shows how urgently a new edition is needed. In the context of a performance of the Violin Concerto Op. 77, Brahms writes that, in his view, for the soloists, 'Hr. Heermann or Herr. Barth are ideal. I think you owe the former the first invitation.' The editor, who was personally involved, chose to reverse the sequence of the two interpreters and simply omitted the second sentence. Typical of Brahms is, of course, the conclusion of the letter:

> But please forgive me this scribble, I have no time, no patience, and – can't think of anything more to say [after three and a half pages!]. Just go ahead and propose something, add as much as possible by my colleagues Beethoven und Bach, and I will certainly agree and even rejoice with you a little![23]

Further Reading

A. Bohnenkamp and W. Wiethölter (eds.), *Der Brief – Ereignis & Objekt, Katalog der Ausstellung im Freien Deutschen Hochstift Frankfurter Goethe-Museum* (Frankfurt am Main and Basel: Stroemfeld, 2008)

A. Bohnenkamp and E. Richter, *Brief-Edition im digitalen Zeitalter* (Berlin: De Gruyter, 2013)

B. Borchard, 'Entwurf eines Künstlerlebens. Max Kalbecks Ausgabe der Brahms-Briefe', in U. Harten (ed.), *Skizzen einer Persönlichkeit. Max Kalbeck zum 150. Geburtstag* (Tutzing: Hans Schneider, 2007), 247–59

W. Sandberger, 'Neue Schätze im Brahms-Institut Lübeck – zur Brahms-Motette "Es ist das Heil uns kommen her" op. 29, Nr. 1', *Brahms-Studien* 13 (2002), 9–24

M. Struck, 'Brahms-Philologie ohne die Briefe des Meisters? Eine Fallstudie', in H. Bennwitz, G. Buschmeier and A. Riethmüller (eds.), *Komponistenbriefe des 19. Jahrhunderts* (Stuttgart: Akademie der Wissenschaften und der Literatur, 1997), 26–56

M. Struck, 'Revisionsbedürftig: Zur gedruckten Korrespondenz von Johannes Brahms und Clara Schumann. Auswirkungen irrtümlicher oder lückenhafter Überlieferung auf werkgenetische Bestimmungen (mit einem unausgewerteten Brahms-Brief zur Violinsonate op. 78)', *Die Musikforschung* 41 (1988), 235–41

---

[23] Letter of 23 November 1880, R. von der Leyen, *Johannes Brahms als Mensch und Freund. Nach persönlichen Erinnerungen* (Düsseldorf und Leipzig: Langewiesche Verlag, 1905), 20. Manuscript, Brahms-Institut an der Musikhochschule Lübeck, Inv.-Nr. 2007.145, Sign: Bra : B1 : Ley : 1.

CHAPTER 7

Holidays

Inga Mai Groote

For Brahms, holidays did not just mean a nice break; they constituted important or even essential periods of composition. This is best seen through the example of his First Symphony Op. 68: as is well known, it had its roots in a birthday greeting of 12 September 1868 to Clara Schumann, in which Brahms notated an alphorn call he allegedly heard during a walk from Grindelwald to Lauterbrunnen. He then worked on the symphony in summer 1874 in Rüschlikon (near Zurich) and in 1876 in Sassnitz on the island of Rügen, where he enjoyed the landscape. As he wrote to his publisher Fritz Simrock, the Symphony 'was dangling' from the Wissower Klinken cliffs, the famous chalk formations on the east coast of the island.[1] The manuscript was finally completed in September 1876 in Lichtenthal, near the fashionable spa town of Baden-Baden, where the composer often stayed.

Brahms's holidays – and the locations he frequently chose to visit – chime with the wider conception of 'holiday', which proliferated through the nineteenth-century middle classes as the expansion of the railway improved the journey to popular vacation resorts such as those on the North Sea, the Baltic Sea or in the Alpine foothills.[2] In particular, the idea of a 'summer holiday' as a type of vacation established itself alongside the known formats of educational tours (*Bildungsreisen*) and spa visits; in such holidays, a relatively settled and stable lifestyle was offered in resorts with charming natural surroundings. Holidaymakers often returned to the same places over many years, sometimes even to identical addresses – as did Brahms, once he had found a place which suited him. Apart from Lichtenthal, as mentioned above (1865, 1866, 1869, 1871, 1876, 1877), these were in the Swiss and Austrian resorts: Bad Ischl (1880, 1882, 1889–94, 1896) and Pörtschach,

---

[1] *Briefe X*, 13.
[2] See P. Prein, *Bürgerliches Reisen im 19. Jahrhundert. Freizeit, Kommunikation und soziale Grenzen* (Münster: LIT, 2005).

60

Holidays

near the Wörthersee (1877–9), Mürzzuschlag in Styria (1884, 1885) and Hofstetten near Thun (1886–8).[3] In addition to Rüschlikon und Sassnitz,[4] Brahms also made one-off stays in Fluntern near Zurich (1866), Tutzing on Lake Starnberg (1873), Ziegelhausen near Heidelberg (1875), Pressbaum near Vienna (1881) and Wiesbaden (1883). To these can be added his visits as a young man to areas near Hamburg (Hamm, Münster am Stein and Blankenese, 1861–3).

In his letters, Brahms often laid emphasis on the beauties of nature; for example, in 1873 he wrote:

> Tutzing is far more beautiful than we could ever imagine. We just had a magnificent storm; the lake was nearly black, the shores wonderfully green. [The lake] is usually blue, but a more beautiful, deeper blue than the sky; and then the chain of snow-capped mountains – one never gets tired of looking.[5]

His choice of destination was guided above all by the beauty of the landscape and, to some extent, also by the proximity of friends and acquaintances. He often invited visitors to see him on his holidays or himself made visits to nearby acquaintances. For instance, in Wiesbaden, he stayed in the studio of the painter Ludwig Knaus and frequently visited Rudolf and Laura von Beckerath in Rüdesheim or Wiesbaden;[6] and in Baden-Baden his visits overlapped with those of Clara Schumann and her family.[7] From Tutzing, he visited Hermann Levi, Julius Allgeyer and Franz Wüllner in Munich; while in Ziegelhausen, he often visited Heidelberg, where he made music in the homes of the piano manufacturer Johann Baptist Trau and Henriette Feuerbach.

Musicians' lives in the nineteenth century were fundamentally characterised by great mobility. Periods of study, professional demands, concert tours and conducting necessitated constant travel, and this also applied to Brahms. His concentration on summer (with its absence of concert activity) as his 'creative period' was therefore very practically orientated around the annual professional cycle. This can be observed in other composers too: Gabriel Fauré, for example, systematically used vacations abroad for

---

[3] See T. Kneif, 'Konzertreisen und Sommeraufenthalte', in C. Jacobsen (ed.), *Johannes Brahms. Leben und Werk* (Wiesbaden: Breitkopf & Härtel 1983), 36–9.

[4] K. Stahmer, 'Brahms auf Rügen. Der Sommeraufenthalt eines Komponisten', *Brahms-Studien* 3 (1979), 59–68.

[5] *Briefe VII*, 134.

[6] See K. Stephenson, *Johannes Brahms und die Familie Beckerath* (Hamburg: Christians, 1979), esp. 21–6.

[7] See J. Draheim & U. Reimann (eds.), *Johannes Brahms in den Bädern Baden-Baden, Wiesbaden, Bad Ischl, Karlsbad* (Baden-Baden: Kulturamt der Stadt Baden-Baden, 1997).

concentrated work, both before and during his employment as director of the Paris Conservatoire. So did Max Reger, who repeatedly took restorative holidays on the Baltic Sea (Kolberg) and near Berchtesgaden. Gustav Mahler established still more concentrated working conditions for himself during his holidays in that, both as a guest in the pension at Attersee and in his own villa at Wörthersee, he made use of a separate 'composition shed'.

Brahms, although he no longer held a fixed official position after relinquishing the directorship of the Singverein and the Gesellschaft der Musikfreunde concerts in Vienna, similarly maintained some divide between his professional journeys and visits, and the summer holidays. The number of significant works developed or brought to completion during his various holidays is correspondingly high. These include the *Neue Liebeslieder* Op. 65 in Rüschlikon, the Fourth Symphony Op. 98 in Mürzzuschlag, the Cello Sonata Op. 99 and Violin Sonata Op. 100 in Hofstetten, and the second version of the First Piano Trio Op. 8, as well as the Clarinet Trio Op. 114 and Quintet Op. 115 in Bad Ischl. However, since for Brahms the creative process was fundamentally characterised by long interruptions and periods of deliberation,[8] there is generally no direct perceptible link between the specific place and the completed works. (The aforementioned, identifiable 'inspiration' of the alphorn melody is the exception.)

Already as a young man, Brahms visited various German regions. In 1853, his first extended journey on foot along the Rhine took him from Mainz to Mehlem, near Bonn; he prepared himself for it thoroughly with the help of a travel guidebook, in which some of his notes are still preserved. He conscientiously observed the landscape, places and tourist attractions on the way and also visited the poet Heinrich Hoffmann von Fallersleben in Neuwied. At that point, he seems to have striven to be the most punctilious tourist possible: 'On the first day (26 August) I went walking in Mainz and saw the cathedral (also inside), the Gutenberg Memorial and another very old church. I was rushed away too quickly to see any more.'[9] In contrast, in later years he preferred a mode of slow, deliberate travel.

The following August, he visited Heidelberg, where, in addition to the ruins of the castle there (an emblematic symbol of Romanticism), he also

---

[8] M. Struck, 'Vom Einfall zum Werk – Produktionsprozesse, Notate, Werkgestalt(en)', in *Brahms Handbuch*, 171–98.

[9] R. Hofmann, 'Johannes Brahms' erste Reise an den Rhein. Ein unbekannter Brief von Johannes Brahms an Arnold Wehner', in M. Gutiérrez-Denhoff (ed.), *Johannes Brahms und Bonn* (Bonn: Stadt Bonn, 1997), 28.

Holidays

sought out the former home of Robert Schumann. Finally, he walked up the Neckar to Heilbronn and travelled on from there by train to Ulm. However, the journey was overshadowed by the knowledge of Schumann's illness ('Throughout the whole trip, I never felt completely, unreservedly happy, as one needs for a walking tour'[10]). In August and September 1856, he then accompanied Clara Schumann, her sons Ludwig and Ferdinand and his sister Elise on a restorative trip to the Vierwaldstättersee.

Some of Brahms's holidays also held personal significance as an opportunity to spend time with his parents. In 1867 and 1868 he went walking with his father in Styria and Switzerland (his stepmother did not accompany them). His father recalled the fortnight-long Swiss journey from Basel in the Bernese Oberland in his memoirs, from the paintings on the Kapellbrücke in Lucerne, to the Reichenbach falls in Meiringen, complete with a firework display. But professional contacts were also made on that trip: during one three-day stay in Zurich, the Brahms men met Friedrich Hegar and Theodor Kirchner, attended concerts in the Tonhalle and even organised a partial rehearsal for *A German Requiem*.[11]

In 1866, during his first extended stay in Switzerland, Brahms similarly combined a tour in the Bernese Oberland with a stay in Fluntern near Lake Zurich. He stayed in an isolated holiday apartment, the first of a type that he subsequently sought time and again. He thereby managed to avoid having to accept an invitation to stay with Mathilde Wesendonck, with whom he had become acquainted earlier that year on a concert tour. On the contrary, his 'delightful composer's refuge' was very modest, as he related to his Winterthur publisher Jakob Melchior Rieter-Biedermann ('the room is situated up high, but the ceilings are all the lower; it has a lovely wide prospect, but is all the narrower'[12]).

Brahms's longer summer stays are documented in his letters as well as the accounts of his circle of friends and acquaintances. Even if some of these hosts' sketches and memoirs have an anecdotal quality, taken as a whole, they reveal a remarkably coherent picture of Brahms's habits and requirements [see Ch. 5 'Personal Habits']. Above all, he needed to be able to withdraw himself; uninvited guests were kept at a distance if possible. Even when he stayed in seaside resorts and spa towns such as Sassnitz, Baden-Baden and Wiesbaden, he kept himself apart from the social life there – he had no use for spa treatments, and he usually preferred

[10] *SBB I*, 8.
[11] W. Zimmermann, *Brahms in der Schweiz. Eine Dokumentation* (Zurich: Atlantis, 1983), 37–40.
[12] *Briefe XIV*, 127.

64 INGA MAI GROOTE

private landlords to large hotels. Or he simply avoided the social scene altogether, as in the case of Baden-Baden; in 1864 he stayed in a hotel and with Anton Rubinstein but, in the following years, preferred suburban Lichtenthal. In Pörtschach, following his first year where he stayed in castle Leonstain with Baron von Pausinger, he subsequently lodged with a private landlord. In 1875 he chose the village of Ziegelhausen rather than Schlierbach near Heidelberg because he hoped for greater seclusion there.

In 1873, Vincent d'Indy visited him in Tutzing. D'Indy was travelling through Germany and, at César Franck's request, was bringing over a score of his *Rédemption*. But he too was put off by Brahms's typical reserve towards uninvited guests; at least, he reported that he rang the bell at Brahms's holiday apartment on a hot day, that the composer opened the door but stayed in the doorway without inviting his guest in and laid the score aside without great interest.[13] Brahms also tended to rent several rooms or entire residences in order to avoid being disturbed by other tenants. He regarded the tranquillity as a precondition for work: 'I need complete solitude, not only to achieve what is possible for me, but in order to be able to think about my things at all. That lies in my nature.'[14]

At every holiday location, Brahms established a similar daily routine – very early rising, morning walks, work throughout the day and relatively simple but good catering, of which, for example, the brewing of his own coffee was a part. The culinary attractions of his stay in Rüschlikon, in a farmhouse opposite Nidelbad (a sulphurous mineral spring) are evoked by Carl Ferdinand Pohl in a letter to Brahms:

> The man who calls me sits far away beside the lake of Zurich, admiring the view of the Nidelbad; he drives to Küsnacht, eats freshwater fish and crayfish in the 'Sun', drinks the excellent red wine at Erlenbach, or even better, lakeside wine at Mariahalden – and saunters along the Horgen, which is one fragrant rose garden in June.[15]

Brahms also took copious physical exercise. In addition to his walks, there were also strenuous hikes and lake or sea bathing. But walking, as a time for reflection, was a feature of his habits in any case, not just on holiday. Nevertheless, Max Kalbeck gives a striking account of one summer in Bad

---

[13] V. d'Indy, 'Impressions musicales d'enfance et de jeunesse', *Annales politiques et littéraires* 94 (15 May 1930), 472. See also L. Vallas, 'The Discovery of Musical Germany by Vincent d'Indy in 1873', *The Musical Quarterly* 25/2 (April 1939), 176–94, who however claims that the exchange between the two may have been more extensive.

[14] Brahms to Ellen Franz, *Briefe XVII,* 75.

[15] Carl Ferdinand Pohl to Brahms, 16 June 1874, M. Musgrave, *A Brahms Reader* (New Haven: Yale University Press, 2000), 202.

Holidays

Ischl, even if it seems a stereotypical image of genius, describing how he saw Brahms in shirtsleeves, with his hat and jacket in his hand, completely out of breath, rapidly striding out of the forest, completely immersed in his thoughts.[16] Even though his failing constitution eventually made exertion difficult, Brahms still undertook some mountain tours; thus, in 1888 he ascended the Niesen and hiked from Kandersteg to Oeschinen Lake in the Bernese Oberland.

In contrast, Brahms's eight longer journeys to Italy (including two visits to Sicily) have a notably different character.[17] These truly count as his only holidays abroad, since Brahms otherwise limited himself to German-speaking territories. He went to Italy with friends or close acquaintances, such as the surgeon Theodor Billroth (1878, 1881 and 1882) and the poet Josef Viktor Widmann (1888, 1890 and 1893). On these trips, sightseeing was the dominant activity; however, Brahms did not make these journeys (like a typical *Bildungsreise*) in his youth, but from his forties onwards. His routes were concentrated on north and central Italy. In previous years, he had already read travel guides and history books such as Jacob Burckhardt's *The Culture of the Renaissance in Italy* (*Die Cultur der Renaissance in Italien*; Brahms's copy is in the 1877/8 edition).[18] His outlook on Italian culture was therefore a combination of direct experience, as can be gleaned from his many exuberant observations, and an informed critique of the relevant factual writings, enriched by his knowledge of literature. Furthermore, Italian art evidently fed Brahms's interest in the Renaissance. Billroth also remarked that Brahms made great (if unsuccessful) efforts to communicate in Italian. Brahms's profound joy in visiting Italy can be seen, for example, in a letter to Clara Schumann:

> If you stood before the facade of Siena Cathedral for just one hour, you would be in a state of bliss, and would feel that this sufficed for the entire journey. And then you go in, but on the floor and in the entire church, there is not a single spot which does not delight in equal measure. And the next day in Orvieto, you would have to concede that *that* cathedral is even more beautiful. And then to land here in Rome, that is a pleasure that can't be described ... Each and every individual thing completely

[16] *Kalbeck III*, 247.
[17] S. Keil, "' ... es ist ja allerorten schön in dem herrlichen Land". Johannes Brahms und seine Italienreisen', *Brahms-Studien* 15 (2008), 23–36; Widmann also offers important information in his *Johannes Brahms in Erinnerungen*, 4th edn (Berlin: Paetel, 1921).
[18] K. Hofmann, *Die Bibliothek von Johannes Brahms. Bücher- und Musikalienverzeichnis*, (Hamburg: Karl Dieter Wagner, 1974), 18, 90–1.

66   INGA MAI GROOTE

justifies the trip, the slower and more comfortable, the more pleasurably.[19]

As with the regulated daily schedule of his summer vacations, Brahms also had in mind a leisurely rhythm for his sightseeing trips, to avoid from the outset, as it were, any possible danger of 'Stendhal syndrome', as might be experienced by travellers confronted with the glories of Italy. He also expressed this in his travel recommendations to Clara Schumann:

> You must make it a firm rule to yourself to see as little and as slowly as possible . . . Another person will recommend to you a different city, and in that city a different church and gallery as the most important. But in Italy one may not ask what one should not see; far too easily, one sees too much far too easily.[20]

However, Brahms's interests were not restricted to historical artworks and attractions but also embraced the contemporary. Thus, he mentioned that the writer Richard Voss was staying in the Villa Falconieri in Frascati, which the addressees would have known from the novella by Paul Heyse of the same name, written in the same place. In 1888, Brahms also visited the Esposizione Internazionale di Musica,[21] which took place in Bologna parallel to the Esposizione Emiliana and a national art exhibition. He attended the exhibition of manuscripts, printed music and instruments. The opening concert, organised by Charles-Victor Mahillon and featuring historical instruments from his Brussels collection, was a disaster which Brahms slated. He met and had an animated exchange with Giuseppe Martucci (1856–1909), the director of the local music school. But, overall, Brahms remained critical about his musical experiences in Italy: for him, Italian music was 'terrible', as he related to Clara Schumann. To Billroth, he criticised a performance of *Barbiere di Sevilla* by Achille Graffigna (1816–96) in Florence as 'bloodless and miserably Philistine'. A mass by Emilio Andreotti (1852–96) in Cremona in 1890 was, according to Widmann's account, an example of 'desire without corresponding ability'. For Brahms, Italy's appeal was illustrated by the fact that the classical

---

[19] April 1881, *SBB II*, 231. See also M. Engelhardt, '"La primavera più bella la vivo qui, per la prima volta in Italia". L'immagine dell'Italia nelle lettere di Brahms', in *Schumann, Brahms et l'Italia* (Rome: Accademia nazionale dei Lincei, 2001), 279–89.

[20] May 1881, *SBB II*, 236; see also 344 (June 1888).

[21] E. Mercadante & D. Tonini: 'Bologna 1888: la grande impresa dell'Esposizione Internazionale di Musica', in B. Basevi and M. Nottoli (eds.), *Expo Bologna 1888. L'Esposizione Emiliana nei documenti delle Collezioni d'Arte e di Storia della Fondazione Cassa di Risparmio in Bologna* (Bologna: Bononia University Press, 2015), 31–41.

Holidays 67

scholar Theodor Mommsen was recognised and greatly admired by an antique dealer and other simple folk at provincial railway station.

In 1888, Billroth suggested a trip to Spain and even Egypt to Brahms – and this plan was received as completely feasible; at least, he read the relevant travel literature, as usual, but ultimately settled on another journey to Italy with Widmann.[22] Thus, on holiday and while travelling, Brahms maintained the essentials of his lifestyle in concentrated form, especially the balance between social participation and retreat; and simultaneously carved out the space in which he could absorb and creatively reflect his impressions of nature and art.

Further Reading

J. Draheim and U. Reimann (eds.), *Johannes Brahms in den Bädern Baden-Baden, Wiesbaden, Bad Ischl, Karlsbad* (Baden-Baden: Kulturamt der Stadt Baden-Baden, 1997)

M. Engelhardt, 'Italien in Brahms' Briefen', in N. Bolin, C. von Blumröder and I. Misch (eds.), *Aspetti Musicali: Musikhistorische Dimensionen Italiens 1600 bis 2000: Festschrift für Dietrich Kämper zum 65. Geburtstag* (Cologne-Rheinkassel: Dohr, 2001), 57–65

A. Fuchs, 'Johannes Brahms: Auf seinen Spuren in Kärnten', *Die Brücke* 2/4 (Autumn 1976), 235–51

T. Kneif, 'Konzertreisen und Sommeraufenthalte', in C. Jacobsen (ed.), *Johannes Brahms. Leben und Werk* (Wiesbaden: Breitkopf & Härtel 1983), 36–9

P. Prein, *Bürgerliches Reisen im 19. Jahrhundert. Freizeit, Kommunikation und soziale Grenzen* (Münster: LIT, 2005)

K. Stahmer, 'Brahms auf Rügen. Der Sommeraufenthalt eines Komponisten', *Brahms-Studien* 3 (1979), 59–68

---

[22] See K. Hofmann, 'Johannes Brahms in Ägypten – eine Spurensuche an den Originalschauplätzen', *Die Tonkunst* 2/2 (April 2008), 221.

PART II

Identities, Environments and Influences

CHAPTER 8

Finances

Jakob Hauschildt

During his lifetime, Brahms accumulated a sizeable fortune. Although the early days were not without difficulties, his finances then accumulated steadily and virtually uninterruptedly. When he died in 1897, he left behind not only manuscripts of his own works, but also an extensive collection of other composers' autograph manuscripts (including of Mozart, Haydn, Beethoven, Schubert, Schumann, etc.) as well as bonds worth over 181,000 Gulden.[1] The size of the sum is evident when one compares the rent that he paid his landlady Coelestine Truxa between 1887 and 1897 for his three-room apartment in Vienna's Karlsgasse, which amounted half-yearly to 347 Gulden and 25 Kreuzer.

Brahms grew up in the Hamburg 'Gängeviertel', an area of workers, small-scale artisans and tradesmen in modest circumstances [see Ch. 1 'Childhood in Hamburg']. Later on, when he could determine his own lifestyle, luxury still held no appeal. Still, as a youth, the introverted young composer sought ways of earning his own keep. Children of his background began to work around the age of thirteen or fourteen; Brahms correspondingly began to play in local venues in 1846 and, somewhat later on, in occasional public concerts as a pianist, for which he received his first fees. We know that in a Bergedorf restaurant on Sunday afternoons he earned 2 Taler (5 Mark Courant) playing dance music (the average weekly wage of a Hamburg artisan in 1848 was roughly 6–14 Mark Courant). From 1847 onwards, Brahms gave piano lessons, but the number of pupils remained modest, and no stable, profitable group of pupils was established.

Indeed, Brahms's most important source of income over this period was musical arrangements, including potpourris from Italian operas. He did this grunt work until at least around 1853/4, occasionally assisted by Joseph

---

[1] The exact sum was 181,473 Gulden, 79 Neukreuzer (*A-Wsa*, Hauptarchiv – Akten – Persönlichkeiten, Akt 3.1.4.A1.B26.3, Nachlassinventar, 29 March 1898).

72 JAKOB HAUSCHILDT

Table 8.1 *Currency equivalencies in relation to the 1871 Mark (1 Mark = $^{1000}/_{2790}$ grams of pure gold)*

1 Louisdor	19.56 Marks
1 Friedrichsdor	16.829 Marks
1 Napoleondor	16.20 Marks
1 Mark Courant, legal tender in North Germany until the founding of the empire in 1871 (divided into 16 Schillings, each of 12 Pfennig)	1.20 Marks
1 Prussian Taler (divided into 30 Silbergroschen, each of 12 Pfennig)	3 Marks
1 Saxon Taler (divided into 30 Neugroschen, each of 10 Pfennig)	3 Marks
1 Austrian Gulden (divided into 100 Neukreuzer)	2 Marks
1 Franc	0.80 Marks
1 Dollar	4.336 Marks
1 Pound sterling	20.4295 Marks

Joachim.[2] He never revealed himself as the author of these arrangements, and his fees for them remain unknown. Only the *Souvenir de la Russie* (Anh. IV Nr. 6 in *Werkverzeichnis*) published by Cranz under the pseudonym G. W. Marks can be identified conclusively as Brahms's. It is known, however, that Cranz's fees, upon Brahms's mother's insistence, were initially paid into a savings account and later used to fund his travels in 1853.[3] Thus, to some extent, Brahms retained his earliest earnings for his own use. Solitary composition was central to his artistic development in the years before 1853. The extent and significance of this deeply private work remained hidden from his father, who expected his son to contribute funds to the household and put pressure on him around 1850 to improve his financial situation.

In late 1853 and February 1854, Brahms's first works were published. For his first six opuses, he received a total of 40 Louisdors and 10 Friedrichsdors, a considerable sum for a novice, achieved not least through Schumann's mediation. Still, his financial situation remained precarious, and he borrowed from Joachim, although when he had any money, he bought himself books.[4] Christiane Brahms advised in 1854: 'You cannot have debts, that won't work ... Art is luxury, the working classes can, indeed must do without it ... Oh, one doesn't go through this world so easily and proudly, one must submit to and endure many things.'[5]

Thus, between 1855 and 1865, piano lessons were Brahms's source of income, even though he did not particularly value this work [see Ch. 13

---

[2] See *Heuberger*, 80.
[3] See K. Stephenson (ed.), *Johannes Brahms in seiner Familie. Der Briefwechsel* (Hamburg: Hauswedell, 1973), 55.
[4] *Avins*, 62–3.   [5] Stephenson, *Briefwechsel Familie*, 56.

Finances

'As Teacher']. Clara Schumann's pupils, who Brahms taught in Düsseldorf in 1855, generally paid him 1 Taler per hour; in Detmold and later Hamburg, this fee doubled.[6] His pupil Susanne Schmaltz, a member of the Hamburg Ladies' Choir, correspondingly paid 'five Marks Courant', and added in her recollections that the 'lessons were very expensive'.[7] In addition, Brahms also began to give regular concerts. Until the end of the 1860s, his pianistic activity served not only to disseminate his own works but also to secure his income. The fee for two concerts in Bremen and Hamburg on 20 and 24 November 1855 is recorded in a letter to Georg Dietrich Otten:

> For my fee I ~~must~~ want to suggest 10 or 8 louis d'ors to you. But I beg you not to speak about it, because I would have to ask for more elsewhere. In Bremen, for example, I receive 12 ld'ors; therefore, as you can imagine, I must stick to the best possible price. Nevertheless, I gladly leave to your discretion the deduction of 2 louis d'ors, if there is no other way. All in all, do whatever you want.[8]

Therefore, already at the start of his public concert career, Brahms could command fees comparable to those he had secured for his newly published first works (e.g. 10 Louisdors for the Piano Sonatas Opp. 1 and 2); in 1862, he requested 15 Louisdors for a concert in Oldenburg under Albert Dietrich.[9] Meanwhile, he rarely received a regular salary. In 1857–9, during which time he published hardly anything, his temporary employment at the Detmold court was his financial support. According to the court accounts, he received 566 Taler 20 Silbergroschen for the period between October and December 1859.[10] He only held a salaried post on two further occasions: as choral director of the Vienna Singakademie in 1863/4, he received a modest 600 Gulden; and as artistic director of the Gesellschaft der Musikfreunde in Vienna in 1872–5, he received 3,000 Gulden annually. Ultimately, however, such employment remained sporadic and Brahms sought to maintain himself as an independent composer.

Consequently, the publishers' fees for his works were his main source of income [see Ch. 24 'Publishers']. While Schumann suggested the fees in

---

[6] Clara Schumann to Brahms, 19 November 1860, *SBB I*, 338.
[7] S. Schmaltz, *Beglückte Erinnerung. Lebenslauf eines Sonntagskindes* (Dresden: Verlag Deutsche Buchwerkstätten, 1926), 24.
[8] K. Stephenson (ed.), 'Johannes Brahms und Georg Dietrich Otten', in H. Hüschen (ed.), *Festschrift Gustav Fellerer. Zum sechzigsten Geburtstag am 7. Juli 1962* (Regensburg: Gustav Bosse, 1962), 506.
[9] *Avins*, 242.
[10] W. Schramm, *Johannes Brahms in Detmold* (1933), rev. edn, R. Müller-Dombois (ed.) (Hagen: Kommissionsverlag v. d. Linnepe, 1983), 51.

74 JAKOB HAUSCHILDT

1853, thereafter Brahms himself had to negotiate the prices for which he sold his works. It was a sensitive area, because it concerned his artistic identity and precisely delineated the boundary between market forces and his self-positioning as a creative artist. Just as Brahms himself could only roughly estimate the material worth of his work and had no idea of the real cost of production and distribution, the artistic worth of his music was only of indirect value to his publishers. Thus, for a long time it remained subliminally problematic to evaluate and ultimately capitalise on the material worth of his artistry. Brahms raised this topic with his main publisher, Fritz Simrock, several times, most explicitly in September 1881:

> That one thing is the confounded relationship to money which, unfortunately, is still customary between musicians and publishers. Regarding that, we musicians are treated like children and incompetents, we don't in the least know for what and how payment is actually made, whether we are giving or getting, whether we rob or are being robbed ... Why can't we musicians have the same relationship to publishers as do authors?[11]

He continued by citing the writer Gustav Freytag as an example of how to share profits, yet Simrock did not want to follow this example – just as Schumann, notably, had done in his negotiations on Brahms's behalf with Breitkopf in 1853. For his part, in September 1881 Brahms regretted not having introduced such a change of terms for composers. Furthermore, as was common in the nineteenth century, he made over the complete rights to his work to his publisher through so-called '*Verlagszessionen*' or publisher's agreements, even though he believed such agreements – in accordance with the gradually evolving intellectual property legislation – to be too drastic. He expressed his reservations to Simrock in 1871 as follows: 'Here is the 'blood bill' [publisher's agreement] along with my thanks for the purchase price for the poor fragment of my soul [Op. 54].'[12]

The development of Brahms's publishers' fees can be sketched as follows: from 1853 to 1868, relatively modest sums were paid, albeit with gradual increases from 1864 onwards. However, from 1868, *A German Requiem* Op. 45 and the first series of *Hungarian Dances* WoO 1 (Nos. 1–10) pushed his fees to a considerably higher level. Brahms demanded a fee of 110 Napoleonsdors (1,782 Mark) from the publisher Jakob Melchior Rieter-Biedermann, observing at the end of his letter: 'I should like to ask most particularly to send me honest-to-goodness Napoleons. A payment of honour must be in gold, not paper.'[13] From 1874, by which time Brahms

[11] *Avins*, 584–5. [12] *Briefe IX*, 105. [13] *Avins*, 359.

Finances 75

was already receiving substantial fees, he secured an exceptional fee for the First Symphony Op. 68. Each of his first three symphonies, including arrangements, was rewarded with 5,000 Taler (15,000 Mark). Brahms did not keep a record of his fees in a book, but he did make many entries in his pocket diaries of his income from published works, concert fees and interest, as well as outgoings including rent and transfers to his family. These were maintained from 1867 to 1897 (1870 is missing). After his fees had grown to a certain size during the 1860s, he noted them in his own catalogue of works.[14]

Throughout his life, the composer sought practical financial advice from his nearest and dearest. The first of these was, as already hinted, his mother Christiane. In contrast to his father, she counselled him not only to earn but to save, was generally familiar with his finances and kept some of his savings for him in Hamburg.[15] Although in those years Joseph Joachim also played a role in financial matters, it was the exchange with Clara Schumann which decisively increased his wealth. She had numerous helpful business connections, such as to Hermann Victor Wendelstadt (the director of the private Cologne bank A. Schaaffhausen) and to the Berlin bank Mendelssohn & Co. Her experience in financial matters was enormously helpful to him. As early as November 1860, she bought bonds for his siblings: 'I did understand correctly, didn't I? 200 Rtl. [i.e. Taler] for Fritz and 100 Rtl. for Elise?'[16] Indeed, she continued to advise Brahms on his finances for many years, until 1868.[17]

Brahms's habit of having some money and 'Austrian securities' handled by Arthur Faber, the successful Viennese textile manufacturer, was established at the latest by 1868 – it probably began soon after 1863 when Faber married Bertha Porubsky. The securities in Hamburg were sent to Faber in 1870 by Brahms's father.[18] Brahms had known and valued Bertha Porubsky since 1859 from the time of the Hamburg Ladies' Choir; Faber later became a closer friend who helped him not only in financial matters but also with other practical things.

Similar to the connection to Faber, a connection developed with Wilhelm Lindeck, a trained singer and later the Mannheim representative of the banking house Ladenburg & Söhne, initially through musical

---

[14] See also J. Hauschildt, '"Ein Calender ist ein gar gutes Geschenk ... " Werkgenetische, publikationsspezifische und biographische Spuren in Johannes Brahms' Taschenkalendern sowie seinem eigenhändigen Werkverzeichnis', in S. Oechsle, M. Struck and K. Eich (eds.), *Brahms am Werk. Konzepte – Texte – Prozesse* (Munich: Henle 2016), 305–25.

[15] See Stephenson, *Briefwechsel Familie*, 83, c. October 1859.   [16] 16 November 1860, *SBB I*, 337.

[17] 30 June 1868, *SBB I*, 586.   [18] Stephenson, *Briefwechsel Familie*, 167.

76   JAKOB HAUSCHILDT

contacts – in this case Hermann Levi, Lindeck's brother. Brahms evidently asked Levi in 1871 for financial advice, at which point, he made the introduction to his brother. In this context, Brahms thanked an unidentified friend in Hamburg in September 1872 for the 'hospitality for my papers! I have just found out that I am losing money on them because they should be cashed!' and added the request to 'send them promptly to Herr Lindeck . . . in Mannheim'.[19] In another letter from the same time to Lindeck himself, who managed some of his money from 1872, it is clear that Brahms was having 'some reservations about having everything in one place'. A desire for security as well as personal independence may have played a role. By depositing money in different places, one could avoid or minimise losses from currency exchanges as well as money transfers, both between German territories before the founding of the empire in 1871 and internationally. In terms of securities, Brahms preferred Prussian government bonds. In the same letter, he asked Lindeck: 'If you would now have the kindness to buy some other securities (Prussian?) for me in place of the unsuitable ones, I would be most grateful to you.'[20]

As mentioned above, in spring 1877, Simrock paid an exceptionally high sum for all the rights to the First Symphony,[21] enabling the composer fundamentally to rethink his financial situation. Brahms now recognised that his financial independence was assured. Since he was inexperienced with financial transactions, did not follow the stock markets and feared risking his capital, he explicitly wished 'to keep it safe for my nearest and dearest, but in the simplest and safest place'.[22] He had already expressed his preference for fees in 'gold or Prussian securities'.[23] Thus, the Prussian Bank, which was incorporated in the newly formed Reichsbank, was an obvious choice. It was at first unclear who should deposit the money there and act as financial manager. He briefly considered Clara Schumann again, who lived in Berlin between 1873 und 1878.[24] She herself suggested her friend and adviser Franz Mendelssohn or her son Ferdinand, who worked in the bank Mendelssohn & Co., as authorised representatives.[25]

---

[19] *A-Wgm,* unpublished letter from Brahms to unidentified recipient.   [20] *Avins,* 513.

[21] Brahms to Lindeck, July 1877. M. Martin (ed), *Johannes Brahms. Briefwechsel mit dem Mannheimer Bankprokuristen Wilhelm Lindeck 1872–1882* (Heidelberg: Heidelberger Verlaganstalt und Druckerei, 1983), 33.

[22] Brahms to Fritz Simrock, c. 12 June 1877, *Briefe X,* 38.

[23] Brahms to Rieter-Biedermann, 18 September 1864, *Briefe XIV,* 103.

[24] 24 April 1877, *SBB II,* 95.   [25] 19 May 1877, *SBB II,* 100.

Finances

Ultimately, upon her suggestion, Brahms decided to dispense tactfully with the help of Wilhelm Lindeck and Arthur Faber, who managed half his fortune each, and to replace them with Fritz Simrock.[26] Presumably the choice of the Berlin-based Simrock was also more practical. Over many years, Brahms had had a close correspondence with his financially competent main publisher, which necessarily and regularly touched on financial matters. Brahms initially asked Levi to prepare his brother for the separation. At the same time, he shared reflections on his financial situation with him:

> I earn what I need. I don't do any kind of speculating with the saved money, I will probably never use it for myself, but can leave it to those who belong to me. I understand absolutely nothing about money matters, am not in the least interested in them; I have no cause to think of increasing the capital through higher interest – so if possible, I don't want to have to think about my money at all, hence I'd rather have it, for example, in the Prussian Bank than with the best brother and friend ... The Prussian Bank pays little interest. I regard it as neither stupid nor wrong if I don't seek to increase my capital through interest – that will happen sufficiently by other means.[27]

Although Brahms had already had most of the money managed by Lindeck transferred to the Berlin Reichsbank by 1877, their business relationship continued until spring 1882 – above all because Lindeck had undertaken this task so gladly and well. In thanks, Brahms sent Lindeck a signed portrait photograph as well as the then unpublished song 'Feldeinsamkeit' Op. 86 no. 2. He wrote the vocal part out in the bass clef for the singer's range, adding 'To Mr Wilhelm Lindeck / offered for a friendly attempt / by / J. Brahms'.[28]

While contact with Lindeck about money remained limited and ended after 1882, the connection to the Fabers in Vienna was already intimate early on, and endured lifelong. Nevertheless, tact was needed in 1877, since Brahms did not wish to upset his friend, and it may be no coincidence that in the spring of that year, Brahms and Faber began addressing one another with the familiar 'Du' in letters. Still, little change had been achieved by March 1878:

> Herr Faber has masses of my money in safekeeping and I have already told him long ago that I want to put that in the same corner where the other lies. Most of this is Austrian government or railway bonds. Now wouldn't it be very nice if he could simply send you the whole load? Maybe the bank will

---

[26] May 1877, *SBB II*, 106.   [27] May 1877, *Briefe VII*, 186f.
[28] The facsimile of the autograph was published by Henle (Munich, 1983).

take the things as they are, and otherwise perhaps Par[r]isius could exchange them? May I ask you to do this?[29]

Somewhat later, the bonds managed by Faber were either added to the Reichsbank account or sold or exchanged if they were not traded outside Austria. With this, Simrock became the main manager of the growing fortune from 1878, and it fell to him to reinvest the interest or dividends or to send cash remittances to Brahms's family in Hamburg. Still, there was a downside to this change, since Brahms could no longer so straightforwardly draw upon the interest from the account Faber had managed.[30]

Although Faber was still available for financial advice, Brahms's finances were largely managed by Simrock from 1878, who occasionally received circulars and Reichsbank statements to sort out when they were unclear to Brahms. From 1888, Brahms knew that he no longer needed his fees to live on, given his frugal lifestyle. In this spirit, he wrote to Clara Schumann: 'I cannot, don't want to, and will not live any other way; it would be useless to give more to my family than I now do, and where my heart demands it, I am able to help and do good to any degree without noticing it.'[31] In other words, he could help his friends financially as he pleased.

Brahms's relationship to money was tested once more in later years. In spring 1895, Fritz Simrock, who had been entrusted to look after the money with as little risk as possible had to reveal that he had lost almost 20,000 Marks in a risky speculation. But it was less concern about the loss of the money, which the relaxed Brahms referred to as the 'great' or 'famous bankruptcy', than concern for his friend that troubled Brahms: 'I would be ashamed and very annoyed if I had wanted to earn money in such a manner. If a good friend has erred, I am sorrier for him than for myself – no, only for him, for I really think about money only as long as it is under discussion.'[32]

Further Reading

G. Ehlert, 'Brahms, Schönberg und ihre Berliner Verleger', in A. Dümling (ed.), *Verteidigung des musikalischen Fortschritts. Brahms und Schönberg* (Hamburg: Argument, 1990), 111–16

---

[29] Brahms to Simrock, probably March 1878, *Briefe X*, 68. The Deutsche Genossenschaftsbank Soergel, Parrisius & Co. was Simrock's own main bank.

[30] Brahms to Simrock, 4 December 1878, *Briefe X*, 97.   [31] *Avins*, 656.

[32] Brahms to Simrock, 5 April 1895, *Briefe XII*, 170.

Finances 79

L. Lütteken, 'Brahms – eine bürgerliche Biographie?', in *Brahms Handbuch*, 24–43
Meyers Konversations-Lexikon, 3rd edn, 16 vols. (Leipzig: Verlag des Bibliographischen Instituts, 1874–8)

M. Martin (ed.), *Johannes Brahms. Briefwechsel mit dem Mannheimer Bankprokuristen Wilhelm Lindeck 1872–1882* (Heidelberg: Stadtarchiv Mannheim, 1983)

K. Stephenson (ed.), *Johannes Brahms und Fritz Simrock – Weg einer Freundschaft. Briefe des Verlegers an den Komponisten* (Hamburg: J. J. Augustin, 1961)

CHAPTER 9

As Pianist

Katrin Eich

Typically for many musicians of his day, Brahms was artistically active in multiple ways, not only as a composer but also as a performer, mainly as a pianist and conductor, piano teacher and director of musical societies. He never perceived himself as primarily a pianist; however, playing the piano – in private and public – was inseparable from his artistic and compositional identity. Schumann remarked on this as early as 9 November 1853 in a letter to the Leipzig publishers Breitkopf & Härtel, to whom he had recommended the young man: 'his playing is truly a part of his music; I cannot recall hearing such unique sound effects'.[1] Brahms received his initial piano training in Hamburg from Otto Friedrich Willibald Cossel and then from Cossel's teacher Eduard Marxsen, who had trained in Vienna and who also advised Brahms in composition (Brahms never attended a conservatory) [see Ch. 1 'Childhood in Hamburg']. His talent as pianist and composer was evident early on; Cossel regretted that Brahms's passion for composition prevented him from fulfilling his pianistic potential. Nevertheless, from his first subscription concert onwards, which according to Florence May took place in 1843 when he was ten years old, he played the piano in public for virtually the whole of his life.

Brahms's pianistic activity fluctuated, inasmuch as there were phases of intensive and sporadic concert activity as well as times when he did not perform publicly at all. To some extent, this depended on external circumstances. In his youth, it was naturally important to introduce himself to the musical world as a performer. This largely began with his first concert tour with the violinist Eduard Reményi in spring 1853 and continued with the private playing that would be hugely significant to his future, for example in April with Joseph Joachim and with Robert and Clara Schumann that autumn. Furthermore, it included his first

---

[1] F. Gustav Jansen (ed.), *Robert Schumanns Briefe. Neue Folge*, 2nd edn (Leipzig: Breitkopf & Härtel, 1904), 486.

performance in the Leipzig Gewandhaus in December 1853, at which he performed his Piano Sonata Op. 1 and the Scherzo Op. 4. The need to earn was also a longstanding preoccupation and, initially at least, could not be met through composition. His salaried posts as choral director, pianist and piano teacher at the court of Detmold (in the final months of 1857–9) and as choirmaster of the Vienna Singakademie (for the 1863/4 season) made him feel too restricted, so piano teaching and freelance concert-giving provided options that he could control in terms of the time they cost him.

A high point, but also a turning point, was the second half of the 1860s. On one hand, this was a particularly active phase of concertising, with artists who included Joseph Joachim and the singer Julius Stockhausen. On the other hand, towards the end of the 1860s, early performances of *A German Requiem* Op. 45 and the first series of his *Hungarian Dances* WoO 1 (Nos. 1–10), finally brought him real recognition as a composer. His resultant financial independence did not mean that concert performances retreated entirely into the background, but their relationship to composing changed; the latter now required unhampered spells of concentration, and Brahms could correspondingly limit his concert activity as needed. It might, then, be more intense over certain periods, for example when he appeared as the soloist in his two piano concertos. It was naturally important for Brahms to promote his music and his aesthetic conceptions both as a conductor and as a pianist, but he could be choosier about his concert-giving than before. Henceforth, he enjoyed considerable personal freedom, a situation enhanced by his lack of family commitments. This situation was entirely different from that of pianists who had no reputation as composers or who could not live from their composing income – for example, Clara Schumann, who was trained as a pianist by her father Friedrich Wieck and who, as a pianist, regarded herself very differently from Brahms. Having greatly reduced her concert activity after marrying Robert Schumann, she had to provide for her family after his death in 1856 and was therefore forced to take on far more concerts and teaching than Brahms (her championing of her husband's and, Brahms's music was an important additional motivation). She regularly undertook demanding tours, including trips to England. Before one such tour in spring 1865, she wrote to Brahms pragmatically: 'You will protest, won't you, dear Johannes, but if you were the father of seven children, you would do as I do.'[2]

---

[2] *SBB I*, 501.

The repertoire that Brahms played publicly also remained within manageable boundaries. For other composers' works, there was a clear emphasis on Bach, Beethoven and Schumann. From the 1860s, he increasingly performed his own works. Altogether, his programmes, when he was in full control of them, were dictated more by his own interests than by any didactic intentions or structural considerations; he gave no explicitly 'historical' concerts and eschewed ideas such as Beethoven cycles, like those offered by Hans von Bülow, in keeping with his deliberate transformation of traditional programmes and broadening of repertoire. Nevertheless, historical aspects and aesthetically meaningful programme concepts were by no means foreign to Brahms. Arrangements of other composers' music played a significant role [see Ch. 11 'As Arranger']. These included J. S. Bach's Toccata BWV 540, the final movement of Beethoven's String Quartet Op. 59 no. 3, marches by Schubert originally for four-hand piano and the Scherzo from his Octet D803, and Schumann's *Studies for Pedal Piano* Op. 56, above all the B minor Canon No. 5. These performances doubtless had an improvisatory flavour, since they were generally neither notated nor published. Thus (with a few exceptions) Brahms remained distant from the nineteenth-century practice, popularised not least by Liszt, of publishing transcriptions of other composers' works.

When it came to venues, Brahms was active as a pianist in many spaces, be it a large concert hall, a noble salon or a middle-class music room. This free movement between public and private performance, with various stages in between, reflected the conditions of his century. But as many friends and acquaintances recalled, he particularly cherished private, intimate music-making with or for close friends, and it was in this context that his piano playing was possibly at its greatest. His actual concert activity did not cover a large geographical area but was mainly limited to German-speaking territories, the Habsburg empire, Switzerland and the Netherlands. It was out of the question for Brahms to travel beyond the mainland, as Joseph Joachim, Clara Schumann or Hans von Bülow did, or to extend to places like Russia or France, let alone America. His aversion to milieus that were linguistically and culturally alien to him was surely significant here [see Ch. 7 'Holidays'].

Brahms's comportment in public piano playing was described as introspective and inward-looking. Many accounts describe how he was not only immersed in himself but had to be forcefully called back to the platform for the applause; he built practically no social relationship with his public, unlike von Bülow, for example, who sought to educate his audiences by

As Pianist

addressing them. Brahms also refused to bolster his musical activity through writing publicly about music (an exception was the Manifesto against 'New' German music, signed by him, Joachim and a few other musicians, which was prematurely published in May 1860). In his performances, he was everything other than self-promoting; self-staging or self-styling as a virtuoso or flirting with the public, as many of his contemporaries did, was alien to him. His friend Richard Heuberger recalled: 'As a virtuoso, Brahms had only the virtuosity, but he had nothing of the theatrical magic with which such artists do not want to, or do not believe they can, dispense.'[3] This view was reinforced by the fact that Brahms paid little attention to his appearance. He nonetheless frequently used the word 'virtuoso', both of others and of himself, in a general sense rather than as a narrow concept, applying it to interpreters who were genuinely technically highly competent together with other pianists who performed publicly, sometimes ironically.

In any case, in 1889 Brahms made himself available for a recording with the Edison phonograph [see Ch. 30 'Science and Technology'], which the German-born Edison representative Theo Wangemann presented during his European trip in 1889/90 in various cities including Vienna (where he also recorded the pianist Alfred Grünfeld). Fascinated by this technical achievement, Brahms wrote in November 1889 to Clara Schumann:

> We live here now under the sign of the phonograph, and I had the opportunity to hear it often and in comfort. You will have read plenty about the new miracle or will have had it described for you; once again it's as though one were living a fairy-tale.[4]

The context of this recording is interesting because Wangemann recorded not only music of varying styles and complexity during his trip but also voices – of family members, as well as of key political figures such as Otto von Bismarck (many of these recordings are now available in the Edison National Historical Park, New Jersey).[5] Through this medium, Brahms can be heard playing parts of his first *Hungarian Dance* and the Polka-Mazurka 'Die Libelle' Op. 204 by Josef Strauss, albeit with very problematic sound quality. Nevertheless, one can gain a sense of the pianist Brahms and, above all, his sometimes improvisatory, paraphrasing style and a certain flexibility in tempo and hand coordination.

---

[3] *Heuberger*, 131.   [4] *Avins*, 671.
[5] Some are available online: www.nps.gov/edis/learn/photosmultimedia/theo-wangemann-1889–1890-european-recordings.htm.

84 KATRIN EICH

Brahms's pianistic ability was described very differently by his friends and contemporaries: the judgements and recollections range from the highest praise to the harshest criticism. These divergent statements can be explained by the fact that Brahms was apparently exceptionally gifted as a pianist, both technically and aesthetically, but was certainly not always in the right mindset and did not practise regularly or intensively enough to retain consistent mastery of the instrument. Already no perfectionist as a young man, his proficiency evidently declined with age. Statements about Brahms as a pianist therefore depend upon context, in particular, the timing, the frequency and the temporal distribution of the experiences which prompted the evaluations and, finally, also the individual listener's attitude and relationship to him. Altogether, Brahms was regarded more as a piano-playing composer than a composing pianist, which aligned with his own preferences; much the same is true for the Norwegian Edvard Grieg, for example. Thus, the Viennese music critic Theodor Helm wrote in the *Musikalisches Wochenblatt* in 1874: 'Alongside all the pianistic achievements of this man, one immediately gains the impression that a significant creative artist is sitting at the piano.'[6]

Brahms did not indulge in negative, competitive thinking; rivalry of the type between Franz Liszt and Sigismund Thalberg, which raged in the late 1830s and which was reported widely in the press, would have been unthinkable (although, among his friends, he did enjoy demonstrating his phenomenal memory). While he did not rate the compositions of figures like Liszt or Rubinstein highly, he evidently praised both as pianists several times. As his biographer Max Kalbeck recalled, Brahms once said: 'People who have not heard Liszt really cannot speak about it. He is the first, and there is a considerable gap before the next. His piano playing was something unique, incomparable and inimitable'; he also said to Klaus Groth: 'We also play the piano ... but all of us together have only a few fingers of his two hands.'[7] In the 1890s, he apparently said to the daughter of his friend Ottilie Ebner, when she was rhapsodising about Rubinstein: 'Yes, I say that too; when I hear Rubinstein play, I always feel that it would be better if keep my hands firmly clasped behind my back and never touch a piano again.'[8] He also wrote to Elisabeth von Herzogenberg in December 1885 acknowledging Rubinstein's demanding series of 'historic' concerts.[9] He is said to have told Clara Schumann that she was 'far superior' to him in

[6] *Musikalisches Wochenblatt* 5/28 (3 July 1874), 344. [7] *Kalbeck I*, 90.
[8] O. von Balassa, *Die Brahmsfreundin Ottilie Ebner und ihr Kreis* (Wien: Franz Bondy, 1933), 118–9.
[9] *Briefe II*, 114.

terms of 'accuracy and purity of playing, and magnificence of sound'.[10] And in later years, he valued the playing of Ilona Eibenschütz, for example, who, along with Fanny Davies, championed his piano music in England, and also Eugen d'Albert, who, from 1887 onwards, under Brahms's leadership, almost as an alter ego, played his piano concertos after the composer himself no longer appeared publicly as a soloist.

While Brahms could be absolutely scathing about other pianists, the ideal situation was an artistic partnership, for example with Carl Tausig, who died young in 1871 and came from the Liszt–Wagner camp. He gave the premiere of Brahms's Sonata for Two Pianos Op. 34bis in Vienna with the composer. According to Kalbeck, Brahms's *Variations on a Theme of Paganini* Op. 35, which he himself played several times in concerts and which characteristically combine pedagogical, pianistic and compositional aspects, were 'truly composed into Tausig's fingers'.[11]

Brahms was also very active as a pianist in chamber music and vocal accompaniment. He did organise his 'own' recitals in which he performed (mostly) as a solo pianist (e.g. his successful Vienna concert on 6 January 1863). However, he was often, as was normal for his time, a co-organiser or participant in other people's concerts, both as a soloist and as a chamber musician. Collaborating with other musicians was a significant part of his identity as a performer, and this is reflected in his works in that solo and chamber works are roughly equal in number. He remained active as a public chamber musician almost until the end of his life, even though he no longer performed publicly as a soloist after the 1885/6 season. In the 1890s, he apparently justified giving up solo playing simply because of the stage fright he suffered from when playing from memory.[12] But the decline in his own abilities and his greater affinity for collaborative music-making may well have also played a part in this decision.

Ultimately, Brahms's ambivalent relationship to performance can be seen in numerous (often-cited) statements. The fact that these are inconsistent is unsurprising, since they arise in various contexts: they appear in letters and in memoirs, date from different periods and relate to private and public situations amassed over an artistic lifetime, which in Brahms's case spanned several decades. In early years, he seems to have suffered from relatively bad performance anxiety. Thus, for example, he wrote to his friend Julius Otto Grimm in autumn 1855: 'I intend to play in public this

[10] K. Huschke, *Johannes Brahms als Pianist, Dirigent und Lehrer* (Karlsruhe: Friedrich Gutsch, 1935), 28.
[11] *Kalbeck II*, 43.   [12] von Balassa, *Die Brahmsfreundin Ottilie Ebner*, 119.

86 KATRIN EICH

winter and notice with horror that my aversion to playing for people has got quite out of hand. How will it go; at times I am seriously frightened.'[13] In the 1860s, especially, and into the 1870s, there were occasions when Brahms derived real pleasure from his concert-giving. He wrote to Clara Schumann in December 1865 after a concert in Switzerland:

> Above all, what pleases me most is that I really have the talent to be a virtuoso. The only thing I am completely dependent on is the piano I have, if it is good I play with the greatest comfort and best of ease. The bigger the pieces, the better.[14]

Still, the need to express himself productively, through works he had himself composed, remained constant. He intermittently led what he described to Joachim in autumn 1868 as an 'amphibious life, half virtuoso, half composer', adding that 'at present, it is the virtuoso who is praised, which doesn't say much for the composer'.[15]

In September 1879, Brahms embarked on a concert tour to Siebenbürgen with Joseph Joachim; from Brahms's perspective, this took place under perfect conditions, combining as it did sociable travelling, the discovery of delightful new places, relaxed public music-making with his friend and gratifying public approval. He was motivated in this by Joachim, to whom he wrote before the trip: 'Your glorious playing has after all awoken in me a fancy for concerts. Next year I'd like to bring my fingers back under control and now and then do something with you, if you'd like to.'[16] Afterwards, he reported to Clara Schumann:

> To travel in the loveliest weather through a strange, interesting, and often very beautiful country, to make a little music on the side and to let others sing and drink to you, I suppose that's fine for a few weeks, one can put up with it . . . I would be happy to make such concert tours more often! . . . But today's virtuosi have need of too much money for that. There has to be a concert every day, one arrives an hour before and leaves an hour after the concert. For me, that would be the most disagreeable and despicable activity.[17]

The irregularity of his performances was a recurring problem, to which he occasionally referred when he wished or was obliged to decline invitations for concerts. He once explained to his friend the doctor Theodor Engelmann in late 1875: 'My biggest mistake as a virtuoso is that I play too seldom in public, so one doesn't easily feel comfortable.'[18] Thus the

---

[13] *Avins*, 112. [14] *Ibid.*, 337. [15] *Briefe VI*, 59. [16] *Ibid.*, 154. [17] *Avins*, 556.
[18] *Briefe XIII*, 32.

As Pianist

close relationship between interpretation and creation, identified so early by Schumann, always led to a conflict that ultimately Brahms could or would not resolve: he was too much the composer to be a full-blooded pianist but too much a pianist to subjugate it completely to his composition.

Further Reading

R. and K. Hofmann, *Johannes Brahms als Pianist und Dirigent* (Tutzing: Hans Schneider, 2006)

R. and K. Hofmann, 'Brahms als Interpret', in *Brahms Handbuch*, 77–86

K. Huschke, *Johannes Brahms als Pianist, Dirigent und Lehrer* (Karlsruhe: Friedrich Gutsch, 1935)

M. Musgrave, 'Brahms the pianist', in M. Musgrave, *A Brahms Reader* (New Haven and London: Yale University Press, 2000), 121–36

CHAPTER 10

As Conductor

Walter Frisch

The earliest evidence of Brahms's activity as a conductor comes from 1847, when as a fourteen-year-old he led a chorus of school children in the small town of Winsen near his native Hamburg. His last reported appearance on a podium was with the Berlin Philharmonic in January 1896, aged sixty-two. Over a span of almost fifty years between these two moments, Brahms conducted a wide range of amateur and professional ensembles in many different locations across the Austrian Empire, Germany and Switzerland.

Brahms's activities on the podium coincide with the steady rise of the professional conductor during the nineteenth century, embodied in the Austro-German sphere at first by Weber, Mendelssohn, Wagner, Spohr and Spontini, and later by Richard Strauss, Mahler, Richter and Bülow. These musicians assumed demanding positions as music directors partly out of necessity to make a decent living but also out of a desire to achieve the best possible performances of what was becoming standard concert and operatic repertory. Like Brahms, many were also composers who conducted and promoted their own works. Brahms was more of an 'occasional' conductor than most of these figures, but he also stands out from them through his strong love of and advocacy for early music that extended back to the Renaissance.

In addition to many guest appearances at which he led performances of his own compositions, Brahms held four longer-term appointments as a conductor or music director: for three seasons (October–December), 1857 to 1859, he led a choral group at the small court of Detmold; from 1859 to 1861, he conducted the Hamburg Ladies' Choir; from 1863 to 1864, he led the Wiener Singakademie; and for three seasons, from 1872 to 1875, he led the concerts of the Vienna Gesellschaft der Musikfreunde. Brahms was offered numerous other positions during his lifetime but turned them down primarily for the same reason he left those listed above: he wanted the time to compose. The one position he desired most, and which he might have held for longer, eluded him: he was twice

88

As a conductor, Brahms's superb musicianship, high standards and ambitious programming, especially of Renaissance and Baroque repertory, earned him the admiration of many musicians who worked with him, as well as critics and listeners who attended the concerts. But these very qualities sometimes incurred disapproval or impatience from others.

passed over for the directorship of the Hamburg Philharmonic in his own hometown.

Detmold

Through a connection made by Clara Schumann, Brahms was engaged in 1857 to work in Detmold at the court of Count Leopold III of Lippe, a small principality in north-western Germany. Brahms served as court pianist, piano teacher to the princesses, and conductor of the amateur choral society. Brahms's repertoire at Detmold reveals what would be a lifelong interest in exploring – and exposing the public to – music from the Renaissance and Baroque eras. Among the works he rehearsed and/or performed at Detmold were Rovetta's *Salve Regina*, Praetorius's *Maria Zart*, Palestrina's *Pope Marcellus Mass*, portions of Handel's *Messiah* and Bach's Cantatas BWV 4 and 21. Brahms also programmed more recent Classical and Romantic music, including his own, for which the Detmold chorus served as a valuable laboratory. 'How little practical knowledge I have!' he wrote to Joseph Joachim in December 1857. 'The chorus rehearsals have shown me great weaknesses, they will not be useless to me. My things are certainly written in an excessively impractical way! I have rehearsed numerous things and fortunately, right from the first hour, with sufficient audacity.'[1]

Brahms was frustrated at Detmold because the resident concertmaster August Kiel would only permit the younger man to conduct the orchestra when the works included chorus. Brahms also felt constrained by the geographic isolation and the restrictions of dress and behaviour at court and, perhaps most of all, by the uneven quality of his singers, who came from the court and the town. 'Half my tenure is over, thank God,' he wrote grumpily to his friend Julius Otto Grimm in early November 1858.[2] In the summer of 1860 Brahms refused the Prince's invitation to return to Detmold for a fourth season.

---

[1] *Avins*, 161. [2] *Ibid.*, 179.

Hamburg Ladies' Choir

In the months before what would be his final season at Detmold, Brahms began to work with the Hamburg Ladies' Choir, a group that grew out of a gathering on 6 June 1859, when twenty-eight women assembled to rehearse Brahms' *Ave Maria* Op. 12, and *O bone Jesu* and *Adoramus* Op. 37 nos. 1 and 2. The event went so well that the choir began to rehearse one morning per week under Brahms's direction at the home of one of the founders, singing mainly works that he wrote for them. Brahms was disciplined but good-natured with the choir, as is clear from the contract or 'Avertimento', as he called it, which the women had to sign. It included such conditions as being fined two shillings if they appeared more than fifteen minutes late for a rehearsal and forbidding them to share the music scores with anyone outside the group.

The ladies of the choir had respect and affection for Brahms. One of them, Franziska Meier, wrote in her diary:

> We sang the Psalm by Schubert, two songs by Brahms, three by Schumann, and then 'Poor Peter' by Grädener, for six part women's chorus – terrifically difficult! It went very badly. I admired Brahms's patience. We practiced only the first two parts, then in conclusion, the Psalm over again. I like Brahms as a conductor exceedingly.[3]

The admiration was mutual. After returning to Detmold in the fall of 1859, he wrote to Clara Schumann longingly of his Hamburg group: 'O my dear girls, where are you! ... I tell you, the ladies' choir is one of my most endearing memories.'[4]

Hamburg

Even as he was working with the Ladies' Choir, Brahms was seeking a more public and prominent role in musical life. In February 1860, he conducted his Second Serenade Op. 16, and played the solo part in Schumann's Piano Concerto Op. 54 with the Hamburg Philharmonic, to considerable acclaim. In 1862, Brahms left Hamburg for his first trip to Vienna, where, during the autumn and winter of 1862–3, he introduced himself and his music to the public of the imperial city with a series of concerts at which he played his piano and chamber works.

---

[3] S. Drinker, *Brahms and His Women's Choruses* (Merion, PA: Musurgia Publishers, 1952), 27.
[4] *Avins*, 199.

As Conductor

The committee that governed the Hamburg Philharmonic was now seeking a new conductor to replace the ageing Friedrich Wilhelm Grund. Brahms strongly desired the position but was passed over in favour of the baritone Julius Stockhausen. Brahms, who had hoped to settle in his native city, was devastated, writing to Clara Schumann from Vienna:

> It is a much sadder event than you may think . . . I am not cosmopolitan, but instead, am attached to my native city as to a mother . . . Now this hostile friend comes along and pushes me away – forever, I suppose. How seldom does someone like us find a fixed abode, how I would have liked to find it in my native city.[5]

Stockhausen, who was not aware that Brahms had sought the Hamburg position, was genuinely puzzled by Brahms's reaction. He wrote to Clara, 'Early on Brahms himself told me he wouldn't be the right man to wrestle with people in order to transform the orchestra . . . Has Brahms all of a sudden acquired talent as a conductor? Earlier on he didn't have any, and the musicians allowed themselves remarks, etc.'[6]

Wiener Singakademie

Stockhausen's comments suggest that despite Brahms's experience in Detmold and with the Hamburg Ladies' Choir, he did not yet have confidence and poise in front of a larger professional ensemble like the Hamburg Philharmonic. In any case, it appears that Brahms's lot was now cast with Vienna. In 1863, he was offered the directorship of the Wiener Singakademie, a group that had been founded in 1858.

Brahms stayed only one season with the Singakademie, but in the six concerts (of which three were subscription events) that he led, Brahms made a strong impact on the musical life of the city. As in Detmold, Brahms's programming mixed Classical and Romantic repertory (including one concert of his own music) with music from the Renaissance and Baroque eras. The first concert began with Bach's Cantata BWV 21 ('Ich hatte viel Bekümmernis'), for which Brahms himself prepared the continuo part. Public and critical reaction was very positive. The powerful Viennese music critic Eduard Hanslick, who would become a strong ally and supporter of Brahms, wrote after the first concert that Brahms was a 'conductor full of understanding', displaying 'a youthful energy, in

---

[5] *Ibid.*, 258.   [6] *Ibid.*, 265–6.

92   WALTER FRISCH

which an unspent freshness is combined with a rare calmness and maturity'.[7]

The second and third subscription concerts of the Singakademie were less successful. The programme of 6 January 1864, which included seventeenth-century a cappella works by Eccard, Schütz, Gabrieli and Rovetta, as well as a Bach motet, was deemed by both the singers and the governing committee too heavy for the holiday season. Hanslick wrote of a monotony that gave the event 'the feeling of an improvisation or rehearsal, rather than a concert'. The critic Rudolf Hirsch called the concert a 'shipwreck'. Among the mishaps: a Bösendorfer piano provided to substitute for an organ was tuned too high and thus unusable.[8]

The 20 March concert was comprised entirely of five movements from Bach's *Christmas Oratorio* BWV 248. This event had the misfortune to be scheduled, by chance, just days before a performance of Bach's *St John Passion* BWV 245 by the Singverein of the Gesellschaft der Musikfreunde across town. Together, the concerts offered too much Bach for Viennese tastes. Brahms wrote to Clara that the concert 'went indeed quite splendidly, I must say. I and the chorus, at least, enjoyed it. Faced with the local critics, a Bach work has a difficult time.'[9]

Despite the many bumps in the Singakademie season, Brahms was offered a three-year extension of his contract. But he decided to give up the position. In a letter to his friend, the music critic Adolf Schubring, Brahms stressed how the political and logistical problems outweighed the musical rewards:

> I have given up my post there! In spite of many joys which the chorus there provides, unfortunately it had to be. The nature and circumstances of the Institute [Akademie] are such that I would be occupied less with musical than with other matters. [The Singakademie] would have to be helped out by means of concerts which taste more agreeable to the public, etc., I would have to pay too much heed to prima donnas, to a thousand things that are no concern of mine.[10]

Although it would be eight years before Brahms took up another professional post, he was not absent from the podium. His most prominent appearances involved introducing *A German Requiem* Op. 45 to the public. Brahms conducted three movements in Vienna in December 1867, and then on Good Friday in April 1868 he led the official premiere in the

---

[7] K. Huschke, *Johannes Brahms als Pianist, Dirigent und Lehrer* (Karlsruhe: Friedrich Gutich Verlag, 1935), 59.
[8] *May II*, 23.   [9] *Avins*, 292.   [10] *Ibid.*, 297.

As Conductor

cathedral of Bremen. In her diary Clara Schumann specifically mentions Brahms's role as conductor of his work: 'As I saw Johannes standing there like that with the baton in his hand, I continually had to think of my dearest Robert's prophecy "let him but once take the magic wand, and work with the orchestra and choir," which is fulfilled today.'[11]

Gesellschaft der Musikfreunde

During the 1860s and early 1870s, even with the expansion of his reputation and activity as a composer, Brahms continued to be on the lookout for professional positions. He considered possibilities in Cologne, Berlin and Amsterdam. But as he became more settled in Vienna, he was reluctant to make a move. In 1872, Brahms was offered the post of artistic director and conductor at the Gesellschaft der Musikfreunde, one of the oldest and most prestigious musical institutions in Vienna.

Brahms was responsible for six concerts per year; he was to work mainly with the chorus, but two events were to include chorus and orchestra. From the start, Brahms sought to impose his high standards and values. He made changes in the traditional rehearsal techniques of the chorus. He called for extra rehearsals, requiring sectionals and placing small groups of singers on a part so that they would learn the music thoroughly. In a first rehearsal, he would run through a piece, then study its structure and musical details.

Needless to say, some of the singers resisted Brahms's techniques. But he earned their respect. The chorus received Brahms enthusiastically. 'Brahms knows superbly how to prepare individual movements, and the members of the society show a lot of enthusiasm and clear interest,' reads a diary log report of the first rehearsal. 'Brahms's distinguished teaching was recognised by everyone.'[12] One singer, Theresa Gügler, recalled in later years:

> Brahms was always serious at a rehearsal, but also very patient and friendly, never harsh or rude. The choir worked very willingly under Brahms's direction. At that time, Brahms was beardless, young, and blond; he was already famous, but still understood to be swiftly on the rise. We had the clear impression of a standing before great personality, and no ordinary choral conductor.[13]

---

[11] Cited in M. Musgrave, *Brahms: A German Requiem* (Cambridge: Cambridge University Press, 1996), 9.

[12] M. Komorn, *Johannes Brahms als Chordirigent in Wien und seine Nachfolger bis zum Schubert-Jahr 1928* (Vienna and Leipzig: Universal, 1928), 30.

[13] *Ibid.*, 48.

94   WALTER FRISCH

In a history of the Gesellschaft, Robert Hirschfeld suggests that 'in Brahms there lived a piece of the great Thomaskantor [Bach], and the vocal textures of powerful choruses comprised his world'.[14]

Brahms's ambitious programming reflected his earlier practices, but now with the greater resources of the Gesellschaft. The concerts included oratorios by Handel (*Saul, Alexander's Feast* and *Solomon*) and cantatas (BWV 4, 8, 34, 50) and the *St Matthew Passion* BWV 244 by Bach. As with Brahms's tenure with the Singakademie in the 1860s, some Viennese audiences and critics had difficulty digesting this fare, but many also appreciated the opportunity to hear unfamiliar works by great masters. When Brahms performed *Saul* in February 1873, the critic Theodor Helm wrote: 'It is incomprehensible that we get to hear this piece ... only 145 years after its composition.' Helm reported that the performance 'was very satisfying. Brahms deserves credit not only for artfully resurrecting the work but also for the very reverent treatment on the part of all involved in this rediscovery. The chorus and the orchestra, so carefully rehearsed and conducted by Brahms, gave a truly superb performance.'[15]

But for all his successes, Brahms also met with resistance, not least from the directorship of the Gesellschaft, who pressured him into programming works (like Berlioz's *Harold in Italy* Op. 16) they felt would temper the heavily Baroque repertory and the massive choral works he favoured. Ultimately Brahms could change the tastes of neither the management nor the Viennese audiences. As he would write somewhat bitterly in 1895 to Richard von Perger, a later conductor of the Gesellschaft concerts: 'The Viennese barely have a clue about great choral music.'[16] Brahms resigned his position in 1875, though he would maintain cordial relationships with the Gesellschaft for the rest of his life. Otto Dessoff, the conductor of the Vienna Philharmonic, noted that Brahms would now have more time to compose – thus making a much greater contribution even than that which he made through directing the Gesellschaft's concerts.[17]

The experience Brahms gained across the three years and eighteen concerts with the Gesellschaft was significant, not least for developing his familiarity with the inner workings of an orchestra. This experience appears to have given him both the confidence and the time at last to bring to completion his First Symphony Op. 68 in 1876, just a year after

---

[14] R. Hirschfeld et al., *Geschichte des K. K. Gesellschaft der Musikfreunde in Wien* (Vienna: Gesellschaft der Musikfreunde, 1912), 148.

[15] Cited in Komorn, *Johannes Brahms als Chordirigent*, 33–4.   [16] *Ibid.,* 52.   [17] *Ibid.,* 46–7.

As Conductor

leaving the Gesellschaft, and to compose his Second Symphony Op. 73 in quick succession.

Final Impressions, Final Years

Although Brahms would never again assume a permanent conducting position after his time at the Gesellschaft, in his later years, as his symphonic and choral-symphonic works multiplied, he was a frequent guest conductor of his own works. Various accounts of Brahms's conducting in his later years emphasise its passion. A relative of Brahms's friend Theodor Billroth reported,

> His manner of conducting is extremely vigorous and full of go. When he wants a *pianissimo,* he bends right forward, while for a *fortissimo* he draws himself up erect, but always with a perfectly natural movement, without any theatrical striving for effect. One can see from the expression of his face, from his every movement, how the throws himself into every note. The passion which emanates from him communicates itself automatically to the members of his choir and orchestra.[18]

Brahms's final appearance as a conductor in Vienna was on 18 March 1895, when he led the Vienna Conservatory student orchestra in the *Academic Festival Overture* Op. 80. His biographer Max Kalbeck reported on the event in what is perhaps the single most vivid extant account of Brahms on the podium:

> I could look directly into Brahms' face – it was a memorable sight. He put his entire soul into it, and the fire of his pathos completely drew in the enchanted young people. Yet he gave the impression he was suffering from demons evoked by his baton. It seemed as if he first had to fight with them before he had control of them. Again and again he pressed his left fist into his heart as if he were in pain and then used it again either to push ahead or slow down. His left hand had more to say than his right hand, because the little that it communicated was of decisive importance. He wore neither nose glasses [*Pincenez*] nor regular ones. His eyes had a strange, foreign, rigid glance, as if they were sometimes communicating fear intensified into fury. Every downbeat shook his heavy body, and the grey streaks of hair were flying around.[19]

It was on this occasion that the artist Willy von Beckerath made his well-known series of drawings of Brahms conducting (see Figure 10.1).

---

[18] W. Niemann, *Brahms,* trans. C. A. Phillips (New York: Tudor, 1937), 195.
[19] *Kalbeck IV,* 400–1. Translation adapted from J. K. Bass, *Johannes Brahms the Conductor: Historical Context, Chronology, and Critical Reception,* DMA thesis, University of Miami (2005), 137.

Figure 10.1. Brahms conducting, drawn by Willy von Beckerath, 1895.

Overall, Brahms's conducting style seems to have fallen comfortably between the extremes of his day, which might be characterised most simply as strict and free. At the strict end of the spectrum fell Hans Richter, the director of the Vienna Philharmonic, whom Brahms found sometimes dull and pedestrian. At the freer end was Hans von Bülow, whose extreme nuances and liberties also sometimes irritated Brahms. Yet Brahms expressed admiration for both Richter and Bülow, recognised champions of his music, as he did for their younger contemporaries Fritz Steinbach and Felix Weingartner. Upon hearing Weingartner perform the Second Symphony Op. 73 in April 1895, Brahms remarked that the young

As Conductor

conductor's 'healthy, fresh personality was uncommonly sympathetic' and that the performance was 'truly wonderful'.[20]

Weingartner's compelling recording of Brahms's Second Symphony Op. 73 with the London Symphony Orchestra in 1940 (on CD as EMI CHS 7 64256 2), though made many years after Brahms heard him, gives not only a good idea of what Brahms may have found 'wonderful' but perhaps also a taste of what Brahms aimed for in his own conducting. Weingartner's tempi are brisk but always fluid; they never seem rushed. His performance has plenty of nuance yet also displays a broader sense of musical time that spans an entire movement.

In the absence of any sound recording of Brahms's conducting, the collective impression – verbal, visual and sonic – of Kalbeck's description, Beckerath's images and Weingartner's performance bring us perhaps as close as possible to a direct experience of Brahms on the podium. At its best, Brahms's conducting was distinguished by the same qualities that characterise his compositions: a blend of fervour and logic, abandon and control, heart and brain.

Further Reading

J. K. Bass, 'Johannes Brahms the Conductor: Historical Context, Chronology, and Critical Reception,' DMA thesis, University of Miami (2005)

S. Drinker, *Brahms and His Women's Choruses* (Merion, PA: Musurgia Publishers, 1952)

K. Huschke, *Johannes Brahms als Pianist, Dirigent und Lehrer* (Karlsruhe: Friedrich Gutich Verlag, 1935)

M. Komorn, *Johannes Brahms als Chordirigent in Wien und seine Nachfolger bis zum Schubert-Jahr 1928* (Vienna and Leipzig: Universal, 1928)

M. Komorn, 'Brahms as Conductor', *Musical Quarterly* 19/2 (April 1933), 151–7

M. Musgrave, 'Brahms the Conductor', in Musgrave, *A Brahms Reader* (New Haven and London: Yale University Press, 2000), 136–47

[20] *Briefe XII*, 169.

CHAPTER 11

As Arranger

Valerie Woodring Goertzen

On 22 November 1883, ten days before Hans Richter was to conduct the premiere of Brahms's Third Symphony Op. 90 in Vienna, Brahms organised a musical evening in the elegant Ehrbar Salon. With the Austrian pianist Ignaz Brüll, he presented the new symphony in his arrangement for two pianos to a distinguished group of invited guests: Hans Richter and his wife Mariska, critic and author Eduard Hanslick and his wife Sophie, historian and composer Carl Ferdinand Pohl, Gesellschaft der Musikfreunde professor Josef Gänsbacher, composer and Vienna Conservatory professor Robert Fuchs, physician Josef Standhartner, critic and later Brahms biographer Max Kalbeck and choral conductor and composer Richard Heuberger. In his *Reminiscences*, Heuberger describes the scene:

> Brahms was almost the last to arrive, and said, 'Now we will put on a Richter Concert.' The small performance, namely, was organised mainly so that Richter could become more familiar with the work. I turned pages for Brahms. He played magnificently and boldly, and droned along with the music as was his habit. It was not really singing, more like grunting. He played from the manuscript, written on heavy bluish paper, the notes quite small and hard to read. As a page-turner, I had my work cut out for me. By request the duo played the work a second time . . . The new work took hold of me immediately, especially the gigantic finale with its powerful opening section that softly dies away.[1]

This trial performance is but one colourful example of Brahms's lifelong occupation with arrangements. Brahms was especially fond of playing four-hand music, and there are many accounts of his playing such arrangements in the homes of friends or salons of aristocrats. With Clara Schumann, for example, he studied Beethoven's Ninth Symphony in Liszt's two-piano arrangement in July 1855, and he and Theodor

---

[1] *Heuberger*, 24; translated by the author.

98

As Arranger

Kirchner played Liszt's symphonic poems and Brahms's Second String Sextet Op. 36 at the home of the surgeon Theodor Billroth in April 1866.[2]

Brahms created twenty-two arrangements for four hands or two pianos of his own compositions (including his revision of Robert Keller's duet arrangement of the Third Symphony Op. 90) and five of works of other composers. He also made piano reductions of orchestral parts in his four concertos and in his own and others' solo vocal and choral works [see Ch. 16 'Genre']. He orchestrated accompaniments to Schubert songs and to several of his own *Liebeslieder* Opp. 52 and 65, orchestrated three of the *Hungarian Dances* WoO 1 and realised figured basses for several vocal works of Bach and Handel. Brahms also crafted technical studies for piano solo and concert showpieces for his own use based on existing music.[3] Underlying all these arrangements was Brahms's wish to enlarge the reach of music by making it more accessible to both amateur and professional musicians, including close friends. The arrangements belong to the story of Brahms the composer, concert pianist, recreational player, conductor and student of music of the past and present. They also yield insights into the musical culture in which he lived.

From the late eighteenth century to the development of recordings and radio in the early twentieth, the piano was the centre of a rich culture of music-making that flourished in the home and within social and civic organisations. In modest venues, piano arrangements could substitute for fully realised orchestral, choral, operatic or chamber works, or serve as tools for study. Arrangements for two pianists afforded the social and intellectual interaction of chamber music. A skilled arranger transmitted outlines of melody, harmony and rhythm, and drew on the piano's ability to suggest details of instrumental colour and effect. Although an arrangement could not fully communicate the details of its model, it allowed musicians to bring to life a composition – in sound and in memory – that they had heard, or to prepare to hear a live performance. A reviewer writing about Robert Schumann's arrangement of his First Symphony Op. 38 observed that 'usually the public has [piano arrangements] to thank for the understanding of our greatest masterworks, and where, for example, the public

---

[2] *Litzman II*, 380; *Briefe V*, 35. R. and K. Hofmann, *Johannes Brahms als Pianist und Dirigent* (Tutzing: Hans Schneider, 2006), 90.

[3] Brahms's arrangements are listed in *Werkverzeichnis*, 777–9. The instrumental pieces for which Brahms indicated an alternative solo instrument are not considered arrangements in the present chapter: the Trio Op. 40, featuring horn or cello (or later viola), the Sonatas for clarinet or violin Op. 120, and the Trio Op. 114 and Quintet Op. 115 featuring clarinet or viola. Kurt Hofmann has made a strong case for Brahms as the author of G. W. Marks, *Souvenir de la Russie* Op. 151 (Hamburg: August Cranz, before 1852); see reprint, ed. K. Hofmann (Hamburg: K. D. Wagner, 1971).

listens attentively in a concert hall to a symphony of Beethoven, it can always be concluded that musical life in the home is directed toward this enjoyment of art'.[4]

By the middle of the nineteenth century, orchestral and chamber works were issued routinely for piano, especially piano solo and four hands, by publishers who, once they paid the honorarium for a given work, were entitled to publish it in any form. Sale of arrangements promoted interest in the original work and helped to cover the costs of printing expensive full scores and instrumental parts. Publishers kept arrangers on staff or engaged freelance musicians to supply the arrangements they deemed profitable. Brahms arranged an unusually large number of his own works for amateur use.[5] Up until the mid-1870s he offered duet arrangements to publishers for an additional honorarium, substantially increasing his income from a given work. Then he started including arrangements in initial offers. He arranged the Third and Fourth Symphonies for two pianos, realising the usefulness of this format for trial performances. Of his own works for instrumental ensemble, Brahms made only one solo arrangement: the variation movement from the First String Sextet Op. 18, which he presented to Clara Schumann and which both she and Brahms performed in their concerts but which Brahms never published.

For four of his compositions, Brahms created alternative versions for piano that he regarded as original works: the Sonata for Two Pianos Op. 34bis, a pair with the Piano Quintet Op. 34; the *Variations on a Theme of Haydn* for Two Pianos Op. 56b, begun before the orchestral variations published as Op. 56a; and the settings of the *Liebeslieder* and *Neue Liebeslieder* for piano duet Opp. 52a and 65a. As the separate opus numbers indicate, Brahms viewed these piano versions as fully authentic expressions of his compositional idea in another idiom.

Brahms's actual arrangements include four-hand (duet) settings of all three of his String Quartets, both String Quintets, both String Sextets, the Piano Quartets Opp. 25 and 26, both Serenades, both Overtures, his First, Second and Fourth Symphonies and the First Piano Concerto Op. 15. He also substantially revised Robert Keller's duet arrangement of the Third Symphony Op. 90. For *A German Requiem* Op. 45 and the *Triumphlied* Op. 55 he created four-hand arrangements with text that were

---

[4] *Allgemeine musikalische Zeitung* 44/52 (28 December 1842): col. 1047.
[5] See V. W. Goertzen, 'The Piano Transcriptions of Johannes Brahms', PhD dissertation, University of Illinois (1987), 12–15.

As Arranger

intended for study and music-making with a partner, not as accompaniments to choral singing. Brahms circulated manuscripts of new arrangements among his friends and directed his publishers to mail them printed copies. These arrangements were greatly prized and frequently played. In a letter to Brahms about his study of the Fourth Symphony Op. 98 in the two-piano arrangement, Theodor Billroth described the value of being able to experience the work in this way:

> One is able to derive full pleasure from your creations only by taking part in them. You are too powerful, too full, too profound for mere listening; one must actually be within them . . . I was unable to recognise the broad lines of the work above the detail. Now I believe I can do this and, as a result, have had a more serene enjoyment.[6]

Whereas Franz Liszt's monumental and technically demanding arrangements (e.g. of Berlioz's *Symphonie fantastique* Op. 14, Schubert lieder and the Beethoven symphonies) drew attention to the creative virtuoso himself,[7] Brahms sought to keep focus on the work and bring it into the music-making of friends, colleagues and the wider public. Thus, the arrangements of Brahms's own compositions are not independent *versions* but rather translations or reanimations of the works in the idiom of the piano. They may serve as surrogates for the original work where its use would be impractical, but they also bring new perspectives. The layers of revisions found in Brahms's sources for his arrangements – autographs, manuscript copies and proofs – show his care in making these settings effective and pianistic (see Figure 11.1).

He nevertheless insisted that he not be identified in print as the arranger of his own compositions, worrying that such 'cud-chewing of one's own works' might harm his reputation.[8] The proliferation of arrangements and the honoraria system that took decisions out of the composer's control provoked Brahms to complain to or gently rib his publishers, as when he, in the midst of arranging his First Symphony for piano duet, suggested to Simrock that they might add to the growing number of arrangements of the popular 'Wiegenlied' Op. 49 no. 4 by crafting some 'in a minor key for naughty or sickly children'.[9]

---

[6] 18 July 1886, O. Gottlieb-Billroth (ed.), *Billroth und Brahms im Briefwechsel* (Berlin: Urban & Schwarzenberg, 1935), 388.

[7] See J. Kregor, *Liszt as Transcriber* (Cambridge: Cambridge University Press, 2010).

[8] 15 October 1870 to Melchior Rieter-Biedermann, *Briefe XIV*, 190–1.

[9] c. 12 June 1877 (corrected date), *Briefe X*, 38–9.

Figure 11.1. Autograph engraver's model of Brahms's arrangement of the First Piano Concerto Op. 15 for piano duet, last page of first movement, with revisions in ink in Brahms's hand.

Other musicians supplied arrangements that Brahms himself did not wish to create. Simrock's editor Robert Keller arranged many of the works, including the symphonies and overtures for piano solo and for eight hands on two pianos, as well as the Violin Concerto Op. 77, Double Concerto Op. 102, Second Piano Concerto Op. 83 and Third Symphony Op. 90 for four hands. Theodor Kirchner set the two String Sextets as piano trios and supplied a four-hand arrangement of the Piano Quintet Op. 34 and solo arrangements of both *Liebeslieder* sets and the *Requiem*. Friedrich Hermann arranged a series of Brahms's chamber works for piano four hands, violin and cello. However, Brahms found that duet arrangements created by others did not suit his taste. He advised Keller to 'jump around very freely with everything as if I were not even here, just so everything sounds as fine as possible for four hands and is playable' and gave similar

As Arranger

encouragement to Kirchner.[10] But Brahms also acknowledged that no arranger could exercise as much creativity and freedom as he himself could.

In arrangements for four hands, Brahms simplified textures and rhythmic structures, remodelled accompanimental figures, used contrasting registers of the keyboard to distinguish separate instrumental voices, and modified melodies and harmonies to clarify structure and intensify expression. He reworked articulation, phrasing, dynamics and tempos, and developed innovative strategies to convey instrumental techniques. Perhaps most importantly, he carefully controlled the pacing of the arrangement, shaping the dramatic trajectory through his handling of texture, register, articulation and pedalling.

Some of Brahms's arrangements show departures from their model works arising from what Robert Pascall has termed 'creative happenstance and renewal'.[11] Brahms acknowledged the necessity of such differences in comments about the First and Third Symphonies Op. 68 and Op. 90. He also endeavoured to convey details of the model work to pianists, for example in his use of differently notated tremolo figures for timpani rolls and unmeasured and measured string tremolos in arrangements of Joseph Joachim's overtures. As several writers have described, sources for the arrangements, when studied in conjunction with sources for the model works, may help to document stages in the genesis and process of these compositions.

An example from the beginning of the development section (bars 57–69) of the Second String Quintet Op. 111, illustrates several of Brahms's transcribing techniques. The section opens with an ethereal passage in which melodic fragments are heard against a fabric of tremolos in groups of nine semiquavers and a pedal point in the cello (Example 11.1a). The passage begins *pianissimo* and grows in volume and intensity from bar 65 to *forte* in bar 69 as the cello brings in the main theme. On the piano Brahms expressed this atmospheric moment of suspended animation through the use of cross-rhythms between triplet arpeggios in the two inner parts and semiquaver tremolos in the bass (Example 11.1b).

By moving the bass down an octave beginning in bar 57 and the first violin line up an octave beginning in bar 61, he created additional resonance (use of damper pedal is implied) and increased the physical space in which the two pianists could encompass the quintet texture. Brahms could then separate the imitative entries in first violin and viola in bars 65–8, both

---

[10] Brahms to Fritz Simrock, 12 December 1879, *Briefe X*, 139; and Rieter-Biedermann, 6 October 1875, *Briefe XIV*, 252–3.

[11] R. Pascall, 'Brahms Arranges His Symphonies', in K. Hamilton and N. Loges (eds.), *Brahms in the Home and the Concert Hall* (Cambridge: Cambridge University Press, 2014), 149.

Example 11.1a. Brahms, Second String Quintet Op. 111, first movement, bars 57–69.

voices set in Primo right hand, through registral changes. For bars 66 and 68, where the quintet's texture becomes more strongly rhythmic and accented through *sforzandi*, the cross-rhythms in the arrangement cease,

Example 11.1b. Brahms, Second String Quintet Op. 111, arrangement for piano, four hands, first movement, bars 57–69.

and steady quavers in the Secondo left hand drive momentum towards the return of the main theme. Two-piano arrangements more easily accommodated complex textures than those for one keyboard and offered a wider

Example 11.1b. (cont)

colour palette and a more powerful exchange between the two players, each of whom commanded an instrument's full resources.

Trial performances of the Second, Third and Fourth Symphonies (Opp. 73, 90 and 98) played a role in Brahms's revising process and helped to lay the groundwork for early performances. In early December 1877 Brahms and Brüll presented the Second Symphony Op. 73 in the Ehrbar Salon in the composer's arrangement for one piano, four hands. Simrock had pre-publication copies of the arrangement printed the following June, before the orchestral score was finalised, to sell in connection with the symphony's performance during the Lower Rhine Music Festival. Brahms and Brüll performed the two-piano arrangement of the Second Piano Concerto Op. 83 on 12 October 1881 for a small group including Billroth, Hanslick, Kalbeck and conductor Richter. Afterwards Brahms, who played the principal, solo part (which also participates in the orchestral tuttis in this arrangement), substantially revised the musical text of the concerto. Since the arrangement was published the following January, eight months before the full score and separate solo part, it was used by pianists as a study

As Arranger

score early on, and editions of it continue to be so used, although most of these do not reflect the revisions that Brahms later made to the full score and solo part.[12]

Brahms arranged the orchestral parts of the Violin Concerto Op. 77 and Double Concerto Op. 102 for piano, to be used for study or for performance where an orchestra is not present. He and Joachim performed the Violin Concerto with piano in Transylvania in September 1879 in venues lacking an orchestra, and Joachim and Robert Hausmann practised the Double Concerto with Brahms at the piano in Baden-Baden in September 1887 in preparation for rehearsals with the orchestra. Also designed for practical use were Brahms's piano reductions of accompaniments to choral works, including the *Ave Maria* Op. 12, *Begräbnisgesang* Op. 13, *Alto Rhapsody* Op. 53, *Rinaldo* Op. 50, *A German Requiem* Op. 45, *Triumphlied* Op. 55, *Nänie* Op. 82, and *Gesang der Parzen* Op. 89. He also revised Hermann Levi's piano-vocal score of the *Schicksalslied* Op. 54 and provided piano reductions for other vocal works, including the *Liebeslieder* and *Neue Liebeslieder* Op. 52 and Op. 65 and the *Gesänge*, Op. 17.[13]

In the early to mid-1850s Brahms created duet and two-piano arrangements of works of other composers, as a means of studying this music and in order to be able to play it with friends: Joseph Joachim's Overture to *Hamlet* Op. 4, Robert Schumann's Piano Quintet Op. 44 and Piano Quartet Op. 47 for duet, and Joachim's Overtures to *Demetrius* Op. 6 and *Heinrich IV* Op. 7 for two pianos. Brahms also crafted a virtuosic solo arrangement of the Scherzo from Schumann's Quintet 'for pianoforte/ Frau Schumann alone'. He intended to publish all but this private arrangement both to promote his friends' compositions and to earn much-needed income. Only the quartet arrangement reached print during Brahms's lifetime, however (and not until January 1887 after the copyright protection covering Schumann's works expired) [see Ch. 25 'Copyright']. There also survives an autograph, dated May 1852, of the physharmonika part (a portable harmonium) of Brahms's setting of Henry Litolff's Overture to *Robespierre* Op. 55 for this instrument and piano. The *20 Ländler* of Franz Schubert, published by J. P. Gotthard in solo and duet editions, both containing arrangements as well as original works, were regarded for some

---

[12] *JBG, Arrangement 2. Klavierkonzert*, xiv–xv.

[13] Brahms also provided publisher J. Rieter-Biedermann with solo and simplified solo arrangements of the Waltzes Op. 39 and two-piano arrangements of Nos. 1, 2, 8, 11, 14 and 15. Books 1 and 2 of the *Hungarian Dances* WoO 1 were arranged for piano solo by Brahms, Books 3 and 4 by Theodor Kirchner; Brahms also orchestrated Nos. 1, 3 and 10.

108 VALERIE WOODRING GOERTZEN

years as Brahms's work; these were arranged by Gotthard himself, who worked from Schubert manuscripts in Brahms's possession.[14]

The solo arrangements of works of other composers reflect Brahms's view that such arrangements were of interest only when 'made by a real virtuoso, something like Liszt's Beethoven symphonies'.[15] Brahms performed several blisteringly difficult arrangements in his concerts, including organ works of J. S. Bach, most famously the Toccata in F major BWV 540 (performed from 1853; see Figure 11.2) and the Fantasy in G major BWV 572, and also the Prelude and Fugue in A minor BWV 543, Pastorale in F major BWV 590 and Prelude and Fugue in B minor BWV 544; the Scherzo from Schubert's Octet D803; two Marches by Schubert originally for four-hand piano D968B and the fugal finale of Beethoven's String Quartet Op. 59 no. 3. Brahms probably never wrote these arrangements down, though pencilled notations in scores of the Toccata and Fantasy once belonging to the Schumanns provide tantalising clues about his performances.[16] Reviewers remarked on Brahms's fearlessness, his ability to simulate sounds of the organ and the sheer power of these arrangements, which could lead them to overshadow the original piano pieces on the programme.[17] The pieces Brahms chose to present in arrangements also show his desire to familiarise audiences with a historical repertory.

Brahms notated his arrangements of the Gavotte in A major and the 'Gratieux sans lenteur' from Gluck's *Iphigénie en Aulide* specifically for Clara Schumann; the Gavotte, which Brahms already had performed in several cities in 1868–9, became a staple of her repertory and was published in Germany in late 1871 and in England early the next year. He also produced Five Piano Studies Anh. Ia no.1. The first two (published in 1869) are etudes based on already difficult piano pieces: Chopin's Etude Op. 25 no. 2 and the finale of Weber's Rondo Op. 24. Studies 3–5 (1878) are based on two movements from J. S. Bach's Sonatas and Partitas for solo

---

[14] J. Behr, 'Franz Schuberts 20 Ländler D 266/D 814 – *nicht* bearbeitet von Johannes Brahms', *Die Musikforschung* 64/4 (2011), 354–63. Regarding the *Robespierre* arrangement, see *JBG, Arrangements fremder Werke 1*, xxv–xxix.

[15] Brahms to Fritz Simrock of 16 March 1880 (date verified), *Briefe X*, 143.

[16] See R. Stinson, 'Clara Schumann's Bach Book: A Neglected Document of the Bach Revival', *Bach: Journal of the Riemenschneider Bach Institute, Baldwin-Wallace College* 39/1 (2008), 1–67, and *JBG, Arrangements fremder Werke 2*, xxxii–xxxviii.

[17] See, for example, accounts in the *Deutsche Musikzeitung* 3/49 (6 December 1862), 389, and *Neues Fremden-Blatt* 3/325 (26 November 1867), 5, also *JBG, Arrangements fremder Werke 2*, xxxii–xxxviii.

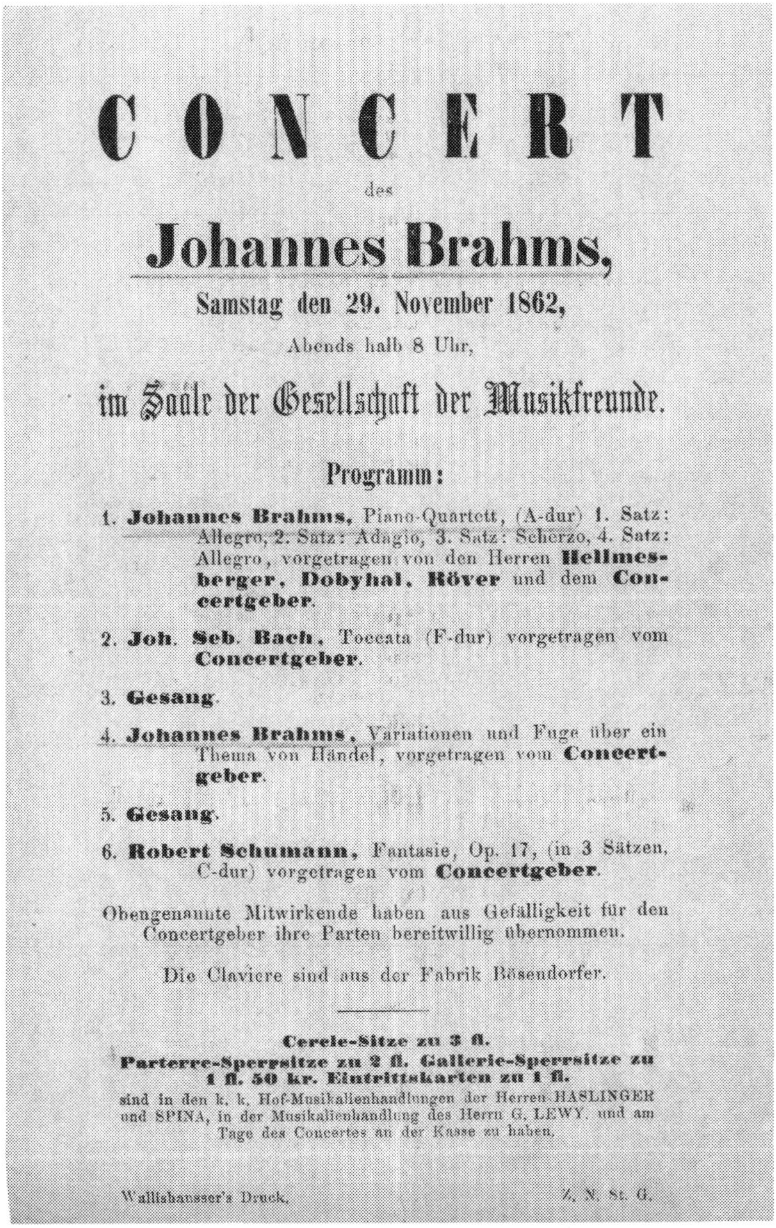

CONCERT

des

Johannes Brahms,

Samstag den 29. November 1862,

Abends halb 8 Uhr,

im Saale der Gesellschaft der Musikfreunde.

Programm:

1. **Johannes Brahms,** Piano-Quartett, (A-dur) 1. Satz: Allegro, 2. Satz: Adagio, 3. Satz: Scherzo, 4. Satz: Allegro, vorgetragen von den Herren **Hellmesberger, Dobyhal, Röver** und dem **Concertgeber.**
2. **Joh. Seb. Bach,** Toccata (F-dur) vorgetragen vom **Concertgeber.**
3. **Gesang.**
4. **Johannes Brahms,** Variationen und Fuge über ein Thema von Händel, vorgetragen vom **Concertgeber.**
5. **Gesang.**
6. **Robert Schumann,** Fantasie, Op. 17, (in 3 Sätzen, C-dur) vorgetragen vom **Concertgeber.**

Obengenannte Mitwirkende haben aus Gefälligkeit für den Concertgeber ihre Parten bereitwillig übernommen.

Die Claviere sind aus der Fabrik Bösendorfer.

Cercle-Sitze zu 3 fl.
Parterre-Sperrsitze zu 2 fl. Gallerie-Sperrsitze zu 1 fl. 50 kr. Eintrittskarten zu 1 fl.
sind in den k. k. Hof-Musikalienhandlungen der Herren HASLINGER und SPINA, in der Musikalienhandlung des Herrn G. LEWY, und am Tage des Concertes an der Kasse zu haben.

Wallishausser's Druck. Z. N. St. G.

Figure 11.2. Concert Programme, 29 November 1862, Saal der Gesellschaft der Musikfreunde. Brahms performed Bach's Toccata in F major (No. 2 on this programme) in early October 1853 during his first visit to the Schumanns in Düsseldorf.

110   VALERIE WOODRING GOERTZEN

violin: the Presto in G major BWV 1001 (two settings, the melody first in the right hand and then in the left) and the Chaconne BWV 1004, which Brahms arranged for left hand alone as a means of capturing the experience of playing this giant work on violin. In addition to arranging a few other small pieces,[18] Brahms revised or recomposed individual movements of a piano reduction of Schubert's Mass in E♭ D950 for J. Rieter-Biedermann and realised figured basses of a chorale from Bach's Cantata BWV 44 (published in Carl Grädener's *System der Harmonielehre* in 1877) and of vocal duets and trios for *G. F. Händel's Werke* edited by Friedrich Chrysander (1870, 1880).

Whether Brahms learned Josef Strauss's Polka-Mazurka 'Die Libelle' Op. 204 from a printed score or from hearing it played by the Strauss Orchestra in Vienna is not known. His recording of the piece on an Edison cylinder in the home of Richard and Maria Fellinger in December 1889 illustrates his practice of extemporising dances, something he could do for hours at a time.[19] The example serves as a reminder that arranging was fundamental to Brahms's orientation to the piano. His notated piano arrangements, too, notwithstanding the critical editions that have appeared recently, should be viewed as essentially fluid, given their lack of status as works and their use in Brahms's day and ours as music for sight-reading and informal music-making. Pianists may find arrangements liberating for this reason.

Brahms's orchestrations of accompaniments to lieder by Franz Schubert were important to the reception of this composer's music in the second half of the nineteenth century. Here Brahms transformed songs designed for use in the home and salon into concert works appropriate for large public venues while leaving the vocal solos untouched. In spring 1862 he arranged several songs, including 'Memnon' D541, 'Geheimes' D719, 'An Schwager Kronos' D369 and 'Greisengesang' D778, for concerts of the great baritone and Schubert champion Julius Stockhausen, who performed these settings

---

[18] See *Werkverzeichnis,* 674, 677–8, 686, 689–91, 742. The authorship of the solo arrangement of Schubert's Impromptu Opus D899 no.2 in Brahms's Nachlass in the Gesellschaft der Musikfreunde (*Werkverzeichnis* Anh. IV, Nr. 2) is uncertain. Brahms's autographs of Carl Czerny's Etude (Anh. Va, Nr. 17) and Gluck's 'Gratieux sans lenteur' (Anh. Va, Nr. 19) transmit arrangements, not copies, of these works. See *JBG, Arrangements fremder Werke 2,* xxvii–xxviii, and J. Draheim, '" . . . für das Pianoforte gesetzt". Die zweihändigen Klavierbearbeitungen von Johannes Brahms', in *Üben und Musizieren* 5/2 (1988), 106–14.

[19] See *Brahms spielt Klavier, aufgenommen im Hause Fellinger 1889,* Casinos Austria Classic OEAW PHA CD 5, with commentary by Imogen Fellinger; also *Kalbeck II,* 454, and *JBG, Arrangements fremder Werke 2,* xlii–xliii.

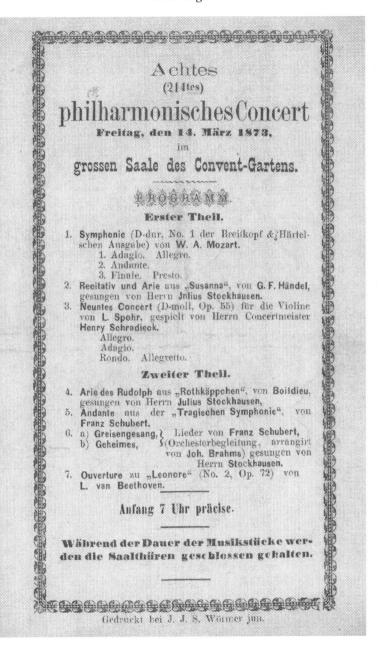

Figure 11.3. Concert Programme, 14 March 1873, Grosser Saal des Convent-Gartens Hamburg.

in Vienna and Germany in the 1860s and 1870s. In a Wiener Singakademie concert on 23 March 1873, Brahms conducted his arrangement of 'Ellens zweiter Gesang' D838, for solo voice, chorus, four horns and two bassoons, the solo part sung by Viennese soprano Marie Fillunger.[20] In another concert in the same year, the Hamburg Philharmonic Orchestra accompanied Julius Stockhausen in two lieder by Schubert using Brahms's orchestrations (Figure 11.3).

In the arrangements discussed in this chapter – many of them published, some notated but unpublished and some never committed to paper – Brahms engaged with close to sixty musical works. Added to this is an unknown number of dances and pieces that he played in social gatherings. In the arrangements for solo piano that he performed or published, Brahms helped to shape the historical narrative, enhanced his stature as a virtuoso and enlarged what was deemed possible on the instrument. Orchestrations and figured-bass realisations also brought music to new venues and audiences. In trial performances of the symphonies and the Second Piano Concerto Op. 83, arrangements were a means of finalising compositional details and communicating these new works to conductors, critics and friends. Brahms's largest group of arrangements, those for piano duet, brought his chamber and orchestral music into the homes of fellow musicians, not only helping to build a public for his music but also sharing with pianists the experiences that Brahms himself relished: those of studying music at the piano and playing it with others.

Further Reading

J. Draheim, 'Brahms als Bearbeiter', in *Brahms Handbuch*, 101–9

M. McCorkle, 'The Role of Trial Performances for Brahms's Orchestral and Large Choral Works: Sources and Circumstances', in G. Bozarth (ed.), *Brahms Studies: Analytical and Historical Perspectives* (Oxford: Clarendon Press, 1998), 295–328

R. Pascall, 'Brahms Arranges His Symphonies', in K. Hamilton and N. Loges (eds.), *Brahms in the Home and the Concert Hall* (Cambridge: Cambridge University Press, 2014), 137–57

H. Paskins, K. Hamilton and N. Loges, 'Brahms and His Arrangers', in K. Hamilton and N. Loges (eds.), *Brahms in the Home and the Concert Hall* (Cambridge: Cambridge University Press, 2014), 178–220

---

[20] J. Draheim, 'Brahms als Bearbeiter', 107–8. See also Peter Jost, (ed.), *Sechs Lieder für mittlere Singstimme und Orchester. Bearbeitet von Johannes Brahms* (Wiesbaden, Leipzig, Paris: Breitkopf & Härtel, 2000. PB 5375).

M. Struck, 'Main and Shadowy Existence(s): Works and Arrangements in the Oeuvre of Johannes Brahms', in K. Hamilton and N. Loges (eds.), *Brahms in the Home and the Concert Hall* (Cambridge: Cambridge University Press, 2014), 110–36

V. W. Goertzen, 'The Piano Transcriptions of Johannes Brahms', PhD dissertation, University of Illinois (1987)

V. W. Goertzen, '"Auch für vierhändige Seelen genießbar": Adaptation and Recomposition in Brahms's Piano Arrangements', in S. Oechsle and M. Struck (eds.), *Brahms am Werk: Konzepte – Texte – Prozesse* (Munich: Henle, 2016), 221–42

Fuller information is provided in volumes of the *Johannes Brahms Gesamtausgabe*: Serie IA, Nr. 1 *Symphonien Nr. 1 und 2*, Nr. 2 *Symphonie Nr. 3*, and Nr. 3 *Symphonie Nr. 4*, all ed. R. Pascall (2008, 2013, 2012); Nr. 4 *Serenaden und Ouvertüren*, ed. M. Musgrave (2012); Nr. 6 *Klavierkonzert Nr. 2 Klavierauszug*, ed. J. Behr (2014); Nr. 7 *Violinkonzert und Doppelkonzert, Klavierauszüge*, ed. L. C. Roesner and M. Struck (2010); Serie IIA Nr. 3 *Streichquartetten*, ed. Jakob Hauschildt (2015); Serie IX, Nr. 1 *Arrangements von Werken anderer Komponisten für ein Klavier oder zwei Klaviere zu vier Händen*, ed. V. W. Goertzen (2012); Serie IX, Nr. 2 *Arrangements von Werken anderer Komponisten für Klavier solo*, ed. V. W. Goertzen (2017).

CHAPTER 12

As Editor

Peter Schmitz

Like many other nineteenth-century composers, Brahms was often approached to edit other composers' works. Publishers strove to attract famous musicians such as Clara Schumann, Franz Liszt and Julius Rietz for editing work, alongside music scholars, not least because their names attracted buyers. Brahms's own preference as editor was to remain anonymous, and we also do not know exactly why he undertook this work. The demands on time (studying the sources, comparing texts, revising, corresponding with the publisher, etc.) were considerable, especially alongside his own daily work of composition and concert duties. Furthermore, the pecuniary rewards were limited [see Ch. 8 'Finances']. Thus, in relation to Brahms's edition of Mozart's *Requiem,* he was told on 12 February 1876 that he, like all the other editors, would have to be content with a 'modest compensation of 1.50 Marks per score plate'. A publisher's note to Gustav Nottebohm written on the same day reveals 'only in the case of exceptional expenses through copies etc. will the price be increased to 3 Taler'.[1]

Brahms's motivation was most likely his documented interest in the creation of reliable scores. He owned a substantial music library of printed editions, autographs and copies. His estate, held in the archive of the Gesellschaft der Musikfreunde in Vienna, also holds numerous editions containing his own written-in corrections which testify to in-depth text comparison and a profound understanding of sources. His exchanges with music scholars such as Friedrich Chrysander, Philipp Spitta and Gustav Nottebohm may also have encouraged his philological interests.

Brahms's editing represents an exceptionally broad range of epochs and genres. It includes works by Couperin, C. P. E. Bach, Mozart, Schubert,

---

[1] Breitkopf & Härtel to Brahms and Gustav Nottebohm, 12 February 1876, D-LEst, Bestand Breitkopf & Härtel 21081. Sig. 202.

As Editor 115

Chopin and Schumann.[2] This chapter will focus on the four complete editions for the Leipzig publisher Breitkopf & Härtel to which he contributed. Although there had been a rift between Brahms and Breitkopf & Härtel in autumn 1865 following some manipulative behaviour regarding the Second String Sextet Op. 36 [see Ch. 24 'Publishers'], they laid their differences aside around ten years later, and he dedicated himself conscientiously to the edition projects.

Breitkopf & Härtel's *Wolfgang Amadeus Mozart's Werke. Kritisch durchgesehene Gesammtausgabe* was made possible thanks to the significant initiative and financial support of Ludwig Ritter von Köchel. It appeared mainly between 1877 and 1883 (with supplements until 1910). Surprisingly, this complete edition initially had little impact: by 1883 it had only ninety-three subscribers. And yet a whole slew of prominent figures had contributed to it: Joseph Joachim, Otto Goldschmidt, Franz Espagne, Gustav Nottebohm, Carl Reinecke, Julius Rietz, Ernst Rudorff, Paul Graf Waldersee, Franz Wüllner, Philipp Spitta and also Brahms, who was allocated a keystone of the edition, the *Requiem* K626. Brahms owned valuable manuscripts (e.g. the autograph score of the Symphony in G minor K550) and first editions of Mozart's works and had already anonymously edited the *Offertorium de Venerabili Sacramento* (*Venite populi*) K260, published by Johann Peter Gotthard in Vienna in 1873.

Judging from the correspondence with the publisher, Brahms evidently approached the task very seriously, consulting the relevant scholarly literature surrounding the *Requiem*.[3] His estate contains a first edition of the score printed by Breitkopf & Hartel in 1800 in which Brahms has made annotations in blue pencil (Sig. I 1704, Q 285), and his copy from the Complete Edition also contains entries (Sig. I 1704, H 27209). Another working copy, namely the revised first edition of 1827, is held in the Brahms Archive of the Staats- und Universitätsbibliothek Hamburg (BRA: Ab24). Brahms noted the deviations from the original manuscript (Codex a and b of the Vienna autograph, ÖNB, Mus. Hs. 17561) meticulously in this document too.

As in the edition published by Johann Anton André in 1827, Brahms attempted to differentiate, through the use of the letters 'M' and 'S', between the passages which were by Mozart and those which were his

---

[2] A full list is in *Werkverzeichnis*, 749–53. Brahms declined to be involved in the old Bach Complete Edition, to which he subscribed, although he may have occasionally offered advice or proofread the work of other editors.

[3] O. Jahn, *W. A. Mozart* (Leipzig: Breitkopf & Härtel, 1856–59), and G. Weber, *Ergebnisse der bisherigen Forschungen über die Echtheit des Mozartschen Requiem* (Mainz: B. Schott's Söhnen, 1826).

116 PETER SCHMITZ

student Franz Xaver Süssmayr's interventions. Brahms judged Süssmayr's work in the 1886 critical report as follows: 'He carefully copied Mozart's conception and completed it with as much diligence as piety.' Brahms's primary objective was therefore 'through an exact rendition of both manuscripts through which the work has survived, to give as faithful and reliable a picture as possible of how Mozart left his work, and how his student immediately after his death completed it'.[4] In contrast, he paid little heed to the unfinished completion of the instrumental parts by Joseph Eybler. In his view, 'this relic is spoiled through the weak and awkward attempts by one or two people to fill out the score'.

As Brahms wrote in a letter to Joseph Joachim on 24 May 1876, the 'dreadful work of revision' ultimately took much longer than he had hoped.[5] The publisher's newsletter *Mittheilungen der Musikalienhandlung Breitkopf & Härtel in Leipzig* (No. 2, December 1876) initially listed the edition for January 1877 at the price of '8 M. 40 Pf', but there was no way Brahms could meet this deadline. At this point, he was still corresponding with the publisher about the handling of the trombone part, which Mozart had left incomplete in the autograph. Friedrich Chrysander and Julius Rietz were called upon to advise. Ultimately, Brahms's first experience of editing for Breitkopf & Härtel was marred by a largely negative review in the *Neue Zeitschrift für Musik*, although its content could be disputed on the grounds of its questionable approach.[6] Still, Brahms's influence on the Mozart Complete Edition extended beyond the *Requiem,* as for example when he advised Ernst Rudorff during his editorial work on the Flute Concerto K314.

While Brahms was still working on the *Requiem,* Breitkopf & Härtel approached him on 31 January 1877 to ask him to contribute to the Chopin Complete Works (*Friedrich Chopin's Werke. Erste kritisch durchgesehene Gesammtausgabe*). This was now viable because the copyright on Chopin's works expired thirty years after his death. Unlike Mozart's *Requiem,* Brahms worked as part of a veritable team of colleagues, in which his was the authoritative voice. His closest colleagues were Ernst Rudorff and Woldemar Bargiel, in whose editions he was actively involved. In addition, August Franchomme, Franz Liszt and Carl Reinecke acted as

---

[4] For details, see Dietrich Berke und Christoph Wolff, *Kritischer Bericht. Wolfgang Amadeus Mozart. Neue Ausgabe sämtlicher Werke* (Serie 1 Geistliche Gesangswerke, Werkgruppe 1, Abteilung 2, Requiem), (Kassel, Basel, etc.: Bärenreiter, 2007), 15–20.

[5] *Briefe VI*, 122.

[6] G. Pressel, 'Brahms' Revision des Mozart'schen Requiems', *Neue Zeitschrift für Musik* 73/32 (3 August 1877), 337–8.

editors in the fourteen volumes (1878–80, Supplement 1902). No overall editorial guidelines to reconcile the work of the various editors have been located. The revised copies of the Mazurkas Opp. 17, 24, 30, 50, 56 and 63 in the Breitkopf & Härtel archives in Wiesbaden show that Friedrich Ferdinand Brissler, the in-house proofreader, exerted considerable influence. The archive also contains a working copy of the Barcarolle Op. 60 (in which Brahms was particularly interested) with handwritten editorial comments which show how the editor marked the results of his textual comparisons (see Figure 12.1).

The Hoboken Collection in the Austrian National Library in Vienna also provides some insight into Brahms's working methods as editor. Among other things, his attitude to the creation of a critically informed hierarchy of the various textual sources, as well as to doubtful interpretations, is revealing. Brahms arrived at the conviction that Chopin's autographs, which were naturally important as a basic benchmark, were nevertheless only relevant to the edition to some extent. If correction proofs with subsequent emendations were available, Brahms accorded these more significance.

During the editing of the piano sonatas, a difference of opinion developed between Brahms and the publisher. In letters to Breitkopf & Härtel on 24 and 31 May, and 11 June 1878, Brahms expressed his hope that the 'Cloverleaf' Sonatas (Opp. 4, 35 and 58) would be published in a single volume; but the publisher argued that even in the thematic catalogue, the Piano Sonata Op. 4 was unpublished (a 'Nachlasswerk'), and that Chopin was against publishing works he regarded as inferior. Still more crucial was a practical consideration: the publisher already owned the Sonatas Opp. 35 and 38 so could publish them immediately. Thus, the three works were spread across two volumes (Op. 35 and Op. 38 in Volume 8, and Op. 4 in Volume 13, 'Unpublished Works').

Brahms also took an ambivalent stance regarding critical reports for the Chopin Complete Edition. Despite emphatically stressing their importance to Woldemar Bargiel, he decided, in a letter to the publisher from 31 October 1878, that the critical report by Ernst Rudorff, despite good content, was too long. And he himself published no such reports for the Chopin Complete Edition. Reports were only provided by Rudorff and published for volumes 1, 2, 9 and 14 (Ballades, Etudes, Waltzes and Songs with Piano). Bargiel prepared corresponding reports for volumes 4 and 5 (Nocturnes and Polonaises).

The most protracted project which Brahms undertook for Breitkopf & Härtel was the Schumann Complete Edition, which appeared in fourteen

118 PETER SCHMITZ

Figure 12.1. Revision copy of Chopin's Barcarolle Op. 60 (prepared for the Chopin-Gesamtausgabe) with annotations by Johannes Brahms.

series between 1879 and 1893 (*Robert Schumann's Werke. Herausgegeben von Clara Schumann*). Brahms had handled the major negotiations in advance between Breitkopf & Härtel and the editor, Clara Schumann [see Ch. 2 'The Schumanns']. According to the contract, this entailed 'a fee towards the complete editing settlement of 10,000 Marks' in two instalments, half

As Editor

on 1 January 1878, the other upon completion.[7] The London publisher Novello & Co. had also tried to persuade Clara Schumann to produce a complete edition of the piano works in 1877, but she ultimately decided in favour of Breitkopf, to whom 'the exclusive and unlimited rights of publication and distribution of the first complete edition of the works of Robert Schumann . . . for Germany and all other countries' were accorded.

The surviving source material does not reveal the exact works in which Brahms was involved; however, he was clearly involved in drawing up the editorial guidelines and also occasionally took on bits of editorial work for Clara Schumann. Only the supplementary volume published in 1893 was issued under his name. For this, he received 100 Marks from the publisher as well as several free copies. In addition, Woldemar Bargiel, Albert Dietrich, Ernst Frank, Julius Otto Grimm, Hermann Levi, Ernst Rudorff, Robert Volkland and Franz Wüllner collaborated on the Complete Edition, which hardly fulfilled the requirements of a critical edition due to its lack of a source list or comparative and descriptive commentaries. Brahms repeatedly argued that they should adhere to the original editions authorised by Schumann and have these re-engraved; any later editions could basically be ignored: 'Just don't look at the newest editions at all! They have nothing to do with us. *Carnaval* must simply be engraved according to the old edition', he declared in a letter to Clara Schumann from February 1878.[8] In this, he took the opposite stance from Breitkopf's proofreader Brissler, who strove for a diverse orthographic modernisation. The full history of this edition can be traced through Clara Schumann's correspondence with the individual editors, the publisher, her diary and the notes in her own copy of the *Thematic Catalogue of the Complete Published Works of Robert Schumann* (*Thematischen Verzeichnisses sämmtlicher im Druck erschienener Werke Robert Schumann's*), published by J. Schuberth & Co. (Robert-Schumann-Haus Zwickau, 13392 – E2/A3), and of course the surviving print templates and correction proofs.[9]

The publication of Schumann's Fourth Symphony Op. 120 in its earlier 1841 version led to a serious conflict with Clara Schumann. Not least on aesthetic grounds, Brahms's wish was for this version to be available as a supplement to the popular re-instrumented version of 1851 in the Complete Edition. Initially, she seemed to agree, but she later protested

---

[7] Historisches Archiv der Wiener Philharmoniker, Sch/29b Nr. 1   [8] *SBB II*, 135.
[9] See M. Heinemann (ed.), *Briefwechsel Clara Schumanns mit dem Verlag Breitkopf & Härtel 1856 bis 1895* (*Schumann-Briefedition* III, 3) (Cologne: Dohr, 2015).

against what she felt to be an edition 'imposed by' Brahms (which Franz Wüllner provided). Wüllner then also performed the early version – albeit mixed with elements from the later version – on 22 October 1889 with the Cologne Gürzenich Orchestra. The edition of the first version from 1841 appeared in November 1891 and was apparently the subject of an argument between Brahms and Clara Schumann in autumn of the following year. In her concern for her husband's posthumous reputation, she was persuaded not to publish various compositions (particularly youthful and late works). When it came to Op. 120, Brahms felt differently, but he too was not really aiming at a strictly 'complete' edition. In that sense, the edition can best be described as a 'selective collected edition'.

Upon the urging of the wealthy Vienna-based Schubert collector Nicolaus Dumba, Breitkopf & Härtel took the decision to create a Schubert Complete Edition (*Franz Schubert's Werke. Kritisch durchgesehene Gesammtausgabe*) in summer 1883. The thirty-nine resulting volumes appeared in twenty-one series between 1884 and 1897. Unlike the Chopin and Schumann Complete Editions, critical reports were planned from the outset (even if these vary widely in quality and scope). The individual editors were largely drawn from the so-called Vienna 'Brahms circle'; Brahms himself undertook the first series (the symphonies). At his recommendation, Eusebius Mandyczewski was appointed the lead editor, and the ten-volume series of songs (No. 20) edited by this Nottebohm student remains highly regarded. Sadly, this did not apply to Brahms's edition of the symphonies: in comparison with the original manuscripts, Ernst Laaff and others have pointed out various editorial mistakes.[10] Brahms approached this editing unenthusiastically, which is astonishing, given the important role he played in nineteenth-century Schubert reception both as a performer and collector of manuscripts. Initially, he did not even want to include the first six symphonies, since they did not accord with his estimation of the composer's artistic ability. On 26 March 1884, he informed the publisher:

> I have not hidden the fact that I have no particular pleasure in the printing of these symphonies. I believe that such works, or indeed preliminary works, should not be published, but only piously kept and perhaps be made available to a few people through copies. Only the artist who sees them in their seclusion and – with great pleasure – studies them, can take genuine, wonderful pleasure in them![11]

---

[10] E. Laaff, *Franz Schuberts Sinfonien* (Wiesbaden: Rauch, 1933), 61–92.   [11] *Briefe XIV*, 353.

As Editor

Although he ultimately submitted to the voices clamouring for a complete edition, he clung to his stance even after publication. But when it came to the symphony fragments, Brahms absolutely insisted on their remaining unpublished. The sole exception was 'Unfinished' Symphony D759, which he edited as No. 8 in the main corpus of the first series, volume 2. Regarding the sketch of the Symphony in E D729, Brahms declared: 'To my mind, the E major Symphony seems in no way or shape suitable for publication (in our Collected Edition). Publishing the sketches has no purpose; it would be a mere curiosity.'[12]

All this confirms that Brahms's statements as well as his philological practice are far from contradiction-free. Consequently, it makes sense to evaluate individual editorial work within its context, including the role of the leading publisher, the proofreader and the general editorial guidelines. Brahms was doubtless gripped by the blossoming scientific spirit of his age, yet still allowed himself plenty of space to exercise his aesthetic sense and judgement. Last but not least, Brahms's extensive experience of having his own compositions edited surely had an impact on his approach to editing the music of others.

Further Reading

D. Brodbeck, 'Brahms's Edition of Twenty Schubert Ländler: An Essay in Criticism', in G. Bozarth (ed.), *Brahms Studies. Analytical and Historical Perspectives* (Oxford: Clarendon Press, 1990), 229–50

W. Dürr and A. Krause, 'Zur Rezeption des Schubertschen Werkes', in W. Dürr and A. Krause (eds.), *Schubert-Handbuch* (Kassel: Bärenreiter 1997), 114–39

I. Fellinger, 'Brahms zur Edition Chopinscher Klavierwerke', in K. Fellerer and H. Hüschen (eds.), *Musicae Scientiae Collectanea. Festschrift Karl Gustav Fellerer zum siebzigsten Geburtstag* (Cologne: Volk, 1973), 110–16

E. Laaff, *Franz Schuberts Sinfonien* (Wiesbaden: Rauch, 1933)

T. Leibnitz, 'Johannes Brahms als Musikphilologe', in S. Antonicek and O. Biba (eds.), *Brahms-Kongress Wien 1983* (Tutzing: Hans Schneider, 1988), 351–60

H. J. Marx, 'Brahms und die Musikforschung', in F. Krummacher, M. Struck et al (eds.), *Johannes Brahms. Quellen – Text – Rezeption – Interpretation* (Munich: Henle, 1999), 291–303

N. Reich, *Clara Schumann. Romantik als Schicksal* (Reinbek bei Hamburg: Rowohlt, 1991)

---

[12] Breitkopf & Härtel to Eusebius Mandyczewski, 30 December 1884, D-LEst, Bestand Breitkopf & Härtel 21081. Sig. 288.

PETER SCHMITZ

L. C. Roesner, 'Brahms's Editions of Schumann', in G. Bozarth (ed.), *Brahms Studies. Analytical and Historical Perspectives* (Oxford: Clarendon Press, 1990), 251–82

L. C. Roesner, 'Evaluating the Chopin sources: Johannes Brahms as a Breitkopf Editor', in I. Fuchs (ed.), *Festschrift Otto Biba zum 60. Geburtstag* (Tutzing: Hans Schneider, 2006), 341–56

W. Sandberger, '"Ich schwelge in Mozart . . . " Mozart im Spiegel von Brahms', in W. Sandberger (ed.), *Mozart im Spiegel von Brahms: eine Ausstellung im Brahms-Institut an der Musikhochschule Lübeck* (Lübeck: Brahms-Institut, 2006), 52–81

P. Schmitz, *Johannes Brahms und der Leipziger Musikverlag Breitkopf & Härtel* (Göttingen: V & R Unipress, 2009)

M. Struck, 'Editor im Doppelspiegel. Johannes Brahms als Herausgeber fremder und eigener Werke', in W. Sandberger and C. Wiesenfeldt (eds.), *Musik und Musikforschung. Johannes Brahms im Dialog mit der Geschichte* (Kassel: Bärenreiter, 2007), 185–206

CHAPTER 13

As Teacher

Johannes Behr

Brahms never studied at a music conservatory, nor did he ever teach at one.[1] However, in private, individually negotiated settings, he was active as a teacher throughout his musical life in many ways. From his youth onwards, he gave piano lessons and sporadic theory lessons [see Ch. 1 'Childhood in Hamburg']; later, he acted as occasional adviser to younger composers on many occasions, and even took on some regular students.

The young Brahms studied piano with Otto Cossel from 1840, changing to Eduard Marxsen in 1843, who also subsequently gave him composition lessons. At the age of fourteen at the latest, he began to give piano lessons himself, initially for free as a favour but soon in order to earn an income [see Ch. 8 'Finances']. The few surviving statements of four of his students reveal that in these years he neither enjoyed teaching, nor was he particularly good at it. In summer 1847, he stayed in Winsen an der Luhe with the Giesemann family and taught piano to their daughter Elise, who was a year younger than him; owing to her lack of progress, this was not repeated the following year.[2] Around 1850 Brahms gave his former schoolteacher Eduard Johann Christian Bode piano lessons, but this too ceased after a short time under some pretext.[3] In May 1851, Brahms was engaged as piano teacher to the eleven-year-old Benedikt Hübbe; this also proved fruitless and soon ended.[4] Kalbeck names another pupil from this time as Brahms's friend and contemporary Alwin Cranz, for whose father's Hamburg publishing house Brahms arranged potpourris [see Ch. 11 'As Arranger'].[5] Of the content of these lessons, it is only known that

[1] This chapter is a revised version of J. Behr, 'Brahms als Lehrer und Gutachter', in *Brahms Handbuch*, 87–92.
[2] *May I*, pp. 71 and 80.
[3] R. Meisner, 'Aus Johannes Brahms' Schulzeit', *Brahms-Studien* 2 (1977), 93. Bode's previously unknown first names were identified in the *Hamburgisches Adreß-Buch für 1855*, 32.
[4] W. Hübbe, *Brahms in Hamburg* (Hamburg: Lütcke & Wulff, 1902), 4–7.
[5] *Kalbeck I*, 57; obviously personal communication from Alwin Cranz.

123

JOHANNES BEHR

Brahms improvised finger exercises for his pupils and invented his own off-the-cuff études as needed.[6]

When he left Hamburg in spring 1853, Brahms gave up his teaching. Two years later, during an extended stay in Düsseldorf, he took it up again for two reasons: firstly, he needed the income, and, secondly, Clara Schumann's pupils needed a replacement when she was away on concert tours. From January 1855, he taught Anna Wittgenstein, Agnes Schönerstedt and one unidentifiable 'little Miss Weil';[7] later that year there followed 'the little Miss Arnold from Elberfeld',[8] Laura von Meysenbug from Detmold,[9] another unidentifiable youth called 'Jung',[10] the Danish violinist Lars Valdemar Tofte[11] and the composer Hermann Adolf Wollenhaupt.[12]

Brahms got his young pupils to play scales, Cramer studies, Bach inventions and Schumann's *Album for the Young* Op. 68, which he himself hardly enjoyed: 'how etudes and scales remind me of Hamburg! It is truly no pleasure teaching children little things.'[13] Work on larger pieces with advanced students, on the other hand, was a real pleasure: 'Today I was with Miss v. Meysenbug, who really plays very well. I like her very much.'[14] A surviving album-leaf from Detmold includes the opening of Beethoven's *Fantasia* Op. 77, and the date 'October 55' suggests that it may have been written as a farewell for Laura von Meysenbug and may have been a piece she had played in lessons.[15]

After Schumann's death in July 1856, Brahms lived mainly in Hamburg until his departure for Vienna in autumn 1862, and part of his income came from piano teaching. Already by the end of 1855, he was teaching Friederike Wagner, who became his 'favourite pupil' and later preserved one of his

---

[6] Meisner, 'Aus Johannes Brahms' Schulzeit', 93; Hübbe, 'Brahms in Hamburg', 6.

[7] 25 January and 22 February 1855, *SBB I*, 64 and 78; 26 January 1855, *Briefe V*, 87; unpublished notebook with Brahms's mention of three pupils, dated January 1855 (Wienbibliothek im Rathaus, H.I.N. 55732).

[8] *Litzmann II*, 373; 14 August 1855, *SBB I*, 124. Presumably this concerns Agnes Arnold (later Bredemeyer), daughter of the publisher Friedrich Wilhelm Arnold in Elberfeld (see: www.musikdrucke.htwk-leipzig.de/wordpress/?p=2792).

[9] 12 to 20 August 1855. *SBB I*, 122–131.   [10] 14 August 1855. *SBB I*, 124.

[11] *Ibid.* The published letter states 'N[?]' because the editor could not decipher it, but in the autograph letter it refers to 'Tofte'.

[12] *Ibid.* In parting, Brahms gave this pupil a photograph of himself with the handwritten dedication 'Herrn H. A. Wollenhaupt zur Erinnerung an Johannes Brahms. Düsseldorf Aug. 55' (Reproduced in David Schulson Autographs, New York, Catalogue 69, Title page).

[13] 25 January 1855. *SBB I*, 64.   [14] 15 August 1855, *ibid.*, 125.

[15] Reproduced in W. Schramm, *Johannes Brahms in Detmold* (1933), rev. ed. R. Müller-Dombois (Hagen: Kommissionsverlag v. d. Linnepe, 1983), 19.

As Teacher

piano exercises.[16] Two other pupils, who (like Friederike Wagner) belonged to the Hamburg Ladies' Choir which Brahms conducted from 1859, were Susanne Schmaltz[17] and Marie Völckers [see Ch. 10 'As Conductor'].[18] The twelve-year-old niece of the latter, Minna Völckers, was taught by Brahms between February 1861 and autumn 1862; and Anna Vorwerk during a five-month stay in Hamburg, was his pupil from March 1862; she was later head of a girls' school.[19] Apparently, Minna Kruse was another of his Hamburg pupils, who like Friederike Wagner, later became a piano teacher herself.[20]

From 1857 to 1859, Brahms spent the last three months of each year as a piano teacher, pianist, choral and orchestral director in the court of Detmold. He mainly taught the prince's sister Friederike, which by his own account gave him 'the greatest of pleasure': 'Giving her lessons is real music-making.'[21] Several court ladies, wishing to keep up with the princess, also had piano lessons with Brahms: Auguste von Donop, wife of the Master of the Hunt; Meta Sophie Luise von Meysenbug, wife of the Court Marshall; and her sister-in-law Laura von Meysenbug, who had already been his pupil in Düsseldorf.[22] Some of these teaching duties, which as a court employee he could hardly avoid, were burdensome; 'They make quite a lot of use of me here', he grumbled in December 1859.[23] He did, however, have at least one talented pupil, the court musician's son Friedrich Müller (b.1847), who later made a name as a music director and composer, though tragically he died aged thirty.[24]

In September 1862, Brahms went to Vienna for the first time. In subsequent years, he spent extended periods of time there, and eventually settled there. Soon after his arrival, he began to teach Julie

---

[16] 3 July 1859, *SBB I*, 264; *Johannes Brahms. 51 Übungen für das Pianoforte mit 30 weiteren, größtenteils erstveröffentlichten Übungen*, ed. J. Behr (Vienna: Wiener Urtext Edition, 2002), 91.

[17] S. Schmaltz, *Beglückte Erinnerung. Lebenslauf eines Sonntagskindes* (Dresden: Verlag Deutsche Buchwerkstätten, 1926), 24, 34–6, 40.

[18] *Kalbeck I*, 442; S. Kross, 'Brahmsiana. Der Nachlaß der Schwestern Völckers', *Die Musikforschung* 17 (1964), 131–6.

[19] M. Stone [née Völckers], 'Johannes Brahms als Lehrer. Zum Gedächtnis an seinen 25. Todestag am 3. April', *Hamburger Nachrichten*, 3 April 1922; partially reproduced in Kurt Hofmann, '*Sehnsucht habe ich immer nach Hamburg . . .*' *Johannes Brahms und seine Vaterstadt. Legende und Wirklichkeit* (Reinbek: Dialog-Verlag, 2003), 39–41; A. Vorwerk, 'Meine Erinnerungen an Johannes Brahms', in R. and K. Hofmann (eds.), *Über Brahms. Von Musikern, Dichtern und Liebhabern. Eine Anthologie* (Stuttgart: Philipp Reclam jun., 1997), 28–35.

[20] I. Schumann-Reye, 'Johannes Brahms im Leben unserer Mutter und Großmutter, berichtet von Gertrud Reye', *Brahms-Studien* 8 (Hamburg 1990), 62.

[21] October 1858, *Briefe IV*, 69.

[22] Schramm, *Brahms in Detmold*, 28, as recalled by the Detmold violinist Carl Bargheer.

[23] *Briefe V*, 255.   [24] Schramm, *Brahms in Detmold*, 30, n. 37.

von Asten, a former pupil of Clara Schumann, to whose mediation he owed his first work opportunities in the unknown city.[25] Through her, Brahms made contact with various ladies in the Vienna Singverein for whom he ran private choir rehearsals, as he had done with the Hamburg Ladies' Choir. Some of these also became his pupils, including Ottilie Hauer, Marie Geisler and Anna Wittgenstein (he had already taught the latter in Düsseldorf).[26] He gained another pupil, Johanna Grassl von Rechten, after his Vienna debut as a pianist at the end of November 1862.[27] And, in spring 1863, he briefly taught the then sixteen-year-old Elisabeth von Stockhausen, who, after her marriage to Heinrich von Herzogenberg, became a lifelong friend. Around 1864 he taught Stephanie Vrabély, who later became a composer and writer.[28] When the pianist Carl Tausig left Vienna in 1865, Brahms took over one of his pupils, the ten-year-old Rosa Neuda-Bernstein.[29] Another pupil from these Vienna years is one 'Frau Rosengarden', who – like Anna Wittgenstein – was taught by Clara Schumann when Brahms was away in February 1866.[30]

From autumn 1865, Brahms went on lengthy, income-generating concert tours as a pianist each winter. Thereafter, he was no longer financially dependent on teaching and completely stopped. When in 1868 *A German Requiem* Op. 45 and the *Hungarian Dances* WoO 1 signalled his break-through as a composer, the pecuniary aspect of concert-giving also retreated into the background; henceforth, he could live from his publishers' fees, and most of his concert activity served to disseminate his own works. In this period, Brahms only gave occasional lessons as a favour. In summer 1871 and 1872, which he spent in Baden-Baden because of Clara Schumann, he gave three of her pupils piano lessons at her request (evidently for free). The first summer, when she was away on holiday, he taught the young Pole Nathalie Janotha and the Englishwoman Florence May, who remained with Brahms even when her original teacher returned.[31] In 1872, Clara Schumann had her daughter Eugenie taught by Brahms during the summer months in order

---

[25] 3 and 21 November 1862. *SBB I*, 411–2 and 417.

[26] O. von Balassa, *Die Brahmsfreundin Ottilie Ebner [née Hauer] und ihr Kreis* (Vienna: Kommissionsverlag Franz Bondy, 1933), 38; *Kalbeck II*, 12; 4 February 1866, *SBB I*, 530.

[27] *Kalbeck II*, 26–7, note 2. [28] *Kalbeck II*, 108 and 114.

[29] R. Neuda-Bernstein, 'Brahms als Lehrer', in *Über Brahms*, 37–9; see also *Kalbeck II*, 107–8.

[30] 4 February 1866, *SBB I*, 530. Amalie Bruch-Vehoffer, mentioned in the same letter, is also regarded as one of Brahms's pupils. See R. Hofmann, '" . . . das nöthige Salz zur großen Wassersuppe" – Ein unbekanntes Schreiben von Johannes Brahms an Elisabeth von Herzogenberg', *Brahms-Studien* 13 (2002), 57, but this cannot be confirmed, and is rather unlikely given that Bruch-Vehoffer described herself only as a 'delighted listener' to Brahms (*ibid.*, 61).

[31] 15 July 1871, *SBB I*, 644–5; see also *May I*, 9–25.

As Teacher

that 'the stimulating influence of a fresh teacher might incite [her] to a more eager pursuit of [her] studies'.[32] We know of no further piano teaching from later years.

Brahms undeniably disliked his teaching in Hamburg, and also to some extent in Düsseldorf and Detmold, because many of his pupils were either still children or simply lacked talent. But, from the mid-1850s onwards, he seems to have taught with genuine pleasure and commitment, as reflected in numerous pupils' published recollections. Some of these reports also offer a more detailed picture of his lessons. Notably, even pupils who were accomplished pianists did fundamental technical studies with him [see Ch. 9 'As Pianist']. For example, Florence May and Eugenie Schumann, who had previously studied with no less than Clara Schumann, began afresh with elementary finger exercises in order to relax the hand and to work on particular problems such as passing the thumb under the hand.[33] Rosa Neuda-Bernstein, whose 'iron fingers' also soon relaxed under Brahms's tutelage, recalled the reason why he laid particular stress on the relaxation of the hand joints and fingers as follows: 'If the attack is soft, and if the hands are extraordinarily light, they can create the finest nuances, the tenderest movements and vibrations of the soul.'[34] In that sense, an elastic, supple technique was not an aim in itself for Brahms but a necessary precondition for artistically sensitive playing. In order to structure the tasks in stages, Brahms followed finger exercises with études, Cramer (as mentioned above) and especially Clementi's *Gradus ad Parnassum* Op. 44. Only after this were students permitted to approach new repertoire. Brahms preferred to go through Bach, Mozart and Beethoven in his lessons, and more seldom Scarlatti, Schubert, Mendelssohn, Schumann and Chopin; according to many accounts, he generally omitted his own works. Apparently, his way of teaching Bach was particularly characteristic, with an elastic tempo, lean and variously shaded in sound quality, and with particular emphasis on syncopations and grace notes.

In the 1850s, Brahms also gave a few theory lessons. In Düsseldorf in 1855, he taught Agnes Schönerstedt 'thoroughbass', Clara Schumann's blind friend Rosalie Leser (who was not his piano student) 'modulation' and Laura von Meysenbug 'theory'.[35] Around 1858/9, he also gave Susanne

---

[32] E. Schumann, *The Schumanns and Johannes Brahms. The Memoirs of Eugenie Schumann* (New York: Dial Press, 1927), 141.

[33] Eugenie Schumann shared some of these exercises; see *ibid.*, 228–31; reprinted and expanded in Brahms, *51 Übungen* (see note 16), 88–90.

[34] Neuda-Bernstein, 'Brahms als Lehrer', 38.

[35] 14 and 17 March, 14 and 20 August 1855, *SBB I*, 95–6, 99, 124, 131.

128   JOHANNES BEHR

Schmaltz 'harmony lessons' in Hamburg, which seem to have been a trial to her.[36] Nothing more is known of these lessons.

The occasional theory lessons cannot be described as composition lessons. However, in later years, Brahms often gave such lessons in the form of one-off, or repeated, discussions of works that were brought to him by people seeking advice from various quarters, for whom he took on different teaching roles.

From the 1850s until the end of his life, Brahms provided advice within his social circle, and the composers who knew him asked him to look through and evaluate their works. Among these was, for example, the Viennese musician Richard Heuberger, whom Brahms met in 1876 and who sought his opinion of various works between 1878 and 1892. Brahms often dispensed quite acerbic criticism, gave detailed suggestions for reworking and recommended to Heuberger that he study basic counterpoint using specific textbooks.

Alongside the growing recognition of Brahms as a composer, from the 1870s onwards, he was increasingly approached by composers he did not know to evaluate the works they brought or sent to him. For example, in March 1879, the young Hugo Wolf visited him and showed him songs and probably part of his String Quartet in D minor. Brahms went through the works with him, revealed deficiencies in his craftsmanship and also recommended contrapuntal studies to him, pointing him to the music scholar Gustav Nottebohm. Unlike Heuberger, however, Wolf did not take his advice.

In his final decade, several young composers came to Vienna with the specific intention of spending time with the highly respected 'master'. Brahms enjoyed the admiration of these 'disciples' and encouraged them to show him their works – but then subjected them to stringent criticism. During his three-month long stay in Vienna in spring 1887, Robert Kahn from Mannheim endured only one such discussion and did not even summon the courage to show him his compositions. Eduard Behm from Berlin, on the other hand, who moved to Vienna for four months in January 1890, took up Brahms's offer and thereafter had virtually weekly lessons.

Towards the end of his life, Brahms enjoyed working in a sustained way, over longer periods with a younger composer, effectively acting as a 'composition teacher' in the truest sense. Brahms invited the twenty-two-year-old Gustav Jenner from Kiel, whose songs he had encountered in summer 1887 via his publisher Fritz Simrock, in order to 'show him all the things he had to change and how one would do it'.[37] Jenner stayed in

---

[36] Schmaltz, *Beglückte Erinnerung*, 24.

[37] Simrock to Klaus Groth, 14 August 1887, J. Behr, *Johannes Brahms – Vom Ratgeber zum Kompositionslehrer. Eine Untersuchung in Fallstudien* (Kassel: Bärenreiter, 2007), 229. Groth had sent Simrock Jenner's songs.

As Teacher

Vienna, with interruptions, from 1888 to 1895, completed his counterpoint studies with Eusebius Mandyczewski and was always allowed to show Brahms new works. Brahms, in turn, did not set his student any fixed exercises but shaped his studies by first suggesting that he compose short strophic songs and variation forms before turning to sonata movements and full sonatas. Jenner's memoir contains the most detailed surviving account of Brahms as a composition teacher.

The surviving sources concerning this wide-ranging advisory and teaching activity (above all notes in diaries and composers' recollections) show that Brahms paid less attention to the artistic content of the works he evaluated than to the mastery of compositional craft. Jenner wrote that during the discussions of his works he learned basically 'nothing about their [artistic] worth', since Brahms 'exclusively concentrated on the extent of the [technical] perfection'.[38] In this spirit, Brahms also drew attention to errors in musical orthography and demanded clear, legible handwriting.[39] Furthermore, he laid great stress on the secure mastery of counterpoint and frequently recommended that such studies be undertaken with the help of textbooks or the teachers he valued. Finally, Brahms believed it to be right for young composers first to work through the forms which had been practised by the classical masters and to tackle freer and larger forms only when their artistry was more developed. Both as a teacher of composition and of piano, Brahms placed the greatest value on the fundamental mastery of technique as an essential precondition for one's own artistic playing and composition.

Further Reading

J. Behr, 'Brahms als Lehrer und Gutachter', in *Brahms Handbuch*, 87–92

J. Behr, *Johannes Brahms – Vom Ratgeber zum Kompositionslehrer. Eine Untersuchung in Fallstudien* (Kassel: Bärenreiter, 2007)

J. Behr, '"Seinen Unterricht kann ich ernstlich empfehlen." Kontrapunkt bei Gustav Nottebohm und Eusebius Mandyczewski', in W. Sandberger and C. Wiesenfeldt (eds.), *Musik und Musikforschung. Johannes Brahms im Dialog mit der Geschichte* (Kassel: Bärenreiter, 2007), 155–83

G. Jenner, 'Johannes Brahms as Man, Teacher, and Artist', trans. S. Gillespie and E Kaestner, in W. Frisch and K. Karnes (eds.), *Brahms and His World*, 2nd edn (Princeton: Princeton University Press, 2009), 381–423

[38] G. Jenner, *Johannes Brahms als Mensch, Lehrer und Künstler* (Marburg: N. G. Elwert, 1905), 25.
[39] *Heuberger*, 15.

CHAPTER 14

Private Music-Making

Katy Hamilton

It is difficult to overestimate the importance of private musical activity as a testing ground, a compositional setting and, indeed, as a pleasurable activity for Brahms. 'Private music-making' deserves a word of explanation first, since private spaces were not always in the home, performers were not always amateurs and repertoire was not strictly divided according to public or private consumption. While Brahms was clearly often concerned to write music suitable for amateur performers, such repertoire was not automatically excluded from the concert platform as a result. Indeed, since the public lied recital was an innovation during his lifetime, some of the pieces which had previously found readier advocates in the domestic space were pushed further into the limelight thanks to pioneering programmers such as Gustav Walter and Amalie Joachim [see Ch. 19 'Singers']. Therefore, this chapter provides an outline of the various ways in which Brahms engaged with performance in, and composition for, private spaces.

Although public concerts became increasingly frequent and affordable during Brahms's lifetime, domestic music-making was a ubiquitous feature of middle-class and upper-middle-class life. The ability to play or sing pointed to good education and *Bildung*, and was thus a desirable skill for those with cultural pretensions. Suitable repertoire was therefore much in demand, as is clear from the ever-increasing quantities of published scores through the century and the countless composers who specialised in catering for this audience (such as Franz Abt, 1819–85, who wrote hundreds of pieces for amateur vocal ensembles).[1] Others composed occasional pieces with a popular slant in order to accrue income and raise their public profile. In addition to original works for domestic forces – piano solos and duets, songs and pieces for small vocal ensembles, and chamber

---

[1] See J. Draheim & W. Kahl, 'Abt, Franz', in L. Finscher (ed.), *Die Musik in Geschichte und Gegenwart* 2, revised edn, 27 vols. (Kassel: Bärenreiter, 1994–2008), Personenteil vol. 1, col. 74–6.

instrumental works – a considerable amount of larger-scale repertoire was also made available to amateur performers at home through arrangements [see Ch. 11 'As Arranger'].

Brahms's interest in this burgeoning scene is clear from his own compositional output. Indeed, his very first published piece, issued under the pseudoym 'G. W. Marks' was a series of Russian and Bohemian melodies for piano duet [see Ch. 1 'Childhood in Hamburg']. In 1866, having established himself as a composer of complex piano works and chamber pieces, he published a set of sixteen Waltzes Op. 39 a few years after his arrival in the waltz-capital of the world, Vienna. The fact that these are dances, short and melodious (if rather more harmonically and rhythmically sophisticated than some) and for piano duet points clearly to their domestic target audience. As Thomas Christensen has remarked of this configuration, 'No other medium was arguably so important to nineteenth-century musicians for the dissemination and iterability of concert repertory.'[2] Furthermore, Brahms also prepared two solo piano versions of the Waltzes: one 'for sensible hands' and one 'perhaps for pretty ones' (i.e. female pianists, in a simplified version).[3] The Waltzes were followed in due course by four books of *Hungarian Dances* WoO 1, also for piano duet (1868 and 1880). In addition, Brahms's continuous engagement with lieder of various kinds – from folk-song collections to original solo compositions, duets and quartets – includes countless examples of simple melodies, grateful part-writing and straightforward piano accompaniments, making them eminently suitable for performance or even sight-reading at a convivial musical gathering. Several of his chamber works also seem geared equally towards the pleasure of the players and the audience, as Marie Sumner Lott has demonstrated in regard to his two Sextets Opp. 18 and 36.[4] And there are numerous examples of Brahms undertaking arrangements of his larger-scale compositions, above all of his symphonic music, for piano duet and two pianos [see Ch. 11 'As Arranger'].

This preoccupation with domestic audiences is not matched by many of Brahms's contemporaries. Anton Bruckner did not make the reductions of his symphonic works, nor did he write many lieder or chamber pieces. Wagner made rather more arrangements of music by other composers, and

---

[2] T. Christensen, 'Four-Hand Piano Transcription and Geographies of Nineteenth-Century Musical Reception', *Journal of the American Musicological Society* 52/2 (Summer 1999), 256.
[3] Brahms to Rieter-Biedermann, 12 February 1867, *Briefe XIV*, 141–2.
[4] See M. Sumner Lott, 'Domesticity in Brahms's String Sextets, Opp. 18 and 36', in K. Hamilton and N. Loges (eds.), *Brahms in the Home and the Concert Hall* (Cambridge: Cambridge University Press, 2014), 43–94.

also wrote songs and some piano pieces, although he was not interested, it seems, in producing workable reductions of his own large-scale compositions. Similarly, Liszt was a prolific composer of keyboard and vocal repertoire, but little of this is suitable for performance by non-specialists.

Brahms's published scores, then, speak to his interest in this wider musical audience – even though he was not always universally positive about it. After all, the publication of any piece of music represents a loss of control for the composer: purchasers could make what they liked of the scores that they bought, while a formal, public event in which some travesty of arrangement or musical forces was proposed could be quashed if he became aware of it. It is thus possible to view the many published arrangements of his own music (which he sanctioned and in some cases produced himself) as both a means of signalling a willingness to cater for amateurs and of marking out what he considered to be acceptable manipulation of an original. The more popular the pieces were, the more numerous the arrangements: between 1868 and 1900, the famous 'Wiegenlied' Op. 49 no. 4 appeared in editions for various vocal ranges as well as for solo piano; piano, flute and violin (or two flutes); piano duet; male voice choir; orchestra; solo harp; cello and piano; mixed chorus; and zither with ad lib. vocal part.[5]

In 1874, writing to Max Abraham of Peters Edition, Brahms commented upon 'the current bad habit that all people, with a greater or lesser lack of taste, would rather play music in ways other than that which the composer wrote'.[6] The remark was made in regard to a suggestion from Abraham that a new set of vocal quartets might include a note that the music was also suitable for performance by larger forces; but Brahms did not wish to codify such flexibility in print. While acknowledging that domestic performance might well, and for perfectly practical reasons (the number of people at a party, the available instrumentalists on a given occasion), lead to changes in instrumentarium and forces, Brahms did not believe that such things should be accommodated in a score description, as this would weaken the original conception of the music as being for certain forces. This is further reinforced by the liberties he was prepared to take in making piano reductions of his orchestral pieces: unlike his paid arrangers, he – as the creator of the work – could freely adjust the presentation of musical ideas to suit their new medium.

---

[5] These arrangements were listed in Friedrich Hofmeister's monthly reports of new publications, the *Monatsberichte*. See www.hofmeister.rhul.ac.uk.

[6] Brahms to Max Abraham, 15 October 1874, *Briefe XIV*, 234.

Private Music-Making   133

One final aspect of practical score adjustments deserves mentioning here, and that is the question of printed language for vocal items. As Brahms's music became increasingly popular abroad, his publishers sought to issue vocal music with translated texts for a non-German-speaking market. Recognising the pragmatic reasons for this decision, Brahms did not object to Simrock and others commissioning such translations (initially in French and English) to increase their sales. But he was also not interested in the results. 'The German song that I compose has absolutely nothing to do with the English translation', he wrote to Simrock in 1887, 'that is only stuck on afterwards by the publisher – there is nothing further to say about it'.[7]

Despite these reservations, Brahms remained interested in both writing for, and performing with, amateur musicians. He enjoyed taking part in musical evenings with friends who were themselves the target audience of his own efforts in this repertoire, and the memoirs of Brahms circle members frequently mention treasured occasions of performing his music and delighting in their connection with the composer. Furthermore, in the late 1850s and early 1860s, Brahms directed and wrote music for the Hamburg Ladies' Choir [see Ch. 10 'As Conductor']. This group of around forty amateur singers met regularly to rehearse and sing for their own pleasure – public performance was not the aim of the ensemble. They worked on folk-songs, music by Schubert, Brahms and Karl Grädener, and occasionally persuaded Brahms to play to them. While Brahms was delighted and embarrassed in equal measure by so much female attention, he was obviously committed to the little group as both their director and composer. He wrote to Clara Schumann in 1860 that in addition to their indoor rehearsals, 'we usually have a lot of fine singing and serenading on the road [on the journey home]. My girls, for instance, will walk quite calmly into a garden and wake the people up at midnight with their singing.'[8] He was sorry to leave the ensemble when he moved to Vienna, and at least one of the choir's members, Ottilie Ebner, went on to found her own domestic vocal ensemble in turn.

The word 'amateur' can have a pejorative ring to it in contemporary usage. But to be a non-professional (an 'amator' in the Latin sense of practising something for the love of it) does not necessarily imply a lower level of ability than that of a career musician. Indeed, Brahms's closest

---

[7] Brahms to Simrock, 27 February 1887, *Briefe XI*, 144.

[8] Brahms to Clara Schumann, 2 April 1860, S. Drinker, *Brahms and His Women's Choruses* (Merion, PA: Musurgia Publishers, 1952), 51.

acquaintances included several extremely able amateurs. Chief among these was Elisabeth von Herzogenberg (née von Stockhausen), the daughter of a cultured diplomat who had learned with Chopin in Paris (and was the dedicatee of Chopin's First Ballade Op. 23). She also studied piano with the noted pedagogue Julius Epstein and, briefly, with Brahms himself in 1862. She married the composer Heinrich von Herzogenberg in 1868, and, from the 1870s onwards, the couple became members of Brahms's inner circle. Indeed, her considerable musical talent led Brahms to seek her comments on his late piano compositions; in this sense she became as important an arbiter of his music as Clara Schumann had been since his earliest opuses. Elisabeth von Herzogenberg's repertoire included Brahms's own solo (often virtuosic) piano music, alongside the works of Mendelssohn, Schumann, Bach, Mozart and Beethoven. She gave several public performances of sonatas and concertos by J. S. Bach in the 1870s and 1880s, alongside professional performers such as Julius Röntgen and Paul Klengel [see Ch. 4 'Leipzig and Berlin'].[9]

Brahms's good friend Theodor Billroth was a proficient pianist and string player who regularly held musical soirées at his home in Vienna. A highly regarded surgeon and professor at the University of Vienna, Billroth's musical interests were almost as important to him as his medical work. He frequently played violin or viola in private performances of Brahms's quartets, quintets and sextets, often alongside professional musicians such as Joseph Hellmesberger, who led a prominent Viennese string quartet. Brahms also played through piano-duet scores of new or recently published works with Billroth. For example, in 1870, Brahms suggested they try his duet arrangement of the First Piano Quartet Op. 25, and in 1877 he teased Billroth that he had made a similar arrangement of his Second Symphony Op. 73 'only because of you', so that they might play it together.[10]

As capable musicians who were personally familiar with Brahms's compositional style, both Billroth and Elisabeth von Herzogenberg were crucial to the composer in his development of new pieces. Trial performances among friends allowed Brahms to test ideas against his most trusted associates while works were still developing. There are numerous examples of this occurring, and the performance space at Ehrbar's, a noted Viennese piano manufacturer, was a favourite venue. Here, Brahms gave trial

---

[9] A. Ruhbaum, *Elisabeth von Hergozenberg: Salon – Mäzenatentum – Musikförderung* (Kenzingen: Centaurus-Verlag, 2009), 90.

[10] Letters of 1870 and 9 November 1877, H. Barkan (ed.), *Johannes Brahms and Theodor Billroth. Letters from a Musical Friendship* (Westport, CT: Greenwood Press, 1957), 12–13 and 57.

Private Music-Making 135

performances for his most trusted friends and advisers of his Second Symphony Op. 73 (for piano four hands), his Second Piano Concerto Op. 83 (for two pianos), his Third Symphony Op. 90 (for two pianos) and his Fourth Symphony Op. 98 (for two pianos), in each case performing alongside fellow pianist and composer Ignaz Brüll.[11] In the case of the Fourth Symphony, the audience consisted of the critics Eduard Hanslick and Gustav Dömpke, the conductor Hans Richter, composer and historian Carl Ferdinand Pohl and Billroth.[12] Important rehearsals of new chamber works, including the Clarinet Quintet Op. 115 and Clarinet Trio Op. 114, were held in the home of the Fellinger family, the audience once again including Billroth, Hanslick, Kalbeck and others. Indeed, the Clarinet Quintet was also performed at the home of Karl and Leopoldine Wittgenstein in Vienna on 5 January 1892 because Brahms wished to hear it performed in a private setting before its Viennese premiere a few days later.[13]

These intimate run-throughs were doubtless pleasurable for both the composer and performers, but they also existed in an interlocking relationship with public performance. For the music-makers (performers and composers), private concerts and rehearsals provided an opportunity to hone their craft; for the intimates of Brahms's circle, they were a mark of the esteem in which Brahms held them to permit them to attend, as friends or colleagues, and were thus treasured even more greatly than the experience of a public premiere.

Finally, in addition to the hard graft of shaping and developing new material with his friends, Brahms also made music with his fellow professionals simply for the joy of it. Billroth's home was a frequent venue for house concerts, in which the likes of Joachim, Gustav Walter, Robert Hausmann, Hermine Spies and Ignaz Brüll would play chamber music with Brahms. In addition to this, there must have been countless occasions on which informal performances took place when friends met and made music, together with conversation. Clara Schumann, who was a part of Brahms's life from his first steps into a musical career, remained a regular collaborator, and her diaries and letters are full of references to their musicmaking: entertaining each other with solo performances and playing duets

---

[11] These performances were given in mid-December 1877, 12 October 1881, 9 or 22 November 1883 and 8 October 1885, respectively. See R. and K. Hofmann, *Brahms als Pianist und Dirigent*, 169, 200, 229 and 249–50.

[12] *Kalbeck III*, 451–2.

[13] See S. Avins, 'Brahms in the Wittgenstein Homes: A Memoir and Letters', in *Brahms in the Home and the Concert Hall*, 228. A picture of the Wittegenstein music room is given on 229.

together. Eugenie Schumann recalled visits from many musicians when she and her mother holidayed in Baden-Baden, 'including the Florentine Quartet, Rubinstein, Jaëll, Ernst, Sivori, Joachim, Stockhausen, Brahms, Levi, and many others. We had music to our hearts' content, and friends were invited to share our enjoyment.'[14] Eugenie further records that the noted singer Pauline Viardot, who also spent her summers in Baden, even constructed a 'charming little theatre' in her garden, writing music for her students to perform before an invited audience which frequently contained leading professional musicians and members of the Prussian court.[15]

While Viardot was writing for a prestigious private assembly (and to show off her students), compositional gifts for private performance could be far more intimate. In a particularly touching gesture, Brahms composed a 'sacred lullaby' ('Geistliches Wiegenlied'), later published as the second of the Two Songs for Alto, Viola and Piano Op. 91 in 1864, for the birth of Johannes Joachim – the son of his dear friends Joseph (who was an able violist as well as violinist) and Amalie Joachim (a professional contralto) and named after Brahms himself. That the first public performance was given only twenty years later points to the privileged private 'ownership' of this piece by the friends and colleagues for whom Brahms wrote it and with whom he must have performed it at home.

The ways in which such occasions brought together both professional and non-professional musicians indicate the flexible interaction between these two categories. Orchestras in Vienna were also frequently composed of both professional and amateur players (once again, the word indicating only the financial implications of music-making, and not ability). The intermingling of career musicians and dedicated enthusiasts was common to both public and private performance. The centrality of music-making to the lives of cultured individuals is evident well into the early twentieth century, for example in the lives of other notable Viennese figures such as Stefan Zweig and Theodor Adorno.[16] The reminiscences of these figures, and the diaries and letters of Brahms's closest friends, make clear that such experiences remained tremendously precious to them – particularly when they were able to play with, or listen to, such first-rank musicians themselves. As Ellen

---

[14] E. Schumann, *Memoirs of Eugenie Schumann*, trans. M. Busch (London: Eulenberg Books, 1927), 105.

[15] *Ibid.*, 108.

[16] See R. Leppert, 'The Cultural Dialectics of Chamber Music: Adorno and the Visual-Acoustic Imaginary of *Bildung*', in *Brahms in the Home and the Concert Hall*, 346–65.

Franz reported to her brother in 1891, 'With Brahms, one makes wonderful music.'[17]

Further Reading

T. Christensen, 'Four-Hand Piano Transcription and Geographies of Nineteenth-Century', *Journal of the American Musicological Society* 52/2 (Summer 1999), 255–98

S. Drinker, *Brahms and His Women's Choruses* (Merion, PA: Musurgia Publishers, 1952)

K. Hamilton and N. Loges (eds.), *Brahms in the Home and the Concert Hall* (Cambridge: Cambridge University Press, 2014)

M. McCorkle, 'The Role of Trial Performances for Brahms's Orchestral and Large Choral Works: Sources and Circumstances', in G. Bozarth (ed.), *Brahms Studies: Historial and Analytical Perspectives* (Oxford: Clarendon Press, 1998), 295–328

M. Sumner Lott, *The Social Worlds of Nineteenth-Century Chamber Music: Composers, Consumers, Communities* (Chicago: University of Illinois Press, 2015)

---

[17] Freifrau von Heldburg (Ellen Franz), *Fünfzig Jahre Glück und Leid. Ein Leben in Briefen aus den Jahren 1873–1923*, 2nd edn (Leipzig: Koehler & Amelang, 1926), 81.

CHAPTER 15

Concert Life

Laurenz Lütteken

The claim that the nineteenth century was the century of the bourgeoisie or middle class (*Bürgertum*) is undeniably a hot topic in research. This claim provokes questions not only about the wider definition of 'bourgeoisie' but also about the accuracy of this claim specifically for music history. Brahms rarely travelled outside German-speaking territories, apart from eight trips to Italy and concerts in the Netherlands. Within this region, the bourgeoisie did not consist of a single, homogenous group but could be described variously in social, political or behavioural terms, with overlaps between these. In terms of social class, the term primarily describes those who practised an established 'craft' in the broadest sense, as Brahms's father did [see Ch. 1 'Childhood in Hamburg']. In political terms, the middle class (*Bürger*) bore a degree of responsibility; however, even after the revolutions of 1848, their real power was still very restricted within a society which was still largely dominated by the aristocracy. Defined in terms of behaviour, the bourgeoisie consisted of those who wished to identify with specific ideologies and ways of being and strove to express these in their lives in ways connected with economic capital.[1] An obvious symptom of this tendency was their gathering together in clubs, associations and societies. These sprung up in all areas of life but took on particularly significant roles within the arts and sciences. After 1848, their original latent or implied political undertones were increasingly suppressed.[2]

Bourgeois music clubs emerged under the influence of the Napoleonic Wars of Liberation and the Congress of Vienna and were, therefore, initially patriotically and politically motivated. Organisations

---

[1] See M. Hettling, *Politische Bürgerlichkeit. Der Bürger zwischen Individualität und Vergesellschaftung in Deutschland und in der Schweiz von 1860 bis 1918.* (Göttingen: Vandenhoeck & Ruprecht, 1999).

[2] For an overview, see F. Becker, 'Bürgertum und Kultur im 19. Jahrhundert. Die Inszenierung von Bürgerlichkeit', in L. Lütteken (ed), *Zwischen Tempel und Verein. Musik und Bürgertum im 19. Jahrhundert* (Kassel: Bärenreiter Verlag, 2013), 14–34.

Concert Life 139

like the Berlin *Liedertafel* or the Vienna Musikverein even explicitly supported the beleaguered monarchy. Such clubs constituted an organised public realm, in contrast to the privacy of domestic music-making (*Hausmusik*) with its distinctive genres like piano pieces or lyric song. This blend of collective self-organisation and individual action was a pattern of behaviour born from aspiration and was also reflected in material things. The bourgeoisie (*Bürgerlichkeit*) was characterised by such behaviour.[3] The number of music associations founded in just the first two decades of the nineteenth century is astonishing: 1806, Hanover; 1808, Frankfurt an Main; 1810, Salzburg; 1811, Munich; 1812, Cologne, Regensburg, Vienna and Zurich; 1815, Bern, Graz; 1816, Münster; 1817, Brünn, Krakow; 1818, Darmstadt, Düsseldorf, Innsbruck; 1819, Bamberg and Erfurt.[4] These all functioned, in a series of complex evolutions, as concert organisations (Brahms had contact with most of them later in the century), and they occasionally extended their remit to establishing conservatoires. Hence, the clubs supported orchestras and choirs initially funded exclusively by subscriptions from members and only gradually professionalised from the second third of the century onwards through the establishment of paid orchestras.

Furthermore, and increasingly in the second half of the century, such societies decided to build their own concert halls, hence the Berlin Singakademie's Incunabula (1821) and the Munich Odeon (1828) in the first instance, and the imposing, lavish halls constructed after 1850: Vienna in 1870, Leipzig in 1884 and Berlin in 1888. In these typically prestigious and programmatically conceived halls (which, unlike the Odeon or Singakademie, tended not to be in the historic centres of cities), the practices of the bourgeois clubs coalesced into virtually religious artistic self-representation. Brahms himself worked in all the significant concert halls of the German and Dutch-speaking realms; as late as 1895 he conducted his *Triumphlied* Op. 55 for the opening of the Zurich Tonhalle, a hall financed exclusively by a bourgeois club. There, he could observe the canonisation of his own portrait among

---

[3] T. Reitz, *Bürgerlichkeit als Haltung. Zur Politik des privaten Weltverhältnisses* (Munich: Wilhelm Fink Verlag, 2003).

[4] See for example, C. Heine, '"Aus reiner und wahrer Liebe zur Kunst ohne äußere Mittel". Bürgerliche Musikvereine in deutschsprachigen Städten des frühen 19. Jahrhunderts', PhD Dissertation (University of Zurich, 2009, http://opac.nebis.ch/ediss/20090646_002427553.pdf), 195ff; see also W. Weber, *Music and the Middle Class. The Social Structure of Concert Life in London, Paris, and Vienna between 1830 and 1848*, 2nd edn (Aldershot: Ashgate, 2004) and P. Küsgens, *Horizonte nationaler Musik. Musiziergesellschaften in Süddeutschland und in der Deutschschweiz 1847–1891* (Frankfurt: Peter Lang, 2010).

Figure 15.1. The 'Komponistenhimmel' in the Tonhalle, Zurich.

his deceased composer-colleagues in the 'heaven of the muses' (see Figure 15.1).[5]

At first glance, it would seem as though Brahms identified with this world of bourgeois music clubs (a world which his father entered only after considerable effort). This is also evident from the fact that he selected an apartment in Vienna close to the new Musikverein building. However, upon closer scrutiny, this connection is revealed as fragmentary, already apparent in the fact that within the selfsame Vienna apartment, he avoided various upper-middle-class conventions. Indeed, he deliberately cultivated a petit-bourgeois setting which drastically differed not only from the typical means of self-representation within the educated middle class but also from his own music and, above all, his financial possibilities.[6]

Also, apart from a short episode, Brahms never allowed himself to be bound to a music institution or club. His hope of being appointed director

---

[5] There is currently no systematic comparative investigation of nineteenth-century concert halls; see, however, R. Kanz, 'Konzertsaalbauten im 19. Jahrhundert', in *Zwischen Tempel und Verein*, 71–91, on the Zurich Tonhalle; and W. Sandberger, *Imagination und Kanon. Der 'Komponistenhimmel' in der Zürcher Tonhalle von 1895* (Winterthur: Amadeus, 2015).

[6] See also M. Pammer, 'Geldgeber und Produzenten: Wirtschaftsbürger in Wien zwischen 1820 und 1873', in R. Hoffmann (ed.), *Bürger zwischen Tradition und Modernität* (Vienna: Böhlau, 1997), 204–23.

Concert Life

of the Hamburg Philharmonic in 1863 was unrealistic, despite his friend Joseph Joachim's indignation that the position was offered to their colleague, the baritone Julius Stockhausen. He rejected the attempt from Hamburg in 1894 to 'make amends', just as he had rejected overtures from the Düsseldorf Musikverein in 1876. It was probably only sentimental reasons that led him to flirt with the idea of the post of Thomaskantor in Leipzig, held over for him in 1879. In any case, this job had long ceased to be that of a city music director and was purely a church position.

In other words, Brahms was more or less detached from the bourgeois concert institutions of his day, apart from a short spell as choirmaster of the Vienna Singakademie in 1863–4 and the brief period as artistic director of the Gesellschaft der Musikfreunde in Vienna from 1872 to 1875.[7] His institutional affiliations were limited to honorary memberships (Lemberg, Krefeld, Dresden, Laibach, Hamburg, Vienna); his public performances as a pianist and conductor were always guest appearances. Even attempts to get him to take on a role in the conservatories in Cologne (through Ferdinand Hiller) and Berlin (through Joseph Joachim) failed. His connections to such significant educational institutions were, again, only through honorary memberships (Klausenburg 1879, St Petersburg 1888).[8]

However, bourgeois music clubs were only one aspect of musical life in the nineteenth century (and possibly not even the most important). The decisive bearers of musical life were largely unchanged from previously: the generally richly endowed, long-established court orchestras (*Hofkapellen*). This was not only because of their regular, established concert activity but also because of the court opera houses which coexisted in nearly every case (especially significant were those in Munich, Berlin, Vienna, Dresden, Stuttgart, Kassel and Karlsruhe). These court institutions, which have not yet been systematically compared, accorded their members numerous privileges both before and after 1848, including a type of tenure or public-employee status, extremely generous pension arrangements and significant tax advantages. These privileges were only jeopardised if one deliberately sought conflict with the ruling houses, as Richard Wagner did in Dresden in 1849, but ultimately even he remained astonishingly tightly bound to this courtly world (and that of the Munich Court Orchestra) through his closeness to the Bavarian King Ludwig II.

---

[7] See O. Biba, 'Brahms und die Gesellschaft der Musikfreunde in Wien', in S. Antonicek and O. Biba (eds.), *Brahms-Kongress Wien 1983* (Tutzing: Hans Schneider, 1988), 45–65.

[8] See J. Behr, *Johannes Brahms – Vom Ratgeber zum Kompositionslehrer. Eine Untersuchung in Fallstudien* (Kassel: Bärenreiter, 2007).

142 LAURENZ LÜTTEKEN

Through their recruitment processes and organisational structures, the court orchestras guaranteed the kind of professionalism which the bourgeois music clubs achieved only gradually, laboriously and, to an extent, with intense conflict. In the first decades of the nineteenth century, for instance, the Kassel Court Orchestra under Louis Spohr was an important model. But even Mahler and Richard Strauss lived out their professional conducting careers as court conductors, enjoying many perks and extremely generous salaries. Apart from his short stint at the court of Lippe-Detmold, Brahms, who ultimately abstained from opera, also remained markedly distant from the world of court music, even if he enthusiastically dedicated his *Triumphlied* to Emperor Kaiser Wilhelm I.[9]

However, if one contemplates the sequence of his premieres from 1870 onwards, one fact becomes evident: Brahms's connections to bourgeois music clubs and court institutions are roughly equal.[10]

The Karlsruhe premiere of the *Schicksalslied* Op. 54 was organised by the local philharmonic society but was run by the court orchestra and the court conductor as part of their responsibilities, along with the symphony concerts. In the case of the Vienna Philharmonic, one must consider the fact that the court orchestra uniquely operated as a music club (albeit under imperial patronage). This balance was then tipped decisively in favour of the courtly world through Brahms's late but profound connection with the Meiningen Court Orchestra. This exceptional situation is especially well portrayed through the 'public' premiere of the Second Piano Concerto Op. 83, which took place on 9 November 1881 in Pest with the (court) National Theatre Orchestra under Alexander Erkel. A few weeks earlier the work had had its first 'real' performance at the Meiningen Court with Brahms as soloist and Hans von Bülow at the podium; however, this performance was not open to the public.

The concert formats which were connected to the music clubs and court orchestras are only comparable to a certain extent, and they were also still generally heterogenous in the second half of the century. Music club events were aimed first and foremost at the members, whose role as active musicians after the middle of the century either ceased or only continued through choral singing. Until well into the second half of the century, such events mixed various musical genres in extremely diverse formats in

[9] See W. Schramm, *Johannes Brahms in Detmold* (1933), rev. edn, R. Müller-Dombois (Hagen: Kommissionsverlag v. d. Linnepe, 1983).

[10] See L. Botstein 'Time and Memory. Concert Life, Science, and Music in Brahms's Vienna', in W. Frisch (ed.), *Brahms and His World* (Princeton: Princeton University Press, 1990), 3–22.

Concert Life 143

Table 15.1 *Locations of premiere performances of Brahms's orchestral works divided into bourgeois music clubs and court institutions*

Music Club	Court Orchestra
Variations on a Theme of Haydn Op. 56a (1870, Vienna)	
Alto Rhapsody Op. 53 (1870, Jena)	
	Schicksalslied Op. 54 (1871, Karlsruhe)
	Triumphlied Op. 55 (1872, Karlsruhe)
	First Symphony Op. 68 (1876, Karlsruhe)
Second Symphony Op. 73 (1877, Vienna)	
Violin Concerto Op. 77 (1879, Leipzig)	
Tragic Overture Op. 81 (1880, Vienna)	
Nänie Op. 82 (1881, Zurich)	Second Piano Concerto Op. 83 (1881, Pest; prior to this, Meiningen)
Academic Festival Overture Op. 80 (1881, Breslau)	
Gesang der Parzen Op. 89 (1882, Basel)	
Third Symphony Op. 90 (1883, Vienna)	
	Fourth Symphony Op. 98 (1884, Meiningen)
Double Concerto Op. 102 (1887, Cologne)	

programmes which did not necessarily fall under the music director's authority but under that of the relevant club committees, which were partially bound by statutory regulations.

Conditions only changed with Felix Mendelssohn's activities at the Leipzig Gewandhaus, which were regarded as exemplary but, even then, this happened gradually and by no means without conflict. The 1871 Karlsruhe concert at which Brahms's *Schicksalslied* Op. 54 was premiered included sections of Schumann's *Scenes from Goethe's Faust* WoO 3, as well as individual Schubert songs. Given that the court orchestra was ultimately responsible for the event, this concise programme can be regarded as an exception. A clearer indication of the possible structure of music club concerts is given by the programmatically orientated concerts at the 1892 Lower Rhine Music Festival. This programme included Weber's *Euryanthe* Overture J291, Mendelssohn's *114th Psalm* Op. 51, Schumann's Fourth Symphony Op. 120, Brahms's *Triumphlied* Op. 55 and the Funeral March from Wagner's *Götterdämmerung*, as well as Beethoven's Ninth Symphony

Op. 125.[11] It therefore involved around two and a half hours of music, without piano or song, in keeping with the character of the music festival.

The programmes of the court orchestras are notably varied, but when directed at a larger public, e.g. as described in Karlsruhe in 1865 as open 'to the general public', could be adapted to suit. The premiere of the *Triumphlied* in Karlsruhe in 1872 was also the conductor Hermann Levi's farewell concert, and the programme included Beethoven's Eighth Symphony Op. 93, Schumann's Piano Concerto Op. 54, a Handel aria, piano pieces and Schubert songs. In 1876 (also in Karlsruhe), the programme in which Otto Dessoff gave the premiere of Brahms's First Symphony Op. 68 was comparable; the second Beethoven *Leonore* overture was followed by the *Euryanthe* cavatina, one of Robert Volkmann's string serenades and three songs with piano.[12]

Even if the court orchestra had sole control, programme formats could still look different. At the premiere of Brahms's Fourth Symphony Op. 98, the work was preceded by Mendelssohn's *Melusine* Overture Op. 32, Brahms's Violin Concerto Op. 77, then, after a short interval, a *Fidelio* Overture (the exact one is unspecified) – and finally, the new symphony. The Duke himself, who must have approved the programme (as planned by von Bülow), led the enthusiastic applause – and, after the concert, had the first and third movements repeated for himself, his court and guests.[13]

From the 1860s onwards, following the Vienna music directorship, Brahms himself more rarely gave concerts and conducted. Since he organised his existence to some extent as a compositional 'corporation', i.e. he lived off his wisely invested composition fees, he preferred to appear in public as a pianist only when he needed additional income. Certainly, the subsequent concert tours might then be lengthy, and they were systematically planned, seemingly via a network he controlled. As a rule, Brahms appeared as a soloist in orchestral concerts. (In contrast, the later concerts with the clarinet works from 1895 were conceived under very different circumstances.) In his appearances as a pianist, he fitted himself into the

---

[11] Both programmes are reproduced in W. Sandberger and S. Weymar (eds.), *Johannes Brahms. Ikone der bürgerlichen Lebenswelt? Eine Ausstellung des Brahms-Instituts an der Musikhochschule Lübeck* (Lübeck: Brahms-Institut an der Musikhochschule Lübeck, 2008), 49 and 60f.

[12] The programmes are reproduced in *Johannes Brahms in Baden-Baden und Karlsruhe. Eine Ausstellung der Badischen Landesbibliothek.* (Karlsruhe: Landesbibliothek Karlsruhe, 1983), 123; see also the Digital Archive of Programmes in the Brahms-Museum Lübeck (www.brahms-institut.de/web/bihl_digital/programme.html).

[13] Report in *Berliner Courier*, 1 November 1885; see also H. von Bülow, *Briefe und Schriften*, 8 vols. (Leipzig: Breitkopf & Härtel, 1907), vol. 7, 386.

Concert Life 145

existing structures of primarily middle-class music societies, but with his growing fame, he also demanded exceptional conditions; for example, in a guest performance at the Hamburg Cäcilien-Verein which took place on 9 April 1886 in the Convent-Garten, he conducted his own works exclusively. This is part of a larger tendency which became firmly established in the late nineteenth century: the dedication of certain festivals to the music of just one composer (thus, there were before and around 1900 not only Brahms festivals but also Reger and Strauss festivals). At the same time, his earlier performances, particularly in chamber-music contexts (with various partners), belonged to the type of evenings generally organised by music societies for soloists and virtuosos who were passing through; the specific conditions of each society dictated the organisation and format.

Since there are still no comparative studies of concert life for the second half of the nineteenth century, it is difficult to build an exact picture of its structures – especially in a case like that of Brahms, who positioned himself in such a tense relationship with the musical life of his era and basically never held a fixed, professional role. As a rule, music societies preferred subscription concerts, which were both socially and financially predictable, and court orchestras ran both subscription concerts (sometimes called 'academies') and other specially organised public performances. While music society concerts ultimately took place in their own, increasingly standardised concert halls, court orchestras not infrequently performed in court theatres. This is particularly evident in Meiningen, where the theatre and orchestra were close, thanks to Duke Georg II's strivings for cultural and political reform. When this was not so, as in Karlsruhe, the parameters were nonetheless unchanged, even though the concerts took place in the Hall of the Museumsgesellschaft (in the Kaiserstrasse), i.e. a music society. However, this society was closely linked to the ducal collection and authorised solely through it.

It is virtually impossible to offer an overview of the audience profile of the various concert formats in their multifarious urban contexts. In the case of the music societies, the representatives of the financial middle class were not only the leading elite but were also part of the paying public (albeit with discounts for society members). While culturally ambitious courts operated a complex politics of recruitment and remuneration, patronage of the societies was left to chance and individual initiative. Furthermore, the music societies did not necessarily guarantee that their performances would all be open to the public; they could operate exclusively, just like the court orchestras. Thus, the six annual concerts of the Karlsruhe

Museumsgesellschaft with the court orchestra (which also regularly performed in Baden-Baden) were, as a rule, closed to the public.[14] Furthermore, the difference between royal ('Residenz') and civil cities ('Bürgerstädten'), between large and small municipalities, between economically strong and weak regions were considerable. In cities like Duisburg or Düsseldorf, where Brahms could have been music director, even the construction of the theatre buildings was due to the patronage of the same middle class which also significantly determined the life of the music societies. This is also true of Zurich, where the supporters of the concert hall and the opera house, which were built practically at the same time (and by the same architect), were largely identical. Only as the state took increasing responsibility for these institutions did the situation change, but this process only began after Brahms's death – and gained special momentum after World War I. At this point, the court orchestras and theatres were transformed into 'neutral', national institutions, e.g. Vienna, Dresden, Berlin and Munich.

Furthermore, the constitution of the concert-going public in individual cities is difficult to reconstruct – especially since alongside the subscriptions, there was always the possibility of freely purchasing a ticket. At the premiere of the Fourth Symphony in Meiningen, the ticket prices ranged from 3 Mark to 50 Pfennig (see Table 8.1 in Ch. 8 'Finances'); this is exceptionally cheap when one considers that, at the same time, the cheapest seat in the Leipzig Gewandhaus cost as much as the most expensive in Meiningen.[15] However, Leipzig was one of the wealthiest cities in the German-speaking territory and therefore could hardly be compared with a small duchy. The Vienna Musikhalle, erected by Hermann Otte in 1892 for the Viennese Theatrical Exhibition had a capacity of 1,800 places; at 50 Kreuzer for a single concert or 2 Gulden for a subscription to twelve concerts, the tickets were exceptionally good value.[16] In comparison, Brahms paid 35 Gulden monthly for his apartment in Karlsgasse 4, a house occupied by lower-middle-class artisans as well as minor civil servants. (Still, his annual income differentiated him drastically from his fellow occupants, in that it was roughly a hundred times higher).

---

[14] See B. Freudenberger, 'Karlsruhe', in L. Lütteken (ed.). *Musik in Geschichte und Gegenwart Online* (Kassel, Stuttgart, New York: 2016ff)., published in this form 18 June 2016, www.mgg-online.com/mgg/stable/14228.

[15] This was the eleventh subscription concert of 1 January 1888, in which Brahms conducted his Double Concerto Op. 102.

[16] T. Antonicek, *Die internationale Ausstellung für Musik- und Theaterwesen Wien 1892* (Vienna: [s.n.], 2013), 100ff.

Concert Life 147

An investment for a concert subscription would have involved not even 6 per cent of the monthly rent for people of this background, 11 per cent for a married couple.

Alongside professional concerts, the numerous choral societies included schemes which enabled not only active participation as a singer but also very cheaply priced attendance at performances; these too played a large role in the musical life of a city. Moreover, if one considers that domestic 'privacy' was no coincidental corollary to these various types of 'publicness', then it follows that piano scores (which Brahms also regularly produced, see Ch. 11 'Brahms as Arranger') had a decisive role to play in exposure to and deeper study of musical works, particularly in places which lacked sufficiently competent music societies. To the piano scores can be added the numerous other arrangements and transcriptions available to any concertgoer. In general, there was a desire to engage with works on more than a superficial level. As late as the start of the twentieth century, programmes for the subscription concerts of Berlin's Hofkapelle (which naturally took place not in the Philharmonie but in the Opera House) stated: 'Upon popular request, scores of works being performed this evening are for sale in the foyer of the Opera House.'[17]

With regard to music, the 'middle-class' century was strongly marked by courtly elements. Although Brahms was technically a representative of middle-class societies, he maintained close links with both spheres, demonstrating a clear preference for the exclusive world of the small court at the end of his life. The concert formats, cycles and festivals of the music societies and the court orchestras made use of Brahms's music, yet the composer had only an indirect influence over it, in that he avoided a music director's post. Nevertheless, through the capital income from the honoraria, the chief source of his wealth, he remained, at least in this respect, connected to the cultivated middle-class aspirations of the second half of the century.

Further Reading

O. Biba, 'Brahms und die Gesellschaft der Musikfreunde in Wien', in S. Antonicek and O. Biba (eds.), *Brahms-Kongress Wien 1983* (Tutzing: Hans Schneider, 1988), 45–65

M. Hettling, *Politische Bürgerlichkeit. Der Bürger zwischen Individualität und Vergesellschaftung in Deutschland und in der Schweiz von 1860 bis 1918* (Göttingen: Vandenhoeck & Ruprecht, 1999)

---

[17] Programme booklet of tenth Berlin *Sinfonieabend*, 4 April 1912, [1].

P. Küsgens, *Horizonte nationaler Musik. Musiziergesellschaften in Süddeutschland und in der Deutschschweiz 1847–1891* (Frankfurt: Peter Lang, 2012)

L. Lütteken (ed.), *Zwischen Tempel und Verein. Musik und Bürgertum im 19. Jahrhundert* (Kassel: Bärenreiter, 2013)

W. Frisch and K. Karnes (eds.), *Brahms and His World*, 2nd edn (Princeton: Princeton University Press, 2009)

W. Sandberger and S. Weymar (eds.), *Johannes Brahms. Ikone der bürgerlichen Lebenswelt? Eine Ausstellung des Brahms-Instituts an der Musikhochschule Lübeck* (Lübeck: Brahms-Institut, 2008)

W. Weber, *Music and the Middle Class. The Social Structure of Concert Life in London, Paris, and Vienna between 1830 and 1848*, 2nd edn (Aldershot: Routledge, 2004)

CHAPTER 16

Genre

Matthew Gelbart

The two passages of music below might be taken, by a musician who had not yet encountered them, to come not only from the pen of very different composers but from very different eras. The first (Example 16.1) seems to be from the early to middle part of the nineteenth century. Its theme – songlike in form but clearly instrumental in tessitura and technique – unfolds exuberantly upward against a cloud of oscillating strings, a sensuous texture retained by at least some of the instruments almost continually until the theme lands on a cadence at bar 16. This opening seems inspired by Felix Mendelssohn's celebrated Octet Op. 20, whose beginning is remarkably similar, although Mendelssohn's theme is presented by violin rather than cello (Example 16.2). In both chamber pieces, too, the outer elements of the texture come to play off each other melodically as the theme unfurls. Meanwhile, Example 16.3 could come from a century earlier. Cast in a style common in Bach's strophic cantatas, it features a cantus firmus (here in the top voice) set against *Vorimitation* in diminution running through the other voices, and it adheres to a chord progression and voice leading that would not be adventurous for Bach. Indeed, in some ways it harkens back to Schein and Scheidt and even earlier music.

These two very different pieces are both examples by Brahms. The former is the beginning of his Second String Quintet Op. 111. The latter is the second stanza of his Motet Op. 74 no. 2 'O Heiland, reiss die Himmel auf'. Other composers have demonstrated a wide variety of styles in their writing, certainly; but during Brahms's lifetime, this level of stylistic tractability was controversial and still raises questions today. Most centrally: at a time when many critics and musicians were promoting a cult of personality around artist-creators whose styles were stamped with novelty and individuality, what would motivate Brahms to demonstrate such chameleon-like attributes? The answer to the question hinges on

149

Example 16.1. Brahms, Second String Quintet Op. 111, bars 1–19.

genre – or more specifically on Brahms's attitude toward the normative function of genres.

During the nineteenth century, the concept of genre came under unprecedented critical scrutiny. For centuries, genres had been seen as natural shaping phenomena. As long as the arts were primarily conceived

Example 16.1. (cont)

in mimetic terms, the imitation of nature had to be channelled through conventions, which were seen either as obeying natural laws in and of themselves or as the logical solutions to artistic material geared toward particular ends. 'Rules', related to genres, were seen generally not as shackles but as the very tools that enabled communication. As Alexander Pope put it: 'Learn hence for Ancient *Rules* a just Esteem; To copy *Nature* is to copy *Them*.'[1] *Styles* were therefore inherently and closely linked to generic norms, indeed more than they were linked to individuals. But as the early Romantics began to attack artistic rules as constrictive and to exalt artistic genius as the transcendence of such rules, the idea of genre itself came to be seen as limiting as well. It was not just that certain genres were becoming obsolete. (That had happened, if sometimes controversially,

---

[1] J. Butt (general ed.), *The Twickenham Edition of the Poems of Alexander Pope*, 6 vols. (London: Methuen, 1961), vol. 1, 255.

Example 16.2. Mendelssohn, Octet Op. 20, bars 1–25.

many times over the centuries, as new demands upon and functions for art dictated new rules and norms.) It was rather that the idea of genre itself was now becoming suspect. Recalling and intensifying earlier literary rhetoric – among the Schlegel brothers, then Victor Hugo and others – and applying

Example 16.2. (cont)

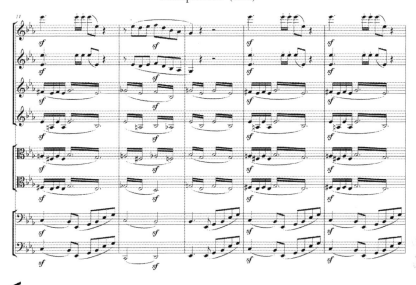

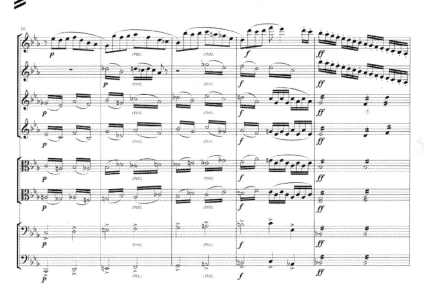

Example 16.2. (cont)

it to music, Wagner, for example, consistently attacked genre in these terms. In one of his baldest formulations, he suggested that the very act of naming a 'genre', even when codifying new, iconoclastic developments such as the 'music-drama', automatically pushed music toward a trite conformity, rendering what had been artistically great or extraordinary, 'ready for the common use of every fumbler'.[2]

It is worth pausing to consider the extent to which Brahms's aesthetic differences from the New Germans – his 'academic' and 'conservative' qualities – can be understood above all as a respect for genres and generic precedent. When Wagner invoked Beethoven and Bach as forebears, he framed their achievement (tied to their Germanness) as their folk-inspired Promethean creativity. To follow in their spiritual footsteps was intrinsically to seek the same wilful originality, and that meant moving *away* from their styles, and from the genres with which they became most closely associated. Conversely, Brahms's reverence for those same forebears began with their *techniques*. And those techniques were intimately related to genres.

[2] R. Wagner, 'Über die Benennung Musikdrama', *Richard Wagner Prose Works*, trans W. Ashton Ellis, 8 vols. (London: Routledge and Kegan Paul, 1896), vol. 5, 303.

Example 16.3. Brahms, Motet Op. 74 no. 2, 'O Heiland, reiss die Himmel auf', bars 18–36.

Thus, when Brahms, motivated by his own vein of nationalism, appealed to past composers as 'German' idols, the genres those musicians wrote in and perfected were as much (or more) a part of the cultural capital

Example 16.3. (cont)

that was to be mined as were their breaks from tradition [see Ch. 26 'Politics and Religion']. In this aesthetic outlook, genres from the past, themselves treasures of national heritage, reached out to current composers for further development. Brahms himself composed four symphonies, four concertos, overtures, a variety of works for different chamber combinations (cello sonatas, violin sonatas, clarinet sonatas, piano trios, piano quartets and a piano quintet, string quartets and quintets) and for solo piano (sonatas, but also variation sets and a variety of character pieces under different labels). His vocal output included over 200 solo lieder, duets and larger ensembles, numerous unaccompanied choral works, as well as choral-orchestral works and many folk-song arrangements. Aside from the evocative titles of his overtures ('Tragic' and 'Academic Festival'), he composed – unlike most of his contemporaries, including his mentor Schumann – no openly 'programmatic' works. And except for some choral-orchestral works discussed below, almost all the genres he worked in had long pedigrees in Germanic music history.

Even as he studied the works of his German forerunners, however, Brahms could not simply build on the techniques passed down to him in the same way that his eighteenth-century predecessors could. The discourse on originality that had murmured in Edward Young's writing, built to a din around the Jena Romantics and become a dogma for Wagner and his followers, meant that a composer could no longer engage with old genres unproblematically. If Haydn could write over a hundred symphonies precisely because he did not feel pressured to make each symphonic composition assure the genre's continued life – pressured to justify the very existence of a symphony or, for that matter, a mass or an opera – Brahms notoriously faced these very challenges. As Reinhold Brinkman, Margaret Notley and others have stressed in their work on Brahms, the composer lived in an era when central Europe was permeated by a sense of historical lateness: a hyper-awareness of the weight of centuries of cultural traditions and an angst about the apparent unravelling of those traditions in the face of industrialisation and decadence.[3] To advocate optimistically, or even ambivalently, on behalf of such traditions meant demonstrating to sceptics their relevance and to supporters their vitality. This is exactly the task that Brahms faced with the past genres he valued, and with their attendant styles.

The most well-worn example of Brahms's position was the burden he felt – growing especially after Schumann's 'New Paths' article of 1853 – from friends and critics who saw him as the saviour of the symphony [see Ch. 31 'Germany']. Schumann had written earlier: 'Just as Italy has its

---

[3] R. Brinkmann, *Late Idyll: The Second Symphony of Johannes Brahms*, trans. P. Palmer (Cambridge and London: Harvard University Press, 1995); M. Notley, *Lateness and Brahms: Music and Culture in the Twilight of Viennese Liberalism* (Oxford: Oxford University Press, 2007).

Naples, the Frenchman his revolution, the Englishman his seafaring, etc., so the German has his Beethoven symphonies.'[4] Those who held up the symphony as the greatest enduring achievement of German music, even of German culture, needed someone to write a symphony that would at once prove not only that the genre was not dead after Beethoven's Ninth, as Wagner loudly proclaimed, but in fact that it could serve as a symbol of German musical prowess even after 1850. Many other genres presented similar challenges on a smaller scale. Brahms's reverent engagement with beloved past genres was a lifelong source for him of both tension and (often consequent) inspiration.

For almost any pre-existing genre to which he was attracted, Brahms sought out 'classics': composers and pieces that set a standard and against which he would need to compete. He would meticulously consider how widely he wished to cast a net of precedent, and when he made deliberate allusions – whether melodic (the rarest type), formal or stylistic – to a model or group of models, he was inherently staking a claim about the genre in hand. In the case of his First Symphony Op. 68, as I have argued elsewhere, Brahms overcame the spectre of Beethoven as sole model by advancing the symphonic genre as a cultural agglomeration, a compendium of Germanness – where Beethoven himself could be viewed as working with models and materials from earlier and where a modern composer might thus create a new synthesis of those materials. In his First Symphony, Brahms thus invoked not only symphonists both before and after Beethoven (notably Mozart, Schubert and Schumann), but he interpreted Bach's techniques too as elements that, by virtue of their Germanness, could be mixed into a symphonic context. Nevertheless, Beethoven remained a sort of yardstick and gatekeeper in this genre. For this reason, although Brahms incorporated Bach's techniques into his symphonies much more extensively than any of his predecessors in the genre had done, he nevertheless justified this by invoking *Beethoven* and a Beethoven *symphony*: when Max Kalbeck balked at the idea that a Bachian passacaglia would 'fit' as the finale of Brahms's Fourth Symphony Op. 98, the composer defended the choice on the grounds that he was only extending what Beethoven had done in the bass-variation finale of the 'Eroica'.[5]

---

[4] See 'Neue Symphonieen für Orchester', *Neue Zeitschrift für Musik*, 11/1 (2 July 1839), 1.

[5] M. Gelbart, 'Nation, Folk, and Music History in the Finale of Brahms's First Symphony', *Nineteenth Century Studies* 23 (2009), 71–2; *Kalbeck III*, 454. On the finale of the Fourth Symphony and genre questions, see also R. Pascall, 'Genre and the Finale of Brahms's Fourth Symphony', *Music Analysis* 8/3 (October 1989), 233–45.

Genre

As the example above suggests, the attention Brahms devoted to the traditions of any genre he approached included engaging both with specific archetypal pieces and composers and with the general development, purposes and meanings of the genre. We can clearly see both types of engagement by looking at his concerto finales. Brahms modelled his First Piano Concerto Op. 15 finale on a carefully chosen precedent within the genre: Beethoven's Third Piano Concerto Op. 37.[6] But the influence of such precedents goes beyond the thematic and formal modelling of one movement on another. Rather, Brahms would telescope the material in the model into a whole idea of the genre, even as he added in the influence of other equally prudently chosen models.

For instance, one aspect that Brahms did *not* take over from Beethoven's concerto into his own concerto finale was the transformation after the cadenza of the simple metre into compound for a gigue-like coda marked 'Presto'. Yet despite having broken, by removing this metrical intensification, with the Beethoven model movement in the one piece he based most closely upon it, Brahms then used that exact device in all of his *later* concertos. In the Second Piano Concerto Op. 83 finale (bar 377) and in the Violin Concerto Op. 77 finale (bar 267) there are explicit 'Poco piu presto' gigue codas; in the Double Concerto Op. 102 finale, the shift is more fluid, Brahms adding running triplets at the end of the movement (from bar 327). The fact that this device was likely modelled for Beethoven himself by Mozart's own Piano Concerto K491, which has the same switch at the coda, is less important than the fact that, as Brahms clearly came to recognise, gigue-like finales and finale codas are common in Mozart and Beethoven concertos and create a field of precedents for Brahms within a genre-bounded canon. Furthermore, the gigue as conclusion is not limited to concertos but is itself a legacy of the Baroque dance suite, suggesting the modern concerto writ large as the culmination of centuries of instrumental tradition. Again, this attention to history set Brahms far from avant-gardists such as Liszt, who bent his concerto-writing toward his general preference for thematic integration and single-movement works. Liszt, while keeping the idea of frenetic, bravura finishes (of course!), was not one to consider details such as metrical traditions for finales.

Brahms's choice of models, and consequently of apposite style and character for a genre, was a function of several factors, from the venue and social setting in which it would be performed to the critical position of

---

[6] See C. Rosen, 'Influence: Plagiarism and Inspiration', *19th-Century Music* 4/2 (Autumn 1980), 87–100.

160   MATTHEW GELBART

the genre. The less a genre was dominated by an archetype critically
elevated as a nationalist symbol or a model for *Bildung*, the more Brahms
was free to mix his influences. Consider the differences between the
'serious' rigour expected of string-quartet writing (whose status was
boosted by Goethe, Haydn and Beethoven) and the slightly more loosely
patrolled set of chamber genres for strings or for piano and strings in
other combinations. The critical position of Haydn, Mozart and
Beethoven as string quartet writers meant that Brahms would need to
live up to those models perhaps partly by being careful to shun less
'wholesome' more recent models, such as the more amateur-oriented
quartets of George Onslow. In other chamber works, as Marie Sumner
Lott has recently argued, a composer such as Onslow might be a prime
forebear.[7] For the chamber works of Brahms's 'first maturity' – none of
them string quartets – Beethoven was not even a primary model.
As James Webster has shown, for those works the dominant precedent
was quite clearly Schubert.[8] Along similar lines, the more melodic and
'light' character of a string quintet (versus a quartet) also explains an
aspect of Example 16.1. Whereas in the opening of his First Quartet
Op. 51 no.1, Brahms breaks the textural tremolo bedding under the
opening theme after only six bars in order to involve all the players
contrapuntally, in the opening of the Second String Quintet Op. 111,
Brahms felt free to continue the 'sensual' patterning for much longer. In
other words, if the quartet was reserved as an austere and intellectual
genre, Brahms's other chamber pieces contain some of his most lyrical,
even carnal, writing in general.

It is helpful to conceive of a spectrum of genres available to Brahms.
At one end sat those most historically freighted, either because they seemed
archaic or because they needed to be proved the opposite despite the fact
that apparently culminating exemplars already existed. We have already
considered the two most classicised and policed of genres, the symphony
and the string quartet, both of which exerted a pressure that led Brahms to
destroy his early efforts and wait to publish until he was in his forties.
The concerto, though a large-scale and technically imposing composition,
remained just a few shades less daunting because it had not been critically

---

[7] M. Sumner Lott, 'Domesticity in Brahms's String Sextets, Opp. 18 and 36', in K. Hamilton and
N. Loges (eds.), *Brahms in the Home and the Concert Hall* (Cambridge: Cambridge University Press,
2014), 43–94. As Lott points out elsewhere, however, Onslow himself was careful to create a more
'serious' style in his quartets than in his quintets.

[8] J. Webster, 'Schubert's Sonata Form and Brahms's First Maturity', *19th-Century Music* 2/1
(July 1978), 18–35, and 3/1 (July 1979), 52–7.

Genre 161

propounded as the apex of a generic hierarchy, and because more than one composer might be argued to be the primary model, so that styles could be combined and experimentally extended at least a bit more freely. (Brahms, as we have seen, tackled the concerto relatively early, if no less reverently.) The piano sonata was dominated by Beethoven again, but allowed various other models.[9] Lieder, meanwhile, seemed to be springing to new life in the nineteenth century but after mid-century were bound to be compared with those of Schubert and Schumann. Character pieces of different types each presented their own histories, or lack thereof (and his piano music of the 1850s allowed Brahms to experiment with a multitude of influences from Schumann to Chopin and even Liszt). All the way at the other end of the spectrum from the symphony and quartet, novel genres could spring forth, topical responses to modernity – blissfully unencumbered but, for that very reason, potentially suspect. For a composer such as Brahms, giving a work a title that suggested blazing a new generic path would require clear efforts to relate the work to *other* (more established) genres that were rife for combination or adjustment into something new.

In fact, the composer's biography in the years following his first encounter with the Schumanns can be read as a series of psychologically predictable, often strategic, decisions about engaging with the generic spectrum posited above. After 'New Paths', there was the famous retreat to counterpoint exercises with Joachim and to composition in small, often truly archaic genres, ones that Brahms knew would be taken, even by his champions, primarily as experiments while he bided his time before fully announcing himself to the world. In different ways, the music for women's voices and the serenades worked this way. Then came the 'first maturity' in which he could revel in Schubert and – remaining a stylistic chameleon – in a variety of genres and predecessors together, but still not through works that would make or break him. Finally, (putting aside the trauma of the First Piano Concerto premiere), the 'major' work he finally used to declare himself on the broadest stage, *A German Requiem* Op. 45, created a 'new' genre – but one in which he could show the fruits of his study of the past.

Brahms's supporters were able to find in his *Requiem* not only originality and freedom (in the face of his 'New German' detractors) but also a rich vein of technique from past masters in order to show what made him different from those New Germans. In earlier works, Brahms had dabbled in directly mixing the ancient and modern. (This combination could be

---

[9] See for example W. Frisch, 'Brahms: From Classical to Modern', in R. L. Todd (ed.), *Nineteenth-Century Piano Music*, 2nd edn (New York: Routledge, 2004), 356–94.

162 MATTHEW GELBART

accomplished through juxtaposing styles, as in the *Variations and Fugue on a Theme of Handel* Op. 24. Or it could involve juxtaposing media, as in his earlier *Vier Gesänge* Op. 17, where the clearly Romantic sonorities of the horn and harp highlight the potential of a women's chorus to sound either archaic or lushly Romantic.) Now, in a free generic domain under a title that both invoked a Protestant musical past stretching from Schütz to Bach and promised a large-scale modern orchestral work (indeed one that would resonate with nineteenth-century patriotic oratorios),[10] that juxtaposition could become a fully hybrid style. That the *Requiem* in fact begins with the instruments working in a modern idiom followed by the entry of the chorus in an archaised idiom, but quickly starts to blur this distinction, is partly a clever response to the text, as Daniel Beller-McKenna has argued.[11] But it is also accomplishing and proclaiming in real time – within the first minutes of a long piece – something that was part of that piece's very purpose in Brahms's oeuvre: the forging from old and new of a combined, personal style. It was through such carefully chosen 'new' genres, including the other choral-orchestral works that came on the heels of the *Requiem*, that Brahms was increasingly able to create a style that 'sounded like Brahms' [see Ch. 38 'Inspiration'].

Nevertheless, as the many examples above show (including the opening examples, which are middle and late works), well after the *Requiem*, Brahms would continue to write passages, even whole smaller works, that plunged fully into styles associated with specific older genres in which he was working. To the end of his life, he continued to study Schütz, Buxtehude, Bach, Beethoven and Schubert, and he retained his chameleon skills, though he often shifted colours more quickly, as in 'O Heiland, reiss', or left more of his personal markings showing through the archaisms. He never lost his veneration for past generic traditions nor ceased to uphold them as cultural capital.

In short, generic considerations influence almost every aspect of Brahms's compositional choices, even down to which works he chose to withhold opus numbers from. As scholars have noted, using various examples, the very act of writing in certain genres was often for Brahms an artistic credo and, by extension, a socio-political statement.[12] That fact

---

[10] See J. Heidrich, 'Zwischen religiösem Bekenntnis und nationaler Emphase: "Ein Deutsches Requiem (Op. 45)" von Johannes Brahms und sein Gattungskontext', *Neues Musikwissenschaftliches Jahrbuch* 8 (1999), 137–57.

[11] D. Beller-McKenna, *Brahms and the German Spirit* (Cambridge, MA: Harvard University Press, 2004), 69.

[12] See for example Notley, *Lateness and Brahms*; M. Vaillancourt, 'Brahms's 'Sinfonie-Serenade' and the Politics of Genre', *Journal of Musicology* 26/3 (Summer 2009), 379–403; and D. Beller-McKenna, 'Brahms's Motet "Es ist das Heil uns kommen her" and the "Innermost Essence of Music"', in D. Brodbeck (ed.) *Brahms Studies 2* (Lincoln and London: University of Nebraska Press, 1998), 31–62.

Genre

should be an invitation to critics as well: we can find 'meanings' in Brahms's music not only through interpersonal and literary references but just as much (often more) by interpreting his works, whether vocal or 'absolute', as 'stories' about the history of music and the charged nature of traditions.

Further Reading

C. Dahlhaus, 'Zur Problematik der musikalischen Gattungen im 19. Jahrhundert', in W. Arlt et al. (eds.), *Gattungen der Musik in Einzeldarstellungen: Gedenkschrift Leo Schrade*, (Bern: Francke, 1973), 840–95

M. Gelbart, 'Layers of Representation in Nineteenth-Century Genres: The Case of One Brahms *Ballade*', in J. Walden (ed.), *Representation in Western Music* (Cambridge: Cambridge University Press, 2013), 13–32

M. Gelbart, 'Nation, Folk, and Music History in the Finale of Brahms's First Symphony', *Nineteenth Century Studies* 23 (2009), 57–85

F. Krummacher, 'Reception and Analysis: On the Brahms Quartets, Op. 51, Nos. 1 and 2', *19th-Century Music* 18/1 (Summer 1994), 24–45

M. Musgrave, *Brahms: A German Requiem* (Cambridge and New York: Cambridge University Press, 1996).

M. Notley, 'The Chamber Music of Brahms', in S. Hefling (ed.), *Nineteenth-Century Chamber Music* (New York and London: Routledge, 2004), 242–86

M. Sumner Lott, *The Social Worlds of Nineteenth-Century Chamber Music* (Urbana, Chicago and Springfield: University of Illinois Press, 2015), 195–202

CHAPTER 17

Folk Music

George S. Bozarth

The dedication of late eighteenth- and early nineteenth-century German intelligentsia to collecting and consuming folk music was fostered by a belief that a repository of wisdom lay with the common people and that, by drawing together the peasant songs of various regions where German was spoken, one could grasp a German national identity [see Ch. 26 'Politics and Religion'] where, politically, none existed. As Philip V. Bohlman writes,

> German folk song became a visible player in the struggle to construct German nationalism. 'Germanness' accrued to folk song as it accompanied the spread of the *Aufklärung*'s constituent parts: *Bildung* (the heightened belief in the achievements possible through education and culture), modernity, and nationalism. German folk songs ... [do] not simply represent German national identity, they were active agents participating in its formation and implementation.[1]

Johann Gottfried Herder's collections of European folk poetry, *Stimmen der Völker in Liedern* and *Volkslieder* (1778 and 1779), inspired not only future collectors but also the writing of folk-inspired poems (*volkstümliche Gedichte*), perfected by Johann Wolfgang von Goethe, who had met Herder in Strasbourg in the early 1770s. Ludwig Achim von Arnim and Clemens Brentano's *Des Knaben Wunderhorn* (1805, 1808) and Andreas Kretzschmer and Anton Wilhelm von Zuccalmaglio's *Deutsche Volkslieder* (1838, 1840, with melodies) followed, as did the *volkstümliche Gedichte* of the Romantic poets Eduard Mörike, Ludwig Uhland, Joseph Freiherr von Eichendorff and Heinrich Heine. Folk-songs with piano accompaniment entered the musical parlours of the German middle class, as well as the pages of music periodicals, by means of collections by such arrangers as

---

[1] P. Bohlman, 'Landscape – Region – Nation – Reich: German Folk Song in the Nexus of National Identity', in C. Applegate and P. Potter (eds.), *Music and German National Identity* (Chicago: University of Chicago Press, 2002), 108 and 110.

164

Folk Music 165

O. L. B. Wolff (*Braga*, 1835) and the prolific Friedrich Silcher, as well as in the masterful arrangements by Brahms.

Actual German folk-songs also inspired composers, both major and minor, from the mid-eighteenth-century onwards, to fashion their own melodies with accompaniments in imitation of this genre (*volkstümliche Lieder*). Haydn (*Lieder für das Clavier*), Mozart (Papageno's songs), Schubert ('Heidenröslein' D257 and many of the songs from *Die schöne Müllerin* D795), Mendelssohn, Schumann, Brahms (the famous 'Wiegenlied' Op. 49 no. 4, among others), and even Beethoven (independent songs and the continuous song cycle *An die ferne Geliebte* Op. 98) all tried their hands at the latter. But of these master composers, only Brahms (to my knowledge) set about collecting folk-songs, German and otherwise, to study their very nature in order to ground and expand his compositional language. His manuscript collections are listed in Table 17.1.

The youthful Brahms knew the publications of the Romantic folk-song collectors, as his pan-European compendium of at least thirty-one folk-songs and dances, written in his youthful hand, attests. Only songs 18–31 are preserved at the Library of Congress (ML30.8b.B7 CASE).[2] The location of the rest of the manuscript, if it survives, is unknown. The fragment begins with two accompanied melodies from Silcher's widely popular *Ausländische Nationalmelodien* (in four volumes, here vol. 1, c. 1840) – one Scottish ('Stumm schläft der Sänger'), the other from Savoy ('Oft wenn verbleicht der Sterne Pracht'), both translations of poems by Thomas Moore. Four Lapland dances and two songs – settings of 'Spring nie snälla reen' in triple and duple metre – then follow, all copied from the *Beilage: Melodien aus Lappland* published in the 25 June 1850 issue of the *Neue Zeitschrift für Musik*. Next comes the well-known Danish royal song 'König Christian stand am Höhe' with accompaniment. Brahms then returned to Silcher's *Ausländische Nationalmelodien* (vol. 4, 1841), to copy the Irish song 'Dem Rothen Röslein gleicht mein Lieb' ('O my Luve's like a red, red rose' by Robert Burns) – set to the flowing tune that Thomas Moore used for 'Believe me, if all those endearing young Charms' – and Silcher's harmonisation of the old French song 'Wild tobt der Sturm'. Brahms found the remaining four accompanied melodies – two Swiss songs, a Finnish Rune and a Spanish love lament – in O. L. B. Wolff's *Braga*. The pattern set here – to find folk material in publications rather

---

[2] For detailed descriptions of Brahms's folksong sources, see *Werkverzeichnis*.

Table 17.1. *Brahms's manuscript collections of folk music*

Date	Current Location	Description	Scribe	Brahms Sources	Notes
Sometime after 1840/41, others after June 1850	US-Wc, ML30.8b.B7 CASE	At least 31 Finnish, French German, Irish, Lapplandish, Savoyard and Scottish folk songs and dances at least (19 folk songs missing)	Brahms, youthful hand	Friedrich Silcher, *Ausländische Nationalmelodien*; *Neue Zeitschrift für Musik*; O. L. B. Wolff, *Braga*	
17 January 1853	A-Wgm, A 130, fol. 28ʳ	2 Hungarian melodies	Brahms, youthful hand	Eduard Reményi?	Cf. *Variations on a Hungarian Song* Op. 21 no. 2 (1856)
April 1853	D-Hs, BRA: Aa8	3 Hungarian melodies (*Magyar dalok*)	Brahms, youthful hand, annotated by Eduard Reményi	Eduard Reményi?	*Hannover*; gift to Joseph Joachim in April 1853; cf. *Variations on a Hungarian Song* Op. 21 no. 2 (1856)
April/May 1854	A-Wgm, A128, ff. 1ʳ–4ᵛ	At least 82 French, German, Bohemian and Swedish folk songs with text incipits	Brahms, youthful hand	Nos. 31–34, 74–76: Andreas Kretzschmer and Anton Wilhelm von Zuccalmaglio, *Deutsche Volkslieder* (1838, 1840); No. 77: Georg Forster (1549); No. 78: Hans Leo Hassler (1601)	*Düsseldorf*; fragment, only Nos. 31–34 and 74–82 extant
April/May 1854	A-Wgm, A128, f. 4ᵛ	15 Hungarian melodies	Brahms, youthful hand	Eduard Reményi?	Cf. *Variations on a Hungarian Song* Op. 21 no. 2 (1856); 'Magyarisch' Op. 46 no. 2; A major and F major *Hungarian Dances* (1869)

June 1854	D-Zsch	34 Danish, German, Hungarian, Swedish folk melodies and 3 Minnelieder	Brahms, youthful hand	Selected by Brahms from melodies he already knew	Gift to Clara Schumann on Robert Schumann's birthday, 8 June 1854; cf. C major Piano Sonata, Op. 1 (1852–3); *Variations on a Hungarian Song* Op. 21 no. 2 (1856); solo and choral arrangements; Chorale Prelude for Organ Op. 122 no. 8 (1896)
Mid-1850s	A-Wgm, A128, ff. 5^r–8^v	28 German melodies and texts	Brahms	Friedrich Wilhelm Arnold	Cf. 'Soll sich der Mond' Op. 14 no. 1; solo and choral arrangements
By 1862	US-private collection	Sketches of two German folk-songs	Brahms	Friedrich Wilhelm Arnold	Brahms's bass line for Friedrich Wilhelm Arnold's harmonisation of 'In stiller Nacht' and a new accompaniment for 'Es war ein Markgraf über'm Rhein'
1864	A-Wgm, A128, f. 9^r–10^v	16 German folk-songs	Brahms	Friedrich Wilhelm Arnold	
Perhaps 1864	A-Wgm, A128, ff. 11^r–12^v	11 early German songs	Brahms	Friedrich Wilhelm Arnold?	Compared by Brahms to various Renaissance and nineteenth-century compendia
After 1877	A-Wgm, A129	*Volkslieder aus dem Siebengebirge gesammelt von Prof. Grimm u. Dr. Arnold*	Franz Hlaváček	Friedrich Wilhelm Arnold and Jacob Grimm	Hlaváček was Brahms's regular Viennese copyist

seeking it directly from the people, as Bartók did – continues throughout the rest of Brahms's manuscripts of folk music.

From these publications, Brahms grasped the styles employed by his predecessors to accompany folk-song, from the simple 'antique' *cantional* style of 'Wild tobt der Sturm' to the responsive setting of the Spanish lament for two sopranos and a cappella SATB choir – a style to which he turned in the final volume of his *Deutsche Volkslieder* (1894). Most of the other settings duplicate the folk melody in the right hand of the piano, but each shows the changing internal textures and interesting bass lines that became hallmarks of Brahms's own arrangements. Some have structures that depart from the standard four-bar phrases of the traditional *Volksliedstrophe*, for example, 'Wild tobt der Sturm' with its phrases of 4 + 5 + 4 + 2 + 2 + 5 bars. The Finnish Rune is in 5/4 metre. When harmonised, the song and dance melodies abound in the parallel thirds and sixths that make Brahms's own compositions so lush.

The definition of *Volkslied* at the time encompassed recently harvested songs of the people and those surviving since the Middle Ages, lowbrow country lyrics and songs expressing the refined sentiments of medieval aristocrats, silly and serious children's ditties, songs of unrequited love by adolescent lads and lasses, and mature reflections on life's odd ways. Sacred as well as secular tunes were included. In his *14 Deutsche Volkslieder* WoO 34 of 1864, Brahms gathered together his four-part harmonisations of eight secular songs, four sacred songs and two folkish *Marienlieder*. And he was not bothered if the melodies had been reworked to make them flow better, as Kretzschmer and Zuccalmaglio had done to some of their folk-songs. Indeed, this was the style of presentation he preferred.

Next come three manuscripts of Hungarian folk music. Brahms's lifelong fascination with the irregular rhythms, triplet figures and use of *rubato* of the *style hongrois* can be traced to the time when, in the wake of the

Figure 17.1. Brahms, 'Ade mein Schatz, ich muß nun fort', German folk-song copied by Brahms into his handwritten collection of folk-songs from different countries, c. 1850.

Example 17.1. Transcription of melody handwritten by Brahms and annotated by Reményi.

Akkor csinos a bakkancsos,
ha gatyája végig rongyos,
tergye kilóg a gatyabol,
mint a rozsa bimbójatol.

Then the man who wears soldier's boots is pretty
if his breeches are torn down,
his knees sticking out of his pants
as the rose from its bud.[4]

suppression of the revolutions of 1848, Hungarian political refugees poured through Hamburg on their way to the USA. Among the expatriates was the violinist Eduard Reményi, who typically closed his concerts with popular Hungarian songs and dances. Brahms met Reményi by early 1853. An autograph manuscript in his estate dated 17 January of that year records two Hungarian tunes, the second being the noble, mixed-metre melody on which he based his set of thirteen *Variations on a Hungarian Song* Op. 21 no. 2 (1856) (A-Wgm, A130, fol. 28[r]).[3] An incipit of the theme also appears as No. 12 in the little catalogue of fifteen Hungarian tunes (two full melodies, eleven incipits) that Brahms copied at the time (A-Wgm, A128, f. 4[v]). Brahms arranged two of these melodies as his A major and F major *Hungarian Dances* (1869); another provided the starting point for the song 'Magyarisch' Op. 46 no. 2. Three of the melodies appear in full on another sheet, written in Brahms's hand and annotated by Reményi (D-Hs, BRA: Aa8, see Example 17.1). The musicians gave this manuscript to Joseph Joachim while

---

[3] See K. Stephenson, 'Der junge Brahms und Reményis "Ungarische Lieder"', *Studien zu Musikwissenschaft* 25 (1962), 523–31, with a facsimile of this sheet facing 529, and W. Horne, 'Brahms's *Variations on a Hungarian Song, op. 21, no. 2*'.
[4] I wish to thank Helen Szablya and Sandra Layman for helping me with this translation.

Example 17.2. Brahms, *Variations on a Hungarian Song* Op. 21 no. 2, bars 1–8.

visiting him at the Hanoverian court in April 1853. One of the melodies is again the theme of Op. 21 no. 2 (Example 17.2), here designated *Glorioso* and supplied with its not-so-lofty Hungarian text.

William Horne has suggested that 'the bold, almost bombastic character of [Brahms's] presentation of the theme' was inspired by 'Reményi's ardent Hungarian nationalism'.[5] However, the mood is already present in the folk-song and reflects the arrogance of its haughty yet shabby protagonist. All three Hungarian melodies in this manuscript made their way, along with seven others, into a manuscript Brahms gave to Clara Schumann on her stricken husband's forty-fourth birthday, 8 June 1854. Brahms provided each melody with a bass line, and some have figures indicating harmonies. Only the melody used in the *Variations* Op. 21 no. 2 was left for unaccompanied violin, with double stopping and string articulation – as Brahms would have heard Reményi play it.

In Clara's manuscript, one also finds the *Minnelied* 'Verstohlen geht der Mond auf', on which Brahms had already composed a set of variations as the slow movement of his Piano Sonata Op. 1 (1852–3). Forty years later he closed his *49 Deutsche Volkslieder* WoO 33, with a setting of this melody with piano – 'thus the snake bites its tail', he wrote to his publisher Fritz Simrock on 17 September 1894.[6] The other two *Minnelieder* in her collection – the lovely 'Ich fahr dahin' from the *Lochheimer Liederbuch*, and 'Mein Herzlein tut mir gar so weh!' – would receive solo song and choral

---

[5] W. Horne, 'Brahms's *Variations on a Hungarian Song*, op. 21, no. 2', 57.   [6] Avins, 722.

Folk Music

settings.[7] Four of the remaining melodies were soon harmonised for the Hamburg Ladies' Choir (1859–62); six would be graced with original piano accompaniments (1858 and 1894) [see Ch. 10 'As Conductor']. Brahms would return decades later to Michael Praetorius's setting of 'Es ist ein Ros' entsprungen', which has pride of place at the beginning of the collection for Frau Schumann, to fashion it into a touching chorale prelude for organ, Op. 122 no. 8, composed shortly after his dear friend's death in May 1896.

Just prior to preparing the manuscript for Clara Schumann, Brahms made a collection of up to eighty-two German folk-songs with text incipits (A-Wgm, A128, f. 1^r–4^v). All that survive are the melodies Brahms numbered 31–4 and 74–82. The first series is from Kretzschmer and Zuccalmaglio's collection; two are sixteenth-century songs (31, 32). Next come fifteen Hungarian tunes, without texts, three of which appear on the *Magyar dalok* sheet (April 1853) and several of which Brahms included in Clara's manuscript. The location of the folk-songs 1–30 and 35–73 is unknown.

The second series begins on a bifolium Brahms inscribed 'Ddf. April 54' (Düsseldorf April 1854) and ends on a single leaf inscribed a month later. Three songs from Kretzschmer and Zuccalmaglio (74–76) – the ceremonial *Landesvater* and two sixteenth-century songs – are followed by two ancient songs (77, 78) from Georg Forster (1549) and Hans Leo Hassler (1601). The sheet closes with the song 'Ich sass auf einem Hüegeli' (79), a craftsman's song or *Handwerksburschen Lied* ('Heut noch sind wir hier zu Haus', 80), two old Bohemian dances (*Alte böhmische Nationaltänze*)[8] and eight Swedish folk tunes (*Schwedische Volksweisen*), which continue onto the single leaf, where one finds two more German folk-songs. The mixture of old and recent, dances and songs, German, Bohemian and Swedish is typical of Brahms's broad and eclectic interests in traditional music.

By February 1855 Brahms had come to know fellow folk-song collector Friedrich Wilhelm Arnold, who lived in Elberfeld, near Düsseldorf and was one of Schumann's publishers. In 'Aus der Sammlung des Hrn. Arnold', as

---

[7] WoO posth. 32, no. 17 (voice and piano; 1858) and 34, no. 9 (SATB; 1865); WoO posth. 36 no. 5 (SSAA; 1859–62) and 38 no. 14 (SSA; 1859–62), respectively.

[8] Although Brahms wrote in this manuscript that these dances came from Friedrich Dionys Weber's *Allgemeine theoretisch-praktische Vorschule der Musik* (Prague, 1828), they do not appear in that publication.

172   GEORGE S. BOZARTH

Brahms labelled his manuscript, he copied twenty-eight melodies and texts
(A-Wgm, A128, unnumbered), supplying four with piano accompaniments –
'Erlaube mir, feins' Mädchen', 'Es sass ein schneeweiss' Vögelein', 'In stiller
Nacht' and 'Soll sich der Mond'. Three of these songs he arranged for solo
voice and piano, and for four-part choir;[9] one was set for accompanied solo
voice.[10] The poem of 'Soll sich der Mond' inspired an original folk-like song,
'Vor dem Fenster' Op. 14 no. 1.

Beginning in 1862 Arnold issued a series of ten volumes of German
folk-songs with piano accompaniments of his own. Prior to publication
he submitted some of his settings to Brahms. In an autograph manuscript now in a private American collection, Brahms suggested
a different bass line for Arnold's harmonisation of 'In stiller Nacht'
and a new accompaniment for 'Es war ein Markgraf über'm Rhein' that
Arnold adopted in its entirety. The first six bars of the song 'Es warb ein
schöner Jüngling' that Brahms wrote out match the reading Arnold
published. In 1864 Brahms once again had access to Arnold's collection
and copied out a number of folk-songs (A-Wgm, A128, f. 9^r–10^v).
Brahms had his regular Viennese copyist, Franz Hlaváček, prepare
a volume for him of 'Volkslieder aus dem Siebengebirge gesammelt
von Prof. [Jacob] Grimm u. Dr. Arnold' (A-Wgm, A129) sometime
after 1877, the earliest year that Hlaváček's address appears in Brahms's
pocket calendar book (A-Wst, Ia 79559).

Another manuscript, perhaps copied from Arnold's collection, reveals
Brahms comparing his new finds to published and original sources
(A-Wgm, A128, ff. 11^r–12^v). On the second leaf of the manuscript,
Brahms studied three settings of 'Ich stund an einem Morgen', by
Ludwig Senfl (c. 1490–1543), Heinrich Finck (1444/45–1527) and from
the *121 New Songs Set by the Famed Ones in this Art* (*Hundert und
ainundzweintzig newe Lieder von berümbtenn dieser Kunst gesetzt*,
Nurenberg, 1534). The latter he cross-referenced to C. F. Becker's *Songs
and Tunes from Past Centuries* (*Lieder und Weisen vergangener Jahrhunderte*,
Leipzig, 1853) and Wilhelm Tappert's arrangement with piano accompaniment in his *Deutsche Lieder aus dem 15. 16. und 17. Jahrhundert* (Berlin,
c. 1870). On the final page of the manuscript, Brahms entered Paul
Hofhaimer's songs 'Nach Willen dein' (1539) and 'Es steht ein Lind in
jenen Thal' from the *68 Lieder* (Nürnburg, c. 1550).

---

[9] 'Soll sich der Mond' as WoO 33 no. 35 and WoO 38 no. 19; 'In stiller Nacht' as WoO 33 no. 42, WoO
34 no. 8 and WoO 36 no. 1; and 'Erlaube mir, feins' Mädchen' as WoO 33 no. 2, WoO 35 no. 3 and
WoO 38 no. 4.
[10] 'Es sass ein schneeweiss' Vögelein' as WoO 33 no. 45.

Folk Music

The heritage of European folk-song and dance that Brahms discovered as a young man took root as deeply in his soul as the compositional lessons he learned from his predecessors in art music. Among Brahms's 197 published songs, Virginia Hancock has identified twenty 'folklike' songs and thirty 'hybrid' folk/art songs.[11] In some songs, such as 'Magyarisch' Op. 46 no. 2 and 'Sonntag' Op. 47 no. 3, the folk melody with which the setting opens is wedded seamlessly to the original material that forms its completion. Little does one realise that in the 'Wiegenlied' Op. 49 no. 4, which still lulls children to sleep, the voice's melody is actually a descant over an Austrian waltz song that the vivacious Viennese Bertha Porubsky had sung to Brahms in the late 1850s and which now came back to her in the piano's right hand as a very private dedication upon the birth of her child.

Brahms's instrumental music often took flight from folk inspirations as well. All the elements of the *style hongrois* enliven the finales of the First Piano Quartet Op. 25, written for Brahms's premiere season as a pianist and composer in the capital of the Austro-Hungarian Empire, as well as the Violin Concerto Op. 77, dedicated to the great Hungarian-Jewish violinist Joseph Joachim. The peasant *doina* of the Clarinet Quintet Op. 115, represents the pinnacle of Brahms's melancholic style, the devastatingly beautiful song of a soul trying to ease itself.

The crowning glory of Brahms's involvement with the study and arrangement of vocal folk idioms was the seven-volume set of *49 Deutsche Volkslieder* WoO 33, which he published as a corrective to the inartistic collection *Treasury of German Songs* (*Deutsches Liederhort*, 1893–4) systematically organised by the folk-tune preservationists Ludwig Erk and Franz Magnus Böhme. Brahms's collection presents his multifaceted solutions to the nineteenth-century agenda of uniting folk simplicity with urban amateur music-making.

Further Reading

J. Bellman, *The Style Hongrois in the Music of Western Europe* (Boston: Northeastern University Press, 1993)

G. Bozarth, 'Johannes Brahms und die Liedersammlungen von David Gregor Corner, Karl Severin Meister und Friedrich Wilhelm Arnold', *Die Musikforschung* 36 (1983), 179–99

---

[11] V. Hancock, 'Volkslied/Kunstlied', in R. Hallmark (ed.), *German Lieder in the Nineteenth Century* (New York: Schirmer Books, 1996), 123–32.

174 GEORGE S. BOZARTH

G. Bozarth, 'Johannes Brahms und die geistliches Lieder von D. G. Corners *Gross-Catolisch Gesangbuch* (1631)', in S. Antonicek and O. Biba (eds.), *Brahms-Kongress Wien 1983* (Tutzing: Hans Schneider, 1988), 67–80

G. Bozarth, 'The Origin of Brahms's *In stiller Nacht'*, *Notes* 53/2 (December 1996), 363–80.

M. Gelbart, *The Invention of 'Folk Music' and 'Art Music': Emerging Categories from Ossian to Wagner* (Cambridge: Cambridge University Press, 2011)

V. Hancock, 'Volkslied/Kunstlied', in R. Hallmark (ed.), *German Lied in the Nineteenth Century* (New York: Routledge, 2010), 119–52

K. Stephenson, 'Der junge Brahms und Reményis "Ungarische Lieder"', *Studien zur Musikwissenschaft* 25, Festschrift für Erich Schenk (1962), 520–31.

CHAPTER 18

Early Music

Virginia Hancock

To define what Brahms thought of as 'early music' is not difficult. It was essentially the same view as that of his musical contemporaries, particularly those in the German-speaking world. For them, it ended with the works of Johann Sebastian Bach and Georg Friedrich Händel (since they thought of him as German); it began roughly in the era that we think of as the mid-Renaissance, in particular with composers who were important contributors to the development of church music. For Catholics, interest centred on the works of Palestrina and his contemporaries, extending to seventeenth-century composers in the religious tradition. For Lutherans, the history that began with Martin Luther and culminated in the works of Bach was a principal thread that included composers such as Heinrich Isaac, Ludwig Senfl, Johannes Eccard, Michael Praetorius and Heinrich Schütz.

Brahms's interests are reflected in both his personal library, which is preserved in the archive of the Gesellschaft der Musikfreunde in Vienna (A-Wgm), and in the works he chose to perform.[1] The published early music in his library is primarily editions that were widely available, and the identifiable sources of his manuscript copies (*Abschriften*) are mostly similar publications.[2] Except for common sacred Latin texts, nearly all the vocal music is in German, the only language with which he was comfortable. In particular, he showed early and sustained interest in the history of the Lutheran chorale. To give two examples: the one fragment of Gregorian chant among the *Abschriften* is the first verse of the hymn 'Veni creator spiritus', which appears on a single sheet along with two versions of Luther's related melody, 'Komm, Gott, Schöpfer, heiliger Geist'.

---

[1] See O. Biba, 'New Light on the Brahms *Nachlass*', in M. Musgrave (ed.), *Brahms 2: Biographical, Documentary and Analytical Studies* (Cambridge: Cambridge University Press, 1987), 39–47.

[2] The types of sources from which he made *Abschriften* are described in V. Hancock, 'Sources of Brahms's Manuscript Copies of Early Music in the Archiv of the Gesellschaft der Musikfreunde in Wien', *Fontes Artis Musicae* 24/3 (July-September 1977), 113–21.

175

Heinrich Isaac's secular lied 'Innsbruck' appears repeatedly, first in connection with its sacred version, 'O Welt, ich muss dich lassen', but later in its own right as a work he performed with several of his choral groups. (His lifelong fascination with folk music, particularly German folk music, is, of course, closely related [see Ch. 17 'Folk Music'].

There are, however, ways in which Brahms's involvement with early music is unusual among his contemporaries. To begin with, he developed a collector's instinct early, rummaging in the Hamburg second-hand bookshops for items of musical interest; a copy of a treatise on figured bass bears his signature and the date, 1848. His earliest surviving *Abschriften* of early sacred music are short pieces by Francesco Durante, Antonio Lotti, Giuseppe Corsi and Palestrina, all taken without attribution from an anthology entitled *Musica Sacra* published by the firm of Schlesinger in Berlin in 1852. (This is one of several collections with that title that appeared in mid-century.) Brahms copied them before 17 January 1853, when he dated a pair of Hungarian melodies (one is the theme he used for the *Variations on a Hungarian Song* Op. 21 no. 2); he added these on empty staves at the bottom of the bifolio that contains three of the sacred pieces. Thus, while some writers have suggested that Robert Schumann first inspired his interest in early music, these copies pre-date their meeting.

However, the Schumanns did certainly help cultivate his knowledge of the music of the past. During 1854 to 1858 in particular, Brahms spent a large amount of time in their library, both in Düsseldorf during Robert's illness and in Berlin after Clara moved there. He copied several extended works to add to his own collection of *Abschriften*, most notably the entirety of Palestrina's *Missa Papae Marcelli*, which he signed and dated June 1856, just prior to Schumann's death in late July. (This and some other works have no identifiable published sources; it is likely that they circulated in manuscript copies.) Other large works he copied in this period include eight- and ten-voice settings of the Crucifixus by Lotti (these dated May 1858) and a 'Salve Regina' by Giovanni Rovetta, which he found in a supplement to an 1813 issue of the *Allgemeine musikalische Zeitung*. Along with manuscript copies, his collection of printed music was growing: Clara Schumann gave him the first volume of the Bach collected edition for Christmas in 1855, and he appeared in the list of subscribers for the first time in 1856.

During this time, possibly because he found them in Schumann's library or the library of his Hamburg friend Theodor Avé-Lallemant, Brahms became acquainted with two sources that helped form the foundation of his knowledge of German music before the time of Bach. These were the

Early Music 177

monumental publications of Carl von Winterfeld – the three volumes of *Der evangelische Kirchengesang* (1843–7), one focus of which was the music of Eccard, and the earlier *Johannes Gabrieli and his Era* (*Johannes Gabrieli und sein Zeitalter*, 1834), in which the music of Schütz was first brought to the attention of the German musical world. Brahms's copies from *Der evangelische Kirchengesang* begin as early as 1854; they include Isaac's 'Innsbruck, ich muss dich lassen' and Hans Leo Hassler's 'Mein G'müth ist mir verwirret' (the original version of the Passion Chorale), both of which demonstrate his longstanding interest in the history of the Lutheran chorale and appear in choral programmes he conducted in Hamburg and Vienna.[3] On the same sheet as the Hassler he copied two versions of its tune (with the sacred text 'Herzlich thut mich verlangen') to illustrate different editorial approaches to notation of its rhythm; his printed volumes also contain many instances of his own rebarring to correspond with text declamation.[4] They show Brahms's awareness of various kinds of rhythmic complexities, such as hemiola, cross-rhythms and obscuring of bar lines, that appear in many of his own compositions. They also demonstrate his interest in aspects of the editorial process and, in general, his unusually academic attitude toward his early-music endeavours.

The musical examples for Winterfeld's *Johannes Gabrieli und sein Zeitalter* are in the third volume; from it, Brahms copied six-, eight- and twelve-voice pieces by Palestrina and Giovanni Gabrieli, reducing them to short score, perhaps to save on expensive paper as well as to facilitate study. In 1858, Avé-Lallemant gave him his own copy of Winterfeld, which he returned to repeatedly, particularly as it contributed to his strong interest in the music of Schütz. Another important gift from Avé-Lallemant was Karl Severin Meister's *The German Catholic Church Song in Its Melodies* (*Das katholische deutsche Kirchenlied in seinen Singweisen*, 1862), in which Brahms made many notes, including marking the locations of Meister's sources in places that he might be able to visit.

The Schumanns and Avé-Lallemant were only among the first of many of Brahms's friends and acquaintances who contributed books, *Abschriften* or advice to his study of early music. In 1855 and 1856 his independent work on canons, along with the study of counterpoint he undertook with Joseph Joachim (who was a less dedicated participant), resulted in some of his

---

[3] For a list of performances of early vocal music that Brahms conducted, see Hancock, *Brahms's Choral Compositions and His Library of Early Music* (Ann Arbor, MI: UMI Research Press, 1983), Appendix I.

[4] See a variety of examples in Hancock, *Brahms's Choral Compositions*, 159–67.

178   VIRGINIA HANCOCK

earliest choral works.[5] Another early supporter was Julius Allgeyer, who, on a visit to a monastery on Lake Constance (Bodensee) in 1856, wrote out the entire contents – mostly monophonic and in square notation – of two sixteenth-century Catholic songbooks for him. Brahms himself visited a Swiss monastery during a trip with his sister Elise and Clara Schumann shortly after Schumann's death and filled a bifolio with copies of keyboard pieces by Girolamo Frescobaldi from editions printed in 1637. In summer 1858 Clara Schumann offered to make copies of pieces that interested him;[6] he asked specifically for music by Eccard and Schütz, although the only copy in her hand by either composer in his library is Eccard's 'Übers Gebirg Maria geht', a piece that he performed with both the Hamburg Ladies' Choir and the Vienna Singverein.

Brahms's first visit to Vienna in 1862 provided him with vast new opportunities opened up by his friendships with the pioneering musicologists C. F. Pohl, librarian of the Gesellschaft der Musikfreunde, and the scholar Gustav Nottebohm, who introduced him to the Hofbibliothek (now the Nationalbibliothek). Brahms made various copies from sources in the Hofbibliothek; these include transcriptions from lute tablature, a copy of parts of an opera by Antonio Cesti and scores compiled from partbooks – neither complete – of Sethus Calvisius's 'Josef, lieber Josef mein' and Schütz's setting of Psalm 23, 'Der Herr ist mein Hirt' SWV 398. A further important group of copies comes from David Gregor Corner's *Gross' Catholisch Gesangbuch* (Nuremberg, 1631), which, together with the Meister collection mentioned above, provided him with material for the sacred folk-song settings he wrote in 1864 as well as the motet 'O Heiland, reiss die Himmel auf' Op. 74 no. 2.[7]

This account has so far concentrated on Brahms as a collector and student of early music and has included only the briefest mention of him as a performer, and specifically as a conductor [see Ch. 10 'As Conductor']. The three aspects are obviously intimately connected. When he took the job at Detmold in 1857, which included conducting the court choir, he was responsible for finding repertoire for that group. His first season included performances of portions of Handel's *Messiah*, an unnamed work by

---

[5] The project is chronicled in *Briefe V* in letters from February to July 1856. See also D. Brodbeck, 'The Brahms-Joachim Counterpoint Exchange; or, Robert, Clara, and "the Best Harmony between Jos. and Joh."', in D. Brodbeck (ed.), *Brahms Studies 1* (Lincoln and London: University of Nebraska Press, 1994), 30–80.

[6] *SBB I*, 221, 224.

[7] See G. Bozarth, 'Johannes Brahms und die Liedersammlungen D.G. Corners, K.S. Meisters, und F.W. Arnolds', *Die Musikforschung* 36/4 (October-December 1983), 177–99.

Michael Praetorius (probably 'Es ist ein' Ros' entsprungen', which he returned to in later years) and Rovetta's 'Salve Regina', which he may well have copied specifically for this purpose. In 1858 the choir performed two Bach cantatas, 'Christ lag in Todes Banden' BWV 4, about which Brahms asked the advice of Joseph Joachim, who had performed the work earlier, and 'Ich hatte viel Bekümmernis' BWV 21.[8] In Brahms's third and final season at Detmold, he conducted several more performances of BWV 21; his own copy of volume 5 of the complete works contains an assortment of analytical and performance markings in the first chorus of this cantata, which were probably made during this period.[9] His choral experience at Detmold, together with his study of canon and counterpoint, inspired the composition of a number of choral works for mixed voices, including the *Begräbnisgesang* Op. 13,[10] the two Motets Op. 29, the *Geistliches Lied* Op. 30 and the three *Gesänge für 6-stimmigen Chor* Op. 42, along with a quantity of folk-song settings.

1859 saw Brahms's last season at Detmold and also the beginning of the Hamburg Ladies' Choir,[11] for which Brahms wrote a large quantity of new music, including the four *Gesänge für Frauenchor* (with two horns and harp) Op. 17, the twelve *Lieder und Romanzen* Op. 44 and the original versions of all but one of the *Marienlieder* Op. 22. He also arranged – or at least transposed – an assortment of older works not originally for treble voices for the young women to copy into their partbooks. These included 'Ecce quomodo moritur justus' by Jacobus Gallus (Jakob Handl), which he had himself transcribed from original partbooks, Isaac's 'Innsbruck' and Eccard's 'Übers Gebirg Maria geht'. A beautifully handwritten score of two Palestrina motets for four-part treble choir in soprano, mezzo-soprano and alto clefs, which could have been either a purchase or a gift, bears his name on the title page. It must be the model from which the young women copied their parts into their own *Stimmbücher* and shows the process: Brahms added rehearsal letters, corrected wrong notes, clarified the text underlay and wrote in treble clefs and the first few notes at important entrances in order to get singers started correctly in the unfamiliar clefs.

In his first visit to Vienna in 1862, Brahms made such a favourable impression on the wider musical community that he was invited to return

---

[8] See *Briefe V*, 191, 214–18 and 221–30.

[9] These are described in Hancock, *Brahms's Choral Compositions*, 86.

[10] See V. Hancock, 'Brahms and Early Music: Evidence from His Library and His Choral Compositions', in G. Bozarth (ed.), *Brahms Studies: Analytical and Historical Perspectives* (Oxford: Oxford University Press, 1990), 30–5.

[11] See S. Drinker, *Brahms and His Women's Choruses* (Merion, PA: Musurgia Publishers, 1952).

in 1863–4 as director of the Singakademie.[12] The group's emphasis on historical music was compatible with his own tastes, and he got off to a good start with a concert that included BWV 21 and Isaac's 'Innsbruck' along with works by Beethoven and Schumann, plus two of his own folk-song arrangements. His second concert, however, was too severe for the Viennese public and the critics; it included the Rovetta 'Salve Regina' from his Detmold days, the first and last movements of Bach's 'Liebster Gott, wann werd' ich sterben?' BWV 8 (he had copied its last movement from Winterfeld's *Kirchengesang* during the Detmold period), Eccard's 'Der Christen Triumphlied aufs Osterfest' from a recently published collection of the *Preussische Festlieder* (1858) and two pieces from Winterfeld's *Gabrieli* – Schütz's 'Saul, Saul, was verfolgst du mich?' SWV 415 and a twelve-voice Benedictus by Giovanni Gabrieli. In both of these, his performance decisions, along with additional annotations, appear in his own copy (he added more to sample parts prepared by a copyist). With his usual attention to detail, he also consulted the original partbooks of Schütz's *Symphoniae sacrae III* (1650) in the Hofbibliothek and entered a few corrections into Winterfeld's edition.

This second concert was a failure, both because of the unusually serious repertoire, which was felt to be inappropriate at the beginning of the Carnival season (it also included Beethoven's 'Elegischer Gesang' Op. 118 and Mendelssohn's 'Mitten wir im Leben sind mit dem Tod umfangen' Op. 23 no. 3), and because of the poor quality of the performance. Brahms redeemed himself to some extent with his third concert – parts 1, 2 and 6 of Bach's *Christmas Oratorio* BWV 248 – and the fourth, made up solely of his own works; he was offered a three-year renewal of the position, but declined.

Once Brahms's reputation was well established and he was financially secure, he could buy whatever he wanted for his library and rarely needed to make manuscript copies. From the late 1860s onward, the surviving *Abschriften* consist primarily of short excerpts that interested him, including passages of unusual voice leading which were added over the years to the collection *Oktaven und Quinten*, started in about 1863 and continued until late in his life.[13] He continued to receive gifts from admirers, and here his reputation as a connoisseur of old music produced some rich rewards. A particularly valuable example is the five volumes of Georg Forster's

---

[12] See *Kalbeck II*, 72–3, 93–104.
[13] See P. Mast, 'Brahms's Study, Octaven u. Quinten u. A., with Schenker's Commentary Translated', *Music Forum* 5 (1980), 1–196.

Early Music   181

sixteenth-century collection, *A Model of Beautiful German Songs (Ein aussbund schöner Teutscher Liedlein*, 1552–60). These, copied from scores made from the original partbooks by a teacher at the local Lyceum, were presented to Brahms by the directors of the Philharmonische Verein of Karlsruhe to mark the first performance there, on 12 May 1859, of *A German Requiem* Op. 45. The instigator of the gift, which must have been planned and prepared well in advance, was probably Hermann Levi, conductor of the Karlsruhe court opera and then a close friend of Brahms.

The original compiler had provided complete bibliographic information, included title pages, registers and introductory material from the originals and had also shown all variations from the original musical material such as clef changes, transpositions and corrections; these elements of a modern critical edition are all faithfully reproduced in the scores made for Brahms. He studied them carefully and annotated them copiously. His bibliographic notes include cross-references to different settings of the same melody and to other collections where they appear; his musical additions include marking hemiolas, adding editorial accidentals, filling in canonic parts from verbal instructions and correcting errors.[14]

In 1872 Brahms agreed to take on the position of artistic director of the Gesellschaft der Musikfreunde in his by-now-adopted home of Vienna; he thus became director of both its Singverein and the professional orchestra. In his first performance, along with a 'Symphony in C major' by Schubert (Joachim's orchestration of the Grand Duo D812) and a Mozart aria, he conducted Handel's *Dettingen Te Deum* HWV 283 and two of his old favourites, Eccard's 'Übers Gebirg' and Isaac's 'Innsbruck'. During the three years he held the position, the other works of early music he conducted were Handel's *Saul* HWV 53, *Alexander's Feast* HWV 75, *Solomon* HWV 67 and one of the organ concertos; and Cantatas BWV 4, 8 and 50 and the *St. Matthew Passion* BWV 244. For a concert in December 1873 that included another favourite, Gallus's 'Ecce quomodo moritur justus', he prepared several additional short works of early music; they include parallel settings of the chorale 'Es ist genug' by Johann Rudolf Ahle and Bach (from Cantata 60).[15] His own *Abschrift* of the Ahle setting (from Winterfeld's *Kirchengesang*) comes from the Detmold era, and he had copied the Bach chorale in 1863 from the newly published volume 12 of

[14] A copy of a page from this source, showing Brahms's annotations, appears in V. Hancock, 'Brahms's Links with German Renaissance Music: A Discussion of Selected Choral Works', in M. Musgrave (ed.), *Brahms 2: Biographical, Documentary and Analytical Studies* (Cambridge: Cambridge University Press, 1987), 95–110.

[15] See Hancock, 'Performances', 140, for a reproduction of Brahms's *Abschrift* of Bach's 'Es ist genug'.

182   VIRGINIA HANCOCK

the Complete Edition, likely considering the pair for the Singakademie. Materials that survive in A-Wgm, along with two pieces that were not performed – a six-voice Palestrina 'Haec dies' and Orlando di Lasso's 'Aus meiner Sünden Tiefe' – contain his detailed performance markings.

Complete runs of the collected works of Bach and Handel were significant additions to Brahms's library of printed music over his entire life. He studied the Bach volumes carefully as they arrived, marking large-scale structures, noting important themes and imitative entries, identifying chorale cantus firmi, supplying a few ornaments, correcting errors, writing in information such as dates of composition from Philipp Spitta's biography of Bach and making rare verbal comments (he wrote 'wie schön!' next to a striking example of chromaticism in BWV 91 and copied the same passage into *Oktaven u. Quinten*).[16] The only performance markings in his own set are in BWV 21 (these were later erased) and the *Christmas Oratorio*, both of which he performed with the Singakademie. A second complete set in A-Wgm contains his instructions for performances at the Musikverein, along with those of other conductors. A similar situation obtains for the complete works of Handel, which evidently interested Brahms less because there is far less evidence of careful study.[17]

In Brahms's own Handel volumes, the most annotations are in the keyboard pieces in volume 2 (1859), which are marked with fingerings, sources, occasional question marks and corrections and subject entrances in fugues. He did, as one would expect, maintain a lively interest in the history of keyboard music throughout his life: he performed a Bach fugue on his first solo piano recital at age fifteen, and his library includes, among many other examples, François Couperin's *Pièces de clavecin*, volumes 1 and 2, in Brahms's own edition, prepared for Friedrich Chrysander's *Monuments of Composition* (*Denkmäler der Tonkunst*) and published in 1871 (his own copy is missing from A-Wgm); and Samuel Scheidt's *Tabulatura nova*, edited by Max Seiffert and published in 1892 as volume 2 of *Denkmäler deutscher Tonkunst*, of which Brahms was a founder, and which he annotated carefully.

Late in his life, Brahms was delighted by the long-anticipated appearance of the complete works of Schütz, edited by his friend Philipp Spitta (1885–94).[18] As with the volumes of the Bach edition, he studied each carefully as it arrived, annotating liberally in his usual manner – supplying

---

[16] Some of these annotations are described in Hancock, *Brahms's Choral Compositions*, 84–8.
[17] See Hancock, 'Performances', 134–7, for reproductions of pages from the Bach and Handel works with Brahms's markings.
[18] See *Briefe XVI*, 88.

Early Music 183

references and cross-references, correcting errors, noting parallels, tracing chorale tunes and texts and marking structural repetitions, ground bass patterns, imitative entries and striking uses of chromaticism and dissonance. He also copied out some short selections from several of the volumes for reasons which are not clear; possibilities include the kinds of disguised parallel motion that appear in *Oktaven u. Quinten* and unusual employment – at least to ears accustomed to Bach – of chromaticism and dissonance.[19] Some features of his last choral works, the *Festival and Commemorative Verses* Op. 109 and the Three Motets Op. 110, show resemblances to details he noted in the music of Schütz.

Taken together, the evidence shows that Brahms was interested in early music in ways similar to at least some other German musicians of his time; he had strong patriotic instincts and valued his sense of his place in the larger sweep of German music history while wishing to give appropriate value to the accomplishments of musicians of the past. In addition, however, as his friends and colleagues recognised, he explored many of its aspects more widely, more academically – and also as a practical performer – than the majority of his fellow musicians. This exploration is reflected in his own compositions, perhaps most obviously in his choral writing, but also in his lifelong fascination with counterpoint and the endless possibilities of rhythmic complexity in all musical genres.

Further Reading

K. and I. Geiringer, 'The Brahms Library in the Gesellschaft der Musikfreunde Wien', *Notes* 30/1 (September 1973), 7–14

V. Hancock, 'The Growth of Brahms's Interest in Early Choral Music, and Its Effect on His Own Choral Compositions', in R. Pascall (ed.), *Brahms: Biographical, Documentary and Analytical Studies* (Cambridge: Cambridge University Press, 1983), 27–40

V. Hancock, *Brahms's Choral Compositions and His Library of Early Music* (Ann Arbor, MI: UMI Research Press, 1983)

V. Hancock, 'Brahms's Performances of Early Choral Music', *19th Century Music* 8/2 (Autumn 1984), 125–41

K. Hofmann, *Die Bibliothek von Johannes Brahms: Bücher- und Musikalienverzeichnis* (Hamburg: Karl Dieter Wagner, 1974)

E. Mandyczewski, 'Die Bibliothek Brahms', *Musikbuch aus Oesterreich* 1 (1904), 7–17

---

[19] Annotations in the Schütz volumes are described in Hancock, *Brahms's Choral Compositions*, 91–3, together with a list of the passages he copied, 29–33, and analysis of some of these passages, 141–6.

PART III

Performance and Publishing

CHAPTER 19

Singers

Natasha Loges

Throughout his lifetime, Brahms accompanied dozens of singers in a variety of settings, ranging from huge public halls to his friends' homes, and conducted many others in choirs. Some of those working relationships were one-offs, arising from the widespread practice of including a set of piano-accompanied songs within most concerts and the expediency and cost-effectiveness of using local talent. Others were deep, enduring partnerships; the timbres and interpretative approaches of those singers are surely ingrained in his vocal music. Overall, Brahms's singers were generally not part of the international operatic elite associated with Verdi, Bizet and Massenet. Figures like Julius Stockhausen (1826–1906) and Raimund von Zur-Mühlen (1854–1931) were almost exclusively concert singers and, later on, teachers. Most hailed from German-speaking territories, reflecting Brahms's own concert career. His deepest professional relationships were with low voices: Stockhausen, Amalie Joachim, George Henschel, Hermine Spies and Alice Barbi; these will be discussed below. Nevertheless, many of Brahms's songs are ideal for the soprano range; conversely, while tenor technique arguably underwent the greatest evolution in his lifetime, he seems to have been less interested in it. (The exception is the rarely heard cantata *Rinaldo* Op. 50, and the associated singer Gustav Walter).

From Brahms's earliest youth, his concerts involved singing.[1] Thus, at the pianist Therese Meyer's *soirée musicale* on 27 November 1847, the fourteen-year-old Brahms played a Thalberg duo with Meyer, and one Herr Lüdert sang. Some of the teenaged Brahms's concerts involved highly reputable singers, such as the soprano Hermine Küchenmeister-Rudersdorf (1822–82), who sang throughout German-speaking territories and beyond in the 1840s–50s (exceptionally, even after her marriage in

---

[1] All references to Brahms's concerts in this chapter are drawn from R. and K. Hofmann, *Johannes Brahms als Pianist und Dirigent* (Tutzing: Hans Schneider, 2006).

187

188 NATASHA LOGES

1844). Adele Passy-Cornet was just eleven when she participated in Brahms's *soirée musicale* in April 1849; after moving to Vienna in the 1860s, she developed a substantial operatic and teaching career (Brahms performed with her again in 1862).[2] In 1860, Brahms shared a concert with the Belgian soprano Desirée Artôt (briefly Tchaikovsky's fiancée) at the Hamburg Musikverein; he played his First Piano Concerto Op. 15 and she contributed songs and arias.

Brahms's early relationships with singers were also shaped by his work as a choral director. This was mainly in Detmold (1857–9), Hamburg (1858) and Vienna (1863/4) [see Ch. 10 'As Conductor'], although already in 1853, while on tour with the violinist Eduard Reményi, he wrote works for the local male-voice choir in Celle.[3] Choral conducting and composition allowed Brahms to indulge his fondness for and deepen his awareness of historic repertoire; it honed his contrapuntal skills; and it brought him into contact with groups of convivial young women, some of whom remained lifelong friends.

Brahms met Alsace-born Julius Stockhausen in 1856. They became longstanding friends, colleagues and recital partners – as well as rivals when the singer was appointed conductor of the Hamburg Philharmonic Society and Singakademie in 1862 over Brahms. Notwithstanding this, their groundbreaking recitals of Schubert's and Schumann's lieder (including the presentations of complete song cycles) established this repertoire on the concert stage. Stockhausen, dedicatee of Brahms's vast *Magelone Romances* Op. 33, also specialised in French arias by figures like Boieldieu and Auber, as well as Schumann's *Scenes from Goethe's Faust* WoO 3. Their concertising peaked in the 1860s, although as late as the 1880s, Stockhausen sang in concerts of Brahms's vocal ensemble works. Stockhausen's pupils, such as Helene Magnus, also shared concerts with her teacher and with Brahms in 1869. Alongside many private performances, Stockhausen gave a significant early performance of *A German Requiem* Op. 45 on 10 April 1868 (excepting the fifth movement) and was involved in the premieres of several other pieces including the *Triumphlied* Op. 55 on 5 June 1872. Many solo songs which Stockhausen premiered eventually became recital favourites. Also, his performances in cities such as London (which Brahms never visited) were crucial in familiarising an English-

---

[2] See A. Ehrlich, *Berühmte Sängerinnen der Vergangenheit und Gegenwart* (Leipzig: A.H. Payne, 1896), 147f.

[3] See H. Lauterwasser, '"Von seinen Jugendstreichen bewahrt man nicht gern die sichtbaren Zeichen": Johannes Brahms' älteste Kompositionen im Stadtarchiv Celle entdeckt', *Brahms-Studien* 16 (2011), 101–12.

Singers 189

speaking audience with Brahms's music (one example is the much-loved 'Sonntag' Op. 47 no. 3 which Stockhausen premiered in London in 1871) [see Ch. 32 'England']. He later gave Brahms's works to his singing students in Frankfurt, thus contributing to their enduring popularity. Notably, Stockhausen was no typical vocal 'star'; his strength lay in interpretation and responsiveness to poetry.

Equally important was Amalie Joachim (1839–99), née Schneeweiss, whose repertoire of Brahms songs included no fewer than 139 songs, according to documented performances. Typically for her day, Joachim's career was shaped by her gender and private circumstances. Although she had her public debut at the Royal Court Opera in Hanover in 1862, her marriage to the violinist Joseph Joachim the following year ended her stage career. A move to Berlin and the arrival of six children severely limited her professional activities for a decade or so although she doubtless continued to sing privately. In 1884, her marriage ended acrimoniously (Brahms took her side against Joachim), forcing her back onto the recital stage to support herself. Her rich, instrumental timbre can be imagined through much of Brahms's music, such as the Duets for Alto and Baritone Op. 28, dedicated to her in the year of her marriage (Brahms sent the newly published copy as a Christmas present); the *Alto Rhapsody* Op. 53; and the Two Songs for Alto, Viola and Piano Op. 91. Like Stockhausen, she advised Brahms on appropriate keys for lower transpositions. Brahms also accompanied her in repertoire not by him, for example on 3 December 1872 in Vienna's Kleiner Musikvereinssaal, at which she sang a selection of songs including six from Schubert's *Die schöne Müllerin* D795. Brahms accompanied her in concert throughout the next two decades, as late as 1895. Like Stockhausen, she exerted enormous influence on the subsequent history of song performance, particularly through her themed, historic recitals which were a model for many subsequent singers' programmes.

In 1869 the tenor Gustav Walter sang at the premiere of Brahms's cantata *Rinaldo* Op. 50 in Vienna's Grosser Redoutensaal. This launched their artistic partnership, and their performances continued into the 1890s. Apart from public performances, they also made music informally in Walter's Vienna flat on the Getreidemarkt. In 1883, Brahms met the alto Hermine Spies (1857–93); she sang his *Alto Rhapsody* more than once in those years, and he accompanied her in many recitals. A pupil of Stockhausen's, she was a committed advocate of Brahms's songs in her recitals. According to surviving documentation, she performed at least forty of them, with surprisingly little overlap between her and Amalie

Joachim's list.[4] Brahms's glorious 'Todessehnen' Op. 86 no. 6 was her favourite encore, and his much-loved 'Sapphische Ode' Op. 94 no. 4 was dedicated to her. However, the main attraction seems to have been personal; both Brahms and his friend Klaus Groth [see Ch. 27 'Literature'] were quite infatuated by her. But the quality of her singing evidently declined, and by the time of her early death, Brahms had noticeably cooled towards her as an artist.

The baritone, conductor, pianist, composer and teacher George Henschel (1850–1934), was (like Stockhausen) an outstanding all-round musician and by all accounts a man of tremendous charm and energy. He met Brahms at the Lower Rhine Music Festival in 1874, and the two soon became colleagues and friends, even spending a holiday together on the island of Rügen in 1876. His subsequently published *Recollections* (1978) offer wonderful insights into the composer's personality, working habits and artistry. In 1877, Henschel sang solo songs accompanied by Brahms at the Leipzig premiere of the First Symphony Op. 68. However, Henschel's stellar career soon took him (and Brahms's music) well beyond Austro-Germany to Great Britain and the USA. He became a teacher at the Royal College of Music in London in 1886, took English citizenship four years later and was ennobled by George V in 1914. His importance as a conductor to Brahms was no less great; he conducted the British premiere of the *Triumphlied* in 1879 and the American premiere of the *Alto Rhapsody* three years later, to name but two examples.

Brahms's fondness for Alice Barbi (1862–1948) is an exception because of her Italian origin and *bel canto* training, but her strengths too lay in concert repertoire. Following successful tours in England, Russia and elsewhere, she first performed in Vienna in 1889. She first sang Brahms's songs in 1892 but retired from the operatic stage just over a year later following her marriage; thereafter she lived in Russia and Italy. Ultimately, their friendship involved hardly any public performance although they remained close and he loved her singing.

This account summarises the best-known singers associated with Brahms, but many other figures were important in different ways. The Leipzig home of soprano Livia Frege (1818–91), who was close to the Schumanns and Mendelssohns, was a centre for private performances of Brahms's music in that otherwise hostile city [see Chapter 4 'Leipzig and

---

[4] Accounts of their repertoires are given in B. Borchard, 'Amalie Joachim und die gesungene Geschichte des deutschen Liedes', *Archiv für Musikwissenschaft* 58/4 (2001), 278; and W. Ebert, 'Die von Hermine Spies gesungenen Brahms-Lieder', in M. Meyer (ed.), *Brahms-Studien* 11 (Tutzing: Hans Schneider, 1997), 73–81.

Singers 191

Berlin']. Brahms had a comparable, if deeper relationship with Ottilie Ebner, née Hauer (1837–1926). When she moved to Vienna in 1860, she joined the recently founded Singakademie, of which Brahms was appointed conductor in 1863. Their friendship continued beyond her marriage in 1864 to Edward Ebner and a move to Budapest where Brahms regularly saw her (as a fascinating aside, Eduard Ebner was acquainted with Wagner through a mutual passion for rowing).[5] When her first child died, Brahms played for her almost daily to console her.[6] Over the years she acquired no fewer than sixteen of his song manuscripts. Ebner was evidently a sufficiently good singer to give premiere performances of Brahms's vocal quartet 'Wechselllied zum Tanze' Op. 31 no. 1 in 1862. She also founded her own choir, which she conducted and accompanied; a good sight-reader, she played the challenging four-hand arrangements of Brahms's larger-scale repertoire with him.

Ebner was friends with Marie Wilt; the two shared singing lessons. A dramatic coloratura soprano, Wilt (1833–91) regularly sang Brahms's works in concerts involving him from 1863 until well into the 1880s. Wilt had initially begun as a choral singer because it was believed that she lacked solo talent; unusually, her career first developed after her marriage to Franz Wilt in 1855. In the following decade, she rose to international fame, singing (for example) *Aida* in the Vienna premiere of Verdi's work. Despite her tremendous success, Wilt was emotionally fragile and died by suicide in 1891. Around the same time as Brahms met Wilt, he also encountered the extraordinary pianist-singer Caroline Bettelheim (1845–1925). The Budapest-born Bettelheim studied with Karl Goldmark and had a successful opera career until her marriage in 1867. She performed Beethoven's arrangements of Scottish folk-songs with Brahms accompanying, among many other works. In 1876, Marie Fillunger's name appears in a concert where she sang Brahms's tumultuous setting 'Wehe, so willst du mich wieder' Op. 32 no. 5. A great recitalist, she familiarised English audiences with Schubert's songs; she also toured Australia and South Africa with Sir Charles and Lady Hallé, and was Eugenie Schumann's partner.

A host of other singers sang for and with Brahms over the years. From the late 1860s onwards, the names Rosa Girzick, Louise Dustmann and Dr Emil Kraus appear regularly in his concert programmes. One can only imagine Brahms's concerts with the operatic *Heldentenor* Heinrich Vogl, who in 1874 sang various Brahms songs in Basel. In 1876, Hedwig

[5] O. von Balassa, *Die Brahmsfreundin Ottilie Ebner* (Vienna: F. Bondy, 1933), 45. [6] *Ibid.*, 55.

Kiesekamp sang the *Alto Rhapsody*, with Brahms accompanying a few solo songs. Similarly, in 1878, Adele Assmann sang the *Alto Rhapsody* alongside a few songs in Breslau, a format she repeated with him in 1880. In the 1880s–90s, Brahms's singers included Max Staegemann, Antonie von Kufferath (with whom he developed a lasting friendship), Jenny Hahn, another Stockhausen pupil Raimund von Zur-Mühlen, Marie Hanfstängl-Schröder, the Hungarian opera singer Vilma von Balás-Bognar, the Viennese operetta singer and actress 'Kathinka' Engel, Clara Bruch (who sang at the concert which included the premiere of the Fourth Symphony Op. 98), Therese Malten (who did the same at the Symphony's Meiningen premiere) and William Shakespeare [see Ch.15 'Concert Life'].

The wonderfully flamboyant tenor Zur-Mühlen, who had worked with Brahms in the 1880s, gave an insight into Brahms's method of song composition, recalling how he 'repeatedly declaimed, with growing intensity, the poems he wished to set, striving to unify the rhythmic particularities of the words and the music, and simultaneously trying to transpose himself into the poem's overall mood (*Stimmung*)'.[7] Zur-Mühlen was also the recital partner of the pianist Hans Schmidt, who wrote the poem to one of Brahms's best-loved songs, 'Sapphische Ode' Op. 94 no. 4. Zur-Mühlen later settled in England.

Brahms's singers do not form a coherent group by any means, but there is strikingly little overlap with Wagner's favourites, such as Wilhelmine Schröder-Devrient, Mathilde Mallinger (in 1868, the first Eva in *Die Meistersinger von Nürnberg*) and the tenors Joseph Tichatschek and Ludwig Schnorr von Carolsfeld. Amalie Materna (the first Kundry and Bayreuth Brünnhilde) did not cross Brahms's path despite being based in Vienna from 1869 until the mid-1890s. The partial exception is Gustav Walter, but he only tackled lighter Wagnerian roles. A different kind of exception is Wagner's first Alberich, the baritone Karl Hill, who sang the solo in the *Triumphlied* in Zurich in 1874 and 1895 under Brahms, as well as upon other occasions.

The concert repertoires of Brahms's singers frequently blurred contexts and genres as we tend to understand them today. Because of the prevailing concert formats, singers would often sing a solo part in a large oratorio or a huge aria followed by a handful of solo songs, and one wonders how the rapid shift from large-scale statement to intimate communication was handled. And there was no tidy divide between the singers who sang solo

---

[7] D. von Zur-Mühlen, *Der Sänger Raimund von zur-Mühlen* (Hanover-Döhren: Harro von Hirschheydt, 1969), 75–6.

Singers 193

or vocal ensemble works for him; the latter repertoire particularly seems to have been a democratic space for singers of a wide range of experience, evoking the conviviality and mutual support of instrumental chamber music. Brahms's singers were also relaxed about issues of gender in repertoire. In Budapest in 1888, Brahms's 'Das Mädchen spricht' Op. 107 no. 3 was sung by Gustav Walter, with its closing lines 'du bist wohl auch noch / Nicht lange Braut?' ('You haven't been / a bride for very long either, have you?'). Amalie Joachim's first public concert with Brahms in 1872 in Vienna's Kleiner Musikvereinssaal included songs from Schubert's *Die schöne Müllerin* D795, and Spies sang Schumann's *Dichterliebe* Op. 48 with Brahms at Widmann's home in Berne; both these cycles have explicitly male protagonists. There is no space here to explore this intriguing gender-neutrality in a century generally associated with a quite rigid separation of gender roles.

What is more elusive is Brahms's definition of 'good' singing, either from a technical or expressive standpoint. The vocal tradition of the great pedagogue Manuel Garcia (1805–1906) loomed large in Stockhausen's singing and was perpetuated in his own extensive teaching practice. Garcia's *Complete Treatise on the Art of Singing* (*Traité complet de l'art du chant*, 1840, 1847) is still in use in modern singing teaching. In some respects, it maintained eighteenth-century practices, but Garcia's understanding of different timbres, the *voix claire* and *voix sombre,* marked a significant change. The darkening of the voice provided the resonance needed to blend with increasingly heavy orchestrations (and which is almost universally audible in performances of Brahms's oratorios today), but the concomitant modification of the vowels led to greater incomprehensibility of the text; this tension still exists.[8] As the century progressed, singing teachers (Stockhausen among them) advocated a more scientific approach to singing. Alongside this was a general shift towards declamation rather than legato, 'at its worst akin to shouting', although such descriptions must be seen in relative terms and cannot be accurately pinned to individual singers.[9]

The picture is complicated by the existence of some very early recordings which suggest the prevalence of a relatively fast, narrow-bored vibrato and

[8] D. Mason, 'The Teaching (and Learning) of Singing', in J. Potter (ed.), *The Cambridge Companion to Singing* (Cambridge: Cambridge University Press, 2000), 212.

[9] D. Shawe-Taylor, 'Wagner and His Singers', in B. Millington & S. Spencer (eds.), *Wagner in Performance* (New Haven & London: Yale University Press, 1992), 20. See also K. Henson, *Opera Acts. Singers and Performance in the Late Nineteenth Century* (Cambridge: Cambridge University Press, 2015), 9ff. for a description of this style in an operatic context.

a more committed sense of legato than is generally heard today, as well as a freer approach to notated rhythm, which makes one wonder what the fuss over declamation was really about. Interestingly, in the many reviews of Stockhausen's singing from the 1850s–70s, the word 'declamation' is absent; more typical is one review from the *Allgemeine musikalische Zeitung* praising his 'brilliant interpretation' overall.[10]

In his late seventies, Henschel – whose voice remained remarkably healthy – made recordings for HMV and Columbia. The recordings of Schubert's songs (accompanying himself!) reveal a perhaps unexpectedly disciplined and restrained approach to the score, along with a relatively light, flexible timbre, often without vibrato but with much rhythmic flexibility. His rendition of Schubert's 'Der Leiermann', the bleak closing song of *Winterreise* D911, remains extraordinarily evocative. Evidence also suggests that singers had smaller working ranges.[11] Henschel recalled that Brahms did not mind him altering high notes in the *Triumphlied* because of a cold. Brahms memorably said:

> As far as I am concerned, a thinking, sensible singer may, without hesitation, change a note which for some reason or other is for the time being out of his compass, into one which he can reach with comfort, provided always the declamation remains correct and the accentuation does not suffer.[12]

Further Reading

O. von Balassa, *Die Brahmsfreundin Ottilie Ebner* (Vienna: F. Bondy, 1933)

B. Borchard, 'Amalie Joachim und die gesungene Geschichte des deutschen Liedes', *Archiv für Musikwissenschaft* 58/4 (2001), 265–99

G. Bozarth, *Johannes Brahms & George Henschel: An Enduring Friendship* (Sterling Heights, Mich.: Harmonie Park Press, 2008)

W. Ebert, 'Die von Hermine Spies gesungenen Brahms-Lieder', *Brahms-Studien* 11 (1997), 73–81

A. Ehrlich, *Berühmte Sängerinnen der Vergangenheit und Gegenwart* (Leipzig: A.H. Payne, 1896)

G. Gaiser-Reich, *Gustav Walter 1834–1910: Wiener Hofopernsänger und Liederfürst* (Tutzing: Hans Schneider, 2011)

---

[10] *Allgemeine musikalische Zeitung* 2/51, (18 December 1867), 410.

[11] A more detailed discussion of this can be found in W. Crutchfield, 'Vocal Performance in the Nineteenth Century', in C. Lawson & R. Stowell, eds., *The Cambridge History of Musical Performance* (Cambridge: Cambridge University Press, 2013), 611–42.

[12] Diary entry, 3 February 1876, Münster. G. Bozarth, *Johannes Brahms & George Henschel: An Enduring Friendship* (Michigan: Harmonie Park, 2008), 24.

Singers 195

D. Mason, 'The Teaching (and Learning) of Singing', in J. Potter (ed.), *The Cambridge Companion to Singing* (Cambridge: Cambridge University Press, 2000), 204–20

J. Wirth, *Julius Stockhausen, der Sänger des deutschen Liedes: nach Dokumenten seiner Zeit dargestellt* (Frankfurt: Englert & Schlosser, 1927)

D. von Zur-Mühlen, *Der Sänger Raimund von zur-Mühlen* (Hanover-Döhren: Harro von Hirschheydt, 1969)

CHAPTER 20

Conductors

Leon Botstein

A symbiosis in music between performance and composition prevailed throughout the nineteenth century. It was particularly evident among conductors. Conducting did not emerge as a distinct profession until the last quarter of the century. But even then, those who sought to make conducting a career either dabbled in composition or harboured lifelong hopes to succeed with their own music. The instincts of a fellow composer dominated the approach to interpretation from the podium.

In Johannes Brahms's circle of close friends and colleagues, there was perhaps no better example of this link between composing and conducting than Otto Dessoff (1835–92). Dessoff is remembered only as a conductor, despite many fine works to his name. It was to Dessoff that Brahms entrusted the first performance, in 1876, of his First Symphony Op. 68. Dessoff was born in Leipzig to Jewish parents; he met Brahms in 1853 but became a close friend in the 1860s, after they both settled in Vienna. During his years leading the Vienna Philharmonic, from 1860 to 1872, Dessoff set a high standard of professionalism. Like Brahms, his aesthetics were rooted in a reverence for Schumann, Mendelssohn and the Viennese Classical tradition. He invited Brahms to play with the Vienna Philharmonic and in 1863 premiered the Second Serenade Op. 16 in that city.

The choice of Dessoff to premiere the First Symphony in Karlsruhe in 1876 was not therefore merely motivated by caution, i.e. Brahms's desire to try the work out, not in Vienna or Leipzig but in a smaller city. Dessoff stood out as an exception in Vienna's musical life because of the seriousness and integrity of his musicianship, as well and his dignity as a person. Nasty intrigues, nativist prejudices and politics in Vienna favoured far lesser talents. Brahms admired Dessoff's surprising decision to leave Vienna in 1872 for Karlsruhe in advance of evident intrigues to oust him. When Dessoff died in 1892 Brahms, in a letter to Clara Schumann, observed, 'He was an exemplary man, lively and sensitive, and a deeply educated

Conductors

musician."[1] Dessoff, like Brahms, was in awe of the history of music that had preceded their generation.

An ardent partisan of Brahms, Dessoff never sought to justify his allegiance to both Brahms and Wagner, unlike Hermann Levi (1839–1900), his predecessor in Karlsruhe, and Johann Ritter von Herbeck (1831–77), Dessoff's *bête noir* in Vienna. Dessoff taught one of Brahms's younger acolytes, Heinrich von Herzogenberg, and became a key member of the circle which also included Joseph Joachim [see Ch. 22 'Other Instrumentalists'], Eduard Hanslick, the pianist Julius Epstein and Max Bruch, whose music Brahms championed as a conductor in Vienna between 1872 and 1875.

Indeed, the rise to prominence of the personality and music of Wagner, particularly in the 1870s, cast a shadow over the connections between Brahms and the leading conductors of the era. The fact that Brahms turned his focus to orchestral music in earnest only in the 1870s was no coincidence. Among the many plausible explanations for why Brahms took so long to write large-scale orchestral works is his alarm at the extent to which Wagnerian drama and theatre began to dominate musical aesthetics and define the essence of German cultural identity.

It is as well, however, to remember that, before the appearance of the string of masterpieces for orchestra beginning with the 1873 *Variations on a Theme of Haydn* Op. 56a (whose premiere Brahms conducted himself), Brahms had completed the First Piano Concerto Op. 15 in 1857, two Serenades Op. 11 and Op. 16 for orchestra in 1859, and his longest work, *A German Requiem* Op. 45 in 1866. Joachim, who was much more of a violin virtuoso than a conductor, was the soloist for the first performances of the Violin Concerto Op. 77 and the conductor of the First Serenade. Brahms himself conducted both the concerto and the premiere of the Second Serenade.

Carl Reinecke, the legendary teacher and head of the Leipzig Conservatory, renowned as a pianist and composer, and an avowed proponent of a conservative musical tradition derived from Mendelssohn, conducted the first completed performance of the *Requiem* in 1869. Despite a shared admiration for Schumann and Mendelssohn and antipathy for Wagner, Brahms had little regard for Reinecke. Herbeck had premiered the first three movements two years earlier in Vienna, and Brahms conducted a six-movement version in 1868 in Bremen. Hermann Levi would conduct subsequent performances in 1869.

[1] *SBB II*, 486.

The spectacular victory by Bismarck and Wilhelm I over the Habsburg Monarchy in 1866 and, four years later, over France, as well as the subsequent unification of Germany under Prussia, changed the political landscape and cultural politics of German-speaking Europe [see Ch. 26 'Politics and Religion']. The restructured multi-ethnic and multi-lingual Austro-Hungarian monarchy (in whose capital Brahms lived since the early 1860s) emerged as a subordinate power. In the new monolingual Imperial German Empire, the Wagnerian and Wagner himself became nearly synonymous with the image of modern Germany. Wagner's accessible and alluring framing of German myth and history in his music dramas gave voice to a new spirit of chauvinism in politics and culture.

To celebrate Bismarck's achievement, Brahms composed the *Triumphlied* Op. 55, using historicist aesthetics: a synthesis of a form evocative of Handel and a contrapuntal texture reminiscent of Bach, as if to counter overtly Wagner's conceits regarding the proper path for the music of the future. For Brahms, the *Triumphlied* was a statement directed at the wider public that Wagner had captured. The conductor Hermann Levi, Brahms's old friend, embraced Brahms's new work. He declared to Clara Schumann that in the nineteenth century, no greater work of church music had ever been written.[2] Levi prepared the piano score, suggested improvements in the orchestration and gave the first performance in Karlsruhe in 1872. Levi himself grasped the paradox that at the very moment he was struck by the power of Brahms's historically rooted tribute to the new German Empire, he was due to conduct several performances of *Die Meistersinger von Nürnberg* – Wagner's most explicit celebration of German culture, whose controversial but triumphant Viennese premiere had taken place in 1870.

From the late 1860s on, gaining the support of conductors became increasingly significant for Brahms. At stake was, in the first instance, the future of *A German Requiem* in the concert repertoire. After turning to composition for the orchestra in the 1870s, finding advocates became indispensable. Wagner's ascendency as emblematic of the present and the future of music and of the German spirit was evident in Vienna throughout the 1870s. Wagner came to Vienna in 1875 to advance his dream of Bayreuth. He conducted concerts and raised money. The entire city was engulfed by a pro-Wagnerian enthusiasm. The comparatively muted success of the *Triumphlied* Op. 55 made Brahms realise that if he were to successfully combat what he regarded as the deleterious influence of

---

[2] F. Haas, *Zwischen Brahms und Wagner: Der Dirigent Hermann Levi* (Zurich: Atlantis, 1995), 153.

Conductors

Wagnerism, even in Vienna, he would have to fight his aesthetic battle against the Wagnerian with symphonic works on a grand scale. The symphony offered a platform for Brahms to claim Wagner's appropriation of the legacy of Beethoven regarding the dramatic in music.

Brahms, for his part, never denied Wagner's talent and originality. He was rather more concerned with Wagner's influence on musical culture and taste. Wagner, on the other hand, responded to Brahms's strikingly successful aesthetic counter-attack with sharpened rhetorical venom and disparagement. Writing in 1879, in 'On Poetry and Composition', in the wake of Brahms's success with his first two symphonies Op. 68 and Op. 73 and the Violin Concerto Op. 77, Wagner made explicit reference to Brahms's new-found stature as the purveyor of a different and more overtly traditional ·aesthetic of musical drama, citing with contempt the *Triumphlied* and the idea that Brahms's First Symphony might be considered 'Beethoven's Tenth'. He slammed the music as sterile, as 'Jewish'.[3] The notion that Brahms might be considered the 'Prince of Serious Music' was an insult to German pride.

Both Brahms and Wagner were keenly aware that new urban concert halls and civic orchestras all throughout Germany rivalled the opera house for public attention. Brahms's career as a performer began in the 1850s, when princely and ducal courts still dominated musical life. But in the mid-1860s new opportunities emerged as a consequence of rapid economic expansion. Brahms hoped for an appointment as a conductor in his native Hamburg. It was during a politicised era of economic growth, between the mid-1860s and early 1880s, when new musical institutions were coming into being, supported by cities, middle-class patrons and amateur societies, that Brahms sought to forge relationships with conductors who would champion his works [see Ch. 15 'Concert Life'].

Among all of Brahms's conductor colleagues Franz Wüllner (1832–1902) was closest to the composer. Wüllner premiered several of Brahms's choral works including the *Marienlieder* Op. 22, 'Darthulas Grabgesang' Op. 42 no. 3, 'Es geht ein Wehen durch den Wald' Op. 62 no. 6 and the Three Motets Op. 110. They met in 1853 and shared a close friendship with Joachim (Wüllner would later help reconcile Brahms and Joachim after their estrangement over Joachim's divorce). Wüllner started, like Brahms, as a choral conductor. He was a highly successful teacher (he taught Max Kalbeck and

---

[3] M. Gregor-Dellin and D. Mack (eds.), *Cosima Wagner's Diaries*, trans. G. Skelton, 2 vols., (New York: Harcourt Brace Jovanovich, 1978), vol. 1, 779; and R. Wagner, 'On Poetry and Composition', in *Prose Works*, trans. W. Ashton Ellis, 8 vols. (New York: Broude Brothers, 1966), vol. 6, 1434.

served as Director at both the Dresden and Cologne conservatories). Ironically, Wüllner's rapid rise to prominence as conductor came courtesy of Wagner. However, Wagner and Cosima, his second wife, disparaged Wüllner as 'evil' and second-rate. The Wagners favoured Levi, Wüllner's rival in Munich. But it was Wüllner who seized the opportunity in Munich to conduct the controversial first performances of *Das Rheingold* and *Die Walküre* in 1869 and 1870, after Hans Richter (see below) was fired. The relentless antipathy shown towards Wüllner by the Wagners (despite the success of Wüllner's performances) secured his ongoing loyalty to Brahms. Brahms trusted him as an editor and adviser, and he was the first to be shown the completed Third Symphony Op. 90. Like Dessoff, Wüllner's restrained approach to interpretation was rooted in a classicist Mendelssohnian tradition: he took few liberties with tempos and phrasing. Loyalty rather than genius recommended him to Brahms.

The centrality of the post-1870 Wagner–Brahms rivalry would engulf three far more prominent Brahms conductors: Hermann Levi, Hans Richter and Hans von Bülow. Levi became friendly with Brahms in the early 1860s after Clara Schumann introduced them during their shared time in Karlsruhe. Levi came from a rabbinical family. He trained in Leipzig, by then already legendary as a bastion of aesthetic traditionalism [see Ch. 4 'Leipzig and Berlin']. He showed early gifts as a composer, but Brahms urged him to focus on conducting. Their close relationship, however, came apart because of Brahms's astonishment at Levi's growing devotion to Wagner's music and his later championing of Bruckner's symphonies. A heated discussion took place in 1875 when Brahms paid a visit to Levi in Munich. Brahms left without saying goodbye. The relationship was never repaired, even though Levi would conduct Brahms's music to the end of his career.

Brahms's harsh reaction to Levi's new allegiances possessed pointed political overtones. Levi never converted to Christianity, despite enormous pressure placed on him by Wagner prior to the first performance of *Parsifal*. Brahms understood that Wagner's notorious anti-Semitism not only masqueraded as an ideology about art and politics but was also an instrument by which to deride Brahms's approach to music. It enabled Wagner to render Brahms the composer and the man as mirroring an anti-German 'Jewish' aesthetic. It was one thing for non-Jews, like Wüllner and Richter, to ignore this aspect of Wagner, but Levi's behaviour seemed incomprehensible. Dessoff and Joachim, who were born Jewish, were hardly oblivious to Wagner's anti-Semitism. Brahms's contempt for anti-Semitism was well known. The Viennese satirist Daniel Spitzer observed

Conductors 201

(with considerable irony) that, owing to Brahms's many Jewish friends (including the composers Karl Goldmark and Ignaz Brüll) and his status in Vienna as the antipode to Wagner, among Viennese adherents of Wagner and the politics Wagner was associated with – particularly the Pan-German movement – Brahms himself became a Jew.[4]

Hans Richter (1843–1916), who performed Brahms with enthusiasm in Vienna and London [see Ch. 32 'England'], was the only Brahms conductor to negotiate the Brahms–Wagner conflict with success. Richter came of age in Vienna and had gone, like Schubert, to the Vienna Boys' Choir School. By the mid-1880s, Richter, as a conductor, dominated Viennese musical life, conducting the opera, the Vienna Philharmonic, the Imperial Chapel and the Gesellschaft der Musikfreunde. Brahms genuinely liked Richter as a person, despite his fame as Wagner's choice to open Bayreuth in 1876 and his close links to the Master of Bayreuth, including his role in the surprise 1870 performance of the *Siegfried Idyll* for Cosima in Wagner's home. Richter remained, however, his own man and advocated the work of Dvořák (whom Brahms supported and admired) and, later in his career, English composers, including Elgar. In 1884, Brahms's friend the surgeon and amateur musician Theodor Billroth commented to Brahms on Richter's incredibly successful performance of the Third Symphony Op. 90 in Vienna, writing that Richter had conducted it with such enthusiasm that one might have thought he had composed the work himself.[5]

Richter, by all accounts, was a consummate craftsman as a conductor. He copied out his scores and conducted from memory. He could spot errors instantly. He also favoured a straightforward approach that highlighted expressive restraint and the long line, all without idiosyncratic distortion. His movements were economical. The key to his ability to put works on the stage with relative ease was an approach that eschewed both accuracy and expressive nuance. Variations in tempos and the use of rubato were not hallmarks of his style. Yet Brahms was relentlessly critical, and Richter's work did not always meet his standards. He could be too undemanding in rehearsals, and the results were thus not always polished – consequently Brahms was known to leave a performance early or even avoid going.[6] But Brahms appreciated Richter's loyalty to his music, evident in Richter's refusal to be swayed by Hugo Wolf's relentless anti-

---

[4] See D. Spitzer, 'Aus Ischl' (1889), in *Wiener Spaziergänge*, 7 vols. (Vienna: Haase, 1894), vol. 7, 2667.
[5] O. Gottlieb-Billroth (ed.), *Billroth und Brahms im Briefwechsel* (Berlin and Vienna: Urban & Schwarzenberg, 1935), 361.
[6] *Kalbeck III*, 412–3; also, *Heuberger*, 88.

Brahms reviews in the 1880s. He proved to be a successful advocate of Brahms's music and helped propel it into prominence; he was entrusted with the first performances of the Second and Third Symphonies Op. 73 and Op. 90.

The career of Hans von Bülow (1830–94) is without doubt among the most notorious in music history. Bülow started out not only as a prized piano student of Liszt but also, with Liszt's encouragement, as a conductor. And he ended up marrying Liszt's daughter, Cosima. His talent was astounding. Bülow entered Wagner's orbit in the 1860s and became his loyal assistant in roles that ranged from rehearsal pianist to conductor. He gave the premieres of *Tristan und Isolde* and *Die Meistersinger von Nürnberg*. An affair blossomed between Wagner and Cosima Liszt, resulting in public scandal and humiliation for Bülow and, for Wagner, a new wife. Bülow, like Levi, had once harboured ambitions as a composer but gave up composition faced with the enormity of Wagner's genius. After the split with Wagner and Cosima Liszt, he returned to piano performance and, most of all, conducting. He toured during the 1870s, and in 1880 was made conductor of the court orchestra in Meiningen, an ensemble of forty-nine musicians. Two years later he remarried.

Bülow was a formidable intellect. He had a sharp wit. He was also a martinet, a fierce nationalist and an ardent anti-Semite of the old school. Unlike Wagner, he did not subscribe to racialist theories but rather argued against the influx of Eastern European Jews to Germany. Bülow advocated the complete assimilation of German Jews. It was in the 1870s and 1880s that he developed an affinity for Brahms's music. He premiered the Fourth Symphony Op. 98 in 1885 and embraced Brahms's music in a pointed, public manner. Bülow's championing of Brahms's music no doubt carried the intensity of an act of revenge. He prepared performances of Brahms in painstaking detail. By championing Brahms, he reclaimed his public dignity. But he never repudiated Wagner's music.

Bülow was an exacting conductor, the very opposite of Richter. His rehearsals were meticulous, rigorous and detailed. This permitted him to integrate into his performances subtle and not so subtle variations in tempo, phrasing, articulation and balance. The result was a transparency and accuracy to which orchestral musicians and audiences were not accustomed. When the Meiningen Orchestra went on tour to Vienna in 1884, the reaction was sheer astonishment. The vaunted superiority of the much larger Vienna Philharmonic under Richter was challenged. The discipline and refinement of the Meiningen orchestral playing was a revelation. Prussian efficiency confronted a smug Viennese relaxed approach to

Conductors

music making. Nonetheless, Bülow's precise but personalised reading of Beethoven, particularly the *Egmont* Overture Op. 84, scandalised critics, notably Ludwig Speidel. At the third performance of the same programme, brandishing a copy of Speidel's review, Bülow announced to the audience that he was replacing *Egmont* with Brahms's *Academic Festival Overture* Op. 80.[7]

Bülow's strict dictatorial control over the ensemble made it possible for him to treat the orchestra as if it were a single instrument. The result was that the performances became famous not so much for their accuracy but for the extent to which Bülow could fashion and deliver a quite idiosyncratic interpretation. In place of workmanlike, straightforward and uninflected performances of a Dessoff, Wüllner or Richter, came polished, highly flexible and, to some, particularly the composer-conductor Felix von Weingartner, highly distorted personal readings.[8] Bülow, however, left lasting impressions on Gustav Mahler, Richard Strauss and Ernő Dohnányi, whose careers as conductors he influenced. He possessed an extraordinary memory and his Prussian emphasis on discipline and accuracy was accompanied by what audiences admired as a baton that seemed itself to sing. Bülow was energetic and displayed intense but flexible physical gestures and minute control.

The irony in Bülow's approach to performing Brahms was that it derived from Wagner's approach to conducting, famously articulated in his 1869 pamphlet 'On Conducting'. Wagner argued (particularly in the performance of Beethoven) for great flexibility in tempo, a wide range of dynamics, an expressive rubato and the avoidance of mechanical regularity. Indeed, Bülow's Wagnerian emphasis on theatrical expressive gesture did not sit well with Brahms. Yet Brahms developed a close bond with the Meiningen Orchestra in the 1880s, performing his Second Piano Concerto with the orchestra and conducting his own music, notably the Fourth Symphony. He remained sceptical of Bülow's focus on orchestral virtuosity, his emphasis on colour and, most of all, his distortions and mannered exaggerations in the delivery of the musical line and structure. Brahms took the view that he would have indicated tempo shifts and other alterations in the score had he wished them. As a defence against Bülow's tampering, Brahms asserted the authority of the composer's expressive and interpretive

---

[7] A. Walker, *Hans von Bülow: A Life and Times* (Oxford and New York: Oxford University Press, 2010), 313.

[8] F. Weingartner, *Über das Dirigieren*, 4th edn (Leipzig: Breitkopf & Härtel, 1913), 715; also, A. Weissmann, *Der Dirigent im 20. Jahrhundert* (Berlin: Propyläen Verlag, 1925), 103.

intention as inscribed in the composer's text as the proper guideline and restraint to excessive personalising.[9]

Brahms's connection to Meiningen through Bülow left a decisive legacy. Fritz Steinbach (1855–1916) succeeded Bülow in 1886. Brahms had been a mentor to Steinbach during the latter's student years in Vienna during the late 1870s. Over his sixteen years as music director, Steinbach sought to establish Meiningen as the definitive venue for the performance of Brahms's orchestral music. Steinbach's notes on the performance of Brahms's symphonies and the *Variations on a Theme of Haydn* Op. 56a were published in 1933 by a protégé of Steinbach's, Walter Blume, in a small pamphlet dedicated to Fritz Busch.[10] In these notes, one encounters an approach presumably reflective of Brahms's opinions. Neither the routine and relatively straightforward approach of Richter nor the excessive personalisation of Bülow is advocated. Rather, Steinbach's instructions are an account of subtle flexibilities, detailed highlighting of dynamics, articulation and phrasing that permit an expressive intensity consistent with respect for the larger structural integrity of the music, the economy of form, as well as the extent to which Brahms's orchestral music pays elegant homage to models from the past, including those of Haydn, Schubert, Schumann, Mendelssohn and, above all, Beethoven. Both Brahms the innovator in terms of music on a grand scale and Brahms the historicist become seamlessly integrated through Steinbach's approach. Among Steinbach's admirers was Arturo Toscanini.

The advocacy of Brahms by Richter and Bülow, two performers closely tied to Wagner, between 1870 and the mid-1890s succeeded in fulfilling Brahms's ambition. The music of Brahms and the respect it displayed for a tradition of musical practice that honoured the Classical style and an early Romantic privileging of instrumental music – the symphony, the concerto and variation form – took hold among musicians and the audience during the last quarter of the nineteenth century. The Wagnerian idea that these practices and forms of musical expression had been rendered obsolete for future generations – a fear that Brahms harboured – was successfully countered. Likewise, in the art of conducting, the path chartered by Wagner and realised by Bülow met its own negative reaction in the

---

[9] See R. Pascall and P. Weller, 'Flexible Tempo and Nuancing in Orchestral Music: Understanding Brahms's View of Interpretation in his Second Piano Concerto and Fourth Symphony', in M. Musgrave and B. Sherman (eds.), *Performing Brahms. Early Evidence of Performance Style* (Cambridge: Cambridge University Press, 2003), 230.

[10] See W. Blume (ed.), *Brahms in der Meininger Tradition: Seine Sinfonien und Haydn-Variationen in der Bezeichnung von Fritz Steinbach*, new edn, M. Schwalb (Hildesheim: Olms, 2014).

Conductors 205

work of Felix von Weingartner, Fritz Busch and Arturo Toscanini, leading conductors in the generation after Bülow [see Ch. 36 'Recordings'].

From the distant perspective of the twenty-first century, given the contemporary state of politics and culture, Brahms and Wagner appear to share, through their use of music, more common ground. Their music reveals to us shared fundamental ways to create meaning and give, in an intensely affecting way, voice to the human condition. The difficult task is to bring their ambition to life for a contemporary audience in the context of the radical discontinuities bequeathed by the twentieth century [see Ch. 34 'The Era of National Socialism']. The habits and practices of the conductors in Brahms's lifetime may offer, at best, only clues on how to do this and few reliable prescriptions.

Further Reading

J. Brahms, *Johannes Brahms im Briefwechsel mit Franz Wüllner*, ed. E. Wolff (Tutzing: Hans Schneider, 1974)

J. Draheim and G. Jahn (eds.), *Otto Dessoff (1835–1892) Ein Dirigent, Komponist und Weggefährte von Johannes Brahms* (Munich: Katzbichler, 2001)

C. Dyment, *Conducting the Brahms Symphonies: From Brahms to Boult* (Woodbridge: Boydell Press, 2016)

C. Fifield, *Hans Richter* (Woodbridge: Boydell Press, 2016)

H. J. Hinrichsen, *Musikalische Interpretation: Hans von Bülow* (Stuttgart: Franz Steiner, 1999)

M. Musgrave and B. Sherman (eds.), *Performing Brahms: Early Evidence of Performing Style* (Cambridge: Cambridge University Press, 2003)

S. Obert and M Schmidt (eds.), *Im Mass der Moderne: Felix Weingartner – Dirigent, Komponist, Autor, Reisender* (Basel: Schwabe, 2009)

A. Walker, *Hans von Bülow: A Life and Times* (Oxford and New York: Oxford University Press, 2010)

CHAPTER 21

Pianists

Michael Musgrave

Although Brahms was a fine pianist and the composer of major repertory for the instrument, he is not normally regarded as having established a 'school' of performance as such; certainly not like his pianist-composer contemporaries Liszt and Anton Rubinstein, whose numerous students promoted their teaching through technical features of performance. Although Brahms wrote an extensive set of exercises – the *51 Exercises* WoO 6 (published in 1893, but apparently dating from the 1850s and 1860s) – which clearly address the technical requirements of his own works, he often showed little interest in public performance and did not especially promote his piano works apart from the concertos (at least on the inconsistent evidence of documented first performances). By comparison, he premiered virtually all his piano chamber music: only one work, the First Piano Quartet Op. 25, was definitely not given by him [see Ch. 9 'As Pianist']. Although Brahms had a core of performer-supporters from many backgrounds and of different abilities, his own circle provided a focus, and these musicians left the most recollections of his playing and recordings of his music. By the time of his death, when his music was more fully established, it was played by most leading performers.[1]

Clara Schumann, Her Circle and Other Early Performers

The pianist most closely associated with Brahms's piano music was Clara Schumann, who, with Robert Schumann, heard Brahms play some of his earliest piano music at their first meeting in October 1853 [see Ch. 2 'The Schumanns'] and remained intimately connected with much of his output for the rest of his life. Some of the earliest public performances were by Clara Schumann. She played the Andante and Scherzo of the Piano

---

[1] Op. 25 was premiered with Clara Schumann at the piano (with J. Böie, J. Breyther and L. Lee) in Hamburg on 16 November 1861.

206

Pianists 207

Sonata Op. 5 on 23 October 1854 and the unpublished two Gavottes WoO 3 on 29 October 1855; she later gave the public premieres of the second and third Ballades Op. 10, on 21 March 1860 in Vienna, and premiered the *Variations and Fugue on a Theme of Handel* Op. 24 in Hamburg in December 1861. She played his works throughout her life including both concertos, though with their wide uncovered leaps, they lay outside her normal technical constraints.[2]

Though Brahms's music was often conceived on a more symphonic scale than the classics and early Romantics in which she excelled, Schumann clearly saw Brahms as a pianist in this broad tradition and taught his piano works to her many students. In turn, many of them came to know Brahms and his playing first-hand. She had begun teaching long before her appointment to the Hoch Conservatory in Frankfurt 1878, from which most records of her teaching date, and these students also left recordings. There was a great deal of musical interchange between Britain and the Germany: many English students studied in Germany and German students came to Britain, where the Royal Academy of Music (RAM, founded 1823) was the main instrumental focus for Brahms in England prior to the opening of the Royal College of Music (RCM) in 1883.

The earliest British student of Clara Schumann appears to have been Franklin Taylor (1843–1919), who studied with her in 1861 in Paris, after learning with various teachers including Ignaz Moscheles. He teamed up with the pioneering Agnes Zimmermann (1847–1925), who was of German birth, but settled early in England and studied at the RAM with Cipriani Potter (a keen supporter of Brahms) to give the British premiere of the *Variations on a Theme of Schumann* Op. 23 at the Monday Popular Concerts on 30 March 1874. Zimmermann had already given the UK premiere of the Second Piano Quartet Op. 26k on 6 July 1865 at Hanover Square Rooms with Ludwig Straus (violin), [S.?] Webb (viola) and Alfredo Piatti (cello). Zimmermann was later the duet pianist with Marie Krebs (1851–1900) in the British premiere of the *Liebeslieder* Op. 52 (on 15 and 27 January 1877) at the Monday and Saturday Popular Concerts at St James's Hall: Krebs, born in Germany and taught by her father Karl A. Krebs, had also come early to England, and gave the second Crystal Palace performance of the First Piano Concerto Op. 15 on

---

[2] See *Werkverzeichnis*, 14, 508, 30, 81.

208 MICHAEL MUSGRAVE

20 February 1875, later playing it at an Euterpe Concert in Leipzig on 5 November 1878.[3]

Even before this, a pioneering performance of the concerto had been given at the Crystal Palace by a student (of Henry Holmes) at the RAM, Agnes Baglehole, who presented it on 9 March 1872 at the Crystal Palace, probably with the encouragement of the director of music of the Crystal Palace, August Manns, who had already given the first UK performance of the First Serenade Op. 11. However, this was soon overshadowed by a performance by Alfred Jaëll (1832–82), a pupil of Moscheles in Vienna, who had travelled widely and now settled in London where he played frequently from 1866. He played a range of difficult new music, giving the First Concerto Op. 15 its second, and more important, UK performance at the Philharmonic Society on 23 June 1873. (The Crystal Palace also claimed the first UK performance of the Second Piano Concerto Op. 83 when the German-born Oscar Beringer (1844–1922), a pupil of Moscheles, and of Reinecke and Richter at the Leipzig Conservatory, later of Tausig in Berlin, gave the first UK performance there on 14 October 1882.)[4]

An early student of Clara Schumann who helped establish Brahms's music as a soloist was Florence May (1845–1923), who was studying with Schumann in Baden-Baden in 1871 when she met Brahms personally and received the lessons she describes in detail in her biography of the composer. She contributed to the establishment of Brahms's music in England by claiming the first public performances in England of the Handel Variations on 12 November 1873 and the *Variations on a Hungarian Song* Op. 21 no. 2 on 25 March 1874, at the Crystal Palace. Bernarr Rainbow in *New Grove* claims her as 'an authoritative player of Brahms piano music', though insufficient records exist to confirm this natural assumption definitely. However, she appears equally to have placed her efforts into her biographical work, which includes invaluable references to first Brahms performances in England.[5]

---

[3] Listed in *May II*, 103; A. Horstmann, *Untersuchungen zur Brahms-Rezeption der Jahre 1860–1880* (Hamburg: K.D. Wagner, 1986), 291. This and all following Crystal Palace references are to *Catalogue of the Principal Instrumental and Choral Works performed at the Saturday Concerts from October 1855 to May 1895* (London, Crystal Palace: F. M. Evans & Co., Ltd., [1895]), here 33.

[4] Alfred Jaëll's performance is recorded in *The Philharmonic Society of London*, compiled by M. Birket Foster (London: John Lane, The Bodley Head, 1912), 341. Beringer's performance is reported in 'Crystal Palace', *The Times* 30639 (16 October 1882), 8; *May II*, 200–1 gives an incorrect date for the first British performance of this work.

[5] B. Rainbow, 'May, Florence', in S. Sadie (ed.), *The New Grove Dictionary of Music and Musicians*, 20 vols. (London: Macmillan, 1980), vol. 11, 851.

Of later pupils of Clara Schumann who lived well into the twentieth century, most notable were Fanny Davies and Leonard Borwick. Fanny Davies (1861–1934) studied with her for two years from 1883, and from her debut in 1883 she included Brahms's works in her programmes. She gave the British premiere of the Fantasies Op. 116 and Intermezzi Op. 117 but was also very prominent in chamber performance; she was pianist in the first British performances of the Third Violin Sonata Op. 108 with Ludwig Straus, the Clarinet Sonatas Op. 120 with Richard Mühlfeld and the Clarinet Trio Op. 114 with Mühlfeld and Alfredo Piatti. Davies is especially remembered for a description of a performance of the Third Piano Trio Op. 101 with Brahms in Baden-Baden (the first performance in England was with Clara Schumann at the piano) and detailed observations of his playing. Leonard Borwick (1868–1925), reputedly Schumann's favourite student, played the First Piano Concerto Op. 15 in 1889 (aged twenty-one) under Richter at the Vienna Philharmonic Society and on 29 November 1890 at the Crystal Palace. Brahms was particularly impressed with him playing this work in 1891, writing to Schumann on 22 January that 'Borwick played quite excellently, with the most perfect freedom, warmth, energy, passion, in short everything that one could desire', and acknowledging her teaching of this.[6] But Borwick was especially associated with a mastery of the Second Piano Concerto Op. 83 which he played frequently after his Frankfurt debut in 1889.

Like Fanny Davies, Ilona Eibenschütz (1873–1967) left important recollections and recordings, though, since she retired on marriage, recordings only survive from very early and late in her life. Born in Budapest she came to London while still a young woman and was an early champion of Brahms in England. A pupil of Schumann in Frankfurt in 1886–9, she was closely connected with Brahms. But she claims significance in having premiered almost all of the two sets of later Piano Pieces Op. 118 and Op. 119 in London at a Popular Concert on 7 March 1894. A recording of a talk she made in England, in which she spontaneously played the Scherzo of the Third Piano Trio, shows a profound feeling for the music and supports Schumann's enthusiasm for her.[7]

Adelina de Lara (1872–1961) studied with Schumann from 1886, who regarded de Lara as one of her best pupils. De Lara continued her career until 1954, performing many works by Brahms. She left vivid descriptions

---

[6] Brahms to Clara Schumann, 22 January 1891, *Litzmann III*, 532–3.

[7] See Mrs Carl Derenburg (Ilona Eibenschütz), 'My Recollections of Brahms', *The Musical Times* 67/1001 (July 1926), 598–600. She delivered this recollection as a BBC talk in 1952. See the CD set *Pupils of Clara Schumann*, Pearl. Gemm CDS 9904–9. CD 6.

210   MICHAEL MUSGRAVE

of his playing and of his practical advice to her in interpreting his own music. In her eighties, she made recordings of the Rhapsody Op. 79 no. 2 and Intermezzo Op. 117 no. 1 in 1951.[8]

Other pupils of Clara Schumann acquainted with Brahms are less well documented. Although Carl Friedberg (1872–1955) came into her circle early and was definitely given lessons by Brahms on his piano music in the 1880s when Friedberg was still a teenager, these are not recorded in any detail [see Ch. 13 'As Teacher']. His importance lies in the fact that he made recordings, though, like others who did so, mainly very late in life.[9]

Other Contemporaries and Later Performers in Germany

Clara Schumann's devotion to Brahms's works was not at first paralleled in other schools of performance (Liszt never apparently played Brahms's music publicly, though he played much Schumann; nor did Rubinstein, who Brahms knew quite well in earlier years in Baden-Baden). However, there were significant exceptions.

Hans von Bülow (1830–94), a pupil of Liszt from 1851, came to know Brahms from 1854 though they did not become close till later, when he made the Meiningen Court Orchestra available for Brahms to rehearse the Fourth Symphony and conducted him in early performances of the Second Piano Concerto [see Ch. 20 'Conductors']. But he is credited with the first public performance of any Brahms piano work other than by the composer: the first Allegro from the Piano Sonata Op. 1 on 1 March 1854 in Hamburg; and he also gave the first recorded public performance of the *Variations on a Theme of Robert Schumann* Op. 9 (though as late as 1879). Perhaps the most famous example of his remarkable musicianship in relation to Brahms's piano music is his directing the First Piano Concerto Op. 15 from the keyboard on 25 November 1884.[10]

However, the fact that Liszt's pupil Carl Tausig (1841–71), one of the greatest players of the time, gave with Brahms the first performance of the Sonata for Two Pianos Op. 34bis (the two-piano version of the Piano Quintet Op. 34) on 17 April 1864 apparently arose through coincidence,

---

[8] De Lara's reminiscences are recorded in Adelina de Lara, *Finale* (London: Burke Publishing, 1955), 49ff. These and other notes are reproduced in the notes to her recordings: *Pupils of Clara Schumann*.

[9] Friedberg's recordings are Scherzo Op. 4, Intermezzi Op. 76 nos. 3 and 4, Intermezzo Op. 119 no. 3, Ballade Op. 118 no. 3 [1953]. Issued on *Carl Friedberg. The Brahms/Schumann Tradition*, Marston 52015–2.

[10] *Werkverzeichnis* gives first performances, 2, 27. The many reviews of this event on 25 November 1884 in Vienna are listed in *Johannes Brahms Gesamtausgabe*, Serie I, Bd. 8 [Klavierkonzert op. 83], Vorwort, xxv, n. 145.

Pianists

as both he and Brahms were involved in the preparation for the Vienna premiere of Wagner's *Die Meistersinger von Nürnberg* in 1863. Likewise, the Boston-born William Mason (1829–1908) was coincidentally present on the only documented occasion that Liszt ever played Brahms's music, when Brahms visited Weimar with Eduard Reményi in June 1853. But Mason retained an immediate interest in Brahms and gave the first performance of his music in the USA soon after – an early performance (probably the second) of the First Piano Trio Op. 8 in New York on 27 November 1855 with two German immigrant musicians, Theodor Thomas and Carl Bergmann.[11]

Brahms's increasing presence in Vienna from 1862 introduced him to a much wider range of performers than Hamburg, and many pianists associated with the Conservatory who were his close contemporaries became close friends and grew to maturity with him and performed his works publicly. The senior figure in his first reception in Vienna was Julius Epstein (1832–1926), a student in Vienna of Anton Halm and Professor at the Vienna Conservatory 1867–1902, whose pupils included Gustav Mahler and Ignaz Brüll (1846–1907): (Brüll himself, a Moravian pianist and composer, taught piano in Vienna and was a close friend of Brahms and frequent duettist with him). Anton Door (1833–1919), a pupil of Czerny and Simon Sechter in Vienna, Professor at the Vienna Conservatory from 1869, played the First Piano Concerto in Vienna in April 1879. The premiere of the *Variations on a Theme of Haydn* for Two Pianos Op. 56b had been given by members of Door's class in Vienna in 1874, Malwine von Benfeld and Gabriele Brauner. A Viennese player of later generation was Alfred Grünfeld (1852–1924), a pupil of Theodor Kullak, who established himself in Vienna from 1872 and was well known to Brahms; he made some of the earliest piano recordings including Brahms's Capriccio Op. 76 no. 2.[12]

---

[11] The first performance took place on 13 October 1855. See M. Struck, 'Zwischen Alter und Neuer Welt. Unbekannte Dokumente zur Uraufführung und frühen Rezeption des Klaviertrios op. 8 von Johannes Brahms in der Erstfassung', in K. Hortschansky (ed.), *Traditionen – Neuansätze. Für Anna Amalie Abert (1906–1996)* (Tutzing: Hans Schneider, 1997), 663–76.

[12] Grünfeld's performance is reproduced on CD: *Alfred Grünfeld. The First Pianist of Note to have made Recordings. 1899–1914*. Pearl. Opal 27031 98502. See also S. Kross, 'The Brahms Repertory 1890–1902', in M. Musgrave (ed.), *Brahms. Biographical, Documentary and Analytical Studies 2* (Cambridge: Cambridge University Press, 1987), 32, and Horstmann, *Untersuchungen zur Brahms-Rezeption*. Door's performance is noted in *Werkverzeichnis*, 236. May claims Door as having given the second Viennese performance of the First Piano Concerto Op. 15 in 1873 but without verification: *May II*, 103. This concerto remained a problematic work throughout Brahms's life: Theodor Leschetizky gave what appears to be its first Russian performance in St Petersburg in 1874; see E. Tsareva, 'Brahms's Kammermusik in Russland 1870–1900', in I. Fuchs (ed.), *Internationaler Brahms-Kongress Gmunden 1997. Kongressbericht* (Tutzing: Hans Schneider, 2001), 218.

By the 1880s, Brahms's piano works were becoming a necessary part of the new repertory of expanding difficulty, and players from a wider range of backgrounds were attracted to them. Most prominent were Robert Freund and Eugen d'Albert. Though the Hungarian Robert Freund (1852–1936) was Liszt's student, he became well known to Brahms (and accompanied him in 1893 on one of Brahms's Italian holiday trips – see Ch. 7 'Holidays'). Brahms admired his playing, and Freund performed the First Piano Concerto on 8 December 1892, under Carl Reinecke, with the Rhapsody Op. 79 no. 1 at the Leipzig Gewandhaus. Freund's much younger sister Etelka Freund (1879–1977) knew Brahms, played for him often and left some recordings made late in life, in 1950–3. Eugen d'Albert (1864–1932), of German and Scottish parentage, who trained under Ernst Pauer at the National Training School, the predecessor of the Royal College of Music, and later with Liszt, also knew Brahms well. He played both concertos in one evening under Brahms (31 January 1895), though Kross says it was not appreciated by the Berlin critics.[13]

The Second Piano Concerto Op. 83 was an inevitable magnet for aspiring pianists, since it was effectively Brahms's greatest assertion of his pianistic command: he unusually premiered and toured it himself from its premiere in Budapest in 1882. After the earlier attempts previously noted, performances became more frequent and displayed greater command from the later 1880s. Brahms's Dutch friend Julius Röntgen (1855–1932) played it at the Leipzig Gewandhaus on 28 January 1886. The Scottish Liszt student Frederick Lamond (1868–1948), born, like d'Albert in Glasgow, played it on 14 May 1891 at the Philharmonic Society. Max Pauer (1866–1945) and Ernő Dohnányi (1877–1960) played it in England and Karl Heinrich Barth (1847–1922), a pupil of Bülow and Tausig, and friend of Brahms, played it at the Crystal Palace on 8 November 1884, as did Marmaduke Barton (1865–1938), trained at the RCM, on 14 March 1891. Frederick Dawson (1868–1940), a pupil of Hallé and Rubinstein, played both concertos in one concert in 1898. Kross asserts that in Germany Willi Rehberg (1863–1937) made a speciality of it, citing that of the twenty verified performances in the 1899–1900 season (reviewed in the *Musikalisches Wochenblatt*) at least half were by Rehberg, while Busoni played it only twice in the same period. In the USA Rafael Joseffy (1852–1915), a Hungarian pupil of Tausig and

---

[13] Listing in J. Forner, *Die Gewandhauskonzerte zu Leipzig 1791–1981*, 2 vols. (Leipzig: VEB Deutscher Verlag für Musik, 1981), vol. 2: Programmstatistik, 401; Kross, 'The Brahms Repertory 1890–1902', 32. Recordings by Etelka Freund include the Piano Sonata Op. 5; *Variations and Fugue on a Theme of Handel* Op. 24, theme and variations 1–12; and the Intermezzo Op.118 no. 6, available on *Brahms: Recaptured by Pupils and Colleagues*, Arbiter 163.

Pianists 213

Liszt, who had settled in New York from 1879, was a pioneer performer of Brahms in the USA. He gave apparently the first USA performance of the Concerto on 9 December 1882 with the New York Philharmonic, and in 1896 with the Boston Symphony Orchestra.[14]

Conclusions and Lines of Descent

The lack of parallel accounts or recordings of the performance of any one work make it difficult to draw conclusions about any one tradition of Brahms playing. Although the pupils of Clara Schumann certainly claimed to follow her precepts, these cannot be demonstrated with regard to Brahms. And though there are clear lines of descent from these and other later contemporaries of Brahms to their students, who were frequently recorded with the highest technical standards, they are defined more by individual musical insights rather than technical features of playing. If one compares the best work of modern recorded artists, whether descended from the Schumann school, like Solomon (born Solomon Cutner, 1902–88: taught by Mathilde Wurm), or independently, like Myra Hess (1890–1965: RAM and Matthay), Artur Schnabel (1882–1951: Leschetizky) or Egon Petri (1881–1962: Busoni), they respond differently to the music itself in equally satisfying ways. And this accords with what we know of Brahms's view of performance: that, allowing for certain natural characteristics of his performances – flexibility of tempo above all – it was always characterised by practicality and the interests of a musically effective result.

Further Reading

G. Bozarth, 'Fanny Davies and Brahms's Late Chamber Music', in M. Musgrave and B. Sherman (eds.), *Performing Brahms: Early Evidence of Performing Style* (Cambridge: Cambridge University Press, 2003), 170–219

W. Crutchfield, 'Brahms, by Those Who Knew Him', *Opus* 2/5 (August 1986), 12–21 and 60

F. Davies, 'Some Personal Recollections of Brahms as Pianist and Interpreter' in the article 'Brahms', in *Cobbett's Cyclopedia Survey of Chamber Music*, 2 vols.

---

[14] Forner, *Die Gewandhauskonzerte*, 387; Foster, *The Philharmonic Society*, 341. Pauer, Dohnyáni and Rehberg are noted in Kross, 'The Brahms Repertory 1890–1902', 32; *The Philharmonic Society of London*, 426. Joseffy is noted in M. Musgrave, 'Brahms-Rezeption in den USA bis 1900', in *Internationaler Brahms-Kongress Gmunden*, 355; Dawson is listed in P. A. Scholes, *The Mirror of Music*, 2 vols. (London: Novello, 1941) vol. 2, 311.

(Oxford: Oxford University Press, 1929. repr. with additional material, 1963), vol. 1, 182

H. P. Greene, 'Leonard Borwick. Some Personal Recollections', *Music and Letters* 7/1 (1926), 17

J. Northrop Moore, Notes to *Pupils of Clara Schumann*, Pearl. Gemm CDS 9904–9

CHAPTER 22

Other Instrumentalists

Heather Platt

Throughout his career, Brahms forged significant professional and personal relationships with a variety of instrumentalists, ranging from talented amateurs to highly accomplished professionals. The violinist Joseph Joachim (1831–1907), cellist Robert Hausmann (1852–1909) and clarinettist Richard Mühlfeld (1856–1907) numbered among Brahms's closest friends. Through their performances and interactions, these men inspired the composer and gave him concrete advice about writing idiomatically for their respective instruments. Because many of their exchanges took place while making music at the homes of friends, we will never know the full extent of the impact that they had on Brahms. Nevertheless, letters, diaries, personal recollections of friends and the few remaining manuscripts revealing Brahms's creative process, all provide us with a window into the multifaceted nature of their influence.

Joseph Joachim

From the very beginning, Joachim played a significant role in Brahms's career. The two first met in 1853 while Brahms was touring as the pianist for the Hungarian violinist Eduard Reményi [see Ch. 1 'Childhood in Hamburg']. Reményi and Joachim had previously met when they were both studying in Vienna. Although Joachim was only two years older than Brahms, he had the musical experience and professional worldview of a more senior man. In 1844, at only twelve years of age, he had achieved iconic status when he performed Beethoven's Violin Concerto Op. 61 in London under his teacher Felix Mendelssohn.[1] Through Mendelssohn's guidance, Joachim performed for some of the most prominent musicians of the era, including Berlioz, Liszt and the Schumanns. Years later,

---

[1] A. Moser, *Joseph Joachim: A Biography (1831–1899)*, trans. L. Durham (London: Welby, 1901). All Joachim biographies rely on Joachim's pupil Moser, whose biography was authorised by the violinist.

215

Joachim, in turn, ushered the young Brahms into the vast network of associates he had established, which included such luminaries as the writer Bettina von Arnim. After meeting Joachim, Brahms visited Weimar, where the violinist had served as Liszt's concertmaster from 1850 to 1853; there he met Joachim's former colleagues Liszt, Peter Cornelius (1824–74) and Joachim Raff (1822–82). With Joachim's encouragement, Brahms then travelled to Düsseldorf to meet the Schumanns.

The 1853 F–A–E Sonata for violin and piano, which Schumann, Brahms and Albert Dietrich composed for Joachim, illustrates the camaraderie Brahms quickly established with his new friends. The letters stood for *Frei aber einsam* (*Free but Alone*), Joachim's personal motto, and the composers wove the corresponding musical motive throughout the sonata. Joachim employed this motive in his own compositions, and Brahms also used it in later works that were also connected to the Schumanns and Joachim, including the finale of his Piano Sonata Op. 5.[2]

Further evidence of the bond that the young Brahms and Joachim established is documented by their 1860 Manifesto [see Ch. 9 'As Pianist']. While working for Liszt, Joachim had participated actively in Weimar's musical culture, and had responded especially enthusiastically to the music of Wagner. In 1857, however, he broke with Liszt, and three years later he joined with Brahms, Julius Otto Grimm and Bernhard Scholz to pen a Manifesto separating their aesthetics from those of the New German School. Unfortunately, this project came to an embarrassing end when an unfinished version of the document was published in the Berlin journal *Echo*.

In the wake of Robert Schumann's final illness and death, Brahms and Joachim provided Clara Schumann with much-needed support. Moreover, the three built a tight professional bond, performing together and promoting Brahms and Robert's compositions. Joachim and Clara also gave Brahms invaluable advice on composition. Indeed, throughout his career, Brahms frequently sent or played Joachim and Clara Schumann early versions of his compositions. Although both men began composing at a very young age, Joachim could draw on a wealth of experience as a performer with and conductor of orchestras and chamber ensembles. Brahms, who lacked this experience, greatly benefited from Joachim's expertise, particularly during the 1850s when he was writing his first orchestral works. Among these was

---

[2] Joachim acknowledged the programmatic and self-referential character of his compositions by labelling them as 'psychological music'. See K. Uhde, '*Psychologische Musik*, Joseph Joachim, and the Search for a New Music Aesthetic', PhD dissertation, Duke University (2014); and J. Daverio, *Crossing Paths: Schubert, Schumann, & Brahms* (Oxford: Oxford University Press, 2002), 103–20.

Example 22.1. Evolution of the solo violin line in the Violin Concerto Op. 77, first movement, bars 102–4, reproduced from B. Schwarz, 'Joseph Joachim and the Genesis of Brahms's Violin Concerto', *Musical Quarterly* 69/4 (Autumn 1983), 514.

Ex. 1a. First version, solo part No. 1

Ex. 1b. Brahms's alternate version in solo part No. 1 and holograph score

Ex. 1c. Joachim's correction in solo part No. 3, entered in holograph score (red ink), final version

a large-scale piece that ultimately became the First Piano Concerto Op. 15. During his tenure as concertmaster at the court of Hanover (1853–68), Joachim conducted a trial performance of this concerto, and he arranged similar rehearsals for the composer's First Serenade Op. 11 and First String Sextet Op. 18. Trials like these became an important part of the composer's creative process because they enabled him to hear a new work and make significant changes to the score before a public debut.

Joachim's time in Hanover was his most active period as a composer. During these years, the two men critiqued drafts of each other's compositions, and in 1856 they exchanged counterpoint exercises. By the time Brahms began his Violin Concerto Op. 77 in 1878, Joachim had composed five works for solo violin and orchestra, including the Hungarian Concerto Op. 11, which he dedicated to Brahms. That Brahms's own concerto has a Hungarian-style finale is no doubt a reflection of Joachim's concerto and heritage as well as of their shared admiration of this style. Joachim offered Brahms advice on the new concerto's solo parts and accompanying orchestral textures. As often happened when requesting his colleagues' input, Brahms decided against some of these suggestions; however, in Example 22.1, Schwarz identified one place where Brahms accepted the violinist's advice. In this passage from the concerto's first movement, Joachim recommended changing one pitch of Brahms's second draft to make the writing more idiomatic.[3] According to John Alexander Fuller Maitland, Joachim's first English biographer:

> Every note that Brahms wrote for violin, whether in chamber or orchestral music, was such as it would have been congenial to Joachim to play; and in the violin concerto, op. 77, and the concerto for violin and violoncello, op. 102, the special polyphonic effects in which Joachim was unrivalled among the violinist of all time are found in abundance.[4]

In a review of the Violin Concerto's premiere, which Brahms conducted, Alfred Dörffel wrote, 'Joachim played . . . with a love and devotion which brought home to us in every bar the direct or indirect share he has had in the work.'[5] Undoubtedly, Joachim did contribute to the composition of the concerto. However, one must also consider that Joachim's audiences commonly reported that he played as though he were channelling the composer whose music he was performing. This phenomenon dates back to his first performance of Beethoven's Violin Concerto, when critics reported perceiving Joachim as Beethoven. Even Brahms experienced this effect when he first heard Joachim playing this work.[6]

In the course of Brahms and Joachim's work on the concerto, Brahms also composed the First Violin Sonata Op. 78. This sonata, and particularly its slow movement, is now understood as Brahms's expression of deep concern for Clara Schumann and her son Felix, an amateur violinist and Brahms's godson, as they grappled with Felix's deteriorating health.[7] As with the concerto, Brahms and Joachim toured with this work together.

Despite the success of these two pieces, the Brahms–Joachim friendship ruptured shortly thereafter. Recognising the darker aspects of his friend's personality, which extended to matters of control and unwarranted jealousy, Brahms took the side of Joachim's wife Amalie during the couple's 1880 separation and subsequent divorce [see Ch. 19 'Singers']. However, in 1884, Brahms once again called on the violinist for assistance. This time he was writing a double concerto for violin and cello in which Robert Hausmann, the cellist of the Joachim Quartet, would team up with Joachim. In response to Brahms's queries, both soloists made numerous

---

[3] B. Schwarz, 'Joseph Joachim and the Genesis of Brahms's Violin Concerto', *Musical Quarterly* 69/4 (Autumn 1983), 514. See also the critical editions of the concerto: *JBG, Violinkonzert*, and C. Brown (ed.), *Konzert in D-Dur für Violine und Orchester* Op. 77 (Kassel: Bärenreiter, 2006).

[4] J. A. Fuller Maitland, *Brahms* (New York: John Lane Company, 1911), 49–50.   [5] *May II*, 178.

[6] Brahms to Joachim, c. 22 February 1855, *Avins*, 91.

[7] M. Struck, 'New Evidence of the Genesis of Brahms's G major Violin Sonata, Op. 78', *American Brahms Society Newsletter* 9/1 (Spring 1991), 5–6.

Other Instrumentalists 219

suggestions for their respective parts, with Joachim increasing the level of virtuosity for the solo violin part. This concerto also employs the Hungarian style that characterises other compositions that Brahms and Joachim had worked on together, including Brahms's Violin Concerto Op. 77, his First Piano Concerto Op. 15 and Joachim's Hungarian Concerto.

From his earliest student years in Vienna, Joachim had performed in string quartets. Upon assuming the role of founding director of Berlin's Königliche Hochschule für Musik in 1869, he formed the Joachim Quartet with other faculty members. Over time the group's membership changed, but at the peak of its fame Joachim was joined by the musicians shown in Figure 22.1: Heinrich de Ahna (1835–92) on second violin, Emanuel Wirth (1842–1923) on viola and Robert Hausmann on cello. Through their concerts in Berlin as well as on tour throughout Europe, the quartet consistently promoted Brahms's music. Indeed, as late as 1906 the ensemble, with the assistance of Mühlfeld and English musicians including Donald Francis Tovey, presented a series of concerts in London's Queen's Hall encompassing almost all of Brahms's chamber works.

Although Joachim's ensemble gave the premieres of Brahms's Second and Third String Quartets (Op. 51 no. 2 and Op. 67), it was Vienna's Hellmesberger Quartet (1849–87) that premiered the First Quartet Op. 51 no. 1. For that occasion, the quartet included Joseph Hellmesberger and his son bearing the same name, Sigismund Bachrich and Heinrich Röver. Like the Joachim group, the Hellmesberger Quartet played a significant role in Brahms's career, performing many of his string chamber works (not just his quartets). Brahms made his first appearance in Vienna giving the premiere of his Second Piano Quartet Op. 26 with this group. Perhaps ironically, Brahms did not dedicate his string quartets to either ensemble but rather to significant friends: he dedicated the Quartets Op. 51 to Theodor Billroth, a surgeon whose home functioned as a salon in which many of Brahms's pieces were heard for the first time [see Ch. 3 'Vienna'], and Op. 67 to Theodor Wilhelm Engelmann, a physiologist and amateur cellist who married Emma Brandes, a pianist whose playing was praised by Clara Schumann.

Other violinists who were both colleagues and friends of Brahms included students of Joachim. For instance, Jenő Hubay (1858–1937) joined Brahms in premiering the Third Violin Sonata Op. 108 (1888); he also promoted Brahms's chamber works with the quartet he established. Richard Barth (1850–1923) performed the Violin Concerto

Figure 22.1. Portrait of the Joachim Quartet. Beethoven Feier in Bonn, 11–15 May 1890.

Op. 77 under the composer and the two also performed many of Brahms's chamber pieces not only in public but also in private gatherings, for instance at the house of Laura von Beckerath. As a conductor in Hamburg, Barth also promoted Brahms's orchestral and choral works. Whereas Joachim introduced Brahms to numerous musicians who would become close friends and collaborators, it was Brahms who introduced the young Marie Soldat-Röger (1863–1955) to Joachim. After studying with Joachim, she collaborated with Brahms in numerous public and private venues. When she first performed the Violin Concerto, Brahms modified a version of Joachim's cadenza especially for her. She also performed the Double Concerto Op. 102 with one of Brahms's favourite cellists, Robert Hausmann.

Robert Hausmann

Robert Hausmann's career was in large part shaped by Joachim. In 1869, Hausmann became one of the first students at the Berlin Hochschule, where he studied with Wilhelm Müller, the original cellist in the Joachim Quartet. Then in 1871 he went to London to study with Alfredo Piatti, a cellist who performed in Joachim's English quartet. After returning to Germany and performing in Graf Hochberg's quartet in Silesia, Hausmann joined the faculty at the Hochschule, and in 1879 he joined the Joachim Quartet. Hausmann's skill was widely recognised; Max Bruch, Heinrich von Herzogenberg, Charles Villiers Stanford and Tovey all wrote solo cello pieces for him. Aside from chamber repertoire, he gave multiple performances of the Schumann, Dvořák and Molique cello concertos. Indeed, during one of his last meetings with Brahms, the two played through a cello-piano arrangement of the Dvořák.

Aside from Joachim, Hausmann was the only member of the Joachim Quartet who established a personal relationship with Brahms. He made music and socialised with many of Brahms's closest friends – including the Herzogenbergs, Klaus Groth and Hermine Spies. During the mid-1880s, Hausmann and Brahms gave several performances of the composer's First Cello Sonata Op. 38 at the homes of Brahms's friends, the von Beckeraths and the Fellingers.

It seems that Hausmann's masterful public performance of this sonata inspired Brahms to respond to the cellist's request for a new sonata. The colouristic effects in the resulting Second Cello Sonata Op. 99, including the use of the high register, pizzicato in the second and fourth movements, and prominent tremolandi in the first movement, have been attributed to Hausmann's calibre as a musician. By contrast, such effects are absent from the First Cello Sonata, written for Brahms's Viennese friend Josef Gänsbacher (1829–1911), an amateur cellist. Prior to the Second Sonata's public premiere in November 1886, Brahms and Hausmann gave informal performances of the work for friends. Joined by Soldat-Röger, they also presented two other new pieces from Brahms's remarkably productive summer of that year: the Second Violin Sonata Op. 100 and the Third Piano Trio Op. 101.

Following the premiere of the Second Cello Sonata, Hausmann and Joachim premiered the Double Concerto Op. 102 with Brahms conducting. The three friends toured through Germany and Switzerland with the work, after which the two soloists took it to London and Vienna. In 1888 Joachim performed the work with cellist Julius Klengel, but sources

HEATHER PLATT

indicate that he preferred Hausmann's warmer tone.[8] In the years that followed, Hausmann continued to perform Brahms's latest chamber works, and joined Richard Mühlfeld in some of the earliest performances of the Clarinet Trio Op. 114 and Quintet Op. 115.

Richard Mühlfeld

Brahms first met Mühlfeld in 1881 while visiting Meiningen at the invitation of Hans von Bülow – a conductor and pianist Brahms had met through Joachim. By this time, Mühlfeld was serving as first clarinettist of the Meiningen Orchestra. Although it was von Bülow who spearheaded the orchestra's growing international reputation during the 1880s, their success was attributed partly to Mühlfeld's influence. Having captured the attention of Wagner when the orchestra played at Bayreuth, Mühlfeld also played solo clarinet at Bayreuth from 1884 to 1896 under Hermann Levi, Felix Mottl and Richard Strauss.

The clarinettist's musicianship stirred Brahms to continue composing even after he had declared retirement. Upon hearing Mühlfeld's 1890 performance of Weber's Clarinet Concerto Op. 73, Brahms was inspired to write a clarinet trio and quintet.[9] The successful premiere of these pieces in Meiningen, with Hausmann playing cello, led Joachim to include both works in one of his quartet's Singakademie concerts in Berlin. This gesture was notable because previously the concert series had featured exclusively music for strings. Prior to the Berlin concert, Mühlfeld met the painter Adolph Menzel, a friend of Brahms. Figure 22.2 displays the sketch Menzel subsequently sent Brahms. His accompanying note described the clarinettist as Brahms's muse.

Both the Quintet and Mühlfeld were highly acclaimed by a wide array of musicians. In a letter to Brahms, Clara Schumann wrote, 'And the man plays so wonderfully, he might have been created for your works. I marvelled at his profound simplicity and the subtlety of his understanding.'[10] Like many other observers, she praised the writing in the Adagio, with its passages that allowed Mühlfeld to showcase the full range of his instrument (see the passage in Example 22.2).

---

[8] F. B. Hausmann, 'Brahms und Hausmann', *Brahms-Studien* 7 (1987), 25. Michael Struck discusses all of the primary sources for this concerto in his edition of the work; *JBG, Doppelkonzert*.

[9] See C. Lawson, *Brahms: Clarinet Quintet* (Cambridge: Cambridge University Press, 1998), particularly 16–20 and 34.

[10] 18 March 1893, *SBB II*, 222.

Figure 22.2. Adolph Menzel's 1891 sketch of Mühlfeld as a Greek god.

In March 1892, Mühlfeld undertook his first tour of England, performing Brahms's new works with Joachim and his English colleagues. In subsequent years, he performed the quintet with the Soldat-Röger, Skalitzki, Kneisel and Halir Quartets. He also performed the work with the Heerman Quartet. Led by the violinist Hugo Heermann, a colleague of Clara Schumann's in Frankfurt, this ensemble played many of Brahms's chamber works, in some cases collaborating with Clara Schumann, Joachim and the composer himself. Performing Brahms's works with members of the composer's extended circle of associates expanded Mühlfeld's career, and this was even more the case after Brahms wrote the two Clarinet Sonatas Op. 120 for him in 1894.

Example 22.2. Brahms, Clarinet Quintet Op. 115, second movement, bars 52–7.

In 1895, Brahms and Mühlfeld premiered these sonatas in Vienna during concerts of the Rosé String Quartet, an ensemble led by Arnold Rosé that had earlier premiered Brahms's Second String Quintet Op. 111 (1890) and

Other Instrumentalists 225

given the Viennese premiere of the Clarinet Quintet (1892). The duo then toured Germany with the sonatas. Collaborating with Mühlfeld was one of Brahms's last great joys; the two bonded musically and personally, with Brahms affectionately referring to the younger man as 'Fräulein von Mühlfeld, my Primadonna'.[11]

Mühlfeld continued to tour Europe until his death in 1907. Aside from Brahms's compositions, he performed works by Weber, Mozart, Beethoven, Schubert and Strauss. Composers who wrote pieces for him included Gustav Jenner (a composition student of Brahms – see Ch. 13 'As Teacher'), Theodor Verhey, Carl Reinecke, Stephan Krehl and Henri Marteau. Hailed as a model for orchestral clarinettists, Mühlfeld has been credited with kindling an increased interest in the instrument.

Above all, Joachim, Hausmann and Mühlfeld shared a crucial aesthetic with Brahms and Clara Schumann. Critics recognised that for each of these musicians, the faithful interpretation of a composition was far more important than sheer instrumental virtuosity. An 1897 *Musical Times* review described Hausmann's 'wonted breadth of phrasing and purity of style', and the journal's 1909 obituary noted, 'His playing was characterised by great power, yet also with artistic restraint.'[12] Words like 'purity', 'subtlety' and 'restraint' similarly pervaded descriptions of Joachim and Mühlfeld's playing. And yet, despite claims that they were steadfastly following a composer's 'intentions', their performances were highly nuanced; they were in no way depersonalised representations of a composer's score. For example, the 1895 *Musikalisches Wochenblatt* reported that Brahms and Mühlfeld's performance of the Clarinet Sonata Op. 120 no. 1 'seemed like two intimately communicating musical souls were spontaneously improvising'.[13]

While scholars have likely identified most of the significant performances of Brahms's compositions by Joachim, Hausmann and Mühlfeld, they are still developing ways to understand these instrumentalists' performing techniques. In addition to studying Mühlfeld's instruments, they are interrogating the early recordings of Joachim and his students, as well as any related contemporary documents that reference performance pedagogy. They focus on interpretative techniques, including the use of vibrato and generous rubato [see Ch. 37 'Historical Performance']. Just as intriguing is the work of scholars such as Karen Leistra-Jones, who is exploring

---

[11] *May II*, 251.
[12] 'Crystal Palace Concerts', *Musical Times and Singing Class Circular*, 38/658 (1 December 1897), 818; 'Obituary: Professor Hausmann', *The Musical Times*, 50/793 (1 March 1909), 173.
[13] F., 'Bericht: Leipzig', *Musikalisches Wochenblatt* 26/7 (7 February 1895), 82.

the extent to which the concept of adhering closely to a composer's score was a highly successful, premeditated marketing strategy, which ultimately impacted the culture of concerts even into the twentieth century.[14] That the repeated claims regarding these performers reproducing a composer's intentions intersect uncomfortably with the intentional fallacy is another thread that could well be further explored. Yet even as scholars cast new light on Brahms's colleagues, what remains uncontested is that Brahms and the instrumentalists who inspired him shared common aesthetics of composition and performance, and that they deeply benefited both musically and personally from each other's friendships.

Further Reading

B. Borchard, *Stimme und Geige: Amalie und Joseph Joachim, Biographie und Interpretationsgeschichte* (Vienna: Böhlau, 2005, rpt. 2007). See also the review of this book by V. W. Goertzen, 'Review', in *The American Brahms Society Newsletter* 29/1 (Spring 2011), 6–8

R. Eshbach, 'Der Geigerkönig: Joseph Joachim as a Performer', *Die Tonkunst* 1/3 (July 2007), 205–17

R. Eshbach, *Joseph Joachim – Biography and Research*, https://josephjoachim.com

R. Eshbach, 'Joachim's Youth – Joachim's Jewishness', *Musical Quarterly* 94/4 (2011), 548–92

M. Goltz and H. Müller, *Der Brahms-Klarinettist Richard Mühlfeld/ Richard Mühlfeld Brahms' Clarinetist*, trans. M. Lemmel (Balve: Artivo, 2007)

K. Leistra-Jones, 'Staging Authenticity: Joachim, Brahms, and the Politics of *Werktreue* Performance', *Journal of the American Musicological Society* 66/2 (Summer 2013), 397–436

K. Leistra-Jones, 'Improvisational Idyll: Joachim's 'Presence' and Brahms's Violin Concerto, op. 77', *19th-Century Music* 38/3 (Spring 2015), 243–71

R. Wilson, 'Style and Interpretation in the Nineteenth-Century German Violin School with Particular Reference to the Three Sonatas for Pianoforte and Violin by Johannes Brahms', PhD dissertation, University of Sydney, Sydney Conservatorium of Music (2015)

---

[14] K. Leistra-Jones, 'Staging Authenticity: Joachim, Brahms, and the Politics of *Werktreue* Performance', *Journal of the American Musicological Society* 66/2 (Summer 2013), 397–436; and 'Improvisational Idyll: Joachim's 'Presence' and Brahms's Violin Concerto, op. 77', *19th-Century Music* 38/3 (Spring 2015), 243–71.

CHAPTER 23

Instruments

Anneke Scott

During the long nineteenth century, the design of most musical instruments changed considerably. While the late nineteenth-century orchestra may be familiar in terms of size, configuration and instrumental design, musicians of Mozart and Haydn's era would be forgiven for not immediately recognising the descendants of the instruments that they themselves played. The industrial revolution generated new technologies and ways of manufacturing which impacted upon the musical world. Woodwind instruments gained more keys, brass instruments acquired new valve technology, strings would eventually transition from gut to metal strings, and metal-framed pianos allowed for more stable instruments with a larger pitch and dynamic range. Within individual histories of these instruments, it is difficult to pinpoint when changes were accepted and adopted. Communities (e.g. soloists, orchestral musicians, amateurs) and countries varied enormously. Furthermore, sections in an orchestra often contained differing styles of instrument alongside one another, for example woodwind instruments with different key systems or brass instruments with different types of valve design.

A driving force was the growth in size of both ensembles and venues. The Viennese Imperial Orchestra comprised fewer than thirty musicians in 1807. By 1842 the earliest form of the Vienna Philharmonic Orchestra consisted of sixty-nine musicians, growing to over a hundred by 1900. In 1870 it moved to its new, purpose-built home, the Musikverein of the Gesellschaft der Musikfreunde. The Grosser Musikvereinssaal seats 1,744 with additional standing room for 300 people, far larger than the 1822 Gesellschaft der Musikfreunde hall, a 500-seat hall attached to the *Roter Igel* (*Red Hedgehog*) restaurant. Larger venues meant that musicians needed instruments with greater carrying power. Seeking to achieve this often altered what many felt were the innate qualities of each instrument. For example, bassoon players and makers questioned whether experiments with the size and material of the bell compromised the instrument's tone.[1]

Of all the instruments in the orchestra, the late nineteenth-century string family is the most unchanged. The strings were still mostly made of gut, familiar to earlier eighteenth-century musicians, since metal strings were regarded as unstable and of a poor tone. Aids such as violin chin rests and cello endpins were not yet standard. The adoption of the chin rest can be seen in portraits of Brahms's close friend, the violinist Joseph Joachim. George Frederic Watts's 1866 portrait appears to depict him playing, like his contemporaries of the time, without a chin rest, while in a later photographic portrait from 1890, he is using one.[2] Concerns were raised that chin rests posed an acoustic disadvantage, damping the resonance of the instrument.[3]

The use of cello endpins had been known since at least the mid-eighteenth century, and, while the short, fixed-length endpins became more common from the mid-nineteenth century, cellists such as Alfredo Piatti and Robert Hausmann preferred not to use them. This development was driven more by the need for the instrument to project than by the need for the performer to ascend the fingerboard to ever higher pitches. Traditionally the instrument had been braced between the cellist's legs, a method which, if holding the instrument by the ribs rather than the edges, risked damping the resonance and projection of the instrument. The debate as to how to ensure the cello projected well extended to whether metal or wooden endpins aided the sonic power of the instrument.[4] Still, students were encouraged to learn without chin rests and endpins, in order to prevent bad habits like extraneous movement. The resultant playing style reflected the practical considerations associated with a more audible changing of position of the left hand; this shaped aesthetic preferences such as the use of portamento, portato and articulation with both the left hand on the fingerboard and the right hand with the bow. Then as now, string players greatly admired Italian instruments of the sixteenth and seventeenth centuries, which would have been altered to suit the playing style of the era; for example, the necks of instruments were altered so that the fingerboard was at a higher angle. Both Joachim and the

---

[1] J. B. Kopp, *The Bassoon* (New Haven & London: Yale University Press, 2012), 126.

[2] 11–15 May 1890. *Portrait of Alfredo Piatti, Carl Reinecke and Joseph Joachim with Musical Quotations. Beethoven Feier in Bonn, 11–15 Mai 1890.* [Sepia photograph] (Royal Academy of Music, Museum & Collections, 2004.604).

[3] L. Auer, *Graded Course of Violin Playing* (New York: Carl Fisher, 1925), 10.

[4] G. Kennaway, *Playing the Cello, 1780–1930* (Farnham, Surrey: Ashgate, 2014) 6–16, 33–4.

Instruments 229

cellist Robert Hausmann, for whom Brahms wrote several works, owned Stradivari.

Brahms uses a woodwind section consisting of the same forces as found in Beethoven's Ninth Symphony Op. 125: two flutes plus piccolo, two oboes, two clarinets and two bassoons plus contrabassoon. Still, the instruments themselves had changed: makers had experimented with additional keys and new key systems to achieve a greater chromatic and dynamic range. Previously, wind players used forked fingerings (opening a hole while closing one or two holes below it) on their instruments to get more chromatic notes; it often caused timbral changes, with some notes more 'covered' or dull than others, something that skilful composers and performers could exploit as an expressive device.

The prolific music press included reports on the latest acoustic research, and makers sought ways to build instruments incorporating this knowledge.[5] More advanced key work allowed performers to open and close holes on their instruments which their fingers could not otherwise reach. New designs appeared for the flute, clarinet, oboe and bassoon. However, the peculiarities of how different wind instruments produce their sound (single reed, double reed, edge blown), meant that often it was not straightforward for the scientific findings of this period to be applied to instrument manufacture. Makers experimented with different materials; softer woods such as boxwood were replaced by the harder cocus wood around mid-century and African blackwood by the early 1900s.[6] Such experiments went hand in hand with adjustments to bore profiles, which could drastically alter an instrument's timbre and playing characteristics. Theobald Boehm designed the first cylindrical metal flute in 1847, instigating the move away from wood. The wooden flute was perceived as softer, more mellow and requiring a tighter embouchure, while the more penetrating silver flute required a more relaxed embouchure. Another advantage of metal was the stability of the instrument, as the humidity of a musician's breath risks cracking a wooden instrument. Makers also experimented with metal clarinets, oboes and bassoons, and created sleeves and other linings for the inner bore of instruments to overcome this problem.

Early woodwind instruments were built in a variety of keys, either to get around the challenges of certain keys by avoiding too many chromatic notes (e.g. clarinets in A, B♭ and C), or as an auxiliary to the regular

---

[5] See, for example, G. Weber, 'Wesentliche Verbesserungen des Fagotts', *Caecilia* 2 (1825), 123–40.
[6] A. Carse, *Musical Wind Instruments* (London: Macmillan, 1939), 81–209.

instrument (such as the lower pitched flute, and the oboe and clarinet d'amore). The expansion of the orchestra can be seen in the extension of the woodwind section. As mentioned above, Brahms extended the flute section only with a piccolo (most notably in the Fourth Symphony Op. 98 and *A German Requiem* Op. 45). He did not extend the oboe section at all, foregoing the cor anglais which Wagner chose for an extensive solo in *Tristan und Isolde* (1865). Nor did he use either the higher E♭ clarinet or bass clarinet, whereas Mahler favoured both in his First Symphony. Adolphe Sax's family of saxophones, developed in the 1840s by attaching a bass clarinet mouthpiece to the body of an ophicleide, was not used by Brahms, but other composers encouraged experimentation: Verdi, for example, tasked his publisher Ricordi with sourcing three 'big flutes' in B♭ and A♭ for his opera *Aida*[7] to add to an exotic scoring which also featured specially invented 'Aida' trumpets by Pelitti.[8] Wagner feverishly sought a new sound for his orchestra, part horn, part tuba, in order to create his 'Wagner Tubas' in 1875.[9] However, Brahms frequently required the contrabassoon, in both his symphonic and large-scale choral compositions.

Among the woodwind instruments that Brahms knew are the stained boxwood clarinets by the Munich maker Georg Ottensteiner belonging to Richard Mühlfeld, principal clarinet of the Meiningen Orchestra, preserved in the Meiningen Museum. The two instruments, in B♭ and A, use the Baermann keywork system, jointly patented by clarinet player and teacher Carl Baermann and Ottensteiner, which aimed to improve intonation by relocating the tone holes. It also allowed more combinations of fingerings for different notes, giving players options in demanding passages. The instrument is softer, lighter and more mellow than the Boehm system instruments preferred in France, which were designed by clarinet player and teacher Hyacinthe Eléonore Klosé and instrument maker Louis-Auguste Buffet in 1843.

Like woodwind instruments, brass instrument designs were reimagined. The average brass section of the early nineteenth century included a pair of natural horns and a pair of natural trumpets. Pairs of cornets were often used alongside pairs of natural trumpets. Trombones had nearly died out in the late eighteenth century, though small pockets of activity, such as

---

[7] H. Busch, *Verdi's Aida: The History of an Opera in Letters and Documents* (Minneapolis: University of Minnesota Press, 1978), 235–246 *passim*.

[8] M. Renato, 'The Pelitti firm: Makers of brass instruments in nineteenth-century Italy', trans. E. Pelitti, *Historic Brass Society Journal* 6 (1994), 320.

[9] W. Melton, *The Wagner Tuba: A History* (Aachen: Edition Ebenos, 2008), 46.

Instruments 231

Vienna, retained the instrument. However, the invention of the valve in 1814 triggered major changes in brass instrument design. Coal miner, Berghautboist ('mine musician') and early inventor of the valve Friedrich Blühmel was inspired by the air pipes in the mine in which he worked and set about applying the valve technology he saw there to brass instruments, initially to the horn.[10] Uptake of this new design was initially patchy as the nascent technology was unreliable. Several early practitioners championed the new valve instruments through solo or chamber repertoire, presumably partially as a spectacle.[11]

The valve is essentially a mechanical way of altering the pathway of the air so that the overall length of the instrument can be changed. Each length allowed an alternative set of harmonics to be played. The three most successful designs are still used today. The trumpet's piston valve first emerged with the work of Heinrich Stölzel (1814) and was later improved by François Périnet (1838). The rotary valve, a development of the early design by Blühmel, is used on horns and was first added by Joseph Riedl and Josef Kail in the mid-1830s. The Vienna valve, used on Austrian Vienna horns, evolved from Leipzig maker Christian Friedrich Sattler's 1821 double-piston valves. The valve trombone became the dominant instrument over the slide trombone across much of Europe. Between 1862 and 1883 the Vienna Philharmonic almost exclusively used the valved instrument, before director Wilhelm Jahn insisted on large-bore alto, tenor and bass slide trombones.[12] Valves provided the brass family with stronger, more evenly toned, bass instruments. On 12 September 1835 Wieprecht and Moritz patented the tuba; the transition from earlier low brass instruments such as the serpent and the ophicleide to the tuba can be seen in Berlioz's reorchestrations of the *Symphonie fantastique* Op. 14 from the original scoring in 1830 of one ophicleide and one serpent to the final 1843 version for two tubas.[13] Sax created a family of saxhorns, a consort of conical valved brass instruments, the invention of which is linked with the emerging brass band movement.[14]

---

[10] R. Meucci and G. Rocchetti, *The Horn* (New Haven & London: Yale University Press, forthcoming).

[11] C. Ahrens, *Valved Brass: The History of an Invention*, trans. S. Plank (Hillsdale: Pendragon Press, 2008), 19–46.

[12] T. Herbert, *The Trombone* (New Haven & London: Yale University Press, 2006) 182–203.

[13] H. Macdonald, *Berlioz's Orchestration Treatise: A Translation and Commentary.* (Cambridge: Cambridge University Press, 2002), 240.

[14] A. Myers, 'Instruments and Instrumentation of British Brass Bands', in T. Herbert (ed.), *The British Brass Band: A Musical and Social History* (Oxford: Oxford University Press, 2000), 155–86.

Brahms was particular in his wishes for the brass instruments. In a letter to Theodor Avé-Lallemant in 1859 regarding a forthcoming performance of the *Begräbnisgesang* Op. 13, Brahms demanded, 'On no account three tenor trombones! One genuine little <u>alto</u> trombone and, if possible, also a genuine <u>bass</u> trombone.'[15] His trumpet writing tends to be conservative, calling for no notes unavailable to natural trumpets and restricting himself to the traditional keys for both horns and trumpets. However, he was radical in his insistence on the natural, rather than valved, horn in his 1865 Horn Trio Op. 40. He was familiar with the instrument, as his father had played the natural horn. Brahms possibly learnt it himself in his youth and expressed a preference for it over the valve horn [See Ch. 1 'Childhood in Hamburg']. Emil Wipperich, the principal horn of the Vienna Philharmonic from 1882 until 1914, is thought to have asked Brahms for a solo work for valve horn, only to be knocked back by Brahms who retorted: 'I do not write anything for your *Blechbratschen*' ('brass viola').[16]

The natural horn player can sound the sixteen or more open notes of the harmonic series and, by manipulating the hand in the flared bell of the instrument, create chromatic stopped notes in the gaps between these notes. These stopped notes had a different sound quality to the open notes, sometimes muffled, sometimes 'brassy'. Brahms's reasoning was that the natural horn aided the balance of the ensemble. However, his instrumental writing is echoed in his larger orchestral works and points to an aesthetic choice rather than merely a pragmatic decision. In Austro-Germany, horn players normally used a rotary or Vienna valved instrument which could also be crooked into various keys. An example of this is an instrument made by the Leipzig maker Penzel, known as the Gumbert-Modell [*sic*] after horn player Friedrich Gumpert, who performed the trio with Clara Schumann and Ferdinand David in December 1866. Clara wrote to Brahms exclaiming 'the hornist was splendid! I think he didn't crack a single note, and that says a lot. Of course, he had a valve horn; he couldn't be convinced to use a Waldhorn.'[17] Gumpert would, however, have known and played the earlier instrument. Like other nineteenth-century Austro-Germanic pedagogues, he believed it necessary to start horn players on the older instrument in order to instil the true horn sound. Starting on the valve horn was thought to risk a coarse timbre.

[15] S. Avins & J. Eisinger, 'Six unpublished letters from Johannes Brahms', in D. F. Scott (ed.), *For the Love of Music: A Festschrift in Honor of Theodore Front* (Lucca: Lim Antiqua, 2002), 127.

[16] A. Ehrmann, *Johannes Brahms, Weg, Werk und Welt* (Leipzig: Breitkopf & Härtel, 1933), 182 n. 2.

[17] J. Humphries, *The Early Horn: A Practical Guide* (Cambridge: Cambridge University Press, 2000), 99–103.

Instruments 233

The nineteenth century saw an explosion in the range of percussion instruments. Brahms, like Beethoven, normally required one pair of timpani, a hand- rather than pedal-tuned instrument with a calf-skin head and wooden beaters. Late nineteenth-century timpani have a softer timbre and a less clearly pitched sound. Janissary (Turkish percussion, as heard in the final movement of Beethoven's Ninth Symphony), also appears in Brahms's works. The triangle features prominently in the Fourth Symphony Op. 98, and Brahms uses a festive combination of bass drum, triangle and cymbals in the *Academic Festival Overture* Op. 80. These sparse forces are in keeping with other Austro-German composers of the period. The French and Russian schools exploited more exotic percussion such as Saint-Saëns's use of the xylophone in *Danse macabre* (1874) and *Le carnaval des animaux* (1886), and Chabrier's use of the tambourine in *España* (1883).[18]

Brahms's century witnessed three main schools of piano design and action: the Viennese (represented by makers like Streicher, Bösendorfer and Blüthner), the English (Broadwood) and the French (Erard and Pleyel). The Viennese piano evolved out of the late eighteenth-century pianos of Johann Andreas Stein. Stein had simplified the action of the first piano maker Bartolomeo Cristofori, placing the hammer in direct contact with the key as well as reversing it so that it faced towards the player. This action enabled a shallow touch which aided fast passagework. Viennese makers used hammer heads covered with leather and their instruments typically had a clarity and brightness to them, despite the instruments favouring the lowest fundamental tones of the individual strings rather than their higher partials. In the late eighteenth century, British maker Broadwood added a screw to regulate the escapement (the way in which the hammer is released: the hammer falls away having hit the string, despite the key still being depressed) and putting the jack (the lifting device) in direct contact with the hammer butt (the opposite end to the hammer head). These developments, aided by felt-covered hammers, and innovations in using metal braces and plates, gave the instrument more power and sonority, but required a deeper touch. Erard developed an action known as the double escapement, a complex piece of craftsmanship which enabled the note to be restruck even if the key had not yet returned to its original position, thus enabling swift passagework. The French used layered felt and leather hammers which helped favour the higher overtones of notes.

---

[18] J. Blades, *Percussion Instruments and Their History*, 2nd edn (London: Faber & Faber, 1984), 309.

The combination of the action and the hammers led to a powerful, bright yet agile instrument.

Throughout his lifetime Brahms had at his disposal Austro-German pianos, performing on instruments by Streicher, Bösendorfer, Bechstein, Steinweg Nachfolgern and Blüthner. He was also familiar with American instruments with Austro-German ancestry, such as Steinway and Knabe as well as French Erards and British Broadwoods. In the early 1870s, Emil Streicher presented Brahms with an 1868 straight-strung Streicher grand piano, and for many years Brahms exhibited a preference for Streicher instruments, encouraging others to choose similarly.[19] Brahms wrote glowingly of his Streicher instrument to Clara Schumann explaining that

> it is quite a different matter to write for instruments whose characteristics and sound one only incidentally has in one's head and which one can only hear mentally, than to write for an instrument which one knows through and through, as I know this piano. There I always know exactly what I write and why I write one way or another.[20]

Brahms's piano would not have had a single-piece metal frame but two cast-iron tension bars attached to a metal string plate. Such a frame cannot stand very high tension. The instrument also had clearly defined ranges of timbre, with an audible difference between the top, middle and bottom ranges of the instrument. Various aspects of Streicher's pianos, such as the 'Viennese action', the straight rather than crossed strings and the leather rather than felt-covered hammers, contributed to the light, fast action and the clear, transparent yet mellow timbre.[21]

Erard and Pleyel were also famed for their harps; many design elements and techniques were common to both instruments. The double-action pedal was developed in the early nineteenth century and forms the basis of modern harp design. These pedals allow each string to be sharpened by either a semitone or a tone, making the instrument more chromatically versatile.

Robert S. Winter has observed that 'the nineteenth century was an era that valued color, contrast, and variety above all else'.[22] Given the

---

[19] See P. McNaulty: Fortepiano.eu (2017). *Fortepiano after Streicher, 1868*. [online]. Available at: www.fortepiano.eu/streicher-1868/; S. Siek, 'Nanette Streicher (Stein)', *A Dictionary for the Modern Pianist* (Lanham: Rowman & Littlefield, 2016), 210; and C. Cai, 'Brahms's Pianos and the Performance of His Late Piano Works', *Performance Practice Review* 2/1 (1989), 60.

[20] August 1887. Cai, 'Brahms's Pianos and the Performance of His Late Piano Works', 58–72.

[21] G. Bozarth & S. Brady, 'The Pianos of Johannes Brahms', in W. Frisch and K. C. Karnes (eds.), *Brahms and His World*, 2nd edn (Princeton: Princeton University Press, 2009), 73–93.

[22] R. Winter, 'Orthodoxies, Paradoxes, and Contradictions: Performance Practices in Nineteenth-Century Piano Music', in R. L. Todd (ed.), *Nineteenth-Century Piano Music*, 2nd edn (New York: Routledge, 2004), 19.

Instruments

enormous variety of instruments, musicians could easily find a maker and instrument that satisfied their desires. Across the orchestra, the wealth of designs that blossomed during the nineteenth century illustrates the musicians' appetite for exploration of different colours and contrasts, with makers seeking to facilitate new techniques and satisfy new demands.

Further Reading

A. Baines, *Woodwind Instruments and Their History* (London: Faber & Faber, 1967)

C. Brown et al., *Performing Practices in Johannes Brahms's Chamber Music* (Kassel: Bärenreiter, 2015)

A. Carse, *The Orchestra from Beethoven to Berlioz* (Cambridge: W. Heffer and Sons, 1948)

A. Carse, *Musical Wind Instruments* (London: Macmillan, 1939)

T. Herbert and J. Wallace (eds.), *The Cambridge Companion to Brass Instruments* (Cambridge: Cambridge University Press, 1997)

C. Lawson, *The Cambridge Companion to the Orchestra* (Cambridge: Cambridge University Press, 2003)

H. Macdonald, *Berlioz's Orchestration Treatise: A Translation and Commentary* (Cambridge: Cambridge University Press, 2002)

University of Leeds Collection of Historical Annotated String Edition website: http://mhm.hud.ac.uk/chase/

CHAPTER 24

Publishers

Peter Schmitz

Since Brahms only had a salaried position for brief periods (as choral director in Detmold, 1857–9, director of the Vienna Singakademie 1863–4 and artistic director of the Gesellschaft der Musikfreunde 1871–5), he had to support himself primarily by other means. Apart from concert fees, he relied on the honoraria his publishers paid him and did not receive royalties. Indeed, his relationships with his publishers are a means of tracing his stratospheric career trajectory. As a young man, Brahms was forced to tout his works to publishers and enter into protracted and wearying negotiations, which jarred against his artistic principles. In later years, he was a universally courted composer who could determine the conditions under which his work would be published. In fact, after 1869, it was virtually only one publisher, Fritz Simrock, who issued all of Brahms's new works.

Robert Schumann not only thrust the twenty-year-old Brahms into the limelight in autumn 1853 with his essay 'New Paths' [see Ch. 31 'Germany']; he also paved the way to publication by recommending his works to Leipzig, the heart of Germany's musical publishing world. Through his mediation, Brahms's first works were issued by the reputable publishers Breitkopf & Härtel. By 1864, Breitkopf had published fourteen opuses in total. The composer accorded them the 'exclusive and unlimited publication and distribution rights ... for Germany and all other countries' (Figure 24.1).[1] The Leipzig publisher Bartholf Senff, who also produced the leading music journal *Signale für die musikalische Welt*, published two of Brahms's works (the Piano Sonata Op. 5 and *Sechs Gesänge* Op. 6). From 1869, Senff also published a few of Brahms's arrangements of works by Chopin, Weber, Bach and Gluck (Five Piano Studies Anh. Ia no. 1 and no. 2).

[1] See Assignation of Rights for Opp. 7–8, held in the Handschriften- und Musikabteilung of the Hessischen Universitäts- und Landesbibliothek Darmstadt, Musikerbriefe Brahms 17.4.

236

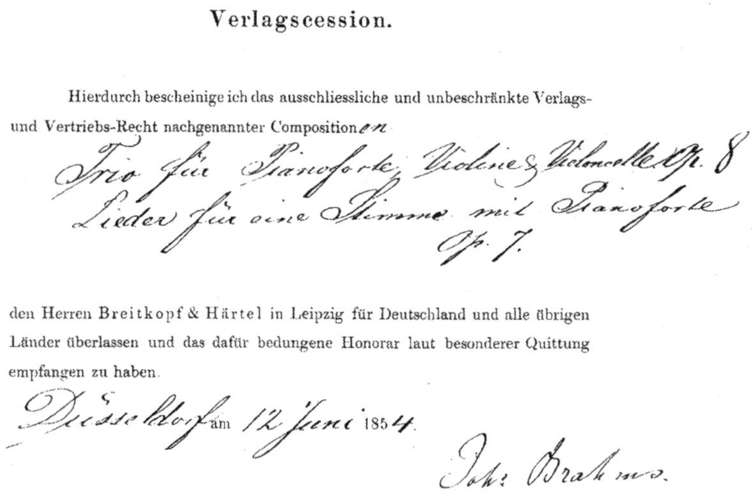

Verlagscession.

Hierdurch bescheinige ich das ausschliessliche und unbeschränkte Verlags- und Vertriebs-Recht nachgenannter Compositionen

Trio für Pianoforte, Violine & Violoncelle Op. 8
Lieder für eine Stimme mit Pianoforte Op. 7.

den Herren Breitkopf & Härtel in Leipzig für Deutschland und alle übrigen Länder überlassen und das dafür bedungene Honorar laut besonderer Quittung empfangen zu haben.

Düsseldorf am 12 Juni 1854.

Joh: Brahms.

Figure 24.1. Assignation of Rights for Opp. 7–8.

Yet despite this headstart, Brahms soon risked losing his advantage. His relationship with Breitkopf & Härtel seems to have been particularly turbulent, probably because of his mixed reception in Leipzig in the 1850s and 60s [See Ch. 4 'Leipzig and Berlin']. The premiere of the First Piano Concerto Op. 15 at the Gewandhaus in January 1859, for example, was a flop. The work was lambasted by much of Leipzig's musical press (led by Eduard Bernsdorf). This damage to Brahms's reputation doubtless affected his relationship with Hermann and Raymund Härtel, whose faith in him was hardly limitless; their judgement was influenced unhelpfully by their advisers. Ultimately, the publishers' manipulative behaviour in relation to the Second String Sextet Op. 36 in autumn 1865 led to a breakdown in their relationship; they had accepted the work unseen, then later rejected it on the advice of an anonymous reviewer. From the mid-1870s, Brahms put aside their earlier disagreements and acted as an editor on several of their collected edition projects [see Ch. 12 'As Editor']. Still, his resentment bubbled up again in 1888 when Simrock attempted to secure publication rights for all of Brahms's works that he had not published. Breitkopf & Härtel was the only publisher to agree, claiming that they did not wish to hinder Simrock's (ultimately unrealised) project for

238 PETER SCHMITZ

a complete Brahms edition – but the composer dismissed this as hypocritical, suspecting that they were only after profit.

The relationship with the Swiss publisher Rieter-Biedermann, based in Winterthur, was considerably more straightforward. Jakob Melchior Rieter-Biedermann wrote to the composer in July 1856 to express his interest in adding a Brahms work to his catalogue, which already included music by Theodor Kirchner, Hector Berlioz, Julius Otto Grimm and posthumous works by Schumann. The first publication with them appeared in 1858, namely the *Volks-Kinderlieder* WoO 31, dedicated to the Schumann children (though published anonymously, at Brahms's request). Rieter-Biedermann published twenty works in total, among them major works like the aforementioned First Piano Concerto, the *Variations on a Theme of Robert Schumann* Op. 23, the *Magelone Romances* Op. 33 and *A German Requiem* Op. 45. The actual printing took place in the prestigious Leipzig workshop of C. G. Röder – whose clients included numerous German and foreign publishers (André, Simrock, Eulenburg, Jurgenson, etc.) – and several particularly beautiful title pages (e.g. that of the *Ave Maria* Op. 12 and the *Begräbnisgesang* Op. 13) were lithographed in Leipzig by Friedrich Krätzschmer.

Brahms's warm relationship with the publisher, who from 1862 maintained a branch in Leipzig headed by Edmund Astor (who would later become Rieter-Biedermann's son-in-law), is evident from the compositional history of *A German Requiem*. Brahms visited the publisher in spring 1866 and worked on the sixth and seventh movements ('Denn wir haben hie keine bleibende Statt' und 'Selig sind die Toten') in the summerhouse of the publisher's country home 'Zum Schanzengarten'. He also enjoyed the hospitality of Rieter-Biedermann's wife Luise and daughter Ida. A surviving publisher's calculation book provides detailed information about the printing costs, fees and supplementary editions (German and English) of *A German Requiem*.[2]

After Brahms settled in Vienna, he still preferred international, financially powerful publishers. This was because Vienna in the second half of the nineteenth century was simply not equal to the music publishing scene in Leipzig and Berlin, in terms of professional advertising and distribution. Only *Psalm 13* Op. 27 and Four Duets for Alto and Baritone Op. 28 were published by the Vienna publisher C. A. Spina in 1863/4 (the duets were acquired by C. F. Peters in 1874).

---

[2] D-LEst, Bestand 21070 C. F. Peters, No. 3970, 366.

Publishers

Fritz Simrock's dogged determination to become Brahms's main publisher by acquiring a monopoly on his works put the composer in a situation enjoyed by virtually none of his contemporaries. This bond meant financial security and basically rendered relationships with other publishers unnecessary. From the 1870s onwards, only Max Abraham at Peters constituted any kind of competition to Simrock. Abraham launched 'Edition Peters' in 1867 and founded the Musikbibliothek Peters in Leipzig in 1893. The following works were first printed by Peters (who would gladly have taken the First Symphony Op. 68 too): the *Lieder und Gesänge* Op. 63, Three Quartets Op. 64 (1874), *Nänie* Op. 82 (1881), Six Quartets Op. 112 and Thirteen Canons for Female Voices Op. 113 (1891). Brahms also greatly admired Abraham's business strategy of publishing larger print runs and selling for lower prices. He repeatedly urged Simrock to adopt the same approach. Two record books of the publisher C. F. Peters provide detailed information on the distribution of Brahms's works between 1911 and 1931.[3]

The origins of Brahms's relationship to the traditional and well-established Bonn publisher Nikolaus Simrock dated from 1860, when Peter Joseph Simrock (the founder's son) asked Brahms whether he would like to offer a work for publication. The first work Brahms entrusted to him was his Second Serenade Op. 16. To these he added, in a very organised fashion, the songs, piano music and chamber works Opp. 17–21, and Opp. 25, 26, 36, 38 and 40. However, Nikolaus Simrock's faith in and admiration of the composer was mixed; this changed fundamentally with his son Fritz, who declared that he personally hung on each and every note of Brahms.

Fritz Simrock took over as head of the publisher Robert Timm & Co. in Berlin in 1864, which he renamed the 'Simrock Music Dealer (Musikhandlung)'. From 1867, he also led 'N. Simrock in Bonn'. In 1868, Brahms's songs Opp. 46–9 appeared under the Berlin imprint; *Rinaldo* Op. 50 followed the next year. After Peter Joseph Simrock's death in 1868, the Bonn head office also was under Fritz Simrock's charge. Two years later, both branches were combined under the name 'N. Simrock in Berlin'. Apart from the aforementioned publications with C. F. Peters, of which Simrock was positively jealous, all of Brahms's works with an opus number thereafter were published by Fritz Simrock. Furthermore, from 1877, Fritz Simrock also acted as Brahms's financial adviser, supplied printed music, books, wine, cigars, tobacco and culinary delicacies. In this way, Simrock spared Brahms the responsibility of pecuniary matters, keeping him free for

---

[3] D-LEst, Bestand 21070 C. F. Peters, No. 4761 and 4764.

PETER SCHMITZ

his composition [see Ch. 8 'Finances']. The friendship as documented in their correspondence evinces exceptional mutual regard and trust. Another interesting aspect of this relationship is that Brahms regularly recommended other composers to Simrock. Following Brahms's endorsements, the Berlin publisher produced works by Antonín Dvořák, Robert Fuchs (1847–1927) and Julius Röntgen (1855–1932) among others. In August 1891, Brahms even sent his publisher and friend his will, requesting that he be executor (because of changes made in 1895, and formal errors, there was unfortunately a protracted dispute over the inheritance).

This completes the catalogue of Brahms's most significant publishers. A few other works appeared elsewhere: August Friedrich Cranz in Bremen, A. Cranz in Hamburg (*Drei Gesänge* Op. 42), Adolph Fürstner in Berlin (an arrangement of Schumann's Piano Quartet for piano duet Anh. Ia no. 8), and Karl Grädener, Boyes & Geisler Nachf. in Hamburg (a realisation of the Bach Cantata 'Ach Gott, wie manches Herzeleid' Anh. Ia no. 9). In 1881 the composer gave an organ work and a vocal canon WoO7 and 25 to the *Musikalisches Wochenblatt,* to which he had subscribed since 1874, published by the Leipzig-based Ernst Wilhelm Fritzsch.

As mentioned above, after Brahms had published his Opp. 1–9 with Breitkopf & Härtel and Bartholf Senff in 1853 and 1854, only a few works appeared in the next years (Ballades Op. 10 in 1856, *Volks-Kinderlieder* WoO 31 in 1858). The fees for the individual works in these early years were generally between 6 and 12 Louisdor (see Table 8.1 in Chapter 8 'Finances'). In comparison, Breitkopf & Härtel paid Schumann 30 Louisdors in 1852 for his Third Piano Trio Op. 110, and 25 Louisdor for his Second Violin Sonata Op. 121 the following year. However, Brahms's early fees as mentioned in the publishers' correspondence as well as in Schumann's requests, differ partially from the entries (in Taler and Groschen) in a Breitkopf & Härtel calculation list held in the Sächsisches Staatsarchiv – Staatsarchiv Leipzig (see Figure 24.2).

This reveals how Breitkopf & Härtel calculated their net profit (described as 'Ordinair' in the list), based on the size of print runs, sale prices, production costs and composer's fee. (The customer and trade discounts, c. 33 per cent, still had to be factored into that amount.) The size of the print runs of Brahms's first works with Breitkopf & Härtel were 250 for the *Sechs Gesänge* Op. 7 and First Piano Trio Op. 8, 300 for the Piano Sonata Op. 2 and the *Variations on a Theme of Robert Schumann* Op. 9, 350 for the Six Songs Op. 3 and Scherzo Op. 4, and 375 for the Piano Sonata Op. 1. These are typical for the period. However, there were other Breitkopf & Härtel publications which were printed in far

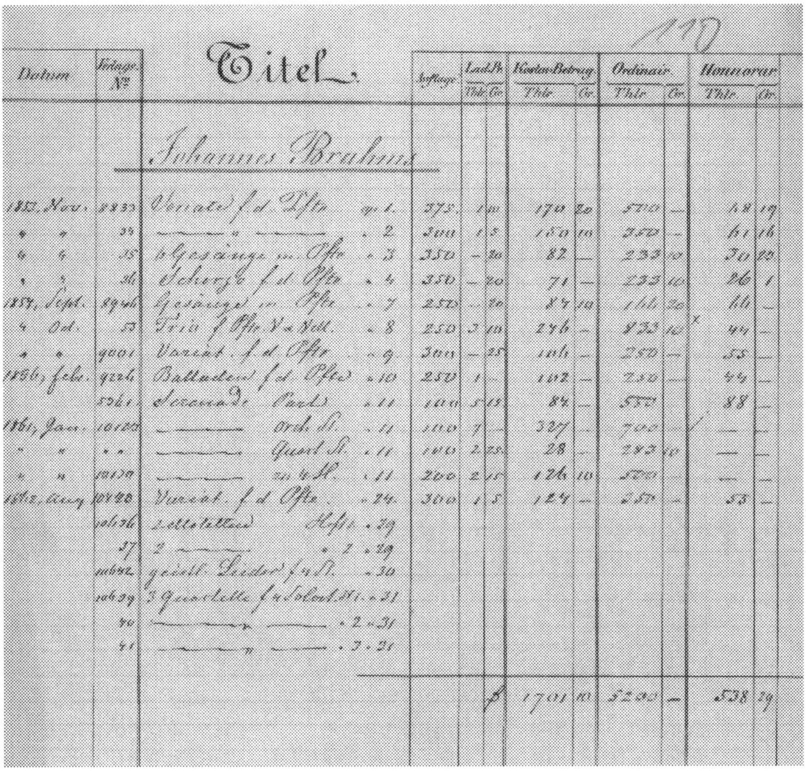

Figure 24.2. Breitkopf & Härtel Calculation List.

higher numbers: the first publication of Chopin's *Grande valse brillante* Op. 18, for instance, appeared in 1834 with a print run of 2,100. Mendelssohn's *Sechs Gesänge* Op. 47 appeared in 1839 with a print run of 1,800.

In 1855, 1857 and 1859, Brahms published no works and thus earned no composition fees. However, from 1860 until 1896, at least one new work appeared annually. In some years, Brahms published as many as seven works. Several years have been presented as a sample below and the concomitant fees added up.[4]

1854: 58 or 60 Louisdor, approx. 336 Taler (Opp. 2, 4, 5, 7, 8 and 9).

1862: 56 Friedrichsdor, approx. 314 Taler (Opp. 19–22 and 24).

[4] All fees are drawn from *Werkverzeichnis*.

1866: 96 Friedrichsdor, approx. 538 Taler (Opp. 35, 36, 39 four-hand version, 40 and 44).

1874: 4,560 Taler (Opp. 52a, 56a, 61–64 and WoO 1 orchestral arrangement of nos. 1, 3, 10).

1877: 9,450 Taler (Opp. 65a, 68–72; it is not known if a fee for Anh. Ia no. 9 was paid).

1882: c. 7,550 Taler (Opp. 83–88, WoO 7).

1884: c. 8,700 Taler (Opp. 90–92, 93a, 94–95).

1891: 10,500 Mark = c. 3,500 Taler (Opp. 8 (revised), 111–113).

Brahms received premium fees for his first three Symphonies Opp. 68, 73 and 90 (the fee for the Fourth Symphony Op. 98 has not been recorded): 5,000 Taler, a fee which included the corresponding four-hand piano arrangements, and for Op. 90, the arrangement for two pianos. For the Violin Concerto Op. 77, he received 3,000 Taler, including the piano scores. The *49 Deutsche Volkslieder* WoO 33 received 15,000 Mark. For the song opuses Opp. 68–72, Brahms demanded 150 Taler per song from Simrock, i.e. a total sum of 3,450 Taler. As can be seen from the figures for the symphonies and the Violin Concerto, the preparation of piano scores and arrangements (primarily for four-hand piano or two pianos) was financially advantageous [see Ch. 11 'As Arranger'].

However, arrangements could potentially create conflict, as can be seen in two cases: in 1868/9, as mentioned above, *A German Requiem* Op. 45 appeared with Rieter-Biedermann (Leipzig and Winterthur). Brahms was paid 110 Napoléons for the full and piano score of this key work; the four-hand piano arrangement attracted 30 Napoléons. However, the publisher wanted the words 'by the composer' to appear on the title page of the arrangement, because it was potentially profitable, and this led to a disagreement with Brahms. Rieter-Biedermann had stated his intentions in a letter from 10 February 1869, but Brahms seems not to have agreed explicitly. He was later incensed, demanding that the words be removed:

> I request urgently (and demand, since I have mentioned this repeatedly), that you now remove my name as arranger of the four-hand version from the *Requiem* as soon as possible! Cost up the title pages you have in stock, and I will gladly pay for new ones. I cannot look at the *Requiem* without feeling annoyed. How can you not understand how absurd this chewing over one's own work is! Indeed, I have never done it by choice, but only to earn the money, and because arrangements made by others make more work for me.[5]

---

[5] Brahms to Rieter-Biedermann, October 1870, *Briefe XIV*, 190–1.

His demand was honoured.

A similar situation arose in relation to his four-hand arrangement of his First Piano Concerto Op. 15. After initially declaring himself against it, he sent Rieter-Biedermann an engraver's copy on 11 February 1864:

> To my own surprise, and possibly also yours, I enclose a four-hand arrangement of my Concerto. I thought of you while making it, and I believe I can be proud of how practical and even easily playable the arrangement has turned out. Still, I request once again: please do not name me as the arranger! It is just some simple scribbling, and it doesn't look nice when the master himself creates such a shapeless monster from his own work, as a four-hand concerto necessarily must be! Furthermore, I frequently thought of your benefit rather than mine, and made it to be played rather than to be read (as is currently the fashion). By the way, you will see, for example, that the Sextet [Op. 18] and Serenade No. 2 [Op. 16] have appeared [in four-hand arrangement] without my name, and both works are popular. I would like to have lots of money for them![6]

If at the start of his career, Brahms was still occasionally awkward and formal when it came to business matters, many later letters in which he stated his demands for fees reveal a fine sense of irony and humour [see Ch. 6 'Correspondence']. Regarding the four-hand piano arrangement of the *Triumphlied* Op. 55, for example, he wrote to Fritz Simrock:

> I really don't know what I am going to get for the four-hand *Triumphlied,* and you are in such a rush that I just can't calculate that quickly. Anything that ends with three zeros sounds fine to me. I'm not so picky about the number in the front![7]

Once Brahms was an established composer, his financial situation and his exceptionally modest lifestyle meant that he hardly needed his fees any more. This is clear, for example, from a notable letter which he wrote in connection with Simrock's aforementioned acquisition of the rights for works which had appeared first with Breitkopf & Härtel:

> To show you my sympathy, I would truly and seriously like to make clear that henceforth I no longer wish to receive any fees, but rather, as I recently suggested, a statement of credit balance on which I can draw if necessary, and which can simply be wiped out after my death. You are familiar with my situation (better than I) and you know that I can live comfortably without any more fees. And I will do this, as far my un-Wagnerian needs permit. But after my death – I should really make over the whole residue to you, so that

---

[6] Brahms to Rieter-Biedermann, 11 February 1864, *Ibid.*, 86–7.
[7] Brahms to Fritz Simrock, May 1873, *Briefe IX*, 142.

244   PETER SCHMITZ

you get something out of this whole Härtel situation. Right then, I congratulate you, but wash my hands with carbolic and everything else possible![8]

Apart from the business and legal implications, Brahms's relationships with his publishers are also of great philological interest since they offer us a glimpse (albeit often at a very late stage) into his compositional workshop and partially document his final interventions prior to publication. In this context, the different stages – from the engraver's copies to sample proofs to the first published printing – are immensely significant [see Ch. 35 'Editing Brahms'].[9] In the frame of the often standardised editorial process, the role of the proofreader was critical. As long as the publisher did not undertake this work in-house, the proofreader had to work closely with the composer for each phase of the correction process. In Brahms's case, Robert Keller, who worked for Simrock, was often praised by Brahms for his meticulousness, for example in the Violin Concerto Op. 77 and the Third Symphony Op. 90 – as was Alfred Dörffel, who worked for Breitkopf & Härtel and later C. F. Peters. It was thanks to this network of professionals – proofreaders, engravers, lithographers and publishers – that Brahms's music was made available to an international audience.

Further Reading

O. Biba, 'Die Simrocks – Verleger für Beethoven wie für Brahms', in W. Ottendorff-Simrock (ed.), *Das Haus Simrock. Beiträge zur Geschichte einer kulturtragenden Familie des Rheinlandes*, rev. ed. I. Bodsch (Bonn: Stadtmuseum Bonn, 2003), 57–68

G. Bozarth, 'Brahms and the Breitkopf & Härtel Affair', *The Music Review* 55/3 (August 1994), 202–13

G. Bozarth (ed.), *The Brahms-Keller Correspondence* (Lincoln and London: University of Nebraska Press, 1996)

R. Hofmann, 'Vier Briefe des Verlages J. Rieter-Biedermann an Johannes Brahms', in M. Struck (ed.), *Johannes Brahms: Ein deutsches Requiem – Stichvorlage des Klavierauszuges* (Kiel: Kulturstiftung der Länder, 1994), 13–26

K. Hofmann, 'Zu den Beziehungen zwischen Johannes Brahms und Fritz Simrock', *32 Stichvorlagen von Werken Johannes Brahms*, (Kiel: Kulturstiftung der Länder, 1995), 7–16

---

[8] Brahms to Fritz Simrock, April 1888, *Briefe XI*, 182.

[9] Kathrin Kirsch in her illuminating study distinguishes between six types of proof. See K. Kirsch, *Von der Stichvorlage zum Erstdruck. Zur Bedeutung von Vorabzügen bei Johannes Brahms* (Kassel: Bärenreiter, 2013), 248–88.

Publishers

H. Joelson-Strohbach, 'Vom Winterthurer Musikverleger Jakob Melchior Rieter-Biedermann', *Librarium: Zeitschrift der Schweizerischen Bibliophilen-Gesellschaft* 34 (1991), 51–66

K. Kirsch, *Von der Stichvorlage zum Erstdruck. Zur Bedeutung von Vorabzügen bei Johannes Brahms* (Kassel: Bärenreiter, 2013)

I. Lawford-Hinrichsen. *Music Publishing and Patronage: C. F. Peters: 1800 to the Holocaust* (Kenton: Edition Press, 2000)

P. Schmitz, *Johannes Brahms und der Leipziger Musikverlag Breitkopf & Härtel* (Göttingen: V & R Unipress, 2009)

K. Stephenson (ed.), *Johannes Brahms und Fritz Simrock – Weg einer Freundschaft. Briefe des Verlegers an den Komponisten* (Hamburg: J. J. Augustin, 1961)

M. Struck, 'Vom Einfall zum Werk – Produktionsprozesse, Notate, Werkgestalt(en)', in *Brahms Handbuch*, 171–98

P. Sulzer, '13 neu aufgefundene Postkarten und ein Brief von Johannes Brahms an Jakob Melchior Rieter-Biedermann', *Brahms-Studien* 6 (1985), 31–60

K. Van Orden, *Music and the Cultures of Print* (New York: Garland, 2000)

CHAPTER 25

Copyright

Friedemann Kawohl

Three days before Brahms was born on 7 May 1833 in Hamburg, the first weekly illustrated magazine, the *Pfennig-Magazin* was published. Following on from the success of the *Penny Magazine,* which had appeared in England since 1832, the *Pfennig-Magazin* also aimed to reach a broad public. A few months later, the Hamburg music publisher Julius Schubert announced a new music periodical, a *Pfennig-Magazin für Pianofortespieler,* which offered 'selected piano compositions for beginners, experienced players and virtuosos'.[1]

Brahms was born at a time in which the market for printed matter, and especially music, was burgeoning as a result of newer, cheaper printing methods and the growing demand from music-making (especially piano-playing) amateurs [see Ch. 14 'Private Music-Making']. Arrangements were very profitable, but since resulting copyright issues were still unresolved, this led to many copyright disputes between publishers from the 1830s onwards [see Ch. 11 'As Arranger'].

Brahms could no longer profit from performance rights. Austrian copyright law in 1846 only allowed for such rights if the work was unpublished. From 1856 onwards, performance rights could be granted after the first edition appeared, but only if the rights were explicitly stated on the cover. This was not in the publishers' interests and so was only applied to stage music – opera, operetta and ballet, i.e. none of Brahms's works. After the copyright law of 1895 came into force, such music was protected even without this provision, but this altered nothing for purely musical works.

After the founding of an association for authors, publishers and composers (which included Brahms's friends Ignaz Brüll and Richard Heuberger)[2] on 5 December 1897, a few months after Brahms's death, change became possible. The State-authorised Association of Authors,

---

[1] *Wochenblatt für Buchhändler, Musikhändler, Buchdrucker und Antiquare* 15/45–6 (1833), 414.
[2] 'Der Autorenverein in Wien', *Signale für die Musikalische Welt* 55/49 (26 October 1897), 769.

Copyright 247

Composers and Music Publishers (Staatlich genehmigte Gesellschaft der Autoren, Komponisten und Musikverleger), later called the AKM, became the second worldwide copyright collecting society, after the French Société des auteurs, compositeurs et éditeurs de musique (SACEM), but failed to get the Austrian government to join the Berne Convention. In the USA, the exclusive performance rights of a musical work were recorded in a central copyright register from 1897. Within the German Empire, performance rights for musical works were granted in 1901. Since the Berlin revision in 1908, this law applied in the whole jurisdiction of the Berne Convention, which Austria only joined in 1920.

So how was Brahms's career as pianist, choral director, composer and editor of musical works affected by copyright law? What did Brahms think of the existing justification for copyright law, for example the term 'intellectual property' or the notion of 'personal rights', which protected the words of authors through copyright? And how did contemporary discussions around the legitimacy of arrangements influence his composition? From recollections, we know that Brahms rated pure inspiration relatively low but enormously valued the composer's craft. He said to George Henschel in February 1876:

> There is no real creating . . . without hard work. That which you would call invention, that is to say, a thought, an idea, is simply an inspiration from above, for which I am not responsible, which is no merit of mine. Yea, it is a present, a gift, which I ought even to despise until I have made it my own by right of hard work.[3]

A few years later, when Max Kalbeck quoted this statement, he added in a footnote a similar recollection from Clara Simrock:

> Brahms once spoke to his publisher Fritz Simrock about the vanity of artists who constantly needed to be surrounded and by disciples and admired. 'Admired!' he cried scathingly. 'What is there to admire about artists? Of course, the public must always admire something, and run after the sensational. People always want to admire something about me too, for example, my invention. But there is little that is admirable about it. People who always have to have a name for everything say that it is "divine inspiration". What has my "invention" to do with me? It is like a seed-corn which lies in the earth; either it grows, or it doesn't, in which case it was worth nothing. If it grows, and I think of a melody – well, I note it down, but don't look at it again until it comes to me of its own accord. If it doesn't come, then it was worthless, and I discard it.'[4]

---

[3] G. Henschel, *Personal Recollections of Johannes Brahms* (Boston: Badger, 1907), 22f.
[4] *Kalbeck II*, 180f.

248   FRIEDEMANN KAWOHL

These statements illustrate the composer's creative process in the 1870s. He also told his student Gustav Jenner, 'if at all possible, do not attempt a working out ... until the whole plan is established in your head or on paper. If ideas come to you, just go for a walk and you will then realise that what you thought were polished thoughts were just the starting points.'[5]

In other words, Brahms distrusted pure musical inspiration, possibly because he had seen that written-out piano improvisations did not later withstand his critical judgements. Henschel recalled Brahms's advice not to lose oneself in unstructured melodies but from the very outset to make use of theoretical tools: 'In writing songs', he said, 'you must endeavour to invent, simultaneously with the melody, a healthy, powerful bass'.[6]

Because Brahms himself approached composition in a rational and structured way, he emphasised the importance of craft. As his marking of the sentence, 'If ingenious creativity is the gift of generous nature, then art is a possession only gained with effort'[7] in Otto Jahn's 1867 Mozart biography shows, it was also important to him to identify precursors for this attitude. But why did he speak so disparagingly about inspiration, which had nothing 'admirable' about it, nothing 'to do with him' and which he despised 'until I have made it my own by right of hard work'? Many authors attribute this to his background, especially his father, who trained as a city wait within the framework of an artisanal guild and who received a journeyman's certificate upon completion [see Ch.1 'Childhood in Hamburg'].[8] Others point out the particular veneration of work within Vienna's liberal intellectual milieu: Brahms's 'liberal identity extended beyond the prejudice against Catholicism he voiced more than once, beyond even his pride in being both a German and a self-made man'[9] and, furthermore, 'not only do hard work and willed achievement characterise Brahms' personal behaviour, but also the concept of work ... shaped his understanding of the compositional process'.[10] Still others remind us that the young Brahms, who was fascinated by Romantic literature, fully appreciated inspiration as the source of art, and his disparaging attitude only emerged as part of an aesthetic change of heart in

---

[5] G. Jenner, *Johannes Brahms als Mensch, Lehrer und Künstler* (Marburg: N. G. Elwert, 1905), 42.

[6] Henschel, *Personal Recollections*, 44.

[7] W. Sandberger, 'Brahms im Dialog mit der Musikforschung seiner Zeit', in *Brahms Handbuch*, 146.

[8] Struck, 'Vom Einfall zum Werk – Produktionsprozesse, Notate, Werkgestaklt(en)', in *Brahms Handbuch*, 174.

[9] C. M. Schmidt, *Johannes Brahms und seine Zeit*, (Laaber: Laaber 1983), 59, quoted in M. Notley, *Lateness and Brahms, Music and Culture in the Twilight of Viennese Liberalism* (Oxford: Oxford University Press, 2007), 18.

[10] Notley, *Lateness and Brahms*, 74.

Copyright

1860, expressed in works such as the *Variations on a Theme of Schumann* Op. 23 and *Variations and Fugue on a Theme of Handel* Op. 24.[11]

Additionally, I would like to suggest that the stark contrast between Brahms's high valuing of work, and low opinion of inspiration suggests something of his attitude to copyright, since there were two conflicting copyright models available at the time. I will show that his positioning was closely connected to the most pressing copyright question of the day, namely the legitimisation of arrangements. As an arranger of his own and other works [see Ch. 11 'As Arranger'], the morally minded Brahms must have considered this question.

During the nineteenth century, two arguments were offered in support of copyright law: the ban on unauthorised reproduction was justified as a means of protecting, firstly, the investment of authors in the form of work and, secondly, the capital investment required to produce the printed work. This was the standard argument behind traditional print privileges and remains the basis for existing copyright law in various places. Since c. 1800, additional new systems around authors' rights were developed, above all in France and German territories, in which authors' rights were based on more than just the work and invested capital. Powerful groups enforced new rights in France: in 1791 and 1793, the first performance rights were legally established, under pressure from playwrights; in the 1820s and 1830s, journalists organised themselves in order to prevent the hitherto free reproduction of articles, and, in 1851, composers founded the Société des auteurs, compositeurs et éditeurs de musique (SACEM) the first worldwide copyright collecting society.

Within German territories, discussions to justify authors' rights centred more on philosophical arguments and general personal rights than in, for example, the United Kingdom. Kant declared in 1785 that unlicensed copies were illegal because someone who published a copy did so in his own name, unlike the original publisher, who was acting in the name of the author.[12] Therefore, in German territories, spoken statements could be protected under copyright law, independently of their printed realisation. This is clear if we compare the 1837 Prussian law protecting authors from the publication of transcripts of speeches[13] and the UK's 1835 Publication of

---

[11] J. Brachmann, *Kunst – Religion – Krise. Der Fall Brahms* (Kassel: Bärenreiter, 2003).

[12] F. Kawohl, (2008) 'Commentary on Kant's Essay *On the Injustice of Reprinting Books* (1785)', in L. Bently and M. Kretschmer (eds.), *Primary Sources on Copyright (1450–1900)*, www.copyrighthistory.org.

[13] F. Kawohl, 'Commentary on the Prussian Copyright Act (1837)', *Primary Sources on Copyright (1450–1900)*, www.copyrighthistory.org.

Lectures Act. The British law protected the 'the Author of any Lecture . . . or the Person to whom he hath sold or otherwise conveyed the Copy thereof',[14] while according to Prussian law, the legitimate owner of the manuscript had to seek the author's permission in order to publish.

The two models underpinning authors' rights corresponded with different theories of property. The core of the labour theory of property stemming from John Locke states: 'Whatsoever then he [man] removes out of the state that nature hath provided, and left it in, he hath mixed his labour with, and joined to it something that is his own, and thereby makes it his property.'[15]

Locke's theory was received late into German territories, at a time when legal philosophy already had begun to count all rights, including the right to own property, as fundamental human rights. In the 1830s, Hegel stated that 'the reasonableness of property consists not in satisfying our needs, but in its superseding and replacing the subjective phase of personality'.[16] In saying this, Hegel regarded property as a means of being acknowledged as a person in a society. Also, both legitimation models raise different subsections of the rights which are collected under the name 'copyright'. The labour theory of property justifies the rights which permit authors to benefit financially from the exploitation of their works, while from general human rights one derives the right to be named as author and assert the integrity of the work.

In his comments on inspiration and work, Brahms of course did not mention copyright protection for composers and, indeed, never directly broached the question of copyright. When he stressed that it was 'hard work' which made his works his own, he did not so much mean a legal as a moral legitimation of his intellectual property. However, through his disregard for melodic inspiration, he touches upon the criteria for permitted arrangements within the copyright dispute. Around 1830, several large publishers demanded ownership of the melodies of their publications, thus attempting to gain control over every type of adaptation. Smaller publishers argued that 'form' was the decisive feature of a musical work and that, therefore, arrangements of melodies should be permitted without agreement from the original authors.[17]

---

[14] Publication of Lectures Act, London (1835), *Primary Sources on Copyright (1450–1900)*, www.copyrighthistory.org.

[15] J. Locke, *Two Treatises of Government*, ed. P. Laslett (London: Cambridge University Press, 1967 [1690]), 305–6.

[16] G. W. F. Hegel, *Hegel's Philosophy of Right*, trans. S. W. Dyde (London: G. Bell and Sons, 1896), 41.

[17] F. Kawohl, *Urheberrecht in Preußen 1820–1840* (Tutzing: Hans Schneider, 2003), 150–65.

Copyright

Brahms's affiliation to the labour theory of property aligns with his anchoring within the liberal Viennese middle class. His friend Eduard Hanslick also evaluated music according to rational criteria and encouraged sparing use of melodic inspiration; common waltzes lacked melodic 'development', leading to 'inartistic prodigality'. The melodies of Johann Strauss I were, in contrast, praiseworthy, because they were suitable for 'further development', particularly the waltz *Herztöne* Op. 203, which consists 'of the working-out of a single motive'.[18] Verdi's *La forza del destino* attracted Hanslick's praise because of its 'considerably longer working period' than the 'otherwise so nimble maestro currently devotes to his operas'.[19] However, he also emphasised musical form because this, unlike feeling, was always the product of work.

Like Brahms, Hanslick never directly mentioned copyright. But as a trained lawyer, he was familiar with the principles of copyright, and his aesthetic criteria for a good piece of music recall its language. When he writes that the 'intellectual power and uniqueness' of the composer's imagination 'is imprinted upon the result as *character*', he describes the criterion called 'originality' within English law, which in German copyright tradition is exactly defined by the term 'geistig' ('intellectual', in contrast to 'mechanical') and 'eigentümlich' ('unique', i.e. marked with the personality of its author). For German law, therefore, 'eigentümlich' ('unique' or 'characteristic') is the crucial term in defining the boundary between permitted and forbidden arrangements. However, Brahms's and Hanslick's views were not shared by all their Viennese contemporaries, as can be seen in an essay from 1864 on copyright by the lawyer and composer Johann Vesque von Püttlingen, who, as Hanslick's correspondent and supporter, presumably also knew Brahms. Like the large publishers who wanted to prevent unauthorised arrangements of melodic themes in their works, he defined 'melody in the narrow sense (the isolated motive – the cantilena') as the 'object of musical copyright'.[20]

The novelty of Brahms's views regarding invention and work is evident in comparison with those of Schumann, who, in 1853 in his eulogy to the young Brahms, expressed the hope that he would be granted 'wonderful glimpses into the secrets of the spirit world' if Brahms would use his 'magic wand', and 'the greatest genius' would help him.[21] Composers like

---

[18] E. Hanslick, 'Johann Strauß', quoted in D. Strauss (ed.), *Eduard Hanslick, Sämtliche Schriften*, 3 vols., (Vienna: Böhlau, 1993–2008), vol. 1/2 *Aufsätze und Rezensionen 1849–1854*, 124.

[19] E. Hanslick, 'La forza del destino', *Neue Freie Presse* 242 (3 May 1865), 354.

[20] J. Vesque von Püttlingen, *Das Musicalische Autorrecht* (Vienna: Braumüller, 1864), 15.

[21] R. Schumann, 'Neue Bahnen', *Neue Zeitschrift für Musik* 39/18 (28 October 1853), 185–6.

Schumann, who ascribed music above all to compositional imagination, legitimate their authorial rights more through association with basic human rights, rather than through the labour involved. As a young composer, Schumann improvised a great deal at the piano and notated the resulting fragments, but much remained undeveloped.[22] Later on, he first conceived his melodies in his mind, only to work them out at his desk afterwards, i.e. to supply them with bass and harmony. 'What the fingers create is a bodge job', he wrote in 1843, 'but what resounds inside, that speaks eternally to all, and survives the frail body'.[23] Despite his subsequent abandonment of improvisation and a certain rationalisation of compositional work, Schumann remained fascinated by the miracle of inspiration.

Schumann regarded himself as a musical poet and accorded his inspiration artistic value. Brahms, in contrast, destroyed most of his sketches and early versions of his works himself, because for him, only works which met his strict standards deserved to survive.[24] Thus Brahms had less in common with the Romantic, inspired artist than with the modern industrialist who only brought complete products to the market and regarded the creative process as trade secrets to be concealed from the public.

Many legal disputes are concerned with the question of what sort of arrangements are permissible without further consent. Since the various German-speaking territories could not agree on a single copyright law, a few large publishers founded a cartel in 1829/30 to exclude smaller publishers.[25] They drew attention to pirated copies in the press, demanding that music-sellers withdraw them and cease trading with the pirates. They also compiled a register, a 'Vereinsarchiv', in which many publishers listed their works. Unlike the register maintained in London's Stationer's Hall, a record in the Leipzig-based register was not a legal requirement for protection against piracy. For this reason, some publishers included the words 'Eintrag in Vereinsregister' on the front cover of Brahms's first editions, including Breitkopf & Härtel and C. A. Spina in Vienna for *Psalm 13* Op. 27 and Four Duets for Alto and Baritone Op. 28, but others, Simrock, Rieter-Biedermann, Senff and Cranz, never did.

---

[22] B. Appel, 'Poesie und Handwerk: Robert Schumanns Schaffensweise', in U. Tadday (ed.), *Schumann Handbuch* (Kassel: Bärenreiter, 2006), 155.

[23] R. Schumann, 'Pianofortemusik', *Neue Zeitschrift für Musik* 18/10 (2 February 1843), 40.

[24] M. Struck, 'Vom Einfall zum Werk – Produktionsprozesse, Notate, Werkgestaklt(en)', in *Brahms Handbuch*, 171.

[25] F. Kawohl (2008) 'Commentary on the Leipzig Music Publishers' Union against Piracy (1830)', *Primary Sources on Copyright (1450–1900)*, www.copyrighthistory.org.

Copyright

The publishers were unable to enforce their demand for rights over the melodies of their works, but they did manage to achieve something. In a Saxon law of 1831, the limit of music piracy was specified: it was not permitted to publish an arrangement when it 'only required mechanical skills, and the creation of an altered form as intellectual product cannot be seen. In musical compositions in which arrangements based purely on mechanical processes may be seen as piracy, the melody can be used as the basis for the evaluation of the publisher's rights in this case.'[26]

Schumann must have been aware of this discussion, as an essay in the journal *Neue Zeitschrift für Musik*, (of which he was then editor) cites this exactly. Prussian law in 1837, which was the model for many laws in other German territories, dispensed with the criterion 'melody' and determined:

> §. 20. It shall be treated as equivalent to reprinting if somebody, without the author's consent, publishes extracts, arrangements for various instruments, or other types of adaptation, which cannot be regarded as original compositions in their own right.[27]

Thereafter, within the important Prussian and Saxon markets, the type of intellectual activity which a musician used to create an arrangement was the decisive criterion for its legality. An arrangement either involved purely 'mechanical skill' – such as transposition into another key or the separating out of a piano texture into other instruments – or it was considered an 'intellectual product' (in Saxony) or 'unique composition' (in Prussia). When Schumann repeatedly argued that musical works were 'intellectual products', he may have deliberately used this terminology, the meaning of which was ambiguous not only in moral and aesthetic terms but also in terms of copyright, which Schumann, as an editor and the son of a publisher, recognised.

Brahms's own work as an arranger is considered elsewhere in this volume [see Ch. 11 'As Arranger'], but in this discussion it is worth pointing out that August Cranz, who published the *Souvenir de la Russie*, was well known for his pirated publications. He was a member of the Leipzig cartel for only one year before leaving so as not to have to follow its strict rules.[28] His main publications were potpourris. Under the term 'Potpourri of the

---

[26] *Neue Leipziger Zeitschrift für Musik* 1/5 (17 April 1834), 18.

[27] Quoted in 'Prussian Copyright Act, Berlin (1837)', *Primary Sources on Copyright (1450–1900)*, www.copyrighthistory.org.

[28] A.B., 'Der Verein deutscher Musikalienhändler', in *Allgemeine Preßzeitung* 6/43 (30 May 1845), 169; see also *Caecilia* 13 (1830), 106f.

254 FRIEDEMANN KAWOHL

most popular operatic themes', Hofmeister's *Handbuch der musikalischen Literatur* in 1844 lists over 100 publications by Cranz – more than any other publisher.[29] In the courts, such potpourris were not regarded as a contravention of copyright law. Still, the knowledge of collaboration between Brahms and a notorious publisher of potpourris would have awakened the suspicion of the larger publishers because, unlike during the previous century, arrangements were now seen as less valuable than 'original' compositions.

Brahms's particular relationship to arrangements of his works can be clarified through comparison with Robert Schumann's. To an extent, Schumann delegated arrangements to musicians he regarded highly.[30] But in the case of his *Drei Sonaten für die Jugend* Op. 118, he made over to the publisher Julius Schuberth the right to print not only the original but also any optional arrangements.[31] Furthermore, he ensured that even unauthorised arrangements were included in his catalogue of works, published by Whistling in Leipzig in 1851.

Although Brahms was aware of the lower status of arrangements, and although he occasionally concealed his own arranging activity from the public, his concept of a work aesthetic was so firm that he could clearly and consciously emphasise his own contribution to an arrangement. Regarding the *Hungarian Dances* WoO 1, he wrote to Simrock that they were 'genuine puszta and gypsy children, in other words, not sired by me, but only nurtured with bread and milk',[32] and on the title page it stated 'gesetzt' (i.e. 'arranged') by Johannes Brahms. The reproach that the melodies were not his (justified to some extent) did not keep him from producing a second series of these dances, indeed they 'even motivated him' to do so, and the set appeared in 1880.[33]

Brahms seems to have been aware of the Prussian copyright law of 1837, according to which arrangements were only permitted when they constituted 'original compositions in their own right'. Brahms's evident sympathy for the legal status of intellectual property through work might have reinforced this attitude. That many of his contemporaries agreed can be seen in this anonymous article from 1876:

---

[29] *C.F. Whistling's Handbuch der musikalischen Literatur*, ed. A. Hofmeister, Dritte, bis zum Anfang des Jahres 1844 ergänzte Auflage. Zweiter Theil: Musik für Pianoforte (Leipzig: Hofmeister, 1844), 218–221. See also digitised catalogue, www.hofmeister.rhul.ac.uk/2008/index.html.

[30] Appel, 'Poesie und Handwerk', 173.   [31] Facsimile of the contract is in *ibid.*, 186.

[32] *Briefe XIV*, 168.   [33] K. Eich, 'Die Klavierwerke', in *Brahms Handbuch*, 356.

Copyright

One cannot impose any foreign elements into the awe of an artwork that stands before one – and one cannot be sensitive or strict enough in this regard. An era which enjoys Henselt's edition of Weber's Sonatas, Tausig's arrangements of the *Aufforderung zum Tanz*, Gounod's meditation on Bach's C major Prelude, and Liszt's paraphrase on *A Midsummer Night's Dream*, is still a long way from the goal to which aesthetic education should strive in this respect. Conversely one should also say: if you want to arrange, leave to the others what is theirs, aspire just to reflect the effect of the original as faithfully as possible, and take care that you are forgotten as fully as possible; if, on the other hand, you want to compose, then try either to stand completely on your own feet, or if your creative powers are ignited by external materials, then do not take Liszt as an example, but Brahms; learn from him, instead of just simulating production, take your borrowed motive so deeply into yourself, that on its basis, a new creation can emerge, which is fully and honestly your own property.[34]

Further Reading

S. Gerhartl, '"Vogelfrei" – Die österreichische Lösung der Urheberrechtsfrage in der 2. Hälfte des 19. Jahrhunderts oder Warum es Österreich unterließ, seine Autoren zu schützen', PhD dissertation, Vienna University (1995)

F. Kawohl (2008), 'Commentary on the Leipzig Music Publishers' Union against Piracy (1830)', in L. Bently and M. Kretschmer (eds.) *Primary Sources on Copyright (1450–1900)*, www.copyrighthistory.org

F. Kawohl (2008) 'Commentary on the Prussian Copyright Act (1837)', in L. Bently and M. Kretschmer (eds.) *Primary Sources on Copyright (1450–1900)*, www.copyrighthistory.org

---

[34] [n.a.], 'Arrangements und Transcriptionen', *Allgemeine musikalische Zeitung* 40/4 (26 January 1876), col. 52.

PART IV

Society and Culture

CHAPTER 26

Politics and Religion

David Brodbeck

We begin our consideration of Brahms's politics and religion with the great historical turn that occurred in the centre of Europe in the year 1870. With the decisive German military defeat of France and proclamation of King Wilhelm I of Prussia as German Emperor, the German Question was at last given its definitive Prussian-dominated Smaller German solution. Brahms probably would have preferred a Larger German solution that included Austria, Prussia's traditional rival for leadership in the loosely bound German Confederation that was established by the Congress of Vienna following Napoleon's final defeat in 1815. But what mattered most was that Germany had at last emerged from its political impotence to become a nation-state possessed of power and influence in the world commensurate with its long-recognised achievements in the cultural sphere.

Although the creation of a unified German Reich had been the goal of liberal nationalists dating back to the Napoleonic era, it took a Junker conservative who was less interested in German unity per se than in Prussian aggrandisement to bring it about. On 22 September 1862, in the midst of a constitutional crisis over a proposed military reform bill that the liberal majority in the Prussian parliament was unwilling to approve, Otto von Bismarck (1815–98) was made Prussia's minister-president and foreign minister. Eight days later, in one of his most famous speeches, and in what the liberals could only view as an attack on constitutional parliamentary democracy, Bismarck proclaimed: 'The position of Prussia in Germany will not be determined by its liberalism but by its power ... The great questions of the time will not be settled by speeches and majority decisions – that was the great mistake of 1848 and 1849 – but by iron and blood.' Events would bear Bismarck out. Through a series of three military conflicts won in six years' time – with Denmark, in 1864; with Austria, in 1866; and with

259

260   DAVID BRODBECK

France, in 1870 – a Smaller German nation state was delivered by means of a stunning revolution from above.[1]

For most Germans, unification was the signal event of their lifetimes. Brahms was no exception, and hereafter his veneration of Bismarck was unreserved.[2] Yet he had by no means always been an admirer of the Iron Chancellor. In his youth he immersed himself in the traditional liberal nationalism that Bismarck loathed, reading the political poetry of the Young Germans and including passages from it in *Des Jungen Kreislers Schatzkästlein*, the anthology of literary and other quotations he began to compile in the early 1850s.[3] Moreover, in the summer of 1853 he struck up a friendship with August Heinrich Hoffmann von Fallersleben, another member of the Young Germany movement, whose iconic 'Lied der Deutschen', with its call to repudiate traditional German particularism (*Kleinstaaterei*) in favour of German unity ('Deutschland über Alles'), embodied the sentiments of the defeated bourgeois revolutionaries.[4] The *Fünf Lieder* Op. 41 for male voices (1860–2), Brahms's only work in a prime medium for the expression of liberal nationalist sentiment, give the most direct musical evidence of these aspirations.

Not long after Brahms completed this pan-German set, he began to divide a good part of his time between Vienna, the city he would eventually call home, and the Grand Duchy of Baden, a liberal bastion in the southwest of Germany. He was in Baden, living in the Karlsruhe home of Julius Allgeyer, a veteran of the Revolution of 1848, when in early 1866 it became evident that Bismarck was itching for a showdown with Austria. Writing to his Viennese friend Josef Gänsbacher, Brahms observed that they were now all in the same boat: 'Berlin and Bismarck! Like you [in Vienna] we [here in Baden] have to lie low!'[5] War came that summer and was over in a matter of six weeks. His next letter to Gänsbacher, written when it had become clear that defeated Austria would no longer be included in German political affairs, took on a subtly different tone: 'You will have experienced how

---

[1] For an excellent concise account, see D. Blackbourn, *History of Germany 1780–1918: The Long Nineteenth Century*, 2nd edn (Malden, MA: Blackwell, 2003), 184–95.

[2] P. Clive, *Brahms and His World: A Biographical Dictionary* (Latham, MD: Scarecrow Press, 2006), 44–5.

[3] C. Krebs (ed.), *Des jungen Kreislers Schatzkästlein: Aussprüche von Dichtern, Philosophen und Künstlern* (Berlin: Verlag der Deutschen Brahmsgesellschaft, 1909); Eng. trans. as *The Brahms Notebooks: The Little Treasure Chest of the Young Kreisler*, trans. A. Eisenberger, annotations by S. Levarie (Hillsdale, NY: Pendragon Press, 2003).

[4] See Clive, *Brahms and His World*, 227.

[5] Quoted in *Kalbeck II*, 219–20. On Brahms's misgivings about the Austro-Prussian War, see also his undated letter to Allgeyer, c. 10 May, *Avins*, 341.

Politics and Religion

261

deeply one's entire self is affected by what has occurred. The mood where you are must be so distressing ... But the world makes progress slowly and meanwhile we can, I suppose, be grateful to the Prussians for the brouhaha they have caused, for nothing moves forward without that.' Brahms clearly empathised with the German Austrians in their plight, but he expressed no grievance with Prussia for having caused the trauma.[6]

This is significant. It has often been noted that in 1866 many liberals went from hating Bismarck to worshipping him as a national hero almost overnight. To be sure, the left wing of the Progressives in Prussia remained implacably opposed, but a larger, more moderate faction, taking the name National Liberals, began to rationalise Bismarck's illiberal actions as the price of obtaining national unity. Besides they were heartened by his restoration of constitutional rule. In the new German political landscape, Brahms found himself falling increasingly into ideological lockstep with this moderate camp, and it was likely around this time that he began what became a lifetime interest in the work of the cultural and political historians of the so-called Prussian School, which held that the Hohenzollern monarchy had historically pursued policies that were in Germany's best interests and that Prussian leadership in Germany was therefore inevitable.

At precisely this moment Brahms was completing a major composition in which the word 'German' was written into its very name. *A German Requiem, to Words from the Holy Scripture* (*Ein deutsches Requiem nach Worten der heiligen Schrift*) Op. 45 (1865–68) is a setting in seven movements for soloists, choir and orchestra, of sixteen passages carefully culled by the composer from the Luther Bible. Although Brahms grew up in a pious home in Hamburg and received traditional Lutheran instruction, he held with no Orthodox belief. He knew the Bible inside and out yet valued it, not as the revealed word of God, but as something central to his German identity.[7] Brahms's rejection of dogma explains why he avoided setting any verse in which Jesus is mentioned by name, much less any having to do with the redemptive power of his crucifixion. Brahms's concern is not with God's promise to the living faithful upon their deaths, much less with the fate of the soul of the deceased, as in the Catholic ritual;

---

[6] Brahms to Gänsbacher, August 1867, A. Orel, *Johannes Brahms und Julius Allgeyer: Eine Künstlerfreundschaft in Briefen* (Tutzing: Hans Schneider, 1964), 40. My thanks to Josef Eisinger for the translation.

[7] For a detailed account of Brahms's annotations in his copy of the Luther Bible, see D. Beller-McKenna, *Brahms and the German Spirit* (Cambridge, MA and London: Harvard University Press, 2004), 37–64.

he seems to have believed in none of that. Rather he sought simply to bring comfort and consolation to the grieving in the here and now.

That the *Requiem* was composed in the midst of significant geo-political change was a matter of coincidence (regardless of how the music may later have been understood); it was inspired by the death of Brahms's mother in 1865, not by the ongoing battle for supremacy in Germany. By contrast, the *Triumphlied (Offenb. Joh. Cap. 19)* Op. 55 (1870–1), composed for double chorus, baritone solo and large orchestra on portions of the nineteenth chapter of the Book of Revelation, was written in direct response to the Franco-Prussian War and the subsequent establishment of the German Reich. Although the work was dedicated to Wilhelm I, its true hero, as we know from the composer's correspondence, was Bismarck. Once one of Brahms's most popular works, it later fell out of the repertory mostly on account of its supposed 'national chauvinism', a topic much discussed in the musicological literature that merits more exploration.[8]

The first movement, written in the immediate aftermath of the Germans' defeat of the French military at Sedan on 2 September 1870, taps into a rich vein of apocalyptic German nationalism that dates back to the Napoleonic era. In the imaginations of the liberal nationalists of that earlier time, desperate to throw off the yoke of French oppression, Napoleon was the Antichrist; his occupying armies, the biblical plague of locusts; and his capital, Paris, the Whore of Babylon.[9] This explains why Brahms insisted on naming his source in the work's title. In the Luther Bible, Revelation 19 is preceded by a gloss: 'Song of Triumph of the Elect on the fulfillment of God's judgement of the Great Whore'. A man of his time, Brahms may well not have been sensitive to the problematic gender implications of this biblical invocation that now seem obvious.[10] What matters most here, however, is that in his Song of Triumph on Germany's apocalyptic victory of 1870, Brahms was rehearsing all the old imagery from the Wars of Liberation of 1813, with Napoleon III, sovereign of the Second French Empire and a figure no less hated than his uncle had been as a man intent on subjugating the German people, now cast in the role as the Antichrist. With this in mind, we can at least put Brahms's 'chauvinism' into some perspective.[11]

---

[8] D. Brodbeck, 'The *Triumphlied* in Context', unpublished paper delivered at the North American Conference on Nineteenth-Century Music (Vanderbilt University, June 2017).

[9] K. Vondung, *The Apocalypse in Germany*, trans. S. D. Ricks (Columbia and London: University of Missouri Press, 2000), 104–41.

[10] For a brief discussion, see L. McManus, 'The Rhetoric of Sexuality in the Age of Brahms and Wagner', PhD dissertation, University of North Carolina, Chapel Hill (2011), 126.

[11] On German attitudes toward Napoleon III, see D. Wetzel, *A Duel of Nations: Germany, France, and the Diplomacy of the War of 1870–71* (Madison: University of Wisconsin Press, 2012), 6.

Politics and Religion

With the French defeated and the German Emperor proclaimed, the National Liberals hoped that a common German national identity could be inculcated by what Heinrich August Winkler has called 'the hegemony of the Protestant principle in German culture, society, and state'. This implied '*both* the continuing secularization of German Protestantism, making religion ideologically of very flexible utility, *and* the increased theologisation of German nationalism.'[12] The second and third movements of the *Triumphlied* can be productively seen in this light. The second implicitly equates the King of Prussia with the 'Almighty God who has taken the realm' (*das Reich einnehmen*), which is to say, made German Emperor. The third equates the Emperor with the 'King of Kings and Lord of Lords', an apt analogy to describe an arrangement whereby the Reich's various constituent polities (monarchies, grand duchies and duchies, principalities and free cities) transferred the most essential powers to Berlin, even if they maintained many of their traditional prerogatives all the same.

The *Triumphlied* thus projects something of the confluence of 'Prussian vitality, the Hohenzollern dynasty, a "high" culture in art, music and literature, and the morality of liberal Protestantism' that would create a set of national values, or so the founders believed, largely synonymous with 'enlightened Prussian Protestantism'.[13] This 'cultural Protestantism' ran like a powerful current through German middle-class consciousness. German culture was understood to be Protestant, and cultural Protestantism was understood to represent progress.[14] By contrast, Roman Catholicism, the religion of approximately one-third of the German population, was politically suspect as an ultramontane institution and, with its 'superstitions, eccentric devotional rituals, [and] pilgrimages to miraculous objects', easy to pillory – as Brahms certainly did – for being 'backward'.[15] National Liberals thus gave their avid support to Bismarck's ill-fated struggle of civilisations (*Kulturkampf*), a set of policies promulgated in the mid-1870s that were designed to reduce Catholic influence in Prussia and to a lesser degree elsewhere in Germany.

---

[12] H. A. Winkler, *Germany: The Long Road West*, trans. A. J. Sager, 2 vols. (Oxford and New York: Oxford University Press, 2000), vol. 1: *1789–1933*, 199 (original emphasis).

[13] J. S. Conway, Review of Helmut Walser Smith, *German Nationalism and Religious Conflict: Culture, Ideology, Politics, 1870–1914*, H-Net Reviews (July 1995), www.h-net.org/reviews/showrev.php?id=113

[14] Blackbourn, *History of Germany 1780–1918*, 221. On cultural Protestantism, see G. Hübinger, *Kulturprotestantismus und Politik: Zum Verhältnis von Liberalismus und Protestantismus im wilhelminischen Deutschland* (Tübingen: J. C. B. Mohr [Paul Siebeck], 1994).

[15] H. W. Smith, *German Nationalism and Religious Conflict: Culture, Ideology, Politics, 1870–1914* (Princeton: Princeton University Press, 1995), 21.

264   DAVID BRODBECK

Nearly two decades later Brahms turned to the Luther Bible once again in search of texts that could be given timely political meaning. In a letter of 28 March 1888, written a few weeks after the death of Wilhelm I at the age of ninety, Elisabeth von Herzogenberg encouraged him to 'write something dear for the dear departed Emperor so that once again a worthy sound will sound in his honor'.[16] Sixteen years earlier Brahms had dedicated the *Triumphlied* to Wilhelm to celebrate the founding of the German Reich; now Elisabeth was encouraging him to pay the late Emperor one final tribute. Whether Brahms was acting on Elisabeth's suggestion or not, that summer of 1888, during his composing holiday in Thun, he set to work on what became the *Festival and Commemorative Verses (Fest- und Gedenksprüche)* Op. 109. By carefully selecting biblical passages that remember 'fathers', evoke the 'people' and admonish against division within the 'kingdom', Brahms aimed to create music appropriate for patriotic occasions. For performances in Germany, he had particular national holidays in mind and asked his publisher, Fritz Simrock, to issue a special edition for that purpose under the title *Deutsche Fest- und Gedenksprüche*. Simrock was unwilling to go to the expense of printing two separate editions, but when Hans von Bülow gave the first performance, in Hamburg on 9 September 1889, he at least made sure to include the adjective 'German' in the billing.[17]

Shortly after Brahms arrived in Thun, the recently crowned Emperor Friedrich III died of cancer after only ninety-nine days on the throne and was succeeded by his eldest son, Wilhelm II. While attending Friedrich's funeral, the late Emperor's brother-in-law, Albert Edward ('Bertie'), Prince of Wales, evidently made known his opinion that Alsace-Lorraine, won from France in 1870–1, ought now to be returned, and it was soon rumoured that Frederick had shared Bertie's opinion. The young Wilhelm II was outraged by this and, in a widely reported speech of 16 August 1888, given during ceremonies held in Frankfurt an der Oder related to the unveiling of a statue of Prince Friedrich Karl, a wartime hero in France, claimed that his father would never have been a party to such a scheme, adding 'we would rather see the whole of our eighteen army corps and our forty-two million inhabitants laid out on the battlefield [*auf der Wahlstatt liegen lassen*] than surrender a single stone of what my father

---

[16] Letter of 28 March 1888, in R. Minor, *Choral Fantasies: Music, Festivity, and Nationhood in Nineteenth-Century Germany* (Cambridge: Cambridge University Press, 2012), 238 n. 20.

[17] Brahms to Bülow, 30 May 1889, in Hans von Bülow, *Die Briefe an Johannes Brahms*, ed. H.-J. Hinrichsen (Tutzing: Hans Schneider, 1994), 129; Brahms to Simrock, 8 June 1889, *Briefe XI*, 219–21.

Politics and Religion 265

and Prince Friedrich Karl gained'.[18] In this context, and during a period of heightened French revanchist agitation, Brahms could do nothing better to honour the late Wilhelm I (and now also Friedrich III) than to compose a work whose texts called for Wilhelm II to strengthen and preserve the Reich's integrity.

The second of the three *Verses*, which Brahms gave Bülow to believe was appropriate for Sedan Day celebrations, is most directly tied to the moment at hand.[19] Later, in a letter to Josef Viktor Widmann sent shortly after the publication of the choruses, Brahms asked: 'Did you not even notice the theological, even Jesuitical sophistry of the second of the *Verses*? I've always wanted to ask you whether something like that is allowed. (Luke 11: 21 and 17.) For fun's sake look back at it again.'[20] The passages in question read: 'Every kingdom divided against itself is brought to desolation' (Luke 11:17) and 'When a strong man armed guards his palace, his possessions are secure' (Luke 11:21). Like Brahms, Widmann was at once a freethinker and a student of the Bible, and he was a friend with whom Brahms enjoyed discussing spiritual and religious matters.[21] The kingdom under discussion in Luke's Gospel, as Widmann noted, is the Kingdom of Darkness and the strong man is Satan. The 'fun' in Brahms's reading lies in his reversal of 'bad' things into 'good'. The 'possessions' of the 'kingdom' become the prosperity and well-being of Germany, and the 'strong man' represents the military power, presumably embodied in the figure of the Emperor, that will ensure Germany's security, above all from its hereditary enemy across the Rhine.

This is an astute reading, but there is more here than meets the eye. If the controversial status of Alsace-Lorraine lay behind Brahms's decision to set the two verses from Luke to music, the position he took with Widmann in expressing his strong support of the Emperor's resolve to hold on to the disputed territory led to a serious row between the two friends.[22] What has gone unnoticed is that the dispute stemmed from inaccurate initial reports of the Emperor's speech. In the telegraphic press notices of 16 August, which Widmann had found disturbing, the phrase '*auf der Wahlstatt liegen lassen*', suggesting a willingness to defend the fatherland to the bitter end, was erroneously given using the huntsman's expression '*auf der Strecke*

---

[18] *National-Zeitung*, 18 August 1888, 2. For discussion, see C. G. Röhl, *Wilhelm II: The Kaiser's Personal Monarchy, 1888–1900*, trans. S. de Bellaigue (Cambridge: Cambridge University Press, 2004), 73–7.

[19] See note 17.   [20] Letter of 19 March 1890, quoted in Minor, *Choral Fantasies*, 177.

[21] See J. Brachmann, *Kunst – Religion – Krise. Der Fall Brahms* (Kassel: Bärenreiter, 2003), 226–41.

[22] See J. V. Widmann, *Johannes Brahms in Erinnerungen* (Berlin: Gebruder Paetel, 1898), 101–2; and letter from Brahms to Widmann, 20 August 1888, in *Avins*, 660–2 (with commentary on 755).

liegen lassen' (laid out in a row), as though Wilhelm were prepared to treat his subjects like animals killed on the hunt. The difference in implication is by no means negligible, and it is understandable that the German press, as Brahms discovered before Widmann did, took measures on 18 August to set the record straight. Again, historical context provides a more nuanced understanding of Brahms's patriotism.

To close, we turn our sights from Imperial Germany to Imperial Austria. As a member of Vienna's German liberal community, Brahms consistently advocated for the German position in the multinational Austrian state, especially when the primacy of the German language and German culture more broadly was under challenge by Slavic nationalism.[23] He was close, of course, to Eduard Hanslick, as well as to other liberal, Austrian-born lapsed Catholics, but the majority of members in his circle were immigrant cultural Protestants and acculturated Jews. Brahms's exceedingly close friendship with the noted physician and surgeon Theodor Billroth rested to some degree on their shared experience of having grown up in devout Lutheran homes in North Germany only to lose their faith as adults.[24] Brahms's cultural Protestantism not only must have led him to support Bismarck's *Kulturkampf* but also fostered his anticlericalism in general, which, living in Catholic Austria, he had many opportunities to express. For example, commenting sardonically on Anton Bruckner, with whom culturally and temperamentally he differed in every respect, Brahms wrote: 'He is a poor, deranged man whom the *Pfaffen* of St Florian have on their conscience. I don't know whether you have any idea what it means to have spent one's youth with the *Pfaffen*? I could tell you stories about that and about Bruckner.'[25] The old-fashioned and nearly untranslatable term *Pfaffen* was Brahms's preferred way of referring to the Catholic clergy. Martin Luther was perhaps the first to use it as a pejorative.

Most notably, Brahms consistently championed the position of Vienna's relatively large community of acculturated Jews, no doubt in part because devotion to German language and culture lay at the centre of their modern social identity. It is not surprising, then, that he was repulsed by the explicitly racialist ideology that emerged in the 1880s under the

---

[23] I discuss a few examples of this in D. Brodbeck, *Defining Deutschtum: Political Ideology, German Identity, and Music-Critical Discourse in Liberal Vienna* (New York: Oxford University Press, 2014), 158–61, 174–7.

[24] N. Grimes, *Brahms's Elegies: The Poetics of Loss in Nineteenth-Century German Culture* (Cambridge: Cambridge University Press, 2019), 166; for a more detailed discussion, see Brachmann, *Kunst – Religion – Krise*, 242–63.

[25] Brahms to Elisabeth von Herzogenberg, 12 January 1885, *Avins*, 619.

Politics and Religion

neologism *Antisemitismus*, which held that Jews could never become German, no matter what culture they professed. To be sure, Brahms, like other liberals, Jew and Gentile alike, felt abhorrence toward the *Ostjuden* whose number in the cities of Central Europe began to grow rapidly in the 1880s, and whose separatist, Orthodox lifestyle was so at odds with the project of progress and modernity that represented, in their minds, *Deutschtum*. But racialist anti-Semitism was anathema. 'I can scarcely speak of it, it seems so despicable to me,' Brahms was quoted as saying in November 1890. 'If the endless reinforcement of Galician Jews in Vienna were hindered, I would be in favour of it; but the rest is vileness.' Five years later, when Vienna's municipal government was taken over by the anti-Semitic Christian Social Party, he lamented: 'Now it's happened and with it we'll have *Pfaffen*-management [*Pfaffenwirtschaft*]. Were there an "Anti-*Pfaffen* Party," that would make some sense. But anti-Semitism is insanity!'[26] [see Ch. 34 'The Era of National Socialism'].

But what about anti-Protestantism? Notably, around this time the composer acquired a copy of *Der Antichrist*, Friedrich Nietzsche's thoroughgoing indictment of Christianity, written in 1888 but published only in 1895.[27] There was much in this controversial tract for the free-thinking Brahms to agree with. Yet he reacted negatively, as Nicole Grimes has shown, to the philosopher's indictment of 'the German monk [Luther]' for having 'restored the Church' in the face of Renaissance Humanism, and to his complaint that, because of this, the Germans would be to blame 'if we never get rid of Christianity'.[28] For Brahms the cultural Protestant, Luther's theology was largely beside the point. Protestantism represented for him freedom from ecclesiastical mandates, secularism and national self-determination; it was the source of modern German culture and, suitably modernised and secularised, the basis for a free and progressive political life.[29] All this was to be valued, not blamed. Still, it evidently was a struggle in those late years of his life for Brahms to maintain much hope in these things.

Max Kalbeck, a younger writer and music critic in Vienna, and an immigrant free-thinking cultural Protestant from North Germany who

---

[26] *Heuberger*, 45 and 82; translations slightly adapted from R. Knox, 'Brahms as Wordsmith', *Gli spazi della musica* 5/2 (2016), www.ojs.unito.it/index.php/spazidellamusica/article/view/2023.

[27] F. Nietzsche, *Der Fall Wagner. Götzen-Dämmerung. Nietzsche Contra Wagner. Der Antichrist. Gedichte*, in *Nietzsche's Werke, Erste Abtheilung*, 8 vols. (Leipzig: C. G. Naumann, 1895), vol. 8. In German, *Antichrist* can mean both 'Antichrist' and 'Anti-Christian'.

[28] Grimes, *Brahms's Elegies*, 163–9; Nietzsche quoted at 168–9.

[29] L. L. Ping, *Gustav Freytag and the Prussian Gospel: Novels, Liberalism, and History* (Bern: Peter Lang, 2006), 211.

268   DAVID BRODBECK

moved in Brahms's circle and eventually became his biographer, wrote this in his diary about six weeks before the composer's death:

> Remarkable conversation [with Brahms] in the coach. Our shared pessimism and the cloudy future of humankind. Crony capitalism and *Pfaffen* rule. The Social Problem. Impossibility of rescuing the masses through education. The miserable average nature of people. Degeneration leads back to the type of apes. (My thought.) The ruling and noble families.[30]

Kalbeck acknowledges that it was he who introduced into the conversation the topic of degeneration theory, the subject of an influential recent book by Max Nordau on the deleterious effects of modernity on culture.[31] It is clear, nevertheless, that Brahms, dying of cancer, was pessimistic about the state of the world he would soon be leaving behind. Yet, in a way that suggests what Kalbeck elsewhere described as the composer's 'heartfelt, stubbornly devoted, and almost childlike patriotism'. Brahms never tired of reliving the glorious days of 1870–1 and continued, until the end, to take comfort in 'what Bismarck had to say to him'.[32]

Further Reading

D. Beller-McKenna, *Brahms and the German Spirit* (Cambridge, MA and London: Harvard University Press, 2004)

D. Blackbourn, *History of Germany 1780–1918: The Long Nineteenth Century*, 2nd edn (Malden, MA: Blackwell, 2003)

D. Brodbeck, *Defining Deutschtum: Political Ideology, German Identity, and Music-Critical Discourse in Liberal Vienna* (New York: Oxford University Press, 2014)

R. Minor, *Choral Fantasies: Music, Festivity, and Nationhood in Nineteenth-Century Germany* (Cambridge: Cambridge University Press, 2012)

H. W. Smith, *German Nationalism and Religious Conflict: Culture, Ideology, Politics, 1870–1914* (Princeton: Princeton University Press, 1995)

---

[30] Diary entry of 22–3 February 1897. I am grateful to Sandra McColl for sharing with me her transcription of this passage from Kalbeck's complete diary for 1897. Kalbeck later included a slightly different version of it in *Kalbeck IV*, 504.

[31] M. Nordau, *Entartung* (Berlin: C. Dunder, 1892).

[32] *Kalbeck IV*, 110, 485; the reference in the latter passage is to the annotated Bismarck Calendar Brahms received as a gift from Simrock's wife at Christmas 1896.

CHAPTER 27

Literature

Natasha Loges

Brahms was among the many avid consumers of the print culture which burgeoned unprecedentedly during his century. The mid-eighteenth century onwards saw a surge in German-language publishing, following the gradual supplanting of Latin as a scholarly language and Johann Gottfried von Herder's advocacy of popular literature as the highest expression of the national spirit. During the long nineteenth century, a vast amount of printed matter was devoured by an eager public. Apart from journalism, there were huge numbers of magazines that serialised popular fiction, science, geography, history and suchlike, as well as handsome bound collected editions of classical authors such as Goethe, Schiller and Shakespeare in translation, aimed at aspirational middle-class households. Literature was crucial to the wider nation-building agenda to unite the various disparate German-speaking territories and principalities under the umbrella of language. It was inseparable from shifts in religion, philosophy and science, and was shaped and re-shaped by successive waves of political censorship. Musicians, including Brahms's idols (Schubert, Schumann) and contemporaries (Wagner, Wolf, Hans von Bülow) also contributed to the literary landscape through their own – often extensive – writings, their reading and the texts they chose to set and thereby popularise for the musical world.

What is lost to the record is the *discussions* of literature that took place; surviving letters offer only tantalising glimpses into this parallel world of conversation. For example, in response to his friend Theodor Billroth's objections to the poet Georg Friedrich Daumer, whose poetry Brahms set more often than any other figure, Brahms wrote: 'But we must discuss Daumer! I'm sensitive about that topic – even though I know myself to be a complete amateur in the art of verse . . . I will bring you a few poems soon, in which you will be able to see what I find beautiful. I'd like to hear more fully what your real objections to Daumer are.'[1] In that sense, the surviving

[1] N. Loges, *Brahms and His Poets: A Handbook* (Woodbridge: Boydell & Brewer, 2017), 86.

269

literary record is surely nothing but a small fragment, preserved on paper, of his generation's lived experience of culture, including literature. After all, Brahms's large social circle included writers, historians, scholars, actors, scientists, as well as other voracious readers who shared his ideal of all-round cultivation, or *Bildung*, in which all the arts – not just music or literature – coexisted, overlapped and mutually fuelled one another, through discussion, exchange of ideas and print. Certainly, Brahms favoured neutral, widely understood titles like 'symphony', 'sonata', 'lieder', etc., in comparison with, say, Schumann's whimsical and evocative titles for works. However, the poetic tags attached to movements of Brahms's early piano sonatas and other later works, his decision to call the four pieces of his Op. 10 'Ballades' (explicitly referencing a literary genre), his mention of Goethe's famous character Werther in relation to his Piano Quartet Op. 60, his youthful identification with E. T. A. Hoffmann's character Johannes Kreisler, and many other instances where text is subtly interwoven into ostensibly 'absolute' music, are significant.[2] With that in mind, the notion of a 'literary age' is too narrow; what is lost is the sense of the enmeshed arts which his generation took for granted before specialisation rendered this impossible.

Broadly speaking, literature in Brahms's lifetime underwent a transition from late Romanticism, with its dependence on fantasy, to the disillusioned, clear-sightedness of Realism, with its investment in the empirical, tangible and specific (however, the shift was neither neat nor complete). Poetry was written in abundance, although the century saw its decline in popularity in favour of prose. Within this changing landscape, a few useful sources give a snapshot of Brahms's relationship with literature at two key points in his lifetime. His love of reading can be traced to his Hamburg boyhood. Already as a very young man, he declared books to be his greatest pleasure.[3] Specifics can be traced in his collections of aphorisms, published shortly after his death under the collective title *Des jungen Kreislers Schatzkästlein* and more recently published in English translation as *The Little Treasure Chest of the Young Kreisler*. The collections date from around 1853–4, possibly in imitation of his hero Robert Schumann, who himself maintained a collection which he called his *Dichtergarten*. Indeed,

---

[2] The tangled webs of literature, music and personal relationships are teased out in studies like P. Berry, *Brahms among Friends: Listening, Performance, and the Rhetoric of Allusion* (New York: Oxford University Press, 2014); and D. Parmer, 'Brahms, Song Quotation, and Secret Programs', *19th-Century Music* 19/2 (Autumn 1995), 161–90.

[3] H. von Holstein, *Eine Glückliche. Hedwig von Holstein in ihren Briefen und Tagebuchblättern* (Leipzig: H. Haessel, 1901), 113.

Literature

271

many of Brahms's entries betray his close reading of his idol's *Neue Zeitschrift für Musik,* in which each issue was given a poetic incipit, usually by a leading poet such as Joseph von Eichendorff or Johann Wolfgang von Goethe.

Four of his notebooks survive; the first was completed in Düsseldorf in 1854 and soon spilled into a second. The third, called *Beautiful Thoughts about Music (Schöne Gedanken über Musik),* was also begun in imitation of Schumann. Begun by September 1853, it gathered and supplemented the scattered quotations about music he had already found; he closed this collection in July 1854 and started a final one which was soon laid aside. In March 1855, he also began a collection of German sayings (*Sprichworte*). Additional aphorisms are scattered through the notebooks in which he copied poetry specifically with a view to musical setting. Some of these inspired haunting, memorable vocal canons like the extraordinary 'Einförmig ist der Liebe Gram', a translation by Friedrich Rückert of a text by the Persian poet Hafis, which Brahms set within his Thirteen Canons for Female Voices Op. 113 to the melody of Schubert's setting of the poet Wilhelm Müller's 'Der Lindenbaum' from *Winterreise* – surely one of the most fascinating instances of intertextuality in music history. According to Kalbeck, Brahms resumed the collection towards the end of his life, adding aphorisms from Hebbel, Goethe's *Farbenlehre* and *Wilhelm Meister*, Schiller, Jean Paul and Bismarck.

It is not possible to know whether the youthful Brahms selected literary aphorisms which simply reflected his worldview or whether that view was in fact formed through his reading. The numerous freely formed quotations from early nineteenth-century Romantic writers such as Jean Paul and Novalis are always counterbalanced by thoughtful statements by Goethe and Schiller, as well as figures who evinced great formal mastery such as Eichendorff and Rückert. These collections perfectly capture Brahms's desire for balance between the Romanticism and Classicism that underpinned his music. For example, one of the earliest quotations is drawn from Shakespeare's *The Merchant of Venice,* Act 5 sc. 1, namely Lorenzo and Jessica's exchange about music, which evokes many Romantic motives including the night, moonlight, open air and the nebulous pleasure of music. It opens:

> And bring your music forth into the air.
> How sweet the moonlight sleeps upon this bank!
> Here will we sit and let the sounds of music
> Creep in our ears; soft stillness and the night
> Become the touches of sweet harmony.

272   NATASHA LOGES

But it is followed shortly after by a quotation from the eighteenth-century scientist Georg Christoph Lichtenberg, which soberly declares: 'In the term 'man of learning' there hides only the concept that one has been taught many things but not that one also has learned something; therefore the French say, sensibly, like everything that comes from these people, not *les enseignés* but *les savans,* and the English say not the *taught ones,* but the *learned.*' Quite a number of aphorisms are religious in nature, advocating moderation, knowledge and wisdom.

Following his stay with the Schumanns, Brahms diligently amassed his literary knowledge alongside his musical craft in the years of his self-directed apprenticeship alongside Joseph Joachim [see Ch. 31 'Germany'], when he withdrew from the public eye. Among Brahms's surviving documents is a rough catalogue of the books he owned; the first part lists the books he owned around 1856–7 (some are crossed out, suggesting that he no longer owned them).[4] The collection is wide-ranging and intellectually demanding; the classical literature includes works by Aeschylus, Ariosto, Homer, Plutarch, Sophocles and Tasso. Romanticism is represented by the writings of Achim and Bettina von Arnim (given to Brahms by von Arnim herself), E. T. A. Hoffmann, Ossian, Jean Paul and Tieck. The writings of Goethe, Schiller (and their correspondence), Lessing, Herder, Cevantes and Dante; the Grimm fairy tales as well as various sagas and other fairy tales and translations of Oriental poetry all foreshadow his lifelong tastes, as does the presence of a Bible and the writings of Luther. Poetry from which he made settings (in some cases many years later), such as by Fleming, Bodenstedt, Hoffmann von Fallersleben, Groth, Reinick and Rückert is also already present. Many items, such as Dante's *Divine Comedy,* the collected works of Jean Paul and Schiller, Sophocles's and Shakespeare's tragedies and poetry volumes of Elisabeth Kulmann, Ossian and Lenau were given to him by Clara Schumann, hinting at her substantial contribution to shaping his literary tastes. Indeed, the number of gifts from friends suggests that his biblio-philia was well known. And the literary lineage of some of his new friends was stellar; in these years he was close to Bettina von Arnim, sister of Achim von Arnim and widow of Clemens Brentano, who together had collected and edited arguably the greatest collection of German folk poetry, *Des Knaben Wunderhorn* (1806–8). She had also known Goethe; her daughter

---

[4] Along with other documents, this collection is described in G. Bozarth, 'Brahms's Lieder Inventory of 1859–60 and Other Documents of his Life and Work', *Fontes Artis Musicae* 30/3 (July–September 1983), 106–7.

Literature 273

Gisela subsequently married Herman Grimm, son of Wilhelm Grimm and nephew of Jakob.

The books that the young Brahms collected remained in Hamburg when he first went to Vienna in 1862 and remained there for over twenty years. (They were housed variously by his parents, then Julius Stockhausen after his parents' divorce and then returned to his father and stepmother before they were finally packed and sent to Vienna in 1883). Naturally, Brahms had acquired many others by then, in addition to a vast music library [see Ch. 18 'Early Music']. Some of those acquisitions can be dated from the letters he wrote to his patient publisher (and general factotum) Fritz Simrock requesting books; Simrock lived in Berlin, which was a vast publishing hub and the intellectual centre of the emerging German nation.[5] There are passing references to literature scattered liberally throughout Brahms's correspondence, and there are his friends' recollections. All these sources are incomplete, in that they give no indication of what he read while away from home, what he borrowed from others or what he simply lost or forgot to document, but they are valuable nonetheless.

Upon his death, his library was given to the Archive of the Gesellschaft der Musikfreunde in Vienna. The items were catalogued by Kurt Hofmann, and the published list of over 850 titles is an invaluable aid to understanding Brahms's relationship with literature. Like any library accumulated over time, and for actual use rather than show, it includes classics in handsome collected sets, numerous gifts, some novels for light entertainment, almanacs, calendars, magazines and newspapers, all of which capture some aspect of his relationship with the written word. As physical objects, Brahms's books are extraordinarily evocative, littered with traces of reading such as the scratchings out of the blemishes in the paper and thick, vigorous underlinings of passages which intrigued or provoked him, but equally there are volumes in which only half the pages are cut, showing exactly where he lost interest.

If one sorts his books loosely into categories, the results are to an extent predictable, such as the large number of items relating to his native city of Hamburg and adopted home, Vienna. His youthful love of a pithy German aphorism evidently endured too, reflected in over twenty volumes of proverbs, adages and such fragments. Indeed, the idea of 'Germany' is

---

[5] Simrock supplied Brahms with books by Willibald Alexis, Franz Kugler, Otto Friedrich Gruppe and many others. See their correspondence, especially *Briefe X and XI, passim.*

manifested in other ways in his library, but one might not reckon with sixty-odd volumes dealing with topics in German history and politics, including many specifically concerned with the Franco-Prussian War of 1870–1. There are also around twenty books on religious topics; these include his five Bibles, including translations of the New Testament into French and Italian, a rendering in Low German dialect, a Hamburg copy from 1833 (the year of his birth) and a concordance. (Rather touchingly, he also owned several grammars, particularly French and Italian, which include his scribbles.)

The collection also includes numerous translations of poetry, literature and mythology from other cultures, and a Koran. And although Brahms himself did not travel far beyond Austro-Germany (excepting Italy), he owned around forty volumes on travel, including guides and travelogues. In wider terms, he also owned around fifty dramas, including contemporary works by figures such as Ibsen and, of course, his heroes – Goethe, Schiller and the great Enlightenment dramatist Gotthold Ephraim Lessing (Brahms owned two sets of complete works, one additional partial set, an illustrated copy of the comedy *Minna von Barnhelm,* a second-hand copy of Lessing's substantial theoretical work from 1769 *Hamburgische Dramaturgie* and an 1890 'explanatory' edition of *Laokoon,* Lessing's 1766 critical study of the nature of painting and poetry). In contrast, Brahms also owned seven plays by the Viennese contemporary satirist Johannes Nestroy (1801–62), showing his keen delight in that master's wit and light touch with contemporary topics such as rail travel and apartment-hunting. Other plays were possibly accumulated in the search for a suitable operatic plot. But he also owned over forty books dealing with visual art, sculpture and architecture, including catalogues, illustrated books and scholarly histories [see Ch. 29 'Visual Arts'], indicating a profound interest in the subject. There are around twenty books on science and medicine but, of these, ten are by or about the surgeon Theodor Billroth and six by the physiologist Theodor Wilhelm Engelmann, both of whom were his friends. He owned relatively few biographies, memoirs and edited collections of letters, and just a handful of books explicitly dealing with philosophy, including works by Nietzsche and Schopenhauer.

Most strikingly, the library includes over two hundred volumes of mainly lyric poetry, including a large amount of translation. This figure excludes over thirty sets of collected works which also contain much poetry, including those of von Arnim, Gozzi, Goethe (multiple sets), Heine, Herder (three sets), Hölderlin, Lessing, Jean Paul, Kleist, Molière, Reuter, Schiller, Shakespeare, Tieck and Wieland. While this

Literature

list is typical of his generation and outlook, the fact that he also owned roughly thirty volumes of literary studies bespeaks a truly searching, intellectual engagement with the written word. In comparison, he owned (or kept) a relatively modest amount of prose fiction, and again we have only the briefest insights into what he admired in that realm; for instance, he adored Paul Heyse's enormously popular novellas. He declared that 'a new novella by Heyse always means a day of celebration for me'.[6] When it came to theatre, it is again hard to identify what he admired beyond Goethe, Schiller and Nestroy.

This collection naturally intersects with the vast corpus of literature he trawled for the purposes of finding texts for musical settings. Brahms copied poetry for setting into notebooks which are preserved in the Wienbibliothek, and these reveal an entirely different cross-section of his reading. These collections were, of course, for a specific purpose and are concerned with the images and above all, rhythms of language. (The actual texts he set were collected and published by Gustav Ophüls.) Because many of the poets Brahms set are no longer highly regarded within literary scholarship, he has gained the posthumous reputation of being undiscerning in his song texts. However, this relatively recent truism perhaps emerges from a persistent desire to commandeer Brahms for the 'absolute music' camp and squares neither with the breadth and depth of his reading, nor contemporary assessments.[7] Brahms's friend, the Swiss writer Josef Viktor Widmann, in a letter to the novelist Gottfried Keller, praised the composer's 'really thorough knowledge of literary matters, which distinguishes him from so many musicians'.[8] Karl Geiringer also described Brahms as a 'fanatic of learning', with a passion for literature and history.[9]

The single figure whose writing infused every layer of Brahms's life was surely Goethe, the complete *Bildungsideal,* the all-rounder *sans pareil.* Goethe shaped the patterns of Brahms's thought; he showed him how to define quality through the perfection of form, how to fuse emotion and intellect in his art, how to relate to antiquity, history, nature and folk culture, and he modelled a disciplined work ethic. Goethe's words are sprinkled throughout the letters of Brahms and his friends. They read his

---

[6] *Heuberger,* 27.

[7] Exceptions to this approach are Heather Platt and Peter Jost, who have encouraged a fuller recognition of Brahms's detailed engagement with texts. See, for example, H. Platt, 'The lieder of Brahms', in J. Parsons (ed.), *The Cambridge Companion to the Lied* (Cambridge: Cambridge University Press 2004), 185–203.

[8] Josef Viktor Widmann to Gottfried Keller, 4 October 1881, in M. Widmann (ed.), *Gottfried Keller und J. V. Widmann. Briefwechsel* (Zurich, Leipzig & Berlin: Orell Füssli, 1925), 75.

[9] K. Geiringer, 'Brahms as a Reader and Translator', *Musical Quarterly* 19/2 (April 1933), 158–62.

276 NATASHA LOGES

plays in private and then saw them again in the theatres they frequently visited. They heard his poems in hundreds of settings ranging from the simplest of folk-songs (Schubert's 'Heidenröslein' D257, for example) to the magnificent expansiveness of Schumann's vast *Scenes from Goethe's Faust* WoO 3; Brahms, of course, also created substantial settings of Goethe's texts, including the cantata *Rinaldo* Op. 50, the *Alto Rhapsody* Op. 53 and the *Gesang der Parzen* Op. 89. Literature, then, was no separable category of amusement, entertainment or even edification; it was the warp and weft of Brahms's mind.

Further Reading

G. Bozarth, 'Brahms's Lieder Inventory of 1859–60 and Other Documents of his Life and Work', *Fontes Artis Musicae* 30/3 (July–September 1983), 98–117

K. Geiringer, 'Brahms as a Reader and Collector', trans. M. D. Herter Norton, *Musical Quarterly* 19/2 (April 1933), 158–68, reprinted in K. Geiringer, *Brahms: His Life and Work*, 3rd edn (New York: Da Capo, 1982), 369–79

R. Heuberger, *Erinnerungen an Johannes Brahms*, 2nd edn (Tutzing: Hans Schneider, 1976)

K. Hofmann, *Die Bibliothek von Johannes Brahms: Bücher-und Musikalienverzeichnis* (Hamburg: Wagner, 1974)

C. Krebs (ed.), *Des jungen Kreislers Schatzkästlein: Aussprüche von Dichtern, Philosophen und Künstlern* (Berlin: Verlag der Deutschen Brahmsgesellschaft, 1909); Eng. trans. as *The Brahms Notebooks: The Little Treasure Chest of the Young Kreisler*, trans. A. Eisenberger, annotations by S. Levarie (Hillsdale, NY: Pendragon Press, 2003)

S. Kross, 'Brahms and E. T. A. Hoffmann', *19th-Century Music* 5/3 (Spring 1982), 193–200

N. Loges, *Brahms and His Poets: A Handbook* (Woodbridge: Boydell Press, 2017)

G. Ophüls (ed.), *Brahms-Texte: sämtliche von Johannes Brahms vertonten und bearbeiteten Texte* (Ebenhausen: Langewiesche-Brandt, 1983)

M. Widmann (ed.), *Gottfried Keller und J. V. Widmann. Briefwechsel* (Zurich, Leipzig and Berlin: Orell Füssli, 1925)

CHAPTER 28

Philosophy

Nicole Grimes

The compositional output of Johannes Brahms contains a wealth of lieder and choral works that attest to the composer's intense engagement with literature and the Bible. Brahms was an avid reader, deeply engaged with the literature of his own time and that of the past. He was also strongly preoccupied with philosophy. Literary figures often provide a much more complex and rich account of the human condition than many of the ideologies of philosophy that dominated the nineteenth century. For instance, we find the philosophical ideologies of Kant and Hegel filtered through the writings of figures such as Hölderlin, Goethe and Schiller. Brahms was aware of this, which is evident in his compositional output in several ways.

The composer's broad intellectual curiosity was often concerned with philosophical issues. From an early age and throughout his life, he read widely and kept a log of proverbs and philosophical sayings that were significant to him.[1] His library testifies to an enduring interest in philosophical matters. Along with the volumes of Herder, Schopenhauer and Nietzsche that he read and annotated were anthologies of philosophy such as Friederike Kempner's volumes, the first of which (1883) contains excerpts of Kant, Locke, Cartesius, Frederick the Great, Marcus Aurelius and Rousseau; and the second (1886) includes passages from Plato, Leibnitz, Cicero and St-Pierre.[2] If Brahms 'preferred to draw his philosophy from literature, of which the Bible was indeed a prime example', then this is only part of the story.[3] Certainly, Brahms was deeply preoccupied

---

[1] See G. Bozarth, 'Johannes Brahms's Collection of *Deutsche Sprichworte* (German Proverbs)', in D. Brodbeck (ed.), *Brahms Studies* (London and Lincoln: University of Nebraska Press, 1994), 1–29; and D. Beller-McKenna, *Brahms and the German Spirit* (Cambridge MA and London: Harvard University Press, 2004), 35–6.

[2] F. Kempner, *Auszüge aus den berühmtesten Philosophen von Plato bis auf unsere Zeit in beliebiger Zeit und Reihenfolge* (Breslau: K. Siegmund in Komm, 1883–6).

[3] M. Musgrave, 'The Cultural World of Brahms', in R. Pascall (ed.), *Brahms: Biographical, Documentary and Analytical Studies* (Cambridge: Cambridge University Press, 2009), 6.

277

with questions regarding the human condition, fate and mortality. As Hans Christian Stekel proposes, he sought out the same difficult questions in his biblical settings as he did in his secular choral orchestral works in order to 'legitimise' them.[4] But his philosophical interests were by no means limited to these areas.

Already at the earliest stage of Brahms's career, in the article 'New Paths' (1853) in which he hailed the young Brahms as the Messiah of music, Robert Schumann carved out a space for Brahms's music that intersects with philosophy and religion [see Ch. 31 'Germany'].[5] Schumann's article directly confronts the question of national identity by specifically addressing the importance of continuing a German musical heritage. The particularly messianic tone of 'New Paths', which relies on a mixture of biblical and mythological imagery, was typical of Romantic writing. Many of its phrases resonate with the Christian Gospels, including 'one would and must appear', 'by whose cradle heroes stand guard' and 'this is a chosen one'. Schumann's nickname of 'eagle' for Brahms had for centuries been an attribute for John the Apostle, the author of the Book of Revelation. The striking imagery of destruction and renewal that is prominent in Revelation (and in apocalyptic literature) underpins Schumann's depiction of Brahms appearing on the musical scene 'fully armed', with musical compositions 'like a rushing current, as if in a waterfall, over whose cascading waves peaceful rainbows were drawn'.[6]

The title 'New Paths' was well observed: it had become a regular phrase for Franz Brendel's promotion of new music. Someone as well-read as Schumann, who was steeped in German philosophical and literary writings, would have recognised that Brendel explicitly positioned himself as a young Hegelian, citing the preface to Hegel's *Elements of the Philosophy of Right* (*Grundlinien der Philosophie des Rechts*, 1821): 'The owl of Minerva spreads its wings only with the falling of the dusk' in his inaugural address to the journal in 1845.[7] Hegel meant that philosophy understands reality only after the event. It cannot prescribe how the world ought to be.[8]

---

[4] H. C. Stekel, *Sehnsucht und Distanz: theologische Aspekte in den wortgebundenen religiösen Komposition von Johannes Brahms* (Frankfurt a. M. and New York, Peter Lang, 1997), 67.

[5] R. Schumann, 'Neue Bahnen', *Neue Zeitschrift für Musik* 39/18 (28 October 1853), 185–6.

[6] See D. Beller-McKenna, 'Brahms, the Bible, and Post-Romanticism: Cultural Issues in Johannes Brahms's Later Settings of Biblical Texts, 1877–1896,' PhD dissertation, Harvard University (1994), 24–34.

[7] *Neue Zeitschrift für Musik* 22/1–2 (1 January 1845). G. W. F. Hegel, *Hegel's Philosophy of Right*, trans. T. M. Knox (Oxford: Oxford University Press, 1967), 103.

[8] P. Singer, *The Oxford Companion to Philosophy*, ed. T. Honderich (Oxford: Oxford University Press, 1995), 638.

Philosophy 279

In choosing to represent Brahms as Minerva, Schumann, arguably, banished Minerva's owl (which can be understood in this context as philosophy), returning to the goddess herself (which can be understood in this context as music) the importance she was due but that had been eclipsed in recent years in the journal in favour of long philosophical exegeses. In other words, Schumann questions the significance Brendel had accorded to his critical writings in the pages of the journal since 1845. 'New Paths' played Brendel at his own game by using Hegelian terminology to promote the one who would 'give the highest expression to the age in an ideal manner'. Banishing philosophy from the role it had been accorded in dictating the progress of music, Schumann returned the focus to music, presenting Brahms as 'fully armed', as independent of Brendel's 'progress' of the age and not reliant on the dictates of Brendel's philosophy.

Stekel suggests that Schumann's essay (and the death of its author) fortified Brahms's interest in the Bible as a philosophical and cultural text that could be drawn upon for spiritual guidance.[9] The consistent absence of dogmatic texts in Brahms's religious output is well documented, for example, *A German Requiem* Op. 45 or the Two Motets Op. 74. In his secular settings of the legends of classical antiquity as mediated through German Idealist poetry such as *Nänie* Op. 82, *Schicksalslied* Op. 54 and *Gesang der Parzen* Op. 89, Brahms confronted the perceived gulf between divine and human, addressing issues of hope, fate, human suffering and death, without relying on religious dogma or drawing on the notion of an afterlife.

Fundamental to many of Brahms's 'fate-related' compositions is the notion of *Bildung*, with its characteristic assimilation of philosophical thought, which applies equally to the individual human life and the individual work of art. The self-education of the mind is a central trope of the Romantic philosophy of consciousness. The figure of the circuitous journey homeward, as the literary critic M. H. Abrams formulates it, is developed into a conduit for Hegel's *Phenomenology of Spirit* (*Phänomenologie des Geistes*, 1807), which recounts a spiritual journey from the 'moment' of departure of an alienated self until it finds itself 'at home within itself in its otherness'.[10] The ultimate goal of this spiritual journey is a recognition of the spirit's own identity.[11]

---

[9] Beller-McKenna, *Brahms and the German Spirit*, 34; see also J. Brachmann, *Kunst – Religion – Krise. Der Fall Brahms* (Kassel: Bärenreiter, 2003).

[10] Hegel, *Phänomenologie des Geistes*, ed. J. Hoffmeister (Hamburg: Meiner Felix Verlag, 1987), 549, as translated and cited in M. H. Abrams, *Natural Supernaturalism: Tradition and Revolution in Romantic Literature* (New York and London: Norton, 1971), 192.

[11] Abrams, *Natural Supernaturalism*, 230.

Brahms was quite taken with the philosophy of consciousness in its literary guise. His frequent annotations in the Schiller-Goethe correspondence testify that he was certainly conversant with this Romantic plot archetype, for example the passage in which Schiller, taking issue with Schelling's *System of Transcendental Idealism* (*System des transcendentalen Idealismus*, 1800), addresses precisely the dichotomies central to Hölderlin's *Hyperion* between the conscious and the unconscious, between what Hölderlin would later term the 'aorgic' and the 'organic', the two extremes of the 'eccentric orbit of all human life'.[12] An example of a composition informed by such philosophical preoccupations is *Schicksaslied* Op. 54. This work, which epitomises Brahms's response to the Romantic philosophy of consciousness, is based upon the composer's nuanced and sophisticated reading of Hölderlin's poem in its narrative context and relies on his familiarity with the spiritual journey of the *Bildungsroman*, or coming-of-age story.

Brahms's markings in his copy of the Goethe-Schiller correspondence also show an awareness of the role of subjectivity within philosophy, art and culture, and its relationship to a Romantic art-religion. His annotations point to his concern with the relationship between the imagination and more abstract faculties of the mind, for instance, 'while the philosopher can let his imagination repose, and the poet his abstracting faculty, I am obliged in this manner of proceeding, to keep both faculties always in equal action, and only by a constant excitement within me can I hold these two heterogenous elements in a kind of solution'.[13] This correspondence also provided a conduit for Brahms's enduring interest in the nature of tragedy. His pencil markings indicate that he took note of the example of the ancients, including Aristotle's definition of tragedy (Letter 498). Here too we get a sense of his preoccupation with the tragic plays of Sophocles. As a corollary to his annotations in the correspondence, there is surely no stronger testament to this interest than the fact that his friend the philologist, Gustav Wendt, dedicated his 1884 translation of Sophocles to Brahms.[14]

Arthur Schopenhauer seems to have exerted a major influence upon Brahms's fate-related compositions, in particular the

---

[12] J. Adler and C. Louth (eds.), *Friedrich Hölderlin, Essays and Letters* (London: Penguin, 2009), 261–4.

[13] Schiller to Goethe, 16 October 1795. J. W. von Goethe and F. Schiller, *Briefwechsel zwischen Schiller und Goethe in den Jahren 1794–1805*, 2nd edn, 2 vols. (Stuttgart & Augsburg: J. G. Cotta'scher Verlag, 1856), vol. I, 100.

[14] Sophokles, *Tragödien*, trans. G. Wendt, 2 vols (Stuttgart: Verlag der J. G. Cotta'schen Buchhandlung, 1884).

Four Serious Songs Op. 121. There is more to Brahms's engagement with Schopenhauer than Musgrave suggests in his claim that Brahms's only interest in Schopenhauer is 'attached to his musical sayings'.[15] Josef Suk reports that when, in 1896, Brahms expressed reservations about the fervour of Dvořák's religious faith, he confessed that 'I have read too much Schopenhauer, and things appear much differently to me'.[16] Beller-McKenna has explored the frequent association of the first two songs with chapter 46, 'On the Vanity and Suffering of Life' in *The World as Will and Representation* (*Die Welt als Wille und Vorstellung*, first edn. 1818–19), which puts forward the view that death or non-existence is preferable to a desolate life.[17] Although *The World as Will and Representation* is absent from Brahms's library, he did own a number of other Schopenhauer books. His copy of *The Two Fundamental Problems of Ethics* (*Die beiden Grundprobleme der Ethik*, 1841) contains relatively few markings and marginalia by comparison with the 1851 *Parerga und Paralipomena*, which is heavily annotated, particularly in the passages where Schopenhauer discusses consciousness, dreams and the intuitively perceiving intellect. Brahms's annotations indicate that he was drawn to Schopenhauer's discussion of the natural and the supernatural. He paid attention to matters regarding reason, the Enlightenment, anti-clericalism and biblical criticism, as much as he considered Schopenhauer's pronouncements on false and artificially produced spirit apparitions. His characteristic blue pencil markings take note of Schopenhauer's pronouncements on the nature of reading and the inner life of the mind. He was also interested in meditations on ageing, such as the following passage (which resonates with Brahms's most often quoted statement on the creative process as later recorded by George Henschel): 'The pen is to thinking what the stick is to walking; but the easiest walking is without a stick and the most perfect thinking occurs when there is no pen in the hand. Only when we begin to grow old do we like to make use of the stick and to take up a pen.'[18]

The relationship between Brahms's music and Nietzsche's writings is equally important to our understanding of Brahms and

[15] M. Musgrave, 'The Cultural World of Brahms', 6.
[16] J. Suk, 'Aus meiner Jugend: Wiener-Brahms Erinnerungen von Josef Suk', *Der Merker* 2 (1910), 149, as cited in Beller-McKenna, *Brahms and the German Spirit*, 31.
[17] A. Schopenhauer, *World as Will and Representation*, trans. E. F. J. Payne, 2 vols. (New York: Dover, 1969).
[18] A. Schopenhauer, *Parerga und Paralipomena: kleine philosophische Schriften*, ed. J. Frauenstädt, 2nd edn (Berlin: A. W. Hayn, 1862), 543. See also G. Henschel, *Personal Recollections of Johannes Brahms* (Boston: Badger, 1907), 22–3.

philosophy.[19] Nietzsche's enthusiasm for Brahms lasted roughly from 1874 to 1884, although in *Human, All Too Human* (*Menschliches, Allzumenschliches,* 1878) he criticises recent music for becoming too intellectual, too 'modern', a censure possibly aimed at Brahms whose First Symphony Op. 68 had received similar rebukes in the contemporary press.[20] In *The Case of Wagner* (*Der Fall Wagner,* 1888), he is just as hostile to Brahms as to Wagner, and it is here that he famously recognised a 'melancholy of impotence' in the music of Brahms.[21] One might assume, along with Kalbeck, that the composer was interested in the philosopher's famous and inflammatory remarks in *The Case of Wagner.* Yet there are no markings at all in Brahms's copy of this text.

He did highlight a number of passages in *On the Genealogy of Morals* (*Zur Genealogie der Moral*), however, which he had been sent in 1887 by Nietzsche himself. These markings are found only in the third of the three essays, called 'What Is the Meaning of Ascetic Ideals'. Here, in a reversal of the familiar trope of reception whereby Brahms was cast as a chaste composer – not least by Wagner – and Wagner was cast as a composer of sensual music, Nietzsche asks:

> What is the meaning of ascetic ideals? – Or, to take an individual case that I have often been asked about: what does it mean, for example, when an artist like Richard Wagner pays homage to chastity in his old age? In a certain sense, to be sure, he had always done this: but only in the very end in an ascetic sense.[22]

In marking this passage, Brahms must surely have been aware that Nietzsche was contributing to an ongoing late nineteenth-century discourse on art, religion and nationalism, in which we may count 'What Is German?' (1878), 'Religion and Art' (1880), and the opera *Parsifal* (1878) as being amongst Wagner's contributions.[23]

---

[19] The 1895 edition of Nietzsche's writings housed at the Brahms *Bibliothek* in Vienna is absent from Kurt Hofmann's 1974 catalogue of the composer's library. See K. Hofmann, *Die Bibliothek von Johannes Brahms* (Tutzing: Hans Schneider, 1974). Brahms's preoccupation with Nietzsche is given sustained consideration in Chapter 4 of my book, *Brahms's Elegies: The Poetics of Loss in Nineteenth-Century German Culture* (Cambridge: Cambridge University Press, 2019).

[20] See W. Frisch, *German Modernism: Music and the Arts* (Berkeley: University of California Press, 2007), 20.

[21] F. Nietzsche, *The Case of Wagner,* in W. Kaufmann (ed. and trans.), *The Basic Writings of Nietzsche* (New York: Random House, 2000), 643. Kaufmann, for reasons he makes clear in this edition, translates 'Melancholie des Unvermögens' as 'melancholy of incapacity'. I have amended this translation.

[22] This translation is from Nietzsche, *The Basic Writings of Nietzsche*, 534.

[23] See *Richard Wagner Prose Works*, trans W. Ashton Ellis, 8 vols. (London: Routledge and Kegan Paul, 1896), vol. 4, 149–69; and vol. 6, 211–52.

Philosophy 283

Brahms's annotations and marginalia indicate that he was drawn to another of the books Nietzsche wrote in 1888 (which was not published until 1895), the attack on Christianity and German culture with the provocative title *Der Antichrist*. Here Brahms marked several passages not only with his usual *Kratzspuren* (the term that Kurt Hofmann uses for Brahms's nail marks that he embedded in the page at a passage that was particularly noteworthy),[24] but also with large exclamation marks. Of note in this regard is Nietzsche's indictment of German Protestantism as articulated through the philosopher's attack on St Paul and Luther. Nietzsche's charge that Luther had robbed Europe of its last great cultural harvest, and his notion that 'If we never get rid of Christianity, the *Germans* will be to blame' elicited an exclamation mark in a heavy hand in Brahms's margin. The last passage that Brahms marked in his copy of *The Antichrist* – also with a large exclamation mark – reads:

> For almost a millennium they have twisted and tangled everything they have laid their hands on, they have on their conscience all the half-heartedness – three-eighths-heartedness! – from which Europe is sick – they also have on their conscience the uncleanest kind of Christianity there is, the most incurable kind, the kind hardest to refute, Protestantism ... If we never get rid of Christianity, the *Germans* will be to blame.[25]

While we must avoid over-interpretation of Brahms's annotations in his books, we can offer an informed speculation as to what these exclamation marks might indicate. Brahms seems not to have believed in any dogmatic aspects of religious faith. During the 1870s and 1880s he carried out an extended correspondence with a number of his friends, including Josef Viktor Widmann, on the question of a 'godless' Christianity. Yet he certainly subscribed to a Lutheran theological and cultural worldview, and revered the Luther Bible as a cornerstone of German patriotism. This is evidenced in many of his compositions that set passages from the Luther Bible. He treats this text as a source of literary and moral edification while avoiding any mention of Christ's sacrifice. Examples include *A German Requiem*, the *Triumphlied* Op. 55, the Two Motets Op. 74 and the *Festival and Commemorative Verses* Op. 109. We might well imagine Brahms to have been intrigued, therefore, by Nietzsche's denouncing of a worldview that is predicated on a future reward and his espousing instead of a return to a focus on this life. We might surmise, however, that when Brahms placed exclamation marks beside passages in Nietzsche's

---

[24] See Hofmann, *Die Bibliothek von Johannes Brahms*.
[25] Nietzsche, *The Basic Writings of Nietzsche*, 198.

284 NICOLE GRIMES

The Antichrist, he did so because they struck at the heart of his patriotic, cultural and artistic identity.

Numerous books in Brahms's library indicate an interest in music aesthetics.[26] Perhaps the greatest figure in music aesthetics of the nineteenth century is Eduard Hanslick. In scholarship on Hanslick and Brahms, the composer is frequently associated with Hanslick's notion of absolute music in which spiritual content (*geistige Gehalt*) is very much reliant on metaphysics, philosophy and religion. Brahms's music concerns all of these attributes. It would be mistaken, however, to associate Brahms narrowly with Hanslick's *The Beautiful in Music* (*Vom Musikalisch-Schönen*). By 1854 when Hanslick wrote this book, Brahms had just been introduced to the musical world through Schumann's 'New Paths', and had set about trying to find a publisher for his first works. When Hanslick wrote *The Beautiful in Music*, he had not yet discovered Brahms's music, and at no point in that book (nor in any of the subsequent nine editions) does Hanslick mention Brahms. Although these two struck up a lifelong friendship following their meeting in 1862, it was not until much later that Hanslick penned the majority of his Brahms reviews in his capacity as the music critic for Vienna's leading liberal daily newspaper, the *Neue Freie Presse*.[27] Rather than ignoring the poetic and expressive aspects of Brahms's oeuvre, Hanslick engages with the extra-musical aspects of Brahms's compositions and with their significant poetic, cultural, patriotic and socio-political elements.[28]

Nicholas Cook has astutely argued that 'Hanslick did not say that music does not, cannot, or should not convey feelings, moods or emotions . . . [T] here should never have been any doubt as to what his basic thesis was – that the objective properties of music, rather than people's subjective responses to it, constitute the proper concern of musical aesthetics.'[29] Mark Burford further clarifies that Hanslick negotiated a 'middle ground between idealism and materialism', suggesting that 'in his attempt to characterize music's essence, Hanslick did not so much reject musical metaphysics as, to a certain extent, reconceptualize it by arguing that the ideal content of

---

[26] For instance, Brahms owned a copy of H. Ehrlich, *Die Musik-Aesthetik in ihrer Entwickelung von Kant bis auf die Gegenwart* (Leipzig: F. E. C. Leuckart, 1881).

[27] Most of these are found in E. Hanslick, *Concerte, Componisten und Virtuosen der letzten fünfzehn Jahre* (1886), with many also appearing in *Aus dem Tagebuch eines Musikers* (1892), *Fünf Jahre Musik* (1896), and *Aus neuer und neuester Zeit* (1900).

[28] See N. Grimes, 'Brahms's Poetic Allusions through Hanslick's Critical Lens', *American Brahms Society Newsletter* 29/2 (Fall 2011), 5–9.

[29] N. Cook, *The Schenker Project, Culture, Race and Music Theory in Fin-de-Siècle Vienna* (New York: Oxford University Press, 2007), 50.

Philosophy

music is a product of a human spirit, not a transcendent one'.[30] In this broader context, then, and widening our lens from Hanslick and Brahms and a narrow definition of 'absolute' music, this holds true for all of the repertoire considered in this chapter. Brahms intricately interwove compositional process with intellectual tradition and philosophical thought. His music is concerned with the notion of *Bildung*, the philosophy of consciousness, issues of cultural pessimism and the human condition. He encounters these issues in philosophical writings ranging from Hegel to Hölderlin and from Schiller to Schopenhauer, and in the Bible. The spirit (*Geist*) of Brahms's music, therefore, is not that of a transcendent spirit. Rather it is of the human mind intended for the edification of the human mind.

Further Reading

D. Beller-McKenna, 'Brahms on Schopenhauer: The *Vier ernste Gesänge*, op. 121, and Late Nineteenth-Century Pessimism', in D. Brodbeck (ed.), *Brahms Studies 1* (Lincoln: University of Nebraska, 1994), 170–88

M. Forster, K. Gjesdal, *The Oxford Handbook of German Philosophy in the Nineteenth Century* (Oxford: Oxford University Press, 2015)

N. Grimes, *Brahms's Elegies: The Poetics of Loss in Nineteenth-Century German Culture* (Cambridge: Cambridge University Press, 2019)

N. Grimes, 'German Liberalism, Nationalism, and Humanism in Hanslick's Writings on Brahms', in N. Grimes, S. Donovan and W. Marx (eds.), *Rethinking Hanslick: Music, Formalism, and Expression* (Rochester: University of Rochester Press, 2013), 160–84

M. Musgrave, 'The Cultural World of Brahms', in R. Pascall (ed.), *Brahms: Biographical, Documentary and Analytical Studies* (Cambridge: Cambridge University Press, 2009), 1–26

D. Thatcher, 'Nietzsche and Brahms: A Forgotten Relationship', *Music & Letters* 54/3 (July 1973), 261–80

---

[30] M. Burford, 'Hanslick's Idealist Materialism', *19th-Century Music* 30/2 (Fall 2006), 167.

CHAPTER 29

Visual Arts

William Vaughan and Natasha Loges

Brahms was a man with wide cultural interests that ranged far beyond his musical practice, as evinced by his circle of friends, as well as the contents of his library. He had close relationships with several leading German artists and art historians of his time. Once he was financially stable, he accumulated a substantial collection of prints that included both modern and classical artists, focussing on German and Italian art (much like his musical interests, and in keeping with prevailing German tastes). He showed little interest in French contemporaries, despite the towering reputation of contemporary painters like Delacroix and Courbet. On a personal level, his interest in art was part of his general thirst for *Bildung,* or all-round cultural cultivation. Already in the late 1850s, he met Herman Grimm through Joseph Joachim. Grimm was a historian of art and literature, and his biography of Michelangelo (which Brahms owned and read) is still consulted today. In 1860–1, Brahms attended talks on art history in the Hamburg home of Johann Gottfried Hallier, a cultured businessman.[1] In the same decade, he befriended the art historian Wilhelm Lübke in Zurich. Various of the poets whose texts Brahms set were also artists, such as Franz Kugler, August Kopisch, Robert Reinick and Gottfried Keller. (This intermingling of skills and talents was characteristic of the earlier generation, in emulation of Goethe; one might also recall the significant artistic gifts of Mendelssohn.) Bertha Porubsky gave Brahms a copy of Kugler's monumental art history *Handbook of Art History* (*Handbuch der Kunstgeschichte*) for Christmas in 1860.

Thus Brahms accumulated many books about art. Some were by his friends, such as Lübke's 1865 *History of Architecture from the Most Ancient Times to the Present* (*Geschichte der Architektur von den ältesten Zeiten bis auf die Gegenwart*), his *Kunsthistorische Studien*, 1869, his

---

[1] See S. Avins and J. Eisinger, 'Sechs unveröffentlichte Briefe von Brahms', *Brahms-Studien* 13 (2002), 34.

286

Visual Arts 287

Monuments of Art (*Denkmäler der Kunst*, in the third, 1879 edition), and his 1885 *History of the Renaissance (Geschichte der Renaissance)*. Some reflected Brahms's interests, such as the Polish-born, Berlin-based eighteenth-century printmaker Daniel Chodowiecki; Brahms owned his *From Berlin to Danzig. An Artist's Journey in 1773 (Von Berlin nach Danzig. Eine Künstlerfahrt im Jahre 1773)*, which included 108 facsimiles of Chodowiecki's drawings as held in Berlin's Akademie der Künste, as well as a copy of Chodowiecki's complete copper engravings and Matthias Claudius's *Collected Works* featuring engravings by Chodowiecki, woodcuts and a musical supplement (in seven volumes, Hamburg 1775–1812). An 1888 biography of Chodowiecki by Ferdinand Meyer contains evidence of much careful reading.

Brahms's appreciation of art was greatly enhanced by the transformations in print culture during his lifetime – from plate engraving (familiar, of course, from musical score production) to chromolithography and photography – evident from the numerous illustrated catalogues, travel guides and magazines in his library. The inclusion of sixty-two colour lithographs in his copy of *Hamburg and Its Charming Surroundings (Hamburg und seine reizende Umgebung)* suggests the kind of glossy visual document very different from what was possible earlier in the century. The two histories of the Great Fire of Hamburg in 1842 which he owned contained lithographs and engravings, as well as a 'Panorama' of the city. His pocket calendars included copper engravings and other illustrations, as did many of his illustrated geographies and atlases. The sale of illustrations and images had long been an important source of the publishing industry's revenue.

Alongside these practical transformations, Brahms' preferences reflected the role the visual arts had come to play in German society during his lifetime. The nineteenth century was a time when painting and sculpture moved from being relatively little regarded in German lands to becoming seen as a central bastion of cultural values. This process began in the mid-eighteenth century with Johann Joachim Winckelmann, the writer who revived the notion of classical purity in the arts, particularly with his celebrated 1755 essay *Thoughts on the Imitation of Greek Works in Painting and Sculpture (Gedanken über die Nachahmung der Griechischen Werke in der Malerie und Bildhauerkunst)*. While Winckelmann celebrated the power of ideal beauty in its own right, he also implied a moral dimension to this, the Grecian form providing the perfect image of humanity. In Brahms's own day, the leading cultural historian to carry this torch was Jakob Burckhardt (1818–97). His 1860 *Renaissance Culture in Italy (Die*

Cultur der Renaissance in Italien) described the Italian Renaissance as defining an original, secular view of the world and attributing to Italian artists the establishment of the work of art as an autonomous impulse. Brahms was an avid reader of this work; he also owned Heinrich Wölfflin's 1888 study of the Renaissance and Baroque in Italy.

Paradoxically, this revival of interest in an art of universal values was also seen in a national context. The rebirth of German nationalism in the Romantic period – which led eventually in Brahms's middle life to the unification of Germany in 1870 [see Ch. 26 'Politics and Religion'] – was accompanied by a sense of revival in German visual arts. This became prominent first with the Nazarene movement, which sought to resurrect German art by taking it back to its medieval roots. In Brahms's youth, the Nazarenes were already a spent force; yet their impact had been felt throughout the German lands, and they had many successors. The field of high-mindedness was occupied largely by the group known as the 'Deutsch-Römer' or 'German Romans', who could be seen as inheriting both Winckelmann's classical ideal and the Nazarenes' moral earnestness.

Four artists are habitually mentioned in relation to Brahms: Adolph Menzel, Anselm Feuerbach, Arnold Böcklin and Max Klinger. These were, indeed, the four that Brahms himself singled out for particular praise in a letter written towards the end of his life to his friend Josef Viktor Widmann in which he declared that Feuerbach, Böcklin and Klinger 'fill house and heart', adding that the thought of Menzel made him realise 'how luxuriously we live'.[2] They represented differing practices and generations. The oldest, Adolph Menzel, was half a generation older than Brahms. Feuerbach and Böcklin were close in age to the composer and arguably the nearest to him in terms of aesthetic interests. Klinger was a younger artist who idolised Brahms and developed a relationship with the composer in his last years that appears to have caused some change in his thought and practice.

Unlike Feuerbach and Böcklin, who were leading figures among the aforementioned Deutsch-Römer, Adolph Menzel (1815–1905) represented a dimension in German art which put observation before theory, and experience before ideals. Like Brahms, he came from a humble background; however, his superlative skill as a draughtsman soon earned him work as an illustrator and lithographer. His most noted early success was his illustrations to Kugler's important *History of Frederick the Great*

---

[2] A. Dietrich & J. V. Widmann, *Recollections of Johannes Brahms.* trans D. Hecht (New York: Charles Scribner's Sons, 1899), 202.

Visual Arts

(*Geschichte Friedrichs der Grossen*, 1840–2). In these he followed the dictum of the great Berlin historian Leopold Ranke to show history 'as it actually was'. Menzel's illustrations were meticulously researched, creating a vivid sense of the period in which the great Prussian ruler lived. Essentially a self-taught artist, his attitude to his profession was pragmatic. Although Brahms did not actually meet Menzel until the mid-1880s, he had long admired Menzel's work. The two shared a sense of bourgeois liberal values, got on well and entertained each other famously.

Another point of connection came through Menzel's own love of music. Already as a young man, in 1836, he had written to a friend that music 'if not perhaps the first art, is indisputably the one that has the most direct effect on the heart'.[3] One of Menzel's most celebrated works was the 1850–2 painting *The Flute Concert* (*Flötenkonzert Friedrichs des Grossen in Sanssouci*), depicting Frederick the Great on his favourite instrument. Menzel also made fine studies of musicians at work throughout his life. One early example is a pastel sketch of the violinist Joseph Joachim performing with Clara Schumann at the Singakedemie in Berlin (Figure 29.1), a record of a concert that was part of an extensive tour the two were making throughout northern Germany. He seems to have captured a profound moment in the performance, with Joachim with his bow poised and Schumann staring intensely at her score. Schumann, however, seems to have taken a dim view of Menzel, who did not seem to fit the elevated view of creative genius that she treasured so much. In one of her last letters to Brahms she wrote expressing surprise at the composer's enthusiasm for the artist. 'Is he really such a great artist?' she asked. 'I know almost nothing about him.' Brahms replied by sending her some drawings and assuring her that Menzel really was one of the greatest artists of the age.[4]

In contrast to Menzel, Anselm Feuerbach (1829–80) was an artist whom Clara Schumann knew well and who met with her full approval. He was the son of an archaeologist and nephew of the philosopher Ludwig Feuerbach. After an initial period of following the French Romantics and Realists – in particular Delacroix and Courbet – he moved to Rome and immersed himself in the classical tradition. He became a leading light among the German Romans. Encouraged by writers such as Kugler and Burckhardt, such artists came to look on themselves as the preservers of the

---

[3] Menzel to Carl Heinrich Arnold, 5 March 1836, in B. Appel et al (eds.), *Clara und Robert Schumann. Zeitgenössische Porträts* (Düsseldorf: Droste, 1994), 94.
[4] *Litzmann II*, 614.

Figure 29.1. Adolph Menzel, *Joachim and Clara Schumann in Concert* (1854), pastel (now lost).

true classical tradition. To some extent Feuerbach aimed to do this visually by a fusion of styles: the severe forms of antiquity were modulated by the more painterly practices of modern times, inspired in Feuerbach's case by Venetian art. He worked broadly, but avoided bravura. His tones are rich but also subdued, with a penchant for drab blues and olive tones. His art was tragic – he concentrated on depicting the heroes from the Greek myths – such as the brooding statuesque image of Iphigenia on Tauris (Figure 29.2), his best-known work.

Brahms was introduced to Feuerbach in Karlsruhe in the spring of 1865, by a mutual acquaintance, the engraver and photographer Julius Allgeyer. Brahms admired Feuerbach's paintings, seeing them in many ways as a visual equivalent to his music in their respect for a classical tradition. Brahms grew closer to Feuerbach when the latter was appointed Professor of History Painting at the Academy in Vienna, in 1872. In his new didactic role, Feuerbach set himself to reform standards in the Austrian capital, particularly opposing the flashy historical dramas of the popular artist Hans Makart.

Figure 29.2. Anselm Feuerbach, *Iphigenia* (1862), oil on canvas.

Feuerbach's time in Vienna was a disaster. He clashed with the architect Theophil Hansen over his major painting *Sturz der Titanen* (*The Fall of the Titans*), destined for the new academy building on the Ringstrasse in 1873. The subject of Titans falling from heaven demanded a degree of action quite alien to Feuerbach, who had a penchant for meditative figures. The result was a tame compromise which was poorly received. Disappointed, Feuerbach resigned his post and left Vienna. He died in Venice three years later. Brahms remained loyal to Feuerbach to the end, writing *Nänie* Op. 82 in his honour, on a text by Friedrich Schiller. Brahms

292 WILLIAM VAUGHAN AND NATASHA LOGES

kept his copies of Allgeyer's various studies of Feuerbach, as well as the published correspondence between Feuerbach and his mother (given to him as a gift in 1887, with a citation of *Nänie* on the flyleaf). In 1894, Allgeyer gave Brahms a copy of his own biography of Feuerbach, which included thirty-eight illustrations.

While Feuerbach's work sought to explore the limits of pure classicism, the Swiss Arnold Böcklin (1827–1901), was more convincingly connected the classical and the earthy. Brahms does not appear to have had any direct contact with Böcklin until 1887 when he visited the artist's studio in Zurich. The writer Adolf Frey, whose poetry Brahms set, mentioned the visits of Brahms and his friend the violinist Friedrich Hegar to Böcklin in his 1903 biography of the painter, evoking the net of friendships across music and art.[5] Böcklin was, from the 1880s at least, one of the most celebrated contemporary artists in German-speaking lands. Although classified as a Deutsch-Römer, and a friend of Feuerbach's from the time when they studied together at the Düsseldorf academy, Böcklin was quite different. Like the other Deutsch-Römer, he shared an obsession with the classical world and contrasted it with the degraded materialism of the modern world. However, his approach was much more congruent with the pessimistic materialism of the age. There appears to be an anarchy about Böcklin, almost a delight in destruction, in the images of cavorting nymphs and satyrs that are among his most popular works. He pitted nature against civilisation, and usually nature won. But in one sense Böcklin was not a materialist: he had as strong sense of the mysterious, which is most apparent in his visions of the antique where landscape dominates. Here the legacy of the early nineteenth-century Romantic Caspar David Friedrich (1774–1840) emerges.

It has been suggested that the sense of struggle that can be found in Böcklin's depictions of nymphs, centaurs and satyrs helped unleash a new emotional dynamic that is evident in particular in Brahms' later songs.[6] He might also be seen as responding to that deeper sense of the mysterious that comes out most strongly in Böcklin's landscapes. The most famous of these mysterious landscapes is the striking *Isle of the Dead* (Figure 29.3), based on the Venetian cemetery island of San Michele. Böcklin called it a picture for dreaming and dismissed all attempts to create a narrative for it. He was emphatically opposed to illustration, stressing the visual as pure

[5] A. Frey, *Arnold Böcklin: nach den Erinnerungen seiner Zürcher Freunde*, 2nd edn (Stuttgart: J. G. Cotta, 1912), 95.
[6] E. Papanikolaou, 'Brahms, Böcklin and the Gesang der Parzen', *Music in Art* 30/1–2 (Spring–Fall 2005), 154.

Figure 29.3. Arnold Böcklin, *Isle of the Dead* (1880), oil on wood.

experience – aspiring to achieve an art that was close to the condition of music. It is not surprising that the intense mood of the *Isle of the Dead* has stimulated so many musical tributes, the most famous being Rachmaninoff's symphonic poem of the same name (1908).

The closest connection between Brahms's music and the visual arts was made not by the composer himself but by a younger artist who venerated him. This was the Leipzig artist Max Klinger (1857–1920), who encountered Brahms when the latter was already a towering figure in the German cultural universe. Klinger's art was developed in relationship to Brahms; and in turn, he offered Brahms the possibility of new and unexpected dimensions, something that the ageing composer responded to with fascination.

Trained in Leipzig, Klinger was initially a master of graphic art. Like Menzel (whom he greatly admired), he addressed a wide public through prints. He was also a keen amateur musician and kept a piano in his studio. Klinger responded enthusiastically to the growing interest in symbolism in art and the related adulation of music as the abstract form of creative expression to which all other arts aspire – the notion most fully expressed in *The Renaissance* (1873) of the English critic Walter Pater. Rather in the same spirit as the American artist James Whistler giving musical titles to his

294 WILLIAM VAUGHAN AND NATASHA LOGES

works, Klinger took the musical association to the point of giving his graphic cycles opus numbers. He saw music as possessing a unique power, following Schopenhauer in believing music to be the virtual equivalent of the Will. It was this Will, with all its darkness – also redolent of the pessimism of Schopenhauer – that Klinger sought to evoke in his graphic work.

From the beginning of his career, Klinger showed an obsession with Brahms. When he was only twenty, he sent Brahms a printed collection of poems with his etchings. He dedicated his cycle *Amor und Psyche Opus V* to Brahms, and prepared frontispieces for Brahms's Lieder Opp. 96 and 97. In 1880 he began his most ambitious engagement with music: the *Brahms-Fantasie*. Technically it was a tour de force, with eighteen intaglio prints and twenty-three lithographs.[7]

Klinger developed his own unique method of interlinking the visual and the aural. It was his contention that graphic art could approach and respond to the suggestive qualities of music more intimately than painting could. His own designs show the variety that graphic art could achieve. They are an intermingling of realistic and abstracted forms in which text, musical notation and imagery flow freely across the page.

Brahms was flattered by the new attention that Klinger brought to his music and showed his appreciation by dedicating his last set of songs, the *Four Serious Songs* Op. 121 to Klinger. He also wrote to the artist:

> Perhaps it has not occurred to you to imagine what I must feel when looking at your images. I see the music, together with the pleasant words – and then your splendid engravings carry me away unawares. Beholding them, it is as if the music resounds farther into the infinite and everything expresses what I wanted to say more clearly than would be possible in music, and yet still in a manner full of mystery and foreboding.[8]

All this is very positive and implies that Klinger had added a dimension to Brahms's music. However, the concluding remarks are striking: 'Sometimes I am inclined to envy you, that you can have such clarity with your pen; at other times I am glad that I don't need to do it. But finally I must conclude that all art is the same and speaks the same language.'[9] The final phrases interestingly retract what has been conceded

---

[7] Klinger's *Brahmsphantasie* has been digitised by the Davison Art Center, Wesleyan University: http://legacyapps.wesleyan.edu/brahmsphantasie/.

[8] W. Frisch, *German Modernism: Music and the Arts* (Berkeley: University of California Press, 2007), 96.

[9] *Ibid.*

Visual Arts 295

earlier on. Seeing all arts as 'speaking the same language' is different from seeing one art as complementing and augmenting the power of another.

Musical association was taken by Klinger in other directions. Despite his claim of the unique power of graphic artist to interpret music, he later developed a parallel career as a sculptor. Here again, the influence of music loomed large, most famously in his Beethoven statue which dominated the Vienna Secession in 1902. He followed this with a Brahms monument for the Hamburg Musikhalle (1905–9). At the time these memorials were seen as heroic triumphs although it is his graphic art which has continued to resonate with later generations.

It must remain an open question how far Brahms's love of art and contemporary artists had serious implications for his musical work. Certainly, he found resonances that could have strengthened certain interests – the idealism of Feuerbach, the unsentimental acceptance of the everyday in Menzel, the fantasies of Böcklin and Klinger – but these are aspects of his music rather than its totality. Perhaps the best conclusion is that Brahms, like all great composers, took inspiration where he could, borrowing and reacting, but always viewing such material from the centrality of his own creativity.

Further Reading

L. Botstein, 'Brahms and Nineteenth-Century Painting', *19th-Century Music* 14/2 (Autumn 1990), 154–68

R. Brinkmann, 'Zeitgenossen: Johannes Brahms und die Maler Feuerbach, Böcklin, Klinger und Menzel', in F. Krummacher, M. Struck et al (eds.), *Johannes Brahms. Quellen – Text – Rezeption – Interpretation* (Munich: Henle, 1999), 71–94

K. Hofmann, *Die Bibliothek von Johannes Brahms: Bücher- und Musikalienverzeichnis* (Hamburg: Karl Dieter Wagner, 1974)

Y. Malin, '"Alte Liebe" and the Birds of Spring: Text, Music, and Image in Max Klinger's Brahms Fantasy', in H. Platt and P. Smith (eds.), *Expressive Intersections in Brahms: Essays in Analysis and Meaning* (Indiana University Press, 2012), 53–79

T. Nelson, 'Klinger's *Brahmsphatasie* and the Cultural Politics of Absolute Music', *Art History* 19/1 (March 1996), 26–43

E. Papanilkolaou, 'Brahms, Böcklin and the Gesang der Parzen', *Music in Art* 30/1–2 (Spring–Fall 2005), 154–65

W. Vaughan, *German Romantic Painting* (New Haven: Yale University Press, 1994)

CHAPTER 30

Science and Technology

Myles W. Jackson and Katy Hamilton

Any tiny discovery, any improvement in everyday gadgets – in short, every trace of human thought, when accompanied by a practical result, pleased him hugely.[1]

Brahms witnessed a period of staggering scientific and technological advances throughout Europe and the burgeoning USA. The nineteenth century offered new modes of transportation: musicians could now travel to distant cities to perform. With this mobility came the need for standardisation, both of technological devices as well as musical parameters, such as concert pitch, which varied considerably among cities. Brahms was both interested in, and delighted by, advances which related to music and its performance, from train travel to new research in the natural sciences. Indeed, he became an interlocutor with a number of leading natural scientists of the period.

By the 1830s, the Industrial Revolution was in full swing in Britain, and German cities were slowly experiencing the effects of mechanisation. A crucial development in both production and communications was the steam engine, which powered factory machinery, facilitating mass production. Furthermore, critical to economic growth was the development of the steam railway. The rail network connected the German states together – indeed, the economist Friedrich List, whose voice was emblematic of the growing German liberal bourgeoisie, famously argued that a national railway would be a critical step in forging a national economy, with the goal of establishing a unified Germany.[2]

On 7 December 1835 the first German steam-powered railway line opened, linking Nuremberg and Furth in Bavaria. It was privately financed and used a British steam engine. Later that decade, locomotives were

[1] Recollection of Josef Viktor Widmann, *Briefe VIII*, 19.
[2] See R. Krause, *Friedrich List und die erste große Eisenbahn Deutschlands* (Leipzig: Eduard Strauch, 1887).

296

Science and Technology

powering through parts of Prussia, Brunswick, Saxony, Hesse and along stretches of the Rhineland. By 1880 Germany had become the leading country in Europe in terms of railway use: some 9,000 locomotives were transporting over 40,000 passengers and 30,000 tons of freight a year.

Brahms regularly travelled by train from Vienna for professional journeys, holidays and visits to friends and family. His correspondence frequently refers to his rail journeys. Among his many professional trips, the most significant was his tour in 1885 with the forty-nine-strong Meininger Hofkapelle and its conductor, Hans von Bülow, giving performances of the Second Piano Concerto Op. 83 in Germany and Holland.[3] Brahms generally sat in second class, the middle of three classes; though in 1887 he joked to his publisher, Fritz Simrock, 'Are you travelling first class? It's all the same to me, I just don't want to pay for 1st class and then come to you in 2nd. But for the long journey and in general: I suppose you'll be in 1st class.'[4] Hamburg was a frequent destination, on visits to his family; he also had close friends in Bonn and Frankfurt am Main. However, the journey from Vienna to Hamburg was not straightforward. In a letter from 1867 to his father, Brahms detailed the itinerary: one needed to change trains four times, namely in Berlin, Dresden, Bodenbach (today Děčín), and Prague. There were two trips daily: one took 33 hours and 26 minutes, the other 31 hours and 42 minutes.[5] Such a journey, on a second-class ticket, cost 30 thaler for a one-way trip – equivalent to 90 Reichsmark, or circa £262 in today's money.[6]

Steam engines also gave rise to a new branch of physics and, during the first few decades of the nineteenth century, leading physicists concentrated their efforts on the science of adiabatic processes, in which heat was neither liberated nor absorbed. The research of Wilhelm Eduard Weber, a leading German physicist, on adiabatic phenomena during the late 1820s led to the construction of compensated organ reed pipes – that is, pipes which did not change pitch regardless of the volume of air flowing through them. This development allowed for the change in volume of an organ pipe without the pitch being affected, a crucial advance that lent far greater stability to the instrument. Since Weber was one of several acousticians with whom Brahms's publisher, Hermann Härtel, was in touch, it seems likely that Brahms would have

---

[3] *Ibid.*, 2; M. MacDonald, *Brahms* (New York: Schirmer, 1990), 241.

[4] T. Quigley, 'Johannes Brahms and the Railway: A Composer and Steam', *The American Brahms Society Newsletter* 30 (Spring 2012), 1; Brahms to Fritz Simrock, 17 April 1887, *Avins*, 641.

[5] Quigley, 'A Composer and Steam', 2–3.   [6] *Ibid.*, 2.

been aware of these developments, particularly given his interest in new technological and scientific discoveries.[7]

Improvements in communication across regions and countries brought about a new urgency to standardise, not only in science but also in music. In the 1810s, numerous essays in the *Allgemeine musikalische Zeitung* debated the merits of a timekeeping piece so that composers' tempos would be followed rather than being subject to the whims and caprices of performers. Early chronometer designs were quickly superseded by Johann Nepomuk Mälzel's metronome, marketed in 1817, which was portable, easy to use, and relatively inexpensive to produce; and its unit of measurement – beats per minute – was universally recognised. By Brahms's lifetime, metronomes had become commonplace. However, Brahms himself remained ambivalent about the usefulness of assigning metronome markings to his compositions. He famously remarked that he provided them on his scores only because 'good friends have talked me into putting them there, for I myself have never believed that my blood and a mechanical instrument go well together', and only a handful of his published works contain metronome markings [see Ch. 37 'Historical Performance'].[8]

Although he remained unpersuaded by the merits of the metronome, Brahms did have a hand in attempting to establish an internationally accepted pitch. In the early nineteenth century, concert pitches could vary by as much as a semitone between cities. Even churches in the same city possessing organs built in different periods did not enjoy the same *Kammerton*. Furthermore, a gradual sharpening was well underway by the 1820s and continued throughout the century. Touring musicians needed to adjust to the pitch the host orchestra had chosen [see Ch. 23 'Instruments'].

In September 1834, the year after Brahms's birth, the Krefeld silk and velvet manufacturer Johann Heinrich Scheibler presented his tonometer, an instrument comprising fifty-six tuning forks, each 4 vps (vibrations per second, or hertz) sharper than the one before it and encompassing a range from 220 Hz to 440 Hz. He worked on the establishment of concert pitch for a' (A4 in modern notation) as 440 Hz by presenting his research on the tonometer to the annual meeting of the Assembly of

---

[7] A. Hui, *The Psychophysical Ear: Musical Experiments, Experimental Sounds, 1840–1910* (Cambridge, MA: MIT Press, 2013), 5.

[8] G. Henschel, *Personal Recollections of Johannes Brahms* (Boston: Badger, 1907), 78, as cited in B. D. Sherman, 'Metronome Marks, Timings, and Other Period Evidence Regarding Tempo in Brahms', in M. Musgrave and B. Sherman (eds.), *Performing Brahms. Early Evidence of Performance Style* (Cambridge: Cambridge University Press, 2003), 99–101.

German Naturalists and Doctors in Stuttgart. Hence, 440 is often referred to as the Scheibler (or German, or Stuttgart) pitch. After conducting experiments with various tuning forks used in Paris, Berlin and Vienna, Scheibler chose his a' as the middle of the extremes of the pitches to which three pianos in Vienna rose and fell due to changes in temperature during the day: that is the origin of 440 Hz.

Not willing to accept a pitch determined by the Germans, the French established a Commission in 1859 to determine a national standard performance pitch. It comprised twelve members, including the composers Hector Berlioz, Gioacchino Rossini, Giacomo Meyerbeer, Daniel-François-Esprit Auber, Jacques Fromental Halévy and Ambroise Thomas; and two physicists, Jules Lissajous and César-Mansuète Despretz. They decided on A4 = 435 Hz as a compromise pitch: not so high as to harm singers' voices, and not so low as to ruin the brilliance of brass instruments. Not to be outdone, the day after the French Commission filed its report, the Society of Arts in London appointed a fifty-member committee to determine a standard pitch for Britain. Their discussions led to an even higher pitch being adopted – among the sharpest in Europe, in fact, much to the outrage of continental sopranos and tenors – of C5 = 528 Hz, the equivalent of A4 = 444 Hz. All this made touring problematic: wind instruments, for example, could not necessarily be adjusted to match pianos or organs in other countries, and pitching, even for more flexible stringed instruments, could not be managed without difficulty. An international agreement was needed.

Over twenty-five years later, in November 1885, delegates from Austria, Hungary, Italy, Sweden, Russia and Germany met in Vienna to establish, for the first time, an international standard pitch. Characteristically, France and Great Britain insisted that they would use their own pitch standards regardless of what was determined in Vienna. The timing was significant, since both Germany and Italy were relatively recently unified, and Italy did not yet even possess a national standard pitch. Just before the conference was due to begin, the Austrian government gathered advice from a plethora of acousticians, composers, musicologists, singers, instrumentalists and musical-instrument makers to choose between the French and various Italian pitches. Those giving their advice included Brahms, as well as his friend, the critic and musicologist Eduard Hanslick, the Austrian physicist Josef Stefan, Belgian physicist Charles Meerens, Court Piano Manufacturer Ludwig Bösendorfer and military musician Leopold Alexander Zellner.

The Austrians hoped to adopt the so-called *diapason normal*, the French pitch of A4 = 435 Hz, already in use in parts of Germany. (Brahms experienced its adoption by the Hamburg Philharmonic in 1864, which forced the orchestra to purchase new wind instruments.) In a letter to his father about the new pitch, Brahms neither seemed angered by the change nor nostalgic for the older, lower *Kammerton* (he simply enquires, 'Do you have the new pitch?').[9] In the event, the International Commission eventually decided upon a slightly lower pitch, A4 = 432 Hz. Given the astonishing variety of pitches that Brahms would have experienced during his career – from the organ of the Jacobi-Kirche in Hamburg (in 1879, recorded as A4 = 494 Hz) to the agreed tuning used by the Vienna Opera (in 1878, recorded as A4 = 448 Hz), such standardisation must have been welcome in the longer term, despite the consequent expense and adjustment.[10] Even the language required for discussing such dilemmas was developing, with the physicist Hermann von Helmholtz (1821–94) codifying his system of note-naming across octaves in his publication, *On the Sensations of Tone as a Physiological Basis for the Theory of Music* (*Die Lehre von den Tonempfindungen als physiologische Grundlage für die Theorie der Musik*, 1863), the most influential work of physiological acoustics for scientists and musicians alike during the second half of the nineteenth century. Brahms owned a copy of this text.

Aside from Helmholtz's prolific research, he was also a gifted amateur pianist, and Joseph Joachim was a frequent visitor to his Berlin home. Helmholtz's *On the Sensations of Tone* is a wide-ranging volume discussing the physics of consonance and dissonance, the physical phenomenon of combination tones, beats, resonance, tonality, equal temperament and the physiology of the ear and auditory perception. The last chapter of the book is dedicated to elucidating the aesthetic qualities of music: Helmholtz argued that scientific principles could neither explain nor analyse aesthetics, since each culture generates its own criteria for defining what constitutes pleasurable music.

Such theoretical discussions were closely linked to practical work and even technological development for Helmholtz. He worked with C. F. Theodore Steinway (whose father had founded Steinway & Sons of Manhattan in 1853) to develop a new patent in 1872. This involved the use of front and back aliquot stringing: the so-called 'dead' sections of piano

---

[9] S. Avins, 'Performing Brahms's Music: Clues for His Letters', in *Performing Brahms*, 15. See also Avins, 304.

[10] A. J. Ellis, 'On the History of Musical Pitch', *Journal of the Society of Arts* 28 (1880), 333 and 336; 400–3; and 29 (1881), 109–12.

Science and Technology

strings, not directly vibrating as part of note production, could be adjusted to vibrate sympathetically with other notes, and this enhanced the power and sustain of the instrument. Helmholtz also experimented with the optimal position of hammers hitting the strings as well as the material composition of the strings and hammers.

Given his particular interest in keyboard instruments (reed pipes and harmoniums, as well as pianos), Helmholtz was also much occupied with the question of temperament and intonation. In his experiments in this field, he worked closely with Joachim, whom he observed to have particularly acute awareness of variations in pitch. During the 1860s and 1870s, Joachim and Helmholtz conducted experiments on a custom-made harmonium built in just intonation. While equal temperament was the established model of tuning at this date – and allowed for smooth modulations to both closely associated and remote tonal areas – this was accompanied by a loss of the unique tonal colour of each key. For this reason, Helmholtz favoured just intonation and pointed to Joachim's instinctive ability to be able to adjust the tunings of his own playing to match the harmonium as proof that the model was workable.

These experiments continued into the 1880s and 1890s. Helmholtz believed that such instruments were particularly beneficial for the training of singers (a useful and potentially lucrative area of research, given the ever-increasing popularity of amateur choral singing in the Austro-German territories). Subsequent research by Helmholtz's protégé and the 1918 Nobel Laureate in Physics, Max Planck, revealed that the harmonium could be used to study how the human ear could accommodate pitch and pitch variation. Joachim was close friends with Planck, a gifted amateur tenor and pianist, whose work was published in the essay *Natural Intonation in Vocal Music* (*Die natürliche Stimmung in der modernen Vokalmusik*) in 1893.

In the mid-1880s, Helmholtz worked with students at the University of Berlin and the Japanese physicist Shohé Tanaka to design a fixed-tone keyboard instrument, the enharmonium, for teaching music theory. The enharmonium was microtonic, containing a twenty-tone-per-octave keyboard. When the instrument was completed, Helmholtz invited Joachim and Brahms to come and see it. Alas, neither of them was enthusiastic. Brahms recalled:

> Joachim and I were once at Helmholtz's, who demonstrated his discoveries and pure harmonics on the instrument he had invented. He claimed that the seventh must sound somewhat higher and the third somewhat lower than is

> customary. Joachim, who is indeed a very polite man, at first wanted to appear to have an entirely proper impression of the intervals, and acted as if he heard them exactly the way Helmholtz heard them. I said to him that the issue was too serious for politeness to decide the point; I consistently heard the opposite of what Helmholtz claimed. Then Joachim admitted that it was actually the same with him.[11]

Despite the enharmonium's failure to impress (the scientist wrote that 'neither Brahms nor Joachim fundamentally understood what it was actually all about for me'),[12] it is significant that Helmholtz consulted these two senior musical figures.

Another close member of the Brahms circle who was following these developments was the baritone Julius Stockhausen. Stockhausen's influential vocal treatise (the 1884 *Gesangsmethode*) introduced singers to the physiology of their craft [see Ch. 19 'Singers'].[13] It was based on three fundamental principles of acoustics describing the characteristics of a tone: the number of vibrations (pitch), the amplitude of the vibrations (volume) and the shape of the vibration (tonal colour). These are determined by three sets of organs: the larynx, with its cartilage, ligaments and muscles, and the glottis govern pitch; the lungs, ribcage muscles, diaphragm, epiglottis and vocal cords are responsible for the volume; and the lips, tongue and palate give rise to the tonal colour. It is notable that while physiologists where studying the organs relevant to the human voice, musicians were incorporating physiology into their pedagogical texts.

The railways had opened new horizons of travel, trade and communication; scientific developments in instrument design and pitch had affected the production of sound and organology. Another major technological breakthrough with profound repercussions for music was the development of devices to record and reproduce sound. Rendering the traces of vibrating tuning forks visible was common practice among experimental natural philosophers of the early 1800s. A stylus was attached to one of the prongs of the fork. After the fork was struck, it would etch out a wave on a soot-coated paper, which was placed on a rotating cylinder. The investigator counted the number of waves per unit time or the time required for the drum to make a complete revolution. This yielded the pitch of the tuning fork. The phonoautograph, patented by the French typesetter Édouard-

---

[11] A. Moser, *Joseph Joachim: Ein Lebensbild* (Berlin: Verlag der Deutschen Brahms-Gesellschaft, 1910), 230, as translated in B. Steege, *Helmholtz and the Modern Listener* (New York: Cambridge University Press, 2012), 210.

[12] Moser, *Joseph Joachim*, 231. As translated in Steege, *Helmholtz*, 210.

[13] J. Stockhausen, *Gesangsmethode* (Leipzig: C. F. Peters, 1884).

Science and Technology 303

Léon Scott de Martinville in 1857, drew upon this earlier form of graphic representation: sounds travelling through the air were funnelled to a needle carving a line into soot-covered paper covering a rotating cylinder. These etchings could not play back sound, but they produced a visualisation of sound waves.

In April 1877, the French poet and inventor Charles Cros proposed a method of reproducing the sound from those traces. By means of photoengraving, one transformed a phonautographic tracing into a groove on a metallic cylinder. A stylus traversed the groove causing it to oscillate, and these oscillations were then transmitted to a diaphragm. The vibrating diaphragm set the sounding air in motion, thereby reproducing the original sound. By October 1877, Cros had improved his technique by having the stylus carve its curve on a thin coating of acid-resistant material on a metallic surface. The surface could be subsequently etched in an acid bath, producing the requisite groove. Too poor to pay artisans to build his contraption, Cros made his plans public at no charge.

In November of that same year, Thomas A. Edison independently invented the phonograph – the physical incarnation of Cros's plans. It arose from his attempts to develop an automatic method to record and play back telegraph messages. The early Edison phonographs employed a stylus, which would travel up and down over a sheet of tinfoil covering a grooved cylinder. Sound was recorded as indentations on the foil which would then generate signals on playback. By 1886 wax-coated cylinders were beginning to appear to record sound, and the technology was primarily used for business correspondence. By the 1890s, phonograph and record manufacturers began to mass produce their technology. Its application to recording musical performance was being explored more fully, although it would be some years before the invention of the condenser microphone made it possible to capture the subtler sonorities of certain instruments.

In 1889, Edison's recording engineer Adelbert Theodor Wangemann travelled to Europe to demonstrate the newly developed phonograph. He visited the Vienna Grand Hotel on 30 October. Brahms attended the demonstration and was thoroughly impressed. A recording of his own playing was organised for 2 December, in the home of Richard and Maria Fellinger. (Richard Fellinger was the head of the Viennese office of Siemens & Halske, the renowned German electrical company.) Brahms played his own *Hungarian Dance* WoO 1 no. 1 and an excerpt of Josef Strauss's Polka-Mazurka 'Die Libelle' Op. 204 on Fellinger's Streicher grand piano. These recordings provide much information about the composer's approach to performance.

In short, Brahms's life was shaped by numerous scientific and technological advances. The dissemination of his compositions, his own international travels, the instruments he played, the training of young musicians and the pitch and pacing of his work were all affected by new discoveries and inventions. With the invention of the phonograph came the possibility of making his music accessible to an infinitely larger audience than could ever previously have been imagined.

Further Reading

L. Botstein, 'Time and Memory: Concert Life, Science, and Music in Brahms's Vienna', in W. Frisch and K. C. Karnes (eds.), *Brahms and His World*, 2nd edn (Princeton: Princeton University Press, 2009), 3–25

E. Hiebert, *The Helmholtz Legacy in Physiological Acoustics* (New York: Springer, 2014)

J. Horvith and S. E. Horvith, *Edison, Musicians and the Phonograph: A Century in Retrospect* (Santa Barbara, CA: Praeger, 1987)

A. Hui, *The Psychophysical Ear: Musical Experiments, Experimental Sounds, 1840–1910* (Cambridge, MA: MIT Press, 2013)

M. W. Jackson, *Harmonious Triads: Physicists, Musicians, and Instrument Makers in Nineteenth-Century Germany* (Cambridge, MA: MIT Press, 2006)

C. Smith and M. N. Wise, *Energy and Empire: A Biographical Sketch of Kelvin* (New York: Cambridge University Press, 1989)

B. Steege, *Helmholtz and the Modern Listener* (New York: Cambridge University Press, 2012)

J. Sterne, *The Audible Past: Cultural Origins of Sound Reproduction* (Rayleigh/ Durham, NC: Duke University Press, 2003)

PART V

Reception and Legacy

CHAPTER 31

Germany

Johannes Behr

The reception of Brahms's music beyond his home city of Hamburg began in 1853, when the young composer made his first extended journey and presented his compositions to some of the leading figures of German contemporary music: Robert Schumann, Robert Franz and Franz Liszt. Each reacted to these unpublished works in distinctive ways.

Robert Schumann, with whom Brahms spent the whole month of October in Düsseldorf, was instantly enthralled. He described Brahms as a 'musical Messiah' to his friends, and published an article, 'Neue Bahnen', in the *Neue Zeitschrift für Musik* in which he proclaimed the twenty-year-old as virtually the most significant living composer:

> I believed . . . there would and must . . . suddenly appear one who was called to give ideal voice to the highest expression of the age; . . . And he has indeed come, a young blood, at whose cradle the Graces and Heroes watched. He is called Johannes Brahms . . . Sitting at the piano, he revealed wondrous regions . . . When he finally lays his wand where the mighty masses will give him their power, in chorus and orchestra, then we will have still more wonderful glimpses into the spirit realm.[1]

A complete contrast was presented by Robert Franz (1815–92) in Halle, whom Brahms visited in December 1853 on the way home from Leipzig. This respected university music teacher, conductor, organist and composer, was tartly dismissive:

> Yesterday, Robert Schumann's declared Messiah Johannes Brahms . . . visited me. Brahms played me his sonata, which appears as his Op. 1 with Härtel. Knock me stone dead if I understood the thing! All short, ragged starts, or tapeworm-like extended contrapuntal passages! . . . Through the wildest, most breakneck harmonic and melodic passagework, motives which are themselves meaningless are bloated into veritable monsters – giants, which by the light of day are really only dwarves! . . . After that, one can

[1] R. Schumann, 'Neue Bahnen', *Neue Zeitschrift für Musik* 39/18 (28 October 1853), 185–6.

308   JOHANNES BEHR

hardly speak of clear and lucid architecture – let he who can, find his way through this muddle; I for my part hereby loudly and clearly declare myself utterly unable to do so.[2]

Brahms made a different impression again on Franz Liszt: he had already visited Liszt for two weeks in Weimar in June 1853, and met him again in December in Leipzig. Regarding the latter visit, Liszt wrote to Hans von Bülow that he was sincerely interested in Brahms and that he believed 'that his "new paths" might lead him closer to Weimar in the future. You will like his Sonata in C major [Op. 1] which I saw in proof stage in Leipzig and which he had showed me here [in Weimar]. Based on this work, I had already formed the highest opinion of his talent.'[3]

Thus, the music of the youthful Brahms inspired various judgements from Schumann, Franz and Liszt, each of which can be explained by their differing conceptions of music. As a composer, Franz, who had been trained in the strict school of Friedrich Schneider in Dessau, remained a lifelong adherent to the old masters. For him, a work's formal beauty ranked fundamentally higher than its expressive truth. 'In art, one can only judge by beauty; everything beautiful is also true, but not everything which is true is also beautiful.'[4] Following these classical principles, Franz could not admire the turbulent Sonata so reminiscent of late Beethoven. For Liszt, precisely these formally adventurous tendencies may have given him hope that Brahms might share the artistic outlook of his Weimar School. This circle of musicians, which since 1859 had called itself the 'New German School', demanded that composers of instrumental music offer not only 'a kaleidoscopic profusion ... of interwoven lines' but also that they could 'unfold a sequence of moods which are unambiguously, clearly present in their consciousness'.[5] Hence, in contrast to Franz's classicism, Liszt believed that the primacy of expressing content justified the abandoning of traditional rules of art, and that the comprehension of this should be aided through a verbal programme.

Schumann, too, required poetic expression from music but for him, this entailed the stimulation of the imagination towards unspecific, abstract ideas. Suggestive titles could well serve as artistic tools, but he rejected concrete programmes as limiting. One verbalisation of this Romantic-

---

[2] E. Müller, 'Robert Franz über Johannes Brahms. Aus einem unbekannten Briefe', *Schweizerische Musikzeitung und Sängerblatt* 66/26 (13 November 1926), 379.

[3] La Mara (ed.), *Briefwechsel zwischen Franz Liszt und Hans von Bülow* (Leipzig: Breitkopf & Härtel, 1898), 61.

[4] W. Waldmann, *Robert Franz. Gespräche aus zehn Jahren* (Leipzig: Breitkopf & Härtel, 1895), 27.

[5] F. Liszt, 'Berlioz und seine Haroldsymphonie', *Neue Zeitschrift für Musik* 43/5 (27 July 1855), 50, 52.

Germany

poetic conception of music is found in E. T. A. Hoffmann's collection of short stories *Kreisleriana*, extracts from which Schumann copied into his anthology *Dichtergarten für Musik* (*A Poet's Garden for Music*): 'Music opens an unknown realm to man, a world which has nothing in common with the surrounding, external world of the senses, and in which he casts off all specific feelings in order to abandon himself to inexpressible longing.'[6]

Schumann was a lifelong adherent to this poetic ideal of music. He also founded the influential music journal *Neue Zeitschrift für Musik* with the explicit aim of 'hastening the advent of a new poetic era'.[7] Brahms in turn called himself 'Johannes Kreisler junior' in the style of Hoffmann's eccentric *Kapellmeister* (concertmaster). When Schumann encountered his highly expressive and formally idiosyncratic works, he was convinced that the younger man embodied 'the highest expression of the age', the longed-for 'new poetic age'. He therefore wrote the article 'New Paths' and, furthermore, published it in the *Neue Zeitschrift für Musik*, even though his former journal, under its new editor Franz Brendel, now sided with the New German School and increasingly criticised or ignored Schumann's works.

After Brahms performed his Piano Sonata Op. 1 and Scherzo Op. 4 at a subscription concert in the Leipzig Gewandhaus on 17 December 1853 and once his first six opuses had been published (in that month and in February 1854), the wider musical public could also pass judgement on him. Contemporary reviews can be divided largely into two camps, in which Liszt's and Franz's aesthetic positions can be identified. Representing the classical view, for example, was the Cologne-based *Niederrheinische Musik-Zeitung*. In 1853 its editor Ludwig Bischoff wrote in the leading article 'What we want':

> We thus take a stand against the trivial ones, but also against the original ones, in other words the pseudo-original ones, who take formlessness for freedom, the excrescences of sickly growth for succulent saplings, the bounds of an overheated imagination for genius, and which in despair of the ability to create good, simple, natural and beautiful things, arbitrarily and intentionally screw themselves onto a scaffold of the striking and outlandish.[8]

---

[6] G. Nauhaus and I. Bodsch (eds.), *Robert Schumann. Dichtergarten für Musik* (Frankfurt am Main and Basel: Stroemfeld Verlag; Bonn: Stadtmuseum, 2007), 304.

[7] R. Schumann, 'Zur Eröffnung des Jahrganges 1835', *Gesammelte Schriften über Musik und Musiker*, 4 vols. (Leipzig: G. Wigand, 1854), vol. 1, 60.

[8] *Niederrheinische Musik-Zeitung* 1/3 (16 July 1853), 18.

Bischoff reproached not only Berlioz and Wagner with 'outlandishness' but also Schumann, 'especially in his later works'.[9] An anonymous review of the Piano Sonata similarly reproached Brahms, stating that instead of 'truly original melodic thoughts', the composer offers material which is 'often pre-existing' and includes 'many blatant imitations', and that his thematic development is unnatural, whimsically random and chaotic. In his view, Brahms had lost a sense of simple beauty. He therefore counts, the review continues, as one of those talents 'which do indeed justify high hopes, but will only fulfil them when they learn, above all, to acknowledge the infinite amount they can learn from the works of the great masters, and that they must turn back to noble simplicity'.[10]

If the conservative faction in the mid-1850s regarded Schumann and Brahms as close to the New Germans, then so did the New Germans themselves. Liszt and his circle saw in Schumann a precursor of their own efforts, as he had 'clearly recognised within his own spirit the need for a closer connection of music, including pure instrumental music, to poetry and literature', even if the consequences for him did not lead to programmatic music.[11] In 1855 the *Neue Zeitschrift für Musik* published its first substantial article on Brahms after the publication of Opp. 1–9. The author 'Hoplit' (i.e. Richard Pohl), defended Brahms against the 'fury of the south German and Rhenish press', but also charged Schumann with 'kind-hearted but premature enthusiasm' and justified his praise of the youthful Brahms as an emerging, not polished talent. Schumann's music, he declared, showed a 'clearly pronounced subjectivity', which 'despite all its profundity, ultimately ended in a spiralling rumination on ideas from which it could no longer free itself'. Brahms, as Schumann's spiritual kin, also innately leaned towards 'inner rumination and the indefinite, the nebulous'. Brahms must therefore 'free himself from his Schumannian nature' and follow the 'artistic currents of the day', characterised above all by a 'tendency towards realism'.[12]

Both factions therefore demanded that Brahms turn away from Schumann, whose music they increasingly regarded as strange (according to the conservatives) or vague (according to the New Germans). Notably, in summer 1854 Brahms himself grew convinced that he could no longer continue on his previous compositional path. The works he had created after meeting Schumann in autumn 1853, with their abundant extramusical

---

[9] *Niederrheinische Musik-Zeitung* 1/2 (9 July 1853), 11.
[10] *Niederrheinische Musik-Zeitung* 2/9 (4 March 1854), 65–6.
[11] F. Liszt, 'Robert Schumann', *Neue Zeitschrift für Musik* 42/13 (23 March 1855), 137.
[12] Hoplit [R. Pohl], 'Johannes Brahms', *Neue Zeitschrift für Musik* 43/25 (14 December 1855), 262–4.

Germany 311

references, were clearly connected with Schumann's poetic music: the Piano Sonata Op. 5 with its poetic mottos heading the slow movement; the First Piano Trio Op. 8 with its 'speaking' quotations from Beethoven's and Schubert's songs; the *Variations on a Theme of Robert Schumann* Op. 9, which through theme, dedication and musical quotations relates in complex ways to both Schumanns; and the Ballades Op. 10 for piano, the 'narrative' intention of which was underlined through the reference to Herder's 'Edward' ballade in the first number. Brahms originally intended to publish both Opp. 9 and 10 (the latter obviously in an earlier version) in two volumes, titled *Leaves from the Diary of a Musician. Edited by Kreisler Junior*; this enigmatic title also recalled Schumann, who in 1836/7 had had *Davidsbündlertänze* Op. 6 and the Piano Sonata Op. 11 printed under the fictitious authorship 'Florestan and Eusebius'. However, Joseph Joachim urgently advised Brahms against this in a letter of 27 June 1854:

> But I must declare myself against the title of the whole set; in Hoffmann's and Jean Paul's day, such riddles were a novelty, an expression of a certain brilliant exuberance which sought to befuddle the Philistines in every way possible – today, such things have degraded into cliché, meaninglessly exploited by practically every youthful versifier . . . ; you shouldn't encourage it by your example.[13]

In this way, Joachim too declared himself against an extended Romantic mystification of music in the Schumannian sense of the 1830s. It is unclear whether Brahms was swayed only by his friend's advice or also by the public discourse around his first printed works; in any case he published the *Variations on a Theme of Robert Schumann* and the Ballades under his own name, and by 1855 had ceased to identify with Kreisler. This was not just the result of abandoning an external symbol but also a sign of fundamental self-doubt about his compositional identity, as evident from a letter to Clara Schumann in 20 August 1855: 'Since I have composed myself out, indeed since I'm already outdated, there is no composition, but still, I have written something for your birthday or for your return. You can guess in the meantime.'[14]

Here, Brahms alludes to two movements of a keyboard suite (now lost). This passage also allows us to see how he extricated himself from his crisis: between late 1854 and late 1860, he published no new works at all, and only the Ballades and the *Volkskinderlieder* WoO 31 appeared. Instead, he

---

[13] *Briefe V*, 50–1. [14] *SBB I*, 131.

dedicated himself for several years to intensive study of strict counterpoint and older forms and wrote – initially without intending to publish them – canons, suite movements, preludes and fugues as well as folk-song and choral arrangements. Only towards the end of this period did he complete several new works in which he sought to make his improved compositional technique and handling of form fruitful. His aims in this can be seen from two statements he made to Joachim at this time: around mid-November 1856 he sent his friend his *Variations on a Hungarian Song* Op. 21 no. 2 and asked him: 'Do write to me with your usual dear honesty about them. Especially in the finale an ill-mannered youth rampages, and I actually want to build forms more tidily, like a journeyman, not rampage like sometimes in the sonatas.'[15]

In a letter of 21 January 1857, he declared more generally: 'Should one not eventually be able to express the most profound thoughts beautifully and in a way which is pleasing to the artistic ear?'[16] Brahms himself now evidently regarded certain 'rampaging' passages from his earlier works critically and, through his studies, had arrived at the conclusion that even the 'profoundest' expression should not impair the beauty of the composition. Seeking a corrective, Brahms had absorbed the central demand of the conservative critics and now strove towards a balance between expressiveness and construction.

After his long silence, Brahms published eight new works (Opp. 11–18) between the end of 1860 and the start of 1862, with which he astonished the musical world. As Adolf Schubring declared in 1862, in a lengthy article about the composer: 'If the name had not been on the front cover, no one would have thought of Brahms, so enormously different are these works in character and in the entire approach from the earlier ones.' Schubring divided Brahms's works to date into three groups: 'The latest works, Op. 11 to 18, are like clear wine in comparison to the brewing must of Op. 1 to 6; between these, Op. 7 to 10 are a transitional group of undecided, changing coloration.'

If the works of the earlier two periods still showed formal weaknesses, 'transgressions of the line of beauty' and (in the songs) 'errors of declamation', 'all was easy, effortless, rounded, mature' in the new ones. The First String Sextet Op. 18 was especially praised by Schubring as the 'most delightful, beautiful and mature' of the new works.[17]

---

[15] *Briefe V*, 158 (here incorrectly dated July 1856).   [16] *Ibid.*, 174.

[17] DAS (= Dr Adolf Schubring), 'Schumanniana Nr. 8. Die Schumann'sche Schule. IV. Johannes Brahms', *Neue Zeitschrift für Musik* 56/12 (21 March 1862), 93–6; 56/13 (28 March 1862), 101–4; 56/14 (4 April 1862), 109–12; 56/15 (11 April 1862), 117–19; and 56/16 (18 April 1862), 125–8.

Germany

While Schubring, who regarded himself as part of the musical 'middle', accordingly emphatically welcomed Brahms's development, those who occupied the extreme positions of German criticism reacted initially with reservations and, later, open rejection. Eduard Bernsdorf, chief critic of the Leipzig-based *Signale für die musikalische Welt* and, like Robert Franz, a member of Schneider's Dessau school, also maintained a lifelong, rigidly classical conception of music [see Ch. 4 'Leipzig and Berlin']. Despite some 'dry' variations in the second movement, the 'insignificant' invention and the occasionally 'raw' sound of the Scherzo, and the altogether 'weak and contrived' Finale, he could still declare the Sextet to be the most successful work that had flowed from Brahms's pen thus far.[18] In the First Piano Concerto Op. 15, however, which Schubring regarded as Brahms's most significant work, Bernsdorf heard only 'truly bleak barrenness and dryness', a 'retching and scrabbling ... straining and tugging ... stitching together and tearing apart of phrases and empty gestures'. In 1882 his judgement of the Second Piano Concerto Op. 83 was only slightly kinder: 'The Second Concerto offers only negative advantages in comparison to the First: there is less which is positively ugly and tasteless, abstruse and confused, overall less which is unhealthy and unnatural.'[19]

If Brahms's music was still too modern for the conservatives, the New Germans criticised his indebtedness to classical models as derivative ('epigonal'). By spring 1860, the Weimar School understood that Brahms was lost to them. In March, Brahms had been working with Joachim on a public declaration – a Manifesto – in which they, along like-minded others, declared that: 'they do not recognise the principles upheld by Brendel's newspaper, and that they can only deplore and condemn the products of the leaders and followers of the so-called "New German" School, which partially realise those principles and partially enforce ever more outrageous theories, as against the innermost being of music' [see Ch. 22 'Other Instrumentalists'].[20]

Before the final, signed version of the Manifesto could be published, a draft was leaked in the press in May 1860. Significantly, the action was explained by a rift 'in the bosom of the so-called party for the music of the future', of which Brahms had previously been regarded a member.[21] Even though the declaration's wider effect was defused, the message was clearly

---

[18] *Signale* 20/3 (9 January 1862), 39.

[19] *Signale* 17/7 (3 February 1859), 71–2; *Signale* 40/3 (January 1882), 34. [20] *Briefe V*, 283.

[21] *Berliner Montags-Post* 6/18 (30 April 1860), [4]; *Signale* 18/23 (3 May 1860), 277; *Berliner Musik-Zeitung Echo* 10/18 (6 May 1860), 142.

understood by the New Germans – and immediately rebutted with a parody in the *Neue Zeitschrift für Musik*.[22] When Brahms's new works started appearing in late 1860, there could be no possible further doubt regarding his position in the dispute. Still, one anonymous review provided a relatively restrained judgement of the Sextet in the *Neue Zeitschrift für Musik,* registering the

> strange tendency in Brahms's newest creations to the simplest melodic construction and harmonic-rhythmic development ... Only rarely does Brahms resort to his earlier rapturous, dreaming, storm-and-stress life. When I hear or read Brahms's recent works, it often seems to me as if this full-blooded Schumannian has become a Haydn-Mozart-derivative in the most modern sense! I'm undecided as to whether this rapid reversal bodes well or ill.[23]

Subsequent, far more drastic examples of New German criticism of Brahms can be found in the numerous concert reviews which Hugo Wolf wrote in 1884–7 for the *Wiener Salonblatt*. In endlessly original formulations of the same idea, Brahms is described as a mere imitator of the classical masters, lacking originality, and is compared with composers such as Franz Liszt, who, in one cymbal crash of his symphonic poems, expressed more 'spirit and sentiment' than Brahms in all his symphonies and serenades together.[24]

Between the two extreme poles of German musical life in that day, Brahms's music attracted constantly growing approval from the 'broad middle', comprising both the public and critics, from the early 1860s onwards. The basis of this success may well have been his balance between expression and structure, the fruit of his intensive studies from 1854. In consequence, Adolf Schubring wrote about *A German Requiem* Op. 45 in 1868, the reception of which was one of the first peaks in Brahms's public recognition, that this work

> must satisfy the musical experts of all parties, because it contains that which each values the most, ... for the musical left, new content and innovative orchestral effects, for the far right, classical form and detailed work, and for us, the musical middle, all of this and far more, complete accord between the contemporary content and the most beautiful form.

---

[22] *Neue Zeitschrift für Musik* 52/19 (4 May 1860), 169–70.

[23] *Neue Zeitschrift für Musik* 60/12 (18 March 1864), 99.

[24] L. Spitzer and I. Sommer (eds.), *Hugo Wolfs Kritiken im Wiener Salonblatt*, 2 vols. (Vienna: Musikwissenschaftlicher Verlag, 2002), vol. 1, 36.

Germany 315

With this modern masterwork, Schubring declared, Brahms had 'given ideal realisation to the highest expression of our time' and thus only now actually fulfilled Schumann's expectations.[25]

Further Reading

M. Calella, 'Gattung und Erwartung: Brahms, das Leipziger Gewandhaus und der Misserfolg des Klavierkonzerts Op. 15', *Ad Parnassum* 2/3 (2004), 31–60

A. Horstmann, *Untersuchungen zur Brahms-Rezeption der Jahre 1860–1880* (Hamburg, K. D. Wagner, 1986)

N. Meurs, *Neue Bahnen? Aspekte der Brahms-Rezeption 1853–1868* (Cologne: Studio, 1996)

U. Romberg, 'Zur Geschichte der Brahms-Rezeption im deutschsprachigen Raum', *Beiträge Zur Musikwissenschaft* 29/1 (1987), 49–58

U. Siegmund-Schultze, 'Zur Geschichte der Brahms-Rezeption im deutschsprachigen Raum von 1853 bis 1914', PhD dissertation, Martin-Luther-Universität, Halle-Wittenberg (1982)

Neue Zeitschrift für Musik: https://de.wikisource.org/wiki/Neue_Zeitschrift_f%C3%BCr_Musik

---

[25] A. Schubring, 'Schumanniana Nr. 12. Ein deutsches Requiem ... von Johannes Brahms ...', *Allgemeine musikalische Zeitung* 4/2 (13 January 1869), 9–11; 4/3 (20 January 1869), 18–20.

CHAPTER 32

England

Katy Hamilton

When Brahms's Violin Concerto Op. 77 received its British premiere at the Crystal Palace on 22 February 1879, George Grove began his programme note to the piece: 'Mr Brahms is no stranger to the Crystal Palace audience; in fact he is very well known here, for his name appears more frequently in the Saturday Programmes than that of almost any other contemporary composer.'[1]

It is certainly true that Brahms's popularity with British audiences increased significantly from the 1870s onwards as initial suspicion of his complex writing was replaced by growing admiration, particularly for his chamber and orchestral works. However, Brahms himself never visited the country – in fact, he turned down at least six separate invitations to do so, from potential festival commissions to performance opportunities, and two attempts to coax him to Cambridge University to receive an honorary doctorate. Rather, he was 'very well known' thanks to an energetic network of performers, writers, publishers and teachers who sought to promote his music in London and further afield, many of whom were personal friends and part of Brahms's own circle in Germany and Austria [see Ch. 21 'Pianists' and Ch. 22 'Other Instrumentalists']. This chapter provides an overview of the roles played by these advocates. Since the overwhelming majority of detailed research into this area has been concerned with performances in England, rather than Britain more generally, the focus here is also limited to England.

While Brahms himself refused to make the journey to England, a number of his closest friends established long-lasting and fruitful working relationships with British musicians and organisations. Clara Schumann made her first visit to England in 1856, shortly before her husband's death, and made regular visits from this date until the late 1880s. One of her

---

[1] Quoted in R. Pascall, 'Frühe Brahms-Rezeption in England', in I. Fuchs (ed.), *Internationaler Brahms-Kongress Gmunden 1997* (Tutzing: Hans Schneider, 2001), 298.

England

earliest concerts, on 17 June 1856 (billed as a solo 'recital' at a time when this term was not yet in general usage), included the earliest public performance of a piece of Brahms in Britain: a Sarabande and Gavotte 'in the style of Bach' (probably WoO 5 no. 1 and WoO 3), which was judged 'extremely difficult, extremely uncouth, and not at all "in the style of Bach"'.[2] It was left to Joseph Joachim, who began a similarly regular pattern of visits to England in 1862, to select a work which was more accessible to the public: the First String Sextet Op. 18, performed on 5 May 1863 in a concert hosted by the publishers J. J. Ewer & Co. (a company which merged with Novello & Co. in 1867). This Sextet, along with the two early Piano Quartets Opp. 25 and 26, became firm favourites in chamber programmes by the 1870s, and Joachim and Clara Schumann were often involved in these performances, along with the cellist of Joachim's British quartet, Alfredo Piatti.

Joachim was beloved of British audiences not only for his chamber performances, but also as a soloist in major concerto repertoire (including Brahms's Violin Concerto, which he performed six times in England between 1879 and 1888) and, on occasion, as a conductor. When Brahms turned down his first invitation to receive an honorary doctorate from Cambridge University in 1877, it was to Joachim – who *did* receive a doctorate – that Brahms entrusted the direction of the British premiere of his First Symphony Op. 68. The ceremony and performance were engineered by Charles Stanford, then the conductor of the Cambridge University Music Society and an ardent Brahmsian, who had met Joachim several years earlier in Bonn (and was no doubt hopeful that in Brahms's absence, he might be permitted to conduct the Symphony himself).[3] In the event, the Symphony was given three performances that spring, firstly in Cambridge and then in London: 8 March, conducted by Joachim; 31 March, conducted by August Manns; and 16 April, conducted by William George Cusins. The reaction was largely positive, although critics pointed to the 'originality of his style' and 'elaborate' nature of the composition as making it difficult to offer a considered response.[4] Despite such difficulties – exacerbated by the lack of a published score that critics might follow – the esteem in which Brahms's music was held by the British cognoscenti is reflected in the make-up of the audience, which included the poet Robert Browning, the painter Frederic Leighton, the

---

[2] *The Musical World*, 21 June 1856, quoted in Pascall, 'Frühe Brahms-Rezeption', 293.

[3] See P. Rodmell, *Charles Villiers Stanford* (Aldershot: Ashgate, 2002), 43–58.

[4] See for example 'Crystal Palace', *The Musical Times and Singing Class Circular* 18/411 (1 May 1877), 219.

businessman and politician Frederic Lehmann and George Eliot's companion George Henry Lewes.[5]

These performances were supplemented by extensive analytical programme notes provided by George Grove, then the secretary of the Crystal Palace and later the first Director of the Royal College of Music. The notes have subsequently proven invaluable to researchers, since the piece they describe is not the work as it was finally issued in print in 1877; and it is thanks to Grove's notes that it has been possible to reconstruct the second movement of the Symphony as it was heard in London, before undergoing substantial revisions for publication [see Ch. 35 'Editing Brahms'].[6]

The Crystal Palace hosted regular orchestral concerts from 1855 onwards, and their principal conductor from that date until 1901 was the German-born August Manns. Manns and his colleague, George Grove, formulated an ever more ambitious series of 'popular' (i.e. non-subscription) concert programmes which did much to introduce the works of Schubert, Schumann, Brahms and others to British audiences. Manns first programmed Brahms's music in 1863 (several movements of the First Serenade Op. 11 and, a few months later, *Ave Maria* Op. 12), neither of which received much critical attention. But between 1872 and 1882, he conducted the British premieres of the First Piano Concerto Op. 15, *Variations on a Theme of Haydn* Op. 56a, *Schicksalslied* Op. 54, *Rinaldo* Op. 50, the Second Symphony Op. 73, the Violin Concerto Op. 77 (with Joachim), *Academic Festival Overture* Op. 80, *Tragic Overture* Op. 81, and the Second Piano Concerto Op. 83. Several of these works were performed on multiple occasions, with the Second Symphony and *Schicksalslied* as particular favourites.

It is clear, then, that British enthusiasm for Brahms's music only took off in the 1870s. This is not so chronologically dissimilar from reception in Austro-Germany, where *A German Requiem* Op. 45 proved to be the defining work to earn him significant recognition in 1868–9 [see Ch. 31 'Germany']. However, this work held none of the same patriotic connotations for a British audience as it did for Brahms's own compatriots, and the reasons for his success in England seem somewhat different. The popularity of the *Schicksalslied* holds a clue: the British amateur choral

---

[5] M. Musgrave, 'Describing and Evaluating: Grove on Technology, Geography Exploration and Literature, in M. Musgrave (ed.), *George Grove, Music and Victorian Culture* (New York: Palgrave Macmillan, 2003), 57.

[6] R. Pascall, *Brahms's First Symphony Andante – The Initial Performing Version* (Nottingham: University of Nottingham, 1992)

England

scene was a major part of musical life, and the singing public were eager for new repertoire. Both the *Schicksalslied* and the *Requiem* itself were taken up enthusiastically, with the latter receiving its first complete performance in London on 2 April 1873 to great acclaim.[7] The *Schicksalslied* was given on 21 March 1874 at the Crystal Palace and repeated just a few weeks later – a reflection, no doubt, of its having been 'recognised by its hearers as a work of genius of the highest order' at its first performance.[8] In addition to these choral works, pieces such as the *Variations on a Theme of Haydn* proved popular (as in Austro-Germany) and no doubt encouraged listeners to explore the more challenging symphonic and chamber works.

While Manns led the way with so many London premieres, he was not the sole conductor at the cutting edge of British Brahms performance. Following a highly successful series of performances for a London Wagner Festival in 1877, the Austro-Hungarian conductor Hans Richter (1843–1916) established an annual series of concerts in the capital from 1879. The most powerful musical director in Vienna by the mid-1880s, Richter was a master politician who successfully balanced his advocacy for Wagner's music with his promotion of Brahms's – an aesthetic battle which played a considerably smaller role in British musical life than it did on the continent. In addition to conducting the world premieres of the *Tragic Overture* Op. 81 and the Third Symphony Op. 90, he regularly featured Brahms's music in his London series, where he introduced *Gesang der Parzen* Op. 89 and the Third and Fourth Symphonies to the British public. He also toured the country, performing these and other pieces in Birmingham, Manchester and elsewhere. Similarly, Charles Hallé (1819–1895, a German who settled in Britain) conducted numerous performances of Brahms's music with his own orchestra in Manchester, and both he and his wife, the violinist Wilma Norman-Neruda, also performed Brahms's chamber works with Joachim and others in the St James's Hall popular concerts.

It should be apparent, even from the relatively small list of musicians mentioned above, that the musical worlds of Britain and Austro-Germany were intimately connected. Joachim, Clara Schumann and a number of Brahms's other close friends organised concert tours to London, Manchester, Oxford, Cambridge, Leeds and elsewhere (e.g. Julius Stockhausen, Robert Hausmann, Hans von Bülow, Richard Mühlfeld,

---

[7] See G. A. Macfarren, *Analytical Remarks on A German Requiem* (London: Lucas, Weber & Co., 1873)

[8] 'Crystal Palace', *The Musical Times and Singing Class Circular* 16/372 (1 April 1874), 447–8.

Antonia Kufferath and Marie Soldat-Röger). Conversely, numerous British-born musicians travelled to Germany and Vienna to study, either with private teachers or at one of the distinguished conservatories. The Royal Academy of Music in London was held in remarkably poor regard by the British musical establishment, and until the Royal College of Music was founded in 1882, most talented young players and composers were encouraged to study in Leipzig, Berlin, Frankfurt or Vienna. Stanford studied in Leipzig after completing his studies at Cambridge; the conductor and pianist Frederic Cowen went to Leipzig, Berlin and Vienna for musical instruction, meeting Brahms along the way. Ethel Smyth attended the Leipzig Conservatory and then learned privately with Brahms's close friend Heinrich von Herzogenberg – though her assessment of Brahms himself, upon meeting him, was not particularly positive (the feeling was probably mutual!). Clara Schumann taught an impressive array of British pianists, including Leonard Borwick, Fanny Davies and Ilona Eibenschütz (who was born in Hungary but ultimately settled in England) [see Ch. 21 'Pianists']. Borwick performed the First Piano Concerto in both London and Vienna (under Manns and Richter respectively), while Eibenschütz gave the British premieres of two of Brahms's late sets of Piano Pieces Opp. 118 and 119, at the Monday Popular Concerts at St James's Hall. Fanny Davies performed frequently with Joachim, Piatti and Mühlfeld, and played in the first British performances of the Third Violin Sonata Op. 108, Clarinet Trio Op. 114 and Clarinet Sonatas Op. 120, as well as selections from the Fantasies Op. 116 and Intermezzi Op. 117 for solo piano.[9]

Davies also played for the British premiere of Brahms's *Zigeunerlieder* Op. 103, which was masterminded by another close Brahms friend, George Henschel (1850–1934). Henschel first worked with Brahms in 1875, by which time he had already befriended Joachim and Clara Schumann. He quickly established himself as a successful performer in Austro-Germany; upon his first performances in London in 1877, he became an overnight sensation and gave what was probably the first public song-recital in Britain in July of that year (including some Brahms lieder in his varied programme) [see Ch. 19 'Singers']. He pursued a highly successful career not only as a singer and pianist but also as a conductor in London, Scotland and the USA, and directed Joachim and Robert Hausmann in the British premiere of Brahms's

---

[9] E. L. A. Woodhouse, 'The Music of Johannes Brahms in Late Nineteenth and Early Twentieth Century England and an Assessment of His Reception and Influence on the Chamber and Orchestral Works of Charles Hubert Hastings Parry and Charles Villiers Stanford', PhD dissertation, Durham University (2013), 66.

Double Concerto Op. 102 in 1888. (He tried, and failed, to persuade Brahms to visit London and conduct a series of concerts in 1887.) Henschel occupies a particularly interesting position in bringing Brahms's music to English-speaking audiences, since he was fluent in both English and German, could sing and accompany himself, composed a considerable amount of vocal music in an idiom rich with Brahmsian influences, toured America as well as Britain (his first wife was from Boston) and conducted major orchestral works as well as singing himself. Although he did not give many first performances in Britain, he frequently included Brahms's songs and orchestral works in his programming and was also regularly invited to perform at private soirées in the homes of music-loving patrons, which was a crucial means of familiarising influential audience members with new repertoire.[10]

In addition to the ever-growing number of performances of Brahms's music, there was a similarly increasing body of literature on his compositions. Grove's lengthy analytical programme notes for the Crystal Palace have already been mentioned – but the circulation of these notes was not restricted to London audiences. Even before Grove completed his first *Dictionary of Music and Musicians* (1879–89), he was prepared to make his programme notes available to other concert series around Britain. By the mid-1890s, his notes were available to audiences in Brighton, Nottingham, Edinburgh, Glasgow, Manchester, Liverpool, Oxford, Birmingham, Sheffield and Bradford.[11] To have such detailed accounts of the repertoire must have been invaluable to new audiences; even at the Monday Popular Concerts at St James's Hall, programmes usually contained musical examples tracing the principal themes of new works, with a short commentary. Since the most common discomfort that British critics seemed to have had with Brahms's music was its 'difficulty', explanatory documents like these must have been of great use to the musically literate.

If some analytical interpretation was required to help British audiences with Brahms's instrumental works, a rather more literal form of translation was also necessary to help would-be singers of his solo and choral music. Concert programmes usually included translations for lieder, but, as Brahms's popularity grew, publishers saw an opportunity to issue singable

---

[10] See G. Bozarth, *Johannes Brahms & George Henschel. An Enduring Friendship* (Sterling Heights, Mich.: Harmonie Park Press, 2008).

[11] C. Bashford, 'Not Just "G.": Towards a History of the Programme Notes', in M. Musgrave (ed.), *George Grove, Music and Victorian Culture*, 125. See also C. Bashford, 'Educating England: Networks of Programme-Note Provision in the Nineteenth Century', in R. Cowgill & P. Holman (eds.), *Music in the British Provinces, 1690–1914* (Aldershot: Ashgate, 2007), 349–76.

English translations of his music for performance at home and by amateur choral societies. The earliest English-language version of *A German Requiem* Op. 45 appeared in 1872, a new vocal score issued by Rieter-Biedermann; and by 1874, Simrock took the decision to issue lieder editions with English text, even of earlier popular opuses. The only composition of Brahms's to appear with English text from its very first printing was the *Neue Liebeslieder* Op. 65, which suggests a particular enthusiasm for such piano-accompanied partsongs in Britain. Indeed, the *Liebeslieder* and *Zigeunerlieder* prompted a number of British imitations, among them pieces by Stanford, Walford Davies and Ernest Walker. It is difficult to ascertain whether or not Brahms's songs were regularly performed publicly in English – surviving programmes seem to suggest that this was rare. Choral works, however, were performed in translation, causing George Macfarren to refer to 'an English Requiem' when the piece was sung in the vernacular in 1873.

These translated volumes are indicative of the partnerships gradually formed between Brahms's German publishers and those in Britain. Initially, German copies were imported for sale in England, but as Brahms's music became more popular, English publishers produced title pages specifically for the national market, worked in collaboration with German publishers on new editions and eventually produced their own. Novello, Ewer & Co. led the field with editions of choral repertoire, while other companies – above all Alfred Lengnick, in official partnership with Simrock – came to dominate in other genres.

As performances, programme notes, scores and translations made Brahms's music ever more accessible to British audiences, British composers began to turn to his works as inspiration for their own. Stanford, in his role as Professor of Composition at the Royal College of Music (RCM) from 1883, exercised considerable influence on younger generations of British composers (including George Butterworth, Samuel Coleridge-Taylor, George Dyson, Ivor Gurney, John Ireland, Ralph Vaughan Williams and Frank Bridge), and his own compositions as well as his advice to his pupils are peppered with references to Brahms. The RCM's second director (from 1895), Hubert Parry, was an enthusiastic Brahmsian whose works also bear his influence. Henschel and Joachim both taught briefly at the college, which held a Brahms memorial concert on 8 June 1897 (conducted by Stanford).[12] Ethel Smyth, Fredrick Cowen, Edward Elgar, William Hurlstone and many other British composers of

---

[12] 'Royal College of Music', *The Times* 35226 (18 June 1897), 5.

England

the late nineteenth century were consciously indebted to his legacy – and some, such as Elgar, were to see their own works premiered by the same musicians, too. Hans Richter conducted the premieres of both Elgar's First Symphony Op. 55 and *The Dream of Gerontius* Op. 38 in the early twentieth century.

The rich cultural exchange between Austro-Germany and Britain was to end abruptly with the outbreak of the First World War in 1914. For musicians such as Stanford and Parry, this was a particularly painful break after decades of fruitful collaboration. As war was declared in 1914, Stanford wrote to Richter, the only surviving advocate from the time of early British Brahms performances, 'I must send you a note on this terrible day. I have not forgotten the old times, and everything that you have done for music in England.'[13]

Further Reading

D. de Val, 'Fanny Davies: "A Messenger for Schumann and Brahms"?', in T. Ellsworth & S. Wollenberg (eds.), *The Piano in Nineteenth-Century British Culture. Instruments, Performers and Repertoire* (Aldershot: Ashgate, 2007), 217–37

C. Fifield, *Hans Richter* (Woodbridge: Boydell & Brewer, 2016)

M. Musgrave (ed.), *George Grove, Music and Victorian Culture* (New York: Palgrave Macmillan, 2003)

M. Musgrave, 'Brahms and England', in M. Musgrave (ed.), *Brahms 2. Biographical, Documentary and Analytical Studies* (Cambridge: Cambridge University Press, 1987), 1–20

R. Pascall, 'Frühe Brahms-Rezeption in England', in I. Fuchs (ed.), *Internationaler Brahms-Kongress Gmunden 1997* (Tuzting: Hans Schneider, 2001), 293–327

P. Rodmell, *Charles Villiers Stanford* (Aldershot: Ashgate, 2002)

E. L. A. Woodhouse, 'The Music of Johannes Brahms in Late Nineteenth and Early Twentieth Century England and an Assessment of His Reception and Influence on the Chamber and Orchestral Works of Charles Hubert Hastings Parry and Charles Villiers Stanford', PhD dissertation, Durham University (2013)

---

[13] Rodmell, *Stanford*, 287.

CHAPTER 33

Analysis

Heather Platt

Within a decade of Brahms's compositions first appearing in print, supporters and proponents began subjecting his music to analysis. From that time onward, commentators across the centuries have continued to scrutinise his compositions, exploring both structural elements (motifs, harmonies, counterpoint, rhythm and form) and the relationship between structure and meaning. Over time, the theoretical frameworks behind these analyses have changed, as have the broader aesthetic and scholarly environments [see Ch. 16 'Genre']. Nevertheless, the origins of some of the more influential analytical approaches can be traced back to Brahms's contemporaries. This essay will focus on the work emanating from three of the most influential theoretical schools, those inspired by Arnold Schoenberg (1874–1951), Heinrich Schenker (1868–1935) and Hugo Riemann (1849–1919).

Although Schoenberg did not formulate specific analytical approaches to Brahms's music until the early years of the twentieth century, the concepts behind his approach were already present in the writings of music critics from Brahms's time and even in comments made by the composer himself. Following Schumann's 1853 benedictory article 'New Paths' [see Ch. 31 'Germany'], Brahms began publishing his compositions with the Piano Sonata Op.1 in 1854. Reviews quickly appeared, including Louis Köhler's brief descriptions of the first eight opus numbers. During the 1860s, critics Selmar Bagge, Adolf Schubring and Carl von Noorden initiated what has become an unbroken line of analytical discussions regarding structural elements in Brahms's music. Although their essays lack the length and theoretical trappings of modern investigations, these writers consistently noted important features that have continued to fascinate analysts. One such feature is Brahms's treatment of motifs. For example, Schubring's analyses demonstrate the many subtle ways Brahms manipulates his initial motifs to create the main themes of entire movements. In the case of the Piano Sonata Op. 2, Schubring claims this

Analysis

material is woven throughout all of the movements, as shown in Example 33.1.[1]

Brahms was aware of these critical reviews; indeed, Schubring struck up a correspondence with the composer before publishing his first review. Although Brahms often equivocated when asked about the veracity of such analytical observations, his comments to friends amount to tacit acknowledgements that initial reviewers were pinpointing important aspects of his compositional techniques. One of Brahms's most frequently cited reflections on his treatment of motifs comes from a letter he wrote to a friend, the singer and conductor George Henschel. Here Brahms describes how his compositions germinate from a 'seed-corn', citing the opening of 'Die Mainacht' Op. 43 no. 2 as an example [see Ch. 25 'Copyright' and Ch. 35 'Editing Brahms'].[2] This image of a germinating seed, also employed by Brahms's critic Selmar Bagge, has moved many writers to analyse the motivic content of both this song and many other compositions by Brahms.

Recently, Nicole Grimes has argued that the motivic analysis of Schubring and his contemporaries is deeply rooted in the nineteenth-century intellectual tradition of organicism. This same tradition forms the backdrop to Schoenberg's concept of developing variations, which first appeared in his writings in 1917.[3] Unlike Schubring, Schoenberg never met Brahms, although his teacher Alexander Zemlinksy, an avid admirer of the older composer, did.

Through Zemlinsky, Schoenberg could lay claim to membership of the extended Brahmsian circle. Moreover, he acknowledged Brahms's influence on his compositions, as attested by his statements in his much-discussed 1933 broadcast lecture 'Brahms the Progressive'. Seeking in part to address the nineteenth-century critics who lambasted Brahms as a mere epigone, Schoenberg discussed the ways in which Brahms had influenced various aspects of his compositional style. He analysed Brahms's approach to harmony (in the First String Quartet Op. 51 no. 1), asymmetrical phrase structures (in lieder and the main theme of the First String Sextet Op. 18) and motivic elaboration. The passages from 'O Tod, o Tod, wie bitter bist du' Op. 121 no. 3 and the Andante of the Second String Quartet Op. 51 no. 2 that Schoenberg parses exhibit his concept of developing variation, in

---

[1] Some of Adolf Schubring's essays are presented in 'Five Early Works by Brahms (1862)', in W. Frisch and K. C. Karnes (eds.), *Brahms and His World*, 2nd edn (Princeton: Princeton University Press, 2009), 195–215. Example 33.1 is taken from 203 to 4 of this volume.

[2] G. Henschel, *Personal Recollections of Johannes Brahms* (Boston: Badger, 1907), 22–3.

[3] N. Grimes, 'The Schoenberg/Brahms Critical Tradition Reconsidered', *Music Analysis* 31/2 (July 2012), 127–75.

Example 33.1. Schubring's diagram of motivic relationships between the movements of Brahms's Piano Sonata Op. 2.

Analysis

that small motifs (much like those the earlier critics discussed) are altered, transposed and combined (in melodic lines and contrapuntal textures) in ever-varying ways [see Ch. 38 'Inspiration'].

During the second half of the twentieth century, numerous scholars explored the meaning and origins of the compositional technique of developing variation. They extended some of Schoenberg's analyses of Brahms's works and applied it to others that Schoenberg had not considered. For instance, in his book *Brahms and the Principle of Developing Variation*, Walter Frisch drew on Schoenberg's ideas to demonstrate how the pitch structures of many of Brahms's works are saturated with motifs. Moreover, these motifs have an impact on rhythmic and metric structures, form (especially sonata form) and text setting.[4] Although most analysts define Schoenberg's concept of the *Grundgestalt* (a piece's basic idea) as a series of pitches – that is, a motif – some theorists have thought of it in terms of other structural elements. David Epstein and Samuel Ng, for example, have demonstrated ways in which an initial harmonic or rhythmic idea can be varied throughout a work, thereby unifying the work in an analogous way to a pitch motif.

While theorists have been examining new ways of implementing Schoenberg's ideas, the concept of developing variation has been widely embraced by historians. For instance, in the 2014 edition of the *Norton Anthology of Western Music II*, one of the most widely used undergraduate music history textbooks in the USA, this concept is utilised in an analysis of the sonata-form first movement of Brahms's Piano Quintet Op. 34.

Heinrich Schenker recalled meeting Brahms during the 1890s, when both men were living in Vienna. He also heard performances by members of Brahms's inner circle, including Joseph Joachim and the clarinettist Richard Mühlfeld [see Ch. 22 'Other Instrumentalists']. An aspiring pianist and composer, Schenker was also publishing music criticism, including reviews of Brahms's works. Particularly significant are his reviews of the *Fünf Lieder* Op. 107 and the *Fünf Gesänge für Chor* Op. 104. In these articles, Schenker engages with the aesthetic debates and practices of his time. In particular, his illumination of the meaning behind the structural aspects of these songs has much in common with Hermann Kretzschmar's hermeneutic approach to Brahms's music. Despite the brevity of these reviews, Schenker delves into specific technical details. For example, in his

---

[4] W. Frisch, *Brahms and the Principle of Developing Variation* (Berkeley: University of California Press, 1984). Other scholars who led the way in applying the concept of developing variation include Christian Martin Schmidt, Klaus Velten, Michael Musgrave, Rainer Wilke, Jonathan Dunsby and Schoenberg's student Patricia Carpenter.

328   HEATHER PLATT

analysis of the opening measures of 'Mädchenlied' Op. 107 no. 5, he interprets the harmonic movement away from and returning to the tonic chord as perfectly mirroring the text's description of the waves of melancholy experienced by the lonely maiden.[5]

During the early twentieth century, Schenker turned away from performing and composing and gave his full attention to developing theories and analytical methodologies to explicate the musical content of what he regarded as the 'masterworks' of the common practice era. His publications referenced many of Brahms's compositions, ultimately encompassing all of the composer's genres. Many of his insights into Brahms's works are lodged in theoretical discussions of specific voice-leading procedures, and his graphs explicate short excerpts such as a theme or phrase, rather than entire movements. In contrast, his analysis of the *Variations and Fugue on a Theme of Handel* Op. 24 is possibly his most detailed and thorough work on Brahms. Employing both detailed prose commentaries and multilevel graphs, Schenker interrogates the entire piece, considering the voice leading of the theme, each variation and the fugue in turn. He then offers suggestions for the performance of each of these sections.[6]

Subsequent Schenkerian theorists – including Carl Schachter, Alan Cadwallader and Peter H. Smith – have analysed almost all of Brahms's instrumental works and a number of the vocal works. Others have extended Schenker's concepts. Most notably, Frank Samarotto, in part building on Schachter's application of Schenkerian principles to rhythm, has explored the metrical conflicts in the trio of the third movement of Brahms's First Symphony. In contrast, some writers have meshed Schenker's approach with that of other theorists. Allen Forte, in his analyses of the First String Quartet Op. 51 no. 1 and the *Alto Rhapsody* Op. 53, led the way in combining Schenker's voice-leading techniques with motivic analyses influenced by Schoenberg. In response to the recent interest in *Formenlehre*, theorists such as Boyd Pomeroy have coupled Schenkerian techniques with those mapped out in the 2006 book *Elements of Sonata Theory* by James Hepokoski and Warren Darcey. But

---

[5] H. Schenker, 'Kritik. Johannes Brahms: Fünf Lieder für eine Singstimme mit Pianoforte, op. 107 ... ', and 'Kritik. Johannes Brahms: Fünf Gesänge für gemischten Chor a capella, op. 104 ... ' *Musikalisches Wochenblatt* 22/40 (1 October 1891), 514–17 [review by Heinrich Schenker]; 23/33–34 (18 August 1892), 409–12; 23/35 (25 August 1892), 425–6; and 23/36 (1 September 1892), 437–8.

[6] H. Schenker, 'Brahms: *Variationen und Fuge über ein Thema von Händel*, op. 24', *Der Tonwille* 4/2–3 (April–September 1924), 3–46. Schenker's references to other works by Brahms can best be accessed via Larry Laskowski's *Heinrich Schenker: An Annotated Index to His Analyses of Musical Works* (New York: Pendragon, 1978).

Analysis 329

there has also been a shift in the tone of some of these analyses; whereas Forte's rich, but dryly articulated analyses reflect the type of near scientific objectivity that was in vogue around the time of the founding of the Society of Music Theory, Samarotto and other recent writers, openly discuss the affect of pieces in ways that for some might recall the hermeneutic essays of early Schenker and other nineteenth-century writers – though, to be sure, others might interpret this style of writing as reacting to the criticisms levelled at music theory by the New Musicology.

In addition to his analytical work, Schenker also played a significant role in formulating the concept of 'Urtext' editions [see Ch. 35 'Editing Brahms']. In this endeavour, Schenker drew on Brahms and his colleagues' practice of consulting composers' manuscripts and original editions. In turn, Schenker's understanding of the value of source studies influenced some of his followers, leading them to integrate manuscript studies with analysis. For instance, in his analysis of the *Variations on a Theme of Haydn* Op. 56a, Timothy Jackson draws on the unusually large number of primary sources, including Brahms's sketches and *Stichvorlagen* as well as Schenker's own unpublished analytical sketches of the work.

Schenker himself employed this integration of manuscript studies and analysis in his edition of Brahms's handwritten collection of examples of parallel fifths and octaves in the music of other composers. To this collection, Schenker added a commentary explaining why some of these passages were more acceptable than others. William Pastille concluded that in this publication: 'Schenker brought Brahms's instinctual judgments into contact with the analytical methods he had developed, thereby demonstrating that his methods were, as he had always maintained, simply detailed verbal and visual descriptions of the practical knowledge possessed by the masters.'[7]

As Robert Wason has persuasively demonstrated, both Schenker and Schoenberg's theories were descendants of the work of Simon Sechter and other nineteenth-century Viennese theorists. During the second half of the century in Germany, Hugo Riemann offered a contrasting perspective. As a proponent of functional theory, he was one of the nineteenth-century theorists that Schenker disparaged.[8] Riemann, who belonged to an earlier

---

[7] W. Pastille, 'Schenker's Brahms', *The American Brahms Society Newsletter* 5/2 (Fall 1987), 2. Johannes Brahms, *Oktaven und Quinten u. a. aus dem Nachlass* (1933); see P. Mast, 'Brahms's Study, Octaven u. Quinten u. A., with Schenker's Commentary Translated', *The Music Forum* 5 (1980), 1–196.

[8] R. Wason, *Viennese Harmonic Theory from Albrechtsberger to Schenker and Schoenberg* (1985, rpt. Rochester, NY: University of Rochester Press, 1995), see especially 134, 135 and 138.

generation than Schenker and Schoenberg, had already begun publishing his theories and commentaries on music during Brahms's lifetime. In fact, Brahms owned copies of Riemann's 1887 *Handbook of Harmony* (*Handbuch der Harmonielehre*) and his 1888 *Textbook of Simple, Double and Imitative Counterpoint* (*Lehrbuch des einfachen, doppelten und imitierenden Kontrapunkts*). Brahms annotated both books and discussed the latter with his friend Richard Heuberger. However, in his examination of Brahms's responses to Riemann, Georg Predota concludes that the composer likely disagreed with Riemann's approach to counterpoint and figured bass.[9]

Riemann's perspective on Brahms can be obtained from several publications, including both his music history and music theory volumes. In addition, he penned an obituary for the composer, defending him against charges of epigonism levelled in an obituary written by the pro-Wagnerian Arthur Seidl. Riemann's most sustained considerations of Brahms's compositions include introductory overviews of Brahms's Third and Fourth Symphonies Opp. 90 and 98, which are addressed to well-read musical amateurs, and an essay on the metrical freedoms in the lieder.

The essay on lieder makes a number of astute observations, describing, for instance, the structural and expressive significance of two features of the opening of 'Immer leiser wird mein Schlummer' Op. 105 no. 2: the four-note double neighbour motif, which is developed nearly constantly and creates much of the song's drama; and the asymmetric phrasing that also captured Schoenberg's attention. But although cited in subsequent dissertations studying Brahms's text settings, this publication has had limited influence due largely to its more speculative claims. In his telling critique, Paul Berry addresses Riemann's understanding of the harmonic progression at the climax of 'Immer leiser wird mein Schlummer' (Example 33.2). This passage, which contains a highly unorthodox succession of three 6-4 chords, has perplexed both Brahms's contemporaries and modern scholars like myself. Riemann rationalises the passage by inserting root-position chords after each 6-4 chord. Although Berry questions this procedure, he makes a somewhat risky conjecture that Riemann's analysis 'might have resonated with [Brahms's] own notions of musical syntax'.[10] This hypothesis rests on

---

[9] G. Predota, 'Johannes Brahms and the Foundations of Composition: The Basis of his Compositional Process in His Study of Figured Bass and Counterpoint', PhD dissertation, University of North Carolina, Chapel Hill (2000), 190–212.

[10] P. Berry, 'Metric Freedoms in Brahms's Songs: A Translation and Commentary', in E. Gollin and A. Rehding (eds.), *The Oxford Handbook of Neo-Riemannian Music Theories* (Oxford: Oxford University Press, 2011), 477.

Example 33.2. Brahms, 'Immer leiser wird mein Schlummer' Op. 105 no. 2, bars 41–7.

somewhat ambiguous annotations found within Brahms's copy of Riemann's *Handbuch der Harmonielehre* (1887). Brahms underlined words and added an exclamation mark to sentences that, in Berry's view, explicate the type of voice leading exhibited in 'Immer leiser wird mein Schlummer'.

Over the years, a small number of researchers (including Walter Hammermann, Ivan F. Waldbauer and Matthias Schmidt) have expanded upon Riemann's analytical work on Brahms, specifically his concepts of rhythm and phrase structure. However, far more writers, and especially German scholars, have been at least indirectly influenced by Riemann's functional theory. Yet only in recent decades have theorists in the USA more thoroughly investigated the applicability of Riemann's theories to Brahms's music.

By the end of the twentieth century, American theorists had developed a new set of theories to interrogate nineteenth-century chromatic harmonies. These concepts, which stem from both Riemann's work and David Lewin's transformational theories, focus on parsimonious voice leading (i.e. rather than referencing conventions of functional harmony, with its emphasis on fifth relationships, these theories focus on common-tone relationships and stepwise motion between adjacent chords, without reference to a prevailing tonic). For instance, Example 33.3 gives Richard

Example 33.3. Score reduction and Richard Cohn's analysis of Brahms, Double Concerto Op. 102, first movement, bars 268–79, reproduced from 'Maximally Smooth Cycles, Hexatonic Systems, and the Analysis of Late-Romantic Triadic Progressions', *Music Analysis* 15/1 (March 1996), 14–15.

Example 33.3. (cont)

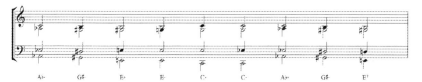

Cohn's analysis of a passage from Brahms's Double Concerto Op. 102 in which each chord progresses to the next by stepwise motion in one voice, while the other two members of each chord remain the same, assuming enharmonic equivalence. (The black note heads in Example 33.3 indicate the pitch that was not present in the preceding chord; plus signs indicate major triads and minus signs, minor triads.) As this example suggests, these types of progressions are often characterised by triads that are a third apart.

Lewin's theories were partly inspired by Riemann and Moritz Hauptmann, a theorist whose influence Riemann himself acknowledged. Moreover, although this field of analysis is often referred to as Neo-Riemannian (rather than transformational), its theoretical concepts stem from a range of other nineteenth-century theorists whose works Brahms may also have been at least somewhat familiar with; they include Adolf Bernhard Marx, Gottfried Weber and Carl Friedrich Weitzmann. Hauptmann, who Brahms met, taught a number of the composer's closest colleagues including Joseph Joachim, Hans von Bülow and Heinrich von Herzogenberg. Brahms owned books by Weber and Weitzmann; however, he did not necessarily support their work. In an 1854 letter to Joachim, Brahms rebuked Weitzmann, who was associated with the Weimar circle. Weitzmann, in turn, penned a satirical response to the 1860 Manifesto [see Ch. 22 'Other Instrumentalists'], in which Brahms and his colleagues had contrasted their aesthetics to those of the Weimar clique.[11]

As with the theories of Schoenberg and Schenker, transformational theories have been integrated with other ideas and expanded in a wide variety of ways, some of which include complex mathematical models. Steven Rings, for example, has developed a pluralist approach. He integrates transformational and Schenkerian theories with ideas by diverse theorists from Rameau of the eighteenth century to Harald Krebs of the

---

[11] For information about the Manifesto see *May I*, 250–3. Brahms's August 1854 letter to Joachim, *Avins*, 196–7.

late twentieth. In particular, he incorporates Schenker's analysis of the Intermezzo Op. 118 no. 2 into his study of the metric and kinetic impulses of the piece's opening motif. Notwithstanding its complexities, Rings's elegant writing ensures the reader is constantly aware that the analysis is deeply rooted in one's hearing and experiencing the piece in real time.

In 1994 Friedhelm Krummacher observed:

> Our store of harmonic, formal, and thematic analytical methodology is the product of late nineteenth-century thought, indebted to the body of teachings ranging from Adolf Bernhard Marx to Hugo Riemann, who were also the leading theorists of Brahms's own time. Our analytical methods are everywhere rooted in their thought, even where we are hardly aware of it.[12]

Yet he also cautions that not all of our analyses are historically informed. Indeed, despite their roots in nineteenth-century thought, most of the analyses referenced in this essay employ techniques that Brahms and his colleagues could not have envisioned. Rather, their techniques are products of the analysts' own cultural contexts. This also applies to the numerous other analytical approaches to Brahms's music that this essay has not considered. Witness, for instance, the proliferation of studies on rhythm that followed the publication of Krebs and Cohn's groundbreaking theories around the turn of the twenty-first century, and their impact on Brahms scholars such as Yonatan Malin. Moreover, scholars who built upon the observations of Brahms's contemporaries (such as his composition student Gustav Jenner) or who invoke the hermeneutic forays of Romantic writers (such as Hermann Kretzschmar) were also responding to stimuli of their own intellectual milieu, and often specifically to the New Musicology of the 1980s and 90s. Thus, just as the richness of Brahms's music continues to enthral listeners, and, for some, to speak to the very essence of our being, so too the metaphors we use to describe its structure and affect will continually evolve.

Further Reading

The complete bibliographic information for all pre-2008 publications referenced in this article is in H. Platt, *Johannes Brahms. A Research and Information Guide*, 2nd ed. (New York: Routledge, 2011)

R. Cohn, *Audacious Euphony* (Oxford: Oxford University Press, 2011), 117–21

---

[12] F. Krummacher, 'Reception and Analysis: On the Brahms Quartets, Op. 51, nos. 1 and 2', *19th-Century Music* 18/1 (Summer 1994), 27.

K. Karnes, 'Another Look at Critical Partisanship in the Viennese *fin de siècle*: Schenker's Reviews of Brahms's Vocal Music, 1891–92', *19th-Century Music* 26/1 (Summer 2002), 73–93

I. Knorr, H. Riemann, J. Sittard, and A. Morin, *Johannes Brahms: Symphonien und andere Orchesterwerke* (Berlin: Schlesinger'sche Buch und Musikhandlung, n.d.)

D. Lewin, 'A Formal Theory of Generalized Tonal Functions', *Journal of Music Theory* 26/1 (Spring 1982), 43–5

H. Platt, 'Text-Music Relationships in the Lieder of Johannes Brahms', PhD dissertation, Graduate Center of the City University of New York (1992)

H. Platt and P. Smith (eds.) *Expressive Intersections in Brahms: Essays in Analysis and Meaning* (Bloomington: Indiana University Press, 2012)

B. Pomeroy, 'The Major Dominant in Minor-Mode Sonata Forms: Compositional Challenges, Complications and Effects', *Journal of Schenkerian Studies* 5 (2011), 75–89

H. Riemann, 'Johannes Brahms (geb. 7. Mai 1833 zu Hamburg, gest. 3. April 1897 zu Wien)', reprinted in *Präludien und Studien III: Gesammelte Aufsätze zur Ästhetik, Theorie und Geschichte der Musik*, 3 vols. (Leipzig: H. Seemann Nachfolger, 1901; rpt. Hildesheim: Georg Olms, 1967), vol. 3, 215–23

H. Riemann, 'Die Taktfreiheiten in Brahms' Liedern', *Die Musik* (Berlin) 12/1 (October 1912), 10–21

S. Rings, *Tonality and Transformation* (Oxford: Oxford University Press, 2011), Chapter 6

S. Rohringer, 'Zu Johannes Brahms' Intermezzo h-Moll op. 119/1', *Zeitschrift für Musiktheorie* 10/1 (2013), www.gmth.de/zeitschrift/artikel/707.aspx

A. Schoenberg, 'Brahms the Progressive', reprinted in L. Stein (ed.) *Style and Idea: Selected Writings of Arnold Schoenberg*, trans. L. Black, (1975; rpt. Berkeley: University of California Press, 1984), 398–441

CHAPTER 34

The Era of National Socialism

Ulrike Petersen

While there is an extensive body of literature on the German reception of Brahms up to World War I, until recently, few scholars have shown an interest in the ways in which National Socialists dealt with this composer. In German publications, there seems to be little acknowledgement of the possible complexities in Brahms reception caused by political influences; most post-war German literature on the composer has simply skirted the issue. Some writers have even suggested that Brahms was not much used for political purposes by the Nazis. Such suggestions are typically supported through direct comparisons with the long-acknowledged appropriations of other composers, notably Wagner.[1]

Indeed, statistics such as those of the Berlin Philharmonic show no change in the frequency of performances of Brahms's works during Hitler's rule, even despite the straitened circumstances towards the end of the war.[2] It seems that with concert-goers the composer's popularity was never in question. Yet, the reception of Brahms during the Third Reich and the immediate post-war period – a time span conveniently framed by his centenary in 1933 and the fiftieth anniversary of his death in 1947 – is still worth investigating. As one of Germany's most prominent musico-historical figures, Brahms was an ideal character for political appropriation. In this chapter, I will show that between 1933 and 1947 the previously disparate and often critical views of the composer gradually gave way to a much more homogenous and favourable image.

1933: Views of Brahms at His Centenary

For the new National Socialist government, the anniversary of Brahms's birth offered the first major opportunity to show its interest in German

---

[1] See, for example, U. Romberg, 'Zur Geschichte der Brahms-Rezeption im deutschsprachigen Raum', *Beiträge zur Musikwissenschaft* 29/1 (1987), 55.
[2] E. Levi, *Music in the Third Reich* (London: Macmillian, 1994), 217.

The Era of National Socialism 337

culture. As part of Hitler's early strategy of 'nationalisation of the masses', the *Volk* was to be presented with national heroes; art became a 'source of power' inspiring national self-confidence.[3] In addition to some Brahms commemorations at established music festivals – for example, the Lower Saxony Music Festival in Osnabrück, which combined this occasion with a celebration of the 'national uprising' – numerous German cities held festivities in honour of the composer, often coordinated by local representatives of the Combat League for German Culture (*Kampfbund für deutsche Kultur*), an influential National Socialist-affiliated organisation. Among these celebrations, those in Vienna and Hamburg were especially ambitious: planned many months in advance, Vienna managed to secure *Reichspräsident* Paul von Hindenburg as patron and Wilhelm Furtwängler as main conductor and speaker. The latter's ambiguous speech, which asserted Brahms's 'Germanness', his genuine affinity with the common people and his extreme anti-Modernist style, caused much debate. While Alban Berg, for example, expressed his disappointment at what he considered a 'Nazi-tainted speech' that ignored recent developments in German music, Heinrich Schenker praised the conductor for his brave stand against the 'delusion of progress'.[4] Furtwängler's speech demonstrates clearly the difficulties of tracing explicitly political intentions in Third Reich literature on Brahms because earlier accounts already displayed a highly nationalistic sentiment.

Hamburg's *Brahmsfest* had originally been planned as a modest series of concerts and speeches. However, in March, three weeks after the National Socialists came to power, *Kampfbund* officials in Berlin declared their intentions to make the Hamburg celebrations a national event. A critical condition was that all Jewish soloists be replaced by Aryans.[5] It remains unclear whether the promise of Hitler's patronage was a tactical move to achieve the removal of Jewish performers or whether it was a serious attempt to provide a German counterpoise to the Austrian festival, for which Furtwängler had engaged several renowned Jewish performers already banned from German stages.

Unlike their Viennese counterparts, Hamburg's organisers stressed the folk-like properties of Brahms's music through their choice of programme

---

[3] T. Mathieu, *Kunstauffassungen und Kulturpolitik im Nationalsozialimus* (Saarbrücken: Pfau, 1997), 63–4.

[4] A. Dümling (ed.), *Verteidigung des musikalischen Fortschritts: Brahms und Schönberg* (Hamburg: Argument, 1990), 56; H. Haffner, *Furtwängler* (Berlin: Parthas, 2003), 158.

[5] For information about the centenary celebrations in Hamburg, see P. Arndt et al (eds.), *Das 'Reichs-Brahmsfest' 1933 in Hamburg: Rekonstruktion und Dokumentation* (Hamburg: Von Bockel, 1997).

338   ULRIKE PETERSEN

and by including a so-called 'open hour of singing'. A local newspaper reported on the event:

> To make most people aware of his significance, it focused on Brahms the man. Comrades from all levels of society had come in masses, and it was deeply moving to see how [the choirmaster, Heinrich] Schumann managed to bring Brahms, whose music isn't accessible to everyone, close in spirit to the crowd by using his folk-song settings.[6]

The importance of folk-song for Brahms's oeuvre continued to be emphasised throughout the Third Reich. Indeed, it resonated with *Reichspropagandaminister* Joseph Goebbels's *Ten Principles for the Creation of German Music* of 1938, in which he stressed that music was 'the most sensuous of the arts' and that melody, rather than formalism, was its essence; in order to secure music's popular appeal, melody had to be reinstated.[7] Like the reviewer at the Hamburg festival, Goebbels considered orchestral works such as Brahms's Second Symphony Op. 73 to be 'too contrived and ... artificial'.[8] Clearly, Brahms's symphonic music, unlike the folk-song settings, was useless for the purposes of mass propaganda.

Despite the efforts of Hamburg's organising committee, Hitler refused to act as patron of their festival – probably because of his personal dislike of Brahms's music, which is well documented in Goebbels's diaries.[9] Ultimately, the event was only partly broadcast, and little was reported in the press. Several scholars have argued that this lack of attention may have stemmed from a rumour at the time that the composer descended from a Jewish family by the name of Abrahamson.[10] Indeed, a foreign newspaper – probably Austrian, judging by the derisive language – reported this rumour, wrongly concluding that all German celebrations had been cancelled as a result. The accompanying caricature, based on Brahms's song 'Feldeinsamkeit' Op. 86 no. 2, shows Brahms lying in the grass with crickets in Nazi uniforms buzzing around him (Figure 34.1.)[11]

---

[6] *Hamburger Nachrichten* 223 (14 May 1933, Morning Edition), reproduced in *ibid.*, 61.

[7] In *Amtliche Mitteilungen der Reichsmusikkammer* 5:11 (1938), reproduced in A. Dümling & P. Girth (eds.), *Entartete Musik: Eine kommentierte Rekonstruktion* (Düsseldorf: Kleinherne, 1988), 123.

[8] J. Goebbels, *Die Tagebücher von Joseph Goebbels – Sämtliche Fragmente* I, 9 vols., ed. E. Fröhlich (Munich: Saur, 1987), vol. 4, 32.

[9] For example, Goebbels, *Tagebücher*, vol. 7, 27 and 325.

[10] D. Beller-McKenna, *Brahms and the German Spirit* (Cambridge, MA: Harvard University Press, 2004), 178–82; *Das 'Reichs-Brahmsfest' 1933 in Hamburg*, 119–20.

[11] Reproduced without information about the original source in Anton Neumayr, *Musik und Medizin – Am Beispiel der deutschen Romantik* (Himberg: Wiener Verlag, 1991), 224–5.

Figure 34.1. Unattributed caricature of Brahms, c. 1938.

Strangely, however, German newspapers did not push the issue. Furthermore, Brahms's origins had already been traced in 1929 as part of Peter von Gebhardt and Johannes Hohlfeld's widely read *Genealogy of Famous Germans (Ahnentafel berühmter Deutscher)*. Had the rumour been believed by Nazi officials, prestigious performances of Brahms's music, such as at the momentous *Tag von Potsdam* (21 March 1933) or at the *Kampfbund*'s first official music festival (July 1933), would surely not have been possible. However, the rumour's existence points to

340 ULRIKE PETERSEN

uncertainty, even anxiety about Brahms's music, intensified by his many Jewish acquaintances [see Ch. 3 'Vienna'].

During the early years of the Third Reich, scholars tended to sidestep Brahms's awkward friendships; however, as the Nazis' grip on power grew stronger, writers increasingly sought to assess and justify these relations. It must have been convenient for Third Reich biographers that Brahms fell out with so many of his friends, as it allowed them to dismiss several Jewish acquaintances with the frequently repeated formula that in the end the 'racial contrasts' were too great. Brahms's friendships with figures like Eduard Hanslick and Hermann Levi could be written off in this way, and ultimately the same argument was used in the case of Joseph Joachim [see Ch. 22 'Other Instrumentalists']. However, in view of his undeniable importance in Brahms's life, all four biographers attested to Joachim's talent as a virtuoso violinist before providing an account of his apparently unsuccessful compositional attempts – a result of the 'creative infertility of his race', which Brahms eventually could no longer ignore. In support of this suggestion, biographers marshalled one of the few comments by Brahms that could be taken as anti-Semitic: '"Joachim has the unfortunate tendency to complain about his lot in life", Brahms once commented, continuing: "Is that perhaps a Semitic characteristic?"'[12]

Brahms's centenary also provided an occasion for academics to voice their thoughts on the composer. As we shall see, there existed an extraordinary number of contradictory images of the composer around 1933; at this tumultuous point in German history he was described as Romantic and Modernist, as conservative and progressive, as Jew and 'pure German', as Liberal and Nationalist.

In 1932, musicologist Willy Reich argued that Brahms's 'bold cadential effects' marked the beginning of a development away from tonality, one completed by Arnold Schoenberg.[13] Oswald Jonas criticised this 'grotesque attempt to drag Brahms, through whose works the breath of eternity blows, into the shabby, stumbling discourse of everyday speech' and accused the Second Viennese School of trying to legitimise itself by claiming roots in Brahms's music.[14] Walter Krug also attempted to dissociate Brahms from younger composers, noting that recent artists like

---

[12] K. Laux, *Der Einsame: Johannes Brahms – Leben und Werk* (Graz: Pustet, 1944), 58; R. Scherwatzky, *Johannes Brahms. Schöpferische Niederdeutsche* 4 (Osnabrück: A. Fromm, 1941), 19–20; R. Litterscheid, *Johannes Brahms in seinen Schriften und Briefen* (Berlin: Bernhard Hahnfeld, 1943), 315; R. Gerber, *Johannes Brahms: Unsterbliche Tonkunst* (Potsdam: Athenaion, 1939), 22.

[13] W. Reich, 'Grenzgebiete des neuen Tons', *Die Musik* 25/2 (November 1932), 120–3.

[14] O. Jonas, 'Ein Auftakt zur Brahms-Feier', *Allgemeine Musikzeitung* 60/1 (6 January 1933), 4.

The Era of National Socialism 341

Schoenberg, Stravinsky and Honegger had shown an antipathy towards Brahms which 'almost tipped over into hatred'. He explained this hatred as the jealousy of 'epigones' who refused to accept their inferior position in history.[15] Indeed, for some time now, scholars had been using Brahms's music as an ideal tool to critique the so-called 'degeneration' of contemporary music. Brahms was portrayed as the first to realise that the 'foundations of the art of sound' were increasingly shaky and the only composer who made an effort to resist this degeneracy, leading a lonely way back to an 'inspired art of moral strength'.[16]

Bound up with the common criticism of the Modernist movement was a 'nostalgia for the lost epoch of bourgeois cultural hegemony' that Brahms represented.[17] Indeed, this nostalgia led to contradictions within the literature that promoted Brahms as an anti-Modernist; while, as we have seen, many scholars found in Brahms the only hope for the future of German music, others considered him a blind alley. Oscar Bie, for example, saw the composer 'not [as] a beginning but an end' and considered it 'unlikely that his music will continue to bear fruit'.[18] Others pointed out elements of 'progressiveness' in Brahms's compositional style without linking the composer to the Modernists. For instance, Herbert Fleischer described Brahms's unprecedented 'variation techniques' and his 'enriched ... range of harmonic colours', while Erwin Stein commented on his 'economy of material', his 'true objectivity', his 'integration of third relationships into the framework of tonality' and the way 'that a sequence of notes emancipated itself from its rhythmic structure'.[19] There are striking similarities here with Schoenberg's now widely known essay 'Brahms the Progressive'; however, it is unclear whether the authors were influenced by Schoenberg's radio lecture broadcast in February 1933 or whether these ideas were more widely accepted than is now acknowledged [see Ch. 33 'Analysis'].

Remarkably, while most scholars in 1933 tended to dissociate Brahms from the Modernists, only a few positioned him in direct opposition to Wagner – a strategy that had been common up until the early decades of the twentieth century. Prompted by Walter Niemann's 1920 biography,

---

[15] W. Krug, 'Brahms unter den Jungen', *Zeitschrift für Musik* 100/5 (May 1933), 426–7.

[16] F. Pfohl, *'Johannes Brahms: Der Mensch und Künstler' – Festrede von Pfohl anläßlich des Staatlichen Festaktes am 7. Mai 1933 in der Musikhalle* (Hamburg: Hamburger Nachrichten, 1933), 31.

[17] M. von der Linn, 'Themes of Nostalgia and Critique in Weimar-Era Brahms Reception', in D. Brodbeck (ed.), *Brahms Studies 3* (Lincoln: University of Nebraska Press, 2001), 237.

[18] O. Bie, 'Brahms: Zu seinem 100. Geburtstage', *Die Neue Rundschau* 44/5 (May 1933), 688.

[19] E. Stein, 'Brahms – ein Bürger?', *Vossische Zeitung* 125 (7 May 1933), 18; E. Stein, 'Bemerkungen zu Brahms' Formgestaltung', *Anbruch* 15/4–5 (April/May 1933), 60.

which argued that 'Wagner and Brahms are symbolic representatives of the German Volk in the period before the [First] World War', the *Völkischer Beobachter*, for example, called the combined importance and influence of the two German composers a Faustian dualism, the 'great intellectual opposition of brilliant minds', which had been distorted by 'minor, small-minded partisans'.[20] By viewing Wagner and Brahms as complementary sides of the German coin, both could be seen to contribute to the glorification and the cultural power of the German nation.[21]

One explanation as to why many Third Reich scholars proclaimed the *Parteienstreit* as long forgotten has been advanced by Margaret Notley, who has argued that because of Brahms's liberal leanings and network of Jewish friends, his music was discredited in the anti-liberal, even anti-Semitic Viennese atmosphere of the 1880s. Many of his critics chose to emphasise those features of his music that were most closely associated with 'his kind': artificiality and intellectualism.[22] These are characteristics from which scholars in 1933 actively tried to dissociate Brahms. While, as already mentioned, arguments about artificiality were met with an emphasis on Brahms's folk-inspired style, intellectualism was justified, for example, by Bie: 'Brahms loses out when he is studied or admired; he has to be inhaled and tasted ... Then even the calculated and calculating passages in his compositions are an acceptable source of calm.'[23]

Notley's argument – that skewed critiques of Brahms's music, usually explained by the aesthetically based *Parteienstreit*, reflected a contemporary political conflict – is remarkable in view of attempts by Third Reich scholars to distance themselves from the issue. The association of Brahms with liberal and Jewish values was clearly contradicted by their image of the composer as a pure German and, at the same time, this could only create further anxiety about his nationalistic credentials.

Although, as I have tried to highlight, images of Brahms at his centenary were remarkably disparate, almost all shared the widespread belief that

[20] W. Niemann, *Brahms* (Berlin: Schuster & Loeffler, 1920), 375; L. Mayer, 'Johannes Brahms zu seinem hundertsten Geburtstag', *Völkischer Beobachter* 46/127–8 (7–8 May 1933), [9].

[21] Yet the *Parteienstreit* was still smouldering: in 1932, Edwin von der Nuell had provoked heated responses because he had compared Brahms's intellectual background unfavourably with those of Wagner and Liszt ('Wie stehen wir zu Brahms?', *Vossische Zeitung*, Unterhaltungsblatt no. 120 (1 May 1932), [1-2]). Adolf Diesterweg, for example, dismissed von der Nuell's arguments in an outraged reply, calling the author a 'rat king of errors and superficialities' ('"Bürger" Brahms', *Allgemeine Musikzeitung* 59/20 (20 May 1932), 271).

[22] M. Notley, 'Brahms as Liberal: Genre, Style, and Politics in Late Nineteenth-Century Vienna', *19th-Century Music* 17/2 (Autumn 1993), 121.

[23] Bie, 'Brahms', 685. Another example is W. Altmann, 'Johannes Brahms', *Allgemeine Musikzeitung* 60/18 (5 May 1933), 249–51.

The Era of National Socialism

343

a 'positive reappraisal' of Brahms's music was necessary, that the composer had not yet been fully appreciated and that something valuable had been lost through this neglect.[24] Furtwängler described him as 'unrecognised, trivialised, portrayed as an irrelevance'; Schoenberg and others argued for Brahms's forgotten 'progressiveness'; even Adorno criticised the 'disrespectful hands' who had neglected the composer's 'real features' by displaying Brahms 'as a genre painting in the living rooms of musical households'.[25]

This image of Brahms as misunderstood gave writers an exceptionally useful base from which to project their own convictions onto the composer: it made Brahms ideal for any kind of appropriation. Doubtless, many of his works fit badly with the Nazis' music aesthetic; however, much effort went into other, subtler kinds of appropriation. Notably, Brahms the man was used as a role model, an *Identifikationsfigur* as Hitler called it when he demanded that the arts should serve as a 'handmaid of the state', educating the *Volk* to be honourable and honest.[26] Indeed, Ferdinand Pfohl, the main speaker at Hamburg's centenary celebrations, considered Brahms a 'paragon of human-artistic virtues'. Accordingly – and in line with a long-established tradition of popular literature – many articles around this time do not mention musical works at all, or, if they do, they often describe them by drawing parallels to the composer's personality. Like many others at the time, Pfohl himself highlighted Brahms's 'manliness' in the face of adversity; Brahms was down-to-earth rather than super-human, modest, industrious, strove for higher causes and, through his work, managed to catch glimpses of eternity – in short, he was a 'model German'.[27]

In later years Goebbels even managed to utilise the sophistication of Brahms's more complex music, namely to reinforce Germany's prestigious position in the Western cultural world. As the Potsdam example shows, Brahms's music was ideal for bolstering the trustworthiness of the Nazi state, showing its high cultural standards as well as the great tradition of the German cultural heritage. Strategically placed in radio broadcasts and presented – especially abroad – by such internationally renowned artists

---

[24] von der Linn, 'Themes of Nostalgia', 231.

[25] W. Furtwängler, *Aufzeichnungen 1924–1954*, eds. E. Furtwängler & G. Birkner (Wiesbaden: Brockhaus, 1980), 90–1; Dümling, *Verteidigung*, 34.

[26] Hitler at an NSDAP meeting in Augsburg, 6 July 1923; reproduced in Mathieu, *Kunstauffassungen*, 63.

[27] Pfohl, *Festrede*, 27–8.

344 ULRIKE PETERSEN

as Furtwängler, Herbert von Karajan and the pianist Elly Ney, Brahms's music could epitomise the continuity of the flourishing German cultural life and at the same time help extend the nation's cultural hegemony.

1947: Celebratory Accounts of Brahms Fifty Years after His Death

BRAHMS
Boldly you embarked on your journey with the fire of dreamy youth,
but reflectively your gaze turned back to your ancestors.
Your acquired discipline and training; they formed the man and the master,
who escaped the day's dangers with a confident stride.

Dr Hans Scholz,
April 1947[28]

Scholz's poem, written in the fiftieth anniversary year of the composer's death, invokes familiar images – Brahms as the forceful renewer of tradition, respectful of his roots, powerful but self-controlled, pure, constant and diligent. But is the immediate post-war picture of Brahms a continuation of earlier views?

Contemporary comments that support such an interpretation are frequent enough. Alfred Orel's biography provides a telling example: 'We can count the rich, flourishing beauty of his work among our proudest intellectual property; but today he isn't only one of the greatest masters of a bygone age, his creations . . . grant us ever new blessings beyond time and space . . . Let us trust in his star!'[29]

This image of Brahms as a leader rather than a comforter had been mostly absent from the Third Reich literature. However, it was hardly new. Niemann had stressed this aspect in his biography, published at a similar point in history – two years after World War I. But while Niemann emphasised that Brahms's music had a deep effect mainly on the 'Germanic world', Orel and his contemporaries avoided such associations and, in an effort to cleanse the composer of possible political stains, argued the opposite: that Brahms was 'beyond time and space'.[30] Such examples show clearly that the post-war tendency to treat Brahms – just like Beethoven – as superhistorical, transcendental and universal rather than as a German was adopted immediately after the end of the Third Reich.

---

[28] *Neue Musikzeitschrift* 1/5 (April 1947), 144.
[29] A. Orel, *Johannes Brahms: Ein Meister und sein Weg* (Olten: Walter, 1948), 231.
[30] Niemann, *Brahms*, 375.

Other aspects of Brahms that scholars revisited in the post-war period show a change of stylistic taste. After the war a strong dislike of Romantic irrationalism – now considered a 'trailblazer' for National Socialism – re-emerged.[31] Rudolf Gerber, for example, wrote of a 'growing alienation of art and life' after Beethoven, which led to the 'loneliness, isolation and deracination of the creative artist'. He singled out Wagner as a central figure for this development and criticised particularly the lack of folk-music elements in his art.[32] Similarly, Rudolf Steglich traced the 'questionable nature, yes, the urge to destruction, [even the] world/life-crisis of our century' back to Wagner.[33] For critics such as these, Brahms again became the ideal counter-example, this time defined advantageously by characteristics in opposition to Wagner, some of which – notably the affinity for folk-music elements – had been praised also by Third Reich authors.

As the examples above suggest, post-war German writings on Brahms continued to be dominated by attempts to engage with his life and character rather than with analytical aspects. In 1947, the imagery of Brahms as a modest, untiring man must have resonated with Germans, who faced years of poverty and travail. Once again, Brahms was valued for the down-to-earth quality of his music, which was seen – for example by Steglich – as confronting rather than avoiding reality: 'This music does not dream of blue skies and rose-tinted existence. Rather, it is music that strives for a humane life on earth; despite death and devil, it is manly music.' Steglich concluded: 'And how necessary this is nowadays!'[34] Clearly, Brahms's function as a role model continued to make him an important figure in the immediate post-war era, when all stable aspects of German identity seemed to have collapsed and only the enduring culture of earlier times could provide comfort and renewed self-esteem.

The Brahms literature around the celebrations of 1947 is characterised by a uniformity that stands in stark contrast to writings at his centenary. Doubtless, this results partly from the limited amount of literature produced during this time of deprivation. However, the hardships of the period also shaped all discourse, as writers attempted to deal with personal convictions moulded by a dark past and considered how cherished cultural

---

[31] M. Schmidt, *Johannes Brahms: Ein Versuch über die musikalische Selbstreflexion* (Wilhelmshaven: Noetzel, 2000), 79.
[32] R. Gerber, 'Brahms und das Volkslied', *Die Sammlung* 3 (1948), 653.
[33] R. Steglich, 'Johannes Brahms: Vermächtnis und Aufgabe', *Neue Musikzeitschrift* 1/5 (April 1947), 135.
[34] *Ibid.*, 144 and 138.

346 ULRIKE PETERSEN

figures and values might be salvaged to give much-needed constancy in an unstable age.

Brahms – helped by both his established position in opposition to the now discredited Wagner and by the convenient timing of his anniversary year – was the perfect focus for such efforts. More than ever, the composer was appropriated to suit the needs of the age: so much so, in fact, that it is difficult to find a single negative comment about him. His position in the canon was now securely established, and his importance in the history and future of music was now beyond doubt. In many ways, then, the German reception of Brahms was affected favourably by National Socialism and its consequences.

Further Reading

P. Arndt et al (eds.), *Das 'Reichs-Brahmsfest' 1933 in Hamburg: Rekonstruktion und Dokumentation* (Hamburg: Von Bockel, 1997)

D. Beller-McKenna, 'Beyond the End', *Brahms and the German Spirit* (Cambridge, MA: Harvard University Press, 2004), 165–94

A. Dümling, *Verteidigung des musikalischen Fortschritts: Brahms und Schönberg* (Hamburg: Argument, 1990)

M. von der Linn, 'Themes of Nostalgia and Critique in Weimar-Era Brahms Reception', in D. Brodbeck (ed.), *Brahms Studies 3* (Lincoln: University of Nebraska, 2001), 231–48

R. Moseley, 'Brief Immortality: Recasting History in the Music of Brahms', PhD dissertation, University of California at Berkeley (2004)

M. Notley, 'Brahms as Liberal: Genre, Style, and Politics in Late Nineteenth-Century Vienna', *19th-Century Music* 17/2 (Autumn 1993), 107–23

A. Podschun, '"Hüte dich nur und bewahre deine Seele wohl" – Der "Tag von Potsdam" und der dritte der *Fest- und Gedenksprüche* von Johannes Brahms', *Brahms-Studien* 17 (2014), 29–50

U. Romberg, 'Zur Geschichte der Brahms-Rezeption im deutschsprachigen Raum', *Beiträge zur Musikwissenschaft* 29/1 (1987), 49–58

M. Schmidt, *Johannes Brahms: Ein Versuch über die musikalische Selbstreflexion* (Wilhelmshaven: Noetzel, 2000)

CHAPTER 35

Editing Brahms

Michael Struck

Is it appropriate to include a chapter on editing Brahms's music in a book about *Brahms in Context*?[1] In fact, it is not only appropriate but indispensable because it concerns what Brahms left for the present day: his notated music. Furthermore, from the first compositional idea through to publication, his works existed in the 'context' of his contemporaries: friends, acquaintances, copyists, publishers, proofreaders, performers, concert organisers, musicians and critics. Finally, the 'context' should not be limited to his contemporaries because we also need to investigate how his now 'historic' scores were edited after his death and continue to be edited today in the light of philological and editorial premises and methods. Naturally, the question of 'suitable' editing arises, and this must reflect knowledge of current Brahms philology. (The question of new modes of presenting scores and texts, i.e. the increasingly important question of digital editions, will not be considered here, since this can be regarded primarily as an issue of presentation.)

In order to consider how compositions by Brahms – and those of his contemporaries such as Dvořák, Bruch and Tchaikovsky – should be edited today, one must reconstruct the 'historical' path of each work from the preliminary idea all the way to the concert hall, the music shelf, the digital library and the tablet screen. This path extends from the point of initial musical inspiration, which often exists only in the mind, to the point where it is captured in notation, itself a creative and intellectual endeavour that may involve the production of sketches, as well as – in an effort to be as comprehensive as possible – more detailed scores, before the music can be translated from handwriting into print. In addition to these, the third and most important state is the representation of the music in sound. This, in turn, has different dimensions: 'invention' at the piano (as practised by

[1] This chapter draws together various observations arising from the editorial work of the New Brahms Edition (*Johannes Brahms. Neue Ausgabe sämtlicher Werke*, Munich 1996ff.).

347

Schumann, for example, before he moved on to what he considered to be the more serious occupation of composing at his desk); private and public rehearsals, which often lead to score revisions; the composer's own performances; and, finally, the 'release' of the score into the wider world beyond the composer's control.

As a scholar, tracing this process can be difficult. One method is the French literary practice of *critique génétique*. Such 'genetic criticism' aims to reconstruct exactly what has happened to a single manuscript, tracing its evolution backwards rather than seeking to generate a new document which synthesises a number of sources. But this method, which concentrates on the process of writing, tends to neglect what is essential to music: its sonic dimension. Without understanding the interplay between these two aspects, it is difficult to capture adequately the totality of the conditions in which compositions are generated.

Unlike, Beethoven, Schubert, Schumann or Reger, for example, Brahms made it difficult to trace the detailed creative process behind his works. Comparatively few sketches, drafts and short scores still exist (the most extensive are those of the *Liebeslieder* Op. 52 and the *Variations on a Theme of Haydn* Op. 56a/b). This might be explained by Brahms's habit of destroying much of his working material, even down to autographs. However, he also told George Henschel, Fritz Simrock and Gustav Jenner that he tended to think out his music as much as possible first, at most notating single themes, and only then embark upon the complete writing out of the work. If the initial idea did not unfold subconsciously of its own accord like a 'seed-corn', in his view, it was worthless.[2] So we have to assume that important early phases of the compositional process took place before pen was put to paper and that sketches might therefore have been far less numerous for Brahms than for Beethoven or Schumann.

Brahms's creative process therefore began and unfolded in his mind, often while he was out walking. For the Brahms philologist, this phase (which could be very protracted indeed) is a type of 'black box'. We may know what happened before (e.g. while working on other compositions, he might notate a phrase, as with the theme of the slow movement of the Second String Sextet Op. 36, which was written down in both a notebook and a letter to Clara Schumann without being assigned to a particular work, many years before the actual composition). We also know what happened after the 'black box' phase. However, we can only

---

[2] M. Struck. 'Vom Einfall zum Werk – Produktionsprozesse, Notate, Werkgestalt(en)', in *Brahms Handbuch*, 174f.

Editing Brahms

guess at the hidden working phase, both in his mind and in destroyed manuscripts. And this 'thinking' naturally includes an important emotional element.

Within this black box, there may be early working documents such as sketches, a draft or a short score. These are generally followed by complete autograph manuscripts, i.e. working autographs which usually contain numerous subsequent amendments. The composer might revise such an autograph so much that he had to write out a clean copy to send to a publisher or copyist. During his stay in Weimar with Liszt in June 1853, Brahms was apparently too shy to play his Scherzo Op. 4 to him, while Liszt – impressively – managed to play it from a barely legible manuscript. However, the surviving autograph of the Scherzo is fairly legible, so Brahms must have copied out the (now destroyed) earlier manuscript from which Liszt had played, before sending this new clean autograph to Breitkopf & Härtel for publication. Here, as in other Brahms autographs, certain corrections reveal that he made mistakes in copying from an earlier manuscript, usually by omitting bars when working from earlier autographs. We can see this in two places in the clean Scherzo autograph.[3] In many other similarly 'clean' manuscripts, passages that Brahms had resumed copying one or more bars too early or too late also reveal them to be second copies, probably intended as clean copies. But even in the preparation of clean copies, Brahms frequently had second thoughts and made emendations in the form of crossings-out or erasures (using a small knife) before notating anew. Thus, a manuscript intended as a clean copy could morph back into a working copy.

Brahms often did not prepare the clean copy himself, but left this task to a professional copyist. As the *Werkverzeichnis* shows, between the 1850s and 1890s, he worked with numerous copyists, reflecting his frequent change of location. However, there were three main copyists, of whom two were important to him from the 1870s onwards, after he settled in Vienna: initially Franz Hlaváček, then later almost exclusively William Kupfer, his fellow Hamburger, who as a cellist could also offer practical suggestions. In terms of the number of copies made, Kupfer and Hlavaczek are followed by Josef Füller from Karlsruhe, who still made far more copies than all other named and unnamed, identified and anonymous copyists.

---

[3] *Johannes Brahms: Scherzo es-Moll op. 4*, ed. M. Wetzstein (Hamburg: Schuberth, 1987), 2f and 8 of this facsimile.

Copyists principally fulfilled two tasks for Brahms. Firstly, they made clean copies of scores. These could serve as conductors' and performance copies before they were sent, following more revisions, to the publisher and, from there, after checking and correction, to the engravers. There are also, however, numerous autograph engraver's copies (the last comprehensive autograph engraver's copy of a complete work was that of the score of the Fourth Symphony Op. 98). Copyists' other main task was the preparation of parts for chamber music, works with and for orchestra and chorus, and vocal ensemble music. Either all the parts were written out separately, or a copy of each was made with special ink on particular paper, a transfer made onto a lithographic stone and copies made from this [see Ch. 24 'Publishers']. (Such choral parts for *A German Requiem* Op. 45 in the original six-part version have survived.) In later years, for works with orchestra, Brahms had the string and choral parts copied out only once by his copyist and then, by arrangement with the publisher, provisionally engraved. Thus, several copies of the same part could be produced for rehearsals and performances – albeit always with the condition that subsequent details could be changed in the engraved plates if experiences during rehearsals and performances necessitated such revisions.

But let us return to the copyists' versions. Although these were meant to provide a legible basis for rehearsals and performances, and later for engraving, printing and publication, in extreme cases, they could also mutate into working manuscripts. An extreme example is the First Piano Trio Op. 8, which was recomposed in 1889. Although its autograph and the engraver's copies have vanished, a copyist's manuscript of the score and parts, which belongs chronologically in between those stages, has largely survived. The earliest rehearsals and performances must have drawn on this first set of copies, prompting Brahms to make many changes. Because of the numerous crossings-out and newly notated passages, he could not send the manuscript to the publisher for use as an engraver's copy. Hence, a copyist had to prepare a new one. Brahms then tore up the earlier score and threw it into his waste-paper basket, but his landlady Celestine Truxa rescued most of the strips and reassembled them, possibly believing that it was an autograph.

During the text's journey into the public world, the autograph or copied engraver's copy was sent to the publisher in full score and – if necessary and available – also in separate parts. Then, the text, which had been revised and had undergone some preliminary editing by Brahms, was edited for engraving and sent on to an engraving workshop. Over the decades, this

Editing Brahms 351

was increasingly that of Carl Gottlieb Röder, who gradually developed a veritable engraving factory; in 1896, it had a workforce of 773.[4]

In many of Brahms's works, the printing stage is yet another 'black box'. It generally included several sub-stages: the preparation for engraving by the copy-editor and the engraver (which one can still see if the relevant engraver's copy survives), the actual engraving, the proofreading phases, the first impression of the edition and the production of copies, both gratis and for sale. Only relatively few correction proofs have survived; these are distinct from other advance copies intended as gifts to friends or which Brahms himself used as temporary copies before a work's official appearance. Brahms's correspondence with publishers and friends, and sometimes also notes on engraver's copies, can give us detailed information about the process of proofreading [see Ch. 6 'Correspondence'].

Traces of corrections in plates of some early printings (above all in plate-printed copies) can be indications of changes made to the galley proofs. Changes, engraving errors and misreadings marked in the corrected proofs were subsequently hammered out of the already engraved original plates in the engraver's workshop, and the new, corrected text versions were re-engraved (an expensive and time-consuming process which did not particularly please the publishers). If the engraver's plates had been used many times, the contours of the original engraving or the corrected templates could break apart. This technical shortcoming can therefore be regarded as an important philological trace which helps explain discrepancies between the engraver's copies and the actual print.

Even after a score had been signed off for printing, the first impression produced and copies sold or given to Brahms and his friends, the compositional history of the work was not necessarily complete. In extreme cases, works like the First Piano Trio Op. 8 or the songs 'Liebe und Frühling' Op. 3 no. 2 and 'Beim Abschied' Op. 95 no. 3 are instances of revised editions or prints which might appear several decades – or just a few months – after the first print. Of course, errors might also be corrected in later prints or tempo indications modified, as in the coda of the first movement of the First Symphony Op. 68.

As Robert Pascall has shown, the journey of a work from the first manuscript, in interaction with its realisation in sound, to the final version authorised and fixed by Brahms (often called the 'Fassung letzter Hand')

---

[4] H. Riemann (ed.), *Festschrift zur 50jährigen Jubelfeier des Bestehens der Firma C. G. Röder Leipzig* (Leipzig: C. G. Röder, 1896), 15.

Figure 35.1. Part of an engraved metal plate for the old Urtext edition by G. Henle Verlag, Munich 1976 of J. Brahms, Intermezzo Op. 117 no. 1, middle section. This shows traces of corrections and musical and verbal text engraved in mirror writing to get the regular image in print. Reproduction by kind permission of G. Henle Verlag Munich and the Brahms-Forschungszentrum Kiel.

was subject to many conflicting forces.[5] On the one hand, the text had to be optimised, a process which concerned editorial improvements as well as Brahms's compositional alterations – for example, to motifs, instrumentation, articulation and dynamics, as well as expressive indications. On the other hand, the integrity of the text was increasingly compromised by hitherto undiscovered errors in writing and copying stemming from the composer himself but, above all, through errors, ambiguities and misunderstandings on the part of the copyists, engravers and copy-editors. Brahms was a committed proofreader, but he was often also under considerable time pressure, with new works in progress demanding his greatest concentration.

The question of editing Brahms today must therefore be understood in the light of all these conflicting currents. As a consequence of the journey I have described for the work and work-text, two things become clear: firstly, it is inappropriate to try to edit Brahms's music according to the old

---

[5] R. Pascall, 'Charakteristika und Probleme des Publikationsprozesses', in *JBG, 1. Symphonie*, xviif.

Editing Brahms

'Urtext' idea, which dominated until well into the twentieth century and which generated numerous 'Urtext' editions and also shaped various historical-critical complete editions. Broadly speaking, this idea followed the premise that the primary authentic and authorised text is that which stems from the composer's hand itself. Of course, this premise is crucial for works that have only survived in manuscript and that moved almost immediately outside the composer's influence, assuming that handwritten copies were only made based on other handwritten copies, without the composer's further involvement. But this kind of 'Urtext' idea becomes increasingly problematic for works from the nineteenth and late eighteenth centuries because, at that point, print was the main medium of dissemination. This increasingly industrialised process, preceded by the stages of autograph copy, a possible further copy, engraving correction phase(s) and publication, was ever more widely standardised.

Bearing all this in mind, it would be fatal to edit Brahms's music according to the old 'Urtext' ideal because this negates all the laborious work of compositional revision. Brahms's ultimate compositional intentions would be rejected in favour of an autograph version – but which? The first? The last? Particularly with working manuscripts, it is not even possible to establish whether a spontaneous correction of an error or alteration of material belongs to a later phase in the work's existence or still to its first 'layer'. Above all, the old 'Urtext' idea ignores the significance of the compositional changes found in copies and correction proofs, which we see as handwritten corrections or can infer through discrepancies between sources.

Equally problematic today are the editorial principles of Brahms's friend Eusebius Mandyczewski and his former student Hans Gál in their first Complete Brahms Edition.[6] They had access to numerous autographs, above all those which Brahms left to Vienna's Gesellschaft der Musikfreunde, but, on the other hand, they almost completely disregarded copyists' manuscripts. Brahms's own *Handexemplare*, i.e. his own personal copies of his printed music, which sometimes also contained annotations, were regarded as particularly important. The editorial premise of the old Complete Edition was that Brahms was a meticulous proofreader and his own printed copies – apart from a few missed errors – definitively reflected his compositional intentions. Therefore, the existence of such copies belonging to him with no corrections was taken as an indication that he

---

[6] E. Mandyczewski and H. Gál (eds.), *Johannes Brahms: Sämtliche Werke. Ausgabe der Gesellschaft der Musikfreunde in Wien*, 26 vols. (Leipzig: Breitkopf & Härtel, 1926–7, rev. 1965).

wanted no further corrections to those scores. Handwritten changes were generally regarded as records of his final intentions. However, Robert Pascall has shown that Brahms's annotations in his own copies need to be evaluated in a more nuanced way.[7]

Since the late 1920s, when the copyright for Brahms's works lapsed, various 'interpretative editions' have appeared, which have completely different intentions, largely follow a text-critical method, sometimes draw on manuscripts, but mainly add performance suggestions such as fingering, dynamics, articulation or tempo indications according to the interpretative conception of renowned musicians. Such editions can also be described as 'didactic' editions.

How, then, should a historical-critical Brahms edition be made today, i.e. an edition which as far as possible approaches not only the *text* critically, but also authoritatively takes into account its sources, the work-genetic perspective, the trial performances and the publication process? Producing such an edition requires the skills and knowledge of a music historian as well as considerable expertise in current methods of editing. Editing Brahms today should first and foremost reconstruct the genesis of the work as precisely as possible, drawing on the available notated sources and with due consideration of missing ones. As mentioned above, Brahms's published and unpublished correspondence offers important information, as do his contemporaries' correspondence about him and his music, his friends' recollections and early biographies of him. This all helps to reconstruct a more or less detailed framework for the sources, their chronological sequence and function. The editions of the individual parts (orchestral, chamber, choral and so forth), as well as the piano scores and arrangements also belong to this framework since, although these reductions sit lower down in the hierarchy of versions, they were nonetheless indispensable for the dissemination of works. (Their significance for a historical-critical edition is limited because Brahms often conceived them as very separate objects.) On the other hand, alternative versions such as the Piano Quintet Op. 34 and the Sonata for Two Pianos Op. 34bis are hierarchically equivalent, as are the orchestral and two-piano versions of the *Variations on a Theme of Haydn* Op. 56a/b; still, even in this case, one has to be cautious about incorporating readings from one version in another.

---

[7] R. Pascall, 'Brahms and the definitive text', in R. Pascall (ed.), *Brahms: Biographical, Documentary and Analytical Studies* (Cambridge: Cambridge University Press, 1983), 59–75.

Within a historical-critical edition, manuscripts and print sources in all their versions must be painstakingly compared, and any discrepancies interpreted as accurately as possible (copyist's error? engraving error? a result of changes in sources now lost, such as corrected proofs?). For works which appeared during Brahms's lifetime, a printing, either a first printing, private copy or a subsequently revised printing, will be the main source. Still, although this reflects Brahms's authorised version, it generally also contains errors that Brahms missed, such as those stemming from copyist, engraver or copy-editor, and these must be amended based on a comparison of sources and text-critical research. The editor must also occasionally intervene in the text without the basis of sources when wrong notes, missing dynamics or articulation cannot be corrected by drawing on a relevant source and one can exclude the possibility of it just being the case of an abbreviated notation typical of Brahms.

In cases of directly visible corrections in manuscripts or personal copies, or those which can be inferred through discrepancies, editors should always seek to understand the cause (timbral precision, avoidance of technical musical errors, notational errors and mistakes in transposing instruments). Therefore, the editor needs the largest possible knowledge of analysis, broader music orthography, Brahms's notational idiosyncrasies, scoring and instrumentation, as well as historical and current performance practice. Editing Brahms also entails acknowledging the 'black boxes' and the 'grey zones', in which no definitively authorised editorial decision is possible.

As a rule, only historical-critical editions are forced to plumb such philological depths. Given the scholarly and financial demands, it is therefore no wonder that only one 'New Complete Brahms Edition' is in existence. (Naturally, complete editions are equally historically contingent in terms of sources, editing method and presentation, including current and future digital formats.) More problematic, however, are current editions primarily concerned with performance-practice methods which claim to be text- and source-critical. They may aim at this but are often superficial in their comparison and interpretation of sources and, in some respects, may become one-sided by privileging some aspect of historical performance practice. 'Practical editions' are most useful when their text is based on a scholarly, historical-critical edition.

In conclusion, editing Brahms is a highly demanding, contextually richly interconnected task, which, since the appearance in 1984 of Margit McCorkle's catalogue of Brahms's works, the *Brahms-Werkverzeichnis*, and

MICHAEL STRUCK

through the ongoing appearance of the New Edition of his complete works (since 1996), demands – and is generating – new principles, methods and standards.

Further Reading

J. Behr and K. Kirsch, 'Ein bislang unbekannter Korrekturabzug zum 2. Klavierkonzert op. 83 von Johannes Brahms', in M. Goltz, W. Sandberger and C. Wiesenfeld (eds.), *Spätphase(n)? Johannes Brahms' Werke der 1880er und 1890er Jahre* (Munich: Henle, 2010), 157–69

K. Kirsch, *Von der Stichvorlage zum Erstdruck. Zur Bedeutung von Vorabzügen bei Johannes Brahms* (Kassel: Bärenreiter, 2013)

K. Kirsch, 'Korrekturphase – Erprobungsphase. Zur Werkentstehung zwischen Redaktion und Interpretation am Beispiel ausgewählter Korrektur- und Aufführungsabzüge von Johannes Brahms' Werken', in U. Krämer, A. Raab et al. (eds.), *Das Autograph – Fluch und Segen. Probleme und Chancen für die musikwissenschaftliche Edition* (Mainz: Schott, 2015), 167–90

F. Krummacher, M. Struck et al. (eds.), *Johannes Brahms. Quellen – Text – Rezeption – Interpretation* (Munich: Henle, 1999)

S. Oechsle, M. Struck and K. Eich (eds.), *Brahms am Werk. Konzepte – Texte – Prozesse* (Munich: Henle, 2016)

R. Pascall, 'Brahms and the Definitive Text', in R. Pascall (ed.), *Brahms: Biographical, Documentary and Analytical Studies* (Cambridge: Cambridge University Press, 1983), 59–75

R. Pascall, 'The Editor's Brahms', in M. Musgrave (ed.), *The Cambridge Companion to Brahms* (Cambridge: Cambridge University Press, 1999), 250–67

M. Struck, 'Progression und Regression: Vom Quellenwert der Autographe für die Edition Brahms'scher Werke', in U. Krämer, A. Raab et al. (eds.), *Das Autograph – Fluch und Segen. Probleme und Chancen für die musikwissenschaftliche Edition.* (Mainz: Schott, 2015), 143–66

M. Struck and K. Eich, *'Zur Edition der Musik von Johannes Brahms'*, in R. Emans and U. Krämer (eds.), *Musikeditionen im Wandel der Geschichte* (Berlin & Boston: De Gruyter, 2015), 564–83

CHAPTER 36

Recordings

Ivan Hewett

The recorded legacy of any composer reckoned to be canonical presents an interesting and revealing set of historical tensions. It has its own narrative, which unfolds in a complicated counterpoint with the story of the performing tradition(s) revealed in live performance. This double narrative is inflected by the changing view of the composer within academe, particularly in matters of performance practice, but not only that. Complicating the picture still further is the stubborn material persistence of the recorded medium itself. Live performances vanish the moment they are over, but LPs and CDs hang around for decades on music-lovers' shelves, enforcing a loyalty to older ways of thinking and feeling, in critics as much as in ordinary listeners. This means that journals which offer critical reviews of recordings, particularly those aimed at musically sophisticated enthusiasts, are peculiarly revealing. They show how recordings, and the discourse around them, work together to create a certain image of the composer, which proves stubbornly resistant to change.

This process is particularly fraught with ironies in the case of Brahms. In this essay, I suggest why that might be, with reference to critical writings aimed at the general public in the English-speaking world, particularly the *Gramophone* magazine, founded in 1923. I also suggest that the recording process itself, in its mature phase, helped to support the image of Brahms that the critical discourse favoured, in a circle of mutual reinforcement that has proved difficult to dislodge.

So what qualities should a fine recording of a piece by Brahms possess, in the view of these opinion-makers? It does not take long to discover the answer: it should be 'Brahmsian'. This peculiar metamorphosis of a proper name into an adjective, as a way of gesturing to the ineffability which belongs to genius, is hardly peculiar to Brahms. We use 'Mozartian' and 'Beethovenian' as adjectives with equal insouciance. However, the concatenation of qualities referred to by the word 'Brahmsian' seems especially complex and particularly resistant to analysis. The fact that such vastly

358   IVAN HEWETT

different conductors as Toscanini and Furtwängler could both be described as 'Brahmsians' is sufficient evidence of that. Recording helped to engender this interesting complexity, partly because Brahms stands in a special relationship to the development of the industry. The performing traditions associated with earlier composers of the Viennese School were already decades old by the time recordings came along. Brahms, on the other hand, actually belongs to a new era, where the composer's own recorded performances, and those of his students and colleagues, offer a model of a performing style with a special claim to be authoritative.

Of course, the authority of these recordings can be contested, on several grounds – the most obvious of which is that composers do not always make the best interpreters of their own works. And the harvest of these recordings is not a rich one. There are just two recordings by Brahms himself, made in Vienna in 1889 by an assistant of Thomas Edison, and only one of them is of a piece by Brahms [see Ch. 30 'Science and Technology']. Then there are recordings by musicians who were close to Brahms and, in some cases, performed with him. They include the pianists Ilona Eibenschütz, Carl Friedburg and Etelka Freund [see Ch. 31 'Pianists'], and the singers Gustav Walter and Anton Sistermans.[1] One would think that these performances would have been treasured by later performers for the insight they offer into a vanished performing style.

These recordings have been available in transcriptions onto LP (in 1989) and CD (in 2004), and yet their influence on Brahms performance has thus far been negligible. One reason may be that the style of these early recordings does not sit well with the received image of Brahms that still dominates discussion of performances of his music in the wider public realm. They are too 'dynamic, restless, carefree and unreservedly impassioned', to quote Anna Scott.[2] They were sidelined by an image of Brahms

---

[1] Etelka Freund (1879–1977), the Hungarian-born, later American pianist, played regularly for Brahms while a student and, in the late 1950s, recorded *Variations on a Theme of Robert Schumann* Op. 9, Ballade Op. 118 no. 3, Rhapsody Op. 119 no. 4 and Intermezzo Op. 76 no. 3; Ilona Eibenschütz (1873–1967), Hungarian pianist, pupil of Clara Schumann, friend of Brahms, recorded the Ballade Op. 118 no. 3 in 1903; Carl Friedberg (1872–1955), German pianist, played for Brahms in 1893, recorded the First Piano Trio Op. 8 in 1939, Rhapsody Op. 79 no. 1 and Ballade Op. 118 no 3 in the late 1940s and Rhapsody Op. 79 no 2 in c. 1951; all on *Brahms: Recaptured by Pupils and Colleagues,* Arbiter Records No. 163 B0186KU0NW (2 CDs, 2015). Gustav Walter (1834–1910), Bohemian tenor, recorded 'Feldeinsamkeit' Op. 86 no. 2 in 1904; Anton Sistermans (1865–1926), Dutch bass, friend of Brahms, gave the first performance of the *Four Serious Songs* Op. 121 in Vienna in 1896 and recorded 'Sapphische Ode' Op. 94 no. 4 in 1906; both on on *Brahms Lieder 1926–1950*, Vol. 8, ArkivMusic Hafg 40008 (2010).

[2] A. Scott, *Romanticising Brahms: Early Recordings and the Reconstruction of Brahmsian Identity*, PhD dissertation, University of Leiden (2014), xiii.

the composer that began to emerge, even during his lifetime, as the Classical antipode of more overtly Romantic composers, above all Wagner. Strong feeling was there, to be sure, but it was feeling of a specifically musical kind, free from the pictorialism and excessive subjectivity that afflicted the music of Wagner and Liszt. Brahms's music could be seen – given a sufficiently strong philosophical *parti pris* – to exemplify the formalist doctrine of his great champion the critic Eduard Hanslick, who insisted that music was 'an end in itself, and not a means for representing feelings and thoughts . . . Of music it is impossible to form any but a musical conception, and it can be comprehended and enjoyed only in and for itself.'[3]

This is why there was a moral tone in writers who praise Brahms, typified by Ernest Walker's assertion that 'to deny that beauty and the passion are to be found in Brahms's work as a whole is, I think, to show oneself . . . incapable of distinguishing between beauty and sensuousness, and between emotion and hysteria'.[4]

I suggest that there is a special affinity between the emotional discipline, even understatement that this view requires of the Brahms performer, and the special discipline required of performers by the recording process – not in its early days, but in its maturity. The transformation whereby recordings changed from being literally a record of a single risky performance to a carefully honed and artificial studio construct, a simulacrum of a performance rather than the real thing, is a well-rehearsed theme in the history of classical music recording (and the recording of other musics).[5] This led in time to a peculiar reversal, whereby recordings of living or long-dead artists became the touchstone against which many listeners measured the quality of the live performance.

This is as true of Mozart and Beethoven as it is of Brahms, but the process whereby recordings usurped live performance took on a particular significance in the case of the Brahms. Recordings lack the thrill of the moment, replacing it with a different thrill, of guaranteed blemish-free perfection. Achieving it requires the privileging of planning and reflectiveness over spontaneity. This was exactly the quality that characterised Brahms, as he was reconceived in the twentieth century. The (alleged) repression of emotion in Brahms fitted hand in glove with the repression

---

[3] E. Hanslick, *The Beautiful in Music*, trans. G. Cohen (London: Novello & Co., 1891), Chapter 3.

[4] E. Walker, 'Brahms', *Proceedings of the Musical Association*, 25th Session (1898–9), 81.

[5] See for example M. Katz, *Capturing Sound: How Technology has Changed Music* (Berkeley: University of California Press, 2010); and R. Philip, *Performing Music in the Age of Recording* (New Haven: Yale University Press, 2004).

demanded by the recording process, as if they were made for each other. The displacement of the impetuous, surgingly Romantic Brahms by this more ambiguous figure is also connected with the profound change in listening habits engendered by the recording process. The depths in Brahms were hidden; what better way to reveal them than through a recording, which in its careful, painstaking manufacture was the analogue of Brahms's own careful sobriety?

We see this peculiarly symbiotic relationship between Brahms's music and recording reflected in the way recordings of Brahms were discussed. In the 1920s and 30s Brahms-lovers were thought of as a sect with enormously refined and lofty tastes. In the pages of the *Gramophone*, Brahms-lovers were referred to as 'Brahmins',[6] and the adjective Brahmsian is made to work strenuously, as in a review of a recording of the Second String Quartet Op. 51 no. 2, where the reviewer refers to 'a grand Brahmsian pull about the opening of the second movement, with its rather dour bass, doubled by the two lowest instruments in octaves'. Or take Joan Chissell's review of Artur Rubinstein's recording of miscellaneous shorter pieces entitled 'The Brahms I Love': 'Every pianist has a special sound world of his own. Rubinstein's is light and translucent rather than deep and saturated, and from that point of view I would not call him the ideal Brahmsian.'[7]

The true Brahmsian sound was rich but not sweet, a point made frequently in reviews. The anonymous reviewer of the 1929 recording by the Budapest Piano Trio of the First Piano Trio Op. 8 complained about the 'excess of lusciousness' in the slow movement' and added, 'but a little of this must be put down to the string players, who have tried to make the music just a little too sweet, I feel. Perhaps this trio is not ideally suited in music demanding a blend of romanticism and austerity.'[8]

Effing the ineffable is always a tricky business, but the frequency of these adjectives in the discourse about Brahms shows that with him it was especially so. Unsurprisingly this 'difficult' composer was a minority taste, even among classical music lovers. It is interesting to note that in the *Gramophone* of 1929, Chopin is ahead of Brahms in terms of the number of index entries, with twenty-two compared to sixteen, and even

---

[6] See, for example, W. R. Anderson, reviewing Alec Robertson's book *Brahms*. 'Book Review: Good Companions', *The Gramophone* 9/105 (February 1932), 402.

[7] J. Chissell, 'Brahms. Piano Works. Artur Rubinstein. RCA SB6845', *The Gramophone* 49/578 (July 1971), 204.

[8] Anon, 'Chamber Music. Brunswick. 10280–10284 – Budapest Trio: Piano Trio in B, Op. 8 (Brahms). (Eulenburg)', *The Gramophone* 7/76 (September 1929), 159.

Debussy is more popular (Verdi is easily the most popular composer, with 110 entries, with Mozart and Beethoven mid-way between him and Chopin).

However, by the 1930s the tide was turning. Longer pieces could be recorded, and record libraries could now be assembled, offering an overview of a composer's work, and rival versions of the same work compared. 'Is it necessary to defend Brahms now?' asked the reviewer W. R. Anderson in the *Gramophone* in 1932. 'Surely not! Not a tenth of his work is really difficult. He has become a best-seller. Among many good results, this has stabilised the feeling for form; we needed that.'[9]

Here we see an early expression of a persistent idea that a recording of Brahms is good if it clarifies the formal process that governs the music; an assumption that reflects the formalism which dominated thinking about music until the advent of New Musicology. Decades later it was expressed again by Stephen Plaistow ('S.P.'), when he praised Clifford Curzon for the way he 'forges the unity of the movement by ensuring that the four-note descending motif can always be sensed as the music's unifying element'.[10] This ability was one thing that distinguished the true 'Brahmsian'. Another was the projection of a lofty high-seriousness, which many thought only German performers, or foreign performers deeply attuned to this quality, could attain. This chauvinist view was not confined to Germans. The distinguished critic Andrew Porter ('A.P.') disparaged Walter Gieseking's recording of the Intermezzo Op. 119 no. 3 for lacking the 'Brahmsian spirit'. His playing, says Porter, 'suggests irresistibly a French pianist's parody of a Brahms performance: the hands not quite together, little swoons over suspensions and so on', even though evidence indicates that this kind of dislocation is precisely what Brahms would have expected.[11]

Yet another pair of antipodes in Brahms's music was that between 'young' and 'late'. Plaistow in that same review of Curzon remarks that 'Rubinstein, though he plays the sonata with a complete command of its heroics, does so almost as if he were interpreting late Brahms, not early. Curzon by comparison seems anxious to stress that this is a young man's music: his performance has a little more personal directness and

---

[9] Anderson, 'Book Review. Good Companions'.

[10] S. Plaistow, 'Brahms. Piano Works. Clifford Curzon (piano). Decca', *The Gramophone* 40/480 (May 1963), 522.

[11] A. Porter, 'Brahms. Intermezzo in E minor, Op. 119, No. 2. Rhapsody in E flat major, Op. 119, No. 4. Walter Gieseking (piano). Columbia LX1581', *The Gramophone* 30/359 (April 1953), 290.

362 IVAN HEWETT

immediacy.'[12] However, some people felt that Rubinstein was simply a non-Brahmsian *tout court,* as in the above-mentioned remark by Joan Chissell. Wiser heads realised that this mysterious Brahmsian essence was not to be found in any one recorded version of a work but in the ability to appreciate and, as it were, hold in one's head the virtues of contrasting versions. Lionel Salter remarked about the famous recording of *A German Requiem* Op. 45 by Klemperer that 'the problem of choice between this version of the Brahms Requiem and [Rudolph] Kempe's will rest largely on your conception of the work: Kempe's is the more humane and expressive, Klemperer's the more virile and stoic. Brahms himself was such a complex character, full of contradictions, that both views are plausible.'[13]

True 'Brahmsians' expressed this tension between contraries in their own performances. Claudio Arrau, for example, was praised for his 'control which comes, not from the fingers, but from the pianist's whole body and spirit, massively poised'.[14] But this impression of 'poise' actually issued from a tempestuously emotional nature, whose preference for deliberate tempos sprung out of a desire to wring the maximum expressivity from Brahms's music, and who once described the slow movement of Brahms's Piano Sonata Op. 5 as 'the most beautiful love-music since Tristan'.[15] Sometimes 'Brahmsian' qualities emerged on record in the most unexpected places. Take Glenn Gould, a pianist more often blamed than praised for his performances of Brahms. In the *Gramophone,* Joan Chissell ('J.O.C.') bewailed Gould's recording of Op. 118 and Op. 119 in which the music is 'not for a single moment left to tell its own tale, but constantly distorted by this pianist's eccentric imagination'.[16]

But one writer's wilful eccentricity is another's cool objectivity. Eugene Narmour actually praises Gould's recording of the Intermezzo Op. 118 no. 1 contained on this LP for revealing the integrity of the falling C, B♭, A, E motive, often ignored by pianists because it is split between two hands. He qualifies this by saying that Gould 'ruins the form in other ways, by

---

[12] Plaistow, 'Brahms. Piano Works'.

[13] L. Salter, 'Choral and Song. Brahms. A German Requiem, Op. 45', *The Gramophone* 39/465 (February 1962) 414–5, on Schwarzkopf, Fischer-Dieskau, Philharmonia Chorus and Orchestra cond. Klemperer, Columbia A SAXS 2430/2431 (1962), and Grümmer, Fischer-Dieskau, Berlin Philharmonic Orchestra and Chorus of St, Hedwig's Cathedral, cond. Rudolf Kempe, Warner Classics T2CD 2013007 (1955, 1993).

[14] E. Greenfield, 'Brahms Piano Works', review of Claudio Arrau, Concertgebouw Orchestra cond. Bernard Haitink, Philips (1) 6768 356 (5 LPs, 1983), in *Gramophone* 61/722 (July 1983), 140.

[15] J. Horowitz, *Conversations with Arrau* (London: Collins, 1982), 152.

[16] J. Chissell, 'Brahms. Intermezzi. Glenn Gould (piano). CBS 73093', *The Gramophone* 50/597 (February 1973), 1530.

Recordings   363

suppressing the repeats', which 'throws the form out of all proportion'.[17] Gould scholar Kevin Bazzana leaps to Gould's defence, saying this suppression springs from Gould's 'organic, dynamical view of musical form ... Gould's suppressing of the repeats actually helps him to impress that overall scheme onto the listener as a single controlling image, almost like an analytical graph'.[18] What neither Narmour or Bazzana seem to have noticed is that Gould is not the first pianist to record the piece as one sweeping gesture. On his wonderful recording from December 1932, Wilhelm Backhaus does the same, in an even more tumultuous performance which comes in a good thirteen seconds shorter than Gould.[19] We can be fairly sure Backhaus was not striving to present an 'analytical graph' to his listeners; rather he grasped the tumultuous nature of the piece, which lends itself to being expressed 'in one breath'.

The freedom of Backhaus's performance harks back to the old, more spontaneous-seeming performance tradition that recordings had by now done so much to repress. It pops up from time to time, like an underground river that occasionally breaks surface, but which performers actually manifested this trait depended partly on who was listening. In the eyes of some, even the great Furtwängler was guilty of 'mannered' tempo fluctuations which were not truly 'Brahmsian'.[20] Another example is the recording made in 1968 by Jacqueline du Pré and Daniel Barenboim of Brahms's Cello Sonata Op. 99.[21] Du Pré turns the little echo figures in the Scherzo into an impassioned outcry, which completely disrupts the rhythmic flow of the piece. It is not 'Brahmsian', but might it not be true to the real Brahms, seen without the distorting lens of 'sober, classical' Brahms that by now was the orthodoxy?[22]

This orthodoxy became more firmly entrenched as the knowledge of old performing practices faded away, and the text exerted an iron grip on performance and recording. A curiously late example of this text-fetishism

[17] E. Narmour, 'On the Relationship of Analytical Theory to Performance and Interpretation', in E. Narmour and R. Solie (eds.), *Explorations in Music, the Arts and Ideas: Essays in Honor of Leonard B. Meyer* (Stuyvesant: Pendragon Press, 1988), 319, quoted in K. Bazzana, *Glenn Gould: The Performer in the Work* (Oxford: Oxford University Press, 1997), 100.

[18] Bazzana, *Glenn Gould*, 100–1.

[19] *Backhaus plays Brahms. Celebrated Piano Solo Recordings 1929–1936* (Music and Arts MACD1132).

[20] See for instance Lionel Salter's reference to Fürtwangler's 'wilful exaggerations'. 'Brahms. Symphony No. 1 in C minor, Op. 68. Symphony No. 2 in D major, Op. 73. NBC Symphony Orchestra (Toscanini). HMV', *The Gramophone* 30/353 (October 1952), 104.

[21] EMI Studio CDM 7 63296 2.

[22] I owe this example to Roger Moseley, 'Between Work and Play: Brahms as Performer', in W. Frisch and K. C. Karnes (eds.), *Brahms and His World*, 2nd edn (Princeton: Princeton University Press, 2009), 158.

364   IVAN HEWETT

is Gunther Schuller's 'The Compleat Conductor'. He casts a beady eye over no fewer than sixty-six recordings of Brahms's First Symphony Op. 68, and any that deviate from the strict letter of Brahms's score are cast into the outer darkness. The idea that fidelity to the written note needs to be tempered with a feeling for performance traditions simply does not occur to him; furthermore, the editing process itself includes many points of ambiguity [see Ch. 35 'Editing Brahms'].[23]

Then in the 1980s something unforeseen entered into the picture of Brahms on record: the period performance movement. In the 1990s Roger Norrington released a recording with his orchestra, the London Classical Players, of all four symphonies,[24] in which his aim was 'to seek to restore as much as possible the relationship between the scores, which have not changed, and the instruments, forces and performing styles, which most certainly have'.[25] Norrington's approach is interestingly ambivalent. On the one hand, he insists that Brahms is 'essentially classical·in his intricate contrapuntal structure, rhythmic precision and interplay of figures, which is so often likened to chamber music'. On the other, he describes the emotional world of Brahms as 'almost Byronic' in its Romanticism, and says he was 'driven to composition by the same forces of desperation, inner conflict, joy and resolution'. Despite his care to recreate the kind of orchestral sound and balance that Brahms would have approved, Norrington insists that music is not made of sound as such, but of sound conceived as gesture [see Ch. 37 'Historical Performance'].

Charles Mackerras would probably have agreed. His recorded version of Brahms's symphonies made with the Scottish Chamber Orchestra in 1998, though advertised as 'authentic', actually uses modern instruments, apart from nineteenth-century brass and timpani. Like Norrington, Mackerras uses sources previously ignored, such as the marked-up scores of the symphonies made by Fritz Steinbach, chief conductor of the Meiningen Orchestra from 1886 to 1902, and a conductor much admired by Brahms.[26] John Eliot Gardiner's complete recording of the symphonies with the Orchestre Révolutionnaire et Romantique followed ten years later, but

---

[23] G. Schuller, *The Compleat Conductor* (New York and Oxford: Oxford University Press, 1997), 306.
[24] Symphony No. 1, EMI CDC 7 54286 2 (1991); Symphony No. 2 EMI CD 554875 (1993); Symphonies Nos. 3 and 4, EMI 7243 5 56118 2 6 (1996), all now deleted.
[25] R. Norrington with M. Musgrave, 'Conducting Brahms', in M. Musgrave (ed.), *The Cambridge Companion to Brahms* (Cambridge: Cambridge University Press, 2006), 232.
[26] Preserved in W. Blume (ed.), *Brahms in der Meininger Tradition: Seine Sinfonien und Haydn-Variationen in der Bezeichnung von Fritz Steinbach*, new ed. M. Schwalb (Hildesheim: Olms, 2014), 89. Brahms's approving remarks on Steinbach are quoted in *Kalbeck IV*, 81, 224.

Recordings

its insistence on 'period' instruments was – ironically enough – starting to seem somewhat dated, given that the philosophy underpinning the historical performance movement was now under attack.[27] The 'new' trend in the early twenty-first century was for recordings that married the knowledge and disciplines of 'period performance' with conventional 'modern' ensembles. An example of this was Nikolaus Harnoncourt's 2011 recording of *A German Requiem* Op. 45 with the Vienna Philharmonic Orchestra and Arnold Schoenberg Choir.[28]

By now we seem to have arrived at the end of history in terms of Brahms on record, in the sense that no dominant trend can be identified. Instead we have a peculiar steady state in which reissues of classic recordings, recordings informed (to a greater or lesser extent) by period performance, and a deliberate recreation of the severe, restrained, dark-brown ambience of certain 'classic'-era Brahms recordings from c. 1930 to 1980, all jostle for attention. However, this is not quite the end of the story. One now sees, finally, a stirring of interest in the thing that was so studiously ignored in the LP era, when the image of 'Brahms the classicist' became so firmly entrenched in recording: the small but telling legacy of recordings made by performers who knew and worked with Brahms.

At present this interest is confined to scholarly circles. In June 2013 Clive Brown and Miaoyin Qu recorded Brahms's Violin Sonata Op. 108 in a style which 'draws upon Clive Brown's research into nineteenth-century performing, and also upon Miaoyin Qu's practice-led PhD research into late nineteenth-century piano playing'.[29] For both musicians, it represents a stage in their investigation of the elements of performance that Brahms and his circle would have expected performers to 'read between the lines' (this refers to the injunction in Otto Klauwell's book *On Musical Execution*, which insists on the necessity for performers to do precisely that).[30] Of course, one swallow does not a summer make. It will take more than a few experiments in reviving old performance practices in university departments to effect a real change in approaches to performing and recording Brahms.

The mindset of critics needs to shift radically too, and there is little sign of that. The 'classical restraint' of Brahms is still regularly invoked.

---

[27] Notably in R. Taruskin, *Text and Act* (Oxford: Oxford University Press, 1995), and C. Rosen, 'The Shock of the Old', *New York Review of Books* 37/12 (19 July 1990), 46–52.

[28] RCA 72066.

[29] University of Leeds of Collection of Historical Annotated String Editions http://chase.leeds.ac.uk/.

[30] http://chase.leeds.ac.uk/article/8-brahms-violin-sonata-op-108-an-experimental-response-to-historical-evidence/.

366   IVAN HEWETT

Murray Perahia's 2010 recording of the Handel Variations on Philips was praised on one reviewing website for displaying 'an appropriate classical restraint that throws a clear light on all of the works.'[31] The *Guardian* reviewer of Lars Vogt's recording of Brahms's piano works Opp. 117, 118 and 119, released in 2004 on EMI, declared that 'there is no hectoring or lecturing, no celebration of virtuosity for its own sake. Lars Vogt is the perfect kind of thoughtful, unflashy pianist for an emotionally contained world; his playing never attempts to impose his own interpretative ideas on music that has its own organic coherence.'[32]

These reviews could have been written seventy years ago, and they show that the apparent revolution wrought by the advent of period performance practice was really only skin-deep. They suggest that in the wider world the old image of Brahms, which the recording industry and its associated critical discourse helped to fix so firmly in the public mind, will be around for some time yet.

Further Reading

K. Bazzana, *Glenn Gould: The Performer in the Work* (Oxford: Oxford University Press, 1997)

M. Chanan, *Repeated Takes: A Short History of Recording and Its Effects on Music* (London: Verso, 1995)

D. Kraus, 'De Mortuis Nihil Nisi Bene: Anmerkungen zu Glenn Goulds Einspielungen der Klaviermusik von Johannes Brahms', *Brahms-Studien* 9 (1992), 23–8

R. Philip, 'Brahms's musical world: Balancing the evidence', in M. Musgrave and B. Sherman (eds.), *Performing Brahms: Early Evidence of Performing Style* (Cambridge: Cambridge University Press, 2003), 349–72

C. Symes, *Setting the Record Straight: A Material History of Classical Recording* (Middletown CT: Wesleyan University Press, 2004)

---

[31] K. Moore, *Classical Music Buzz*, http://cnycafemomus.com/kevin_moore.html, accessed 29 June 2017.

[32] A. Clements, 'Brahms: Intermezzi Op 117; Piano Pieces Op 118 and 119: Lars Vogt', *The Guardian* (March 5, 2004), www.theguardian.com/music/2004/mar/05/classicalmusicandopera.shopping1.

CHAPTER 37

Historical Performance

Michael Musgrave

Brahms holds a special place among the major instrumental composers in that not only does his life straddle major changes in instrumental design and performance practices, but that recollections and sound recordings exist by younger contemporaries to illustrate these. Indeed, there is sufficient evidence to encourage many different perspectives, and the field has become one of lively debate. In this, there are two extremes of interpretation: first the historically driven view that stresses fundamental differences of instruments and performing styles; second, a traditional view of continuity from the past that accepts modern adaptation and expression of these factors. Although the latter is not essentially concerned with historical issues, it cannot be ignored because it represents a permanent counterweight to the historical approach, which remains problematic for many in its implications for modern performance style and social function [see Ch. 23 'Instruments'].

Two drivers lie behind the historical movement in relation to Brahms: firstly, the development of the modern critical edition of Brahms's texts, which places focus on accurate and thorough reproduction of details of articulation and expression affecting performance;[1] and second, the extension of historical performance practice from the Baroque and Classical eras which were more radically concerned with differences in instruments and performance. The demonstration of historically informed performances in Brahms has been through two channels: documentary records and recordings. This outline of the subject summarises recent pro and contra views of the issues through representative commentators and performers in the most prominent spheres of innovation.

---

[1] *Johannes Brahms Gesamtausgabe (JBG)*, Munich, Henle, 1996–; this succeeds the *Johannes Brahms Sämtliche Werke*, ed. E. Mandyczewski and H. Gál (Leipzig: Breitkopf und Härtel, 1926–8), which had minimal source information.

368 MICHAEL MUSGRAVE

Large-Scale Works

The pioneering figure in the application of historical scholarship to the performance of Brahms's large-scale orchestral and choral music has been Roger Norrington (b. 1934) in his recordings of the four symphonies and *A German Requiem* Op. 45 from 1991 to 1996.[2]

Three broad topics are drawn from the records as focus, and guide his approach: tempo issues, the nature of instruments and performance style. Though Norrington notes that Brahms disliked providing metronome marks (only seven works were published with them), his previous devotion to source indications (his notes to all his recordings of Beethoven, Mendelssohn and Schumann symphonies and other early Romantic works all cite the first published marks) leads him to seek other documentary evidence, finding it, for example, in the timings recorded by Hans von Bülow. Bülow gives thirty-seven minutes for the First Symphony Op. 68, thus indicating brisk tempos that relate closely to the Classical era. And even in a case where the published tempo is completely unclear, as in the 'un poco sostenuto' at the beginning of the First Symphony, he inclines to this tradition.[3]

Of instruments, as well as using those of the period (with strings of gut or wound gut tuned to a lower pitch around A = 435), his focus is especially on the 'pure sound' of non-vibrato and use of portato bowing for the strings, for which his source is the treatise of Joseph Joachim, who reserved vibrato for moments of special expression only, and sparingly. But, although he accepts that Brahms preferred and wrote for the natural horn, Norrington also admits that Brahms never expected to hear it; thus he concludes that 'the sound of early valve horns using the whole, rather lighter, instrument, is considerably different from today's heavier compartmentalized version'.

With regards to orchestral size, he emphasises that most German orchestras in the 1870s still used the smaller ensembles of the time of Mendelssohn

---

[2] R. Norrington, Recordings (1985–96): Symphony No.1 and *St. Anthony Variations* (*Variations on a Theme of Haydn* Op. 56a): EMI CD 754286 2; Symphony No.2 and Tragic Overture: EMI CD 077 7 5487 2; Symphony Nos. 3 and 4: EMI CD 7243 5 56118 2; *Ein deutsches Requiem* and *Begräbnisgesang*: EMI CD 0777 7 54658. Norrington's recording career illustrates the transition from Baroque choral music through the Classical era (with the period orchestra The London Classical Players), into the early Romantics, then Brahms (and later Bruckner and Mahler).

[3] Bülow is quoted in Roger Norrington's notes to his recording of the First Symphony Op. 68 and *St. Anthony Variations* (*Variations on a Theme of Haydn* Op. 56a), as above, 7. Numerous issues in relation to Norrington's performance decisions are covered by Robert Pascall, who advised on the performance issues: see R. Pascall, *Playing Brahms. A Study in 19th-Century Performing Practice* (Nottingham: University of Nottingham, 1991).

Historical Performance

at the Leipzig Gewandhaus (eight or ten violins, though bigger orchestras were used for the festivals), stressing that they make an entirely different balance with the winds and brass. For disposition, he particularly follows the pattern illustrated by Henschel to Brahms during Henschel's early Boston experiments, with first and seconds on opposite sides of the stage and 'in our case horns and trumpets too, with double basses divided either side of the woodwind in the manner described by Henschel'.[4]

Recent recordings of the symphonies (2008–10) and the *Requiem* (1991) by John Eliot Gardiner (b.1943, who also began his career in early choral music), follow these principles, though with individuality as regards choice of instruments, less strict use of vibrato and differences of nuance in interpretation. A more general historical influence is discernible in the recent tendency to play the orchestral music with smaller orchestras, as by Neville Marriner and the Orchestra of St Martin the Fields, and Charles Mackerras with the Scottish Chamber Orchestra.[5]

Norrington and Gardiner's performances of the *Requiem* also extend these issues into choral music. But here, as well as incorporating their approach to the orchestra and its performance, they confront the issue of choir size. Although they both cite the size of choirs in Brahms's time (the first performance in Bremen was of 250 singers) and Pascall quotes other performances under Brahms with larger choirs (e.g. at the 1884 Lower Rhine Festival with 704 choir members and an orchestra of 123), both Norrington and Eliot Gardiner use small, specialist professional choirs rather than larger choral societies.

Solo and Chamber Music

The issues of technical performance become much more precise in relation to solo instruments, especially the issues of string technique like tone

---

[4] J. Joachim and A. Moser, *Violinschule*, 3 vols. (Berlin: Simrock, 1905), vol. 2, 96–96a; Norrington, *Symphony No.1 and St. Anthony Variations* (*Variations on a Theme of Haydn* Op. 56a), 5. Henschel's seating is illustrated in Pascall, *Playing Brahms*, 13.

[5] In addition to his input to the notes to the Norrington recording, Pascall also provides the notes for the Mackerras recordings. He and Philip Weller provide a study of nuance which points out how few modifying markings exist in Brahms's marked scores with reference to the Concerto Op. 83. They are largely concerned with the big sectional aspects of the music. See their 'Flexible tempo and nuancing in orchestral music; understanding Brahms's view of interpretation in his Second Piano Concerto and Fourth Symphony' in M. Musgrave and B. Sherman (eds.), *Performing Brahms: Early Evidence of Performance Style* (Cambridge: Cambridge University Press, 2003), 220–43; Symphonies Nos. 1 and 2: Neville Marriner/Academy of St Martin's in the Fields (1999), Hänssler DDD 98. 186/044; Symphonies Nos. 1–4: Charles Mackerras/Scottish Chamber Orchestra (1997) Telarc CD 80643, 80644; 80645.

370 MICHAEL MUSGRAVE

production and fingering. Vibrato and bowing have particularly become matters of dispute. Joachim's point about the use of vibrato is obviously easier to realise in the greater intimacy as well as frequency of solo performance. Bernard Sherman notes that the violinist Joseph Szigeti, whose teachers had trained him in the older style, wrote in 1964 of 'the liberation which modern chromatic fingering has brought to us', mentioning passages that had been 'practically impossible to negotiate neatly in the requisite tempo'. Sherman comments that it seems an obvious advance. But, as Sherman notes from personal communication, 'Clive Brown asserts that something is lost with newer fingerings. He says that by adopting nineteenth-century methods of fingering that often involve moving from one position to another with the same finger, and by using the same finger for consecutive chromatic notes "one can achieve a seamless legato, combined with a range of portamento effects ... one cannot get a real feeling for the sound and feeling [of Brahms's contemporaries] without abandoning modern styles of fingering".'

But as Sherman further observes, the change in bowing habits has musical implications. Nikolaus Harnoncourt was trained in the older approach to bowing in mid-twentieth-century Vienna. He writes of this 'spinning out of notes, with the bow barely moving at all, and the rich tone that was inevitably produced when the same bow stroke was used for a whole minute at a time ... With the old bowing technique you can produce great melodic paragraphs that sound fantastic but that are also comparatively quiet.'[6]

Of earlier playing methods in brass and wind instruments attention has naturally been drawn to Brahms's archaic scoring for natural horns. Though Norrington chooses early valve horns rather than hand horns for practical reasons, there is no controversy about Brahms's scoring of his Horn Trio Op. 40 for 'Waldhorn', with its intended tonal contrast between stopped and open notes, and this is how it is often played today, with a piano and violin of commensurate tonal character.

In solo piano performance, however – given the centrality of the instrument in Brahms's output – the issue of his attitude to the pianos he knew, and the question of what influence this should have on modern performance, has become controversial. Camilla Cai observes that the study of contemporary pianos 'can reveal a different expectation of

[6] B. Sherman, 'How Different Was Brahms's Playing Style from Our Own?', in M. Musgrave and B. Sherman (eds.), *Performing Brahms: Early Evidence of Performing Style* (Cambridge: Cambridge University Press, 2003), 5–6

Historical Performance

sound and way of understanding his music than what we have become accustomed to', observing Brahms's earlier devotion to the Viennese Streicher, a tradition later extended by Bösendorfer. Most emphatic in asserting this historical influence is Robert Winter, who comments as follows:

> Though his career extended to the end of the nineteenth century, Brahms wrote consistently to the characteristics of the Viennese pianos. The Paganini Variations of 1866 are a showcase for instruments by Streicher and Bösendorfer, whether their registral variety and clarity, or the sweetness and expressiveness of the extreme treble. The clarity of the octave doubling [in variations 7 and 11] is a welcome byproduct of the registral variety. Convincing performances of many of the late character pieces face serious obstacles on our modern instrument, for example the opening of . . . Brahms's Intermezzo in E minor Op. 118 no. 6. No modern pianist can hope to replicate Brahms's disembodied (but clear!) bass response to the plaintive solo opening, not to mention the *una corda* at measure 5ff.

He draws a similar point with regard to the bass octave at the opening of the ninth Paganini Variation: 'the execution of a *fpp* and sustained tremolo in this register is inconceivable on a modern instrument'.[7] In opposition to this, Styra Avins stresses that Brahms welcomed the latest developments, as in the pianos of the Steinway company (founded in Germany in 1853):

> The idea that Brahms wrote his piano music 'consistently to the characteristics of the Viennese pianos' seems logical enough in theory, but it is not supported by the evidence of Brahms's letters. They show that he would not have agreed that his late piano pieces faced serious obstacles on our modern pianos. On the contrary they prove that he went out of his way to make sure that he performed, at least, on just those instruments.[8]

Recordings

Performance from an accurate text with instruments of their time or reproductions (and with their playing methods, forces and disposition)

---

[7] See C. Cai, 'Brahms's Pianos and the Performance of His Late Works', *Performance Practice Review* 2/1 (Spring 1989), 58–72; R. Winter, 'Orthodoxies, Paradoxes, and Contradictions; Performance Practices in Nineteenth-Century Piano Music', in R. L. Todd (ed.), *Nineteenth-Century Piano Music*, 2nd edn (New York: Routledge, 2004), 33, 38.

[8] S. Avins, 'Performing Brahms's Music: clues from his letters', in *Performing Brahms*, 14; see also the extensive discussion of Brahms's pianos by Stephen Brady and George S. Bozarth: 'Brahms's Pianos', *The American Brahms Society Newsletter* 6/2 (Fall 1988), 1–7, who also stress his 'progressive' interest in newer instruments.

372   MICHAEL MUSGRAVE

still leaves great room for interpretation of every parameter [see Ch. 36 'Recordings' and Ch. 20 'Conductors']. Rather than as imagined reconstructions, early recordings bring all the elements alive as real music, even if with profound limitations of reproduction in most cases. Most recent scholarly efforts have been directed towards interpreting such evidence through the conductors Brahms knew and admired. Although recordings of this kind are rare (only recordings by Felix Weingartner survive), extremely detailed verbal descriptions survive of Fritz Steinbach, the conductor he admired most and who is regarded by many contemporaries as conveying the Brahms tradition at the Meiningen Court Orchestra most clearly. These were made by his pupil Walter Blume and published in typescript with numerous music examples.

Recent writings by Walter Frisch have explored this material. Of the two extremes of approach noted of Brahms's contemporaries apparently disliked by Brahms – metronomic rigidity (Richter) and over-controlled nuance (Bülow), Frisch places Weingartner and Steinbach as follows:

> Weingartner is the more moderate and restrained, but far from rigid; Steinbach, who was Bülow's successor at Meiningen and was understood as carrying forward the best of Bülow's style, is more given to individual nuances and momentary adjustments of tempo. Weingartner's performance of the Second Symphony with the Berlin Philharmonic was deemed 'truly wonderful'. The composer described Weingartner has having a 'healthy, fresh personality' that was 'uncommonly sympathetic', as revealed in his book on conducting of the following year. Weingartner saw his own style in opposition to – or at least, as a corrective to – what he called the 'tempo rubato' conductors of recent years. He does not name many names, but suggests that these conductors modelled themselves after Bülow, who he described as 'truly great', but whose gestures and nuances were exaggerated by poor imitators.
>
> Steinbach was also held in high esteem by Brahms; in turn, according to Kalbeck, Steinbach took Brahms's conducting as a *Vorbild* for his own. Bülow was also enthusiastic about Steinbach. In a letter to Brahms of October 1884, Bülow said to Brahms that Steinbach and Mottl were his favourite younger conductors. For the Meiningen tour to London of 1902, the *Musical Times* critic wrote that the 'four Brahms symphonies were rendered with such life and impulse, with such a spirit of romance, that one felt their power in quite unaccustomed degree; the conductor seemed to be recreating rather than giving a rendering of the music'.[9]

[9] Weingartner's recordings were made between 1838 and 1940. See, for example, the issue of the entire set with the LSO and LPO on EMI References CHS 7 64256 2; W. Frisch, 'In Search of Brahms's First Symphony. Steinbach, The Meiningen Tradition and the Recordings of Fritz Steinbach', in *Performing Brahms*, 281. See also W. Blume (ed.), *Brahms in der Meininger Tradition: Seine Sinfonien*

Historical Performance 373

In the absence of Steinbach recordings as possible models for the continuation of a Brahmsian tradition, Frisch proposes the recordings of Steinbach's successor Hermann Abendroth, which he compares in detail.[10]

However, we can never know exactly how close Abendroth came to how Steinbach actually performed by seeking to match live recordings to verbal descriptions. The ultimate stage in reproducing how things really were can only be to copy an actual recorded performance of Brahms's time in a genre that permits very detailed expressive imitation; or on the basis of very detailed description of exact points in performance editions by those who knew Brahms's performances or those of his contemporaries. This territory has recently been explored in Neal Peres da Costa's book on piano performance *Off the Record* and by Clive Brown, Peres da Costa and Kate Wadsworth in Bärenreiter editions of the solo sonatas and the book that accompanies them, *Performance Practices in Johannes Brahms' Chamber Music.*

The necessary observation and imitation is only barely possible in Brahms's own case, however. His one recording – including the first *Hungarian Dance* WoO 1, made in 1889 – is only just about aurally decipherable. So it can only relate in a limited way to points drawn from a much wider range of early performances and editions by contemporaries. Brown, Peres da Costa and Wadsworth provide copious references to a wide range of performance tutors and reminiscences as well as examples from early recordings by younger contemporaries who lived into the recording era, especially illuminating piano performances that significantly complement Blume's comments on Steinbach's orchestral performances.

Peres da Costa's book has summarised the technical features of piano performance in categories. As well as the ever-present characteristic of tempo modification, he identifies what he describes as 'dislocation', 'unnotated arpeggiation' and 'metrical rubato and other forms of rhythmic alteration'. Dislocation is defined as:

> a momentary separation between the left and right [hands]; this expressive technique is not exclusive to, but is particularly noticeable on, early recordings of solo pianists. The usual method is to delay a melody note in the right hand, placing it directly against the corresponding accompaniment note in the left hand. In fewer cases the right hand precedes the left.

As regards 'unnotated arpeggiation',

---

und Haydn-Variationen in der Bezeichnung von Fritz Steinbach, new ed. M. Schwalb (Hildesheim: Olms, 2013).

[10] Frisch, 'In Search of Brahms's First Symphony', *Performing Brahms*, 286–301.

374 MICHAEL MUSGRAVE

early recordings show that many pianists frequently made unnotated arpeggiations, playing the notes of chords separately where not indicated in the
musical text. These arpeggiations caused the separation of vertically aligned
material comprising two or more notes, variously described as double notes,
octaves and chords. The speed of these arpeggiations varies according to
function, mood and context, creating different effects. Early recordings also
show that certain pianists made unnotated arpeggiations far less frequently,
or not at all. This more synchronised style of playing, however, did not
become the rule until the second half of the century.

In terms of 'metrical rubato' and other forms of rhythmic alteration, 'early
recordings reveal that many pianists ... displace single melody notes or
multiple adjacent notes within a bar by lengthening or shortening them'.[11]
As applied to chamber music, Brahms's expression markings are seen as
offering many opportunities for the deployment of these features. As well as
the varied alternatives for bowings and positions, Da Costa and his fellow
editors especially seek the expressive implications of Brahms's crescendo/
diminuendo wedge hairpins and use of portato dots in either the solo or
piano parts, notably suggesting dislocation and arpeggiation in various
degrees and citing nineteenth-century performance sources in support.[12]

Conclusions

The striking differences between the freer features identified by Brown,
Peres da Costa and Wadsworth and the precise values espoused by earlier
proponents of historical performance illustrate not only the present scope
of the subject but its significant faultlines too. Central to these is the very
relationship between notation and performance. Thus, the rebuke to piano
performers exhibiting too much freedom from the score – for example
from Brahms himself or Clara Schumann: that 'it is all there' – merely
refers to their own assumptions framed by their own traditions of what the
notation encompassed in performance terms. But performance in the past
was clearly very different. In string technique, the most striking technical
illustration is the use of portamento, studiously avoided in all the orchestral
performances noted because its current effect is more reflective of convivial
music – but clearly stylistic in many early recordings.

[11] N. Peres da Costa, *Off the Record* (Oxford: Oxford University Press, 2012), 45, 101, 189; see also
C. Brown, *Classical and Romantic Performing Practice 1750–1900* (Oxford: Oxford University Press,
1999), 45–50 and 83.
[12] C. Brown, N. Peres da Costa, K. Wadsworth, *Performance Practices in Johannes Brahms' Chamber
Music* (Kassel: Bärenreiter, 2015).

Historical Performance

Thus, great room opens up for discrepancy between notation and performance. But just how far different features can be integrated by a modern performer is unlikely ever to be resolved easily, if at all. On the one hand, even if it is assumed that the few surviving useful early recordings are representative, the reproduction of such effects and the social setting in which they were produced are so alien to modern conditions that they cannot escape a profound self-consciousness which makes widespread acceptance difficult. On the other, historical practices adapted to modern sensibilities are not necessarily historical, however 'clean' and 'vibrant' they may appear by comparison with the approaches they seek to supplant.

The only rational demand that must be made of performance is that it be true to what the performer regards as the essence of the music itself, as captured in older performances. Robert Pascall's expression cannot be bettered: 'Today's historically informed performances only work because we as musicians feed this historical data into our own musicianship; formulaic performances could not possibly be authentic in any case! Interpretation remains of the essence: Brahms's way was expressive, and ours should be too.'[13]

Further Reading

C. Brown, *Classical and Romanic Performing Practice 1750–1900* (Oxford: Oxford University Press, 1999)

C. Brown, N. Peres da Costa, K. Wadsworth, *Performance Practices in Johannes Brahms' Chamber Music* (Kassel: Bärenreiter, 2015)

C. Cai, 'Brahms's Pianos and the Performance of His Late Works', *Performance Practice Review* 2/1 (Spring 1989), 58–72

M. Musgrave and B. Sherman (eds.), *Performing Brahms: Early Evidence of Performing Style* (Cambridge: Cambridge University Press, 2003)

R. Pascall, *Playing Brahms. A Study in 19th-Century Performing Practice* (Nottingham: University of Nottingham, 1991)

N. Peres da Costa, *Off the Record* (Oxford: Oxford University Press, 2012)

R. Winter, 'Orthodoxies, Paradoxes, and Contradictions; Performance Practices in Nineteenth-Century Piano Music', in R. L. Todd (ed.), *Nineteenth-Century Piano Music*, 2nd edn (New York: Routledge, 2004), 16–54

[13] R. Pascall, notes to the Mackerras recording of Symphonies 3 and 4: CD 80465 (1997), 7.

CHAPTER 38

Inspiration

Markus Böggemann

Brahms as a point of reference for contemporary music is somewhat over-shadowed by other composers. While, for example, Johann Sebastian Bach's music is a constant subject of adaptation as well as an inspiration on different compositional levels, contemporary composers seem to be less inclined to approach Brahms's music in this way.[1] Whereas a composer like Helmut Lachenmann published a third voice to one of Bach's two-part inventions and grappled with Mozart's Clarinet Concerto K622 in his own *Accanto* (1975–6), he left Brahms's music almost untouched. Even where the instrumentation suggests Brahmsian models, as in his *Allegro sostenuto* for clarinet, cello and piano (1986–8), a specific relationship cannot be identified. And while Brian Ferneyhough refers to Elizabethan consort music in some of his string quartets, he apparently does not consider Brahms's contributions to this genre, such as his String Quartets Op. 51 and Op. 67. Thus, Wolfgang Sandberger's observation that 'contrary to Schoenberg and his circle, many contemporary composers today seem to have a more distanced relationship with Brahms and his music' is hardly surprising.[2] Schoenberg and his contemporaries had to position themselves as composers within – or against – a still vital tradition of which Brahms was an important part, while today's composers are free to choose their affiliation to, or their reexamination of, any precursor's musical language. Brahms ranges less prominently among these, but he is still considered.

As Sandberger also points out, there are numerous works written in the last five decades in which Brahms's music is explicitly present in a number of ways. And there are also avowed avant-garde composers for whom Brahms is of great musical significance. Mauricio Kagel's 1972

---

[1] A. Krause, 'Eine Bach-Umfrage 1905/2005 – und dazwischen: Komponisten über Bach (1950/1985)', in M. Heinemann and H.-J. Hinrichsen (eds.), *Johann Sebastian Bach und die Gegenwart. Beiträge zur Bach-Rezeption 1945–2005* (Cologne: Dohr 2007), 405–75.

[2] W. Sandberger, 'Bilder, Denkmäler, Konstruktionen – Johannes Brahms als Figur des kollektiven Gedächtnisses', in *Brahms Handbuch*, 18.

Inspiration

Variationen ohne Fuge for large orchestra based on Brahms's *Variations and Fugue on a Theme of Handel* Op. 24 for piano can serve as an example: Brahms's work supplies both the musical material and the framework for the piece. Kagel alters the music substantially by applying a set of strict transformational techniques to it but remains largely within the formal boundaries of the older work. Indeed, his handling of Brahms's work is comparable to how Brahms himself dealt with Handel: he brings him up to date, that is, confronts him with the compositional possibilities of post-war avant-gardism, while also constantly highlighting the historical distance.[3] Kagel's approach to Brahms is a composed-out reflection on historicity in music and thus a 'trans-historic dialogue' on historical consciousness – and surely no better partner in this dialogue than Brahms could be imagined.[4]

While interacting with Brahms's music is therefore not restricted to composers who still adhere to models of nineteenth-century symphonism or who refuse to take into account the changes of musical language during the twentieth century, it is most often related to a critical revision of the avant-garde with its emphasis on unilinear progress, and its preoccupation with structure and technology. This is true for György Ligeti's *Horn Trio* (1982) which is explicitly called a 'Hommage à Brahms' and has been described as following a 'third way' beyond avant-garde and (neo-)tonality.[5] Although the homage to Brahms lies mostly in the instrumentation, it seems no coincidence that Ligeti explores a more traditionally oriented musical language, particularly in this piece. This is equally true for the music of Detlev Glanert, who, as a prolific opera composer and former student of Hans Werner Henze, seeks in his work a balance between artistic sophistication and popular appeal. For him, these qualities are combined in an exemplary way in Brahms's music, and so it is no surprise that Brahms figures prominently as a reference for several of Glanert's compositions.[6] Besides the orchestral arrangements of the *Four Serious Songs* Op. 121 and of four of the *Chorale Preludes* Op. 122, there is also Glanert's *Brahms-Phantasie. Heliogravure for Orchestra* (2011–12), a work based on the introduction to the first movement of Brahms's First Symphony Op. 68. The tense atmosphere and the tightly woven counterpoint of this opening have attracted other composers too: Krzysztof

---

[3] See B. Heile, *The Music of Mauricio Kagel* (Aldershot: Ashgate, 2006), 114–17. [4] *Ibid.*, 117.

[5] See M. Searby, 'Ligeti's "Third Way": 'Non-Atonal' Elements in the Horn Trio', *Tempo*, New Series, 216 (April 2001), 17–22.

[6] See D. Glanert, 'Zum 175. Geburtstag von Johannes Brahms', in S. Drees (ed.), *Neugier ist alles. Der Komponist Detlev Glanert* (Hofheim: Wolke, 2012), 241–2.

378 MARKUS BÖGGEMANN

Meyer, for example, includes strong motivic, rhythmic and timbral allusions to it in his *Hommage à Johannes Brahms* Op. 59 (1982), and Hans Werner Henze quotes it, along with Wagner, in his monumental piano concert piece *Tristan* (1973). Above all, this introduction, together with its counterpart in the finale, figures as the *locus classicus* of Brahms's struggle with a dominating tradition. The labour and the outcome of his thorough historical awareness are directly palpable here, and even though composers today might not face the problem of directly confronting Beethoven's symphonic legacy, they still cannot ignore the vast musical accumulation of previous generations. Since one no longer automatically inherits a shared musical language and compositional technique, the problem of relating oneself critically to the past is of crucial importance for any composer today. That Brahms faced this problem so directly has also informed the way his music is present in contemporary compositions.

For the same reasons, the majority of composers choose his late works when referring to Brahms. Glanert's arrangement of the *Chorale Preludes* and the *Four Serious Songs* Op. 121 has already been mentioned; another case is Avner Dorman's *After Brahms* (2015), a reminiscence of the Intermezzo Op. 119 no. 1, and Jörg Widmann's *Intermezzi* (2010), a set of four pieces ranging from eight to 250 bars in length, of which the last, 'Wiegenlied', comes across as a faint, distorted version of Brahms's Intermezzo Op. 117 no. 1. The motives of memory, retrospect and, linked to it, melancholy and loss displayed here are topical figures central to the image of (not only) the late Brahms. Indeed, this image is pervasive, as a glimpse at some other works makes clear: Manfred Trojahn's . . . *mit durchscheinender Melancholie. Ein Brahms-Portrait* for orchestra (1995) with its emphasis on fragmentation (already present through the ellipsis in the title), melancholy and loss obviously evokes some typical motives of the 1990s intellectual discourse around Romanticism. The piece uses a quotation from Brahms's song 'Ich sah als Knabe Blumen blühn' Op. 63 no. 9. Brett Dean's *Etude: Hommage à Brahms* for piano (2013) is a set of three interludes to be interleaved between the piano pieces of Brahms's Op. 119. Inspired partially by Brahms's relationship with Clara Schumann, melancholy here, too is a prevailing motive. Dean explains that 'these homage-pieces emerge out of the idea of a line or part that's absent, the person *not* by his side. It is music that grows out of accompanying figurations yet takes on a life of its own, shining a light on Brahms' poignantly melancholic Op. 119 pieces.'[7]

---

[7] www.boosey.com/pages/cr/catalogue/cat_detail?=&musicid=100415&langid=1.

Inspiration 379

Indeed, a jolly, light-hearted Brahms seems hard to imagine, even where the music would allow for it: Wolfgang Rihm's *Brahmsliebewalzer* (1985–8) and, in particular, his *Mehrere kurze Walzer* for four-hand piano (1979–88) only half-heartedly hint at this side of Brahms's character, before rapidly returning to a more sombre tone [see Ch. 39 'Mythmaking'].[8] The topoi of melancholy and self-inhibiting historical consciousness are so well-established that a radically decontextualised Brahms reception, making an ahistorical or meta-historical figure like Bach out of him which focuses on his music exclusively in terms of structure, seems inconceivable. At least, there seem to be no such endeavours from today's composers. Quite the contrary, there is a tendency to portray Brahms, to rely on metaphors of his visual representation. 'Heliogravure' from the subtitle of Glanert's *Brahms-Fantasie* hints at the idea of an old photograph, as do Trojahn's *Brahms-Portrait* and also Wilhelm Killmayer's *Brahms-Bildnis* for piano trio (1976). Even the outright comedic instruction in Kagel's *Variationen ohne Fuge* should be mentioned: an actor, dressed as Brahms, can (*ad libitum*) appear on stage near the end of the piece and speak to the audience, followed by another actor representing Handel. However, it was Thomas Adès who pushed this idea still further: his *Brahms* for baritone and orchestra (2001), on a text by Alfred Brendel, summons the composer by endlessly falling thirds in the orchestra and portrays him as a sad, smelly spectre, who cannot let go of his music and piano playing.

These references to a visual representation of Brahms without doubt depend on the fact that we have numerous photographs which show his characteristic appearance. They act as traces connecting our present with the bygone present of the picture, and invite us to perceive it in a genuinely aesthetic way as a representation, that is, as the absent made present again. The same form of aesthetic representation takes place with music, which through performance always creates a compelling, unmediated presence, regardless of the time gone by since it was composed. Reflection on this fundamental condition of musical experience may have helped to shape concert programmes in which classical works are brought together with contemporary compositions written explicitly for the programme as a companion piece or as interpolations. Aside from Dean's aforementioned *Etude: Hommage à Brahms*, a similar work of greater dimensions is Wolfgang Rihm's *Das Lesen der Schrift. Four pieces for orchestra* (2001–2), which were originally commissioned as interpolations for Brahms's

---

[8] But a light-hearted Brahms certainly exists; see K. Hamilton and N. Loges (eds.), *Brahms in the Home and the Concert Hall* (Cambridge: Cambridge University Press, 2014).

380 MARKUS BÖGGEMANN

A German Requiem Op. 45. And Stuart McRae's *Gravity* for orchestra
(2009), conceived as a companion piece to Brahms's Second Symphony
Op. 73, is also not a mere filler but a reflection on some features of the
larger work. Even if there are no direct allusions, quotations or overt
references, a distinct sort of relationship is implied here simply by the
occasion and by the similar instrumentation. Another case of such
intertextual relationships worth mentioning are the *Other Love Songs*
(2010) by pianist-composer Stephen Hough. These were written to supplement Brahms's two sets of *Liebeslieder* Opp. 52 and 65, and do so by
confronting the Brahmsian works with contrasting conceptions both tex-
tually and musically. As Stephen Hough explains, he chose 'to avoid
waltzes, and to avoid setting poems about romantic love between a man
and a woman. *Other Love Songs* explore other kinds of love; and, as
a symbol of this, the accompaniment is for three rather than four hands
at one piano.'[9]

In all these cases, the intended effect is one of cracking the surface
of canonical works by listening to them from another angle and within
a new context. From a theoretical point of view, Schoenberg tried just
this when he was among the first to challenge the view of Brahms as
a late-born conservative of consummate craftmanship without a future.
His plea for 'Brahms the Progressive' has been of considerable influence, even though it turned out to be much more about his own
compositional preoccupations than about Brahms's [see Ch. 33
'Analysis'].[10]

Nevertheless, in the long run, his highlighting of the progressive aspects
of Brahms's music did not overcome the well-known notions of belated-
ness, melancholy, loss and of summing up the musical tradition. These
topoi are still at work when contemporary composers refer to Brahms's
music. And as the examples presented here suggest, they are actually
productive: the composers' appropriation of Brahms adopts the notions
of historical reflection, melancholy and representation in various ways.
Persistent as they are, they seem to be more than just some well-known
motives of the customary reception of Brahms. They leave their imprint on
the music itself: both that of Brahms and that of his contemporary
recipients.

---

[9] S. Hough, liner notes to The Prince Consort, *Other Love Songs. Songs by Brahms and Steven Hough*,
CD Linn Records, CKD 382 (2010), 21.

[10] See R. Brinkmann, 'A "Last Giant in Music": Thoughts on Max Reger in the Twentieth Century',
The Musical Quarterly 87/4 (Winter 2004), 631–59, especially 641f.

Inspiration 381

Works by Contemporary Composers Based upon or Referring to Brahms's Music

Compiled by Thomas Hofmann and Markus Böggemann

This – by no means exhaustive – list focusses mainly on works which refer to Brahms's music on a compositional level. Some transcriptions with special significance for the reception of Brahms by contemporary composers are included, but transcriptions for purely practical purposes (like the innumerable versions of the *Hungarian Dances* WoO 1) are left aside.

Thomas Adès (b.1971), *Brahms* for Baritone and orchestra (2001)

Samuel Adler (b.1928), *Brahmsiana for 8 Horns* (1997)

Samuel Adler, *Concerto for Viola or Clarinet and Orchestra* based upon the Sonata in F minor, Op. 120 no. 1 by Johannes Brahms (2003)

Luciano Berio (1925–2003), *Johannes Brahms: Opus 120 No. 1*. Sonata for clarinet (or viola) and piano (1894), transcribed for clarinet (or viola) and orchestra (1986)

Brett Dean (b.1961), *Etude: Hommage à Brahms* for piano (2013)

Jean-Michael Defaye (b.1932), *À la manière de Brahms* for trombone and piano (2011)

Avner Dorman (b.1975), *After Brahms* for piano (2015)

Eric Ewazen (b.1954), *Variations and Fugue on a Theme by Brahms* for trumpet (or flugelhorn) and piano (2012)

Sebastian Fagerlund (b.1972), *Licht im Licht, fantasia for piano after Brahms's variations on a theme of Haydn* (2007)

Harald Feller (b.1951), *Fantasie über ein Thema von Brahms* for trumpet (or clarinet) and organ (2015)

Michael Finnissy (b.1946), *Brahms-Lieder* for piano (2015)

Michael Finnissy, *In Stiller Nacht* for piano trio (1990, rev. 1997)

Michael Finnissy, *Sehnsucht* for string quartet (1997)

Detlev Glanert (b.1960), *Brahms-Fantasie*. Heliogravure for orchestra (2011–12)

Detlev Glanert, *Vier Präludien und Ernste Gesänge* for bass baritone and orchestra, based on the *Four Serious Songs* Op. 121 by Johannes Brahms (2004–5)

Detlev Glanert, *Vier Choralvorspiele*, orchestration from Brahms's Op. 122 no. 1 ('Mein Jesu, der du mich'), Op. 122 no. 7 ('O Gott, du frommer Gott'), Op. 122 no. 9 ('Herzlich tut mich verlangen'), Op. 122 no. 3 ('O Welt, ich muss dich lassen') (2016)

Detlev Glanert, *Weites Land (Musik mit Brahms)* for orchestra (2013)

Hans Werner Henze (1926–2012), *Tristan*. Préludes for piano, electronic tape and orchestra (1973)

Stephen Hough (b.1961), *Other Love Songs* (2010) for voices and piano 3 hands

Mauricio Kagel (1931–2008), *Variationen ohne Fuge* for large orchestra (with 2 actors, *ad lib.*) based on the *Variations and Fugue on a Theme by Handel* for piano Op. 24 by Johannes Brahms (1971–2)

Wilhelm Killmayer (1927–2017), *Brahms-Bildnis* for piano trio (1976)

Volker David Kirchner (b.1942), 1. *Sinfonie 'Totentanz'* for large orchestra (1980)

Bernhard Lang (b.1957), *Monadologie XXVII 'Brahms-Variationen'* for clarinet, violoncello and piano (2013)

Lowell Liebermann (b.1961), *Four Etudes on Brahms Songs* Op. 88 for piano (2004)

György Ligeti (1923–2006), *Trio* for violin, horn and piano (1982)

Stuart MacRae (b.1976), *Gravity* for orchestra (2009)

Siegfried Matthus (b.1934), *Piano Concerto* after the piano quartet Op. 25 by Johannes Brahms (1992)

Missy Mazzoli (b.1980), *Bolts of Loving Thunder* for piano (2013)

Krysztof Meyer (b.1943), *Hommage à Johannes Brahms Op. 59* for orchestra (1982)

Alexander Müllenbach (b.1949), *Aimez-vous . . . (Brahms)?* Capriccio for violin solo (2002)

Jan Müller-Wieland (b.1966), *Trio-Ballade* for clarinet, viola and piano (2015)

Andrew Norman (b.1979), *Suspend. A Fantasy for Piano and Orchestra* (2014)

Wolfgang Rihm (b.1952), *Brahmsliebewalzer,* No. 2 from '3 Walzer' for orchestra (1985–8).

Wolfgang Rihm, *Mehrere kurze Walzer* for piano 4 hands (1979–88)

Wolfgang Rihm, *Das Lesen der Schrift*. 4 pieces for orchestra (2001–2)

Poul Ruders (b.1949), *Horn Trio* for violin, horn and piano (1998)

Enjott Schneider (b.1950), *Brahms-Metamorphosen* for violin, viola, violoncello and piano (1994)

Enjott Schneider, *Aimez-vous Brahms?* An almost-Hungarian Dance for orchestra or chamber ensemble with 12 musicians (2008)

Enjott Schneider, *Brahms Occasionally Relooped*. Variations on the finale of the Fourth Symphony Op. 98 (2009)

Wolfgang-Andreas Schultz (b.1948), *Gethsemane (Variations on a Theme by Brahms)*, Motet for mixed choir (2016)

Bright Sheng (b.1955), *Prelude and Black Swan. After Johannes Brahms' Intermezzo Op. 118, No. 1 & 2* for orchestra (2010)

Miroslav Srnka (b.1975), *Kráter Brahms* for solo violoncello and string orchestra (2007)

Manfred Trojahn (b.1949), *... mit durchscheinender Melancholie. Ein Brahms-Portrait* for orchestra (1995)

Wolfram Wagner (b.1952), *Variationen für Orchester* (2001)

John Woolrich (b.1954), *... with Land in Sight ...* for violoncello (1994)

John Woolrich, *My Box of Phantoms* for oboe, violin, viola and violoncello (1995)

Udo Zimmermann (b.1943), *Brahms-Fanfare* for 4 horns, 2 trumpets, 3 trombones, bass tuba and timpani (2010)

Further Reading

J. P. Burkholder, 'Brahms and Twentieth-Century Classical Music', *19th-Century Music* 8/1 (Summer 1984), 75–83

E. Gallon, 'Narrativities in the music of Thomas Adès: The Piano Quintet and Brahms', in M. Klein and N. Reyland (eds.), *Music and Narrative since 1900* (Bloomington: Indiana University Press, 2013), 216–33

M. Kagel, 'Die missbrauchte Empfindsamkeit. Johannes Brahms zum 150. Geburtstag', *Worte über Musik. Gespräche, Aufsätze, Reden, Hörspiele* (Munich: Piper, 1991), 174–83

W. Sandberger, 'Bilder, Denkmäler, Konstruktionen – Johannes Brahms als Figur des kollektiven Gedächtnisses', in *Brahms Handbuch*, 2–22

A. Schoenberg, 'Brahms the Progressive', reprinted in L. Stein (ed.) *Style and Idea: Selected Writings of Arnold Schoenberg*, trans. L. Black, (1975; rpt. Berkeley: University of California Press, 1984), 398–441

CHAPTER 39

Mythmaking

Natasha Loges and Katy Hamilton

During his lifetime, Brahms witnessed a veritable explosion in biographical writing and related publications of letters, memoirs and diaries. The monumental *Allgemeine deutsche Biographie* (1875–1912) was edited by Rochus von Liliencron (1820–1912), a personal acquaintance of his; a comparable project in Great Britain was the *Dictionary of National Biography* (1885–1900). Significant biographies of famous Austro-German composers also appeared in those years, often written by Brahms's friends: Otto Jahn's Mozart (1856–9), Friedrich Chrysander's Handel (1858–67), Philipp Spitta's Bach (1873–80) and Carl Ferdinand Pohl's Haydn (1875–82). But one might also think of the biography of Beethoven (1866–79) by the American Alexander Wheelock Thayer, a project which was taken up in German by Hermann Deiters, Jahn's pupil and Brahms's colleague and contemporary. It was Deiters who in 1880 wrote the first book-length biography of Brahms, when the composer still had seventeen years to live. These writers' social and scholarly identities, which embraced the quick and the dead, are virtually impossible to disentangle. There were also the highly creative writings of Marie Lipsius (La Mara, 1837–1927) which included Haydn, Mozart, Beethoven, Henselt, Mendelssohn, Brahms and others. Furthermore, Brahms witnessed at first hand Clara Schumann's efforts towards – and anxieties about – the documentation of her husband's biographical and musical legacy.

Nevertheless, this era has been identified as a period of decline in biographical writing.[1] The historian Nigel Hamilton argues that the market forces of 'commemoration and human curiosity' have shaped biographical writing from the classical age to this day. (Hamilton has also pointed out that biography was for centuries a particularly Western, Christian phenomenon, with its focus on the individual self, in comparison with

---

[1] For this, and the following discussion, see N. Hamilton, *Biography: A Brief History* (Cambridge MA: Harvard University Press, 2010), 105ff.

384

Mythmaking

Islam, in which the graphic depiction of individuals was forbidden, and Hinduism, in which the individual soul has almost no importance in comparison with the greater whole of which it is part.) In other words, although the second half of the century might be regarded as a golden age of biography in terms of sheer quantity, the quality ranged from anodyne hagiography to sensationalist semi-fiction.

Brahms himself grew increasingly private during his lifetime. He scrupulously destroyed sketches as well as works with which he was dissatisfied, thereby ensuring lasting control of his professional legacy. Despite a vast surviving correspondence, his own letters tend towards the cryptic [see Ch. 6 'Correspondence'], and he generally avoided committing personal reflection to the page. Late in his life, he demanded that the many letters between himself and his lifelong friend Clara Schumann be returned and destroyed. His collection of aphorisms, *Des jungen Kreislers Schatzkästlein*, which might provide a clue to his private views, was largely discontinued past his early twenties, and he kept no diary (in contrast to the Schumanns, whose domestic accounts (*Haushaltsbücher*) provide an extraordinarily intimate view of their daily lives). What written records he maintained were as unrevealing as possible – catalogues of works, notebooks in which he collated poetry for potential setting, account books and address books. Somewhat disingenuously, he told Clara Schumann that he spoke through his music.[2] Such statements (also made by Mahler) suggest a desire to discourage closer probing. Clara Schumann herself told Brahms's friend and biographer Max Kalbeck, 'Would you believe that Johannes, despite our long and intimate friendship, has never spoken of that which moved him? He is still so puzzling to me today, I would almost say, as unknown to me as he was twenty-five years ago.'[3]

A glance at the numerous biographical writings, novels and film treatments of Brahms's life suggest that his caution was justified. Although different elements have bubbled to the surface and subsided as overall preoccupations have shifted, the big myths about Brahms have persisted despite longstanding evidence to challenge them and the efforts of 1990s New Musicology to bring in wider perspectives. Brahms's life is generally recounted according to the dominant nineteenth-century 'great man' narrative. This 'fetishism of greatness' loomed over the century.[4] In this scenario, an inevitably male, often military protagonist overcomes early

---

[2] Brahms to Clara Schumann, September 1868, *Litzmann I*, 270.   [3] *Kalbeck I*, 298.
[4] J. Samson, 'The Great Composer', in J. Samson (ed.), *The Cambridge History of Nineteenth-Century Music* (Cambridge: Cambridge University Press, 2001), 259.

travails through strength of character and fortitude, to tread a path to eventual glory. This trajectory is familiar from countless films and novels. However, there was an overall shift in approach between the nineteenth and early twentieth centuries. Where weakness, failure or moral turpitude tended to be omitted from 'great man' narratives, by the early twentieth century, post-Freud and post-World War I, a reaction had set in. Depicting the complexities and psychological depth of a biographical subject was now seen as more desirable than creating an 'an idealized Victorian examplar'.[5]

In all this, Beethoven was a complicating factor; the notion of Romantic struggle associated with him was projected onto his successors. In the absence of deafness, syphilis, loss of children or other tragedies, financial and social disadvantage have loomed large within Brahms biography, along with a sharp focus on sex. Fuller Maitland's observation that Brahms 'lived a quiet uneventful life unlike that of many of his predecessors' and that, upon reaching maturity the 'history of Brahms's life' becomes 'little but a chronicle of his works', would simply not do.[6] However, such shifts were not tidily linear or consistent. Constantin Floros has noted the enduring misalignment between the nature of biographical scholarship and the ways in which musical works were approached by scholars on non-verbal terms; thus, while Kalbeck was penning his biography, both Hugo Riemann and Guido Adler eschewed biographical writing in favour of the what is called the 'style-critical method'.[7]

Specific to the Brahms-Schumann circle – and especially tantalising to biographers – was the fondness for musical ciphers which cryptically encoded life into works. Michael Musgrave has noted that these are prone to conjecture; he has challenged one of the best-known and widely accepted, namely the reading of the notes F–A–F as a cipher for 'frei aber froh', meaning 'free but happy', as a reference to Brahms's rejoicing in his bachelorhood.[8] (Indeed, Musgrave points out that this interpretation had been challenged as early as 1932 by Henry Drinker.) The cipher stems from Kalbeck's biography, but Musgrave reminds us that he does not provide any direct evidence that Brahms mentioned the motto and that Kalbeck

---

[5] Hamilton, *Biography*, 136.

[6] J. A. Fuller Maitland, 'Brahms', in G. Grove et al. (eds.), *Grove's Dictionary of Music and Musicians*, 5 vols. (London: The Macmillan Company, 1911), vol. 1, 383.

[7] See C. Floros, 'Aspekte der Brahms-Biographie', in F. Krummacher, M. Struck et al (eds.), *Johannes Brahms. Quellen – Text – Rezeption – Interpretation* (Munich: Henle, 1999), 43.

[8] See M. Musgrave, 'Frei aber Froh: A Reconsideration', *19th-Century Music* 3/3 (March 1980), 251–8.

Mythmaking

relied heavily on second-hand accounts for the early period of Brahms's life with which the cipher is associated.[9]

In 1999, Ingrid Fuchs assembled an account of posthumous images and stereotypes of Brahms as a composer.[10] Drawing on approximately 400 sources located in the Archive of the Gesellschaft der Musikfreunde in Vienna, she concludes that although Brahms is reconstructed slightly differently in each account, certain in emerge, including the enduring power of Robert Schumann's article 'New Paths', which thrust Brahms prematurely into the limelight, and the irksome polarisation of musical life into progressive and conservative factions which coloured Brahms (and Wagner) reception until well into the following century. Related to this is the idea of Brahms as Beethoven's inheritor, the last 'classicist', North German, towering, assured, serious, complex, misunderstood, but ultimately epigonal (see Figures 39.1 and 39.2.)

Fuchs has also provided a valuable account of Brahms's image overseas at the time of his death, which gives a more nuanced picture of how different nations viewed him.[11] Based on a survey of press articles from 1897 in England, Scotland, France (also reprinted/circulated in journals in Constantinople and Cairo), Belgium, Italy, the Netherlands, Denmark, Russia and the USA, she reveals that the English press (for example) was evidently uninterested in the progressive/conservative question, although an interest in 'New Paths' is detectable, as well as mention of Brahms's relationship to Bach (above all as the starting point for Hans von Bülow's coining of the 'Three Bs'). The English press suggests overall that there was a real affinity with Brahms [see Ch. 32 'England'], particularly with students of the Royal College of Music.

Needless to say, Brahms does present real challenges to the biographer, which explains the endurance of the beautifully simple hero narrative. He was, first and foremost, contradictory, both sociable and independent, and, in an era which sacralised married love, he was single and childless. He was doubtless sometimes lonely; he was primarily – if incompletely – associated with absolute music and according to his friend Albert Dietrich, rejected programmatic interpretations of his works.[12] Yet his composition, and

---

[9] *Kalbeck I*, 98.

[10] I. Fuchs, 'De mortuis nil nisi bene – oder doch nicht? Das Brahms-Bild in den Nachrufen', in F. Krummacher, M. Struck et al. (eds.), *Johannes Brahms. Quellen – Text – Rezeption – Interpretation* (Munich: Henle, 1999), 495–509.

[11] I. Fuchs, 'Das Brahmsbild des ausgehenden 19. Jahrhunderts im Ausland am Beispiel ausgewählter Nachrufe', in I. Fuchs (ed.), *Internationaler Brahms-Kongress Gmunden 1997* (Tutzing: Hans Schneider, 2001), 161–73.

[12] Dietrich quoted in Floros, 'Aspekte der Brahms-Biographie', 55.

Figure 39.1. Portrait of the youthful Johannes Brahms, a gift to Sir George Grove in the early 1890s.

indeed his very thinking, was suffused with poetry, following the example of Robert Schumann.

Max Kalbeck (1850–1921), translator, poet and author of what remains the largest biography of the composer, met Brahms in 1874. It is not clear how close this friendship was, but their social circles certainly overlapped, and Brahms was characteristically fond of Kalbeck's wife.[13] Kalbeck has been much criticised, but it is worth recalling the extent of his achievement

---

[13] See, for example, M. Musgrave, 'Brahms und Kalbeck. Eine mißverstandene Beziehung?', in S. Antonicek & O. Biba (eds.), *Brahms-Kongress Wien 1983* (Tutzing: Hans Schneider 1988), 397–404.

Figure 39.2. Portrait of the elderly Johannes Brahms.

as well as the challenges he faced. Firstly, the leading Brahms organisations were established with great speed following the composer's death in 1897.[14] The Brahms-Gesellschaft in Vienna was created in 1904, the Deutsche Brahms-Gesellschaft in 1906. Kalbeck and Eusebius Mandyczewski, not only friends but also devotees of Brahms, were on the Viennese executive committee. The Deutsche Brahms-Gesellschaft acquired author's rights to all known unpublished compositions, much correspondence and rights to royalties. In other words, the legacy of a ferociously private man was put into the hands of his ferociously loyal friends. Kalbeck approached his task with great scrupulousness and thoroughness, given the surfeit of sources.

In addition to his four-volume biography, Kalbeck also edited many volumes of Brahms's correspondence. Although this directly contravened

[14] D. and M. McCorkle, 'Five Fundamental Obstacles in Brahms Source Research', *Acta Musicologica* 48/2 (July–December 1976), 253–72.

Brahms's stated wish that all correspondence in his possession at his death be destroyed 'without reservation' if it could not be returned to its authors, the composer was evidently aware that such volumes might well appear.[15] As he remarked to George Henschel, 'One should be careful when one writes letters; one fine day, they appear in print!'[16] Kalbeck's approach to Brahms's letters would have been recognisable from the mid-nineteenth century: he omitted and shortened letters without acknowledgement, drawing a boundary between private and public letters, the latter penned with an eye to posterity.[17] His combination of selection and speculation is understandably frustrating today, and the subsequent dispersal of his estate makes it difficult to retrace his steps. Yet, regardless of objections, his work is still largely regarded as a primary source.

What, then, are the juiciest myths in Brahms biography, reinforced in virtually every concert programme note and not a few scholarly studies? The first, and possibly the most important, is the claim that Brahms played the piano in bars or even brothels as a child in Hamburg. A number of scholars, including Kurt Hofmann, Laurenz Lütteken and Styra Avins have presented compelling evidence that Brahms's family background was not poverty-stricken, but 'kleinbürgerlich' or lower-middle-class.[18] But the story, with its tinge of child abuse and its compelling suggestion of ensuing trauma, was restated without qualification in Jan Swafford's popular biography of 1997 and other studies; and it has underpinned several interpretations of Brahms's song-cycle the *Magelone Romances* Op. 33.[19] Swafford argues that Brahms himself apparently conspired with the idea of poverty and a pathologised relationship to sex; he points out that Brahms told the story to his friend Klaus Groth. Another figure who considerably amplified it was Robert Haven Schauffler in his 1933 *The Unknown Brahms*. Swafford's argument still relies heavily on the veracity and accuracy of second- and

---

[15] From his will in May 1891. See *Briefe XI*, 218 n.1. [16] Quoted in *Briefe VII*, preface, vii.

[17] Discussed in B. Borchard, 'Entwurf eines Künstlerlebens. Max Kalbecks Ausgabe der Brahms-Briefe', in U. Harten (ed.), *Max Kalbeck zum 150. Geburtstag. Skizzen einer Persönlichkeit* (Tutzing: Hans Schneider, 2007), 247–59.

[18] See also S. Avins, 'Myth in Brahms Biography, or, What I learned from Quantum Mechanics', *Fontes Artis Musicae* 62/3 (July–Sept 2015), 183–202, which summarises earlier research refuting the 'Poverty Myth' (including poor living standards, impoverished parents, lacking education and playing in brothels). This includes an appendix of biographies from La Mara (1874) to Wikipedia (2015) for traces of the Poverty Myth and whether it is refuted, developed from Kalbeck and so forth.

[19] See J. Swafford, *Johannes Brahms* (New York: Knopf, 1997) and 'Did the Young Brahms Play Piano in Waterfront Bars?', *19th-Century Music* 24/3 (Spring 2001), 268–75; T. Boyer, 'Brahms as Count Peter of Provence: A Psychosexual Interpretation of the Magelone Poetry', *Musical Quarterly* 66/2 (April 1980), 262–86; and B. Desai, 'The Boy Brahms', *19th-Century Music* 27/2 (Fall 2003), 132–6.

Mythmaking 391

third-hand reports, hardly enough to justify the extraordinary claim 'certainly, Brahms's personality was consistent with a history of sexual abuse'.[20]

The story colours almost all subsequent accounts of Brahms's relationships with women in general, and Clara Schumann in particular. Much has been made of Brahms's broken engagement to Agathe von Siebold [see Ch. 2 'The Schumanns'] but a broken engagement, and even a broken heart, were hardly unusual (the baritone Julius Stockhausen experienced both in the same decade as Brahms). Brahms's youthful passion for Clara Schumann is used to interpret not only the man but also a wide range of musical works. Such myths are extremely useful to both musicians and audiences, providing an interpretative key to works which do not need to be true to be effective.

The pathologised artist is also excellent fodder for both fictional and film treatment. Numerous novels, from murder mysteries to romantic narratives, treat Brahms's life, including a 2004 novel by Boman Desai, *Trio: A Novel about the Schumanns and Brahms*. The furthest limit of fictional treatment is surely Ken Russell's *Brahms Gets Laid,* while the most extreme filmed treatment is Tony Palmer's 1996 'documentary' *Brahms and the Little Singing Girls.* The film is replete with explicit scenes, such as the Brahms and Agathe von Siebold frolicking naked in a stream, or Brahms licking whisky from a prostitute's breasts. The various films in which Brahms plays a main character inevitably position him in a love triangle with Robert and Clara Schumann, and Schumann's incipient insanity is given equal priority. These include *Geliebte Clara* (2008), the television film *Robert Schumann–Clara Wieck–Johannes Brahms* (2006), *La forêt noire* (1968), the unforgettable *Song of Love* (1947) in which Clara Schumann is played by Katharine Hepburn, and *Träumerei* (1944). It was not possible to locate copies of *Guten Abend, gute Nacht* (1936) and *Rosen aus dem Süden* (1934). Only János Darvas's 1997 television documentary *Wären nicht die Frauen . . . Dr. Brahms. Johannes Brahms* (1997), avoids all biographical speculation.

More problematically, these myths have resulted in a tendency to privilege the emotional world of Brahms's more intimate music over other parts of his oeuvre such as his large-scale, public-facing choral works. Nationalism, especially German nationalism, has been understandably subdued since 1945, and while Brahms's patriotic feelings are acknowledged in scholarship, they are downplayed in wider consciousness. The exception is *A German Requiem* Op. 45, but in this case, the

---

[20] Swafford, 'Did the Young Brahms Play Piano in Waterfront Bars?', 272.

association with the death of the composer's mother reinforces the narrative of suffering and triumph over adversity. The situation is further complicated by the political implications of selfhood in the nineteenth century; at a time when artists were frequently identified with their geographical background as a short-hand for classifying their personality traits, Brahms's North German roots were frequently cited as a reason for his putative melancholy and misanthropy. Finally, there is the undeniable influence of nineteenth-century German patterns of thought, particularly the tendency to understand phenomena dialectically and therefore construct oppositions which lead to oversimplifications. The tendency to understand Brahms in opposition to Liszt, Wagner and Bruckner resulted in his being denied the possibility of sharing or approving of any of their attributes, despite scholarship which demonstrates otherwise.

While mythmaking provides a powerful means of making certain artists (and their artworks) memorable, its simplicity flattens out the nuances of an individual life lived. Maynard Solomon reminds us that every artwork is only 'partly an individual creation', and that different kinds of biographical events bear upon artistry.[21] Therefore, we need to be critically aware of the act of selecting and interpreting information and artefacts when producing our own narratives of the past. By examining the granular – and sometimes apparently contradictory – information surrounding a creative figure such as Brahms, we may dispense with the myths and wrangle with the genuine complexities of history. This aim has guided the creation of this volume throughout.

Further Reading

S. Avins, 'The Young Brahms: Biographical Data Reexamined', *19th-Century Music* 24/3 (Spring 2001), 276–89

B. Desai, 'The Boy Brahms', *19th-Century Music* 27/2 (Fall 2003), 132–6

K. Hofmann, '*Sehnsucht habe ich immer nach Hamburg . . .': Johannes Brahms und seine Vaterstadt: Legende und Wirklichkeit* (Reinbek: Dialog-Verlag, 2003)

M. Musgrave 'Frei aber Froh: A Reconsideration', *19th-Century Music* 3/3 (March 1980), 251–8

J. Swafford, 'Did the Young Brahms Play Piano in Waterfront Bars?', *19th-Century Music* 24/3 (Spring 2001), 268–75

---

[21] See M. Solomon, 'Thoughts on Biography', *19th-Century Music* 5/3 (Spring 1982), 268–76.

Further Reading

Along with the items in the List of Abbreviations at the start of this volume, this reading list draws together some of the most important general texts of Brahms studies that are relevant across multiple chapters of this book. They include surveys, biographies, letter volumes and editions of Brahms's works spanning English and German-language scholarship. A complete online catalogue of Brahms's correspondence, the *Brahms-Briefverzeichnis*, is available via the website of the Brahms-Institut, Lübeck: www.brahms-institut.de/web/bihl_projekte/pro jekt_bbv.html

L. Botstein (ed.), *The Compleat Brahms: A Guide to the Musical Works of Johannes Brahms* (London: W.W. Norton & Co., 1999)

P. Clive, *Brahms and His World: A Biographical Dictionary* (Lanham, MD: Scarecrow, 2006)

E. Evans, *Historical, Descriptive and Analytical Account of the Entire Works of Johannes Brahms*, 4 vols. (London: William Reeves, 1912)

M. Friedlaender, *Brahms' Lieder. Einführung in seine Gesänge für eine und zwei Stimmen* (Berlin & Leipzig: Simrock, 1922)

M. Friedlaender, *Brahms's Lieder: An Introduction to the Songs for One and Two Voices*, trans. C. L. Leese (London: Oxford University Press, 1928)

O. Gottlieb-Billroth (ed.), *Billroth und Brahms im Briefwechsel* (Berlin: Urban & Schwarzenberg, 1935)

E. Hanslick, *Aus dem Concert-Saal: Kritiken und Schilderungen aus 20 Jahren d. Wiener Musiklebens 1848–1868* (Vienna: W. Braumüller, 1897)

R. and K. Hofmann, *Johannes Brahms. Zeittafel zu Leben und Werk* (Tutzing: Hans Schneider, 1983)

R. and K. Hofmann, *Johannes Brahms als Pianist und Dirigent. Chronologie seines Wirkens als Interpret* (Tutzing: Hans Schneider, 2006)

J. Joachim and A. Moser (eds.), *Briefe von und an Joseph Joachim*, 3 vols. (Berlin: Julius Bard, 1911–13)

B. Litzmann, *Clara Schumann, ein Künstlerleben nach Tagebüchern und Briefen*, 3 vols. (Leipzig: Breitkopf & Härtel, 1918–1920)

M. MacDonald, *Brahms* (Oxford & New York: Oxford University Press, 2001)

FURTHER READING

E. Mandyczewski and H. Gál (eds.), *Johannes Brahms: Sämtliche Werke. Ausgabe der Gesellschaft der Musikfreunde in Wien*, 26 vols. (Leipzig: Breitkopf & Härtel, 1926–7, revised repr. Wiesbaden, 1965)

M. Musgrave, *A Brahms Reader* (New Haven and London: Yale University Press, 2000)

M. Musgrave, *The Music of Brahms* (Oxford: Clarendon Press, 1994)

H. Platt, *Johannes Brahms. A Research and Information Guide*, 2nd edn (New York: Routledge, 2011)

K. Stephenson (ed.), *Johannes Brahms und Fritz Simrock – Weg einer Freundschaft. Briefe des Verlegers an den Komponisten* (Hamburg: J. J. Augustin, 1961)

Index

Page numbers in *italics* refer to a figure or table. The abbreviation JB refers to Johannes Brahms. Birth and death dates have been supplied wherever available.

Abendroth, Hermann (1883–1956), 373
Abraham, Max (1831–1900), 132, 239
absolute music, 284–5
Abt, Franz (1819–85), 130
Adès, Thomas (b.1971), 379, 381
Adler, Guido (1855–1941), 386
Adler, Samuel (b.1928), 381
Adorno, Theodor W.(1903–69), 343
aesthetics, 154–7, 196, 197, 198–9, 200–1, 225, 228, 248, 251, 254, 284–5, 300, 308–10, 312
Ahle, Johann Rudolf (1625–73), 181–2
Ahna, Heinrich de (1835–92), 219
Allgemeine musikalische Zeitung, 194, 298
Allgeyer, Julius (1829–1900), 61, 178, 260, 290, 292
amateur music-making *see* private music-making
analytical approaches, 324–34
André, Johann Anton (1775–1842), 115
Andreotti, Emilio (1852–96), 66
anticlericalism, 266, 267
anti-Semitism, 30, 48, 199, 200–1, 202, 266–7, 337, 338–40
anti-Wagnerism, 41, 42, 197, 198–9, 204–5
Arnim, Bettina von (1785–1859), 216, 272–3
Arnim, Ludwig Achim von (1781–1831), 164
Arnold, Friedrich Wilhelm (1810–64), 171–2
arrangers and arrangements, 98–112, 147
   JB as arranger of others' work, 8–9, 71–2, 82
   JB as arranger of his own works, 56–7, 98–9, 100–1, 103–12, 131–2, 168, 179, 236, 240, 242–3, 253–5
   of JB's works by others, 101–3
   and copyright, 246, 249, 250–1, 252–5
Arrau, Claudio (1903–91), 362
art (visual arts), 286–95
Artôt, Desirée (1835–1907), 188
Assmann, Adele, 192
Asten, Julie von (1841–1923), 126

audiences, 145–7, 317–18
Austria, 28, 260–1, 266–8 *see also* Vienna
Avé-Lallemant, Charlotte (1843–1929), 45
Avé-Lallemant, Theodor (1806–90), 11, 14, 45, 177, 232

Bach, Johann Sebastian (1685–1750)
   arrangements by JB, 108–10
   JB's teaching of, 127
   influence of, 149, 154, 158, 182, 198
   performances of, 91, 92, 94, 179, 180, 181–2
Bachrich, Sigismund (1841–1913), 219
Backhaus, Wilhelm (1884–1969), 363
Bad Ischl, 21, 25, 46, 60, 62, 65
Baden-Baden, 18, 50, 61, 63–4, 107, 126–7, 136, 208
Baermann, Carl (1818–85), 230
Bagge, Selmar (1823–96), 324, 325
Baglehole, Florence (1852–1927), 208
Balás-Bognar, Vilma von (1845–1904), 192
Bamberg, 139
banks, 75, 76, 77
Barbi, Alice (1862–1948), 190
Barenboim, Daniel (b. 1942), 363
Bargiel, Woldemar (1828–97), 116, 117, 119
Barth, Karl Heinrich (1847–1922), 212
Barth, Richard (1850–1923), 13, 219–20
Barton, Marmaduke (b. 1865), 212
Basel, 143, 191
Bayreuth, 198, 201, 222
Becker, Carl Ferdinand (1804–77), 172
Beckerath, Laura (1840–1921), 61, 221
Beckerath, Rudolf von (1833–88), 54, 61, 221
Beckerath, Willy von (1868–1938), 95
Beethoven, Ludwig van (1770–1827)
   arrangements by JB, 108, 124
   Bülow's interpretation of, 203
   folk music as inspiration for, 165

395

396 Index

Beethoven, Ludwig van (1770–1827) (cont.)
  influence of, 28, 29, 154, 158, 159, 160, 311, 386
  Joachim's playing of, 218
  performances of, 41, 42, 143, 144, 180, 203
  popularity compared with JB, 361
  prank concerning, 47
Behm, Eduard (1862–1946), 128
Benfeld, Malwine von, 211
Berg, Alban (1885–1935), 337
Bergmann, Carl (1821–76), 211
Beringer, Oscar (1844–1922), 208
Berio, Luciano (1925–2003), 381
Berlin, 38–43, 139, 141, 176, 240, 273, 301
  Hofkapelle, 147
  Königliche Hochschule für Musik, 40–2,
    219, 221
  Singakademie, 139, 222, 289
Berlin Philharmonic, 336
Berlioz, Hector (1803–68), 94, 231, 310
Bern, 139
Bernsdorf, Eduard (1825–1901), 38, 237, 313
Bettelheim, Caroline (1845–1925), 191
Bible, the, 261–2, 264, 265, 274, 277, 278, 279,
  283
Bie, Oscar (1864–1938), 341, 342
Bildung, ideal of, 39–40, 130, 160, 270, 275, 279,
  285, 286
Billroth, Theodor (1829–94), 24–5
  books by, in JB's library, 274
  cremation discussed, 31
  dedicatee of String Quartets, 219
  Lutheran background, 266
  on piano arrangements, 101
  on Daumer, 269
  on Richter conducting Third Symphony, 201
  private music-making with JB, 99, 106, 134, 135
  travel with JB, 65, 66, 67
biographical writing, 384–92
Bischoff, Ludwig (1794–1867), 309–10
Bismarck, Otto von (1815–98), 198, 259–61, 262,
  263, 268
Blühmel, Friedrich (1777–1845), 231
Blume, Walter (1883–1933), 204, 372
Böcklin, Arnold (1827–1901), 288, 292–3
Boehm, Theobald (1794–1881), 229
Böhme, Franz Magnus (1827–98), 173
Bonn, 239
Borwick, Leonard (1868–1925), 21, 209, 320
bourgeoisie *see* middle-class society
Brahms, Christiane (née Nissen) (mother)
  (1789–1865), 4–7, 16, 72, 75, 262, 273
Brahms, Elise (1831–92), 5, 63, 75, 178
Brahms, Fritz (1835–86), 5, 75
Brahms, Johann Jakob (father) (1806–72), 3–7, 8,
  24, 63, 72, 75, 232, 248, 273, 300

Brahms, Johannes (1833–97)
  appearance and dress, 14, 49–50, 379, *388*, *389*
  as arranger, 8–9, 56–7, 71–2, 82, 98–112, 131–2,
    147, 168, 179, 236, 240, 242–3, 253–5
  biographies of, 384, 385–9
  birth and childhood, 3, 5–10, 53, 71, 80, 88,
    123–4, 182, 187–8, 270, 390–1
  his books and literary tastes, 270–6, 277–8,
    279–84, 286–7, 288, 300, 330, 331,
    333, 385
  on brass instruments, 231–2
  centenary celebrations, 336–44
  compositional technique, 192, 311–12, 324–7
  as conductor, 88–97, *96*, 141, 178–9, 181–2,
    188, 197
  as correspondent, 52–9, 385, 389–90
  creative process, 247–9, 250, 252, 281, 285,
    348–9, 364
  death and burial, 25, 30–1, 268
  and early music, 175–83
  as editor, 114–21, 177, 374
  finances, 71–8, 81, 114, 118, 119, 126, 144, 146,
    236, 239, 240–4
  and folk music, 165–73, 337–8
  genealogy, 3, 4, 338–40
  genres, 154–63, 270
  Manifesto against New German Music, 83,
    216, 313–14, 333
  G. W. Marks pseudonym, 9, 72, 131
  performance anxiety, 85
  personal habits, 44–51, 63–5
  personality, 11–13, 18, 47–8, 50–1, 54, 57, 64,
    82–3, 378–80, 385, 391, 392
  as pianist, 71, 73, 80–7, 90, 98–9, 108, 141, 142,
    144–5, 189
  politics, 260, 264–8
  pranks and jokes, 47
  relationship with women, 15–22, 58, 385, 391
  religion, 261–2, 265, 272, 274, 279, 283–4
  as teacher, 71, 72–3, 81, 123–9
  rivalry with Wagner, 197, 198–9, 200–5, 392
  works
    Anh. Ia, Five Piano Studies, 108–10
    Anh. IV no. 6, *Souvenir de la Russie*, 72,
      131
    Op. 1, Piano Sonata, 15, 73, 81, 170, 210, 240,
      307–8, 310, 312
    Op. 2, Piano Sonata, 15, 17, 73, 240, 312,
      324–5
    Op. 3, Six Songs, 15, 240, 312, 351
    Op. 4, Scherzo, 15, 81, 240, 312, 349
    Op. 5, Piano Sonata, 207, 216, 236, 311,
      312, 362
    Op. 6, *Sechs Gesänge*, 236, 312
    Op. 7, *Sechs Gesänge*, 240, 312

Index

397

Op. 8, First Piano Trio, 62, 211, 240, 311, 312, 350, 351, 360

Op. 9, *Variations on a Theme of Robert Schumann*, 17, 210, 240, 311, 312

Op. 10, Four Ballades, 207, 270, 311, 312

Op. 11, First Serenade, 197, 208, 217, 312, 318

Op. 12, *Ave Maria*, 90, 107, 238, 312, 318

Op. 13, *Begräbnisgesang*, 107, 179, 232, 238, 312

Op. 14, *Lieder und Romanzen*, 172, 312

Op. 15, First Piano Concerto, 19, 34, *102*, 159, 188, 197, 207–8, 209, 210, 211, 212, 217, 237, 238, 243, 312, 313, 318, 320

Op. 16, Second Serenade, 34, 58–9, 90, 196, 197, 239, 243, 312

Op. 17, *Vier Gesänge für Frauenchor*, 107, 162, 179, 239, 312

Op. 18, First String Sextet, 100, 102, 217, 239, 243, 312, 313, 314, 317, 325

Op. 21 no. 2, *Variations on a Hungarian Song*, 169, 170, 176, 208, 239, 312

Op. 22, *Marienlieder*, 179, 199

Op. 23, *Variations on a Theme of Schumann*, 10, 17, 207, 238, 249

Op. 24, *Variations and Fugue on a Theme of Handel*, 10, 162, 207, 208, 249, 328, 377

Op. 25, First Piano Quartet, 10, 134, 173, 206, 239, 317

Op. 26, Second Piano Quartet, 10, 207, 219, 239, 317

Op. 27, *Psalm 13*, 238, 252

Op. 28, Four Duets for Alto and Baritone, 189, 238, 252

Op. 29, Two Motets, 179

Op. 30, *Geistliches Lied*, 179

Op. 31 no. 1, 'Wechselllied zum Tanze', 191

Op. 32 no. 5, 'Wehe, so willst du mich wieder', 191

Op. 33, *Magelone Romances*, 10, 188, 238, 390

Op. 34, Piano Quintet, 10, 36, 100, 102, 327, 354

Op. 34bis, Sonata for Two Pianos, 85, 100, 210–11, 354

Op. 35, *Variations on a Theme of Paganini*, 85, 371

Op. 36, Second String Sextet, 58, 99, 102, 131, 237, 239, 348

Op. 37 Three Sacred Choruses, 90

Op. 38, First Cello Sonata, 221, 239

Op. 39, Waltzes, 131

Op. 40, Horn Trio, 232, 239, 260, 370

Op. 42, *Drei Gesänge für 6-stimmigen Chor*, 179, 199, 240

Op. 43 no. 2, 'Die Mainacht', 325

Op. 44, *Lieder und Romanzen*, 179

Op. 45, *A German Requiem*, 10, 19, 34, 55, 56–7, 63, 74, 81, 92, 100, 102, 107, 126, 161–2, 181, 188, 197, 198, 230, 238, 242–3, 261–2, 279, 283, 314–15, 318–19, 322, 350, 362, 365, 368–9, 380, 391

Op. 46 no. 2, 'Magyarisch', 169, 173, 239

Op. 47, *Fünf Lieder*, 173, 239

Op. 49 no. 4, 'Wiegenlied', 101, 132, 173

Op. 50, *Rinaldo*, 11, 107, 187, 189, 239, 276, 318

Op. 51, Two String Quartets, 160, 219, 325, 328, 360

Op. 52, *Liebeslieder*, 99, 102, 107, 207, 348, 380

Op. 52a, *Liebeslieder* for piano duet, 100

Op. 53, *Alto Rhapsody*, 19, 107, 143, 189, 190, 192, 276, 328

Op. 54, *Schicksalslied*, 74, 107, 142, 143, 279, 280, 318–19

Op. 55, *Triumphlied*, 100, 107, 139, 142, 143, 188, 190, 192, 194, 198, 199, 243, 262–3, 283

Op. 56a, *Variations on a Theme of Haydn*, orchestral version, 100, 143, 197, 204, 318, 319, 329, 348, 354

Op. 56b, *Variations on a Theme of Haydn* for Two Pianos, 100, 211, 348, 354

Op. 60, Third Piano Quartet, 270

Op. 62 no. 6, 'Es geht ein Wehen durch den Wald', 199

Op. 63, *Lieder und Gesänge*, 20, 239, 378

Op. 64, Three Quartets, 239

Op. 65, *Neue Liebeslieder*, 62, 99, 102, 107, 380

Op. 65a, *Neue Liebeslieder* for piano duet, 100

Op. 67, Third String Quartet, 219

Op. 68, First Symphony, 10, 38, 60, 75, 94, 103, 144, 158, 190, 196, 199, 242, 317–18, 328, 351, 364–5, 368–9, 377–8

Opp. 69–72, song collections, 20, 242

Op. 73, Second Symphony, 57, 75, 95, 96–7, 106, 134, 135, 143, 202, 242, 318, 364–5, 368–9, 372, 380

Op. 74, Two Motets, 149–50, 178, 279, 283

Op. 76 no. 2, Capriccio, 211

Op. 77, Violin Concerto, 21, 59, 102, 107, 143, 144, 159, 173, 217–18, 220, 242, 244, 316, 317, 318

Op. 78, First Violin Sonata, 218

Op.79, Two Rhapsodies, 210, 212

Op. 80, *Academic Festival Overture*, 95, 143, 203, 233, 318

Op. 81, *Tragic Overture*, 143, 318, 319

Op. 82, *Nänie*, 107, 143, 239, 279, 291

Index

Brahms, Johannes (1833–97) (cont.)

Op. 83, Second Piano Concerto, 102, 106–7, 142, 159, 203, 208, 209, 212–13, 297, 313, 318

Op. 86, *Sechs Lieder*, 20, 77, 190, 338

Op. 87, Second Piano Trio, 58

Op. 89, *Gesang der Parzen*, 107, 143, 276, 279, 319

Op. 90, Third Symphony, 75, 98, 100, 102, 103, 106, 143, 200, 201, 202, 242, 244, 319, 330, 364–5, 368–9

Op. 91, Two Songs for Alto, Viola and Piano, 136

Op. 94 no. 4, 'Sapphische Ode', 190, 192

Op. 95 no. 3, 'Beim Abschied', 351

Op. 96, *Vier Lieder*, 294

Op. 97, *Sechs Lieder*, 294

Op. 98, Fourth Symphony, 62, 100, 101, 106, 135, 144, 146, 158, 192, 202, 203, 230, 233, 319, 330, 350, 364–5, 368–9

Op. 99, Second Cello Sonata, 62, 221, 363

Op. 100, Violin Sonata, 62, 221

Op. 101, Third Piano Trio, 209, 221

Op. 102, Double Concerto, 102, 107, 143, 159, 218–19, 220, 221–2, 321, 333

Op. 103, *Zigeunerlieder*, 320

Op. 104, *Fünf Gesänge für Chor*, 327

Op. 105 no. 2, 'Immer leiser wird mein Schlummer', 330–1

Op. 107, *Fünf Lieder*, 193, 327, 328

Op. 108, Third Violin Sonata, 209, 219, 320, 365

Op. 109, *Festival and Commemorative Verses*, 183, 264, 283

Op. 110, Three Motets, 183, 199

Op. 111, Second String Quintet, 103–6, 149–50, 160, 224

Op. 112, Six Quartets, 239

Op. 113, Thirteen Canons for Female Voices, 239, 271

Op. 114, Clarinet Trio, 62, 135, 209, 222, 320

Op. 115, Clarinet Quintet, 62, 135, 173, 222–3, 225

Op. 116, Fantasies, 209, 320

Op. 117, Intermezzi, 209, 210, 320, *352*, 366, 378

Op. 118, Piano Pieces, 209, 320, 362–3, 366

Op. 118 no. 2, Intermezzo, 334

Op. 118 no. 6, Intermezzo in E minor, 371

Op. 119, Piano Pieces, 209, 320, 361, 362, 366, 378

Op. 120, Clarinet Sonatas, 25, 209, 223, 225, 320

Op. 121, *Four Serious Songs*, 22, 281, 294, 325, 377

Op. 122, Chorale Preludes, 171, 377

WoO 1, *Hungarian Dances*, 74, 81, 83, 99, 126, 131, 169, 254, 303, 373

Scherzo, F–A–E Sonata for violin and piano, 216

WoO 3, Two Gavottes, 207, 317

WoO 5, Two Sarabandes for Piano, 317

WoO 6, *51 Exercises*, 206

WoO 31, *Volks-Kinderlieder*, 17, 238, 311

WoO 33, 49 *Deutsche Volkslieder*, 170, 173, 242

WoO 34, 14 *Deutsche Volkslieder*, 168

WoO 38, 20 *Deutsche Volkslieder*, 168

Brahms-Gesellschaft, 389

'Brahmsian' as adjective, 357–8, 360, 361–6

Brandes, Emma (1853–1940)

Brandt, Auguste (1822–87), 45

Brandt, Clara (1848–1919), 45

brass instruments, 230–2, 299, 368, 370

Brauner, Gabriele, 211

Breitkopf & Härtel, 10, 20, 21, 55, 80, 115–21, 236, 237–8, 240–1, 244, 252

Bremen, 73, 93, 197, 240

Brendel, Franz (1811–68), 278–9, 309, 313

Brentano, Clemens (1778–1842), 164

Breslau, 143, 192

Brissler, Friedrich Ferdinand (1818–93), 117

Bruch, Clara (1854–1919), 192

Bruch, Max (1838–1920), 197, 221

Bruckner, Anton (1824–96), 42, 53, 131, 266

Brüll, Ignaz (1846–1907), 48, 98, 106, 135, 211, 246

Brünn, 139

Budapest, 193, 212

Buffet, Louis-Auguste (1789–1864), 230

Bülow, Hans von (1830–94), 39, 82, 96, 142, 202–4, 210, 212, 264, 265, 297, 333, 368, 372

Burckhardt, Jakob (1818–97), 287–8

Busch, Fritz (1890–1951), 205

Busoni, Ferruccio (1866–1924), 212

Calvisius, Sethus (1566–1615), 178

Cambridge University, 317

Catholics and Catholicism, 175, 263, 266

cellists, 221–2, 349, 363

cellos, 228–9

Cesti, Antonio (1623–69), 178

Chabrier, Emmanuel (1841–94), 233

chamber music, 41–2, 85, 99, 131, 135, 145, 160, 206, 209, 219–20, 222, 369–71, 374

children, 49, 50, 71, 101

Chodowiecki, Daniel (1726–1801), 287

choirs and choral societies, 147, 369 *see also* Hamburg Ladies' Choir, *see also* Vienna:Singverein

Index

Chopin, Frédéric (1810–49), 108, 116–17, 134, 241, 360
Christian Social Party, 30, 267
Chrysander, Friedrich (1826–1901), 110, 116, 182, 384
ciphers, musical, 386–7
clarinetists, 222–5
clarinets, 229, 230
collaborative music-making, 85 *see also* chamber music, private music-making
Cologne, 44, 139, 143
concert life, 138–47, 199, 318
concert pitch, variety of, 298–300
concert ticket prices, 146–7
concert venues, 139–40, 141, *143*, 145, 146, 199, 227–8
concertos (as genre), 159, 160–1, 204
conductors, 88, 96–7, 190, 196–205, 317, 318, 319, 320–1, 364–5, 368–9
copyists, 349–50
copyright, 74, 107, 246–55
Cornelius, Peter (1824–74), 216
Corner, David Gregor (1585–1648), 178
correspondence, 52–9
Corsi, Giuseppe (?–1690), 176
Cossel, Otto Friedrich Willibald (1813–65), 7–8, 53
Couperin, François (1668–1733), 182
court music and musicians, 17, 23, 28, 39, 46, 73, 81, 88–9, 125, 136, 141–4, *143*, 145–6, 178, 181, 189, 202, 210, 217, 372
Cowen, Frederic (1852–1935), 320
Cranz, Alwin (1834–1923), 123
Cranz, August (1789–1870), 9, 72, 240, 253–4
creativity, 25–7, 30, 31, 61–2, 103, 154, 247–9, 250, 251–2, 281, 285
cremation and burial, 30–1
Cremona, 66
Cros, Charles (1842–88), 303
Curzon, Clifford (1907–82), 361–2
Cusins, William George (1833–93), 317

D'Albert, Eugen (1864–1932), 85, 212
D'Indy, Vincent (1851–1931), 64
Darmstadt, 139
Daumer, Georg Friedrich (1800–75), 269
David, Ferdinand (1810–73), 232
Davies, Fanny (1861–1934), 85, 209, 320
Dawson, Frederick (1868–1940), 212
De Lara, Adelina (1872–1961), 209–10
Dean, Brett (b.1961), 378, 381
Debussy, Claude (1862–1918), 361
Defaye, Jean-Michael (b.1932), 381
Deiters, Hermann (1833–1907), 384
Dessoff, Otto (1835–92), 94, 144, 196–7, 200

Detmold, 73, 88, 89, 124, 125, 178–9
Deutsche Brahms-Gesellschaft, 389
Deutsch-Römer, 288, 292
Dietrich, Albert (1829–1908), 73, 119, 216, 387
F–A–E Sonata for violin and piano, 216
Dohnányi, Ernő (Ernst von) (1877–1960), 203, 212
domestic music-making *see* private music-making
Dömpke, Gustav (1853–1923), 135
Donop, Auguste von (1810–83), 125
Door, Anton (1833–1919), 211
Dörffel, Alfred (1821–1905), 218, 244
Dorman, Avner (b.1975), 378, 381
Dresden, 141
du Pré, Jacqueline (1945–87), 363
Duisburg, 146
Durante, Francesco (1684–1745), 176
Düsseldorf, 9–10, 14–15, 50, 73, 108, 124, 127, 139, 146, 171, 176, 307
Dustmann, Louise (1831–99), 191
Dvořák, Antonín (1841–1904), 53, 201, 221, 240, 281

early music, 175–83
Ebner, Eduard (1821–1906), 191
Ebner, Ottilie (née Hauer) (1836–1926), 126, 133, 191
Eccard, Johannes (1553–1611), 178, 179, 180, 181
Edison, Thomas A. (1847–1931), 303–4
editing, 244, 329, 347–56, 374
Edward VII ('Bertie'), as Prince of Wales (1841–1910), 264
Eibenschütz, Ilona (1873–1967), 85, 209, 320, 358
Eichendorff, Joseph von (1788–1857), 271
Elgar, Edward (1857–1934), 201, 322–3
Engel, 'Kathinka' (1856–1930), 192
Engelmann, Emma (née Brandes), *see* Brandes, Emma, 219
Engelmann, Theodor Wilhelm (doctor) (1843–1909), 86, 219, 274
Engelmann, Wilhelm (publisher), 37
England, 85, 189, 190, 207–9, 212, 223, 316–23, 387
engravers, 350–1, *352*
Epstein, Julius (1832–1926), 134, 211
Erfurt, 139
Erk, Ludwig (1807–83), 173
Erkel, Alexander (1846–1900), 142
Ewazen, Eric (b.1954), 381
Eybler, Joseph (1765–1846), 116

F–A–E Sonata for violin and piano, 216
Faber, Arthur (1839–1900), 75, 77–8
Faber, Bertha *see* Porubsky, Bertha
Fagerlund, Sebastian (b.1972), 381

400   *Index*

Fauré, Gabriel (1845–1924), 61
Feller, Harald (b.1951), 381
Fellinger, Richard (1848–1903) and Maria
    (1849–1925), 54, 110, 135, 221, 303
Ferneyhough, Brian (b.1943), 376
Feuerbach, Anselm (1829–80), 288, 289–92
Feuerbach, Henriette (1812–92), 61
Fillunger, Marie (1850–1930), 112, 191
finances, 71–8, 72, 146–7, 236, 239, 240–4,
    297
Finck, Heinrich (1444/5–1527), 172
Finnissy, Michael (b.1946), 381
First World War, 323
Fleischer, Herbert, 341
Florence, 66
Fluntern, 61
folk music, 164–73, 337–8
Forster, Georg (?1510–68), 171, 180
Franchomme, August (1808–84), 116
Franck, César (1822–90), 64
Frank, Ernst (1847–89), 119
Frankfurt am Main, 139, 189, 209
Franz, Anna *see* Wittgenstein, Anna
Franz, Ellen (later Helene Freifrau von
    Heldburg) (1839–1923), 46, 137
Franz, Robert (1815–92), 307–8
Frascati, 66
'Frazeni, Titus' *see* Schumann, Alfred
Frege, Livia (1818–91), 37, 190
Frescobaldi, Girolamo (1583–1643), 178
Freund, Etelka (1879–1977), 212, 358
Freund, Robert (1852–1936), 212
Frey, Adolf (1855–1920), 292
Friedberg, Carl (1872–1955), 210, 358
Friederike of Lippe, Princess (1825–97), 125
Friedrich III, Emperor (1831–88), 264–5
Friedrich, Caspar David (1774–1840), 292
Fritzsch, Ernst Wilhelm (1840–1902), 240
Fuchs, Robert (1847–1927), 98, 240
Füller, Josef, 349
Fuller Maitland, John Alexander (1856–1936),
    218, 386
Fürstner, Adolph (1833–1908), 240
Furtwängler, Wilhelm (1886–1954), 337, 343, 344,
    358, 363

Gabrieli, Giovanni (c.1554/7–1612), 177, 180
Gál, Hans (1890–1987), 353–4
Gallus, Jacobus (1550–91), 179, 181
Gänsbacher, Josef (1829–1911), 98, 221, 260–1
Garcia, Manuel (1805–1906), 193
Gardiner, John Eliot (b.1943), 364–5, 369
Geiringer, Karl (1899–1989), 275
Geisler, Marie, 126
gender in repertoire, 193

genres, 27–8, 149–63, 192–3, 204
Georg II, Duke of Saxe-Meiningen (1826–1914),
    46, 144, 145
Gerber, Rudolf (1899–1957), 345
German folk-songs, 164–5, 168, 170, 171–2
German identity and nationalism, 164, 197, 198,
    260, 262–3, 278, 288, 391
German Romans (Deutsch-Römer), 288, 292
Germany, 259–66, 273–4, 296–7, 299,
    336–46 *see also* Hamburg, Leipzig,
    Berlin
Gieseking, Walter (1895–1956), 361
Giesemann family, 8, 123
Girzick, Rosa (?1850–1915), 191
Glanert, Detlev (b.1960), 377, 379, 381, 382
Gluck, Christoph Willibald (1714–87), 108
Goebbels, Joseph (1897–1945), 338, 343
Goethe, Johann Wolfgang von (1749–1832), 164,
    270, 271, 275–6, 280, 286
Goldmark, Karl (1830–1915), 48, 191
Gotthard, Johann Peter (1839–1919), 107–8, 115
Göttingen, 18
Gould, Glenn (1932–82), 362–3
Grädener, Karl (1812–83), 47, 90, 110, 240
Graffigna, Achille (1816–96), 66
Gramophone magazine, 360–2
Graz, 139
Grimm brothers, 273
Grimm, Herman (1828–1901), 286
Grimm, Julius Otto (1827–1903), 85–6, 89,
    119, 216
Groth, Klaus (1819–99), 84, 190, 221, 390
Grove, George (1820–1900), 316, 318, 321
Grün, Jakob Moritz (1837–1916), 46
Grund, Friedrich Wilhelm (1791–1874), 10–11
Grünfeld, Alfred (1852–1924), 83, 211
Gügler, Theresa, 93
Gumpert, Friedrich (1841–1906), 232
Gutmann, Albert (1851–1915), 53

Hahn, Jenny, 192
Halle, 307
Hallé, Charles (1819–95), 212, 319
Hallier, Johann Gottfried (1804–82), 286
Hamburg, 3–13, 6, 12, 71, 73, 123–5, 128, 220,
    286, 390
    Brahms centenary celebrations, 337–8
    Brahms memorial, 295
    JB first meets the Schumanns, 14
    JB's library, 273
    pitch variations, 300
    pranks at a party, 47
    premieres and concert firsts, 207, 210, 264
    publishers, 9, 240
Hamburg Cäcilien-Verein, 145

Index

401

Hamburg Ladies' Choir, 10, 17, 45, 73, 88, 90, 125, 133, 171, 178, 179
Hamburg Philharmonic, 10–11, 89, 90, 91, 141, 300
Handel, Georg Friedrich (1685–1759), 94, 110, 144, 178, 181, 182, 198
Hanfstängl-Schröder, Marie (1848–1917), 192
Hanover, 139, 217
Hansen, Theophil (1813–91), 291
Hanslick, Eduard (1825–1904), 24, 25, 91–2, 98, 106, 135, 251, 266, 284–5, 299, 340, 359
Harnoncourt, Nikolaus (1929–2016), 365, 370
harps, 234
Härtel, Hermann (1803–75), 297
Hassler, Hans Leo (1564–1612), 171, 177
Hauer, Ottilie *see* Ebner, Ottilie (née Hauer)
Hauptmann, Moritz (1792–1868), 333
Hausmann, Robert (1852–1909), 107, 135, 215, 218–19, 220, 221–2, 225, 228, 229, 320
Haydn, Joseph (1732–1809), 41, 157, 160, 165
Heermann, Hugo (1844–1935), 223
Hegar, Friedrich (1841–1927), 63, 292
Hegel, G. W. F. (1770–1831), 250, 278–9
Heidelberg, 61, 62
Heldburg, Helene Freifrau von *see* Franz, Ellen
Hellmesberger Quartet, 219
Hellmesberger, Joseph (1828–93), 134, 219
Helm, Theodor (1843–1920), 84, 94
Helmholtz, Hermann von (1821–94), 300–2
Henschel, George (1850–1934), 44–5, 190, 194, 247, 248, 281, 320–1, 322, 325, 348, 369, 390
Henze, Hans Werner (1926–2012), 378, 382
Herbeck, Johann Ritter von (1831–77), 197
Herder, Johann Gottfried (1744–1803), 164, 311
Hermann, Friedrich (1828–1907), 102
Herzogenberg, Elisabeth von (née von Stockhausen) (1847–92), 20, 35, 35–7, 39, 42, 48, 54, 56, 58, 84, 126, 134, 221, 264
Herzogenberg, Heinrich von (1843–1900), 35–7, 36, 39, 41, 134, 197, 221, 333
Hess, Myra (1890–1965), 213
Heuberger, Richard (1850–1914), 83, 98, 128, 246, 330
Heyse, Paul (1830–1914), 66, 275
Hill, Karl (1831–93), 192
Hirsch, Rudolf (1816–72), 92
Hirschfeld, Robert (1857–1914), 94
historical performance, 193–4, 225–6, 228, 364–5, 367–75
Hitler, Adolf (1889–1945), 336, 337, 343
Hlaváček, Franz (1806–89), 172, 349
Hoffmann von Fallersleben, August Heinrich (1798–1874), 62, 260

Hoffmann, E. T. A. (1776–1822), 270, 309
Hofhaimer, Paul (1459–1537), 172
Hofstetten, 61, 62
Hölderlin, Friedrich (1770–1843), 280
holidays, 8, 17–18, 21, 60–7, 190, 212, 264
Holstein, Franz von (1826–78) and Hedwig von (1819–97), 37
Honegger, Arthur (1892–1955), 341
Hough, Stephen (b.1961), 380, 382
Hubay, Jenő (1858–1937), 219
Hübbe, Walter, 47
Hungarian folk music, 168–70, 171

Industrial Revolution, 296
Innsbruck, 139
instrument makers, 28, 229, 230–1, 232
instruments, 227–35, 297–8, 299, 300–2, 364–5, 368–71
intellectual property rights *see* copyright
Isaac, Heinrich (c.1450–55–1517), 176, 177, 179, 180, 181
Italy, 65–7, 299

Jaëll, Alfred (1832–82), 208
Jahn, Otto (1813–69), 384
Jahn, Wilhelm (1835–1900), 231
Janotha, Natalie (1856–1932), 126
Jean Paul *see* Richter, Jean Paul
Jena, 143
Jenner, Gustav (1865–1920), 128–9, 225, 248, 334, 348
Joachim Quartet, 41–2, 218, 219, 221, 222
Joachim, Amalie (1839–99), 38, 39, 136, 189, 193, 218
Joachim, Johannes (1864–1949), 136
Joachim, Joseph (1831–1907), 40–3, 215–20
  at the Berlin Königliche Hochschule für Musik, 40–3, 219
  as composer, 103, 107, 217–18
  as conductor, 179, 317
  correspondence with JB
    JB to Joachim, 16, 52, 86, 89, 116, 312
    on tobacco and smoking, 50
  as dedicatee of JB's works, 17, 173
  in England, 317, 319, 320, 322
  and folk music, 169, 173
  friend and mentor of JB, 9, 72, 86, 135, 136, 177, 179, 215, 311, 312, 333, 340
  friend of Helmholtz, 300, 301–2
  friend of Planck, 301
  friend of Schumanns, 15, 216
  as a Jew, 200, 340
  Manifesto against New German Music, 216, 313
  marriage, 189, 199, 218

402 Index

Joachim, Joseph (1831–1907) (cont.)
as violinist, 107, 135, 197, 221–2, 225, 228, 289, *290*, 317, 320, 368, 370
as violist, 136
Jonas, Oswald (1897–1978), 340
Joseffy, Rafael (1852–1915), 212–13

Kagel, Mauricio (1931–2008), 376–7, 379, 382
Kahn, Robert (1865–1951), 128
Kail, Josef (1795–1871), 231
Kalbeck, Florentine (Flora) (1882–1948), 45–6
Kalbeck, Max (1850–1921)
as biographer, 35, 36, 37, 58, 64–5, 84, 85, 95, 123, 247, 271, 386–7, 388–90
as friend, 45–6, 98, 106, 135, 158, 267–8
Kant, Immanuel (1724–1804), 249
Karajan, Herbert von (1909–89), 344
Karlsruhe, 141, 142, 143, 144, 145, 146, 196, 198, 200, 260, 290
Kassel, 141
Keller, Gottfried (1819–90), 286
Keller, Robert (1828–91), 100, 102, 244
Kempe, Rudolf (1910–76), 362
Kempner, Friederike (1836–1904), 277
keyboard instruments, 300–2 *see also* pianos, organs
Kiel, Clemens August (1813–71), 89
Kiesekamp, Hedwig (1846–1919), 192
Killmayer, Wilhelm (1927–2017), 379, 382
Kirchner, Theodor (1823–1903), 18, 63, 99, 102, 103
Kirchner, Volker David (b.1942), 382
Klauwell, Otto (1851–1917), 365
Klemperer, Otto (1885–1973), 362
Klengel, Julius (1859–1933), 221
Klinger, Max (1857–1920), 288, 293–5
Klosé, Hyacinthe Eléonore (1808–80), 230
Knaus, Ludwig (1829–1910), 61
Köchel, Ludwig Ritter von (1800–77), 115
Kopisch, August (1799–1853), 286
Krakow, 139
Krätzschmer, Friedrich (1806–86), 238
Krauss, Emil (1840–89), 191
Krebs, Marie (1851–1900), 207–8
Kretzschmer, Andreas (1775–1839), 164, 171
Krug, Walther (1875–1955), 340–1
Kruse, Minna, 125
Küchenmeister-Rudersdorf, Hermine (1822–82), 187
Kufferath, Antonie von (1857–1939), 192
Kugler, Franz (1808–58), 286, 288
Kupfer, William (1840–1914), 349

Laaff, Ernst (1903–87), 120
Lachenmann, Helmut (b.1935), 376

Lachner, Vincenz (1803/11–93), 57
Lamond, Frederick (1868–1948), 212
Lang, Bernhard (b. 1957), 382
Langhans-Japha, Louise (1826–1910), 8
Lasso, Orlando di (1530/2–94), 182
Leipzig, 34–8, 42–3, 139, 143, 146, 190, 200, 208, 293, 308, 320
Conservatory, 208, 320
Gewandhaus, 34, 38, 81, 143, 146, 212, 237, 369
publishers, 236, 237, 238, 239, 240, 253–4
Lengnick, Alfred (publisher), 322
Leser, Rosalie (1812–96), 127
Lessing, Gotthold Ephraim (1729–81), 274
Levetus, Amelia (1853–1938), 47, 49
Levi, Hermann (1839–1900), 55, 61, 76, 107, 119, 181, 197, 198, 200–1, 340
Leyen, Rudolf von der (1851–1910), 59
liberal nationalism, 260, 262
Lichtenberg, Georg Christoph (1742–99), 272
Lichtenthal, 60, 64
Liebermann, Lowell (b.1961), 382
lieder, 131, 161, 188, 321–2, 325, 330–1
Ligeti, György (1923–2006), 377, 382
Lindeck, Wilhelm (1833–1911), 75–6, 77
Lipsius, Marie (La Mara) (1837–1927), 384
List, Friedrich (1789–1846), 296
Liszt, Cosima (later von Bülow, then Wagner) (1837–1930), 200, 201, 202
Liszt, Franz (1811–86), 9, 53, 84, 98, 101, 108, 116, 132, 159, 202, 206, 210, 211, 212, 216, 308, 310, 314, 349
literature, 269–76
Litolff, Henry (1818–91), 107
Litzmann, Berthold (1857–1926), 56, 58
Locke, John (1632–1704), 250
London, 189, 207–8, 209, 212, 219, 316, 317, 318–19, 372
Lotti, Antonio (c.1667–1740), 176
Lübke, Wilhelm (1826–93), 286–7
Lueger, Karl (1844–1910), 30
Luithlen-Kalbeck, Florentine *see* Kalbeck, Florentine (Flora)
Luther, Martin (1483–1546), 48, 175, 266, 267, 283
Lutheran chorales, 175–6, 177
Lutheranism, 175, 261–2, 266, 283–4

Macfarren, George (1813–87), 322
Mackerras, Charles (1925–2010), 364, 369
MacRae, Stuart (b.1976), 382
Magnus, Helene (1840–1914), 188
Mahillon, Victor-Charles (1841–1924), 66
Mahler, Gustav (1860–1911), 30, 62, 142, 165, 203, 230
Mainz, 62
Malten, Therese (1855–1930), 192

Index

Mälzel, Johann Nepomuk (1768–1838), 298
Mandyczewski, Eusebius (1857–1929), 120, 129, 353–4, 389
Manns, August (1825–1907), 208, 317, 318
Marriner, Neville (1924–2016), 369
Martucci, Giuseppe (1856–1909), 66
Marx, Adolf Bernhard (1795–1866), 333
Marxsen, Eduard (1806–87), 5, 7, 8
Mason, William (1829–1908), 211
Matthus, Siegfried (b.1934), 382
May, Florence (1845–1923), 37, 38, 49, 50, 80, 127, 208
Mazzoli, Missy (b.1980), 382
McRae, Stuart (b.1976), 380
Meier, Franziska, 90
Meiningen, 142, 145, 146, 204, 222
Meiningen Court Orchestra, 142, 202–3, 222, 230, 297, 364, 372
Meister, Karl Severin (1818–81), 177
Mendelssohn, Felix (1809–47), 53, 56, 143, 144, 149, *152*, 165, 180, 215, 241, 286
Mendelssohn, Franz (1829–89), 76
Mendelssohn, Lily *see* Wach, Lily
Menzel, Adolph (1815–1905), 222, 288–9
metronomes and metronome markings, 298, 368
Meyer, Krzysztof (b.1943), 378, 382
Meyer, Therese (1815–68), 187
Meysenbug, Laura von (1818–87), 124, 125, 127
Meysenbug, Meta Sophie Luise von (1819–1906), 125
middle-class society, 138–41, 145–7, 263, 269, 390
Miller zu Aichholz, Olga von (1853–1931), 46
Mommsen, Theodor (1817–1903), 67
money *see* finances
Moore, Thomas (1779–1852), 165
Moritz, Johann Gottfried (1777–1840), 231
Moscheles, Ignaz (1794–1870), 207, 208
Moser, Andreas (1859–1925), 42
Mozart, Wolfgang Amadeus (1756–91), 41, 114, 115–16, 159, 160, 165, 361
Mühlfeld, Richard (1856–1907), 209, 215, 219, 222–5, 320
Müllenbach, Alexander (b.1949), 382
Müller, Friedrich (1847–?), 125
Müller, Wilhelm (1797–1827), 221, 271
Müller-Wieland, Jan (b.1966), 382
Munich, 27, 61, 139, 141, 200
Münster, 139
Mürzzuschlag, 61, 62
music aesthetics *see* aesthetics
music criticism, 28, 84, 91–2, 202, 203, 225, 284, 307–15, 317, 340–4, 372
music festivals, 44, 143–4, 145, 190, 337
music societies, 138–41, 142–4, *143*, 145–7, 199
musical ciphers, 216, 386–7

musical criticism *see also* analytical approaches
musical instrument makers, 28, 229, 230–1, 232
musical instruments, 227–35, 297–8, 299, 300–2, 364–5, 368–71
Musical Times, 225, 372
Musikalisches Wochenblatt, 84, 225, 240

National Liberals, 261, 263
National Socialism, 336–44, 345
Nazarene movement, 288
Nazism *see* National Socialism
Nestroy, Johannes (1801–62), 274
Neuda-Bernstein, Rosa (1850–1940), 126, 127
Neue Freie Presse, 25, 31, 284
Neue Zeitschrift für Musik, 10, 15, 116, 165, 253, 271, 307, 309, 310, 314
New German School, 42, 308, 309, 310, 313–14
New York, 211, 213
newspapers, 28
Ney, Elly (1882–1968), 344
Niederrheinische Musik-Zeitung, 309–10
Niemann, Walter (1876–1953), 341–2, 344
Nietzsche, Friedrich (1844–1900), 267, 281–4
Noorden, Carl von (1833–83), 324
Nordau, Max (1849–1923), 268
Norman, Andrew (b.1979), 382
Norman-Neruda, Wilma (1838–1911), 319
Norrington, Roger (b.1934), 364, 368–9
Nottebohm, Gustav (1817–82), 47, 114, 178
Novalis (1772–1801), 271
Novello & Co., 119
Novello, Ewer & Co., 322

Oldenburg, 73
Onslow, George (1784–1853), 160
opera houses, 141
Ophüls, Gustav (1866–1926), 275
orchestras, 139, 141–4, 145, 199, 202–3, 227–8, 364–5, 368–9 *see also* instruments
Orel, Alfred (1889–1967), 344
organs, 297–8
Ottensteiner, Georg (1815–79), 230

Palestrina, Giovanni Pierluigi da (1514 or 1529–94), 176, 177, 179, 182
Palmer, Tony (b.1941), 391
Parry, Hubert (1848–1918), 322
Passy-Cornet, Adele (1838–1915), 188
Pauer, Max (1866–1945), 212
Pausinger, Baron von, 64
percussion instruments, 233
performance practice, 193–4, 225–6, 228, 364–5, 367–75
performance rights, 246, 247, 249
Perger, Richard von (1854–1911), 94

404 Index

Périnet, François (fl. 1829–60), 231
period performance, 193–4, 225–6, 228, 364–5, 367–75
Pest, 142
Peters, C. F. (publisher), 238, 239, 244
Petri, Egon (1881–1962), 213
Pfohl, Ferdinand (1862–1949), 343
philosophy, 277–85
phonographs, 83, 303–4
pianists, 84–5, 106, 127, 206–13, 358, 373–4
pianos, 28, 233–4, 300–1, 370–1
Piatti, Alfredo (1822–1901), 207, 209, 221, 228, 320
pitch and tuning, 298–300, 301–2
Planck, Max (1858–1947), 301
poetry, 269, 272, 274–5
Pohl, Carl Ferdinand (1819–87), 64, 98, 135, 178, 384
Pohl, Richard (1826–96), 310
politics, 259–68 see also National Socialism
Pope, Alexander (1688–1744), 151
Pörtschach, 60, 64
Porubsky, Bertha (1841–1910), 48–9, 75, 173, 286
Potter, Cipriani (1792–1871), 207
Praetorius, Michael (1569/71–1621), 171, 179
Pressbaum, 61
print culture, 269, 287
private music-making, 27, 34, 37–8, 39–40, 61, 80, 82, 99–100, 130–7, 189, 190, 220, 321
programme notes, 318, 321
programming, 82, 89, 91–2, 94, 108, 143–4, 177, 178–9, 180, 181–2, 188, 192–3, 318
proofreaders, 117, 119, 244, 352, 353
Protestantism, 263, 266, 267, 283–4
publishers, 73–5, 100, 236–44, 250, 252–4, 322

Raff, Joseph Joachim (1822–82), 47–8, 216
railways, 296–7
Rainbow, Bernarr (1914–98), 208
Rechten, Johanna Grassl von (1841/2–1932), 126
recordings, 83, 97, 110, 193–4, 209, 210, 211, 212, 302–4, 357–66, 371–4
Regensburg, 139
Reger, Max (1873–1916), 62
Rehberg, Willi (1863–1937), 212
Reich, Willi (1898–1980), 340
Reinecke, Carl (1824–1910), 115, 116, 197, 208, 212
Reinick, Robert (1805–52), 286
religion, 30, 200, 261–4, 265, 272, 274, 278, 279, 283–4
Reményi, Eduard (1828–98), 9, 169–70, 188, 211, 215
repertoire see programming
Richter, Hans (1843–1916), 96, 98, 106, 135, 200, 201–2, 204, 208, 319, 323, 372
Richter, Jean Paul (1763–1825), 271, 272

Riedl, Joseph (1814–75), 231
Riemann, Hugo (1849–1919), 329–33, 386
Rieter-Biedermann, Jakob Melchior (1811–76), 55, 56–7, 63, 74, 110, 238, 242–3, 322
Rietz, Julius (1812–77), 115, 116
rights, 74, 246–55
Rihm, Wolfgang (b.1952), 379–80, 382
Rochus von Liliencron (1820–1912), 384
Röder, Carl Gottlieb (1812–83), 238, 351
Roman Catholicism, 175, 263, 266
Röntgen, Julius (1855–1932), 212, 240
Rosé, Arnold (1863–1946), 224–5
Röver, Heinrich (1827–75), 219
Rovetta, Giovanni (c.1595–1668), 176, 179, 180
Royal Academy of Music (RAM), 207, 208, 320
Royal College of Music (RCM), 190, 212, 320, 322, 387
Rubinstein, Anton (1829–94), 64, 84–5, 206, 210, 212
Rubinstein, Artur (1887–1982), 360, 361–2
Rückert, Friedrich (1788–1866), 271
Ruders, Poul (b.1949), 382
Rüdesheim, 61
Rudorff, Ernst (1840–1916), 41, 115, 116, 117, 119
Rügen, 60, 190
Rüschlikon, 60, 62, 64

Saint-Saëns, Camille (1835–1921), 233
Salter, Lionel (1914–2000), 362
Salzburg, 139
Sattler, Christian Friedrich (1778–1842), 231
Sax, Adolphe (1814–94), 230, 231
Scheibler, Johann Heinrich (1777–1837), 298–9
Scheidt, Samuel (1587–1654), 182
Schenker, Heinrich (1868–1935), 327–30, 334, 337
Schiller, Friedrich (1759–1805), 271, 272, 280, 291
Schmaltz, Susanne, 73, 125, 128
Schmidt, Hans (1854–1932), 192
Schnabel, Artur (1882–1951), 213
Schneider, Enjott (b.1950), 382, 383
Schneider, Friedrich (1786–1853), 308
Schoenberg, Arnold (1874–1951), 324–7, 329, 340, 341, 343, 376, 380
Scholz, Bernhard (1835–1916), 216
Schönerstedt, Agnes (1833–96), 124, 127
Schopenhauer, Arthur (1788–1860), 280–1, 294
Schubert, Franz (1797–1828)
  arrangements of, 107–8, 110–12
  edited by JB, 120–1
  folk music as inspiration for, 165
  influence of, 28–9, 160, 271, 276, 311
  performances of, 41, 143, 144, 181, 188, 189, 193
Schuberth, Julius (1804–75), 246, 254
Schubring, Adolf (1817–93), 92, 312, 314–15, 324–5
Schuller, Gunther (1925–2015), 364

Index

Schultz, Wolfgang-Andreas (b.1948), 383
Schumann, Alfred, 15
Schumann, Clara (1819–96), 14–22
  and artists, 289
  on JB as conductor, 93
  correspondence with JB, 55–6, 57–8
    JB to Clara, 53, 65–6, 78, 83, 86, 90, 91, 92,
      133, 196, 234, 348
    Clara on Gumpert's playing, 232
    Clara on Menzel, 289
    Clara on Mühlfeld's playing, 222
  as editor and custodian of Robert's work, 20–1,
    118–20
  in England, 209, 316–17, 319
  as friend of JB, 15–22, 38, 47, 75, 76, 135–6,
    170–1, 176, 178, 200, 218, 272, 378,
    385, 391
    books and music given to JB
    early music copied for JB
    financial advice to JB
    folk melodies manuscript gift from JB
    Leipzig reception of JB
    introduces Levi to JB
    music-making in Baden-Baden
    nature of the relationship
    prank played by JB on
    Violin Sonata an expression of concern
  and the Heerman Quartet, 223
  and Hermann Levi, 198, 200
  as pianist, 19–20, 81, 84, 98, 100, 108, 206–7,
    209, 216, *290*, 316–17
  pupils of, 73, 126–7, 207–10, 320
Schumann, Elise (1843–1928), 16, 21
Schumann, Eugenie (1851–1938), 15, 16, 21, 49, 50,
  126, 127, 136, 191
Schumann, Felix (1854–79), 15, 20, 218
Schumann, Ferdinand (1849–91), 16,
  63, 76
Schumann, Julie (1845–72), 16, 17, 19
Schumann, Ludwig (1848–99), 16, 63
Schumann, Marie (1841–1929), 14, 16, 18, 19,
  21, 56
Schumann, Robert (1810–56), 9–10, 14–15
  arrangements of, 107, 254
  on JB's piano playing, 80
  composition and creative process, 251–2, 253
  concept of music, 157, 270, 308–9, 310
  early music, shared interest in
  editing by JB and Clara, 20–1, 117–20
  F–A–E Sonata for violin and piano, 216
  fees from Breitkopf & Härtel, 240
  illness and death, 19
  letter-writing compared with JB's, 53
  literary influence, 259, 265
  musical influence, 15, 18, 102

'New Paths' article, 10, 15, 19, 33, 42–3, 93, 161,
  278–9, 307, 309
  performances of, 143, 144, 188, 193
  publishers, help with
Schütz, Heinrich (1585–1672), 177, 178, 180, 182–3
science and technology, 296–304
Scott de Martinville, Édouard-Léon (1817–79),
  302–3
Sechter, Simon (1788–1867), 329
Seiffert, Max (1868–1948), 182
Senff, Bartholf (1815–1900), 236
Senfl, Ludwig (c. 1490–1543), 172
Shakespeare, William (playwright) (1564–1616),
  271, 272
Shakespeare, William (tenor) (1849–1931), 192
Sheng, Bright (b.1955), 383
Siebold, Agathe von (1835–1909), 18, 58, 391
Signale für die musikalische Welt, 21, 38, 313
Silcher, Friedrich (1789–1860), 165
Simrock, Clara (1839–1928), 247
Simrock, Fritz (1837–1901)
  1st class travel joke by JB, 297
  as source of books for JB, 273
  correspondence from JB, 55, 58, 60, 101, 133,
    170, 254, 273
  as executor, 31, 240
  and JB's finances, 74, 77, 78, 243–4
  Leipzig reception of JB, 38
  private music-making, 39
  as publisher, 25, 236, 237, 238–40, 242, 244,
    264, 322
  'seed-corn' comment of JB, 247, 348
Simrock, Peter Joseph (1792–1868), 239
singers, 187–94, 299, 358
singing technique, 193–4, 301, 302
Sistermans, Anton (1865–1926), 358
smoking, 50
Smyth, Ethel (1858–1944), 37, 48, 320
Soldat-Röger, Marie (1863–1955), 220, 221
Solomon (Solomon Cutner) (1902–88), 213
Speidel, Ludwig (1830–1906), 203
Spies, Hermine (1857–93), 135, 189–90, 193, 221
Spina, C. A. (1827–1906), 238, 252
Spitta, Philip (1841–94), 37, 39, 41, 115, 182, 384
Spitzer, Daniel (1835–93), 200–1
Srnka, Miroslav (b.1975), 383
Staegemann, Max (1843–1905), 192
Standhartner, Josef (1818–92), 98
Stanford, Charles Villiers (1852–1924), 221, 317,
  320, 322, 323
Steglich, Rudolf (1886–1976), 345
Stein, Erwin (1885–1958), 341
Steinbach, Fritz (1855–1916), 96, 204, 364,
  372–3
Steinway, C. F. Theodore (1825–89), 300–1

406 Index

Stockhausen, Julius (1826–1906), 38, 39, 81, 91, 110, 112, 187, 188–9, 193, 194, 273, 302, 391
Stölzel, Heinrich (1777–1844), 231
Straus, Ludwig (1877–1942), 207, 209
Strauss, Adèle (1856–1930), 25, 30
Strauss, Johann, I (1804–49), 251
Strauss, Johann, II (1825–99), 25, 30
Strauss, Josef (1827–70), 110, 303
Strauss, Richard (1864–1949), 142, 203
Stravinsky, Igor (1882–1971), 341
Streicher, Emil (1835/6–1916), 234
string instruments, 228–9, 368, 369–70
string quartets (ensembles), 219, 221, 223, 224–5
string quartets (genre), 160, 376
Stuttgart, 141
Suk, Josef (1874–1935), 281
summer holidays see holidays
Süssmayr, Franz Xaver (1766–1803), 116
Swedish folk music, 171
Switzerland, 44, 63, 86, 178
symphonies (as genre), 157–8, 199, 204
Szigeti, Joseph (1892–1973), 370

Tanaka, Shohé (1862–1945), 301
Tappert, Wilhelm (1830–1907), 172
Tausig, Carl (1841–71), 85, 126, 208, 210–11, 212
Taylor, Franklin (1843–1919), 207
temperament (keyboard), 301–2
texts for setting, 269, 272, 275, 286
texts, translation of, 133, 321–2
Thalberg, Sigismund (1812–71), 84
Thayer, Alexander Wheelock (1817–97), 384
theatres, 28
Third Reich, 336–44, 345
Thomas, Theodore (1835–1905), 211
Thun, 44, 264
tobacco, 50
Tofte, Lars Valdemar (1832–1907), 124
Toscanini, Arturo (1867–1957), 204, 205, 358
Tovey, Donald Francis (1875–1940), 219, 221
transcriptions see arrangers and arrangements
translation of texts, 133, 321–2
Trau, Johann Baptist (1845–1921), 61
travel, 72, 82, 86, 178, 188, 274, 296–7 see also holidays
Trojahn, Manfred (b.1949), 378, 379, 383
Truxa, Coelestine (JB's landlady) (1858–1935), 71, 350
Tutzing, 61, 64

USA, 211, 212–13, 247

Verdi, Giuseppi (1813–1901), 230, 251, 361
Vesque von Püttlingen, Johann (1803–83), 251

Viardot-Garcia, Pauline (1821–1910), 136
Vienna, 23–31, 44, 49, 95, 136–7, 139, 140, 141, 146, 188, 190, 191, 327
anti-Semitism in, 266–7
Brahms centenary celebrations, 337
JB's final appearance as conductor, 95
JB's first visit, 11, 90, 91, 178, 179–80
JB's pupils, 125–6, 128–9
Bülow and the Meiningen Court Orchestra in, 202–3
Conservatory, 95, 211
Ehrbar Salon, 98, 134–5
Feuerbach in, 290–1
Gesellschaft der Musikfreunde, 24, 30, 31, 48, 73, 88, 92, 93–5, 139, 175, 181–2, 201, 227, 273
Grosser Redoutensaal, 189
International Commission on standard performance pitch, 299–300
Musikhalle, 146
Musikverein, 30, 139, 182, 189, 193, 227
Philharmonic, 142, 196, 201, 202, 227, 231, 232, 365
phonograph demonstration, 83, 303–4
piano manufacturing, 28, 233
premieres in, 85, 143, 189, 196, 197, 207, 219, 224–5
publishers, 238, 252
Richter in, 201
Singakademie, 11, 73, 88, 91–3, 112, 180, 182, 191
Singverein, 126, 178
Theater an der Wien, 28
Wagner and Wagnerism, 28, 198–9
violinists, 215–20, 319, 370
violins, 228–9
visual arts, 286–95
vocal technique, 193–4, 301, 302
Vogl, Heinrich (1845–1900), 54, 191
Vogt, Lars (b.1970), 366
Völckers, Marie, 125
Völckers, Minna, 125
Volkland, Alfred (1858–1901), 37
Volkland, Robert, 119
Volkmann, Robert (1815–83), 144
Vorwerk, Anna (1839–1900), 125
Voss, Richard (1851–1918), 66
Vrabély, Stephanie (1849–1919), 126

Wach, Adolf (1843–1926), 37
Wach, Lily (née Mendelssohn) (1845–1910), 37
Wagner, Cosima see Liszt, Cosima
Wagner, Friederike (Friedchen) (1831–1917), 124–5

Index

407

Wagner, Richard (1813–84), 28, 40, 53, 54, 131–2, 141, 143, 154, 191, 192, 197, 198–9, 200–5, 222, 230, 282, 310, 341–2, 345, 359 *see also* anti-Wagnerism
Wagner, Wolfram (b.1952), 383
Walker, Ernest (1870–1949), 359
Walter, Bruno (1876–1962), 40, 42
Walter, Gustav (1834–1910), 135, 187, 189, 192, 193, 358
Wangemann, Adelbert Theodor (Theo) (1855–1906), 83, 303–4
Watts, George Frederic (1817–1904), 228
Weber, Carl Maria von (1786–1826), 53, 108, 143
Weber, Gottfried (1779–1839), 333
Weber, Wilhelm Eduard (1804–91), 297–8
Weimar, 211, 216, 308, 313, 333, 349
Weingartner, Felix (1863–1942), 96–7, 203, 205, 372
Weitzmann, Carl Friedrich (1808–80), 333
Wendt, Gustav (1827–1912), 46, 280
Wesendonck, Mathilde (1828–1902), 63
Widmann, Jörg (b.1973), 378
Widmann, Josef Viktor (1842–1911), 44, 50, 65, 66, 67, 193, 265–6, 275, 283
Wiener Salonblatt, 314
Wiener Singakademie, 11, 73, 88, 91–3, 112, 180, 182, 191
Wiener Zeitung, 31
Wieprecht, Wilhelm (1802–72), 231

Wiesbaden, 61
Wilhelm I, Emperor (1797–1888), 264
Wilhelm II, Emperor (1859–1941), 264–6
Wilt, Marie (1833–91), 191
Winckelmann, Johann Joachim (1717–68), 287, 288
wind instruments, 228, 229–32, 299, 368, 370
Winsen an der Luhe, 8, 88, 123
Winterfeld, Carl von (1784–1852), 177, 180
Wipperich, Emil (1854–1917), 232
Wirth, Emanuel (1842–1923), 219
Wittgenstein, Anna (1840–96), 124, 126
Wittgenstein, Karl (1847–1913) and Leopoldine (1850–1926), 135
Wolf, Hugo (1860–1903), 128, 201, 314
Wolff, Otto Ludwig Bernhard (1799–1851), 165
Wölfflin, Heinrich (1864–1945), 288
Wollenhaupt, Hermann Adolf (1827–63), 124
woodwind instruments, 228, 229–30, 299
Woolrich, John (b.1954), 383
Wüllner, Franz (1832–1902), 61, 115, 119, 120, 199–200

Zemlinksy, Alexander (1871–1942), 325
Zimmermann, Agnes (1847–1925), 207
Zimmermann, Udo (b.1943), 383
Zuccalmaglio, Anton Wilhelm von (1803–69), 61, 64, 164, 171
Zurich, 63, 139–40, 140, 143, 146, 192, 286, 292
Zur-Mühlen, Raimund von (1854–1931), 187, 192